THE VICTORIA HISTORY OF THE COUNTIES OF ENGLAND

A HISTORY OF MIDDLESEX

VOLUME XII, CHELSEA

INSCRIBED TO THE MEMORY OF HER LATE MAJESTY

QUEEN VICTORIA

WHO GRACIOUSLY GAVE THE TITLE TO AND

ACCEPTED THE DEDICATION OF THIS HISTORY

THE VICTORIA HISTORY OF THE COUNTIES OF ENGLAND

THE UNIVERSITY OF LONDON

INSTITUTE OF HISTORICAL RESEARCH

A HISTORY OF THE COUNTY OF MIDDLESEX

EDITED BY PATRICIA E.C. CROOT

VOLUME XII

CHELSEA

PUBLISHED FOR THE

INSTITUTE OF HISTORICAL RESEARCH

BY BOYDELL & BREWER · 2004

First published 2004

A Victoria County History publication
in association with The Boydell Press
an imprint of Boydell & Brewer Ltd
PO Box 9 Woodbridge Suffolk IP12 3DF UK
and of Boydell & Brewer Inc.
668 Mt Hope Avenue Rochester NY 14620 USA
website: www.boydellandbrewer.com
and with the
University of London Institute of Historical Research

ISBN 1 904356 24 9

A CiP catalogue record for this book is available from the British Library

Typeset by Pru Harrison, Hacheston, Suffolk
Printed in Great Britain by
St Edmundsbury Press Ltd, Bury St Edmunds, Suffolk

CONTENTS OF VOLUME TWELVE

LIST OF ILLUSTRATIONS IN THE TEXT

Thanks are rendered to the following for permission to reproduce material in their possession: City of London, Guildhall Library; Mr A.F. Kersting; London Metropolitan Archives (LMA); English Heritage for material in the National Monuments Record (NMR) and for photographs taken in 2003; the Royal Borough of Kensington and Chelsea for material from the Local Studies Collection in Chelsea Library (CL); the marquess of Salisbury for the plan of Chelsea Great House in Hatfield House Archives.

LIST OF COLOUR PLATES between pages 142 and 143

All the photographs below were taken in 2003 by Derek Kendall of English Heritage, especially for this volume

LIST OF MAPS AND PLANS

The maps in figures 1, 3, 6, 10, and 46 were drawn by Jamie Quinn of the Drawing Office, Department of Geography, University College, London, from drafts prepared by Patricia E.C. Croot. The sections of the OS maps 1:2500 (1st edition), surveyed between 1862 and 1869, are reproduced by permission of the Guildhall Library.

MIDDLESEX
VICTORIA COUNTY HISTORY
COMMITTEE

As at 1 March 2003

Chairman

ALAN CLINTON

Representatives of the following London Boroughs

Camden
Hammersmith and Fulham
Kensington and Chelsea
Hackney
Islington
Tower Hamlets
Westminster

Representatives of

London Metropolitan Archives
The London and Middlesex Archaeological Society
The Institute of Historical Research

Co-opted Members

JOHN GREENACOMBE, Survey of London

MATTHEW DAVIES, Centre for Metropolitan History

Hon. Secretary: R.J. SWINDELLS

Hon. Treasurer: R. HARRISON

FOREWORD AND ACKNOWLEDGEMENTS

THE PRESENT volume is the fifth to have been compiled for the Middlesex VCH Committee formed in 1979 to complete the Middlesex History. The University of London gratefully acknowledges the help of the Committee, which has continued under the chairmanship of Dr Alan Clinton, with Mr Roy Harrison as Treasurer. Mr R.J. Swindells succeeded Mr C.J. Koster as Secretary in 1999. The University also records its gratitude for the continued generosity of the City of Westminster and the London Boroughs of Kensington and Chelsea, Islington, and Hackney in supporting the Committee's work. However, due to pressures on local government funding Hackney had to cease contributing from 2001, and both Islington and Kensington and Chelsea from 2003; Westminster is continuing with a reduced contribution. The completion of the present volume has been made possible by a very generous contribution from Cadogan Estates, who are thanked warmly for their support.

In 2001 the County Editor, Mr T.F.T. Baker, and one of the two Assistant Editors, Miss D.K. Bolton, retired, having worked on the Middlesex History since 1967 and 1965 respectively. Dr P.E.C. Croot, previously Assistant Editor, was appointed to the post of County Editor in 2001. Work on the present volume was also assisted by three temporary appointments: Dr R.M. Kemsley, a full-time Assistant Editor from November 1999 until early 2001; Dr C.R.J. Currie as part-time Consultant Editor for a year in 2001/2; and Dr C. Insley as part-time Assistant Editor from January to August 2002. Reduction in funding prevents the appointment of a permanent Assistant Editor at present.

The general editing at VCH Central Office was carried out by Dr A.T. Thacker (Executive Editor) and Ms Elizabeth Williamson (Architectural Editor).

Those who have provided information for the volume are named in the footnotes, and they are sincerely thanked for their help. We are especially grateful to the staff of Kensington and Chelsea's Central and Chelsea libraries, in particular Carrie Starren, Nicholas West, and Dave Walker, for their assistance over several years, and also to the staff of the London Metropolitan Archives and the Guildhall Library for their help in various ways. We would also like to record our thanks to Mr Stuart Corbyn and his staff at Cadogan Estates for their kind assistance.

The structure and aims of the Victoria County History as a whole are set out in the *General Introduction* (1970) and its *Supplement* (1990). The contents of the first seven volumes of the Middlesex History are listed and indexed in outline in a booklet, *The Middlesex Victoria History Council*, which also describes the work of the precursor of the present Middlesex Victoria County History Committee. Further information about the history and present work of the Middlesex VCH and about the contents of the volumes is available on the county website, www.middlesexpast.net.

ABBREVIATIONS AND COMMONLY CITED WORKS

BC	Borough council
BL	British Library
Bacon, *Atlas of London* (1910)	*New Large-Scale Atlas of London and Suburbs*, ed. G.W. Bacon (1910)
Beaven, *Aldermen*	A.B. Beaven, *The Aldermen of the City of London temp. Henry III to 1912* (2 vols, 1908, 1913)
Beaver, *Memorials*	A. Beaver, *Memorials of Old Chelsea* (1892)
Bignell, *Chelsea 1860–1980*	J. Bignell, *Chelsea seen from 1860 to 1980* (1978)
Blunt, *Chelsea*	R. Blunt, *An Illustrated Historical Handbook to the Parish of Chelsea* (1900)
Booth, *Life and Labour*	C. Booth, *Life and Labour of the People in London* (17 vols. revised edn 1902–4). Chelsea surveyed in 1899
Booth's Map (1889)	*Charles Booth's Descriptive Map of London Poverty, 1889* (London Topographical Society 1984)
Borer, *Two Villages*	M.C. Borer, *Two Villages. The Story of Chelsea and Kensington* (1973)
Bowack, *Antiquities*	J. Bowack, *The Antiquities of Middlesex* (1705)
Bradley, 'Gothic Revival'	S. Bradley, 'The Gothic Revival and the Church of England, 1790–1840' (London Univ. Ph.D. thesis, 1996)
Bryan, *Chelsea*	G. Bryan, *Chelsea in the Olden & Present Times* (1869)
CCC	Council for the Care of Churches (formerly Council forPlaces of Worship).
CL	Chelsea Library
CLRO	Corporation of London Record Office
Calamy Revised	*Calamy Revised*, ed. A.G. Matthews (1934)
Cal. Middx Sess. Bks	Calendars of Sessions Books, 1638–1752, at LMA
Cal. Middx Sess. Rec.	Calendar of Sessions Records, 1607–12, at LMA
Chantry Cert.	*London and Middlesex Chantry Certificate, 1548*, ed. C.J. Kitching (London Record Society, XVI, 1980)
Chelsea BC, *Mins*	Chelsea Borough Council, *Minutes*, in CL
Chelsea Chars 1862	*The Chelsea Charities, 1862. Report of the Committee of the Vestry* (1863)
Chelsea cuttings	at Chelsea Library
Chelsea Dir. *(1878)*	*Chelsea, Pimlico and Belgravia Directory* (1878)
Chelsea Misc.	at Chelsea Library
Chelsea Scraps	at Chelsea Library
Chelsea Settlement Examinations 1733–66	*Chelsea Settlement and Bastardy Examinations, 1733–1766*, ed. T. Hitchcock and J. Black (London Rec. Soc. xxxiii, 1999)
Chelsea Soc. Rep.	*Chelsea Society Annual Reports*
Clarke, *London Chs*	B.F.L. Clarke, *Parish Churches of London* (1966)
Clunn, *London Marches On*	H.P. Clunn, *London Marches On* [1947]
Clunn, *London Rebuilt*	H.P. Clunn, *London Rebuilt, 1897–1927* (1927)
Colvin, *Brit. Architects*	H. Colvin, *Biographical Dictionary of British Architects, 1600–1840* (1978)
Croker, *Walk from London to Fulham*	T.C. Croker, *A Walk from London to Fulham* [*c.*1845], enlarged by B. Horne (1896)
Cruchley's New Plan (1826, 1829)	[G.F.] *Cruchley's New Plan of London and Its Environs* (1826, 1829)
DNB	*Dictionary of National Biography*
Davies, *Chelsea Old Ch.*	R. Davies, *Chelsea Old Church* (1904)
Davies, *Greatest Ho.*	R. Davies, *The Greatest House at Chelsey* (1914)
Dean, *Royal Hosp.*	C.G.T. Dean, *The Royal Hospital, Chelsea* (1950)
Denny, *Chelsea Past*	B. Denny, *Chelsea Past* (1996)
Edwards, *London Street Improvements*	P.J. Edwards, *History of London Street Improvements, 1855–97* (1898)
Endowed Chars London (1897)	*Endowed Charities (County of London)*, I (Parl. Papers, 1897 (394), LXVI(2))
Endowed Chars London (1901)	*Endowed Charities (County of London)*, IV (Parl. Papers, 1901 (133), LI)

Endowed Chars London (1904)	*Endowed Charities (County of London)*, (Parl. Papers, 1904 (333-II), LXXIII)
Educ. Enquiry Abs.	*Education Enquiry Abstract, 1833* (Parl. Papers, 1835 (62), XLII)
Educ. of Poor Digest	*Digest of Returns to Committee on Education of Poor* (Parl. Papers, 1819 (224), IX(1))
Faulkner, *Chelsea*	T. Faulkner, *Historical and Topographical Description of Chelsea and its Environs* (2 vols. 1829)
Faulkner, *Chelsea* (1810)	Single volume edition, mainly superseded by the above
Freshfield, *Communion Plate*	E. Freshfield, *Communion Plate of the Parish Churches in the County of London* (1895)
GLC	Greater London Council
Guildhall MSS	City of London, Guildhall Library. Contains registers of wills of the commissary court of London (London Division) (MS 9171), bishops' registers (MS 9531), diocesan administrative records (MSS 9532–9560), and registers of nonconformist meeting houses (MS 9580)
Hamilton, *Map* (1664–1717)	J. Hamilton, *Map of Chelsea* (1664, continued to 1717)
Hist. London Transport	T.C. Barker and M. Robbins, *History of London Transport* (2 vols. 1975)
Hist. King's Works, IV	*History of the King's Works*, vol. IV, *1485–1660 (Part II)*, ed. H.M. Colvin *et al.* (1982)
Hist. King's Works, V	*History of the King's Works*, vol. V, *1660–1782*, H.M. Colvin *et al.* (1976)
Hist. King's Works, VI	*History of the King's Works*, vol. VI, *1782–1851*, ed. J.M. Crook and M.H. Port (1973)
Hennessy, *Novum Rep.*	G. Hennessy, *Novum Repertorium Ecclesiasticum Parochiale Londinense* (1894)
Holme, *Chelsea*	T. Holme, *Chelsea* (1972)
Hug. Soc.	Huguenot Society of London
Hunting, *Manor Ho. to Mus.*	P. Hunting, *From Manor House to Museum* (1995)
Hutt, *Royal Hosp.*	G. Hutt, *Papers Illustrative of the Origin and Early History of the Royal Hospital at Chelsea* (HMSO 1872)
ILEA	Inner London Education Authority
Images of Chelsea	E. Longford, *Images of Chelsea* (1980)
Improvement com. mins.	MS volumes at Chelsea Library
KL	Kensington Library
Kens.	Kensington
Dr King's MS	'An Account of Chelsea', bound MS vol. in CL, with original pagination from p. 145
LAARC	London Archaeological Archive Research Centre, Museum of London, 46 Eagle Wharf Rd, London N1 7ED
LB	London Borough
LCC	London County Council
LCC, *London Statistics*	LCC, *London Statistics* (26 vols. 1905–6 to 1936–8, beginning with vol. xvi). Followed by ibid. new series (2 vols. 1945–54 and 1947–56) and by further new series from 1957
LCC, *Names of Streets*	LCC, *List of the Streets and Places within the County of London* (1901 and later edns)
LMA	London Metropolitan Archives. Formerly the Greater London Record Office (GLRO), and contains the collection of the former Middlesex Record Office (MRO)
Lambeth Pal. Lib.	Lambeth Palace Library
Loobey, *Chelsea*	P. Loobey, *Images of England: Chelsea* (1999)
Lysons, *Environs*	D. Lysons, *The Environs of London* (4 vols. 1792–6 and Supplement 1811)
MB	Metropolitan Borough
MBW	Metropolitan Board of Works
MCS	Metropolitan Commission of Sewers
MLR	Middlesex Land Registry. The enrolments, indexes, and registers are at LMA
Mackeson's Guide	C. Mackeson, *A Guide to the Churches of London and Its Suburbs* (1866 and later edns)
Middx County Rec.	*Middlesex County Records* [1550–1688], ed. J.C. Jeaffreson (4 vols. 1886–92)
Middx County Rec. Sess. Bks 1689–1709	*Middlesex County Records, Calendar of the Sessions Books 1689–1709*, ed. W.J. Hardy (1905)
Middx Sess. Rec.	*Calendar to the Sessions Records* [1612–18], ed. W. le Hardy (4 vols. 1935–41)

Middleton, *View*	J. Middleton, *View of the Agriculture of Middlesex* (1798)
Mudie-Smith, *Rel. Life*	R. Mudie-Smith, *The Religious Life of London* (1904). Census taken 1903
N&Q	*Notes & Queries*
NMR	English Heritage (formerly Royal Commission on Historical Monuments of England), National Monuments Record
NRA(S)	National Register of Archives for Scotland
Newcourt, *Rep.*	R. Newcourt, *Repertorium Ecclesiasticum Parochiale Londinense* (2 vols. 1708–10)
Old OS Map	Old Ordnance Survey Maps: edition published by Alan Godfrey, Gateshead, from 1983 (reduced facsimile reproductions of 1:2,500 maps *c.*1865–1914). Chelsea is covered by London sheets 87 (1865, 1894), 88 (1869, 1894), 74 (1871, 1894), 100 (1894).
ONS	Office for National Statistics, Birkdale. Formerly the General Register Office (GRO)
PO Dir.	*Post Office Directory*
PRO	Public Record Office
Pearman, *Cadogan Est.*	R. Pearman, *The Cadogan Estate: The History of a Landed Family* (1986)
Pevsner, *London*, ii.	N. Pevsner, *Buildings of England: London except the Cities of London and Westminster* (1952)
Pevsner, *London NW.*	B. Cherry and N. Pevsner, *Buildings of England, London 3: North West* (1999)
P.N. Middx (E.P.N.S.)	*Place-Names of Middlesex* (English Place-Name Society, vol. xviii, 1942)
Places of Worship	*Places of Worship in Chelsea* [Chelsea Soc. and RBKC exhibition catalogue (2001)]
Poor rate bk	MSS in CL, covering 1695–1705, 1707–16, 1716–27, 1728–42, 1748–51
Pop. bk (1801)	In Chelsea Library
RBKC	Royal Borough of Kensington and Chelsea
Reid, *Hundred Yrs in Chelsea Par.*	H. Reid, *One Hundred Years in a Chelsea Parish. A history and survey of Christ Church* [1939]
Regency A to Z	*The A to Z of Regency London*, intro. P. Laxton (1985). Reproduction of R. Horwood's *Plan of the Cities of London and Westminster* (1813 edn)
Rep. on Bridges in Middx	*Report of the Committee of Magistrates Appointed to make Enquiry respecting the Public Bridges in the County of Middlesex* (1826). Copy at LMA
Rep. of Com. on London Sqs	*Report of Royal Commission on London Squares* (Parl. Papers, 1928–9 [Cmd. 3196], VIII), App. III
2nd *Rep. Com. Met. Improvements*	2nd *Report of the Commissioners . . . to inquire into . . . improving the Metropolis* (1845), copy in CL
5th *Rep. Com. Met. Improvements*	5th *Report of the Commissioners . . . to inquire into . . . improving the Metropolis* (1846), copy in CL
Richardson's Map (1769)	Cadogan Estate Office, Richardson's Map of Chelsea, 1769
Rocque, *Map of London* (1741–5)	J. Rocque, *Exact survey of the cities of London, Westminster, and the borough of Southwark, and the country near ten miles around* (1746, facsimile edn 1971)
Stroud, *Smith's Char.*	D. Stroud, *The South Kensington Estate of Henry Smith's Charity* (1975)
Stanford, *Map of London* (1862–5)	*Stanford's Library Map of London and Its Suburbs* (1862 edn with additions to 1865)
Survey of London, II	LCC, *Survey of London*, vol. II, *Parish of Chelsea* (Part I) (1908)
Survey of London, IV	LCC, *Survey of London*, vol. IV, *Parish of Chelsea* (Part II) (1913)
Survey of London, VII	LCC, *Survey of London*, vol. VII, *The Old Church, Chelsea* (Part III) (1921)
Survey of London, XI	LCC, *Survey of London*, vol. XI, *Chelsea, The Royal Hospital* (Part IV) (1927)
TLMAS	Transactions of the London and Middlesex Archaeological Society (1856 to date). Consecutive numbers are used for the whole series, although vols. VII–XVII (1905–54) appeared as NS I–XI.
Thompson, *Map* (1836)	F.P. Thompson, *Map of Chelsea* (1836)
Vestry mins	MS volumes in Chelsea Library
Vestry mins	Printed vols. 1881 to 1900, in Chelsea Library
Vestry orders	MS volumes in Chelsea Library
Vestry orders, 1662–1718	Vol. entitled 'Orders of Vestry and Poor rates 1662–1718, in Chelsea Library
Vestry rep.	Printed vols in Chelsea Library, 1856–7 (1st rep. of vestry appointed under Metropolitan Local Management Act, 1855) to 1899–1900 (44th and last rep.)

WAM	Westminster Abbey Muniments, in the Chapter Library
WCS	Westminster Commission of Sewers
Walker and Jackson, *Kens. and Chelsea*	A. Walker and P. Jackson, *Kensington and Chelsea: a social and architectural history* (1987)
Walker Revised	*Walker Revised*, ed. A.G. Matthews (1948)
Walkley, *Artists' Hos in London*	G. Walkley, *Artists' Houses in London 1764–1914* (1994)
Westm.	Westminster
Westm. Dom.	Westminster Domesday in Westminster Abbey Chapter Lib.

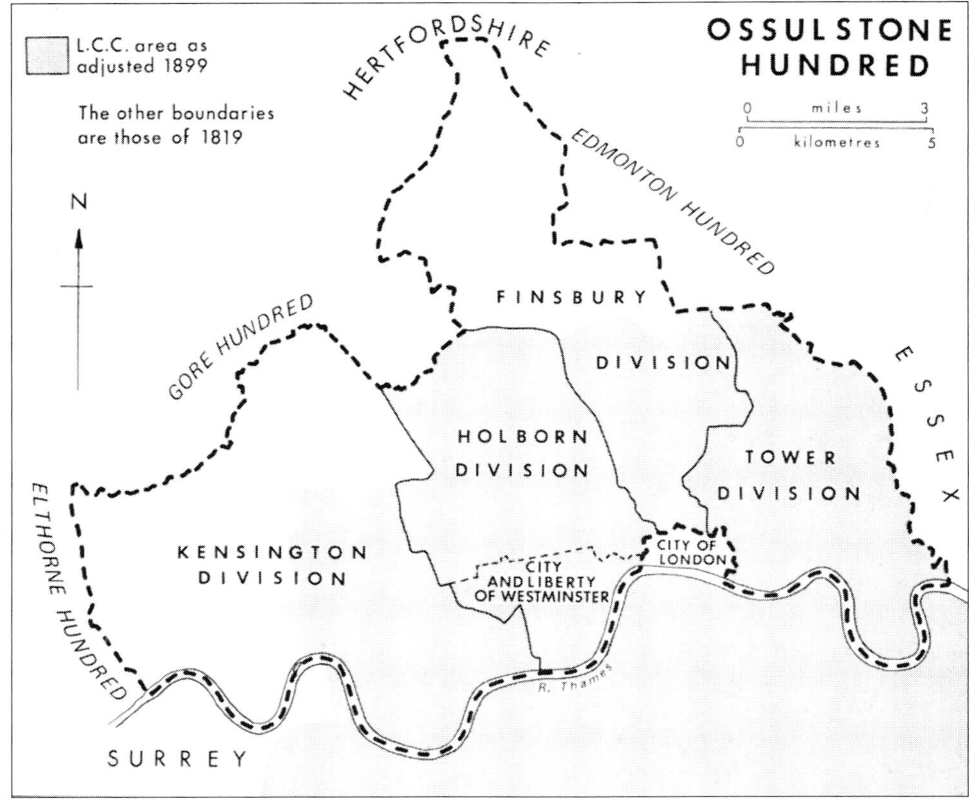

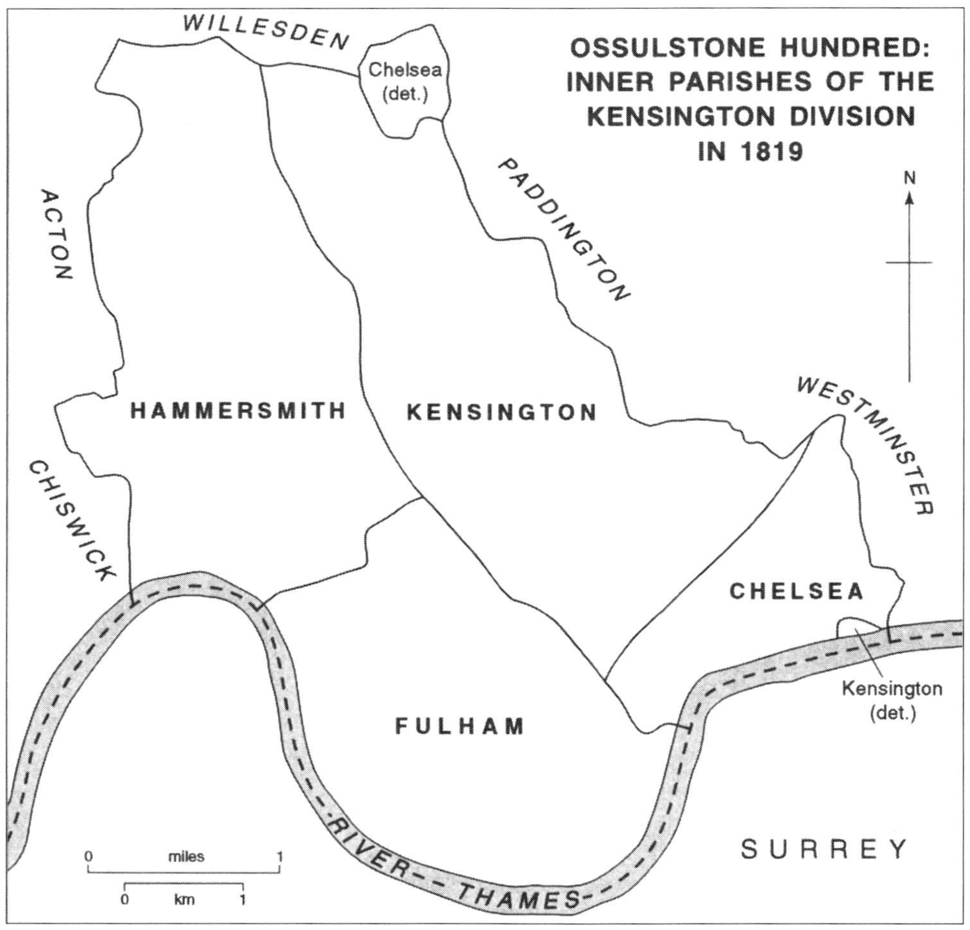

1 *Hundredal Maps*

THE PARISH OF CHELSEA

CHELSEA, a small village on the Thames, developed as a riverside resort, first for courtiers and wealthy Londoners from the 15th to the 17th centuries, and then for a wider section of London's residents in the 18th.[1] It became known from the later 19th century as a centre of artistic life in London, with a socially mixed and rather bohemian society, but by the end of the 20th was again largely an enclave of the rich and fashionable. It is one of the smaller inner London parishes, lying in the Kensington Division of Ossulstone Hundred, and bounded by the detached part of St Margaret Westminster on the north, St George Hanover Square on the east, the river Thames and Fulham on the south, Fulham on the south-west, and Kensington on the north-west. In addition to the Thames, water formed the boundaries on two other sides, with the Westbourne river on the east, and Counter's Creek (its lower stretch known as Chelsea Creek) on the west;[2] in 1900 the eastern boundary of Chelsea MB was straightened to run along Chelsea Bridge Road and other roads to the north. Fulham Road formed the north-western boundary from the western end of the parish for three-quarters of the distance, but where Fulham Road turns north as Brompton Road the parish boundary continues in more or less a straight line north-eastwards towards Knightsbridge; it runs just south of Knightsbridge road itself.

Chelsea's position and links with land in Kensington suggest that it may originally have formed the southern end of a larger land-holding, and later became a separate unit from which the parish was created. Until 1900 the parish included a detached portion of about 120 a. which lay at the northern end of Kensington, possibly once part of a single Anglo-Saxon unit comprising both Kensington and Chelsea parishes.[3] In 1900 the area was allotted to Paddington and Kensington MBs under an Act of 1899. Settlement, churches, and schools of the 19th and 20th centuries which later lay within Paddington (Queen's Park) have been treated under Paddington,[4] and similar building which later fell within Kensington (Kensal New Town) are reserved for treatment under Kensington.

The parish is wedge shaped, only about a quarter of a mile wide in the west and just over a mile in the east; east-west through the centre the parish is about 1¼ miles long from boundary to boundary.[5] In 1664 the area of the parish was estimated by James Hamilton at 631 a., presumably excluding Chelsea detached,[6] and in 1831 the area was given as 780 a.,[7] presumably including the detached portion. Ten acres by the river near the Royal Hospital belonged to Kensington parish, which may account for the 770 a. given as the area under the tithe award.[8] In 1900, after Kensal had been transferred to Paddington and Kensington, the remainder of Chelsea, now a metropolitan borough, was 660 a.[9]

Geology

Like similar settlements on the Thames, Chelsea owed its existence to the proximity of firm gravel to the water's edge, which allowed easy landing. Nearly all of Chelsea lies on Kempton Park gravel drift over London clay. The exceptions are two patches of Langley Silt brickearth at Markham Street and Square south to Smith Terrace, and lying either side of Fulham Road by Elm Park Gardens east to the Royal Marsden hospital. A wide band of alluvium along the eastern side of the parish marks the course of the Westbourne down to the Thames by Ranelagh Gardens, and a narrow band on the west marks Counter's Creek, widening out at the southern end to include the land on the south side of Lots Road. The parish lies beneath the 10 m. contour.[10]

Derivation of Place-name

Chelsea, originally *Chelcehithe* and variants, is apparently an early Anglo-Saxon place-name derived from the Old English words for chalk and a landing-place, the last part in common with nearby Lambeth, Stepney, and Rotherhithe.[11] The usual meaning of a settlement located on such rock is considered unlikely, given the local geology, although a recorded sense of 'coarse sand mixed with pebbles' may well have applied to the Thames foreshore.[12] The other possibility is that Chelsea was a transshipment point for building stone or lime for fertilizer, perhaps brought upriver from Kent, although

1 This Article was written between 1999 and 2003.
2 R. Trench and E. Hillman, *London under London* (1984), 44–6.
3 Below, Settlement, to 1680 (Anglo-Saxon).
4 *VCH Middx*, IX.
5 See fig. 10, map of Chelsea *c.*1700.
6 Faulkner, *Chelsea*, I. 9.
7 *Census*, 1831.
8 CL, tithe award.
9 *Census*, 1901.
10 *British Geological Survey, Solid and Drift edn* (1995), 1:10,000 series, sheet TQ27NE.
11 *P.N. Middx* (E.P.N.S.), 85–6.
12 A.H. Smith, *Place-Name Elements* (1956), I. 77.

2. *Cheyne Walk* c.*1840, from the Old Church looking east to Cadogan Pier*

there is a problem over the derivation from the word for chalk.[1] The older form was still in use in the 16th and 17th centuries, though by this time the form 'Chelsey' was becoming common.

COMMUNICATIONS

THE RIVER THAMES

The Thames, central to Chelsea's development, was probably its earliest means of communication with London and other settlements along the Thames valley, and the river's importance to Chelsea was marked by the number of wharves belonging to private residents, which allowed them to use their own barges to travel along the river. The rector had a wharf next to his rectory in 1388,[2] and in 1399 Master Nicholas Stoket had a wharf in front of his dwelling, formerly that of John Stoket, a local landholder and brewer.[3] Sir Thomas More had acquired a wharf *c.*1525 and kept a barge to travel to Westminster,[4] and the body of John, Lord Bray, was taken by barge to Chelsea church for his funeral in 1557.[5] In 1543–4 the wharves of the queen and the rector both needed repair.[6] Watermen were available for hire for those without a boat of their own, and in 1705 the journey to London by water or by coach took less than an hour.[7]

Ferries

To cross the Thames before 1771, when Battersea Bridge was opened,[8] travellers were carried by watermen or used the ferry. The passage over the Thames at 'Cenlee' mentioned in 1292–3 was perhaps Chelsea,[9] but the earliest positive reference to a passage across at Chelsea was in 1550, named as Chelsea ferry in 1564, when the owners in both cases were William Wylkyns and his wife Alice.[10] Chelsea was included in a list of horse ferries across the Thames in 1592.[11] The ferry was held freely of the manor of Chelsea, and in 1587 the heirs of Francis Bowes owed a quitrent of 10s. a year to the manor for the ferry.[12] It seems likely that the ownership of the ferry escheated to, or was bought by, the Crown as lord of the manor, as prior to 1618 the Crown granted away Chelsea ferry and its landing place, with 9 a. meadow called Thames mead and 47 a. in Kensington, to hold of the king in chief. The grant was probably to Thomas Fiennes, 3rd earl of Lincoln, John Eldred, and Robert

1 *P.N. Middx* (E.P.N.S.), 85–6.
2 WAM 4810, m. 3.
3 WAM 4805, m. 3d.
4 PRO, C 1/540/78; below, Landownership, More.
5 Chelsea Scraps, 603v.
6 PRO, SC 2/188/42–3, SC 2/205/40.
7 John Bowack, quoted in Faulkner, *Chelsea*, I. 406.
8 Below, river crossings.
9 Beaver, *Memorials*, 223.
10 PRO, CP 25/2/61/474/4EDWVIMICH; CP 25/2/171/6ELIZIHIL.
11 Beaver, *Memorials*, 223.
12 BL, Harl. Roll L.26.

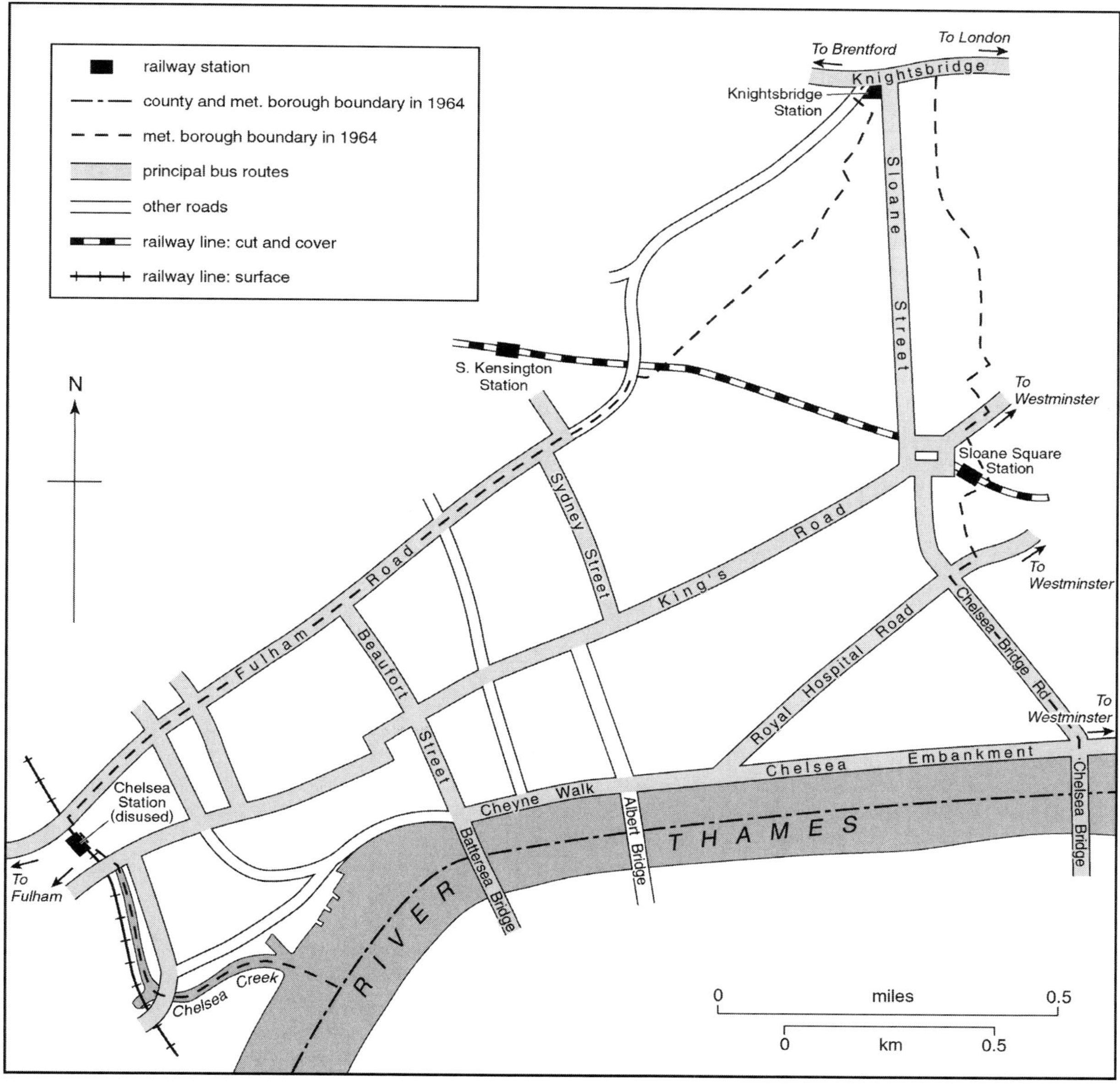

3. *Chelsea Communications, 2002*

Henley, as the three were granted a licence in 1618 to alienate all the property to William Blake.[1] In 1623 William Blake and his wife Mary sold Chelsea ferry and its appurtenances in Chelsea to Oliver St John, 1st Viscount Grandison (d. 1630),[2] who in 1607 had acquired the manor of Battersea, also served by the ferry, through his wife.[3] The ferry and the lands, but not the title, passed to his nephew, Sir John St John, Bt (d. 1648), and to Sir John's grandson Sir John, Bt (d. 1657), whose heir was his uncle Sir Walter St John, Bt (d. 1708). The ferry continued to pass with the estates to Sir Walter's son Sir Henry, created Viscount St John in 1716, to the latter's son Henry, created Viscount Bolingbroke in 1712, and to Bolingbroke's nephew Frederick, 2nd Viscount Bolingbroke, who in 1763 sold the Battersea estate including the ferry to John Spencer, Viscount Spencer (Earl Spencer from 1765).[4]

The right to operate the ferry was leased out by the owners. In 1665 Thomasina Cootes, widow of a waterman, left the ferry and boats to her father Laurence Chase,[5] and in 1668 the lessee was Samuel Chase.[6] In 1696 and 1704 Bartholomew Nutt paid rates for the ferry; John Medley paid in 1735, and George Ludlow in 1750.[7]

1 PRO, C 66/2193, no. 78; below, Landownership, later ests (Blake).
2 PRO, CP 25/2/324/21JASITRIN.
3 *Complete Peerage*, VI. 74.
4 GEC, *Complete Baronetage*, I. 24; *Complete Peerage*, II. 208; *VCH Surrey*, IV. 12.
5 PRO, PROB 11/319, f. 161v.
6 PRO, C 8/161/113.
7 Vestry orders, 1662–1718, f. 67v.; Poor rate bks, 1728–42, f. 388; 1748–51 (not pag.); BL, Add. MS 2934, f. 17.

By statute the Corporation of the City of London appointed watermen to oversee all wherrymen and watermen on the Thames as far as Windsor, and in 1668 Sir Walter St John and Samuel Chase brought a suit against the City's appointees and about 34 watermen of Chelsea, who claimed that the plaintiffs' exclusive rights to operate the ferry from Chelsea's 'Ferry Place', opposite Danvers Street, to Battersea only extended to the horseboat and not to footboats. They also claimed that the ancient ferry was near the Crown on the Chelsea side, and that long before the ferry there was a dock for dredging and trimming boats used by watermen, perhaps referring to the public draw dock at the east end of Cheyne Walk. The charges at that time were 1d. for every horse or beast and horseman in the horseboat, and ½d. for everyone on foot.[1] A ferrymen's petition in 1726 for compensation for loss of business to the proposed Putney Bridge was rejected.[2] In 1808 and 1812 plying places on the river where watermen could pick up passengers included a stretch under the trees opposite the Yorkshire Grey by Manor Street, where there were wooden stairs and a good causeway, opposite Lawrence Street where there were small stairs, and the original ferry place opposite Danvers Street and the White Hart, where there were 8-ft wide brick stairs alongside a brick wall and a 20-ft wide dock.[3]

Steam and Motor Boat Services

A steamboat service serving Chelsea seems to have operated by 1816, and boomed in popularity in the 1830s.[4] Chelsea was served by the London and Westminster Steamboat Company *c.*1835, the Iron Steamboat Company from 1837, the Chelsea Steamboat Company from 1841, and the City (or Citizen) Steamboat Company from 1845. Traffic peaked in the early 1840s, with intense competition between the companies: in 1844 eight steamboats travelled between London Bridge and Chelsea, four times an hour, and traffic was increasing. Chelsea vestry saw steamboats – quick, cheap, and comfortable – as potentially the common transport of residents of the densely-populated shore, but by the 1850s improved railways and roads had begun the decline in both commuter and recreational traffic on the river. Despite benefits to navigation and the improved access to riverside thoroughfares for steamboat passengers brought about by the creation of the embankment in the 1870s,[5] winter services were gradually withdrawn in the 1880s, and commuting was negligible. Successive companies failed to maintain the service, which was minimal by 1900, although a summer service continued.[6] Under the Thames River Steamboat Service Act the LCC operated a service from 1905, but no winter service was offered in 1906–7 and the service was not restarted in 1908. Subsequently river travel was sporadic and recreational, primarily by private initiative.[7] In 1914 steamers, presumably privately operated, called at Cadogan and Carlyle piers.[8] A request in 1933 for a service by the London Passenger Transport Board was unsuccessful,[9] and river services ran only in summer in 1952.[10] In the 1990s, however, the rediscovery of the Thames as a public highway through London led to the introduction of regular motorboat services. In 1992 a private service between Chelsea Harbour (Fulham) and Canary Wharf (Poplar), which called at Cadogan pier every 20 minutes, proved more successful than the Festival of Britain boats had been in 1951 which, underpowered, could not fulfil a timetable. Even so, the backers soon failed,[11] but another service from Cadogan pier to Westminster and the City began in 2000.

4. *Cadogan Pier with a passenger steamboat with the Pier Hotel* (left)

Piers

There was insufficient accommodation on the riverbank for the boats in the 1840s and piers were built into the Thames to accommodate them. Cremorne Gardens had its own landing place, with a regular service from London.[12] In 1840 Old Swan pier and Chelsea Mall pier served the steamboats, but by 1841 Earl Cadogan had erected Cadogan pier in Cheyne Walk, designed by N. Handford, catering for a large number of summer passengers.[13] In 1846 Chelsea improvement commission believed that additional piers were still needed,[14] but provision for piers in plans for the embankment *c.*1852

1 PRO, C 8/161/113.
2 J. Pudney, *Crossing London's River* (1972), 44.
3 Guildhall MSS 6327, 6413A.
4 Except where stated, section based on F.L. Dix, *Royal River Highway* (1985), 50, 60, 63–4, 66–7, 77, 80, 82, 86, 89, 99–100, 105–6, 110; *2nd Rep. Com. Met. Improvements*, 4, 16, 18, and p. lxiv; *Handbk to Chelsea* (1840), 4 (CL, SR 254/1); *5th Rep. Com. Met. Improvements*, 10, 13, 18.
5 MBW, *Chelsea Embankment 1874* (copy at LMA), 4–5, 9–10.
6 e.g. *PO Dir. London* (1902), II. 3139.
7 *Hist. London Transport*, II. 330–3.
8 E.W. Carter, *Chelsea* (1914), 20.
9 *Chelsea Soc. Rep.* (1933–4), 27, 29.
10 Chelsea MB, *Official Guide* [1952], 57.
11 *Chelsea Soc. Reps* (1992), 23, 35; (1993), 21–2.
12 Chelsea cuttings: Cremorne Gardens (pamphlet, 25 Mar. 1982); Thompson, *Map* (1836).
13 *Handbk to Chelsea* (1840), 32; ibid. (1841), p. iv and frontis. (CL, SR 185); Chelsea cuttings: Cadogan pier (drawings 1841); see Fig. 4.
14 Improvement com. mins, 1845–6, pp. 309, 311, 315–16.

was not put into effect.[1] Another pier was built east of Battersea Bridge by 1865,[2] known as Chelsea and later as Carlyle pier; it was presumably rebuilt following completion of the embankment in 1874.[3] Cadogan pier was also rebuilt *c.*1875 to accommodate Albert Bridge.[4] By 1894 Victoria pier had been put up near the Royal Hospital, just outside the parish's eastern boundary,[5] but was disused in 1901.[6] The LCC acquired Cadogan pier from the Thames Conservancy Board and Carlyle pier from the Thames Steamboat Company and repaired them in 1905; passengers travelling higher up the river changed boats at Cadogan pier, but services operated from Carlyle for only a few months.[7] All three piers survived in 1963,[8] but only Cadogan pier still stood in 1996 when it was bought by Cadogan Pier (Chelsea) Limited from the Port of London Authority.[9] Public and private charter services operated from it in 2000.

THE MAIN ROADS AND THEIR BRIDGES

Royal Hospital Road

Chelsea village was reached from the east by a road from Ebury and Westminster, presumably that mentioned in 1433.[10] It ran to the riverside, then turned northward by Chelsea church by 1620 before resuming a western course to Fulham; that latter part was later taken over by the King's Road.[11] After the Royal Hospital was built, the route in front was diverted northward, westward, and southward around Burton's Court in 1687–8:[12] the diversion was unpopular and inhabitants claimed a right of way across the Court. When that footway was closed at night in 1761, it added half a mile for pedestrians, and from 1762 Burton's Court was periodically perambulated. There were concerns about the danger of the longer route in 1785, and the Colonnade of the south front of the hospital was used as a public thoroughfare at night, to the annoyance of the Royal Hospital in 1804. In 1816 a new footpath across Burton's Court replaced the existing one, and public use by night of the Colonnade – which the vestry considered safer – was discontinued. However, the desire for a carriage road on that route was not fulfilled until the 1840s.[13] The closure of the road across Burton's Court in the 1680s meant that by 1836 much traffic to London used the longer route via Sloane Street and Knightsbridge.[14] The Metropolis Improvements Commission recommended re-opening a route between Royal Hospital Row and Paradise Row, and this was undertaken by Chelsea improvement commission in 1846: the road was called Queen's Road, later changed to Royal Hospital Road.[15]

Bridges The road from Westminster to Chelsea village was carried over the boundary by a stone bridge, documented from 1587;[16] it is probably the stone bridge which the vestry paid to mend in 1682.[17] By the early 19th century a single-arch brick bridge in Grosvenor Row (later Pimlico Road) had replaced the stone one. There was also a bridge over the watercourse at the Cheshire Cheese public house; to the south, a bridge built by the proprietors of Ranelagh gardens was by 1826 inaccessible for public use.[18]

Another stone bridge, recorded from 1409, is identified as carrying the highway across the western boundary, later Bull bridge or Stanley bridge on the King's Road.[19] A new bridge stood there at Sandy End by 1717,[20] in 1826 a single-arch brick bridge said to have been built by the Crown, who had maintained it to that date.[21] Under its Act Kensington Canal Company completed a new brick bridge in 1826.[22] In 1908–9 Chelsea MB contributed to the LCC's reconstruction of Stanley Bridge, which by then also crossed the railway.[23]

Fulham Road

London's major route westward bypassed Chelsea's northern tip at Knightsbridge,[24] but was connected to the parish by the Fulham Road, which coincided with all but the easterly stretch of the northern parish boundary and ran through the settlement of Little Chelsea.[25] The way from Fulham to London, presumably that road, was mentioned in 1372.[26] Parts of the road had various names, for example Little Chelsea Street in 1671,[27] while the section near Stamford bridge was Bridge Street in 1811.[28] The highway was connected to Chelsea village by one principal north–south route, Church Lane, and its continuation to Kensington (later Old Church Street)

1 LMA, MBW/OW/CB6/1.
2 LMA, MR/UP 831.
3 Chelsea Misc. 1042.
4 LMA, MR/UP 724; *Ann. Rep. of MBW* (Parl. Papers, 1877 (225), LXXI), p. 17.
5 Old OS Map, London 88 (1894 edn).
6 *Builder*, 2 Nov. 1901, p. 383.
7 LCC, *Rep.* (1905–6), 162–5; LMA, LCC/CE/RB/3/15.
8 *Bartholomew's Reference Atlas of Gtr London* (1963).
9 Chelsea cuttings: Cadogan pier (planning application 1997).
10 *Cal. Close*, 1429–35, 286–7.
11 Beaver, *Memorials*, 131, 311, 313; below, King's Rd.
12 Along the later Franklin's Row; St Leonard's Terr.; and Durham Pl./Ormonde Gate.
13 Hamilton, *Map* (1664–1717); Dean, *Royal Hosp.* 83–4, 230–1; Vestry orders, 1745–71, pp. 245–6, 266, 280, 303; 1771–90, f. 14; 1809–22, pp. 203-5, 213; below, Loc. Govt, pub. svces (pub. order).
14 Vestry mins, 1833–9, p. 146.
15 *2nd Rep. Com. Met. Improvements*, 12–13, 32, 37–8; improvement com. mins, 1845–6, pp. 4, 25, 91, 130, 133–5, 157–8, 177–80, 212–13, 327.
16 BL, Harl. Roll L.26; ibid. Add. Ch. 18205; *Acts of PC* 1626, 179, 269.
17 Vestry orders, 1662–1718, ff. 29, 38v.
18 LMA, WCS PR/37; *Rep. on Bridges in Middx*, 175–6, 183.
19 C.J. Fèret, *Fulham Old and New* (1900), II. 86, 226.
20 Hamilton, *Map* (1664–1717).
21 *Rep. on Bridges in Middx*, 182–3.
22 5 Geo. IV, c. 65 (Local and Personal); Faulkner, *Chelsea*, I. 54.
23 LMA, LCC/CL/IMP/1/22; LCC/CE/RB/3/4.
24 *London Topog. Rec.* VIII. 5.
25 Hamilton, *Map* (1664–1717).
26 WAM 4816.
27 *Survey of London*, XLI. 162.
28 BL, Add. MS 31326.

mentioned in 1566.[1] By 1717 another route (later Milman's Street and Park Walk) also extended from the highway at Little Chelsea to the river, and an irregular route ran from Fulham Road to the Royal Hospital via Blacklands.[2]

In 1672 the Fulham road had long suffered neglect, but in 1673 Chelsea's inhabitants claimed they could not make repairs owing to the wet season.[3] In 1687 two surveyors were amerced for not mending the highway from Queen's Elm, presumably to Stamford bridge. In 1689 the inhabitants repaired the highway between Queen's Elm and the King's Gate (presumably between Fulham Road and King's Road) and between Queen's Elm and the Dog Kennel after being presented.[4] By 1829 the high road had 'become a great thoroughfare',[5] presumably reflecting increased traffic on this route of long-standing importance.

Stamford Bridge 'Samfordbregge', mentioned in 1410 and referring to a sand ford, carried Fulham Road over Chelsea's western boundary. From 1590 the spurious Stamford and variants occur, and it was sometimes known as Little Chelsea bridge. Repair of the bridge was to be shared equally by the bishop of London and the lord of Chelsea in 1582.[6] In the early 17th century Sir Walter Cope, who lived in Kensington, enlarged the waterway,[7] and Stamford bridge (or 'two bridges') was widened. In 1635 inhabitants of Fulham and Chelsea were ordered to repair the bridge but thought that the lord of Kensington and the bishop were responsible, having repaired it for some 40 years;[8] in 1718 inhabitants complained of its condition.[9] It was rebuilt with a single arch of brick and stone in 1762 by Kensington turnpike trust, with contributions from the manorial lords of Fulham and Earl's Court, and was maintained thereafter by the trust. The Kensington canal proprietors failed to secure a contribution for rebuilding the ruinous bridge in 1824 as it was not a county bridge,[10] but it was rebuilt when the canal was made in 1828.[11] Stamford bridge was rebuilt again in 1860–2 and later partly reconstructed.[12]

The King's Road

In 1590 a causeway was to be made at Bloody Gate, a footway into the parish from the east. Under Charles II the king's private road, later simply known as King's Road, was formed from Westminster via Chelsea to Hampton Court along the route of this footpath through the fields, taking over an existing road to Fulham at the western end of Chelsea. King's Road was briefly opened to the inhabitants in 1718 while Stamford Bridge was under repair.[13] In 1719 Sir Hans Sloane led property owners in successfully petitioning for access via King's Road, which had been agreed when the road was formed but denied some years before. The Surveyor of the King's Private Roads argued that 50 to 60 vehicles using the road daily without right had inconvenienced 'persons of quality' under his predecessor; the inhabitants disclaimed knowledge of these 'foreigners'.[14] Tollhouses built in 1720 included three in Chelsea (north of the Royal Hospital; at Church Lane, later Old Church Street; and at World's End); three years later the keepers petitioned for payment.[15] Passes to use the road were issued,[16] and many counterfeits made, so that by 1783 the road was hardly private: the king had also granted permission for local roads to be cut into it, usage could not be limited to gentlemen ticket-holders, and commercial traffic increased, including hackney and stage coaches in the early 19th century. Scuffles between travellers and gatekeepers occurred frequently at junctions between royal and public routes.[17] A proposal to straighten the line of the road by Millman Row and otherwise improve it in the early 1820s was not carried out, and the three bars also remained.[18] From *c.*1827 the road went unrepaired, and as it was recognized that the road had become public, responsibility was transferred from the Crown to the parish in 1830, which resulted in heavy expense. Controversial attempts by the Grosvenor Place trustees (Westm.) to limit commercial traffic (including omnibuses and stagecoaches) by a bar just outside the eastern boundary of Chelsea, inconveniencing the inhabitants, continued until 1836.[19] The gatehouse of 1720 north of the Royal Hospital was demolished in 1833,[20] and from 1843 the vestry, and from 1845 to 1855 the Chelsea improvement commission, solicited funds from the Crown to widen the stretch near the Royal Military Asylum which was too narrow for carriages to pass and lacked a footway: the resulting tendency of pedestrians to keep on the opposite side was said to disadvantage shopkeepers along the entire south side. The work was in progress in 1861.[21] By 1869 the formerly narrow King's Road had been

1 PRO, C 66/1021, m. 27.
2 Hamilton, *Map* (1664–1717).
3 Cal. Middx Sess. Bks, V. 183; ibid. VI. 12.
4 Faulkner, *Chelsea*, I. 42; II. 156, 158–61; LMA, MJ/SP 1689 Dec/12–13.
5 Faulkner, *Chelsea*, I. 138.
6 Fèret, *Fulham*, II. 225–6.
7 *DNB.*
8 PRO, E 192/14/16 (order for repairs, 1635), E 192/15/3 (presentment, n.d.), E 192/15/8 (jury's verdict, n.d.).
9 *Cal. Treas. Bks*, 1718, 530.
10 *Rep. on Bridges in Middx*, 181–2; LMA, MJ/SPB/132.
11 Faulkner, *Chelsea*, I. 138.
12 *Survey of London*, XLI. 241.
13 *Cal. Treas. Bks*, 1718, 530, 540.
14 Faulkner, *Chelsea*, I. 43–8.
15 *Cal. Treas. Papers*, 1720–8, 202–3; PRO, MPE 1/482.
16 Examples at CL, SR 205p, 205s (1731, 1737).
17 *Hist. King's Works*, V. 459–60; VI. 635.
18 PRO, MR 1/1519.
19 *A few plain facts relative to obstructed thoroughfare of King's Road* (1836) (CL, SR 259/6); H. Hobhouse, *Thos Cubitt* (1995 edn), 126–7; Chelsea Scraps, 412; Vestry mins, 1833–9, pp. 61–2, 74–5, 98, 156–8.
20 Dean, *Royal Hosp.* 85.
21 Vestry mins, 1843–56, pp. 4–6; Improvement com. mins, 1845–6, pp. 5, 26, 224–5, 237; PRO, WORK 6/357/3.

5. *Old Battersea Bridge and Chelsea's riverside houses, before the embankment was built. The buildings and trees of Cremorne Gardens can be seen in the distance (*right*)*

transformed by numerous improvements.[1] The road, occupied in the early 19th century by few businesses except nurseries,[2] became the centre of building and commercial development in the parish,[3] altering the focus of the settlement away from the river.[4]

Bloody or Grosvenor bridge[5] The existing Blandel or Bloody bridge, presumably so-called by 1590, was reconstructed to carry the King's Road over the Westbourne. The single-arch brick structure built by the Office of Works before 1723 survived in 1826; it was later known as Grosvenor bridge.[6]

Turnpike Trust

An Act of 1725 formed a trust, usually known as the Kensington trust, which from 1726 maintained Chelsea's roads from Knightsbridge to Fulham ferry (Fulham Road); Westminster to Chelsea ferry (later Royal Hospital Road); and Chelsea church to Kensington (later Old Church Street);[7] turnpike gates were erected at Queen's Elm.[8] In 1728 the trust maintained almost two miles in Chelsea and around a quarter of a mile at the Royal Hospital, leaving over a mile of Chelsea's roads outside its care. The trustees compounded with Chelsea for £50 and with the Royal Hospital for £8 in lieu of statute work on the roads.[9] The trust's attempts to dig gravel on Chelsea Common, in dispute from 1726, were thwarted in 1736 by Sir Hans Sloane and other proprietors.[10] A further Act renewed the trust from 1741 and added Blacklands Lane (later Draycott Avenue), because of its poor condition caused by increased use by carriages.[11] The trust did not meet all the needs of the parish regarding the roads however. In 1770 the vestry had to get the trust to remedy the bad condition of the turnpiked roads, and in the 1780s Hans Town residents were unsuccessful in getting the trust to take over Sloane Street, though from 1795 the trust paid a composition to the Hans Town commissioners for its repair.[12] In 1794 the parish considered demanding concessions including watering to counter a feared increase in tolls, but in the event did not oppose the trust's Bill.[13] In 1825 the trust had gates at Chelsea Bunhouse, Queen's Elm, and Little Chelsea, and under its Act of 1825 set up a new gate in Royal Hospital Row (later part of Royal Hospital Road).[14] A proposal to replace the trust in 1821 was opposed by Chelsea vestry which was satisfied with its management,[15] but under an Act of 1826 the Metropolitan Roads Commission (MRC) succeeded the trust.[16] A Kensington trust post survived in Godfrey Street in 2000.

In 1838 the vestry wanted the MRC to remove the toll gate in Royal Hospital Row,[17] in 1841 claiming that

1 Bryan, *Chelsea*, 160, 166, 169, 176, 209.
2 Ibid., 169; PRO, MR 1/1519.
3 Pevsner, *London NW.* 582. 4 *Survey of London*, II, p. xv.
5 For name: below, Loc. Govt, pub. svces (pub. order).
6 *Rep. on Bridges in Middx*, 175; Faulkner, *Chelsea*, I. 43–5, ii. 139, 353; *Middx and Herts. N&Q*, II. 145, 194–6.
7 12 Geo. I, c. 37. 8 *Kens. Soc. Ann. Rep.* (1969–70), 36.
9 P. Neil, 'Kens. Turnpike Trust', 15 (copy at KL).
10 Faulkner, *Chelsea*, II. 57–9.
11 14 Geo. II, c. 16. For the trusts' roads: CL, maps 10, 13; BL, Add. MSS 31326–7.
12 Vestry orders, 1745–71, p. 344; 1771–90, ff. 170v., 173–173v.; *Kens. Soc. Ann. Rep.* (1969–70), 41.
13 Vestry orders, 1790–1809, pp. 48, 59–60.
14 *Rep. of Sel. Cttee on Metropolis Turnpike Trusts* (Parl. Papers, 1825 (355), V), p. 55; 6 Geo. IV, c. 157; E. Ffooks, 'Kens. Turnpike Trust', 13 (TS at KL).
15 Vestry orders, 1809–22, pp. 380–1.
16 7 Geo. IV, c. 142 (Local and Personal).
17 Vestry mins, 1833–9, pp. 216–17.

traffic avoiding the gates there and at Queen's Elm increased the cost of highway repairs.[1] The Hans Town commission argued in 1844 that the Royal Hospital Row bar diverted traffic onto its roads.[2] Turnpike gates were removed throughout the parish in 1845.[3]

RIVER CROSSINGS

Battersea Bridge

Battersea Bridge, the first road to cross the Thames from Chelsea, was built after an Act was obtained in 1766 under John, Earl Spencer.[4] After a delay apparently caused by disputes among riparian landowners,[5] a wooden bridge 28 ft wide, paid for by subscription, was built by Mr Phillips, carpenter to George III, to Henry Holland's designs, opening in 1771 for foot passengers and in 1772 for carriages.[6] A commentator opined in 1771 that a toll-free stone bridge constructed by the Crown would be preferable to the 'mean' wooden bridge of an 'avaricious' proprietor.[7] The site, west of the ferry landing near Church Lane (later Old Church Street), was thought preferable for river navigation,[8] though in 1842 *Punch* thought that the bridge had been built with little regard to those passing under it.[9] Two piers were later removed to improve navigation.[10] The Battersea proprietors were compensated when Vauxhall Bridge (1811–16) was constructed, and they opposed proposals to remove tolls on Chelsea Bridge in the 1850s.[11] They secured a requirement that the Albert Bridge company acquire and maintain Battersea Bridge when Albert Bridge opened (1873).[12] Under the Metropolis Toll Bridges Act the MBW freed bridges including Battersea in 1879.[13] In 1883 vehicular use was discontinued.[14] Under Acts of 1881 and 1884 the MBW was empowered to erect a new bridge:[15] following demolition of the old bridge, construction began in 1887 of the new five-arch structure 40 ft wide, of iron on granite piers, designed by Sir Joseph Bazalgette; it opened in 1890.[16] It remained vulnerable to damage from shipping because of strong currents.[17]

Beaufort Street The Act of 1766 also authorized the creation of approaches to the bridge, probably leading to the building of Beaufort Row *c.*1766, as the bridge was planned in line with it.[18] In 1839 proposed completion of the route between Battersea Bridge and Kensington was to include a road between Camera Street and Fulham Road.[19] In 1845 the bridge proprietors and improvement commission supported that improvement, the latter blaming the inanimate state of some neighbourhoods on its absence.[20]

Chelsea Bridge

Although Chelsea Bridge lay just outside the parish boundary,[21] it is treated here because of its name and significance for parochial communications.[22] Its site may have been an ancient ford.[23] The embankment and connecting road proposed in 1845 stimulated a private initiative for a Thames crossing,[24] also recommended by the Metropolis Improvements Commission, to make Battersea park (Surrey) more accessible. However, an Act of 1846 authorized construction by the Commission of Woods and Forests of a suspension bridge, as being compatible with river navigation. Work on Thomas Page's ornate iron bridge, begun under the Commission of Works in 1851, suffered various interruptions,[25] and Chelsea Bridge, 47 ft wide, opened in 1858. An attempt in 1857 to prevent the imposition of tolls, thought to negate its usefulness, was unsuccessful,[26] but an Act of 1858 for the abolition of foot passenger tolls after payment of the capital and interest was amended in 1875 to allow their abolition on Sundays and certain holidays;[27] all tolls were abolished in 1879.[28] Doubts about the bridge's strength resulted in modifications in 1863–4,[29] and periodic repairs included fixing additional

1 Vestry mins, 1839–43, pp. 226–30, 236, 241–3; Chelsea Scraps, 454.
2 PRO, WORKS 14/3/5: letter, 30 Nov.
3 *The Times*, 12 Nov. 1845.
4 6 Geo. III, c. 66.
5 Chelsea cuttings: Battersea Bridge (*Middx Jnl*, 11/13 July 1771).
6 *Builder*, 2 Nov. 1901, p. 384; Faulkner, *Chelsea*, I. 32. Company recs are at LMA, B/PBB, MBW/BC/B; Battersea Lib. (NRA list 1089); see Fig. 5.
7 Chelsea Misc. 30.
8 LMA, B/PBB/1, pp. 5, 7–8, 13–14.
9 Quoted in M. Searle, *Turnpikes and Toll-bars* [1930], I. 10.
10 *Ann. Rep. of MBW* (Parl. Papers, 1880 Sess. 2 (212), LXII), p. 82.
11 Pevsner, *London S.* 713–14; LMA, O/265/1.
12 27 & 28 Vic. c. 235 (Local and Personal); below, this section.
13 40 & 41 Vic. c. 99 (Local); MBW, *Programme on opening bridges 1879* (copy at LMA).
14 Rest of para. based, unless otherwise stated, on: MBW, *Opening Hammersmith Bridge and laying memorial stone in Battersea Bridge 1887*, 8–9; LMA, MBW 2594, MR/UP 1464; *Ann. Rep. of MBW* (Parl. Papers, 1884 (186), LXVIII), p. 15.
15 44 & 45 Vic. c. 192 (Local); 47 & 48 Vic. c. 228 (Local).
16 *Builder*, 26 July 1890, p. 67.
17 Chelsea cuttings: Battersea Bridge (*Evening Standard*, 8 Feb. 1993).
18 LMA, B/PBB/1, p. 5.
19 LMA, MR/UP 197.
20 Improvement com. mins, 1845–6, pp. 102–3.; Chelsea Scraps, 466; cf. PRO, RAIL 989/27.
21 It lay partly within Chelsea MB.
22 An inland Chelsea bridge of *c.*1724 (*Rep. on Bridges in Middx*, 177) lay in Westm.
23 LCC, *Opening of Chelsea Bridge 1937*, 5.
24 *2nd Rep. Com. Met. Improvements*, 13, 16; Chelsea Misc. 1027.
25 9 & 10 Vic. c. 39 (Local and Personal); *5th Rep. Com. Met. Improvements*, 4–6, 13–14, 21–2; *Reps. to Com. of Works by Page and Pennethorne* (1856), 9–13 (copy at CL).
26 *The Times*, 31 July 1857; Chelsea Misc. 1033. It was sometimes known as Victoria Bridge.
27 21 & 22 Vic. c. 66 (Local and Personal); 38 & 39 Vic. c. 177 (Local).
28 Above, Battersea Bridge.
29 PRO, MT 6/58/3.

chains in 1880; weight restrictions were imposed. The pinnacles on the towers were removed in 1921–2. Usage almost doubled between 1914 and 1929 to over 12,600 vehicles in one day's survey. The royal commission on cross-river traffic in 1926 recommended rebuilding to accommodate all traffic: in 1931 the LCC improvements committee advised reconstruction to give six lanes, and a Ministry of Transport contribution was eventually agreed for a four-lane bridge. Demolition proceeded in 1935. The new self-anchoring steel suspension bridge, 83 ft wide, opened in 1937, a plain design engineered by Rendel, Palmer, & Tritton, with the LCC architect G. Topham Forrest (succeeded by E.P. Wheeler in 1935); the Royal Fine Art Commission was also consulted.[1] Circa 1961 the bridge carried *c.*16,000 vehicles a day.[2]

Chelsea Bridge Road Following the Metropolis Improvements Commission's recommendation in 1845 for a road to the proposed embankment,[3] an Act of 1846 empowered the Commissioners of Woods and Forests to form it,[4] but the line was only prepared in 1854, to join the embankment at Chelsea Bridge, and the road, originally called Bridge Road, was laid out in 1857–8 to James Pennethorne's designs.[5] The vestry took over its section of the road in 1862 following unsuccessful demands that the Office of Works pave the footpath.[6]

Albert Bridge

Proposals for a bridge between Cheyne Walk and Battersea were made from at least 1842,[7] but a scheme of 1843 was apparently transferred to form the original proposal for Chelsea Bridge.[8] The proposal to build Albert Bridge eventually secured its Act in 1864, although further Acts were necessary in 1869, 1871, and 1873;[9] construction was delayed by arrangements for the embankment.[10] Work progressed from 1870 on an earlier plan for an ornate three-span iron bridge by R.M. Ordish, supported by rigid bands radiating from the towers, according to his patented system; it opened in 1873.[11] Tolls were abolished in 1879.[12] Alterations planned by Sir Joseph Bazalgette, which involved adding new chains, were carried out by the MBW in 1887.[13] A five-ton weight limit was imposed in 1935 and a two-ton limit *c.*1970. Proposed replacement by the LCC met opposition in 1957, and the GLC's proposal to prop the central span provoked debate about whether the bridge should be replaced, maintained for motor traffic, or reserved for pedestrians. Supporting piers were inserted in 1972.[14] A public inquiry of 1974 considered closure to vehicles,[15] but the bridge stayed open.

NEW MAJOR ROUTES

Thames Embankment

The riverbank was an uncertain responsibility in 1685. Disputes between the manorial lord and tenants, parish, turnpike trust, and neighbouring householders often left the walls out of repair. In 1815 the vestry required the lord and neighbouring freeholders to repair the dangerous wall opposite Lindsey Row (later part of Cheyne Walk) and Millman Row (later Milman's Street). Although the turnpike trust's claim that the lord of the manor was responsible for repairs was upheld in 1822, the question was not finally resolved. By 1829, however, the walls were repaired and the trust had improved the road and paved some footpaths. A long-standing scheme to widen Cheyne Walk by extending the embankment into the river, which would include removal of buildings south of Lombard Street and Duke Street (east of Battersea Bridge), was again considered in 1829 but not carried out.[16] In 1836 the vestry suggested improving the route from Battersea Bridge via the riverside and Royal Hospital to Westminster, as communication from lower Chelsea was inconvenient and lowered property values, and also suggested a new riverside route between Chelsea and Fulham, proposals which had local support.[17]

A proposal was drawn up in 1839 for embanking the north shore of the Thames between Vauxhall Bridge and Battersea Bridge, which would aid navigation and sanitation, provide a riverside road improving communications and opportunities for recreation, and benefit neighbouring areas. This was considered by the Metropolis Improvements Commission in 1843, and plans prepared by its engineer, Thomas Page, in 1845. Chelsea vestry supported the proposal, believing the embankment, which it wanted continued to Fulham, would stimulate other improvements.[18] The Commissioners of Woods and Forests were empowered to form

1 *Inst. of Civil Engineers Jnl* (1937–8), 384–5, 421, 432, 441 (copy at LMA); LCC, *Opening of Chelsea Bridge 1937*, 8, 10–13.

2 *Chelsea Soc. Rep.* (1961), 52.

3 *2nd Rep. Com. Met. Improvements*, 13, 21, and plan 1. For embankment see below.

4 9 & 10 Vic. c. 39 (Local and Personal).

5 *Reps. by Page and Pennethorne*, 12–13; G. Tyack, *Sir James Pennethorne* (1992), 66, 112.

6 PRO, WORK 6/139/3. Southern stretch was outside the par.

7 LMA, MR/UP 215.

8 LMA, MBW/OW/CB6/29; *5th Rep. Com. Met. Improvements*, 14.

9 LMA, MR/UP 667, 668, 724; MBW/OW/CB6/7; 27 & 28 Vic. c. 235 (Local and Personal); MBW, *Programme on opening bridges 1879* (copy at LMA), 9.

10 Below, this section.

11 Chelsea Misc. 1034; PRO, BT 356/1183; G. Phillips, *Thames Crossings* (1981), 192–3.

12 Above, Battersea Bridge.

13 LMA, MBW 2820/19, MBW 2535/774; *Ann. Rep. of MBW* (Parl. Papers, 1888 (159), LXXXVII), p. 19.

14 Chelsea cuttings: Albert Bridge (1957, 1970–3); *Chelsea Soc. Reps* (1957), 7–11; (1971), 9–10; (1972), 24–5.

15 Recs listed at LMA, GLC/TD/TP/4.

16 Faulkner, *Chelsea*, I. 30–2, 170; Chelsea Misc. 1681–3; Vestry orders, 1809–22, pp. 133–4, 201.

17 Vestry mins, 1833–9, pp. 145–7; Chelsea Scraps, 359; Chelsea cuttings: roads (cutting 14 Feb. 1838).

18 *2nd Rep. Com. Met. Improvements*, 3–8, 16, 23, and pp. lxiv–lxv and plan 1.

the embankment, but as agreement was not reached with some proprietors the work was deferred.[1] The Commissioners of Works were substituted in 1852, but only empowered to construct an embankment as far as Chelsea Hospital's western boundary.[2] Chelsea improvement commission, however, campaigned for the full scheme, highlighting the inadequacy of communications, which were blamed for the defective condition of much of Chelsea, and arguing that the parish's improvement Act had been founded on the expectation of the full embankment.[3] The partial embankment was made *c.*1853–7; foul mudbanks remained west of Battersea Bridge in 1859.[4] The embankment terminated with a turning place (which survived in 2001) in front of the Royal Hospital, just inside the parish boundary.

The MBW pressed to extend the embankment to Battersea Bridge, resulting in the Thames Embankment (Chelsea) Act, 1868. Engineered by Joseph William Bazalgette, the new embankment was built 1871–4, reclaiming 9½ acres from the river and extending three quarters of a mile with a 70 foot-wide road and river wall faced with hammer-dressed granite. The original route survives as Cheyne Walk. It transformed the riverside, involving the demolition of buildings south of Duke Street and Lombard Street (including Arch House which spanned the latter), and the removal of wharves and stairs: the MBW made three new sets of stairs *c.*1875 on the river wall in lieu of former landing places.[5] When it opened, the embankment became an agreeable promenade for carriages and pedestrians,[6] but in separating Chelsea from the river it altered the focus of the parish and by the early 20th century its creation had become a source of regret.[7]

The vestry made several attempts to get the embankment extended still further: from 1872 they urged the MBW to extend it to Cremorne, and from 1889 they solicited extension by the LCC, to improve the narrow thoroughfare west of Battersea Bridge and remove unhealthy accumulations in the river. A vestry contribution was eventually agreed in 1896, but some inhabitants opposed the plan, and a parliamentary committee rejected it in the LCC (Improvements) Bill of 1897, principally on aesthetic grounds. The vestry continued to support the scheme.[8]

The growth in motor traffic in the 20th century led to proposals for new or enhanced routes through Chelsea, one of them along the riverside. By 1931 the Chelsea Society was concerned by the volume of traffic on the embankment which had become an arterial route through London,[9] but the Bressey report in 1937 advocated its extension to Putney Bridge to relieve other westbound routes in Chelsea and Fulham, a scheme which would have had far wider effects than the one of 1889. The subject again featured in the LCC plan of 1943. In 1951 the borough council's proposal to embank the stretch west of Battersea Bridge towards Lots Road, and perhaps to Fulham, was opposed by the Chelsea Society and others. The council rebuilt the river wall along the existing alignment in 1953–4,[10] but in 1954 it was felt unfair that it should have to maintain roads like Chelsea Embankment, which carried heavy through traffic but were of little local use.[11]

West Cross Route

The growth in motor traffic also led to proposals for a new route on Chelsea's western boundary. From 1951 a west cross route for Greater London was proposed to run north–south near the boundary to relieve Kensington and Chelsea, and from 1965 this was to form the western side of a larger motorway network (Ringway I) projected by the GLC. However, without a Thames crossing it was unacceptable to Chelsea residents, who feared that the traffic would be decanted onto Chelsea Embankment, and after a public inquiry in 1972 concluded that benefits would not justify the detrimental effects, planning permission was refused. A similar scheme in 1978 raised similar fears, but was scrapped in 1981.[12]

PUBLIC ROAD TRANSPORT

Coach Services

In 1822 coaches operated from Chelsea to St Paul's, the Strand, Charing Cross, Fleet Street, and Coventry Street (Leicester Sq.).[13] The caricaturist Thomas Rowlandson drew the Chelsea stagecoach at Paradise Row (later part of Royal Hospital Road) in 1824.[14] In 1825 ten coaches operated on the short stagecoach route from the City which terminated at Chelsea, making 25 return journeys a day.[15] In 1826–7 six operators ran coaches from

1 9 & 10 Vic. c. 39 (Local and Personal); *Reps by Page and Pennethorne*, 5.

2 15 & 16 Vic. c. 71 (Local and Personal).

3 Chelsea Scraps, 769.

4 PRO, WORK 8/60; Chelsea cuttings: Chelsea Embankment (1857); *Builder*, 16 July 1859, pp. 465–6.

5 *Ann. Rep. of MBW* (Parl. Papers, 1876 (290), LXIII), pp. 20, 78.

6 31 & 32 Vic. c. 135 (Local and Personal); Edwards, *London Street Improvements*, 127—9, frontis., and plans following p. 124; MBW, *Chelsea Embankment 1874* (copy at LMA); LMA, MR/UP 831, 855, 876; LMA, MBW 2525; Bignell, *Chelsea 1860–1980*, 57, 60–1, 70–3, 76, 80–4.

7 e.g. *Survey of London*, II, pp. xv–xvi.

8 Edwards, *London Street Improvements*, 261, and plan opposite p. 161; LMA, LCC/CL/IMP/1/80; Chelsea Misc. 37–43.

9 *Chelsea Soc. Reps* (1930–1), 20; (1932–3), 24–5; (1933–4), 19, 21, 23.

10 PRO, MT 39/349; *Chelsea Soc. Reps* (1936–7), 26–7; (1951), 12–13, 37–47; (1954), 23–5.

11 *The Times*, 1 Jan. 1954.

12 Chelsea cuttings: roads, West Cross; *Chelsea Soc. Reps* (1969), 14–21; (1970), 13–28; (1971), 12–16; (1972), 26–32; (1979), 18–19, 25–31.

13 *Pigot's London and Provincial New Commercial Dir.* 1822–3, App. pp. 26, 47.

14 Chelsea Misc. 1519.

15 *Hist. London Transport*, I. 391.

Chelsea, ranging from twice to five times daily.[1] The stagecoaches started from Lawrence Street and Old Church Street, where there was extensive stabling.[2]

Omnibuses

In 1835 two omnibus conductors on a Chancery Lane–Chelsea route fought over the custom of two servant girls.[3] In 1838–9 ten omnibuses were licensed to run between Blackwall and Sloane Street and one between West Ham and Sloane Street; two between Bromley and Chelsea; one each to Bank, Leadenhall Street, and Whitechapel church; and 27 to Mile End Gate.[4] Traffic which in 1830 was carried on by 18 coaches (out and back) making 108 journeys daily was by 1845 operated by 72 omnibuses making 694 journeys.[5] The removal of turnpike gates throughout the parish in 1845 included that at Queen's Elm, enabling omnibuses to proceed beyond Brompton to Little Chelsea.[6]

The Man in the Moon was the starting place for the Chelsea and Brompton omnibuses, also allowed to wait at the Goat in Boots (Little Chelsea) and at the Cricketers (Cheyne Walk).[7] In 1847 the improvement commission allowed the Hoxton and Holborn omnibuses to start from the Colvill tavern (King's Road).[8] By 1857 omnibuses to Chelsea ran every five minutes from Hoxton, Bethnal Green, and Bank, via Fleet Street and Piccadilly; and from Angel (Islington) via New (later Euston) Road and Regent Street.[9]

In 1856 68 omnibuses were delivered to the London General Omnibus Company (L.G.O.C.) for routes having Chelsea or Sloane Street as a terminus. The L.G.O.C. had a depot and stabling at Chelsea, where in 1857–8 large-scale processing of horse feed began,[10] and also several cab-yards in Lawrence Street in 1900.[11] L.G.O.C. premises at the east end of Lots Road dated from 1894.[12] In 1952 it also had a training school and catering department in Milman's Street.[13]

In 1911 the L.G.O.C. ran three routes along Fulham Road (nos 5, 14, 15) and two along King's Road (nos 11, 19). In 1913 there were also buses along Edith Grove, Sydney Street, Oakley Street, and along the Embankment to Battersea Bridge, and by 1930 additions ran along Royal Hospital Road. Nine daytime routes served Chelsea in 1937.[14] From *c.*1987 the C1 minibus service between Westminster and High Street Kensington ran via Sloane Square and Knightsbridge.[15] Eleven routes served Chelsea in 1993.[16]

Trams

Tramways were not introduced when first suggested,[17] and in 1878 the vestry opposed proposals for various routes through Chelsea: local opinion was particularly against the Chelsea Embankment and Royal Hospital Road route, fearing noise, damage to roads and annoyance to other users, and the impact on residences and recreational use of the embankment.[18] Further abortive proposals were made in the 1880s.[19] The LCC were empowered to construct a tramway from Battersea to the junction of Beaufort Street and King's Road in 1909: lines were laid over Battersea Bridge and the electrified route, no. 34, operated from 1911. In 1933 weekday services to and from south London operated about every four minutes.[20] In 1937 the London Passenger Transport Board sought powers to extend the route, for use by trolleybuses, to Fulham Road, returning via residential roads. Residents and Chelsea MB opposed the scheme, but an alternative via Paultons Square and Danvers Street was also unpopular and the scheme was dropped.[21] Trams continued to operate until the no. 45 motorbus replaced route 34 in 1950.[22]

CANAL AND RAILWAYS

Kensington Canal

Counter's Creek, also known as Chelsea Creek, the New Cut River, or Bull Creek, was the parish's western boundary.[23] Sir Walter Cope widened the river, presumably while living at Kensington, 1607–14, to the inhabitants' benefit,[24] and in 1673 Chelsea landowners were presented for failing to scour the watercourse, used by vessels from the Thames.[25] Canalization of the creek by a private company was authorized under Acts of 1824 and 1826, and the Kensington canal opened in 1828 with capacity for craft of 100 tons.[26] However traffic was poor,

1 *Pigot's London and Provincial New Commercial Dir.* 1826–7, 409.
2 Bryan, *Chelsea*, 90.
3 *The Times*, 12 Aug. 1835.
4 *Hist. London Transport*, I. 37–8, 393–4, 403.
5 Chelsea Scraps, 466.
6 *The Times*, 12 Nov. 1845.
7 Improvement com. mins, 1845–6, pp. 67, 81, 85, 97, 104, 146, 164, 166, 190.
8 Improvement com. mins, 1846–8, p. 106.
9 *PO Dir. London* (1857), 2416.
10 *Hist. London Transport*, I. 84, 404.
11 Blunt, *Chelsea*, 35.
12 J. W. Figg, *Hidden Chelsea* (1996), 37.
13 Chelsea MB, *Official Guide* [1952], 82.
14 *Hist. London Transport*, II. 169, 230; LCC, *Municipal Map of London* (1913, 1930); Chelsea MB, *Official Guide* [1937], 54.
15 *Chelsea Soc. Rep.* (1987), 12.
16 *All London Bus Map* (Feb. 1993).
17 e.g. *Ann. Rep. of MBW* (Parl. Papers, 1871 (431), LVII), pp. 45–7. Cf. *Hist. London Transport*, I. 185, 258.
18 Chelsea Misc. 1379–95; CL, map 86; LMA, MR/UP 1207, 1214, 1217.
19 LMA, MR/UP 1312, 1448; *Ann. Rep. of MBW* (Parl. Papers, 1884–5 (186), LXVII), p. 45.
20 9 Edw. VII, c. 75 (Local); *Boro. Guide to Chelsea* [1910], 26; *LCC Tramways Handbk.* (1977), 6, 18, 22, and map.
21 *Chelsea Soc. Rep.* (1936–7), 31, 33; Chelsea cuttings: trolleybuses.
22 *Hist. London Transport*, II. 302; Chelsea cuttings: Battersea Bridge (*Star*, 13 Jan. 1951; *The Times*, 13 Jan. 1951).
23 Fèret, *Fulham*, I. 15–16, 18.
24 *DNB*; PRO, E 192/15/3 (presentment, n.d.), E 192/15/8 (jury's verdict, n.d.).
25 LMA, WCS 332/99.
26 5 Geo. IV, c. 65 (Local and Personal); 7 Geo. IV, c. 96. Acct

and the Birmingham, Bristol, and Thames Junction (after 1840 the West London) Railway was incorporated in 1836 to build a railway line over the northern stretch, outside Chelsea.[1] The company took the canal over, its muddy condition a source of concern. After the West London Extension Railway company was formed in 1859 the canal was transferred to it, and the section north of King's Road was used for the line in 1863 (below). The southern stretch remained in use by businesses with wharves along its banks. It passed to the British Transport Commission after nationalization in 1947. Right of navigation from King's Road southward to the gasworks dock in Fulham was extinguished in 1959, and a dam was formed. From 1963 the remaining stretch was managed by the British Waterways Board, but after 1967 traffic was minimal. The borough council's proposal in 1981 to fill in the derelict stretch between King's Road and the dam provoked opposition,[2] but by 2001 a stretch south of King's Road had been filled.

Railways

The West London railway built 1844 between the Great Western and London and North-Western lines in Willesden and the canal basin at Kensington was not a success, and in 1859 the two companies, with the London and South-Western and the London, Brighton, and South Coast Railway, promoted its extension to Clapham Junction. The line built in 1863 along the canal by the ensuing company, the West London Extension Railway, ran close to Chelsea's western edge with a stretch south of King's Road within the parish, but the line diverged from the boundary towards the Thames; Chelsea station, between Fulham and King's roads, was mostly outside the parish.[3] It was served from 1863 but the fabric apparently dated from 1866;[4] there may have been rebuilding in 1883.[5] The station was renamed Chelsea and Fulham from 1903.[6] The route, connecting northern and southern lines, was important for freight traffic; through passenger services operated only from 1904, and were not extensive. The line also catered for suburban passengers,[7] but suffered from competition with other modes of transport, and passenger services ceased in 1940, when Chelsea and Fulham station closed;[8] it was mostly demolished *c.*1955. Freight traffic continued and from the 1960s use of the line for through passenger routes increased.[9]

Underground Railways

The Metropolitan District Railway Company opened the South Kensington–Westminster stretch of the District line in 1868,[10] with a station at Sloane Square on Chelsea's eastern boundary.[11] The line was electrified in 1905.[12] The station, which served some 150,000 passengers a week, was remodelled in 1940 to include a new ticket hall and escalators,[13] but was bombed later in 1940 and reconstructed in 1951.[14] The flats above ground level, by R. Seifert & Partners, were added in 1965.[15] The line was among London's busiest in 1985 with 24 trains an hour rising to 36 in peak periods.[16]

Proposals for tube lines through Chelsea *c.*1901 failed,[17] but the northern end of the parish was served by the Piccadilly line's Knightsbridge station just outside the parish boundary, which opened in 1906; an entrance and ticket hall at the corner of Sloane Street opened in 1934.[18]

In 1989 the Central London Rail Study proposed a scheme for a Chelsea–Hackney line,[19] which was still awaiting financial backing in 2003.

Lots Road Power Station, on nearly 4 acres just east of the mouth of Chelsea Creek previously occupied by wharves, was built to supply the power which enabled the electrification of the Metropolitan District Railway, and also powered three other lines which formed the Underground Electric Railways Company of London (in 2000 the Northern, Bakerloo, and Piccadilly lines), controlled by the American financier Charles Tyson Yerkes. When built (1902–4) it was the largest electric traction station in the world. The 453-ft long structure in neo-classical style, probably designed by the company's engineer J.R. Chapman with its architect Leslie Green, comprised a steel frame clad in brickwork with terracotta detailing, enlivened by large glazed arches and four 275-ft chimneys. Boilers, fed with coal brought up the Thames and later also by rail, supplied steam to turbo-generators in the adjoining turbine hall.

based, unless otherwise stated, on C. Hadfield, *Canals of E. Midlands* (1966), 140, 238–9; M. Denney, *London's Waterways* (1977), 118–28; J.B. Atkinson, *W. London Joint Rlys* (1984), 8–10, 24.

1 Although Chelsea vestry believed the rly would benefit the par.: Vestry mins, 1833–9, pp. 124–5.

2 Chelsea cuttings: Chelsea Creek (1981).

3 *Hist. London Transport*, I. 127, 145; Old OS Maps, London 87 and 100 (1894 edn). It was within the boro.: PRO, RAIL 732/63.

4 H.V. Borley, *Chronology of London's Rlys* (1982), 50; Fèret, *Fulham*, II. 84.

5 PRO, RAIL 732/61. Cf. CL, print 2085A.

6 Borley, *Chron. of London's Rlys*, 51.

7 Cf. *Boro. Guide to Chelsea* [1910], 9, for destinations.

8 H.P. White, *Regional Hist. of Rlys*, III (1963 edn), 127–8; Borley, *Chron. of London's Rlys*, 50.

9 Atkinson, *W. London Jt Rlys*, 26, 38, 103, 109; White, *Regional Hist.* III (1991 edn), 135.

10 C.E. Lee, *100 Yrs of the District* (1968), 8–10.

11 Borley, *Chron. of London's Rlys*, 32.

12 Lee, *District*, 22.

13 Chelsea cuttings: Sloane Square sta. (*The Times*, 28 Mar. 1940).

14 Lee, *District*, 31, and photo facing p. 13.

15 Chelsea cuttings: Sloane Square Ho. (*Chelsea News*, 1 Oct. 1965).

16 White, *Regional Hist.* III (1987 edn), 99.

17 *Hist. London Transport*, II. 65, 79, 81; PRO, TS 18/271.

18 *Survey of London*, XLI. 13–14; Borley, *Chron. of London's Rlys*, 66–7.

19 *Chelsea–Hackney Line* (1995) (copy at CL).

The station began supply in 1905. Current was distributed via Earl's Court station to substations in various parts of London. Reconstruction from 1927 renewed the machinery and increased capacity. Operated by the London Passenger Transport Board, in 1937 Lots Road supplied electricity to much of the Underground and to trams and trolleybuses. Following nationalization in 1948 the power station was controlled by London Transport. Further modernization (1963–9) included a change from coal to fuel oil, and two of the chimneys were removed in 1966. Gas replaced fuel oil in 1975.[1] In 2000 the power station was due to be decommissioned in 2001, and it finally shut down in October 2002, its output being replaced by electricity from the National Grid. Conversion to residential use was planned for the building.[2]

POPULATION

In 1548 75 communicants (16 years and over) were certfied in the parish.[3] By the 1720s there were said to be 461 families in the parish and about 20 in the Royal Hospital.[4] In 1801 there were 2,746 families and a total population of 11,604.[5] The Table below gives decennial population totals, taken from the censuses, for the area equivalent to the main parish of Chelsea, and excludes the figures for Kensal New Town, transferred to Paddington and Kensington MBs in 1900.[6]

Table of Population 1801–1991

Year	*Total Population*	*Year*	*Total Population*
1801	11,604	1901	73,842
1811	18,262	1911	66,385
1821	26,860	1921	63,697
1831	32,371	1931	59,031
1841	39,796	1951	50,957
1851	53,725	1961	47,256
1861	59,881	1971	n/a
1871	67,717	1981	29,215
1881	73,079	1991	32,850
1891	74,466		

1 Pevsner, *London NW.* 569–70; NMR, file 95412; Chelsea MB, *Official Guide* [1937], 111.

2 *Sunday Times*, 21 May 2000; BBC, London News, 21 Oct. 2002. Fig. 54 shows power sta. in 1956.

3 *Chantry Cert.* p. 73.

4 Guildhall MS 9550, s.v. Chelsea.

5 CL, SR 61, 'Population Bk of St Luke's Par., Chelsea, 1801'.

6 *Census*, 1801–1841; LCC, *Statistical Abstract for London*, IV (1901); XIV (1911–12); XXI (1917–26); XXIX (1927–37); XXX (1937–46); XXXI (1939–48); LCC, *Stats. of MBs, 1956–7, 1962–3.*

SETTLEMENT AND BUILDING

FOR much of Chelsea's history, its main settlement lay by the riverside, the early history of which, up to 1680, is covered below in a single section. From 1680 building began to increase and also to appear in hitherto unsettled areas of the parish. The main developments took place between 1680 and 1865 and are covered with a general introduction and five topographical sections: Chelsea Village; South-East Chelsea and the Royal Hospital; Hans Town; Chelsea Park to Blacklands; Little Chelsea and World End. The period 1865 to 1900 saw the last main areas of open ground built over and new developments in eastern Chelsea and along the embankment. The last section covers the twentieth century, a period of further rebuilding and radical social change in the parish.

CHELSEA UP TO 1680

Evidence for prehistoric settlement in Chelsea has in the past largely consisted of finds taken from the Thames, such as an elegant Neolithic flint sickle, indicating harvesting in the area, and an early Neolithic wooden club, resembling a cricket bat with a rounded handle and a knob, which was found just west of Battersea Bridge and dated to 3540–3360 BC; several flint axes have also been retrieved.[1] More recent excavations have found flint flakes and burnt flint near Chelsea common, and worked flints and pottery fragments, probably from the Late Bronze Age, and other prehistoric material in later features near Chelsea Old Church. Similarly, Roman material has been found in later features on the east side of the church, and a Roman ditch with Roman pottery of the 3rd century AD on the north side.[2]

ANGLO-SAXON CHELSEA

Chelsea's Old English name may indicate some kind of settlement in the early Anglo-Saxon period,[3] but more concrete evidence of settlement emerges in the 8th century. Chelsea, first mentioned in 785, is one of the few places in Middlesex to have a recorded history before 1066.[4] Ten synods of the English Church were held there between 785 and 816, some of them also meetings of the Mercian royal council,[5] and other, unrecorded, church councils may have met there, probably also in the half century after 770. The synods were meetings of the province of Canterbury and as such promulgated canons for the whole of England south of the Humber, that of 816 being of special importance. They coincided with the ascendancy of the Mercian kings and are part of a wider pattern of holding such meetings within the diocese of London, and more particularly within the area of the ancient kingdom of Middlesex.[6] Though the presence of church councils does not necessarily mean the existence of a minster church in Chelsea, the Mercian kings, notably Offa, Egfrith, and Coenwulf, whose reigns covered the period 757–821, were frequently at Chelsea and are thought to have had a residence there.[7] A possible link between Chelsea and these kings is suggested by the name given to a detached portion of Chelsea parish lying north of Kensington: Kensal derives from the Old English *cyning holt*, 'king's wood'.[8] Given the small area of Chelsea and the seemingly artificial boundary separating it from Kensington along the line of Fulham Road, it seems likely that the whole of the territory had once formed a single unit. The hypothesis

1 *VCH Middx*, I. 29, 34; *British Archaeology*, no. 38, Oct. 1998. (website version at www.britarch.ac.uk).

2 LAARC, Catalogue of archaeological sites, Site summaries CSK94, CHY96, OCR97.

3 Above, Intro.

4 Thanks are due to Dr K.A. Bailey for his contribution to this section.

5 C. Cubitt, *Anglo-Saxon Church Councils c. 650–850* (1986), 269–85; *Handbk of British Chronology* (1986), 583–8.

6 e.g. Anglo-Saxon Chronicle s.a. 785 (*recte* 787), in *English Historical Documents, I, c. 500–1042*, ed. D. Whitelock (1979), 180; N. Brooks, *Early Hist. of Church of Canterbury* (1984), 118–19; Cubitt, *Church Councils*, chaps 6–7 and pp. 27–8.

7 Cubitt, *Church Councils*, 32–8.

8 *P.N. Middx* (E.P.N.S.), 162.

is given some support by the presence of a small detached portion of Kensington parish by the river, later in the grounds of the Royal Hospital.[1] Charters granting estates to church and laity were sometimes recorded as having been issued at Chelsea, although the only remotely local properties involved were Stanmore in 793,[2] and Harrow *c.*800.[3]

In 898 Chelsea was the scene of a council attended by King Alfred, Archbishop Plegmund of Canterbury, Aethelred the leader of the Mercians and his sister Aethelflaed, and Bishop Waerferth of Worcester, concerning the refounding of London after the Danish wars. At that council adjacent lots of land at 'Aethelred's hyth' (Queenhythe) within the city were granted to Plegmund and Waerferth. The presence of Aethelred and Aethelflaed and the name of the wharf suggest that the Mercian rulers played an important role, and also suggests that the Mercian royal house had an important estate at Chelsea, which served for meetings in their dealings with the Church and London.[4]

Chelsea's attraction for Offa and his successors lay in its convenient riverside site and its proximity to the important trading centre of London,[5] which could be reached easily by water; it also lay close to Roman roads from London to the west and south-west.[6] Fertile riverside sites such as Chelsea were also attractive to more ordinary residents, however, and some archaeological evidence now exists for pre-Conquest settlement in Chelsea, particularly near Chelsea Old Church. On the east side of Old Church Street, at the rear of nos 6–16, some mid Saxon features have been found with a possible timber structure which may date from the same period, and also a Saxo-Norman ditch, possibly indicating continuity of use of that site, which in the medieval period was part of the manor house and its grounds and outbuildings.[7] Timbers found in 1996 in the Thames about 40 m. from the shore just west of Battersea Bridge, dating from the period 700–900 AD, were at first thought to be part of a mid Saxon wharf, but on further examination were reinterpreted as an Anglo-Saxon fish-trap.[8]

MEDIEVAL CHELSEA

The Anglo-Saxon settlement by the church and the river remained the heart of the only known area of settlement in the parish until the 17th century. Most of the parish was covered by two large open arable fields, Eastfield and Westfield, with Church Lane marking the division between them. A single reference to the north field[9] may refer to the westerly part of Eastfield, which lay north of the village. Within Eastfield were areas called Gosepool, found in the later furlong name of Gospelshot, adjoining the Westbourne, and Thamesshot also in the south-east; the location of Medshot and Crosshot in Eastfield are not known.[10] In the north-eastern part of the parish lay closes known by 1393 as Blacklands,[11] and closes called Landmedes, which lay next to Gospelshot and so probably lay between that part of Eastfield and Blacklands. The name does not appear in records after the 15th century and the closes, at least five in 1454 of which two contained 20 acres, were probably later also known as Blacklands, and may have been the area called Bloody Meadow *c.*1700. Other meadows lay at Eastmead, probably in the south-east corner of the parish by the Thames and the Westbourne, where Thamesmead lay in the early 17th century, and in Westfield, where West meadow lay, in the south-west corner of the parish by Counter's Creek. Next to it by the creek and the Thames was the common meadow called the Lots, divided into portions of about a quarter of an acre each.

The existence of the celebrated 'great houses' of Chelsea and their occupants in the 16th century and later has overshadowed the community that existed there earlier. Alongside the famous and the outsiders Chelsea had several long-established families owning and working land, many of them also involved in trades and crafts.[12] By 1300 locals were seeking opportunities elsewhere: a spurrier and two tanners in London had Chelsea as a surname.[13] The population was probably small, however, for in 1334 Chelsea had the lowest total assessment, at £1 15s. 4d., in the hundred of Ossulstone.[14]

Though less is known about the residents of Chelsea in the Middle Ages compared with later periods, there are several indications of the presence of important figures in the parish well before the arrival of Thomas More and Henry VIII in the 16th century, and it is probable that

1 Old OS Map, London 88 (1869 edn).

2 P.H. Sawyer, *Anglo-Saxon Charters, Annotated Handlist and Bibliography* (1968), no. 136.

3 K.A. Bailey, 'Aspects of Anglo-Saxon Middx: Harrow and Hayes', *Anglo-Saxon Studies in Hist. and Archaeology*, IX (1996, publ. 1998), 66–9.

4 Birch, *Cartularium Saxonicum*, II, no. 577; Sawyer, *Anglo-Saxon Charters*, no. 1628; A. Vince, *Saxon London. An Archaeological Investigation* (1990), 21–2, 56; Brooks, *Early Hist. of Ch. of Canterbury*, 154.

5 Vince, *Saxon London*, 13–26. See also S. Kelly, 'Trading Privileges from 8th-century England', *Early Medieval Europe*, I pt 1 (1992), 5–28.

6 Vince, *Saxon London*, fig. 2 and chap. 10; I.D. Margary, *Roman Roads in Britain* (1967), 53–9.

7 LAARC, Catalogue of archaeological sites, Site summary: OCR97.

8 *British Archaeology*, no. 19, Nov. 1996; no. 27, Sep. 1997; no. 31, Feb. 1998 (website version at www.britarch.ac.uk)

9 BL, Harl. Roll L.26.

10 WAM 4804.

11 WAM 4809.

12 Some are mentioned below under Landownership; Econ. Hist.

13 *Cal. Mayors' Ct R. 1298–1307*, ed. A.H. Thomas (1924), 52, 60.

14 *Lay Sub. of 1334*, ed. R.E. Glasscock (1975), p. 190.

from an early period Chelsea attracted the nobility, gentry, and court officials who wanted country houses near Westminster, especially those accessible by river. Letters and orders of Edward I dated at Chelsea in 1294 and 1305 suggest either the presence of the king or at least of his chancellor, and the king's brother, Edmund, also dated a letter at Chelsea in that period.[1] Thomas Beauchamp, earl of Warwick, wrote his will at Chelsea in September 1369 before going to France, and also wrote a letter there dated in January of an unknown year,[2] suggesting either periodic visits or a period of residency. The 'lord of Latymer', whose servant was presented at the manor court in 1374 for drawing blood,[3] may also have been resident rather than passing through. By the end of the 14th century a number of London citizens and professional men not only owned land in the parish but also had houses there. John Haverbarght, holder of a rectory in Lichfield diocese, was buried in the parish church and left 2 quarters of barley to the priest; Master Nicholas Stoket, a free tenant of the manor, was buried in the parish church,[4] and at least one lord of the manor was often resident and was buried in the parish: John Shoreditch junior and his wife Helen were both buried in the church in Shoreditch's chapel on the north side of the chancel.[5] During the 15th century the number of residents with occupations in the City of London or in the law courts and royal administration increased, though for most the location of their houses is unknown. Thomas Garthorp, citizen and fishmonger of London, died in 1412 holding lands in Chelsea;[6] John Aleyn, citizen and vintner, died *c.*1449 leaving sums to both Chelsea and Kensington for tithes, for the church buildings, and for the poor;[7] and Reginald Boulers, bishop of Coventry and Lichfield, left a house in Chelsea to be sold in 1459.[8] John Palyng, citizen and goldsmith, died *c.*1428 with property in Chelsea,[9] and one of his executors, John Frenshe, also a goldsmith, had a holding in Chelsea by 1447. Frenshe paid 12s. 10d. assized rent in 1453,[10] so it is almost certain that his house was one of those with commoning rights in the 17th century,[11] and it was evidently a house of some importance, since by 1464 the holder was Richard Beauchamp, bishop of Salisbury,[12] who died in possession of it in 1481: the duchess of Somerset, a distant cousin of the bishop's, was living there in 1477.[13] John Beauchamp, Lord Beauchamp of Powick (d. 1475), bequeathed a pair of organs he had left in Chelsea church towards his funeral in Worcester: he was a first cousin of the bishop of Salisbury and may also have lived in his house.[14] In 1484 Elizabeth Mowbray, the widowed duchess of Norfolk, was granted that property for life.[15] Sir Thomas Haseley (d. *c.*1450), chancery clerk of the Crown, had an estate in Chelsea with a house which included a chapel and may have been sited not far from the rectory at the west end of the village.[16] In 1453 his widow Agnes paid the highest of the assized rents.[17] In 1465 Master Robert Kirkham, chancery clerk and Master of the Rolls, acquired a newly-built house in Chelsea from Haseley's successor, and leased some land there.[18] William Berkeley, Earl Marshal and marquess of Berkeley (d. 1491), had freehold property in Chelsea which he left to his wife for life and then to John Whiting, one of his supervisors.[19] Many of the freeholders in the parish were similar outsiders building up estates in Chelsea and Kensington.

MEDIEVAL HOUSES

The core of the medieval village lay around the church. On the north and east sides of the church lay the manor house with gardens, courtyard and outbuildings, which with an adjoining close covered a compact area of 4 acres. The close lay on the east side of the site, north of Lordship Yard, probably with stables and outbuildings in the Yard to the south: yet further south stood a wharf by the Thames which belonged to the house in the 1630s,[20] and doubtless earlier. This all suggests that the manor house itself lay on the western side of the site, perhaps with a main entrance into Church Lane rather than by the riverside; there was a passage through from Church Lane into Lawrence Street just north of the church in 1706.[21] The belief that the manor house lay on the site of houses known in the 18th century as Monmouth House, at the north end of the later Lawrence Street, is unfounded: that narrow site adjoined the boundary pale of the manor house property and would be an unlikely location for the main house.

The medieval parsonage, mentioned in 1388 but implied in 1230 from the existence of a rector,[22] is presumably the one replaced in 1566 by a new house and land north of the medieval manor house. It lay strangely distant from the church, at the western extremity of the

1 *Cal. Pat.* 1292–1301, 61–2; 1301–7, 382; *Cal. Close*, 1302–7, 451; PRO, SC 1/22/198.
2 *Complete Peerage*, XII(2), 374; PRO, SC 1/41/4.
3 WAM 4811, m. 2d.
4 Guildhall MS 9171/1, ff. 95v., 429.
5 Ibid., /2, f. 109v.
6 Ibid., f. 220v.
7 PRO, PROB 11/1, f. 98v.
8 PRO, PROB 11/4, f. 122v.
9 PRO, PROB 11/3, f. 67v.
10 WAM 4804; below, Landownership, other medieval (Frenshe).
11 Below; Econ., agric.
12 *Cal. Close*, 1461–8, 246.
13 *Stonor Letters*, II (Camden Soc. 3rd ser. XXX), p. 26, no. 183.
14 PRO, PROB 11/7, f. 99v.; *Complete Peerage*, II. 47.
15 *Cal. Pat.* 1476–85, 503.
16 *Cal. Close*, 1429–35, 286–7; 1447–54, 134–5; *VCH Middx*, V. 59; PRO, C 1/20/13.
17 WAM 4804.
18 PRO, C 54/317, mm. 7d., 21d., 25d.; below, Landownership, other medieval (Haseley).
19 Lysons, *Environs*, II. 78; III. 173; Dugdale, *Baronage*, I. 364; PRO, PROB 11/9, f. 88.
20 BL, Add. MS 11056, ff. 292–4.
21 Hunting, *Man. Ho. to Mus.* 16–17, plan of 1706.
22 WAM 4810, m. 3; below, Rel. Hist., par. ch.

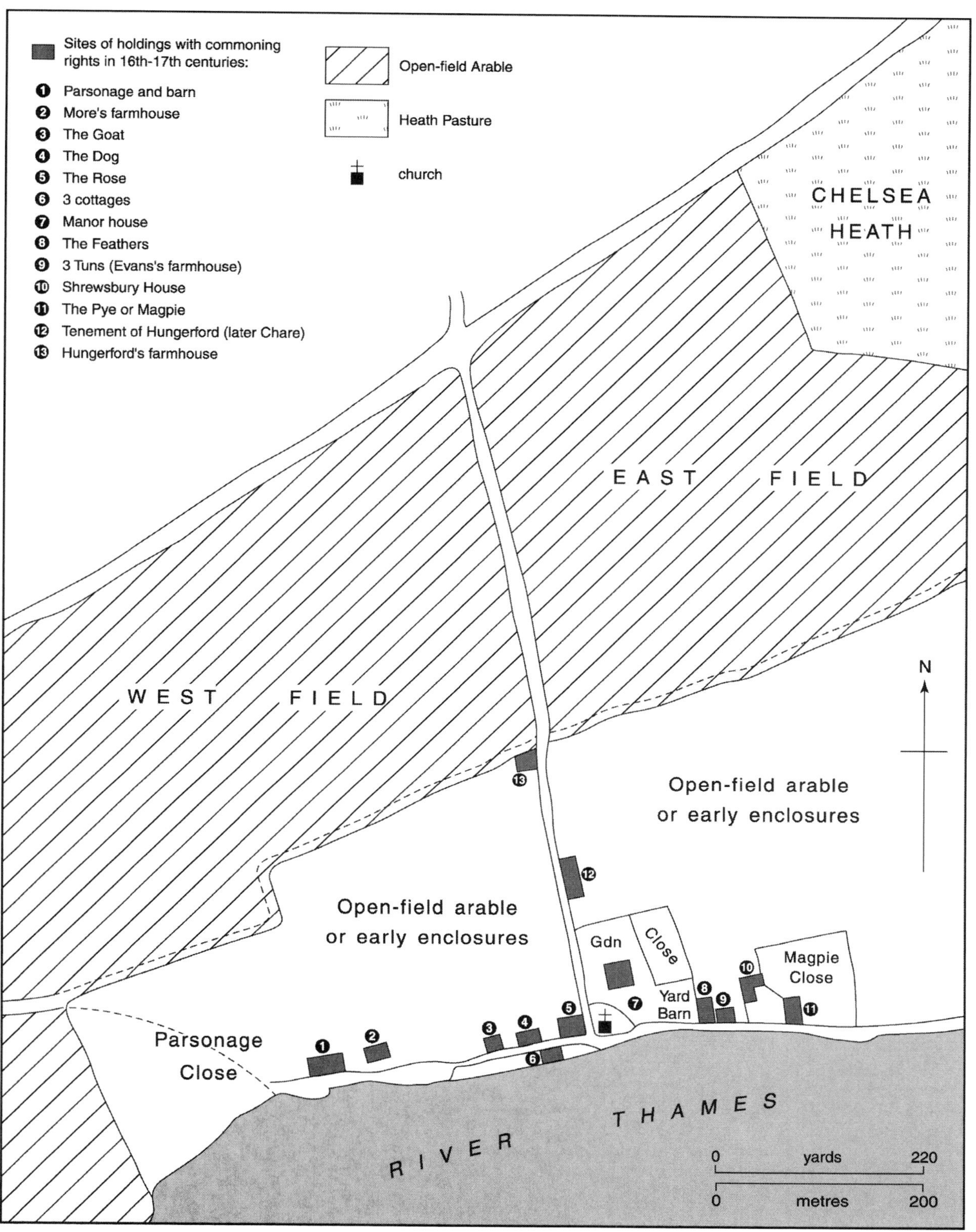

6. *Plan of the medieval village, showing probable house sites*

riverside road through Chelsea, and almost certainly fronted that road and the Thames, so it probably lay at the southern end of the present Milman's Street with Parsonage Close lying north and west of it.[1] The rector had a wharf on the Thames, presumably near to the house.

Houses which had rights of common of pasture in the late 16th and 17th centuries were almost certainly medieval in origin. The old parsonage had such rights which were transferred to the new one in the 16th century, but there is no evidence that other rights were transferred, though some may have been divided between parts of a property. Although obscure, the link between the assized rents and commoning does at least give some indication of the whereabouts of the main medieval houses. The other properties with such rights were the farmhouse on More's estate, later Lindsey House; a tenement belonging to Hungerford, later the Chare family's property, on the north side of the medieval manor house in Church Lane; the farmhouse on Hungerford's estate, later known as Wrennall's farm, opposite the new parsonage; the Pye or Magpie, next to Winchester House; Shrewsbury House; the Feathers next to Lordship Yard; the Goat in Duke Street by Danvers House; the Dog in Lombard Street with Waterman's Court; cottages next to the Dog owned by Thomas Creake in 1616; and the freeholding later known as Evans's farm, which may also have been near Lordship Yard.[2]

7. *Shrewsbury House, from the south*

The river also played an important part in Chelsea's life in the Middle Ages. Chance references, such as four people falling from a boat at Chelsea in 1235,[3] or the flooding which bought a drifting boat into the manor in 1379,[4] reveal little of how important river transport may have been at that time, nor how the river was used by Chelsea's inhabitants, but the wharves belonging to several individuals, mentioned from the 14th century, show a strong permanent link with the river. In the 15th century, and probably earlier, the availability of the river to reach London was probably a factor in attracting royal officials, lawyers, and London merchants to seek a residence in Chelsea: this was certainly the case in the 16th century.

16th AND 17th CENTURIES

Chelsea was one of a number of villages around Westminster which were popular in the 16th and 17th centuries with courtiers and royal officials who needed suitable residences near Whitehall but who could not find space in the limited and increasingly overcrowded settlement of Tudor Westminster. Alongside the famous, however, Chelsea also had an increasing population of farmers, craftsmen, and those providing food and services to the population, such as brewers and victuallers. In 1528 the population of Chelsea was reported to be 190 adults and children, including 16 households which grew no corn, and Sir Thomas More reported that 100 were fed daily in his household,[5] though not all those would have been living in the parish. In 1548 there were 75 communicants (16 years and over).[6]

The evidence for new building to accommodate increased demand is limited, but some older houses were undoubtedly enlarged or improved: illustrations of Shrewsbury House, for example, indicate an earlier timber-framed building refronted in brick in the Tudor period. Since few old buildings survive in Chelsea, and none of those are from the 16th century, the evidence for Chelsea's medieval and early modern houses is slight. Until the end of the 17th century, new building which took place in Chelsea was almost all on existing house sites or gardens or small plots of land associated with existing houses, and this limited both the number and the quality and size of individual houses. Even when building took place on new sites *c.*1700 the new building tended to be ribbon development along existing roads, with only a few, very short, new streets.[7]

While a handful of farmhouses and mansions were built by the early 17th century along Fulham Road at Little Chelsea, inclosing open field as gardens,[8] the main settlement at Chelsea remained concentrated in the limited area of Chelsea village, in Church Lane and along the riverside. Two houses in particular played an important part in Chelsea's fame, but both are surrounded by some doubt.

HENRY VIII AND CHELSEA

Henry VIII's desire to live at Chelsea has always been emphasized by local historians. A visit he made to Sir Thomas More's house there is held to have inspired him

1 Dr King's MS, p. 19; see Fig. 6.
2 Below, Econ., agric.; see Fig. 6.
3 PRO, JUST 1/536, m. 7d.
4 WAM 4815, m. 2.
5 PRO, E 36/257, f. 55.
6 *Chantry Cert.* p. 73.
7 Below, Settlement, 1680–1865 (Village; SE Chelsea); see Fig. 7.
8 Below, Little Chelsea.

with a love of the place, so that he obtained the manor from William Lord Sandys in an exchange to provide, it is said, a suitable nursery for his children. When he discovered that the manor house had been leased out he built, so the tradition goes, a new manor house, usually called Chelsea Place, a little to the east.[1] This tradition, however, exaggerates Henry's connection with Chelsea and in particular with the building of the manor house. It is clear that a manor house, which had been built a little to the east of the original one and possibly on a virgin site, was standing before Lord Sandys granted the manor to Henry VIII in 1536, because the Pye, a house which lay on the west side of it, was described as lying next to Lord Sandys' place, as late as 1538.[2] The Tudor house had probably been built by 1519, when the original manor house was leased out, and it is most likely to have been built by Sandys or his predecessor as owner of the manor, Sir Reginald Bray.[3]

There are also several anomalies in the traditional account of Henry and Chelsea. In fact, he showed little interest in getting a house there, disregarding More's own house, which had been forfeited to the king in 1535. The impetus for the exchange of property with Sandys may even have come from Sandys himself, who thereby acquired Mottisfont priory, which lay near his main seat and on which he lavished time and money and made his main residence to the end of his life.[4] Chelsea manor was one of several manors and houses acquired by the king by exchange or forfeit: during the period 1535–40 alone he acquired 15 such properties. The considerable work carried out on some former monastic properties, which provided staging posts on his journeys around the country, was dwarfed by the enormous alterations and additions at the king's principal houses, Greenwich, Whitehall, and Hampton Court.[5] No major building work was recorded at Chelsea, casting doubt on the tradition that Henry built the Tudor manor house.[6] It is most unlikely that Henry had anything in mind for the house when he first acquired it. The idea that he wanted to use the house as a nursery for his children apparently stems from the heading 'Chelsea Nursery' in one account for repairs in 1601, possibly a reference to the garden, and a statement in a letter by Sir John Lawrence in 1621 that Henry VIII built a nursery in Chelsea.[7] The places of residence of the royal children are very well documented, and there is no contemporary indication that Henry ever intended to use Chelsea as a nursery, nor that the royal children were ever resident there during his lifetime.[8]

Only in 1538 is there any evidence of interest by Henry in the house, when he made his only recorded visit to the parish since acquiring the manor, travelling from Hampton Court to Chelsea by river in May 1538, but only remaining a couple of days.[9] In July of that year the French ambassador wrote from Chelsea that Henry VIII had given him a house which had belonged to the late Master More for the summer, to avoid the plague in London, and that in the same village was lodged 'my lord privy seal' (Thomas Cromwell). Cromwell, who also dated letters there in June and July,[10] was probably occupying the king's house in order to avoid the plague also. It may be no coincidence that in that year the king bought the adjoining Pye from a freeholder, almost certainly to add more land on the west side of the house, as the Pye had a close attached.[11] The accounts for the garden that year[12] suggest that Henry may have had improvements in mind, but he does not seem to have spent any time in residence. In May 1541 Queen Katharine Howard and Princess Elizabeth are recorded as travelling by barge to and from Chelsea on various occasions,[13] and the king may have used Chelsea as a convenient stopping place on the river for journeys to Hampton Court, or as a pleasant garden to visit during the summer. Nevertheless, Henry's connection with Chelsea, however slight, was an important one for Chelsea's history. As a Crown possession for a hundred years the house was used as a residence for members of the royal family or highly-placed courtiers and royal ministers, which gave Chelsea a pre-eminent place in the locality.

In 1544 the king granted the manor of Chelsea to his wife Queen Catherine Parr for life as part of her dowry.[14] Catherine is said to have been interested in gardens and concerned herself with those of her dower manors, particularly at Chelsea.[15] After Henry's death she moved there from the court, and spent much of her time there, as a widow and as the wife of Sir Thomas Seymour, until her death in 1548. Princess Elizabeth lived with her there for several months until Catherine sent her away to protect her from the political consequences of Seymour's indiscretions with the princess.[16]

After Queen Catherine's death in 1548, the manor was occupied until 1638 by Crown lessees or those to whom the sovereign gave occupancy of the house. These included John Dudley, duke of Northumberland, 1551–3, who held meetings of the king's council at Chelsea; his widow Jane from 1554 until her death in 1555; Anne of Cleves who died there in 1557; Anne Seymour, duchess of Somerset, until her death in 1587; and from 1591 the Lord High Admiral Charles Howard,

1 e.g. Dr King's MS, p. 3, followed by Faulkner, *Chelsea*, I. 311, and virtually all writers on Chelsea thereafter.
2 PRO, E 326/12183.
3 Below, Landownership, Chelsea man. (med. man. ho.); see Fig. 47.
4 *Complete Peerage*, XI. 441.
5 S. Thurley, *Royal Palaces of Tudor England* (1993), 49–50.
6 *Hist. King's Works*, IV. 64.
7 BL, Add. MS 34195, f. 16v.; *N&Q*, 2nd ser., XI. 13–15.
8 Thurley, *Royal Palaces*, 79–81.
9 *L&P Hen. VIII*, XIII(1), pp. 332, 343,
10 Ibid., pp. 465, 428, 501–2, 508, 513, 518, 520–1, 534–5.
11 PRO, E 326/12183.
12 Below, Landownership, Chelsea man. (Tudor man. ho.).
13 *L&P Hen. VIII*, XVI, p. 391.
14 Ibid., XIX(1), p. 644.
15 S.E. James, *Kateryn Parr: Making of a Queen* (1999), 145; below, Landownership, Chelsea man.
16 James, *Kateryn Parr*, 300, 317.

Lord Howard of Effingham and later earl of Nottingham, whose wife Catherine was a close friend of the queen. During the Nottinghams' residence at Chelsea Queen Elizabeth made frequent visits to dine with them.[1]

SIR THOMAS MORE'S HOUSE

Sir Thomas More moved to Chelsea in 1524, having previously lived in Bucklersbury in the City of London. As king's secretary he needed larger accommodation more in keeping with his position, doubly so when he became chancellor of the Duchy of Lancaster in 1525; Chelsea provided courtiers with space while being only 2½ miles by river from the palace of Westminster.[2] More bought at least three properties to create his estate in Chelsea and Kensington, but the known purchases do not account for all he held nor make clear where his principal house was located.[3] There is no contemporary evidence that More built the house he occupied, and since he had lost most of his income when he gave up his law practice to serve the king, and was therefore dependent on fees and royal gifts, he was unlikely to have had the resources to build a large new mansion. More's son-in-law, William Roper, mentioned only that More had constructed a new building containing a chapel, library, and gallery at a good distance from his mansion, where he could find solitude for prayer and study.[4]

The activities of later owners have complicated the problem of where More's house and new building were located. More's successor in the property, William Paulet, marquess of Winchester (d. 1572), carried out substantial building at his Chelsea house, as at his other properties: when he died Chelsea was described as his 'new buildings, chief mansion, capital messuage and manor house',[5] and his grandson maintained that by 1575 the house had cost £14,000 in building work.[6] In 1566 Winchester also acquired the parsonage and close which adjoined the western boundary of More's grounds, presumably to give more room for his mansion; his stable yard, which juts west from its grounds, was probably built on part of that close. The earliest depiction of Winchester's mansion, the core of the building later known as Beaufort House, is in what appears to be a survey plan of the house and grounds before alterations were made by Sir Robert Cecil *c.*1597. The plan, reproduced in figure 8, shows a house set away from the road and on display to the river, progressive for the 1560s and certainly not characteristic of the 1520s.

More's mansion is much more likely to have been a building of medieval origin, close to the road running along the riverbank, and formerly one of those belonging to one of the 15th-century residents noted above. Since it is also unlikely that it was the house and Butts close and wharf that More gave outright to William and Margaret Roper in 1534, where Danvers House was later built,[7] it probably lay west of that site. The survey plan includes buildings at the south-east corner, which were entered through courtyards from the walled grounds and appear to have been service buildings, mainly timber-framed. Their complex arrangement and the fact that they are shown in plan form, like the main house, rather than in elevation like the stables and wharf buildings, suggest that these buildings provided significant accommodation. They may have been the remains of More's property, the rest perhaps having been demolished by Winchester to open up the view to and from the river. The site chosen by Winchester for his large mansion may have been that previously occupied by More's chapel, library, and gallery: this retired location, away from the busy riverbank and roads, would have been appropriate for a scholarly retreat, and its raised position accords with Roper's description of More 'going up into his aforesaid new building'.[8]

There has always, in fact, been some doubt about the location of More's house. The first resident of Chelsea known to have commented on the location was Sir John Danvers (born in the 1580s), who told the young John Aubrey that the marble chimney-piece in his chamber was the chimney-piece of More's chamber, and that where the gate to Danvers House stood, adorned with two pyramids, there had been a gatehouse with a pleasant prospect of the Thames and beyond from the leaded roof, where More had walked and contemplated.[9] This anecdote has led to the supposition that this or Danvers House itself was the site of More's new building,[10] but such a location, in the centre of the village a stone's throw from the church and the ferry, would hardly have given him quiet and solitude. Moreover, Danvers House and presumably its gate were on the land given by More to the Ropers and so unlikely to have included either More's house or study. By the late 17th century no-one had any certain idea where More had lived, and Arch House and Shrewsbury House were being mooted in addition to Beaufort and Danvers houses.[11]

The buildings and grounds formerly belonging to Sir Thomas More had by 1595 acquired the general layout shown on later plans and illustrations,[12] and the first detailed description in 1620 lists some additional embellishments. The two forecourts between the mansion and the riverside were walled in brick; a wharf by the

1 Below, Landownership, Chelsea man., for later hist. of ownership.

2 J. Guy, *Thos More* (2000), 62–3.

3 Below, Landownership, More.

4 W. Roper, *The Life of Sir Thos Moore, Kt*, ed. E.V. Hitchcock (E.E.T.S. 197, 1935), 26.

5 BL, Add. Ch. 16153.

6 PRO, SP 12/110, no. 30.

7 Below, Landownership, More; later ests (Sloane Stanley).

8 Roper, *Life of Sir Thos Moore*, 28.

9 A. Clark ed., *Brief Lives . . . set down by John Aubrey* (1898), II. 82.

10 Borer, *Two Villages*, 28.

11 Faulkner, *Chelsea*, I. 119.

12 Cf. Fig. 8 (plan 1595), and Fig. 11 (view *c.*1708).

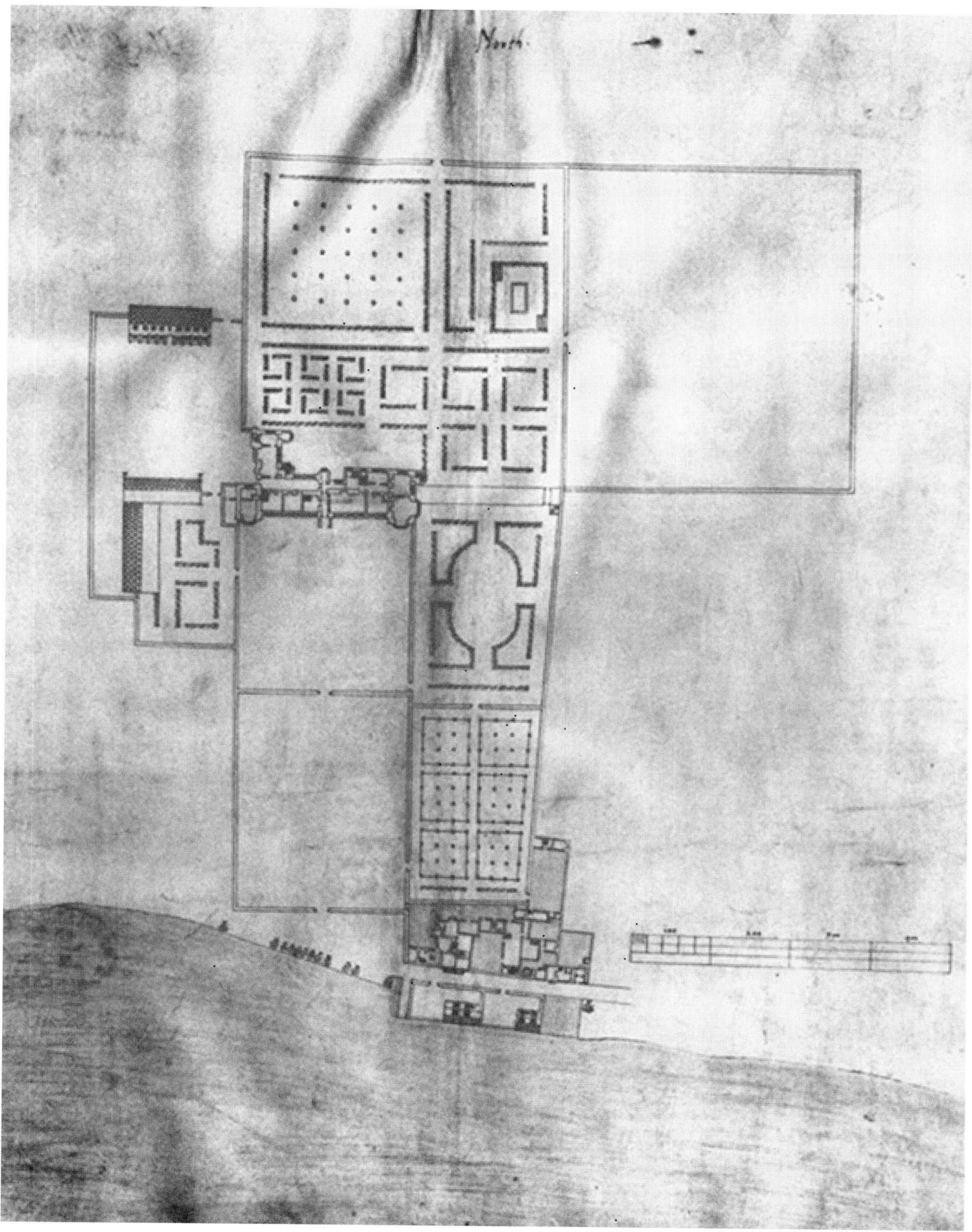

8. *Plan of Sir Robert Cecil's Chelsea Great House and its grounds,* c.1595, *stretching north from the Thames*

riverside had brick towers at east and west ends and a high water tower on the west corner supplying a watercourse; on the east side of the forecourts, and also walled with brick, were an orchard, and a garden which had a pyramid in the centre and a terrace on the north side leading to a banqueting house. North and east of the house lay another garden called the great garden, also enclosed with a brick wall; east of that was Dovecote Close, and west of it was the great kitchen yard with stables and ground with a brick barn on it. Some of the 16th-century brick walling has survived.[1] North of the kitchen yard and garden was Brickbarn close, stretching northwards to Fulham Road. South of the orchard, on the site of the service buildings shown on the survey plan, was another house with a yard in front and a garden beside it, occupied by a tenant.[2]

CHELSEA VILLAGE

Chelsea had no more large mansions and famous or aristocratic residents than any other village around London, but their concentration in the village along the riverside emphasized their presence, which was commented on by visitors and topographers. The quiet backwater nature of the village, at a distance from the main highway and effectively at the end of a cul-de-sac for those without a boat, gave Chelsea peaceful qualities which a house by the river in Westminster or by a main highway into London lacked, yet for those who could afford a well-manned barge it was only a short journey by river to Westminster and Whitehall. Although Chelsea's emergence as a popular residence for courtiers did not start with Sir Thomas More and Henry VIII, the Crown's acquisition of More's estate and the manor did put Chelsea among the locations where the Crown could reward courtiers with property and house ministers, and thereby brought Chelsea's name into national history.

The peak for noble residents in Chelsea was the late 16th and early 17th centuries. The occupants of the Tudor manor house, discussed above, were all close to the Crown, and a succession of prominent residents followed the marquesses of Winchester at the mansion on More's estate: Lord and Lady Dacre, the earl of Lincoln, Sir Arthur Gorges, Lionel Cranfield, earl of Middlesex, George duke of Buckingham. Shrewsbury House saw the earl and countess of Devonshire after the earls of Shrewsbury. The use of Chelsea by courtiers as a pleasant and convenient residence near Westminster continued up to the Civil War, but the presence of such influential residents was not without problems. Sir John Lawrence not only had to complain about his pew being taken by Edward Cecil, Viscount Wimbledon, in 1621, but also that several persons of quality holding lands valued at £260 a year had been taken off the Ship Money assessment in 1638 with the result that he, the countess of Devonshire, and Sir John Fearne had had to make up the difference.[3] Chelsea was also vulnerable to the plague carried by refugees from the City and Westminster, and a draft proclamation of 1630 threatened to punish inhabitants encouraging disease by entertaining strangers. A pest house suggested by the king's physicians in 1631 was not built, though one existed by 1666. Otherwise, the village had a healthy reputation which contributed to its status as a fashionable suburb in the 17th and 18th centuries and it was favoured for convalescence.[4] More visitors of all ranks came to Chelsea, and from the 17th century there are frequent references to watermen, who carried passengers on the river, and whose poorer members received many bequests.[5] Most of the principal houses and some brewhouses and other commercial premises on the riverside included private wharves as part of their property.[6]

Demand for accommodation led to the building of a handful of new mansions or country houses in Chelsea,[7] though most building effort before the 1680s went into rebuilding and improving existing houses or adding gardens to them. Information on more humble residences is erratic but suggests steady infilling and increase in smaller houses in the village.

Riverside

Chelsea had two principal streets in its main settlement, the highway by the river and Church Lane. Buildings known in the early to mid 16th century included a house called the Rose or Great Rose which stood 'next to the church', probably meaning facing the river on the opposite corner of Church Lane from the church, which was surrounded by property belonging to the manor house. It belonged in 1549 to Thomas Beane, who also owned three other houses, that occupied by Thomas Sander, a butcher's house next door, and a house occupied by John Colman, gardener to Queen Catherine at the Tudor manor house in 1547.[8] The Great Rose probably stood on the site of the later nos 64–7 Cheyne Walk, and the house or a later building on this site, which included two gardens and a wharf by the river opposite, formed all or part of the building where Richard Fletcher (d. 1596), bishop of London, lived from at least 1592 until his death. It was later occupied by Sir Thomas Baker, and sold by his widow Constance in 1625, possibly to Sir Edward Powell, Bt, whose wife lived there from 1636 to 1651. Powell also bought the house with gardens and stables in Church Lane which adjoined the north side of his mansion in 1646 and incorporated them into his property. Further alterations were made by Sir Edward's

1 Below, Rel. Hist., foreign chs (Moravians).
2 PRO, C 54/2440, no. 38.
3 *Cal. SP Dom.* 1637–8, 336.
4 Vestry orders, 1662–1718, ff. 6, 8v.; Beaver, *Memorials*, 38–40, 47, 49.
5 *Middx Sess. Recs*, NS, I. 11, 350; II. 171; III. 28, 86, 199, 252–3; IV. 16, 96; LMA, Cal. Middx Sess. Rec. 1612, pt 2, pp. 126–7; PRO, C 10/416/5; PROB 11/239, f. 330v., PROB 11/338, f. 24v., PROB 11/272, f. 47, PROB 11/455, f. 113.
6 Above, Intro., comms (river); below, and 1680–1865 (SE Chelsea).
7 Below, riverside.
8 Guildhall MS 9171/14, f. 109; James, *Kateryn Parr*, 145.

nephew, Sir William Powell *alias* Hinson, Bt, in 1679, and it was possibly then that the mansion was turned into four houses. At some point the westernmost of the four houses was extended across Lombard Street onto the wharf by the riverside, and was known thereafter as Arch House.[1]

West of Arch House some houses on the north side of the riverside road were probably medieval in origin: the Dog tavern, later renamed the Sun, at no. 68 Cheyne Walk, was with Waterman's Court a freeholding of the manor with rights of common.[2] To the west the later no. 72 Cheyne Walk was possibly 16th-century, and may have been part of the gatehouse or outbuildings of Danvers House or part of earlier buildings on Butts close, with another house adjoining to east; it apparently had a pre-existing passage on the west side, which had been built over. Before 1892 it had a narrow plastered street front with two storeys and another window in the single gable, which retained the remains of terracotta classical ornament. It is said to have had rights of common, and may have been the property belonging to Thomas Creake in the early 17th century.[3] By 1595 the westernmost end of the street was also built up on the northern side.[4]

The riverside road also had private property on the south side, which seems to have consisted in the late 16th century of wharves, surrounded by pales or brick walls, with a few buildings standing on them. In 1624 Sir John Danvers bought 'waste ground' with new buildings on it next to the river, formerly part of the Hungerford estate, which adjoined ground built with houses by the late 16th century.[5] Some wharves, such as the horseferry place, remained open, but gradually other sites became built up with houses, and eventually the river lay hidden from the street behind the houses and shops on the south side of the road. The western end of the street was called Beaufort Street by 1735;[6] after the modern Beaufort Street was so-named in the later 18th century, the riverside road was known as Duke Street, and the part between Danvers Street and Church Lane was known as Lombard Street by 1795.[7]

Church Lane

As part of the main settlement of the village, piecemeal rebuilding took place constantly in Church Lane, leaving little trace of earlier dwellings. On the east side the southern half was part of the grounds of the medieval manor house, belonging to the Lawrence family from 1584.[8] By 1665 their property consisted of the old manor house with its outbuildings and gardens, three adjoining cottages on the north side of Lordship Yard, and probably eight cottages on the east side of Church Lane.[9] A partially legible tablet naming Church Lane and the year, later placed on the south wall of a rebuilt no. 9 on the east side, suggests some rebuilding in the street in the 1660s, and nos 11–15 were also built or rebuilt in the 17th century.[10] The medieval manor house was occupied by the family until at least 1675, and possibly 1685, and it may have been divided and occupied by others as well.[11] Between the north side of the Lawrence property and the south side of the rectory estate in Church Lane was a house which had been part of Thomas Hungerford's estate in 1566 and had rights of common.[12] Robert Chare, citizen and fletcher of London, who bought it from Elizabeth Young in 1611, was presented in 1617 for converting the house into four dwellings,[13] and by 1642 his son John Chare, a London tradesman, had 6 or 7 houses on the site, one of which he occasionally occupied, especially in summer. He leased an acre of glebe behind his houses to give access to the rear and better gardens. By *c.*1660 his heirs had leased the acre to Thomas Collett, who enclosed three-quarters of it, dug sand, built a wall, and laid gravelled walks in the garden.[14] Coins of 1610 and an iron plate dated 1652 were recorded at houses on the west side at nos 16 and 18 Church Street.[15] At the junction of the lane with King's Road, opposite the rectory, William Arnold built four new brick houses beside the former Wrennall's farmhouse, garden and barn before 1676.[16]

ADDITIONS TO THE VILLAGE AREA

East and west of the village centre, some major houses were built in the 17th century as well as lesser buildings. At the west end of the village, Gorges House was constructed south of the stableyard of Lord Winchester's mansion, probably between 1617 and 1619. On the east side of the mansion's grounds Danvers House was built *c.* 1624.[17] Some indication of the development of this area is given by a settlement made by Sir Arthur Gorges in 1622. The properties included 4 houses and gardens, an orchard, a wharf, a lane and commoning rights. Significantly, they also including part of a ruined building, possibly part of the former parsonage, already in the course of redevelopment. This structure was fifty feet long, of five bays with a walled courtyard in front, and bounded by the Thames to the south, a common way to the north, and Gorges's coachhouse to the east. It continued westwards, where a house had recently been built on this part of the structure by William Whitehand.[18]

1 Below, Landownership, Hungerford; see Fig. 75.
2 Faulkner, *Chelsea*, I. 170–1.
3 *Survey of London*, IV. 7.
4 See Fig. 8.
5 CL, deed 2989.
6 Poor rate bk, 1728–42, f. 388.
7 CL, deed 17552.
8 Below, Landownership, later ests (Lawrence).
9 PRO, C 10/87/21; C 7/330/22.
10 *Survey of London*, IV. 51.
11 Below, Landownership, later ests (Lawrence).
12 Ibid., Hungerford.
13 *Middx Sess. Rec.*, NS, IV. 288.
14 PRO, C 9/38/10.
15 *N&Q*, 7th ser., VI. 247.
16 CL, deed 3009; see Fig. 46, map of estates.
17 Below, Landownership, More; later ests (Sloane Stanley).
18 PRO, C 66/2268, no. 24.

9. *Nos 55–9 (odd) Milman's Street, at the southern end of the east side, probably built in the mid 17th century*

In 1646 Sir Arthur Gorges junior with his wife and son leased a brick barn and adjoining ground where a dovehouse formerly stood, enclosed with a brick wall, to William Cox, bricklayer of Chelsea, for 41 years, on condition that Cox spent £50 in converting the barn into dwelling houses. Cox converted the barn into, or built, five houses on the site, claiming he had spent more than £100. Three of the houses were later assigned to Thomas Rosse.[1] The site seems to have been near Lindsey House and Gorges House, and may account for some of the smaller houses recorded in the Hearth Tax assessments as lying near Lindsey and Gorges houses, some of which belonged to Rosse. These probably included the three brick cottages, of two storeys with dormers in the tiled roofs, which appeared to date from the middle of 17th century, and were later incorporated into the east side of Milman's Street as nos 55–9.[2] The farmhouse on More estate was apparently rebuilt during the 17th century and later known as Lindsey House: it was occupied by Sir Theodore Mayerne 1639–55, who may have rebuilt it,

1 PRO, C 8/331/196; C 7/456/40.

2 *Survey of London*, IV. 45; see Fig. 9.

before alterations or rebuilding by the 3rd Earl of Lindsey.[1]

At the east end of the village at Chelsea Place, the Tudor manor house, the new owner James, duke of Hamilton, began extensive building soon after acquiring the manor in 1638. He repaired it and extended it by almost doubling the width of the Tudor west range and adding three ranges to form a second courtyard. With the outbreak of the Civil War in 1642 the Hamiltons left Chelsea and the house was later let, probably as two separate dwellings; it was certainly two houses in 1655, divided between Charles Cheyne and Sir Henry Herbert. Cheyne bought the whole manor and sold the freehold of the new part of the house in 1664 to the bishop of Winchester to become Winchester House.[2]

East of the Tudor manor house and garden the highway left the riverside and led through the fields to Westminster. At the beginning of the 17th century the road ran through the open Eastfield, with meadows by the river, and possibly some closes. In 1606 James I granted part of Eastfield called Thamesshot, lying between the road and the river, as the site for King James's Theological College, laying the foundation stone of the college building himself in 1609. The college was discontinued during the Commonwealth and was empty in 1652, when it was described as a brick and tile building 130 ft from east to west and 33 ft deep: on the ground floor was an entry, kitchen, two butteries, two larders, a hall, and 2 large wainscotted parlours with a closet in each; above were six rooms and 4 closets, and over the whole a very large gallery with a little room at each end and turrets above. It had a yard enclosed by a brick wall at the east end and on part of south side, within which was a kitchen, stable and lofts, again in brick and tile. A walled garden lay on the other part of the south side and the west side. On the north was a yard with walls at the east and west ends, fenced with pales on the north side. The whole site was estimated at one acre.[3] The building was used for various purposes, including as a prison for Dutch prisoners, until in 1667 the lease was granted to the Royal Society. In 1682 they conveyed it back to the Crown for the Royal Hospital.[4]

Possibly encouraged by the building of the college, the part of Eastfield west of the college lying between the highway and the Thames also saw some building by the mid 17th century. The Swan Inn and wharf with other buildings had been built on an acre of arable between the highway and the Thames by 1664, and belonged to Francis Smith, maltster, and his son Samuel Smith, citizen and weaver of London.[5] Samuel Smith was assessed for a property of 7 hearths between the college and Chelsea Place in 1674.[6] In 1672 John Baker took a lease from Charles Cheyne of two brick messuages lying towards the college, one of them called Sweed Court, and two plots of land, one enclosed with a wall, on which he built premises for glass-making, which continued until *c.*1681.[7] A plot of *c.*4 a. towards the west end of the highway was leased to the Society of Apothecaries, who built a wall around it in 1674 and three barge-houses by the river, and created their physic garden there.[8] Daniel Wayte of St Martin-in-the-Fields had a half acre of freehold east of the Apothecaries' garden with a house built on it by the highway before 1684, and was granted a long term of years in another half acre by Charles Cheyne with houses built there. He spent £300 on building a new house on part of the freehold adjoining the Thames.[9]

Charles Cheyne granted a 31-year lease from 1675 to Richard Robinson of London, clothworker, of ground in Chelsea and all the buildings on it or to be built during the lease, at a peppercorn rent. Robinson built five houses there and obtained an 11-year extension to the lease; at his death in 1687 he was in possession of eight houses and gardens in Chelsea and property elsewhere.[10] He probably gave his name to Robinson's Lane (now Flood Street) and may have been the builder of the countess of Radnor's house at the corner of the later Paradise Row and Robinson's Lane.[11] William Cox leased a close nearby, also on the north side of the highway, and built houses there; it was still known as Cox's close in 1862 when it was the site of George Place.[12]

LITTLE CHELSEA

By the early 17th century a small settlement, called New Chelsea in 1631 but more usually Little Chelsea, had grown up along Fulham Road, with buildings on both the Chelsea and Kensington sides separated by fields from other settlements in the two parishes. The reason for the growth of a settlement here is not known, though two major farms with lands in both parishes had farmhouses here on the Kensington side.[13] By 1631 some 14 acres in Chelsea's Westfield at the rear of houses in Little Chelsea had been enclosed for gardens.[14] A house had been built on 5 acres adjoining Fulham Road which were let to Richard Stocke by 1618,[15] and between 1634 and 1644 Johanna Abell built or rebuilt a mansion and three other houses on the site of two houses and gardens fronting Fulham Road, probably on 5 acres on the west side of Stocke's house.[16] In 1666 there were 7 houses at Little Chelsea rated for hearth tax under Chelsea, the main one belonging to Sir James Smith with 18 hearths,

1 Below, Landownership, later ests (Lindsey).
2 Below, Landownership, Chelsea man.
3 PRO, E 317/MIDDX/8.
4 Below, Landownership, later ests (Royal Hosp.).
5 PRO, C 10/488/248.
6 PRO, E 179/143/370, m. 5.
7 PRO, C 8/249/81; below, Econ., trade.
8 Below, Landownership, later ests (Physic Gdn).
9 PRO, C 5/195/54; C 8/580/22.
10 PRO, C 7/84/68; C 5/108/21.
11 CL, deed 3007.
12 Below, Soc. Hist., chars.
13 *Survey of London*, XLI. 162.
14 PRO, SP 16/193, f. 101 and v.
15 PRO, C 54/2376, no. 5; below, Landownership, later ests (Blake).
16 Below, Landownership, later ests (Arnold; Boevey); PRO, C 6/62/16.

followed by Dr Baldwin Hamey with 13, two houses with 8, and three others with 6, 4, and 3 hearths respectively. There were two or three more houses by 1674, all of 4 hearths.[1]

Also enclosed out of Westfield were the gardens attached to the house later known as Stanley House, which stood isolated on the north side of King's Road close to Counter's Creek; its 7 acres of grounds stretched from King's Road to Fulham Road. The house seems to have been that sold to Dudley, Lady Lane, by her mother Lady Elizabeth Gorges by 1630, and extended by Lady Lane, who had taken part of an 11-acre inclosure in Westfield for a garden.[2] In 1643 Lady Elizabeth Gorges sold the house and grounds to another daughter, Elizabeth Stanley, later the wife of the 4th earl of Lincoln. The house had 11 hearths in 1666.[3]

CHELSEA BY 1680

In 1674 there were 172 houses in Chelsea chargeable for hearth tax, 8 of which were listed as lying at Little Chelsea; the exempt were not apparently listed. 50 of the houses were marked as empty, including some of the largest: Buckingham's house (formerly Lord Winchester's), with the most hearths at 61, the house thought to be Danvers House with 48, and Chelsea college with 12.[4]

It is clear that though a few substantial country mansions were built or created in Chelsea in the early 17th century, by the middle of the century the demand for housing in Chelsea was more for substantial or middling town houses rather than for great mansions. In the 1650s the enlarged Tudor manor house was divided into two separate dwellings, occupied as though they were semi-detached mansions, one of which became Winchester House. Shrewsbury House had also become two dwellings by 1674, and by 1695 one part was a school. This was also the use that Gorges House had been put to by 1676, while Danvers House was demolished by 1700.[5] The owners of the duke of Buckingham's mansion had difficulty in selling it at the Restoration, and when it was up for sale again the 1st duke of Beaufort, who bought it in 1681, had difficulty persuading his wife that such an old house could be given modern comforts.[6] After the duke and duchess died, it remained largely empty until it was demolished.[7]

FROM 1680 TO 1865

GENERAL INTRODUCTION

The building of the Royal Hospital from 1682 in the south-eastern fields of Chelsea marked a significant point in the parish's history, as it generated a wave of speculative building on formerly unbuilt land, on a scale which was new to Chelsea. The Hospital's presence seems to have attracted aristocratic and eminent residents to the area because of the grandeur of its buildings and its setting and the neighbours who from the 1690s had built mansions on land leased from the Crown. The few speculative houses built in Paradise Row in the 1690s, quickly increased to rows of houses lining the roads either side of the Hospital and leading down to the river at Chelsea village. So much building was taking place that in 1694 a complaint was made that trade at the White Horse near Chelsea church had declined disastrously because of the number of houses being built near 'Chelsea College'.[8]

The old village, too, shared in the desire to build. In the year he died, 1698, Charles Cheyne wrote to the rector about the growing population in Chelsea and the need for a new gallery in the church to accommodate them, saying he would be glad to help by building himself, or getting others to, and would be glad to let land for that purpose and in particular pull down a tavern and a bowling green for the designs of better and more sober purpose.[9] Since building more houses would increase the possible number of churchgoers, he presumably meant that using pleasure grounds to house more sober middle-class residents would augment the contributions to the church rate, and he also presumably had in mind the bowling green attached to the Three Tuns, though it was left to his son to lease that for building in 1708.[10] The growth in Chelsea from this period was demonstrated by the average number of recorded baptisms in the parish church: in the 1560s there were about 5 a year, and 8 in the first decade of the 17th century; in the 1630s it was 16, but by the 1680s it had risen to an average of 43, and by the 1730s had become 108. By the 1780s it was 158, and it continued to climb steeply thereafter.[11] The number of houses rose from about 172 in 1674, to 350 in 1717, 741 in 1777, and 1,350 in 1795.[12] At the beginning of the 18th

1 PRO, E 179/252/32, no. 40, f. 25v.; E 179/143/370, m. 5.
2 PRO, SP 16/193, f. 101 and v.
3 Below, Landownership, More; later ests (Stanley Ho.); PRO, E 179/252/32, no. 40, f. 25v.
4 PRO, E 179/143/370, m. 5.
5 Below, Landownership, later ests (Shrewsbury; Gorges; Sloane Stanley); Soc. Hist., educ. (private schs).
6 M. McClain, *Beaufort: the Duke and his Duchess, 1657–1715* (2001), 103.
7 Below, Landownership, later ests (Beaufort).
8 PRO, C 5/619/126.
9 Dr King's MS, preface.
10 Below, Chelsea village.
11 Lysons, *Environs*, II. 116.
12 PRO, E 179/143/370, m. 5; G. Rudé, *Hanoverian London: 1714–1808* (1971), 3; CL, deed 17553.

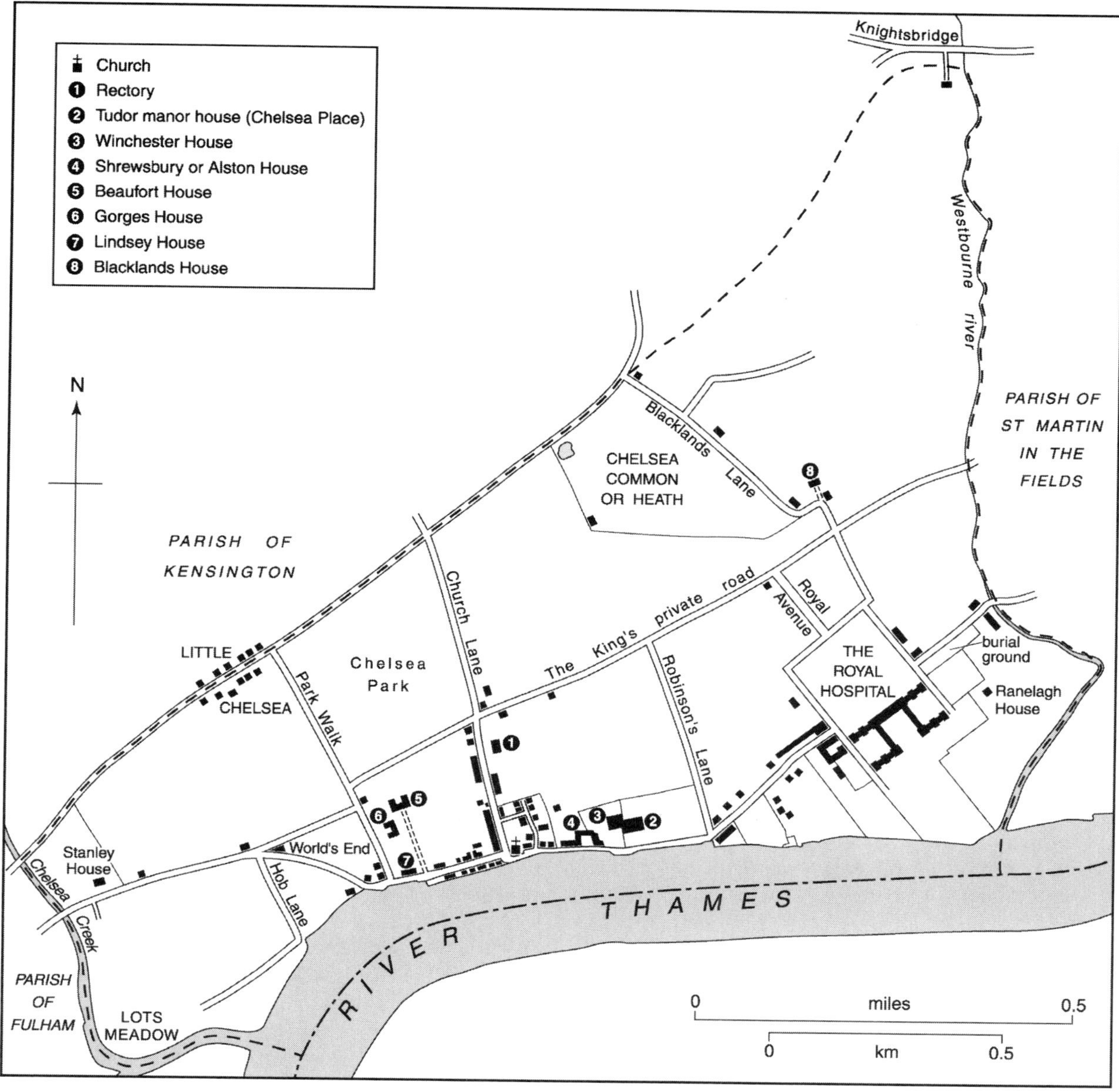

10. *Chelsea* c.*1700*

century Chelsea was praised for its situation on rising ground which sloped gently down to the Thames, to which it had a four-mile frontage, adorned with a handsome church and several stately buildings, especially the Royal Hospital; it was noted as the residence of many of the nobility.[1] Most of its buildings were concentrated close to the river: the body of the town lay near the church, with two rows of buildings extending northwards in Church Lane, and rows reaching to either side of the church, facing the river, from the duke of Beaufort's in the west to the Royal Hospital in the east; west beyond Beaufort House lay many scattered houses and good seats, and beyond the Hospital a row of houses stretched a considerable way towards London. The writer emphasized that it had always been the resort of 'persons of good fashion: Henry VIII, the marquess of Winchester, Sir Thomas More, Princess Elizabeth'. The 'sweetness of its air and pleasant situation' attracted the eminent and it was filled with worthy families. In addition there were many schools with a great number of boarders, and in the 20–30 years before 1705 Chelsea had grown from a small straggling village into 'a large, beautiful and populous town', with *c.*300 houses and more than 300 families, about three times the number in 1664. Its growth was attributed to its proximity to London with easy access by water or coach to the Court, the City, or place of business. Good conversation was available at the coffee house (Don Saltero's) near the church; rare plants grew there and nowhere else, and the Apothecaries' Garden was proof of good soil.[2] The

1 Bowack, *Antiquities*, 1.

2 Ibid., 13.

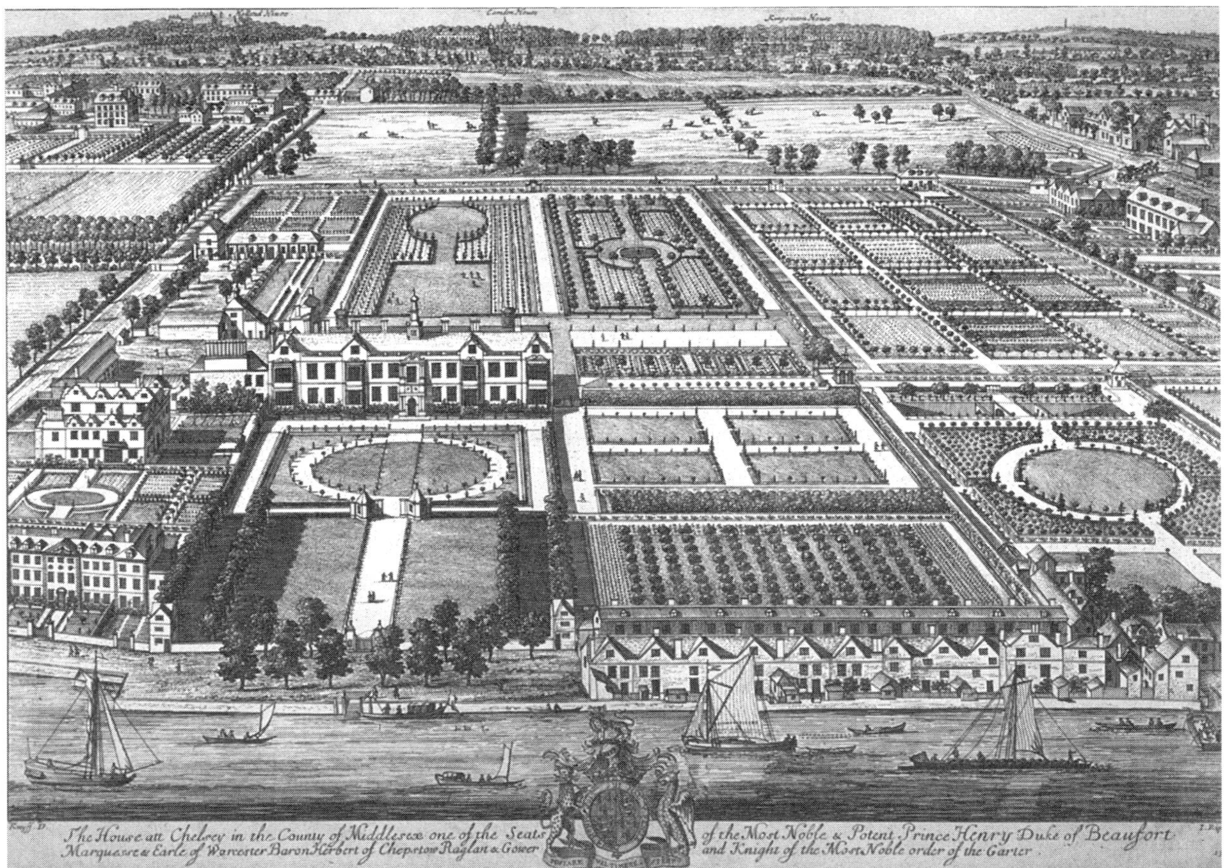

11. *A depiction of Beaufort House and grounds* c.*1708, with Lindsey House (*extreme left*), Gorges House (*behind*), gardens of former Danvers House (*extreme right*), and Little Chelsea showing the 4-storeyed Shaftesbury House (*top left*)*

author lived in Chelsea and, like many resident writers who succeeded him, could not praise his local village enough. The many large seats and houses that had grown up during the 16th and 17th centuries were also emphasized: the Royal Hospital, Beaufort House, Lindsey House, Shaftesbury House, Chelsea Manor House, Blacklands House, Winchester House, Gorges House, and several others, but even in 1705 many of these were let as boarding schools; the number of aristocrats living in Chelsea was by then declining, while the more urban rows of red brick houses in Church Lane and in Paradise Row near the Hospital were the residences of MPs and government officials.

In 1724 Daniel Defoe's *Tour* was published in which he described 'Chelsea, a Town of Palaces', a remark apparently provoked by the Royal Hospital, and which, he presciently says, by its new extended buildings seemed 'to promise itself to be made one time or another a part of London'. He described the Royal Hospital and 'a little Palace' formerly the home of the earl of Ranelagh, describing the house and the charm of its situation and prospect. He then had to cease describing private houses and gardens as there were so many around London in the county of Middlesex.[1] He may not even have seen the Tudor manor house which later writers considered a palace because of its link with Henry VIII, or Winchester House, the palace of the bishops of Winchester, but his phrase has subsequently been echoed in almost every book written about Chelsea, though since Chelsea has become part of London, as Defoe thought it might, the 'town' has been changed to a 'village of palaces'.[2]

Like other villages separated from London by fields, Chelsea had problems with robberies on the highways leading through the parish, mentioned from the 16th century. In 1613 three yeomen had allegedly robbed a man in the highway at Chelsea; in 1692 one Parson Smith, reader or lecturer of Chelsea, stood accused of assisting highwaymen; John Verney found journeys from Little Chelsea to the City tedious in 1680, partly because 'rogues' made the road unsafe.[3] In the 18th century robberies by footpads and highwaymen were common. The Five Fields, just outside Chelsea's eastern boundary,

1 D. Defoe, *Tour Thro' Great Britain*, ed. G.D.H. Cole (1927), I. 391.

2 Perhaps originating with A.G.K. L'Estrange, *Village of Palaces, or, Chronicles of Chelsea* (1880).

3 *Middx Sess. Rec.* NS, I. 299; Beaver, *Memorials*, 52; *Survey of London*, XLI. 162.

were particularly notorious, although the situation improved by the early 19th century. The area around the Royal Hospital was also considered dangerous.[1] In 1761 the parishioners opposed the closure of the Hospital's grounds in the evening, necessitating a detour attended with dangers including frequent robberies.[2] In 1816 the vestry's application to have a road for carriages, rather than only allowing people to walk through Burton's Court after dark,[3] was unsuccessful.[4]

Though Chelsea had been one of the villages around London and Westminster which housed eminent residents in the 17th century, it developed a more particular role and gained more fame as an 18th-century riverside pleasure resort, where people could come for the day or take lodgings for the summer. The main focus of this was Ranelagh Gardens, opened in 1742 and for about 40 years the height of fashion for entertainments, but visits by boat to Chelsea to dine at a riverside tavern were a quiet but pleasant way to escape from the crowds, noise and smells of London. The main street in the village along the river was lined with inns, while some isolated taverns in the fields and along the highways, like World's End, provided more rural surroundings.[5] The new houses of Cheyne Walk included at least two taverns.[6] By the second half of the 18th century Chelsea was attracting greater artistic attention as well, its riverside, picturesque old buildings, and stately mansions and grounds by the river all being favoured subjects for paintings and engravings.[7]

In 1693 the Crown made a payment towards building a road between Kensington and Chelsea,[8] presumably for Royal Avenue from the Royal Hospital to King's Road, thought to be the only section actually built of a grand route planned by William III to run between the Royal Hospital and Kensington Palace.[9] In 1717 just four roads connected Fulham Road with King's Road and five routes ran south from King's Road to the river,[10] but from the 18th century building gradually opened up further north–south routes through the parish. In 1778 George III granted permission for Sloane Street and Lower Sloane Street to be opened up into the king's private road.[11] There were already many houses built along King's Road from the late 17th century, such as on freeholds south of Chelsea common, and on the glebe near the rectory, though many also had some kind of access from other directions. Local use must already have been heavy by the time the road passed into public ownership in 1830 and was open to all. This was a pivotal moment in Chelsea's history: Chelsea already had a new parish church north of King's Road and several public facilities around it; the convenient highway into and through the middle of the parish inevitably became the focus for commercial life and also for new building, and diminished the role of the old centre by the former parish church on the riverside.

The shift from an 18th-century village resort to a 19th-century metropolitan suburb sometimes moved faster than the vestry and parish officers could deal with. The vestry were reluctant to incur expense in connection with highways and footpaths: they refused to take on the recently-constructed Sloane Street in 1782,[12] and roads at Queen's Elm used for some years were only adopted as parish highways in 1799 after proprietors had constructed drainage and paved the footpaths. Riley Street was taken on following drainage work in 1800.[13] The parish feared the expense of taking on roads requiring work, for example in 1828–9 when a road across Chelsea Common which required drainage had been adopted.[14]

Paving also assumed importance when from 1774 the vestry submitted names for the appointment of two surveyors by magistrates. Piecemeal improvements included paving crossways at Swan Walk and Bull Walk near the river in 1781, like those in Manor (later Chelsea Manor) Street and Lawrence Street already done. In 1788 the vestry acted to keep Justice Walk open and in 1789 ordered that the enclosure of part of Millman Row be reversed.[15] In 1801 the parish was responsible for 3½ miles of road and three-quarters of a mile of footways; the turnpike roads totalled 3¼ miles.[16] In 1815–16 the vestry sought exclusion from a Bill for paving metropolitan streets, as the extent of Chelsea's foot- and carriageways would make paving expensive, and also resisted a local scheme for paving outside Hans Town. In 1816 the vestry made a paved crossing near the King's Road burial ground.[17] Following an Act of 1821 to improve collection of the highway composition, administrative improvements were attempted in 1822 and the streets were better regulated by 1829.[18] In 1823–4 drainage was improved and paving was in progress in the late 1820s,

1 Faulkner, *Chelsea*, II. 354; Beaver, *Memorials*, 51–2, 311, 314; Chelsea Misc. 1090–5, 1097–1100, 1102; Chelsea cuttings: crime (18th-cent. news cuttings).

2 Vestry orders, 1745–71, p. 245; Dean, *Royal Hosp.* 230.

3 Vestry orders, 1809–22, pp. 203–5.

4 Dean, *Royal Hosp.* 231.

5 Rudé, *Hanoverian London*, 50–1, 62; below, Soc. Hist., social.

6 Below, Chelsea village.

7 *Two Capitals: London and Dublin 1500–1840*, ed. P. Clarke and R. Gillespie (2001), 247.

8 *Cal. Treas. Papers*, 1557–1696, 332.

9 Pevsner, *London NW.* 554, 565, 582. Dean contests this interpretation: *Royal Hosp.* 84–5.

10 Hamilton, *Map* (1664–1717).

11 *Hist. King's Works*, V. 459.

12 Vestry orders, 1771–90, ff. 75v.–76.

13 Ibid., 1790–1809, pp. 186–7, 189, 198–9, 201–2.

14 Chelsea Scraps, 362–3.

15 Vestry orders, 1771–90, ff. 20v., 67, 157v.–159, 159A, 160, 163v.–164, 170.

16 Ibid., 1790–1809, pp. 248–9. Figs. exclude Hans Town.

17 Vestry orders, 1809–22, pp. 56–8, 71, 159–62, 174–6, 195–8, 208–10, 216–18.

18 1 & 2 Geo. IV, c. 67 (Local and Personal); Vestry mins, 1822–33, pp. 60–6; Faulkner, *Chelsea*, II. 27.

funded partly by private contributions.[1] In 1829 the vestry thought few districts had better roads and footpaths, although surveyors were urged to continue curbing footpaths.[2] In 1833 expenditure on paving was controversial,[3] and in 1834, despite opposition, a highways board was appointed to avoid partiality and the continual reversal of work by succeeding surveyors.[4] The old system was revived in 1836–7, only to return to the board system in 1838.[5]

In 1792 Chelsea inhabitants formed an association to aid the magistrates in preserving order, which directed the constables and watchmen to suppress inflammatory writings, and tried to prevent seditious assemblies. Patrolmen from Bow Street attended when a riot was feared; journeymen at a manufactory in Church Lane (later Old Church Street) were discouraged from burning an effigy of Tom Paine.[6] That year John Martin and others, indicted for seditious talk and assault and said to belong to the Free and Easy or Arthurian Society, a political club, were suspected of being behind a planned riot which was prevented by the Chelsea association.[7]

As a measure of its new urban status, the London Building Act of 1774 added Chelsea and three other parishes to the cities of London and Westminster and parishes in the bills of mortality, to regulating building there.[8] Chelsea also acquired some other urban features, such as hackney coaches which plied at the Royal Hospital in 1771.[9]

In 1825 three private Acts received royal assent allowing the Cadogan trustees to grant building leases on the Cadogan settled estates, and to demolish Winchester House and grant building leases of the site, and allowing the rector to grant building leases for 33 acres of glebe.[10] Despite new building steadily taking place, however, in the 1830s much of Chelsea was perceived as a rather down-at-heel locality. In 1834 Carlyle wrote of his affection for his 'excellent old house': Chelsea was unfashionable and had numbers of old houses, 'at once cheap and excellent'.[11] Another writer contrasted Chelsea's 'barbarism' with the 'aristocratic pavements' of neighbouring Belgravia in 1839.[12] In 1839 the highway board was ordered to water the roads in summer to keep the dust down; not only comfort but the value of property was thought to depend on the quality of the roads. Considered a success, summer watering was ordered to be extended in 1841, and was carried out again in 1843–4, despite doubts about the legality of using the highway rate for this. By 1843 the highway board had improved footpaths and made stone crossings on principal streets, but in 1844–5 paving was partly financed by private contributions.[13] A complaint of 1844 from a King's Road business about new pavements which narrowed the carriage road revealed tensions between tradesmen sympathetic to parishioners' interests and those more interested in wheeled traffic from farther afield.[14]

The prospect of an embankment along the Thames was a stimulus to the Chelsea Improvement Act (1845) for maintaining the parish's streets and footways (excepting Hans Town and Fulham Road).[15] Under the Act a board of 50 commissioners replaced the existing boards of highway surveyors and lighting inspectors and were given extra powers to make, pave, clean, water, and drain streets, collect waste, and deal with nuisances, and to levy rates for the purpose.[16] Its implementation was contentious. An improvement society argued that the commission would regenerate Chelsea by paving throughout, removing obstructions, and, above all, by creating new thoroughfares, particularly around the Royal Hospital and in southern Chelsea west of Church Street. A ratepayers' association, however, feared that rates would be squandered.[17] The commissioners, first elected in August 1845, began work energetically that autumn, meeting far more often than the monthly minimum.[18] By November it was reported that the results of the rate levied on local householders could be seen: tollgates had been removed, allowing buses to serve Little Chelsea, and many footways, especially in King's and Fulham roads, had been paved.[19] The commission maintained, cleansed, watered, and improved roads; paving was laid down, sometimes in response to complaints about particular streets;[20] a uniformed street-keeper was appointed whose duties included dealing with obstructions.[21]

Meanwhile sewage was causing concern as medieval ditches struggled to cope with the effluent from the many new houses discharging into the natural watercourses. In 1854 50 householders and residents in the neighbourhood of Sloane Square complained that the

1 Chelsea Scraps, 335, 362–3; Chelsea Misc. 833; Vestry mins, 1822–33, pp. 208, 210.

2 Vestry mins, 1822–33, pp. 254–5; Faulkner, *Chelsea*, I. 39.

3 Vestry mins, 1822–33, p. 323; Chelsea Scraps, 379, 381.

4 Chelsea Scraps, 413–16; Vestry mins, 1833–9, pp. 62–3, 76.

5 Vestry mins, 1833–9, pp. 135, 168, 174–5, 181–6, 202.

6 CL, SR 62; Vestry orders, 1790–1809, pp. 35, 54–5.

7 PRO, TS 11/1118; below, Soc. Hist., social (political clubs).

8 *LJ*, XXXIII. 434a–b, 456a; *Two Capitals*, ed. Clarke and Gillespie, 74.

9 Chelsea Misc. 1099.

10 Act 6 Geo. IV, c. 16 (Private); Act 6 Geo. IV, c. 17 (Private); Chelsea Rectory Act, 6 Geo. IV, c. 18 (Private).

11 *The Times*, 9 Dec. 1927.

12 Chas. Dickens, quoted in Denny, *Chelsea Past*, 87.

13 Vestry mins, 1839–43, pp. 26, 143, 155–6, 200, 204, 261–6, 283; ibid. 1843–56, pp. 14–20; Chelsea Misc. 841–v., 846v.

14 PRO, CRES 2/548: letter, 16 Sep. 1844.

15 *2nd Rep. Com. Met. Improvements*, p. lxv; PRO, RAIL 989/27; above, Intro., comms.

16 8 & 9 Vic. c. 143 (Local and Personal).

17 Chelsea Scraps, 457–60, 465–6.

18 Improvement com. mins, 1845–6, 1846–8.

19 *The Times*, 12 Nov. 1845.

20 Improvement com. mins, 1845–6, *passim*; ibid. 1846–8.

21 Improvement com. mins, 1845–6, pp. 111–13, 116, 121.

petition which they with local incumbents and surgeons had presented to the Metropolitan Commissioners of Sewers regarding the Westbourne or Ranelagh Sewer had been ignored. The sewer had been covered as far as Sloane Square, but thereafter was open down to the Thames, and by 1854 each side was lined with dwellings densely crowded by the poorest classes, who had suffered great sickness the previous year, presumably because of the filthy stream. The petitioners wanted it covered the whole way, since cholera and fever had again appeared.[1]

The parish also resisted a proposal in 1863 to build new barracks in Chelsea on Quailfield (later the site of Lennox Gardens) to replace Knightsbridge Barracks: residents and the rector of Upper Chelsea strongly opposed the barracks, as the parish would be deprived of a large number of ratepayers if barracks were built instead of houses, and the parish already had three great military establishments.[2]

The number of new houses built in Chelsea between 1831 and 1842 averaged nearly 91 a year, despite a slump in the mid 1830s. Well over half were 4th class, the mid point in the range.[3] As building increased more streets were taken over by the parish, for example William Street in 1837,[4] and others declared public by the improvement commission between 1846 and 1853,[5] although it still wished to ensure that the promoters, not the commission, paid for making up new roads.[6] In 1847 when it proposed a new road between Marlborough Road (later Draycott Avenue) and Hans Place to improve communications to Hans Town, a minority in the vestry felt that the road should be made by the proprietors.[7] In 1854 Chelsea improvement commission had over 19 miles of roads; Hans Town commission had four miles.[8] From 1864 the parish took over responsibility for the one mile of turnpike road still running through Chelsea, included in its 22 miles in 1872. The vestry continued to pave and improve streets, in 1856–72 flagging over 420,000 ft of footways. In 1872 all the roads were watered.[9] The vestry still considered that the embankment through Chelsea to Fulham was necessary, and calls for its extension continued.[10]

CHELSEA VILLAGE OR GREAT CHELSEA

The area between the modern Flood Street in the east and Milman's Street in the west, and from King's Road to the river Thames, formed the main settlement of Chelsea in the Middle Ages, and for a long time was the heart of the parish. After the creation of Little Chelsea, the village was often called Great Chelsea.

LAWRENCE ESTATE

Serious speculative building in Chelsea village began in the late 17th century on the 4-acre site of the old manor house, belonging to the Lawrence family. In 1687 Sir Thomas Lawrence leased to Cadogan Thomas of Southwark, merchant, for 62 years the manor house with its grounds and outbuildings, and adjoining close of 3 a., then let to a butcher: Thomas was to build four ranges comprising in all at least 30 substantial brick houses, with a total frontage of 850 ft; the houses were to be two storeys high plus cellars and garrets, each to have a depth of at least 2 rooms on each floor and to be at least 16 ft across; the agreement also specified in detail the measurements for the window openings.[11] It is not entirely clear what the four ranges referred to, but this could mean two ranges on the east side of Church Lane divided by a new side road called Johns Street (below), and two ranges on either side of the new Lawrence Street: the detail given in the agreement suggests that development of the manor house site had been planned as a whole before work began.

Thomas acted as a contractor, surrendering many sites back to Lawrence's trustees to lease to other builders or purchasers after building; by 1689, when Thomas died, individual houses had been built by John Collett, carpenter, Henry Margetts, plasterer, and Thomas Hearne, bricklayer, all of Westminster.[12] One lease to Collett in 1688 was of a house 20 ft wide fronting Church Lane on a plot stretching back 116 ft to the garden wall of Sir Thomas Lawrence; it lay on the south side of a new street to be called Johns Street, presumably the later Justice Walk.[13] Houses in Lawrence Street and Church Lane had been built by 1689, and the gardens adjoining Lawrence's house had been divided and built on by 1691:[14] in 1705 there were *c.*33 newly-erected houses on the site of the ancient house and adjoining close.[15] The old manor house was probably demolished soon after 1687: John Bowack, who was living in Church Lane by 1704, did not mention it,[16] and though Sir Thomas Lawrence was assessed for an empty house in 1704 the middling rate given suggests it was not for the

1 *The Times*, 1 Sep. 1854.
2 Ibid., 23 Nov., 3 Dec. 1863.
3 LMA, MR/B/SR/18.
4 Vestry mins, 1833–9, p. 149.
5 *London Gaz.* 3 Mar. 1846, p. 824; ibid. 14 Dec. 1847, p. 4604; ibid. 15 Jul. 1851, p. 1844; ibid. 27 Sept. 1853, p. 2631.
6 Improvements com. mins, 1845–6, p. 182.
7 Vestry mins, 1843–56, pp. 79–82.
8 *Returns of Paving, Cleansing, and Lighting Metropolitan Dists.* (Parl. Papers 1854–5 (127), LIII), p. 15.
9 *Returns from Vestries on Improvements since 1855* (Parl. Papers 1872 (298), XLIX), pp. 23–4.
10 Below, 1865–1900.
11 PRO, C 10/511/74.
12 Ibid.
13 MLR 1715/1/79.
14 PRO, C 7/330/22.
15 Guildhall MS 1809; CL, deed 2994.
16 Bowack, *Antiquities*; *DNB*; BL, Sloane MS 2938, f. 5.

12. *Section of OS 1st edition map showing Chelsea village*

manor house itself.[1] Dr King referred in 1704 to the tithe paid by Sir Thomas 'before his house was pulled down and now built into many tenements'.[2] The new houses on the site also included a row of five facing the Thames, later known as Church Row or Prospect Place (nos 59–63 Cheyne Walk), which stretched between the churchyard and Lawrence Street and were all probably built by 1689 when the easternmost was leased; all were rated in 1695.[3] Three old houses on the north side of Lordship Yard belonging to the Lawrence estate were sold in 1706 to William Cheyne, Viscount Newhaven, who leased them for rebuilding.[4]

In 1695 there were four houses rated on the western side of Lawrence Street, followed by two on the eastern side. In 1704 John Lawrence leased to Samuel Chase of St Giles-in-the-Fields, bricklayer, two pieces of land at the northern end of the Lawrence property adjoining the glebe, presumably the site of the four houses which closed off Lawrence Street on the north and were later collectively known as Monmouth House. Chase also leased some glebe land in 1704 on the north side to create gardens for the two central houses, which were larger than the rest and faced down Lawrence Street, with a passage between them to the garden, hidden behind a pair of doors with a pedimented doorcase.[5] They were first rated in 1705–6 as two houses at £28 each and two at £18. The centre house on the east was let from 1715 to Anne, duchess of Buccleuch (d. 1732), widow of James Scott, duke of Monmouth (d. 1685), and from 1718 she also took the adjoining house at right angles:[6] her residency there gave the house its popular name of Monmouth House, but that led later writers to assume that the block had originally been built as a single mansion. The duchess was in Chelsea from at least 1714, and entertained royalty there in 1716, but spent her later years in Scotland.[7] The house was rated to her daughter, Lady Isabella Scott, in 1735.[8] The westernmost house of the group, occupied by Alexander Reid in 1722 and empty in 1735, was rated to Nicholas Sprimont in 1751 when the next house, presumably the western central house, was rated to Tobias Smollett, and the Duchess of Buccleuch's former house to Sprimont as a house and outbuildings, which he used as a showroom for the Chelsea Porcelain works.[9] Smollett lived in Chelsea from 1750 to 1763, though he never identified his house in his letters.[10]

Nos 23 and 24 Lawrence Street, facing Justice Walk and still standing in 2003, had twin doorways in a single

1 BL, Sloane MS 2938, f. 9.
2 Dr King's MS, pp. 3, 16.
3 LMA, AC.79.55; *Survey of London*, II. 84–6.
4 CL, deeds 2995, 3015, 3031; below.
5 MLR 1715/6/131; Dr King's MS, pp. 13, 24–5; see Fig. 13.
6 *Survey of London*, IV. 58–9; Poor rate bk, 1716–27, p. 360.
7 Lysons, *Environs*, II. 92; Chwdns accts quoted in Faulkner, *Chelsea*, I. 266; *Complete Peerage*, II. 366.
8 Poor rate bk, 1728–42, ff. 388 seqq.
9 Ibid., 1748–51, rate 22 Feb. 1750/1; below, Econ., trade.
10 *The Letters of Tobias Smollett*, ed. L.M. Knapp (1970), 14.

13. *The 4 houses at the top of Lawrence Street, known as Monmouth House*

doorcase, similar to the arrangement shown on Monmouth House *c.*1833,[1] and probably date from the development of *c.*1690, which has otherwise left no trace, except for the stuccoed remains of Church Row at nos 62 and 63 Cheyne Walk.[2] Perhaps because of lack of demand, not all the site was built over in the late 17th century. A factory was built for the Chelsea Porcelain works in 1750 on the west side of Lawrence Street on an empty site between the house at the corner of Justice Walk and Chase's houses at the top of the street,[3] while a plot of land opposite at the top of Lawrence Street on the east side was still not built on by 1836. In 1714 Richard Culliford bought the lease of the house on the east side near the top, on a site 32 ft to Lawrence Street and 145 ft back to Cheyne Row, built by Thomas Hearne in 1688, and in 1720 he obtained a 20-ft wide strip of the vacant land which lay between him and the wall of the Duchess of Buccleuch's house at the northern end.[4] The illustration of 'Monmouth House' in 1833 shows the ground still unbuilt, although with a high wall around it.[5]

About nine houses of the estate fronted Church Lane between Justice Walk and the parish church and about seven north of Justice Walk, all of which John Offley sold in 1750 in ones and twos, mainly to the occupiers.[6] Offley's successor Francis Needham sold off further property, including the site of Justice Walk to a builder in 1788: the vestry then had to act to prevent it being built over, despite having been a public highway for over 70 years.[7] Part of the block of Monmouth House was demolished in 1835 to allow Lawrence Street to be extended.[8]

MANORIAL ESTATE

In the 1690s new building also increased on parts of the manorial estate in the village. In 1695 Charles Cheyne, Viscount Newhaven, granted to John Clarkson of Chelsea, carpenter, a 41-year lease of the Magpie inn with stable and coachhouse, and Magpie Yard with buildings fronting south onto the road by the Thames; Clarkson paid a fine of £152 and £5 a year rent. He demolished the old buildings, built two new houses, and converted the coachhouse to a dwelling, spending £600. In 1701 he negotiated with Newhaven to buy the freehold for which he paid £203, but in 1705 his son William, also a carpenter, had to bring a case against Charles Munden and his son-in-law John Goodwin, who claimed the property under a previous lease: Munden claimed he was seized of five messuages, three of which had been laid into one and called the Magpie, with the other two on the west side.[9]

Improvements to existing properties were made in 1706 when William, Lord Cheyne, granted a 99-year lease to John Clarkson of three cottages and gardens, 49 ft by 86 ft, on the north side of Lordship Yard, which adjoined Cheyne's land and had recently been bought from the Lawrence family: Clarkson was to demolish them and use the materials to build three new brick cottages the same size as the old ones.[10] John Clarkson benefited from his association with Cheyne and from the growth of building in Chelsea: in 1763 his heirs divided free and leasehold property including four houses, gardens, and wharves at Swan Walk, let to a timber merchant; the Magpie and a house and buildings

1 See fig. 13.
2 *Survey of London*, IV, 59.
3 Below, Econ., trade.
4 PRO, C 113/85.
5 *Survey of London*, IV, plate 57. See fig. 13.
6 MLR 1750/1/160–6, 201–2, 349, 532–3, 540.
7 MLR 1788/6/392; Vestry orders, 1771–90, f. 164.
8 *Survey of London*, IV. 58–9; Thompson, *Map* (1836).
9 PRO, C 10/416/23; /64.
10 CL, deeds 2995, 3015.

adjoining it in Cheyne Walk; a house in Cheyne Row; a house and buildings at the corner of Little Cheyne Row; and a row of 5 houses and gardens near Cheyne Walk; the total rental was £247 a year.[1]

New speculative building on the manorial estate began with the 11 houses of Cheyne Row, nos 16–36 (even), built halfway up the modern street on land leased from Lord Cheyne in 1708, the date being marked on a tablet on no. 16. The terrace of three-storeyed houses with basements was originally quite plain, only doorcases and eaves cornice being enriched. It was also regular despite having apparently been built by several different lessees, including John Clarkson, Francis Cook, who held adjoining glebe land, Francis Taylor, carpenter, Francis Parker, plasterer, and Oliver Maddox, bricklayer.[2] The site was the former bowling green at the rear of the Three Tuns: nos 16–26 backed eastwards onto the old Tudor brick wall of Shrewsbury House, and the remainder onto part of the glebe. No. 14, Cheyne Cottage, was added 50 years later.[3] Land on the west side of the bowling green was retained for a 30-foot way from the houses to the highway by the Thames, and also gave access to Lordship Yard.[4] Cheyne bought back the lease of former garden ground on the west side of the Feathers in 1707, which allowed him to create the road from Cheyne Row to the riverside.[5] The block facing the river between Cheyne Row and Lawrence Street was quickly filled with many small houses, taverns, and commercial premises, such as the malthouse leased to Thomas Harris in 1725 which included granaries, a kiln for drying malt, and the use of an oven and common yard adjoining the malthouse.[6] The Three Tuns tavern, which adjoined the western wall of Shrewsbury House, and a little house next to it were demolished shortly before March 1711,[7] and rebuilt as three houses, nos 46–8 Cheyne Walk, by William or John Clarkson; no. 48 was remodelled *c.*1750. The Feathers, no. 49 Cheyne Walk, on the corner of Cheyne Row, was later renamed the Princes' Arms.[8] Nos 8–12 Cheyne Row, near the southern end, were apparently built in the later 18th century on part of the garden of the former Three Tuns.[9]

Lord Cheyne also allowed land for a 22-foot way near the north end of the bowling green, which marked the end of Cheyne Row, and in 1709 Oliver Maddox and John Clarkson took a building lease from Cheyne of ground between the 22-ft way, later called Upper Cheyne Row, and part of the glebe on the north side.[10] This road ran eastwards to the boundary between land of the manor and of the glebe. The land, 40 feet deep, on the north side of Upper Cheyne Row was originally intended for stables and a coachhouse, but instead the lessees built houses, renting some glebe on the north side to provide gardens.[11] The land was apparently still unbuilt in 1715 when John Clarkson drew up his will,[12] but a continuous row of five individual houses, more modest than those in Cheyne Row but with front courts, was built *c.*1716 eastwards from the junction with Cheyne Row as nos 8–16 (later nos 20–8). Nos 4 and 6 (later 16 and 18) were added later, appearing in rate books from the end of the 18th century.[13] Thomas Hill, mason, and Francis Cook were also lessees of property there, and may have built some of the houses.[14]

After acquiring Chelsea manor in 1713 Sir Hans Sloane leased out the whole of the great garden west of the manor house for building: Manor Street was laid out through the middle from the riverside northwards as far as the northern wall of the garden, and leases for most of the houses built on the garden were granted 1717–18, many to John Witt. Eighteen houses faced the Thames in a continuous row, broken by Manor Street, to form Cheyne Walk, screened from the road by handsome wrought-iron gates and railings enclosing small entrance courts in French taste. Those on the west side of Manor Street had very long gardens stretching to the northern wall of the great garden, while the gardens on the east side were cut off by plots fronting Robinson's Lane and Manor Street; no. 6, however, had a garden which incorporated one of those plots, giving it access to Robinson's Lane behind the gardens of nos 1–5.[15] To different degrees all the houses relied on their expertly cut and moulded brickwork and their enriched doorcases for effect. Some of them, such as nos 1–3, were built as speculations, usually 3 or 4 bays wide and with two rooms on each floor, but a few were built to the requirements of the ultimate tenants, such as the five-bayed no. 6, built in 1718 for Joseph Danvers, and no. 16, called Tudor House and later renamed Queen's House. No. 16 was the second largest of the houses, built in 1717 by John Witt for Richard Chapman of St Clement Danes, apothecary, and distinguished by a pediment and projecting rear wings.[16] Immediately west of Manor Street nos 13 and 14 were built on a plot 40 feet wide leased in 1717 to John Witt and Jeremiah Gray; it was formerly one four-bayed house called the Yorkshire Grey tavern, but was later rebuilt as two.[17] No. 18, built 1717, was occupied until his death in 1728 by James Salter, who ran his

1 CL, deed 19892; MLR 1732/3/111–13.
2 MLR 1709/2/214; 1711/1/134; 1715/4/116, 118.
3 *Survey of London*, IV. 60. See Plate 9.
4 MLR 1715/4/116.
5 Faulkner, *Chelsea*, I. 262n.
6 CL, deed 3040.
7 MLR 1711/5/8.
8 *Survey of London*, II. 82.
9 *Survey of London*, IV. 60.
10 CL, deed 3034.
11 CL, deed 19892.
12 MLR 1732/3/111.
13 *Survey of London*, IV. 73.
14 MLR 1714/6/36; 1725/1/113.
15 *Survey of London*, II. 31–64; MLR 1717/3/171–6; 1717/4/256; 1717/5/198–9; 1717/6/215; 1718/2/180, 216, 264–7; 1718/3/93, 165; 1718/4/60–3; 1718/5/68–9; Horwood, *Plan* (1792–5); see Plate 2.
16 *Survey of London*, II. 54; MLR 1718/5/130; 1720/4/340.
17 *Survey of London*, II. 50.

coffee house and museum of curiosities there, popularly known as Don Saltero's Coffee House. It continued in that form until 1799, when the museum was dispersed, but continued as a tavern until 1867.[1]

It was not until the late 1750s that the Tudor manor house itself was demolished and Cheyne Walk continued westward, with nos 19–26 built 1759–65 in a standard London row on the site: some Tudor brickwork surviving at the base of the façades, and vaults at no. 24, suggest that the foundations of the old house were used.[2] Two of the houses, nos 21 and 26, had extended gardens which included between them the former manor gardens that lay on the north side of the house, preserving a Tudor wall.[3] No. 24 incorporated an archway leading to stables, later Cheyne Mews, behind the houses.[4] By 1769 a row of small cottages had been built in Manor Street behind no. 14 Cheyne Walk and a row of ten houses with good-sized gardens on the opposite side of Manor Street at it furthest extent with other building on the corresponding part of Robinson's Lane to the east.[5]

Little more new building took place on the manorial estate in the old village until into the 19th century. By 1808 a strip of land on the east side of Dairyhouse field and adjoining Robinson's Lane north of existing building had been leased by the owners of the manor to Lancelot Wood on a building lease,[6] and by 1813 the existing building had been extended northwards with a row of 16 small houses. Further building had also taken place near the northern end of Robinson's Lane and along the south side of King's Road, where pairs of houses called Manor Row and Manor Terrace spread westwards from the junction with Robinson's Lane.[7]

In 1813 Manor Street still only extended across the former Great Garden, but by 1836 it had been extended to King's Road, and the northern half was lined with houses on both sides and in some side streets: Wellington and Collingwood streets, and Manor Gardens, a cul-de-sac of small houses with the gardens in front. The west side of Robinson's Lane, now called Queen Street, was also filled, mainly with terraces but with a few pairs of villas near the northern end.[8]

Along the riverside, one of Chelsea's old mansions, Winchester House, was dilapidated and out of fashion by 1821, when the bishop obtained an Act enabling him to sell it,[9] and the house and the grounds of 2½ a. were sold to the Cadogan Estate trustees. In 1825 the trustees obtained an Act to enable them to pull down the House, sell the materials, and grant building leases of the site.[10] The house had been cleared by 1836,[11] and the site was apparently still vacant in 1847,[12] but Oakley Street was laid across the site and adjoining glebe from Cheyne Walk to King's Road *c.*1850, and by 1850 ten houses at the northern end were occupied, and four at the southern end by 1851. Oakley Street was linked to existing streets such as Upper Cheyne Row, and gave access to Margaretta Terrace on the glebe, where similar terraced houses were being built by 1851.[13] The land on the west side of Manor Street had been filled by the creation of Grove Cottages and Oakley Crescent, the latter enclosed by smaller Italianate houses in brick and stucco, linked to Oakley Street by Phené Street. By 1865 the southern end of Oakley Street and adjoining parts of Cheyne Walk on the former Winchester site had been built up with terraces of large stuccoed Italianate houses, including a public house which became the Pier Hotel, as was part of the east side from the northern end, though land in the centre belonging to the glebe and the former Shrewsbury House was still unbuilt.[14]

DANVERS HOUSE ESTATE

West of Church Lane the house and land belonging to Danvers House also saw new building in the 1690s. Danvers House with its gardens, orchards, and stables, two houses nearby held by Francis Gilford and Thomas Gilbanck, and Dovehouse Close of 5 acres north of the house, used as an orchard or garden, all belonged to Thomas Wharton, Lord Wharton.[15] In 1696 Wharton leased part or all of the house and gardens to Benjamin Stallwood, bricklayer, who sub-let sites to the builders of individual houses, such as Nathaniel Hillyard, as well as to the purchasers of houses he had built, with Wharton issuing individual building leases: in 1696–9 leases were granted for three or four houses on each side of the southern end of Danvers Street, and houses either side facing towards the river including that on the site of the Goat.[16] It is likely that Stallwood put up the plaque once attached to no. 77 Cheyne Walk which recorded that Danvers Street had been started in 1696 by Benjamin Stallwood.[17] Danvers House was probably demolished at this time, though the street never extended beyond the first seven houses or so on each side until the 19th century. Dovehouse Close, with stables, coachhouse and land which had formed a coachway from the mansion to the stables, ground where the house had stood, and garden ground on the north side surrounded by a brick wall, were all leased by Wharton to Matthew Hutchins, gardener, in 1697. The leases were assigned to another gardener in 1729.[18]

Of the first houses to be built on the Danvers estate,

1 Ibid., 61–3; below, Soc. Hist., social (inns).
2 *Survey of London*, II. 65–7.
3 Ibid., 69.
4 Ibid., 70.
5 Richardson's Map (1769).
6 KL, deed 6408.
7 *Regency A to Z.*
8 Thompson, *Map* (1836).
9 Below, Landownership, Chelsea man.
10 Act 6 Geo. IV, c. 17 (Private).
11 Thompson, *Map* (1836).
12 CL, Tithe Map and Award.
13 *PO Dir. London* (1848, 1850, 1858); PRO, HO 107/1472/2/1/6; /2/1/14.
14 Old OS Map, London 87 (1865 edn).
15 CL, deed 3030; below, Landownership, later ests (Sloane Stanley).
16 CL, deeds 2991–3; MLR 1719/1/7–8; 1718/5/26–9.
17 *Survey of London*, IV. 8.
18 CL, Ar.4/76/11.

only no. 7 Danvers Street near the south-west corner still survived when that part of Danvers Street was demolished in 1909, but even then it had been refronted and was undatable. The four houses adjoining it to the north, nos 9–15, were apparently built some years later, most probably by 1722.[1] In 1717, when the estate was sold to Sir Hans Sloane,[2] it included 11 new brick houses built by Stallwood, in Danvers Street or facing the river, where one called the Black Boy was occupied by Valentine Arnold and had the Goat's grazing rights in 1719. Another of the houses, in Danvers Street, was occupied by James Salter, owner of the coffee house.[3] West of the houses in Danvers Street was the White Hart and its small alley, which ran north from the street facing the river. It may have been part of the Danvers estate, but could be part of the buildings belonging to Beaufort House.

Sir Hans Sloane's nephew William bought up the leases of the houses and sites from Stallwood's heirs and other assignees in 1718 and 1722,[4] and leased ground to William Clarkson in 1724 for 61 years; by 1725 Clarkson had built four new brick houses on a plot 75 ft square west of the White Hart.[5] The Danvers estate remained largely unchanged from the early 18th century until the 1840s,[6] when building began again in Danvers Street with about 12 houses built in the street and at the rear in 1846–8, mainly by W. Winks.[7] Dovehouse Close was laid out with the elongated Paultons Square, already partially inhabited by 1851, and Danvers Street was extended northwards to meet it.[8] In 1865 Paultons Square and Street and Danvers Street were complete with long terraces of stucco-trimmed white brick houses of moderate size.[9]

CHURCH LANE AND THE GLEBE ESTATE

Apart from the west side owned by the Lawrence family and the part belonging to the rectory, Church Lane was held by several freeholders and subject to piecemeal rebuilding rather than large-scale development. Nos 29 and 31 on the west side of Church Street were built or rebuilt *c.*1700, as possibly was no. 53. No. 17 was built or rebuilt in the second half of the 18th century, and on the east side nos 24, 26, 38 received new doorcases in the late 18th century. In 1707 the building for Petyt School was erected just north of the church.[10]

The rector continued to let glebe for gardens to the six houses in Church Lane, which in 1694 belonged to Mr Nichols, as well as five similar gardens let to Sir Thomas Lawrence, and a small garden by King's Road to John Gitto.[11] He also let some glebe for commercial gardens, and two of the lessees, the Frenchmen Francis Duneau, gardener, and John Narbonne, merchant, each built a house and walled additional land as gardens. By 1704 the rector was able to let his glebe with increased rents for commercial gardens and for building.[12]

On the glebe on the north side of Upper Cheyne Row the earliest part of Cheyne House was built in 1715 for the duchess of Hamilton, probably set back from the road within the large grounds, which extended east for rest of the row and north to Glebe Place. An additional block of 2 storeys, with dormers in the attic and a deep bay facing east onto the garden, was built on the south side of the house fronting Upper Cheyne Row *c.*1750, and became the principal part; gates were added from Glebe Place into the grounds. The house was not, however, shown on maps of 1745 and 1769.[13]

In 1716 the rector let to Francis Cook of St Martin-in-the-Fields, gardener, 6 acres on the west side of Great Conduit Field, stretching from King's Road to the wall of the Shrewsbury House estate, for 3 lives at £20 16s.[14] Cook also leased adjoining land called the Pindle south of Upper Cheyne Row from Lord Cheyne. He may have already started building on the glebe, as a house on his leasehold, The Cottage (no. 1 Upper Cheyne Row), built freestanding on the part of the glebe that lay at the east end of Upper Cheyne Row on its south side, was occupied by 1715. It had an unusual two-storey, simple-pile plan with a brick vaulted cellar and 4 rooms on each floor above it. What may have been stabling, demolished by 1912, was attached in line with the house.[15] In 1724 Cook was making leases of the sites of individual houses on the glebe, between 15 and 16 ft wide and 85 ft long, fronting King's Road, and the houses were built there within 10 months.[16]

In 1719 the rector let to John Narbonne 2½ a. of glebe in Great Conduit Field fronting King's Road and adjoining the land let to Cook. In 1722 Narbonne sublet a piece 50 ft wide by the road and 130 ft deep to John Peirene (or Pierene) of Westminster.[17] For Peirene, Giacomo Leoni, a Venetian architect, designed Argyll House in 1723, one of a small group of early 18th-century houses that survive on the King's Road between the later Oakley Street and Glebe Place, and are comparable in their size and quality with the superior houses that had been built along Cheyne Walk. Described by Leoni as a little country house, the two-storeyed no. 211 is of grey stock brick, the only enrichment being the linked Doric doorcase and pedimented window above. The

1 Poor rate bk, 1716–27, pp. 357–8; *Survey of London*, IV. 8–10.
2 Below, Landownership, later ests (Sloane Stanley).
3 MLR 1717/4/130.
4 MLR 1718/5/26–9; 1719/1/7–8; 1722/1/63.
5 MLR 1725/1/383.
6 Thompson, *Map* (1836).
7 LMA, MR/B/SR/1846/132, no. 233–4; 1847/45, nos 46–7; 1847/113, nos 176–9; 1848/50, no. 39; 1848/307, nos 380–2.
8 PRO, HO 107/1472/2/1/3.
9 Old OS Map, London 87 (1865 edn); see plate 9.
10 *Survey of London*, IV. 51–3.
11 Dr King's MS, p. 8.
12 Ibid., pp. 13, 24–5.
13 *Survey of London*, IV. 71.
14 MLR 1724/6/190.
15 *Survey of London*, IV. 69–70.
16 MLR 1724/1/425–6; 1724/6/162–4.
17 CL, deed 3037.

kitchen and offices were in the basement, and at the far end of the garden behind the house were the stable and coachhouse with lodgings for servants. The small courtyard towards the road was surrounded with an iron palisade. It was named after the duke of Argyll, occupant 1769–70.[1] On its west side, probably also on Narbonne's land, a pair of identical 3-storeyed houses had already been built in 1720, of warm-coloured stock brick with red brick dressings.[2] No. 217 at the corner of the later Glebe Place was built *c.*1750, of 2 storeys with attic rooms within a mansard roof, and back buildings beside Glebe Place.[3]

By 1745 more buildings had appeared on the south side of Upper Cheyne Row, and a right-angled road called Cook's Ground, later renamed Glebe Place, had been laid out:[4] by 1769 it linked into Cheyne Row and had a smattering of buildings around it, including cottages at the south-east angle, one of brick with a tiled mansard roof, standing by gates into Cheyne House grounds, with another building of the same date on the west side of the gates.[5] Away from King's Road, however, little building took place until the 1820s. Under the Chelsea Rectory Act, 1825, the rector obtained powers to grant 99-year building leases on all the glebe except the rectory house and its grounds. From 1826 the rector issued leases for various houses and land, especially in Cook's Ground, Upper Cheyne Row, and Glebe Place.[6] In 1836 Cook's Ground still had only a few buildings, and a variety of small terraces, pairs of villas, and individual houses were dotted along King's Road. On the south side of Upper Cheyne Row, the owner of Oakley Lodge (no. 9) leased land adjoining it in 1854 to a builder who had built Dudley Lodge or Villa (no. 7) adjoining.[7]

BEAUFORT HOUSE ESTATE

The mansion that had belonged to the duke of Buckingham in the mid 17th century was in 1681 bought by Henry Somerset, 1st duke of Beaufort, as his London residence. He and his wife Mary spent much time and money improving the house and the gardens: the Kip view of *c.*1700, though it distorts the width, gives an idea of the gracious and fashionable lay-out of the grounds. The duke died in 1699, and the duchess spent her final years at Beaufort House after a quarrel with her grandson, the 2nd duke, but after her death there in 1715 the house remained largely empty, and having been purchased by Sir Hans Sloane in 1737, was demolished in 1740.[8]

Count Zinzendorf, who bought Lindsey House as a residence 1750–1, also leased the site and grounds of Beaufort House, with a view to building a large Moravian settlement. The stableyard of Beaufort House was turned into a burial ground for the Moravian Church in 1751, with a chapel and minister's house designed by Sigismund von Gersdorf, completed in 1753 and retaining the 16th-century walls on the east and south. A pathway connected the burial ground with Lindsey House.[9] The Moravian settlement, however, never materialized, and Beaufort grounds were let as garden ground for several years. The narrow street of small houses and commercial premises which lay by the riverside to the east of the Beaufort House forecourt was known as Beaufort Street in 1745, and later renamed Duke Street.[10] In 1751 it was rated with 30 people, all at less than £10 with some listed as poor and rated at £4; one man was rated for the ferry and two men for part of Beaufort Gardens.[11]

Beaufort Row, lying approximately in the middle of the line of the later Beaufort Street, was begun in the 1760s, and a short row existed in 1769.[12] It may have been built in anticipation of the opening of Battersea Bridge, planned in 1766 and opened in 1771;[13] Beaufort Street was presumably laid out to King's Road in connection with the bridge. Houses facing the river were built at the southern end of Beaufort grounds from *c.*1771. Some survived in 2003: no. 91 Cheyne Walk on the west corner of Beaufort Street, with its principal front onto the latter, was first occupied in 1771 and called Belle Vue Lodge or Cottage in the 19th century;[14] adjoining it on the west no. 92, Belle Vue House, was built in 1771 of stock brick with central bay windows front and back;[15] and nos 93 and 94 were both built in 1777.[16] In 1781 the estate, referred to as Beaufort Garden or Street, consisted of *c.*7 a. on which a row of ten houses had been built, all uninhabited; three houses adjoining the row were leased to Edward Anderson, who also occupied several parcels of ground used as wharves, and five other houses were all occupied, mainly by tenants at will. The house and garden in the north-west corner of the Beaufort estate by King's Road was occupied by Edmund Howard.[17] The open ground by the river was known as Beaufort green in 1788.[18]

In 1836 Beaufort Street was largely filled on the west side, with a variety of terraced rows of houses. The east side was still partially open ground, with a few pairs of villas at the northern end and scattered buildings at the southern end. The long period of building the street

1 *Survey of London*, IV. 83–4; Pevsner, *London NW.* 576.
2 Pevsner, *London NW.* 576.
3 *Survey of London*, IV. 80.
4 Rocque, *Map of London* (1741–5).
5 *Survey of London*, IV. 76.
6 Chelsea Rectory Act, 33 & 34 Vic. c. 1 (Private).
7 CL, deed 20115.
8 Below, Landownership, later ests (Beaufort).
9 *Survey of London*, IV. 46; below, Rel. Hist., foreign chs (Moravians).
10 Rocque, *Map of London* (1741–5).
11 Poor rate bk, 1748–51, 22 Feb 1750/1.
12 Richardson's Map (1769).
13 Above, Intro., comms.
14 *Survey of London*, IV. 29–30. Shown with neighbouring hos in Figs. 38 and 51.
15 *Survey of London*, IV. 31–2.
16 Ibid., 33–4.
17 MLR 1835/4/726 (deed 5 July 1781).
18 MLR 1788/6/30.

14. *Backs of houses by the Thames between the Old Church and Battersea Bridge, before the embankment was built*

affected its overall appearance, and in 1865 the street had a mixture of types including some detached houses with large gardens, pairs of large semi-detached houses, and, especially on the west side towards the southern end, a terrace of large houses.[1]

CHELSEA RIVERSIDE

Before the creation of Chelsea Embankment, the riverside from the Royal Hospital to Battersea Bridge was crowded, mainly with commercial premises. In the 1840s, west of the terraces and gardens of the Royal Hospital and Gordon House, lay Druces' no. 2 wharf, with a shed and open ground, the public Paradise Walk, then Bull wharf, Swan wharf (also belonging to Druces), Swan brewery and a shed occupied by Messrs Lyall, boat-houses occupied by the Goldsmiths' and Skinners' companies, the Apothecaries' and their landing place; Old Swan Wharf, with a malthouse, garden, and causeway leased to the Old Swan public house. At the east end of Cheyne Walk was a public draw dock and a public causeway and stairs, and then the privately-owned Cadogan Pier with stairs and landing place; the public stairs and causeway owned by the Watermen's Company; the buildings, stables, and wharf occupied by Henry Alldin called Arch House wharf. West of the latter the small cottages on the south side of Lombard Street, nos 19–16, backed onto the river, no. 16 being the Waterman's Arms beerhouse, and no. 15 had a passage from the street. Next to it stood a building and wharf occupied by Chaplain & Company; another wharf occupied by Gladdish; a causeway, the old Ferry wharf house and counting house occupied by John Davis, then the cottages of nos 1–23 Duke Street again backing onto the river with a piece of vacant ground in front of two cottages of Beaufort Place.[2] West of Battersea Bridge stood Lindsey House wharf, mentioned in 1777 and presumably the one listed as Davis's Place in 1795.[3] By 1829 there was a large trade in coals, particularly at the wharves at the east end of Cheyne Walk, where coal was transferred from barges to wagons; timber was also handled.[4]

There was some opposition to the riverside activity. An application was made *c.*1842 to stop up the free dock (the Watermen's public stairs) at the end of Old Church Street, though unsuccessfully.[5] In 1845 residents near the draw dock at the east end of Cheyne Walk protested about the foul language of the carters, their brutality to horses, and the number of carts awaiting the tide, arguing that many users were not ratepayers. The dock was not closed, but a street-keeper was to regulate its use.[6] Use of the dock also brought great wear to the adjacent road.[7] In 1846 the improvement commission

1 Thompson, *Map* (1836); Old OS Map, London 87 (1865 edn).
2 Embankment Act, 9 & 10 Vic. c. 39; Guildhall MS 21329, copy of schedule; see Fig. 14.
3 CL, deeds 3156, 17552.
4 Faulkner, *Chelsea*, II. 172–3, 189.
5 Chelsea Misc. 846v.
6 Improvement com. mins, 1845–6, pp. 58–9, 62, 74, 78, 82–3, 97, 112, 137–8, 146.
7 Ibid., 1846–8, p. 16.

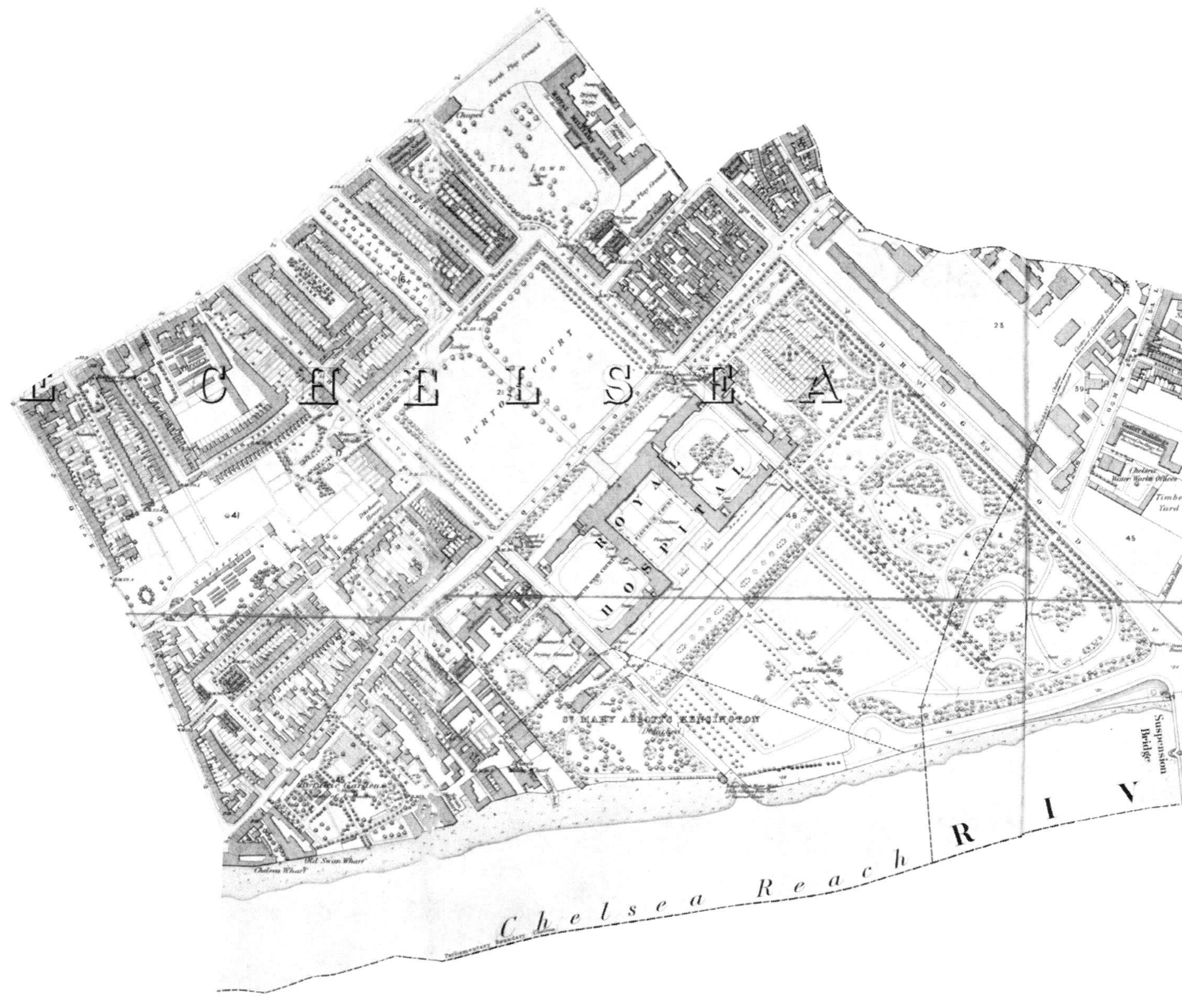

15. *Section of OS 1st edition map showing South-east Chelsea and the Royal Hospital*

wished to terminate use of a wharf at the east end of Cremorne Road.[1] In the 1860s the artist Daniel Maclise protested about the noise and cruelty to horses at the draw dock.[2]

In 1836, despite much piecemeal building and the laying out of new streets, the old village centre was still largely open ground behind the houses lining the principal roads. Between Beaufort Street and Church Street and between the rectory and Manor Street the land that was not being used as the gardens to houses was used as market and nursery gardens, and the early 18th-century Danvers and Lawrence streets and Cheyne Row were largely unchanged apart from a few additional houses.[3] By 1865, however, the street pattern of the village had been completed by the creation of Oakley Street, linking Cadogan pier in Cheyne Walk to King's Road, the expanses of open ground had been covered by new streets, and unbuilt land was confined to small and erratic patches.

1 Improvement com. mins, 1845–6, p. 144.
2 Beaver, *Memorials*, 210.
3 Thompson, *Map* (1836).

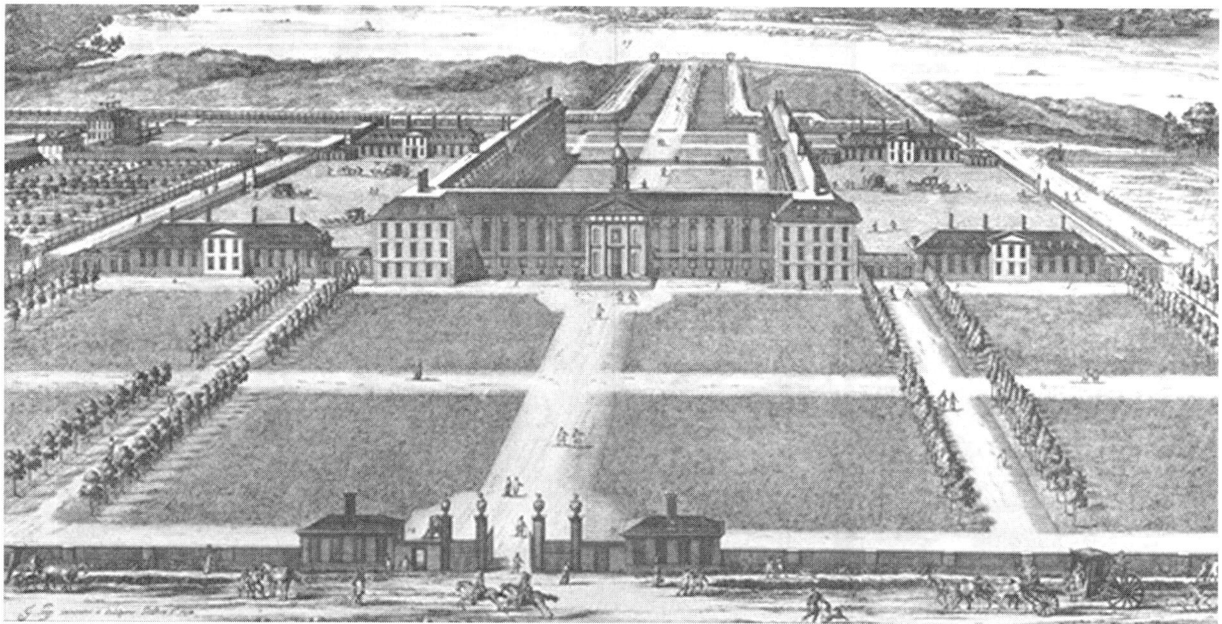

16. *The Royal Hospital from the north 1694, with Ranelagh House in distance* (top left)

SOUTH-EAST CHELSEA AND THE ROYAL HOSPITAL

The area from Flood Street eastwards to the parish boundary and south of King Road was mainly open fields in 1680, apart from King James's College and the premises to the west of the college between the road from Westminster and the Thames. In 1682, however, the college was sold to the Crown with adjoining land as the site for the Royal Hospital, which triggered the growth of new building in the area.

THE ROYAL HOSPITAL

The building of the Royal Hospital, which continued occasionally to be called Chelsea College, had a striking effect on Chelsea's development. It was the first major new royal building since the Restoration, and gave Chelsea a cachet to counter the aristocracy's dwindling interest in residences in the riverside village. Royal patronage and architectural grandeur almost immediately attracted speculators and ambitious individuals to build houses in its immediate vicinity, the superior houses in the reticent brick Dutch-influenced style used by Wren for the Hospital.

Charles II founded the hospital in 1681 for maimed and aged soldiers following its promotion by Sir Stephen Fox, Paymaster-General of the Army: it was hoped that the Hospital could be funded by charitable contributions, but despite assistance by the king out of the Privy Purse only a few thousand pounds were raised, and Fox had to assist by the creation of a fund from deductions from army pay. The foundation stone was laid in February 1682 and work continued until the central lantern was completed in 1689: 476 non-commissioned officers and men were admitted from that year, and the Hospital was completed in 1691 with the consecration of the chapel and burial ground. Sir Christopher Wren, one of those involved in its foundation, chose the site and, using the Doric order, designed an establishment on appropriately austere masculine lines.[1] Wren's planning, with one quadrangle facing south to the Thames, continued the fashion, begun in the late 16th century, for Chelsea's prestigious buildings to acknowledge the river, and gardens with avenues and an access canal, designed by London and Wise, extended from the building to the riverside.[2] On the north side the large open rectangle of land called Burton's Court, created by 1688,[3] preserved an open aspect to the Hospital; the carriage drive from the central gate across Burton's Court to the north side was linked to King's Road by the Royal Avenue by 1700.[4] On the east side of the Hospital, south of the burial ground which bordered the south side of the highway, was the walled physic garden with fruit trees and herbs, a small two-storeyed Apothecary's Laboratory, and a 2-acre kitchen garden.[5]

The building history of the Hospital is well known,[6] and several craftsmen connected with building in

1 Hutt, *Royal Hosp.* 13–14; J. Summerson, *Architecture in Britain, 1530–1830* (1970 edn), 239–41.
2 Pevsner, *London NW.* 565; see Fig. 16.
3 Above, Intro., comms (main rds).
4 Below, west and north of Burton's Ct.
5 Dean, *Royal Hosp.* 88.
6 Pevsner, *London NW.* 562–5.

Chelsea were involved, including Thomas Hill, mason, and Henry Margetts, plasterer.[1]

BUILDING WEST OF THE HOSPITAL

The steady development after the Restoration of mainly industrial premises by the Thames close to Chelsea village continued in the 1680s. In 1686 Lord Newhaven leased to William Kemp junior of Chelsea, brewer, land east of the Physic Garden and stretching between the road and the Thames, with a covenant to spend £600 on building within 10 years. Kemp was prosecuted by the City of London, as Conservators of the Thames, for inclosing 15 feet of the river foreshore into his premises, and by 1689 had built a brewhouse, contrary to his agreement with Cheyne which forbade buildings for brewing, sugar-making, or other offensive trades.[2] By 1695 there were not only several houses built in this area between the Physic Garden and the College, but also a dye house and wharf by the Thames, and a passage ran back to give tenants access to a stairs or causeway to the river.[3]

With the building of the Hospital, residential building began away from the mainly industrial developments by the Thames, and became concentrated by the end of the 1680s in the highway leading past the Hospital, called Jew's Row or Royal Hospital Row on the east side of Burton's Court, and Paradise Row on the west side; the highway in front of the hospital was diverted to go around the north side of Burton's Court in 1688, taking about an acre of ground, and remained thus until 1846 when it was relaid straight across the front of the Hospital and renamed Royal Hospital Road.[4] The reasons why the Hospital generated growth in building are complex. Building work at the hospital probably created demand for accommodation, and some builders may also have seen the prospects for growth in the area. By the early 18th century accommodation was also needed near the Hospital for the out-pensioners who had to attend the Hospital regularly. However, the presence of the Hospital also seems to have attracted notable and aristocratic residents, particularly in Paradise Row: the imposing setting of the Hospital and its royal connections may be partly the reason, as well as the fact that two substantial suburban mansions were created when land east and west of the Hospital was leased by the Crown to favoured officials. On the west side of the Hospital's outbuildings, a lease of 4½ acres of Great Sweed Court was granted by the Crown in 1690, and in the late 1690s rooms in the south-west corner of the stables, which adjoined the leasehold land, became a residence used in association with the leasehold, which was laid out as a garden; the entrance to the house, however, was from the Hospital's stableyard. The house was occupied first by its creator, Edward Russell, earl of Orford, and then by Sir Robert Walpole, Paymaster-General, from 1714.[5] Walpole employed Sir John Vanbrugh to enlarge the house, and design stables and coachhouse and garden buildings including the surviving orangery. Another wing was added to the main house in the early 1720s. After Walpole's death in 1745 the house was the residence of a number of noblemen, before being sold to George Aufrere, a London merchant and art connoisseur, but in 1808 the lease was surrendered back to the Crown and reoccupied by the Hospital.

The buildings of the Hospital, and consequently its surroundings, were much changed after the American War of Independence, when the infirmary premises had proved inadequate. From 1778 temporary premises had been taken on,[6] until in 1809 John Soane, Clerk of the Works to the Hospital from 1807, built a new infirmary on the site of Walpole House, incorporating part of the house; it was destroyed in 1941. The stables and offices were also rebuilt to Soane's design between 1814 and 1824. Soane's more extensive buildings presented a new, stately, neoclassical and stock brick face to adjacent roads. South of the stables the former orangery of *c.*1725 of Walpole House was used for the pensioners' library and RC chapel in 1991.[7] The southernmost portion of the garden of Walpole House was leased in 1810 for 80 years to Sir Willoughby Gordon, Bt, who built Gordon House there. After the lease expired the building was used for the infirmary nursing staff.[8]

North Side of Paradise Row

Even before building began on the Crown leaseholds, speculative building was beginning along the highway to the Hospital, particularly on the Chelsea side. In 1691 Lord Cheyne granted several building leases for land on the north side of the highway: Paradise Row, a terrace of ten houses which later gave its name to the stretch of highway there, was built by George Norris in 1691 on the north side near the eastern end and opposite the Hospital stables. The houses, demolished in 1906, were all of two storeys with attic rooms lit from dormers, but some had five bays each and others three. All lay behind walled and railed forecourts.[9] The large corner site at the eastern end of the Row, 287 feet by 210, was leased to Thomas Hill of Chelsea, principal mason of the Hospital, who built Ormonde House on the site. It received its name when it was occupied by the Duchess of Ormonde, 1720–33; other occupants included Sir Thomas (later Lord) Pelham 1700–3, and the countess of Bristol, 1704–8. It was later used by a naval academy

1 *Survey of London*, XI. 27–9.
2 PRO, C 8/410/12.
3 MLR 1722/4/271, reciting lease of 1695.
4 Hutt, *Royal Hosp.* 95, 327.
5 Below, Landownership, later ests (Royal Hosp.).
6 *English Hosps. 1660–1948*, ed. H. Richardson (1998), 76; Dean, *Royal Hosp.* 254.
7 Pevsner, *London NW.* 565; below, Landownership, later ests (Royal Hosp.).
8 Below, Landownership, later ests (Royal Hosp.); *Survey of London*, II. 3–7; above.
9 *Survey of London*, II. 23–4; see Fig. 17.

17. *Paradise Row, Royal Hospital Road, built in the 1690s and photographed shortly before demolition in 1906*

1777–1829 and then Mrs Elizabeth Fry's School of Discipline.[1] At his death in 1713 Thomas Hill held building leases in St James Westminster and in London, as well as three leases in Chelsea, on one of which he had built *c.*1693 the house in Paradise Row where he was living at his death. This had two rooms on the ground floor plus kitchen, closet, and cellars, three rooms on the first floor and three garrets over, with a brewhouse in the yard, and his possessions at his death included 55 maps and prints, as well as his masonry stock of marble, Portland stone, and several chimney pieces. He was owed money for work by Sir William Milman, Francis Cook, Henry, earl of Rochester, the Royal Hospital, Dr Hans Sloane, the countess dowager of Lindsey, Narcissus Luttrell, Jonathan, bishop of Winchester, Oliver Maddox, and Richard, late earl of Ranelagh; he was also owed £1668 by William III for work done, presumably on the Hospital, a debt classed as desperate.[2] At the western end of Paradise Row, at the corner of Robinson's Lane, stood Radnor House, which obtained its name from Laetitia Isabella, countess of Radnor, who was living there by *c.*1704 and continued there until 1714:[3] the house existed for some years before 1704, and may have been built in the late 1670s.[4]

Between Radnor House and Paradise Row were several other houses and garden ground by *c.*1704.[5] By 1745 the north side of Paradise Row is shown as solid rows of houses which turned the corner northwards up Robinson's Lane.[6] Between 1794 and 1813 one or more houses was demolished to give access to George Place, a row of 11 small cottages.[7]

South Side of Paradise Row

On the south side of Paradise Row, a mansion later known as Gough House was built by John Vaughan, 3rd earl of Carbery, by *c.*1704,[8] on the site of Little Sweed Court west of Lord Orford's Crown leasehold, with a garden laid out in terraces down to the Thames. Carbery lived there until his death in 1713, when the property was sold to the Gough family. Sir Richard Gough also held Lord Orford's leasehold 1714–19, building stables at the northern end by the highway, but in 1719 Sir

1 CL, Ar4/76/13; Davis, *Chelsea Old Ch.* 274; *Survey of London*, II. 24n.
2 PRO, 32/68/57.
3 Dr King's MS, p. 16; *Survey of London*, II. 31–2.
4 Above, Settlement, to 1680.
5 Dr King's MS, pp. 44–5.
6 Rocque, *Map of London* (1741–5).
7 *Regency A to Z.*
8 Dr King's MS, p. 16.

Robert Walpole took over most of that land, leaving only the stables and Lord Orford's gazebo by the river with Gough House.[1] By 1792 the owner, Sir Henry Gough-Calthorpe, let the western half of his estate from the highway to the river west of the house and garden to James Beattie, jeweller, for building: five houses fronting Paradise Row had been built by 1792, and behind them 17 small cottages either side of the narrow Calthorpe Place, running towards the river, had been built by 1794.[2] Between 1814 and 1836 Paradise Wharf was built at the southern end of Calthorpe Place.[3] Gough House remained more or less unaltered until it was converted into the Victoria Hospital for Children in 1866. As part of the embankment scheme, Tite Street was laid out along the south-west wall of the house and garden, obliterating the east side of Calthorpe Place.[4]

Further west along the south side of Paradise Row at least four houses (later nos 71–4 Royal Hospital Road) were built in the early 18th century west of Bull Walk,[5] as were possibly the two or three houses in Swan Walk which stood by 1745 and survived in 2003. Philip Miller, curator of the Physic Garden, lived in a house in Swan Walk 1733–40, and at no. 1 Swan Walk 1741–62. No. 3 Swan Walk was built in 1776; the rest of the land formed gardens to the houses. The Old Swan Inn on the riverside at the southern end of Swan Walk became famous as the finish of the annual watermen's race instituted by Thomas Doggett in 1715, but it was converted into a brewery later in the 18th century and another inn called Old Swan was opened on the west side of the Physic Garden.[6] In 1745 the area still mainly consisted of houses along the highway and wharves and buildings by the river at the end of Swan Walk and Bull Walk, with only a little building in between.[7] By 1794 Paradise Row from Gough House to Cheyne Walk was lined with houses, except at the Physic Garden. In addition to the cottages and gardens in Calthorpe Place, Bull Walk, renamed Paradise Walk about this time, had two rows of houses at the north and south ends with a few individual buildings including an Independent chapel opened *c.*1793. Swan Walk had a large timber yard behind its houses, but both here and in the other alleys was still much open ground. West of the Physic Garden, however, the area was filled with houses and commercial buildings.[8] The east side of Paradise Walk was nearly filled with cottages by 1813,[9] and though by 1836 a few more had been added on the west side, most of the remaining open ground was used in connection with the wharves and commercial buildings by 1865.[10]

BUILDING EAST OF THE HOSPITAL

On the east side of the hospital all the land on the south side of the highway as far as the parish boundary belonged to the Crown in 1690. The Hospital burial ground was created along most of the south side in 1691, with gardens for the Hospital behind. In 1688 Richard Jones, earl of Ranelagh, Paymaster-General of the Army and treasurer of the Hospital, began building an official residence for himself near the south-east corner of the Hospital, laying out gardens on the 7½-acre site of which he was granted a Crown lease in 1690; another 15 acres were added in 1693, also laid out with walks and orchards.[11] Access to the house was via Wilderness Row, a lane running south from the highway near the Westbourne, which had a row of cottages by *c.*1700,[12] but by 1745 an avenue later called Ranelagh Walk or Grove had been created to run to the house across the Westbourne from Ebury (Westm.).[13] The house and gardens were greatly admired by topographers and visitors:[14] Defoe lavished praise *c.*1724 on Ranelagh House, its situation, gardens, and pictures.[15]

In the early 1730s the estate was sold off in lots, and the main portion including the house and *c.*12 acres were sold partly as building land but were mainly used to create the Ranelagh pleasure gardens; an enormous timber rotunda was built in 1741 linked to Ranelagh House, and the gardens opened in 1742 to become one of the most fashionable pleasure resorts of the 18th century, attracting royalty and nobility as well as a host of lesser visitors, with access by river as well as by road.[16] In the 1760s Sir Thomas Robinson, one of the proprietors of the pleasure gardens, built a mansion east of the rotunda to his own designs called Prospect Place, where he lived until his death in 1777; by the 1790s the house had been divided. In 1803 the pleasure gardens closed and Ranelagh House, the Rotunda and other features were cleared. This part of the estate then became gardens in the ownership of the Hospital. Another of the proprietors, Edward Wilford, held land east of Prospect Place, which his son General Richard Wilford acquired and demolished, building a new mansion nearby where he lived until 1822,[17] which seems to be that called Ranelagh House in 1836.[18] In 1857–8 Chelsea Bridge Road was laid in a straight line from a widened White Lion

1 Below, Landownership, later ests (Gough; Royal Hosp.).
2 MLR 1792/6/449; Horwood, *Plan* (1792–5).
3 *Regency A to Z*; Thompson, *Map* (1836).
4 *Survey of London*, II. 8–9; below, Loc. Govt, pub. svces (medical).
5 *Survey of London*, II. 10.
6 Ibid., 11–14.
7 Rocque, *Map of London* (1741–5).
8 Horwood, *Plan* (1792–5); below, Rel. Hist., prot. nonconf. (Congs).
9 *Regency A to Z.*
10 Old OS Maps, London 87 (1865 edn), 88 (1869 edn).
11 Below, Landownership, later ests (Ranelagh; Royal Hosp.).
12 Dr King's MS, p. 39.
13 Rocque, *Map of London* (1741–5).
14 Dean, *Royal Hosp.* 157–8.
15 D. Defoe, *Tour thro' Gt. Britain*, ed. G.D.H. Cole, I. 391; see Fig. 16.
16 Below, Soc. Hist., social (Ranelagh).
17 Below, Landownership, later ests (Ranelagh; Royal Hosp.).
18 Thompson, *Map* (1836).

Street to the new Chelsea Bridge, sweeping away the later Ranelagh House, Wilderness Row and the eastern end of the burial ground; all the land west of the road was thrown into the Hospital's gardens, including land lying in Westminster.[1] The land between the new road and the Westbourne was taken for Chelsea Infantry barracks 1860–2.[2]

On the north side of the highway there was little building *c.*1700: at the extreme eastern end of the parish by the Westbourne was Fleet's garden including a house; a few houses stood at the corner of the highway by Burton's Court; and the half dozen houses of Franklin's Row faced the east side of Burton's Court.[3] The houses at the corner presumably included a tavern, later the site of the Royal Hospital public house, a picturesque plastered building coloured white with a large bay window on the first floor.[4] Franklin's Row, six houses facing the centre of the eastern side of Burton's Court north of the main highway was said to have been built in 1699 by a Chelsea farmer and contractor, Thomas Franklin, who also built the Angel and Soldier nearby, the first tavern in the neighbourhood.[5]

The well-to-do may have taken the houses in Paradise Row, and possibly in Franklin's Row, but they were not the only people wanting accommodation near the Hospital. Old soldiers seeking admission or claiming a pension had to apply in person to the Hospital, a regulation which was not relaxed until 1816 and only finally abolished in 1845. Even after being placed on the pension lists, they had to come up to Chelsea regularly for the half-yearly payments or could be summoned for medical examinations or posting.[6] The rapid increase in building in the first half of the 18th century, including several taverns, seems to be intended to meet the soldiers' requirements.

Gospelshot in Eastfield on the north side of the highway opposite the burial ground was let as garden ground by the 1680s, but in 1693 three parcels of this land were let for building by Charles Cheyne.[7] Sir Hans Sloane granted building leases for parcels here from at least 1716 to the late 1720s, to builders including Thomas Harding of St Clement Danes, Sampson Biddle of St Giles-in-the-Fields, Henry Tregeare of Chelsea, John Turner, and Robert Luing of London, who built brick houses and a few shops, mainly on 36-ft wide plots fronting the highway with long gardens behind. On the east side of the land a new 30-ft street called Princess Street ran northwards from the highway by 1726, later renamed White Lion Street.[8] By 1722 10 feet at the north end of each parcel was reserved to create a new 20-ft wide street,[9] by 1745 known as Turk's Row, running parallel to the highway, which was known as Jew's Row,[10] both presumably a popular reference to the fleecing of soldiers said to go on there.[11] By 1745 Morgan's Ground had been built on the remaining land on the east side of the White Lion Street.

In 1723 land on the north side of Turk's Row was let for building, to John Ward, carpenter, and Ralph Appleton, bricklayer, both of Westminster,[12] and on part of their land Garden Row was built in 1733 facing Burton's Court,[13] consisting in 1794 of seven houses with long gardens behind.[14] The rest of Gospelshot north and east of Garden Row up to King's Road was leased for 91 years from 1747, and was the site of a mansion, stable and gardens, held with a parcel of leasehold meadow containing 6½ acres. The house was built by 1745,[15] and by 1788 the leases belonged to Charles Lord Cadogan; the house was said to have been used by the Cadogan family in the 1770s. In 1788 the mansion was sold at auction and bought by Sir Walter Farquhar, Bt, to whom the owners of the manor granted new 99-year leases.[16]

Many old, poor soldiers obviously lived more or less permanently in the Jew's Row area, and their funerals had to be paid for by the parish. The Royal Hospital refused to pay parish rates for the gentlemen's houses on the Crown land, until a court case brought by the parish resulted in a fixed assessment of £100 being made in 1751. By 1781 this only covered about a fifth of the amount it cost the parish to maintain poor pensioners and their families. The demand for accommodation seems to have caused building to spread eastwards by 1745 across the Westbourne into Five Fields and Ebury (Westm.), where the famous Chelsea Bun House stood. Many of the buildings fronting the road were taverns and alehouses, and in 1734 the Board which managed the Hospital unsuccessfully requested the local JPs not to licence gin-shops nearby.[17] By 1794 at least four of the plots between Jew's and Turk's rows had alleys running along their length with rows of tiny cottages and other buildings, and half a dozen narrow courts giving access to more buildings including a second row of houses inserted behind part of the frontage to Jew's Row;[18] several more courts and yards had been added by 1836. In 1829 the block was condemned as the worse eyesore in the parish.[19] The remaining frontage to Franklin's Row had been filled with courts adjoining the public

1 G. Tyack, 'James Pennethorne and London Street Improvements', *London Jnl*, XV (1990), 51; Old OS Map, London 88 (1869 edn).
2 Below, Landownership, later ests (Ranelagh; Royal Hosp.).
3 Dr King's MS, p. 37.
4 *Survey of London*, IV. 93.
5 Dean, *Royal Hosp.* 33–4.
6 Ibid., 228.
7 MLR 1713/4/2; 1724/6/171.
8 CL, deeds 3038, 3041, 3043; MLR 1717/2/229–30; 1718/2/101; 1719/6/276; 1722/4/78; 1724/1/151.
9 MLR 1722/4/78.
10 Rocque, *Map of London* (1741–5).
11 Dean, *Royal Hosp.* 228–9. Both occasionally given as plural.
12 MLR 1724/6/294.
13 *Survey of London*, IV. 92.
14 Horwood, *Plan* (1792–5).
15 Rocque, *Map of London* (1741–5).
16 Pearman, *Cadogan Est.* 66, 79; MLR 1789/3/78–9; 6 Geo. IV, c. 16 (Private).
17 Dean, *Royal Hosp.* 228–9.
18 Horwood, *Plan* (1792–5).
19 Faulkner, *Chelsea*, II. 316.

house on the corner by 1794, and on the east side of that block White Lion Street, called Little Sloane Street in 1794, was lined with cottages, as was George Street near the Westbourne, a short street with some cottages facing the Westbourne and open ground behind. On the south side of Jew's Row, now renamed Royal Hospital Row, several houses and other buildings stood at the eastern end of the Hospital's burial ground by Wilderness Row.[1]

WEST AND NORTH OF BURTON'S COURT

Land north and west of Burton's Court was largely unbuilt *c.*1700: on the north side the Royal Avenue had been laid down and a house and garden called Robins Garden stood at the corner with the King's Road.[2] By the north-west corner of the Court stood two or three buildings called 'Mr Franklin's houses',[3] standing on part of the Greene estate of which Thomas Franklin was the tenant,[4] and facing the west side just north of the gardens of Paradise Row stood a tavern called the Ship with garden and orchard behind.[5] By 1745 a couple of houses and gardens stood each side of the junction of Blacklands Lane and King's Road, inclosed from the adjoining fields, and a couple more at the south-western end. More buildings had been added behind Mr Franklin's houses, and possibly an access lane running north to King's Road. On the west side of Burton's Court an alley between the gardens of Paradise Row and the Ship was lined with small buildings and led to a few more at the end of the Ship's grounds.[6] By 1769 buildings fronting King's Road and called the Royal Dairy had been built midway between Blacklands Lane and Royal Avenue.[7] They seem to be those later known as Whitelands, which housed a girls' school in 1772 and Whitelands House School in 1797;[8] by 1836 the buildings had been enlarged.[9] In 1842 the lease was purchased by the National Society for the Training of Schoolmistresses and it was thereafter known as Whitelands Training College.[10] Also by 1769 a large house had been built on the Greene estate fronting King's Road, and the five houses called Green's Row, which survived in 2003 as nos 26–30 St Leonard's Terrace, had been built on the north side of the highway facing Burton's Court and the Hospital:[11] they were said to have been built in 1765.[12] Another house had been built close to the west side of Mr Franklin's houses, while at the western side of this area in Robinson's Lane the line of houses at the southern end had been extended a little way northwards.[13]

By 1794 considerable building had taken place, especially on the former Greene estate, which had been divided and sold off by that date.[14] Thomas Smith acquired a large portion of the land north of Green's Row and laid out Smith Street across the site of Mr Franklin's houses of *c.*1700, extending the road on the west side of Burton's Court northwards to join King's Road. Building leases for land on both sides of Great Smith Street from King's Road to the south side of Little Smith Street were granted from 1794 to 1801 and in 1812.[15] Land in Smith Street leased by Thomas Smith for building in 1801 included six unfinished houses on the west side, a vacant plot 260 ft by 80 ft, and another 1½ a.[16] In 1812 Smith leased to Jacob Franks land at the south-east corner of Smith Street, bordered on the east by Green's Row, on which Franks was building a house.[17] Terraced rows of houses on either side of Smith Street had been started at the northern end and near the southern end on the west side, while on the east Little Smith Street ran eastwards with small cottages on the south side and the two buildings of Morley's floorcloth factory on the north lying behind the Smith Street houses. A detached house fronting King's Road lay on the remaining land east of the factory.[18] By 1813 Smith Street had been completed, and on the land between Smith's development and the Royal Avenue another builder had begun the houses at the southern end of Hemus Terrace facing Royal Avenue and a group of five houses facing Burton's Court near the junction with Royal Avenue,[19] called Rayner Place in 1836.[20] By 1859 in addition to houses Smith's former ground included a slaughterhouse, the Phoenix public house, and a stable.[21] On the west side of Burton's Court a large mansion in its own grounds was built in 1780 by Thomas Richardson facing east down the road on the north side of Burton's Court, and called Manor House by 1836.[22] Next to that on the south side was a terraced row of seven houses called Durham Place facing Burton's Court; the tavern called the Ship had been renamed Durham House by 1813. South of that the grounds north and east of Ormonde House had been filled by another terraced row of 15 fairly small houses, with another two facing Paradise Row.[23]

Along King's Road the detached house standing west of Smith Street in 1794 had apparently disappeared by 1813, when another house called Manor House stood further west in King's Road facing Jubilee Place, with

1 Horwood, *Plan* (1792–5).
2 Dr King's MS, p. 37.
3 Dr King's MS, pp. 44–5.
4 *Survey of London*, IV. 88
5 Dr King's MS, pp. 44–5.
6 Rocque, *Map of London* (1741–5).
7 Richardson's Map (1769).
8 *Survey of London*, IV. 90.
9 Thompson, *Map* (1836).
10 *Survey of London*, IV. 90.
11 Richardson's Map (1769).
12 *Survey of London*, IV. 88
13 Richardson's Map (1769).
14 Below, Landownership, later ests (Arnold).
15 CL, deed 21853.
16 CL, deed 3294.
17 CL, deed 3289.
18 Horwood, *Plan* (1792–5).
19 *Regency A to Z.*
20 Thompson, *Map* (1836).
21 CL, deed 21853.
22 NMR, Red box LB Kensington & Chelsea: Chelsea Man. Ho.; Horwood, *Plan* (1792–5); Thompson, *Map* (1836).
23 Horwood, *Plan* (1792–5); *Regency A to Z.*

another detached house on the west side, and a terraced row of 7 houses called Sidney Place fronted King's Road next to the junction with Robinson's Lane. At the southern end of Robinson's Lane a row of seven more terraced houses had been added by 1794 north of the existing row, and a large building, possibly a farm, had been built to the north of the houses, the gap being filled with more small houses by 1813.[1]

Sir Walter Farquhar's house and land between Turk's Row and King's Road were acquired for the Royal Military Asylum for the Children of Soldiers of the Regular Army,[2] founded by Frederick Augustus, duke of York, and a building with two long side wings designed by John Sanders was built 1801–2 across the site from north to south, with the entrance in Franklin's Row, at a reported cost of £40,000.[3] The brick building had a stone balustrade in centre of the western front ornamented with a Doric portico of 4 columns, pediment and frieze, and the north and south wings were joined to the main building by a colonnade: the latter contained the dining halls with school rooms over, and apartments for officers and for boys and girls in the wings. The Asylum was opened by 1805. The girls were moved to Southampton in 1823, and in 1829 the Asylum had 1,000 boys.[4] Blacklands or Whitelands Lane ran along the western boundary of the school site, and a strip of glebe belonging to the rector of Chelsea, which lay on the west side of the lane, was bought on behalf of the Crown, confirmed by Act in 1815. In 1816 the lane (later renamed Cheltenham Terrace) was moved to the west of this addition in order to enlarge the school's grounds.[5] A triangular piece of land on the east side of the school was nursery ground in 1836, but was occupied by the Asylum in 1865.[6]

In the mid 1840s St Jude's church and a National school were built on the north side of Turk's Row.[7] By 1847 building along King's Road virtually filled the whole frontage between Robinson's Lane, now called Queen Street, and Royal Avenue, though much land behind the main streets remained open as market or nursery gardens, or the grounds to larger houses.[8] In King's Road between Sidney Place and Manor House more rows of houses fronted the road with Shawfield Street running southwards and partially built up. Queen (later Flood) Street also had rows of houses at its northern end, leaving only a small portion of unbuilt land in the middle of the east side. Manor House in King's Road had extensive grounds laid out behind it, and to the east houses lined King's Road to Smith Street with Little's Botanic Nursery behind. The floorcloth factory behind Smith Street had been demolished and the area awaited redevelopment. The terrace on the west side of Royal Avenue was nearly complete, but land on the east side was still unbuilt. Facing Burton's Court, Green's Row had been extended to join Rayner Place.[9] In 1845 the approach from King's Road to the Royal Hospital had been improved by removing old chestnut trees and laying out a garden instead, giving an unrestricted view of the Hospital. A terraced row of houses was being built on the east side on the site of a former nursery garden.[10] At the same time Radnor Street was being laid out and building leases granted.[11] In 1847 George Place, north of Paradise Row, was swept away to give access to Christ Church built on former garden ground.[12]

By 1865 the garden ground occupied by Henry Little in 1847 was a nursery, as was the ground occupied by William Puvey. The grounds of Manor House, Smith Street, stretching west to Queen Street were still unbuilt, but elsewhere the whole area was covered in building or about to be so. The former garden ground around Christ Church was built up with small terraced houses in Elizabeth and Caversham streets and Christchurch Terrace. The Manor House in King's Road had either been demolished or radically altered to allow Radnor Street to run south from the main road filled with terraced houses either side; from the southern end a passage led into Smith Terrace built eastwards to Smith Street over former garden ground. The three sides of Wellington Square had been built on the site of the floorcloth factory between Smith Street and Royal Avenue, open to King's Road. Both sides of Royal Avenue were filled with substantial terraced houses, Walpole Street with similar houses had been built to the east, and St Leonard's Terrace to the south fronting Burton's Court. The grounds south of Whitelands School had also been built over.

HANS TOWN

Until the 1770s the large eastern area of the parish stretching from Knightsbridge in the north to King's Road was still fields and market gardens, with few buildings apart one or two along King's Road, and on the small Lowndes estate in the extreme north-east corner of the parish. The Lowndes estate consisted in the 17th

1 Horwood, *Plan* (1792–5); *Regency A to Z.*
2 6 Geo. IV, c. 16 (Private).
3 *The Times*, 22 June 1802.
4 *Survey of London*, IV. 91; Faulkner, *Chelsea*, II. 327–9, 331, 333.
5 55 Geo. III, c. 66 (Private); LMA, MJ/SR 3933/121.
6 Thompson, *Map* (1836); Old OS Map, London 88 (1869 edn).
7 Below, Rel. Hist., ch. extension; Soc. Hist., educ. (pub. schs).
8 Thompson, *Map* (1836); CL, Tithe Map and Award.
9 Thompson, *Map* (1836).
10 *The Times*, 12 Dec. 1845; 8 May 1846.
11 CL, deed 3242.
12 CL, Tithe Award and Map.

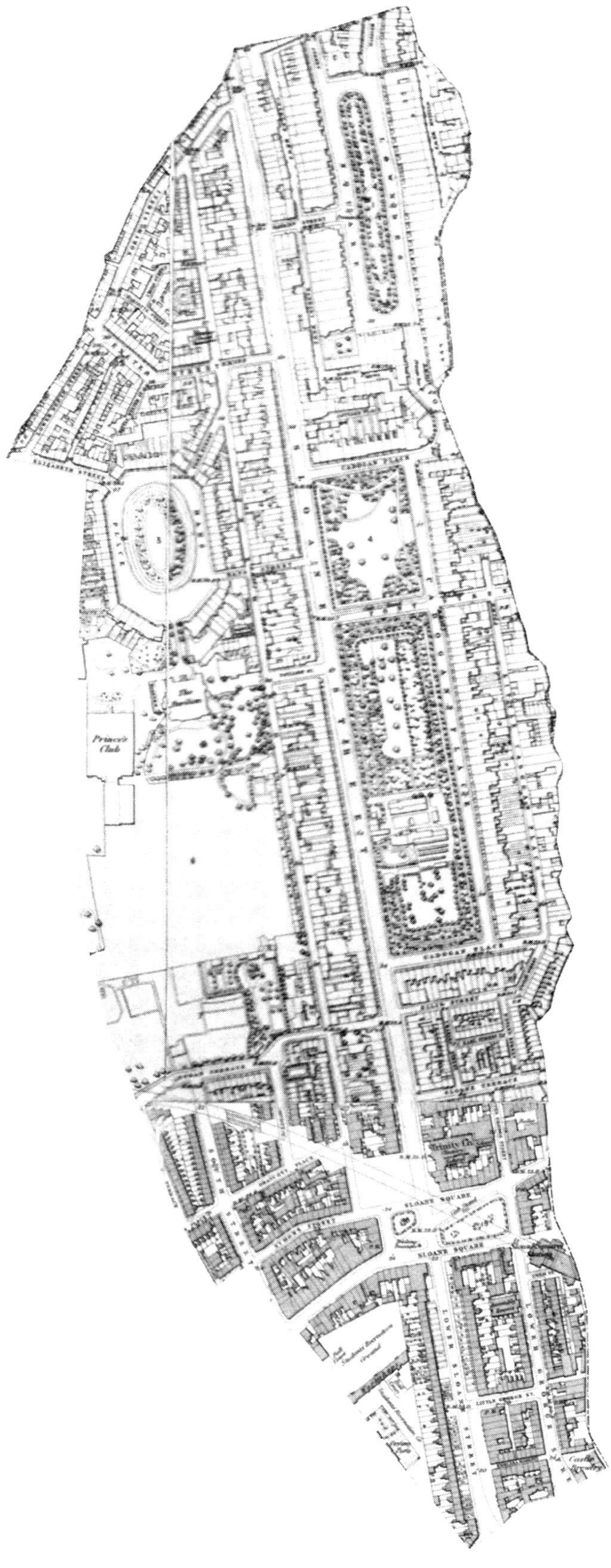

18. *Section of OS 1st edition map showing the Hans Town area, including Hans Place (*west*), Cadogan Place (*east*), and Sloane Square (*south*)*

century of a close of pasture held in the 1660s under a Crown lease,[1] and in or soon after 1670 Henry Swindell, the sub-lessee, built a house there with extensive grounds which became a well-known pleasure resort, originally called Spring Gardens. In the 18th century the large building on the site was called Rural Retreat and later Grove House, where Theresa Cornelys, who had once held fashionable balls and masques in Soho Square, as Mrs Smith tried to restore her fortunes by opening a suite of breakfast rooms, a venture which had failed by 1797. Her successor, William Ick or Hicks, had an archery ground at the rear, still there in 1813.[2] On King's Road a building stood on the north side by 1745, probably in conjunction with the garden ground which lined the road there.[3]

In 1771 Henry Holland the elder, builder, and his son Henry the architect put forward an ambitious scheme for the 89 acres of fields along the eastern boundary of the parish, which then belonged to the heirs of Sir Hans Sloane and was later part of the Cadogan estate,[4] and an agreement was drawn up between the owners and Henry Holland junior.[5] Hans Town, as it was originally known, became the model for the many new 'towns' which sprang up around central London. The agreement covered the land from Knightsbridge in the north to the backs of the houses in Turk's Row and White Lion Street in the south, and included a short lane which led from the highway at Knightsbridge into the fields. Building was delayed, however, and in 1776 Holland proposed a building lease for *c.*34 a. on which he would spend £15,000 on buildings, with a lease to him for the rest of the land with liberty to build. By late 1777, when this arrangement was confirmed in a new agreement, Holland had already spent a large sum on buildings which were about to be completed along the new north-south street he had laid out running from the old lane at its junction with the highway at Knightsbridge south to King's Road. Holland agreed that before 1784 he would build a uniform street of houses without bow windows or any other projections except door-cases, porticoes, and iron rails, on 23 of the 34 acres, which took in a strip 150 ft deep on both sides of Sloane Street from Knightsbridge approximately to Sloane Terrace. By September 1783 he would build other similar uniform houses on both sides of Sloane Street at the southern end where it met the King's Road, and before 1785 would build similar buildings on each side of the extension of Sloane Street south of the King's Road, in all covering another 10 acres. Sloane Street was to be 80 ft wide, narrowing to 70 ft at the northern end; the street

1 *Survey of London*, XLV. 19; below, Landownership, later ests (Lowndes).

2 *Survey of London*, XLV. 30–1; PRO, PROB 11/447, f. 331v.; Horwood, *Plan* (1792–5); *Regency A to Z*.

3 Rocque, *Map of London* (1741–5); Richardson's Map (1769).

4 Below, Landownership, Chelsea man.

5 D. Stroud, *Hen. Holland* (1966), 43.

19. *Nos 33–4 Hans Place, surviving examples of the original 18th-century houses, later heightened*

accounted for nearly 8 acres of land. Holland's rent was to start at £367 a year for 4 years, rising in three stages to £705 after 8 years, with an additional £10 an acre if he took any of the remaining 47 acres for building. Neither the street acreages nor the plan in the agreement show Sloane Square laid out nor Hans Place or the other side streets, though the square for Cadogan Place was delineated, so it is unclear whether the street plan for the whole area had in fact been decided by then.[1]

Holland intended an estate of moderately-sized houses along Sloane Street, and himself built some of the first groups of houses, of white brick, in Sloane Street. Most sites, however, were taken by others to build on and subleases were granted by Holland for one or two houses as they were completed. Many of those taking plots from Holland included his cousin Richard Holland, his nephew Henry Rowles, and several men who had worked with him elsewhere. In 2003 few of the houses, mostly of stock brick with 2 bays and 2 or 3 storeys with basements and attics, and a variety of doorcases, survived and none unaltered. One group on the west side of Sloane Street at the south end was superior, with houses of 3 bays which had more unusual enriched timber doorcases, none of which apparently survived in 2003.[2] Leases for houses on the west side of Sloane Street date from 1777 and by 1780 nearly all the plots had been taken,[3] though the leases followed a few years later. Leases and agreements were granted in 1783 and 1786 for the west side of Sloane Street,[4] for houses on south side of North Street 1788,[5] land at the corner of North and Exeter streets in 1790,[6] the west side of Lower Sloane Street in 1790,[7] and George Street in 1792.[8]

1 CL, deed 25970.
2 Stroud, *Hen. Holland*, 45–6; Pevsner, *London NW*. 581.
3 Stroud, *Hen. Holland*, 45–6 (plan).
4 CL, deeds 2904, 3173–4.
5 CL, deed 3224.
6 CL, deeds 13655, 25971.
7 CL, deed 2917.
8 PRO, C 54/8538, m. 10.

Sloane Square was laid out where Sloane Street crossed the king's private road, and was largely occupied by 1780. Lesser streets were laid out on the west side of the street, and some leases for houses in the mews behind Sloane Street (now Pavilion Road) date from 1788.

The most unusual feature of the scheme was Hans Place, a rectangle with the corners cut off, entered by streets on north-west, north-east and east, and with a wide opening on the south. It was laid out by Holland on part of the 47 acres he held in reserve, and he took 3 acres to the south of it to build for himself a house, framed by the southern opening of Hans Place, which he occupied by 1789; it was initially called Sloane Place but later the Pavilion, a reference to Holland's work for the Prince of Wales at Brighton. The entrance to the house was on the north side and two narrow wings, which housed coachhouse, stable, and drawing office on the east, and laundry, dairy, and scullery on the west, extended northwards enclosing a courtyard. When it was built the house was approached by a short avenue from Sloane Street on the east, with a covered entrance to the courtyard through the ground floor of the wing. A dung-heap was shown on the plan of 1790 at the northern boundary of the site near the west wing,[1] which suggests that the later approach and entrance from Hans Place, which existed by 1794,[2] had not then been planned.

On the south side the simple, 5-bayed villa, faced in timber tiles, had an iron-railed balcony running the length of the house above a loggia, looking out over 3 acres of gardens. The kitchen garden on the west had hothouses, a vinery, and walls lined with fruit trees. Beyond the immediate grounds was a meadow of 16 acres, which was laid out with a small lake between 1813 and the 1830s.[3] In 1829 it had a Gothic ice-house on the west side of a lawn and ruins of an ancient 'priory' with shrubberies and walks, and a courtyard had been formed on the west side of the priory ruins with a gateway leading to a private carriage-road to the west which ran into the green lane (Green Lettuce Lane) connecting with Blacklands Lane.[4] A square was planned to lie south of the park, but this was not built.[5]

Except for a few houses at the north end there was no development on the east side of Sloane Street before 1790. Holland had initially planned an Anglican chapel to face the approach to his house, but though he had the support of the rector of Chelsea, opposition came in 1791 from the chaplains of three existing chapels outside the parish at Ebury, Brompton, and Knightsbridge, who feared diminished congregations. Holland stated that 340 houses had already been built with a population of *c.*1500, making a chapel necessary, and he had the support of the bishop of London, but the plan was dropped;[7] it took some 40 years until Holy Trinity church was opened at the southern end of Sloane Street.[8] Also in 1791 the decision was made to lay out unbuilt land on the east side of Sloane Street in a long narrow garden divided by Pont Street, with terraces of houses on the north, east, and south, many of which survive on the east side. At the north side lay Upper Cadogan Place with 12 houses plus another larger one with a garden at the east corner. By 1804 this terrace and nine similar houses on the east side had been completed, with six more south of Pont Street. In 1804 Holland leased to Henry Rowles

Hans Town in 1795[6]

Location	*No of Properties (mainly houses)*	*Including:*
Great Sloane St (W side)	*c.*134	stables, school, workshop, pub. ho., coachhos.
Great Sloane St (E side)	16	plus land
Sloane Terrace	5	
Sloane Square	55	sheds, bakehouse, workshop
Great George Street	16	stables and warehouse, shop, 2 lodging-houses
Union Street (by par. boundary)	3	plus row of 22 properties by the brook with a slaughter ho.
Little George St	10	a lodging-house
Lower Sloane St E	33	plus vacant land
Chelsea Market	18	
Lower Sloane St W	46	
King's Rd in Hans Town	8	2 gardens and cottage
New Road (Pavilion Road)	44	6 coachhouses and stables, workshop
Wonder What Place	12	hos rated very low at £5
Exeter Street	19	4 coachhouses and stables
Exeter Place	10	
New Street	3	1 coachhouse and stables
North Street	57	2 shops, 4 coach-houses or stables, 1 warehouse, 1 milkhouse
Elizabeth Street	12	
York Street	11	
Hans Place	42	10 unlet or unfinished. Henry Holland rated at £188.

1 BL, K 28 4.dd.4.
2 Horwood, *Plan* (1792–5).
3 Ibid.; *Regency A to Z.*
4 Faulkner, *Chelsea*, II. 344–5.
5 Stroud, *Hen. Holland*, 46–7 (plan).
6 CL, deed 17552.
7 Ibid., 47–8.
8 Below, Rel. Hist., ch. extension.

the garden ground and other premises on the east side of Sloane Street, to be called Cadogan Place, for 80 years, and three months later Rowles made an agreement with the Hans Town Commissioners to enclose the ground in the centre of Cadogan Place with an iron railing and not to build there for the duration of his lease.[1] The gardens in the two halves of Cadogan Place were laid out separately, the northern part to a design by Repton, the larger southern part in 1807, occupied by Salisbury's Botanic Garden, which had moved from Lambeth Marsh.[2] Leases were granted from 1791 for Ellis and D'Oyley streets, south of Cadogan Place, and Sloane Terrace and Charles and Earl streets were built at about the same time.[3] Plots south of Sloane Square had also been laid out by 1791 as far as Turk's Row.

The properties rated in Hans Town in 1795, summarized in the table above, show the mixed nature of the Hans Town development. Premises in many of the streets, for example those north of Hans Place and north-east of Sloane Square, were utilitarian in character: stables to serve the larger houses, and workshops and modest houses for local tradesmen. The social mix of the area was further emphasized by the opening of a Methodist chapel in Sloane Terrace and an Independent one in Pavilion Road, both in 1811.[4]

The land in Holland's 1777 agreement formed the district of Hans Town, for which an Act was obtained in 1790 for the creation and repair of the public streets and passages with powers to light, clean, repair and pave, and to appoint watchmen, with commissioners given powers to raise rates for the purpose. Thereafter the residents of Hans Town were excluded from the rating for highways in the rest of Chelsea on payment of a total of £4 a year to the vestry. The powers of the commissioners in respect of cleaning and repairing of streets were enlarged by an additional Act in 1803.[5]

Following the creation of Sloane Street, some terraced houses were built along the west side of Spring Gardens, and by 1810 Henry Rhodes, surveyor to the Lowndes estate, was making plans to exploit the property in conjunction with the adjoining Grosvenor estate in Belgravia (Westm.). An Act was obtained in 1813 to allow parts of the Lowndes estate to be sold or let on long leases, but only in 1819 did the process begin with a joint application by the two estates for permission to lay drains. In 1823 shops, houses, and the floorcloth factory, which lay just outside Chelsea's boundary, were demolished,[6] but Lowndes Terrace fronting Knightsbridge, on the part of the estate lying in St Margaret Westminster, and openings out of the south side of Knightsbridge road which became William Street and Charles (later Seville) Street were the only development carried out before Thomas Cubitt took over the work in 1826.[7] He received approval for William Street in 1827,[8] but most of his work there took place in the 1830s and 1840s when he finally built up much of Lowndes Square and the rest of the estate in Westminster.[9]

The link with Knightsbridge made Hans Town part of the metropolis rather than part of Chelsea village, but it also brought less desirable problems with the proximity to the capital's barracks. In 1824 three Life Guards who had been drinking and playing skittles at the Bedford Arms in Pont Street wrecked the public house and then attacked the watch sent to stop them; a posse of 15 watchmen and the two Hans Town constables were unable to apprehend them, and they had to get men from Knightsbridge barracks to assist them.[10] The creation of Hans Town district reinforced the separateness, and the Cadogan Estate managed and developed the area in a similar way and with similar objectives to other West End landowners such as the neighbouring Grosvenor Estate. Hans Town also increased the desire of local property owners for the creation of the embankment, which would open up the rest of Chelsea and hopefully lead to a similar demand for high-class residential use.

CHELSEA PARK TO BLACKLANDS

The area between Fulham and King's roads, stretching from Park Walk in the west to the edge of Hans Town in the east was still mostly fields in the 1680s. On the western side lay Chelsea Park, enclosed from Westfield in the 16th century and bounded on the east by the upper end of Church Lane. On the east side of the lane were the open strips and closes of Eastfield stretching to Chelsea common, and then, on the east side of Blacklands Lane (Draycott Avenue), lay the closes of Blacklands. The growth in this period is treated below under three headings: Chelsea Park, land between Upper Church Street and Blacklands Lane, and land between Blacklands Lane and Hans Town.

CHELSEA PARK

In the 1680s the 40-acre Chelsea Park was made up of pieces of pasture or arable enclosed overall with a brick wall and leased to John Thorley, victualler.[11] By 1724 land had been taken along the western boundary of the park to create a road between King's Road and Little

1 KL, deed 35429.
2 Stroud, *Hen. Holland*, 49.
3 e.g. KL, deeds 50268–9, 50279, 50289, 50310, 50331.
4 Below, Rel. Hist., prot. nonconf.
5 30 Geo. III, c. 76; 43 Geo. III, c. 11 (Local and Personal).
6 *Survey of London*, XLV. 30–1.
7 Ibid., 20.
8 LMA, MJ/SR 4445.
9 *Survey of London*, XLV. 32.
10 *The Times*, 16, 18 Oct. 1824.
11 CL, deed 3030.

20. *Section of OS 1st edition map showing the area from Chelsea Park to Blacklands*

Chelsea at Fulham Road, lined with elms and called Twopenny Walk;[1] it was later renamed Park Walk. The park was still apparently without buildings in 1717,[2] but the following year it was leased to patentees for silk production who intended growing mulberry trees there.[3] A large house had been built 'for nursing silk-worms' by 1724 when it was leased to Sir Richard Manningham, MD, famous man-midwife, who was permitted build as he thought fit and take gravel, but had to replace any elms he took down in Twopenny Walk. His lease was subject to the lease of the silk producers' house and ground during the term of their patent, but if their lease was not renewed, Manningham was permitted to sell the mulberry trees growing there.[4] The

1 CL, deed 3006.
2 MLR 1717/4/130.
3 MLR 1718/4/89; Beaver, *Memorials*, 143–6; below, Econ., trade.
4 CL, deed 3006.

Continuation of fig. 20

proprietary Park Chapel, halfway along Park Walk, was said to have been built by Manningham in 1718,[1] which if true would indicate that he had acquired some interest from the silk undertakers that year. Although he died and was buried in Chelsea, he apparently never had a house there.[2]

Manningham leased land on the east side of the park for building in 1724 to Thomas Scott of Walham Green, brickmaker, for 52 years; by 1733 one or more houses had been built there on plots assigned to Robert Cook.[3] A short row of houses was built at north end of Park Walk on the east side soon after 1725 and occupied by 1729,[4] and the row continued with a few houses on the north side fronting Fulham Road.[5] On the east side of the park a parcel 55 ft wide fronting Church Lane and 200 ft deep with a house built on it was leased in 1725 by Manningham,[6] probably one of several similar plots laid out for building at the same time. The silk undertaking failed in the 1720s; workshops to weave tapestries were set up in 1732 near the south-west corner of the park, but also soon closed,[7] and a house was built on the adjoining plot at the south-west corner *c.*1733,[8] known as the Man in the Moon alehouse in 1769.[9] In 1737 at least two houses, one of them the Coach and Horses public house, had been built fronting Fulham Road, next to a passage that ran south behind the houses in Twopenny Walk and gave access to their stables and coachhouses.[10] By 1745, in addition to the inclosures with houses at the south-west corner of the park fronting the King's Road, there were inclosures, mainly for garden ground, all down the east side fronting Church Street.[11]

In 1750 John Hutchins of Chelsea received a building lease for 61 years of the parcel of land on the south side of Fulham Road that he had inclosed out of the park with all buildings to be built there, one of a number of parcels there,[12] and by 1769 there were a handful of houses along the Fulham Road side.[13] Later in the 18th century William Bromfield (d. 1792), surgeon to the queen's household,[14] built a mansion called Chelsea Park at the north end of the park,[15] with access to Fulham Road, occupied by Sir Henry Wright Wilson in 1829.[16] Park Chapel was repaired and enlarged in 1810,[17] and building was underway on the north side of Camera Square in 1821, continuing there and in Little Camera Street in 1826.[18] The houses on the north side of Camera Square were a terraced row of 2 storeys and basements with strikingly long gardens in front and small yards behind.[19] By 1829 the square was linked to King's Road by Camera Street, which one observer thought ought to have been continued to Fulham Road and Kensington to give better access to the old town, but that access had to wait until the 1870s. At the south side of the park The Vale, a cul-de-sac with a narrow entrance from King's Road, had several small villas and cottages 'in the Italian style'.[20]

By 1836 there was building all round the periphery of Chelsea Park but still much open ground in the interior.[21] The housing built varied greatly in style and occupant, from 2-storeyed terraced rows to Chelsea Park mansion with 11 acres of grounds and meadow to the south of it; in 1847 it was occupied by Mrs Henniker Wilson.[22] On the west in Park Walk north of Park Chapel were terraced rows of 3-storeyed houses; south of the chapel, the National school, and the entrance to Camera Square were a few pairs of villas. Behind the northern end of Park Walk was a market garden of 2 acres occupied by William Salmon in 1847. Behind the southern end of Park Walk were terraces in Camera Square and Little Camera Street, and Park Terrace fronting King's Road, but the east side of Camera Street was still not completely built up. Further east The Vale had about 4 houses, while the southern half of it was bordered by the deep plots fronting King's Road with a variety of houses and terraces. At the north end of The Vale lay over an acre of orchard or garden ground, which continued in existence until 1912. On the east side of the park fronting Upper Church Street were one or two large detached houses and their grounds, large houses in twos or threes, and a terraced row. At the north end Laburnam Cottage or House had nearly an acre of garden ground attached to it and the five houses to the south of it also had grounds running back a long way. Bolton Place, a terraced row, had gardens curtailed by part of Chelsea Park meadow, but between that and Park Place was a cul-de-sac later also called Park Place which had a small terraced row at its western end. South of that two large houses and grounds stood fronting Upper Church Street, Park House and Vale Grove, the latter standing back with a lodge at the street.[23]

In 1851 the social and economic mix was as great as the mix of houses: from the landed proprietor in Chelsea Park with 11 servants, City merchants and professionals in the detached houses and large terraces in Upper

1 Lysons, *Environs*, II. 178; illus. in Fig. 78.
2 *DNB.*
3 MLR 1737/1/250; 1778/4/118.
4 *Survey of London*, IV. 49.
5 Richardson's Survey (1769).
6 MLR 1750/3/292, reciting earlier lease.
7 Below, Econ., trade.
8 MLR 1733/1/274.
9 Richardson's Map (1769).
10 MLR 1737/1/542.
11 Rocque, *Map of London* (1741–5).
12 MLR 1750/1/328.
13 Richardson's Map (1769).
14 *DNB.*
15 Beaver, *Memorials*, 146.
16 Faulkner, *Chelsea*, I. 151.
17 *Survey of London*, IV. 48; below, Rel. Hist., dau. chs (Park chapel).
18 KL, BRA 2720.
19 See Fig. 21.
20 Faulkner, *Chelsea*, I. 150.
21 Para. based on Thompson, *Map* (1836).
22 CL, Tithe Map and Award.
23 Ibid.; *Survey of London*, IV. 50.

21. *Cottages on the north side of Camera Square built* c.1821

Church Street, to the small craftsmen and tradesmen in the terraces around Camera Square. Hortulan House in King's Road was occupied by Henry Warren, watercolour painter.[1] On the 2-acre market garden west of Chelsea Park house, Park Road and Park Road East were laid out with pairs of villas and Park Road West with terraced housing between 1854 and 1862, and the ground was all built over by 1865; a couple of houses were demolished in Camera Square to allow Camera Street to run into Park Road East.[2]

UPPER CHURCH STREET TO BLACKLANDS LANE

In the late 17th century most of the area from Upper Church Street eastwards was unbuilt ground, mainly in agricultural use. Chelsea common occupied 37 acres in the north and east of the area, bounded by Fulham Road on the north and Blacklands Lane on the east; the later Cale Street ran along its southern boundary and Pond Place along the western. The common had a pond and gravel pits in the north-west corner, and possibly some poor-houses in the south-west;[3] a pond in the south-east corner by the late 18th century was probably also the result of gravel-digging.[4] Apart from the common the area was part of Eastfield, divided into portions according to ownership but apparently mostly still uninclosed. The curve of the boundaries of the portions between the common and King's Road was later reflected in the street pattern, for example Jubilee Place. An inclosure in the south-west corner contained Mr Mart's detached house and a house or houses at the corner of King's Road and Church Lane.[5] Also in existence presumably was a 17th-century building called Box Farm, which had a datestone of 1686, and stood on part of the Greene estate at the corner of the later Markham Street.[6] In 1733 land on the north side of King's Road was given for a new parish burial ground, consecrated in 1736,[7] and, on the north side of the burial ground, a new parish workhouse opened in 1735.[8] The site was later bounded by Arthur (later Dovehouse) and Britten streets. In 1769 Fulham Road had a couple of isolated houses and a small group by the common. The King's Road side had a sprinkling of detached houses in addition to the new burial ground and workhouse. On the east side of the latter stood a detached house. Further east, on land south of the common, stood two more detached houses, one of them Box Farm with another west of it.[9]

1 PRO, HO 107/1473/2/2/2–5.
2 KL, deed 35374; Old OS Map, London 87 (1865 edn).
3 Dr King's MS, p. 33.
4 Horwood, *Plan* (1792–5).
5 Dr King's MS, p. 35.
6 *Survey of London*, IV. 89; below, Landownership, later ests (Arnold).
7 Below, Loc. Govt, pub. svces (burial).
8 Below, Loc. Govt, par. govt to 1837.
9 Richardson's Map (1769).

In 1792 a 3½-acre close called Queen's Elm Field at the corner of Upper Church Lane and Fulham Road, formerly part of the Warton estate and occupied as garden ground, was sold to Charles Owen of Westminster, who granted building leases of part; several houses had been built by 1794.[1] Owen had let part in 1793 to John Williams, builder, who in 1794 sold a plot which later became the site of Upper York Place, on the east side of Charles Street, with four partly-built houses to a carpenter, James Clarke. By that date York Place to the west was being built, Owen had built some houses in Charles Street, and 8 houses had been built by Thomas Powell.[2] Six houses had been built by Thomas Deacon by 1794 at the adjoining Queen's Elm.[3] Owen's land and houses were auctioned in 1815 in 10 lots, including the houses in Upper York Place, fronting Fulham Road, on the east side of Charles Street, and the north side of South Parade; the occupier in 1815 was Henry Holland. One of the lots, at the western end of the field adjoining Upper Church Lane, was sold to form a Jewish burial ground for subscribers from the Westminster synagogue, and a building for the keeper was built by 1816 when it opened.[4]

Building on Chelsea Common

In 1794 most of the common was still open ground,[5] but on the fifth which then belonged to the manorial estate a lease had been granted to run from 1790 and two others from 1795, probably for property fronting Fulham Road or the top of Blacklands Lane.[6] The common was still undivided at the beginning of the 19th century and generally let for grazing by the commoners; it was also used for public meetings and other gatherings. In 1802 a complaint was made to the magistrate about the great assembly which gathered on a Sunday to watch two pitched battles on the common, and constables were sent to break up the meeting and arrest the principals.[7] The pressure to build soon became irresistible, however, and most of the common was subject to building leases from 1808. While in 1794 there was apparently no building on the east side of the common,[8] a network of roads had been proposed for the site by 1813: the later Keppel Street and Whitehead's Grove are shown on the line that was built, and possibly also College Street; other streets shown were not built. Houses are shown on each side of Whitehead's Grove, probably the detached houses and pairs of villas in spacious grounds which were standing there in 1836, and a terrace of four houses at the extreme southern end of College Street, which was named. Another couple of houses stood further north along Keppel Street and fronting Blacklands Lane near the junction with the later Leader Street.[9]

The rector of Chelsea and the trustee for another Chelsea freeholder, who were both entitled to shares of Chelsea common, made an agreement with William Whitehead, James Bonnin, William Smith, and Nathaniel Fulcher, carpenters, bricklayers, and builders of Chelsea, for building on their shares, and granted 99-year building leases for 32 a. of the 37-acre common, running from 1808–10; they obtained an Act to confirm the leases in 1813.[10] On the share belonging to the manor 13 leases ran from the period 1808–11, with another 7, granted later, from 1820–3.[11] One of the leases was to William Blizard in 1808, for land adjoining Fulham Road on which a house was being built in 1814,[12] probably the land which had a terrace of about ten modest houses fronting Fulham Road by 1833 known as Blizards Place; two other similar terraces, Amelia Place and Kimbolton Place, also fronted Fulham Road nearby by that date.[13] Many of the same builders were involved in both estates and also elsewhere in Chelsea, and in addition to those named above included Peter Denys, Joseph Couzens, John Morbey, John Bennet, James Potter, and Thomas Charlton.

Building leases were granted in 1821–2 for plots for 3 or 4 houses, each 16 ft wide, to front Pond Place, stretching 100 ft back towards the pond, on what was called Little Common, part of Chelsea common,[14] and by 1836 not only the frontages to the roads around the pond were built up but also the land between those houses and the pond was filled with alleys of small houses. In 1836 the whole common had been laid out and nearly all built over apart from the pond and a triangular garden at the junction of College Place and Keppel Street in the south-east.[15] William Whitehead's lease was presumably for the land which included Whitehead's Grove, the only area of the common with houses in large grounds in 1836, and it had some space for infilling. In that year Henry Whitehead leased ground in the Grove to George Todd, builder, who had built 2 houses on it.[16] By 1847 the north side of the Grove was filling up; the south side and its villa-type houses remained, apart from one plot which in 1865 contained the Brompton County Court, and behind it a cul-de-sac called Bucks Place with small terraced houses. By 1865 the open triangle of land opposite Bucks Place had been ringed with small houses with commercial premises in the centre. In the north-west, the pond may have gone by 1847, though its

1 LMA, BRA 641/1/15.
2 MLR 1794/1/759.
3 MLR 1794/1/805.
4 LMA, BRA 641/1/17; PRO, C 54/9678, no. 13; below, Loc. Govt, pub. svces (burial).
5 Horwood, *Plan* (1792–5), shows the south and east parts of the common.
6 6 Geo. IV, c. 26 (Private), schedule.
7 *The Times*, 8 Apr. 1802.
8 Horwood, *Plan* (1792–5).
9 *Regency A to Z.*
10 Act 53 Geo. III, c. 190 (Local and Personal).
11 6 Geo. IV, c. 26 (Private), schedule.
12 CL, deed 3010.
13 Stroud, *Smith's Est.* 23; Thompson, *Map* (1836).
14 KL, deeds 35737–9.
15 Thompson, *Map* (1836).
16 CL, deed 16683 (cal. only).

22. *Houses and shops on west side of Sydney Street, next to workhouse, built between 1810 and 1836. All but the 4 shops were demolished and form the site of The Chelsea Gardener garden centre in 2003*

area had still not been built over then.[1] By 1865, however, it was the site of Onslow Model Dwellings, built *c.*1862 by C.J. Freake for working-class residents, two rows of 12 small cottages facing each other and another row of 12 built at the east end of the gardens of houses in Pond Place and facing east, with a small garden; they seem to have been on the 'associated' model, with WCs grouped for several houses. A hall also built by Freake housed St Luke's National school, opened in 1864 to take children from the Dwellings.[2]

South and West of Chelsea Common

Widespread building on the open field also began around 1808. Jubilee Place, which ran from the King's Road north-east to the common, was begun about 1809,[3] and building was continuing on the east side in 1811;[4] it was almost completely filled by 1813, when there was a short row of houses on the west side as well.[5] To the west of the common the Nineteen Acres, lying between South Parade and King's Road and bounded on the west by Church Lane (Upper Church Street) and the Field House plot (below), was leased in 1809 by the holders of the manor to John Fielder. By 1813, when another lease was made to Fielder, the ground had been divided into eight allotments and two of the lots bordering Upper Church Street had a house on each. In 1813 Fielder covenanted to build within three years one or more substantial brick houses on two of the lots bordering the street; within four years to build two houses on the lot which later became Trafalgar Square; and within five years to build houses on the parcel to the east which became Arthur Street, and the remaining two to the south. There were restraints on carrying on offensive trades, but Fielder was granted a licence to build a forge behind the houses in Arthur Street.[6] In 1814 building had started on the west side of Arthur Street.[7] Trafalgar Square was laid out by 1836, with nearly 2½ a. of garden in the centre, but little building had taken place by 1847.

To the east of Arthur Street, Robert Street (later part of Sydney Street) was also laid out in the 1810s,[8] and Upper Manor Street was completed in 1824.[9] The land, 4½ a., which later formed the site of Oakley Square and bordered Church Lane and King's Road, had a miscellany of buildings in 1835, possibly by 1826: a large house called Field House set back from King's Road with a garden in front stretching to the road and a large paddock behind, and along the Church Lane side Kelly House and garden near the corner with various outbuildings, a row of 6 cottages called Regent Row, and 2 more houses further north along Church Lane. The Rose and Crown public house stood at the corner itself but was not part of this land. The name Regent Row suggests an earlier date for some of the building. The land was sold in 1835,[10] to Lord Cadogan,[11] and was quickly cleared and laid out with Oakley Square in 1836;[12] some building had started at the southern end by 1837.[13]

In 1836 almost all the area south and west of the common had been laid out for building, and most of it built over. A new street, in 1836 called Bond Street at the west end and College Place at the east (later all renamed Cale Street), followed the boundary of the former common and joined a street from King's Road called Robert Street which ended at that junction, leading into a large square called The George Field. At the corner of Robert Street and Bond Street the new parish church of St Luke, built in 1824, stood in the burial ground with the

1 CL, Tithe Map and Award.
2 Old OS Map, London 87 (1865 edn); below, Soc. Hist., educ. (pub. schs: St Luke).
3 RBKC, *Chelsea Conservation Area: Proposals Statement* [1986], 4.
4 CL, deed 2939.
5 *Regency A to Z.*
6 CL, deed 2974.
7 CL, deed 2942.
8 LMA, P74/LUK/274, pp. 30–1, 34–5, 158–60; CL, SR 94, pp. 14–15; see Fig. 22.
9 Faulkner, *Chelsea*, I. 407.
10 MLR 1835/4/67.
11 CL, Tithe Map and Award, no. 18.
12 Thompson, *Map* (1836); see Plate 7.
13 Cadogan Est. Office, estate map 1837.

parochial school at the east end fronting King Street. Most of the area was filled with streets with small terraced houses, and several small courts and alleys of houses led back from King's Road. In Russell Street stood a large brewery with some unbuilt land east and south of it, and Blenheim and Godfrey streets were only partially built. Jubilee Place was erratically built up with some terraces of houses, a pair called Jubilee Cottages and some other slightly larger houses. Markham Street was also only partially built, but incorporated at its northern end the infant school built 1827–8; the land on the east had not yet been built over. Though some houses fronted College Place, the land behind to King's Road was still occupied by a nursery garden and its buildings, and there was open land around the neighbouring floorcloth factory. Another small terrace separated the factory from Colvill's large nursery garden and buildings.[1]

In 1841 houses were being built on the west side of Blenheim Street at the lower end on land belonging to the Archer brewery,[2] next to which a new little street called Brewer Street was laid out, with houses on the south side built in 1842,[3] and on the north side in 1849.[4] In addition to Markham Street, the small Markham estate let plots on building leases in 1846 which were later on the west side of Markham Square,[5] and in 1847 the estate had some building on the east side of Markham Street and the south side of College Place. Markham Square had been laid out and built up by 1852 when the 3-acre site was divided among the heirs of Matthew Markham;[6] most houses in the square were occupied in 1851.[7]

By 1851 Robert Street, called Robert Terrace for the stretch opposite St Luke's, had been continued northwards to Fulham Road as Sydney Street. In 1851 the area had a mixture of residents. Sydney Street, with its Spartan 2- and 3-storeyed terraces, housed a range of professionals and tradesmen, including a cowkeeper, schoolmasters, and artists. The smaller streets had correspondingly more craftsmen, labourers, and laundresses; Britten Street included many Chelsea pensioners and some paupers. Upper Church Street had a middle-class population, with professionals, teachers, annuitants, and merchants: the street was not fully built up especially the southern end towards King's Road. Trafalgar and Oakley (later renamed Carlyle) squares still had few houses; in 1851 Catharine Lodge at the south-west corner of Trafalgar Square, which it pre-dated, was a girls' school. Other inhabitants of the square included several professional men. York Place on Fulham Road again was largely middle-class including 2 curates and a schoolmaster. Charles Street included more tradesmen, especially shopkeepers and craftsmen.[8]

BLACKLANDS LANE TO HANS TOWN

Blacklands Lane ran from King's Road to Fulham Road with a small settlement, known as Blacklands by the later 17th century, by the dog-leg at its southern end. Some houses stood along the east side by *c.*1700. At the northern end where the land joined the Fulham to Brompton road, was a close with a house or barn by the lane, probably that with 4 hearths occupied by widow Buckmaster in 1666.[9] This seems to be the freehold messuage, barn, stable and 8 acres of land belonging to Thomas Child (d. 1686) of Inner Temple, and his son William (d. 1698) of London, surgeon. In 1700 the property, which then had two houses in addition to the land, had three tenants and the major part, the barn and land, was held by Jeremiah Wiltshire.[10] About halfway along the lane Lady Matthews, who has not been identified, had a house fronting the lane,[11] the history of which is obscure. It may be the two houses, barn, and 1½ a. of garden belonging to the manorial estate which was leased to William Francis by 1696 together with a 5-acre close, probably that along the lane between the house and Green Lane; Francis still leased it in 1724. Further south fronting the lane by the dog-leg stood a house occupied by John Tovey *c.*1700,[12] and by 1710 Thomas Franklin leased from the manor three houses and gardens covering *c.*1 acre, and 6 acres of arable and garden ground in the adjoining part of Eastfield: in 1717 the property was described as a messuage called the Longhouse and the old farmyard, and may have been a much older property; it may have stood at the northern end of the short part of the lane near King's Road. Standing back from the lane by the outer corner of the dogleg was Blacklands House, another building whose early history is unknown. It seems to be the house and garden occupied by Count Montefeltro in 1684 and his countess in 1696. By 1702 the house was occupied by Mrs Judith Nezerauw, who ran a French boarding school for young ladies there until the late 1720s.[13] A few other cottages also stood in this group.

In 1724 Sir Hans Sloane was leasing land for building fronting King's Road and close to the east side of Blacklands Lane, some plots running back 200 feet to the property in the lane, others only 100 feet.[14] By 1769 there were about half a dozen houses fronting King's Road near the junction with Blacklands Lane with long gardens running northwards, and another building halfway towards the Westbourne, and the part of Eastfield north

1 Thompson, *Map* (1836).
2 CL, deed 2926.
3 CL, deeds 2928, 2933, 2935.
4 CL, deed 2936.
5 KL, deed 42758.
6 CL, Tithe Award, alterations; below, Landownership, later ests (Arnold).
7 PRO, HO 107/1473/2/2/11.
8 PRO, HO 107/1473/2/2/7–11.
9 PRO, E 179/252/32/40, f. 25.
10 PRO, PROB 11/385, ff. 72v.–3; C 8/464/31; C 10/261/18; Vestry orders, 1662–1718 f. 67v.; BL, Sloane MS 2938, f. 16.
11 Hamilton, *Map* (1664–1717).
12 Dr King's MS, p. 31; BL, Sloane MS 2938, f. 15.
13 Below, Soc. Hist., educ. (private schs).
14 CL, deeds 3039, 3042.

23. *Donne Place, looking east towards rear of Marlborough Buildings, typical of the houses built in the streets off Blacklands Lane in the mid 19th century*

of King's Road had all been converted to garden ground. The house once occupied by John Tovey had probably been enlarged and was called Whitelands, and the garden ground on the north side along the lane seems to have been laid out as private gardens by 1745. Blacklands House continued to be used as a boarding school.[1]

In 1794 the northern end of Blacklands Lane, north of Green Lettuce Lane, still consisted of open land, mainly nursery gardens; by 1813 the nursery included some large outbuildings, while at the top of the lane the beginning of Cumberland Street was laid out on part of the former Child property and a terrace of houses fronted Blacklands Lane.[2] The house halfway down Blacklands Lane was known as the Marlborough Tavern in 1794, with pleasure grounds laid out behind it, and the close between the house and Green Lettuce Lane had become a cricket ground in association with the tavern. By 1828 most of Blacklands Lane was called Marlborough Road,[3] the old name being retained for the part south of the junction with Cadogan Street.[4]

In 1829 Blacklands House was used as an asylum for the insane, and Whitelands, described as a large and spacious old mansion, was being used as a stained-paper factory, established in 1786.[5] Thomas Birks of Marlborough Road, tallow chandler, in 1828 let ground formerly part of the Warton estate with 2 brick houses, stables, and workshops on the east side of Marlborough Road and the north side of Green Lettuce Lane, on which Smith (later Ives) Street was built; further leases were made 1829–30,[6] and 12 houses in Smith Street were let in 1836.[7] In 1836 a wide band along the east side of Marlborough Road was completely built up as far east as Bull's Gardens and Princes Street, with the exception of the grounds of Blacklands House, and most of the streets were filled with small terraced houses, built of brick with stucco trim, some of it in neo-Grecian style. Whitelands, still a paper factory, had extra buildings behind it, and further north a candle factory stood on the north side of Green Lettuce Lane fronting Marlborough Road, with other commercial buildings; a national school stood at the corner of Marlborough Road and James Street.[8]

In 1851 residents of the streets between the parish boundary and James Street had a great range of trades, crafts and labouring occupations; Marlborough Road had a wide range of shops of all kinds and had become a major retail street serving the needs of local residents. From James Street southwards some of the occupants of Marlborough Road and Cadogan Street were professionals, especially teachers, or substantial men such as George Todd, builder of many houses in the area, who employed 60 men.[9]

East of that band of housing and other buildings up to the boundary of the Hans Town district lay 32 acres which until the mid 19th century remained arable and meadow land, with the greater part converted to market gardens. On the north side of Green Lettuce Lane 4 acres of Blacklands Field had been converted to a market garden, possibly by the lessee William Powell. His widow Mary sublet the premises to John Bull, gardener, by 1817 and Bull was granted a new lease for 52 years from 1825 at £20 a year by the holders of the manorial estate. By 1836 he had built 22 small houses in a curving terrace following the line of a small stream or ditch bounding

1 Rocque, *Map of London* (1741–5); Richardson's Map (1769).
2 Horwood, *Plan* (1792–5); *Regency A to Z.*
3 KL, deed 50167.
4 Thompson, *Map* (1836).
5 Faulkner, *Chelsea*, II. 337; below, Econ., trade.
6 KL, deeds 50167–9, 50171.
7 KL, deed 50178.
8 Thompson, *Map* (1836).
9 PRO, HO 107/1474/2/3/5; /2/3/12.

the property on the west, known as Bull's Gardens, and a dwelling house by 1839.[1]

In 1836 Green Lettuce Lane, later Green Street, continued as a private road after the junction with Princes Street, giving access to the grounds of the Pavilion and Hans Town, and to the south Cadogan Street had been laid across the area from Sloane Street to Marlborough Road, but no building had taken place. In 1839 William Davies or Davis, market gardener, had taken over the remainder of Bull's lease of the market garden, known as Green Lettuce Gardens, together with the business and Bull's Gardens. In 1845 Lord Cadogan leased to Davis just under an acre of the land within Green Lettuce Gardens for 99 years for building: Davis was to spend at least £800 in building 40 houses with at least six rooms each.[2] Davis's market garden also included 2 acres on the south side leased from another freeholder.[3] Between 1845 and 1848 Davis issued building leases for First Street for the remainder of his 99-year term, nine of which were for individual houses, the rest for two or four houses; the total ground rents reserved on these leases was £133 6s. They were mainly granted to local residents but included two leases to Edward Davis, gardener, of Buckinghamshire, one to two ironmongers of Birmingham, and one to a spinster of Cheltenham; he took the lease of no. 47 First Street himself. The terraced houses were modest, just 15½ ft wide with small front basement areas and yards behind.[4] Davis also made leases of Richards Place in 1847–8, mostly for small cottages which were built on land held under the 1825 lease.[5] In 1851 Davis assigned a small sliver of land at the south end of First Street to James Miles, the owner of houses in Richards Place, to form gardens or forecourts to Miles's houses. Miles issued a building lease for land abutting the backyard of no. 1 Richards Place on which no. 31 First Street was built.[6] First Street and some adjoining streets survived in 2003.

The 14-acre Quailfield belonging to the Henry Smith charity estate between the parish boundary and Hans Town was nursery ground in 1836, but in 1837 the trustees granted the site for St Saviour's church at the north-eastern corner. The church designed by George Basevi was built by 1840,[7] and Basevi also laid out Walton Place next to the church, with two facing terraces each consisting of nine 4-storeyed houses with stuccoed façades, pilastered porches, and continuous iron-railed balconies at first floor, built 1843–4. In 1841 William Pocock applied to the trustees to build a row of houses facing south-eastwards towards the church, and built 16, presumably the stuccoed group with linked Ionic porches now nos 2–32 Walton Street. The corners of Beauchamp Place are marked by taller pavilions. Walton Street itself was laid out beside the parish boundary in 1847 by the vestry under the Chelsea Improvement Act of 1846 to link Sloane Street and Fulham Road, lying about half on Lord Cadogan's land, the remainder on Smith's estate, and opening up access to both estates.[8] Towards the west the houses became progressively smaller, those nearest to Fulham Road being no more than a single bay wide and without basements. By 1848 land on the east side of Hasker Street, which in 2003 still had 2-bayed houses like those in First Street, had been leased to George Todd, builder, who sub-let part to another builder, John Perrin.[9]

Building over much of the remaining open ground proceeded quickly in the late 1840s and early 1850s. The 2½ a. north of Green Lettuce Gardens was let to George Todd by 1847, who presumably was responsible for building there after Walton Street was laid through it. To the south of the nursery gardens the land belonged to the heirs of Benjamin Tate, apart from *c.*2½ a. on the south side of Cadogan Street sold to trustees for Roman Catholics.[10] The land was settled for a Roman Catholic cemetery and other purposes in 1842, and in 1845 St Joseph's convent was opened there with boys' and girls' schools. Almshouses were built in 1850 on the west side of the convent, and a new church was opened on the east in 1879.[11] The buildings in Cadogan Street, with additions that included St Thomas More's school, thereafter remained a centre of Roman Catholicism in Chelsea.

In 1851, although Cadogan, Princes, Halsey, and Moore streets were partially occupied, houses, slightly larger and more Italianate, were still being built in Moore and Halsey streets; the residents were a mix of professional and tradesmen, and Halsey Street included a stableyard.[12] Further building leases were granted for Moore and Halsey streets in the early 1850s, several by Luke Trapp Flood, who sublet to the builders.[13] To the north First Street, Richards Place, and Bull's Gardens were complete, Hasker Street was finished but some houses were not yet inhabited, while Stanley Street was only half built. The north side of Walton Street was built up, but Walton Villas (possibly on the south side of Walton Street) were still being built. The residents of the northern part were again a mix, though rather more trades and crafts were in evidence, with some labourers. Bull's Gardens included a pig merchant and a watercress seller, perhaps a residue of the gardens' former use. The open ditch bounding Bull's Gardens had been covered by 1871 as the lane called Bull's Gardens.[14] In 1862 Smith's trustees conveyed to St Saviour's a site for a school on the south side of Walton Street.[15] The site took a small plot at the western side of Prince's cricket ground, the only ground still open and unbuilt in 1871.

1 KL, deeds 22293–5; Thompson, *Map* (1836).
2 KL, deeds 22293–4.
3 CL, Tithe Map and Award.
4 CL, deeds 22298–300; see Plate 8.
5 CL, deeds 22296–7.
6 Ibid., 22314–15.
7 Stroud, *Smith's Char.* 16, 38–9.
8 Ibid., 25–8.
9 CL, deed 4975.
10 CL, Tithe Map and Award.
11 Below, Rel. Hist., rom. cathm.
12 PRO, HO 107/1474/2/3/12.
13 CL, deeds 16790, 22045; KL, BRA 2749.
14 PRO, HO 107/1474/2/3/4; Old OS Map, London 74 (1871 edn).
15 PRO, C 54/15791, m. 43.

24. *Section of OS 1st edition map showing the area of Little Chelsea and World's End*

LITTLE CHELSEA, SANDY END, AND WORLD'S END

LITTLE CHELSEA AND STANLEY HOUSE

The western end of Chelsea, from Fulham Road to the Thames and from Park Walk and Milman's Street west to the parish boundary, was still largely fields in the late 17th century, with the small settlement at Little Chelsea rather cut off from the main settlements in Chelsea and Kensington. The isolation of the hamlet was mentioned in 1680 by John Verney, who lived there for a while and found difficulty in travelling to his merchant's office in the City: the road was unsafe because of rogues, while travel by water was cold and involved a dirty, dark, and often wet walk home to Little Chelsea from the riverside at Great Chelsea. In 1712 the residents seem to have succeeded in obtaining an order from the magistrates in petty sessions for a watch or policing service at Little Chelsea independent of the watch provided by the two parishes, on both sides remote.[1]

Despite its remoteness, Little Chelsea had some distinguished residents. By 1682 Sir James Smith had sold his 18-hearth mansion and land there to Charles Morgan (d. 1682), grocer,[2] and by 1700 it was the residence of

1 *Survey of London*, XLI. 162.

2 Ibid., 165.

Anthony Ashley Cooper, 3rd earl of Shaftesbury, who remained there until *c.*1706. Just to the east was the house built by William Mart, which *c.*1700 was the residence of Sir John Cope, Bt. One family had a long association with Little Chelsea. Dr Baldwin Hamey, a Huguenot emigrant from the Low Countries, after the plague in 1666 moved from London to Little Chelsea to a house on the Chelsea side, rated for 13 hearths; his nephew Ralph Palmer already lived in the hamlet, having a house on the Kensington side.[1] Palmer's daughter Elizabeth married John Verney in 1680, and their son Ralph was born there in 1683. Ralph Verney succeeded his father as 2nd Viscount Fermanagh in 1717, and was created Earl Verney in 1743.[2] In 1720 Ralph and his wife Catherine leased a house at Little Chelsea from William Burchett so that Ralph could attend Parliament more readily. They developed an increasing attachment to the area, finding it a centre of much good society and convenient for the education of their children, and they eventually spent much of the year there; both died in Little Chelsea, Catherine in 1748 and Ralph in 1752.[3] The hamlet had a number of other well-known residents in the late 17th and early 18th centuries, though it is not always clear whether they lived on the Chelsea or the Kensington side.[4]

Kip's drawing of Beaufort House *c.*1700 shows the houses at Little Chelsea in the background, all lying west of the junction with the later Park Walk; one of them, probably Shaftesbury House, was a substantial mansion with gardens laid out on the south side.[5] Maps of 1745 and 1769 showed a grouping of about a dozen houses stretching along the south side of Fulham Road from Park Walk westward, and some building nearer the bridge. To the south near King's Road Stanley House, rebuilt in the early 1680s, but left unfinished until the 1690s,[6] stood virtually alone, with only a turnpike house and another near World's End on the King's Road side. In 1745 the rest of the area remained open ground, forming the gardens and grounds around Stanley House and stretching south of the houses at Little Chelsea, with some market gardens laid out along King's Road near Park Walk.[7]

Little additional building took place until the 19th century, though some changes in use occurred, chiefly when the parish of St George Hanover Square purchased Shaftesbury House in 1787 as an additional workhouse for their poor.[8] The use of the area for market and nursery gardening also intensified. In 1808 Joseph Knight opened his Exotic Nursery on 2 acres stretching between Fulham and King's roads, with buildings including hothouses; by 1836 the buildings covered the southern half of the nursery.[9]

By 1836, though building had taken place fronting the main roads, most of the land was still open and apart from a ten-acre pasture close to Park Walk, that not used for the grounds of houses was used for market and nursery gardens. Between Stanley House and Knight's nursery a house or houses called Stanley Place had been built fronting King's Road, with gardens behind. Along Fulham Road west of Little Chelsea, an area had been divided off for building by Robert Gunter, who created an 8-foot pathway and leased adjoining land to George Godwin, who built nos 1–2 Hollywood Place in 1828, and took adjoining land in 1836.[10] By 1836 six houses had been built and a space left for a street running southward. Some larger houses at Little Chelsea were replaced by the mid 19th century, and Fulham Road either side of the workhouse was filled with irregular building, including Sycamore Cottage on the west, and a rope walk, Odell's Place, which had replaced Cope's houses, the start of George Street, and Albion Place to the east. The west side of Park Walk was also completely built up, with Devonshire Place, the alley of Winterton Place, Winchester Terrace, and, in the southern half, the pairs of villas of Park Place. At the southern end Britannia Place fronted King's Road for the length of the gardens of Park Place.[11]

With much new building to the east in Chelsea Park and on the Kensington side, Little Chelsea was beginning to lose its separateness and becoming just part of the development of Fulham Road. The mixed nature of its housing was evident: for much of its history sizeable private houses occupied by distinguished residents were mingled with cottage terraces, lodging-houses, private mad-houses, and private schools, the latter noted by travellers in 1840s as the 'unceasing work of education' with a sequence of schools finally ending near the later Redcliffe Gardens (Kens.). Despite the mixed social character of the houses strung out along Fulham Road by 1811, there was no rapid decline and people of some standing still lived there as late as the 1870s.[12]

Development on the Gunter estate in Chelsea, west of the workhouse, after a desultory beginning with Hollywood Place in 1828 proceeded rapidly in the 1840s with short terraced rows along Fulham Road,[13] and by 1851 some pairs of villas had been built in Gunter Grove, laid out between Fulham Road and King's Road, when like the villas of Park Walk they were occupied by solid

1 *Proc. of Huguenot Soc. of London*, XIX. 52–3; PRO, E 179/252/32, no. 40, f. 25v.; E 179/143/370, m. 5

2 *Complete Peerage*, V. 295.

3 *Verney Letters of the Eighteenth Century*, ed. Margt Maria, Lady Verney (1930), II. 93; below, Landownership, later ests (Boevey).

4 Faulkner, *Chelsea*, I. 143–7.

5 See Fig. 11.

6 *Survey of London*, IV. 43–4; D. Stroud, *Sir John Soane, Architect* (1984), 196–8, 200.

7 Rocque, *Map of London* (1741–5); *Richardson's Survey* (1769).

8 Faulkner, *Chelsea*, I. 142.

9 Below, Econ., mkt gdns; Thompson, *Map* (1836).

10 KL, deed 19549; see Plate 3.

11 Thompson, *Map* (1836).

12 *Survey of London*, XLI. 162.

13 KL, deed 41443.

25. *Linked pairs of villas on the west side of Limerston Street*

middle-class residents,[1] and continued in 1853,[2] again with pairs of villas on the west side. Development on the pasture south of St George's workhouse, belonging to the Sloane Stanley estate, was also taking place at this time, again with short terraces fronting King's Road: there the houses were in terraced rows, fronting King's Road (1845–7), and in Hobury Street (1846, 1848), and the southern end of Limerston Street, occupied by 1851.[3] Stanley Villas, later Gertrude Street, was laid out in the 1850s south of the workhouse grounds with 12 pairs of villas built on the north side with the Victoria Tavern at the western end.[4] Pairs of linked villas were built on both sides of Limerston Street (originally called Chelsea Villas, then George Street) in the late 1850s.[5] St George's workhouse itself was rebuilt in 1856.[6] By 1865 the area between the workhouse and Gunter Grove had been laid out with streets of large semi-detached and detached villas stretching south from Fulham Road as far as Stanley Villas, though some nurseries remained. More building had also taken place in the streets between Stanley Villas and King's Road, with building on the south side of Stanley Villas in 1859.[7]

SANDY END AND CREMORNE

On the south side of King's Road just before it crossed Chelsea Creek at Stanley Bridge, an industrial and residential enclave grew up alongside the creek. A farmhouse and 8 acres, which belonged to the Greene family of Westminster, was in the tenure of John Burchett by 1712, and Jane Burchett, widow, in 1729, and was reached by a lane which ran south from King's Road.[8] North of the farmhouse and adjoining King's Road, a small parcel of meadow belonging to the manorial estate and known as the Pingle was leased in 1729 to William Green of Fulham, brewer, for 61 years, on which he had built a house, brewery, and outhouses.[9] In 1747 Green sold the lease with the brewery and its equipment to John Poole, of the Strand (Westm.), staymaker,[10] in whose family it remained and whose name was given to the lane. Samuel Gower Poole, brewer, also had a storehouse at World's End in 1785.[11]

Although most of this area was still fields, by the early 18th century a few individual houses had also been built in connection with the more intensive agriculture of market gardening. In 1712 26 acres out of 34 of arable in Westfield belonging to the manorial estate were garden ground, 14 acres of it 'lately' converted, and another 6 acres of arable were occupied by gardeners. The 34 acres were held by six tenants and included five houses on the land.[12] All the manorial holdings abutted on King's Road, but at least two of the houses had access through Lots Lane, which ran from Hobgate at the bottom of Hob Lane westward to Lots meadow. In the 1740s two small country-house estates had been created from the

1 PRO, HO 107/1473/2/2/1.
2 CL, deed 3221.
3 KL, deed 35374; PRO, HO 107/1473/2/2/1.
4 CL, deed 3259; see Plate 6.
5 KL, deed 38483; see Fig. 25.
6 Croker, *Walk from London to Fulham*, 117–18.
7 Old OS Map, London 87 (1865 edn); KL, deed 35374.
8 MLR 1712/4/50; 1730/2/261.
9 MLR 1730/2/261. No known relationship to Greene fam. of Westm.
10 MLR 1747/3/54.
11 MLR 1785/2/186; below, Econ., trade (brewing).
12 MLR 1711/1/130.

manorial holdings, Chelsea Farm and Ashburnham House. Chelsea Farm was built for Theophilus, earl of Huntingdon, in 1745 at southern end of the demesne he leased, with access via Hob Lane and Lots Lane; in 1781 the grounds covered nearly 10 acres from King's Road to the river, with Hob Lane forming its eastern boundary. It remained a suburban country house until the 1820s, acquiring the name Cremorne House from Thomas Dawson, Lord Dartrey and Viscount Cremorne, its owner from 1778 to 1812.[1] West of Chelsea Farm a mansion later known as Ashburnham House, also reached via Lots Lane, was traditionally said to have been built *c.*1750 by Dr Benjamin Hoadley on former garden ground leased to him in 1747. It was bought in 1767 by John Ashburnham, 2nd earl of Ashburnham, and it also remained a suburban country house until added to Cremorne Gardens in 1859.[2] At the western end of Lots Lane in the 1740s was a house and 3 acres belonging to the Greene estate and later known as Ashburnham Cottage. Apart from those three houses the land around was used for garden ground, osier beds, or meadow.

Major changes to the far western end of Chelsea began in the 1830s, when difficulties in finding private occupants for the large houses such as Cremorne led to a change of use. Cremorne House was sold with some difficulty and in 1831 was opened as a sports club, but Thomas Bartlett Simpson, who bought it in 1845, turned the grounds into the successful Cremorne Gardens pleasure grounds. The gardens were enormously popular, but as time went on were blamed for vice and disorder in the neighbourhood and generally lowered the attraction of the area as a residential one.[3] Apart from the 18th-century houses, Cremorne Gardens, and the industrial enclave by Stanley Bridge, the area between Hob Lane and the creek remained in use as market and nursery gardens until the second half of the 19th century. The industrial buildings by Stanley Bridge included a house and wharf by 1835, when the Cadogan Estate leased the buildings by King's Road and behind to Thomas Ferguson; by 1866 it included a row of cottages. In 1837 Thomas Christie took a lease of the mill, cottage, and stable on the south side of Ferguson's buildings, and in the same year a piece of ground between the cottage and the canal. In 1856 the Cadogan Estate leased to William Christie a piece of ground on the south side of Thomas Christie's property for 99 years, and added another smaller piece in 1859.[4] In 1862 Poole's Lane gave access to Christie's mill, Dudmaston House and some workmen's cottages, and the Cadogan Iron Foundry. At some point, apparently after 1851, Cremorne Road was laid along the Thames linking Davies Place and Cheyne Walk to Lots Lane (at Hobgate). By 1862 Poole's Lane had been extended south to the Lots meadow to give access to land along the canal,[5] and between 1851 and 1863 Lots Lane, now all renamed Cremorne Road, had been extended to meet it. Also by 1863 the Cremorne Arms public house had been built on the south side of Cremorne (Lots) Road at the junction with Hob Lane.[6]

WORLD'S END

East of Hob Lane lay the nine-acre Parsonage Close, which adjoined Gorges House on the east and stretched from King's Road to the Thames; a footpath ran diagonally between pales from the river by Lindsey Wharf on the south-east to the World's End tavern on King's Road *c.*1700, and was known in the 19th century as World's End Passage. There may also have been a pathway along the river bank from the southern end of the World's End footpath to the southern end of Hob Lane: this was shown in 1700 and may have been a way to Fulham, but no public way was indicated on later maps making it unlikely to have been more than a footpath.[7] The creation of Millman Row may have made it superfluous.

Millman Row, later Milman's Street, was being built over the site and grounds of Gorges House by 1726: this lane, running from the river to King's Road, probably originated as an access road to Gorges House and Beaufort stables, though it is uncertain when it was created. It appears on Kip's View of *c.*1700, and is called the footpath to Little Chelsea by Dr King,[8] and the way from the ferry to Little Chelsea in 1720.[9] In 1726 an agreement was made with Charles Killmaster and Thomas Norris to build a new row of houses on the site of Gorges House and its grounds, to be called Millman Row.[10] Individual plots were 18 ft wide and 100 to 140 ft long,[11] and a tablet formerly attached to the north end of the houses was inscribed 'Millman Row 1726'. Nos 21–33 Milman's Street were part of this row.[12] In 1727 Killmaster and Norris assigned to Charles Carne, glazier, the lease of the corner piece of garden formerly belonging to the mansion at the southern end abutting south on Bertie (Lindsey) House and east on the garden of Beaufort House.[13]

Parsonage Close included a bowling green *c.*1700 which was held in conjunction with a tavern, later called the King's Arms, facing the river; there was a small group of houses where World's End path joined the riverside, and a few more on the western side of the lower end of the later Milman's Street.[14] By 1750 several more houses

1 Below, Landownership, later ests (Chelsea Farm); see Fig. 50.
2 Below, Landownership, later ests (Ashburnham); see Fig. 49.
3 Below, Soc. Hist., social (Cremorne).
4 MLR 1866/18/640, 642.
5 Stanford, *Map of London* (1862–5).
6 CL, Chelsea Maps 41.
7 Dr King's MS, p. 49; Richardson's Map (1769); Thompson, *Map* (1836).
8 Dr King's MS, p. 49.
9 CL, Maps drawer 1, no. 5, Survey of King's Rd.
10 CL, Ar.4/76/7.
11 MLR 1750/2/391; 1750/3/749.
12 *Survey of London*, IV. 45.
13 CL, Ar.4/76/8.
14 Dr King's MS, p. 49.

had been built and the area was developing as a pleasure resort by the river. The eastern half of the close, sold to Richard Davis (or Davies) of Chelsea, shoemaker, had in all 23 houses: on the north side of the World's End footpath in addition to the World's End tavern and the bowling alley held with the King's Arms, there were eight houses with sheds and a former smith's shop. The King's Arms tavern lay on the south side of the footpath with a garden and 13 other houses.[1] East of Davis's property the Hole in the Wall had been built on former garden ground at the western corner of the later Milman's Street and Cheyne Walk, with more garden ground north of it.[2] Opposite the Hole in the Wall was a wharf by the Thames which was sold with a covenant not to build on it nor obstruct the open view of the Thames from the ground which lay on the north side of the wharf.[3] On the western half of Parsonage Close there were another four houses.[4]

By 1776 Davis's ground included a shed used as a foundry by Thomas Janaway, and a house which had been divided into two.[5] By 1805 nine of the houses on the south side of the footpath were part of Davis's Place (nos 5–13),[6] and were leased to two carpenters to demolish and rebuild; by 1808 three had been demolished and being replaced by four new houses.[7] Davis's Place, later simplified as Davis Place, also apparently referred to the road facing the Thames (now part of Cheyne Walk): at the extreme west end lay the later no. 119 Cheyne Walk, a small two-storeyed cottage built in late 18th century, which became famous as the residence and death-place of J.M.W. Turner.[8]

Davis's estate had passed to Stephen Riley, who laid out Riley Street between King's Road and the southern end of World's End Passage and made an agreement in 1792 with John Moore of Chelsea, carpenter, and William Kent of Surrey, bricklayer, to build there: houses had been built on the west side by 1793,[9] in King's Road in 1794,[10] on the east side of Riley Street and on the west side of his house and garden in Davis's Place. In 1807 Riley leased a plot on the west side of the King's Arms with a 60-ft frontage to the river to the directors of the Friendly Pipe Manufactory for 61 years, and by 1815 it had six cottages on it.[11] By 1829 there was a tobacco-pipe factory in or near Riley Street and adjoining the Rising Sun Brewery. Bowling Green Row, facing the river, probably took its name from the bowling green belonging to the tavern once called the Cumberland Arms, converted into a private house by 1829.[12]

In 1829 it was commented that the fine open space belonging to the Norris family between Davis's Place and Hob Lane had 'long been considered very eligible for building a crescent or square, since it would have such a fine prospect over the river'.[13] However, the trend was against elegant middle-class housing in this area, with its industrial premises, taverns, and alleys of small houses. By the 1820s any control over the type of housing was lost when in 1823 the Riley estate, including the site of Janaway's foundry, was auctioned in lots,[14] and building proceeded on a piecemeal basis thereafter. On the north side of the former Riley estate, adjoining King's Road, a terraced row called York Buildings was built by 1824 at the corner of Riley Street,[15] and by 1829 the site of the foundry was occupied by small newly-built tenements.[16] Charles Jackson built five small cottages on the north side of World's End Passage, known in 1824 as Jackson's Buildings, and further houses in Riley Street by 1851;[17] two additional houses were built on the north side of World's End Passage in 1833,[18] and the Lord Clyde beershop, no. 10 Davis Place (later no. 39 World's End Passage), was built before 1844.[19]

By 1836 the part of the former Riley estate fronting the river was heavily built up with Davis's Place, Little Davis's Place, and the courts behind, and Riley Street was built up on the west side and partially on the east, where Riley's own former house and garden lay.[20] Lacland Place had been laid out and some buildings erected on the west side by 1836, as was the north-east side of World End Passage, largely filling the triangular site they made with King's Road. Along King's Road were several terraces and one or two villas between Lacland Place and Milman's Street: Albion Terrace, Rose Cottage, Maynard Place, York Buildings. The land between Riley Street and Milman's Street was still open, however, apart from a small amount of building at the north-east corner.[21] The ground east of Riley's former house was still open in 1847, by which time it had been acquired by the Cadogan Estate, and was described as a botanic garden.[22] Strewan House was built at the northern end by 1862.[23] In 1836 Milman's Street was built up on the east side with rows of terraced houses and a police station, and smaller cottages in a cul-de-sac behind called Ann Place, though the small nursery garden at the junction with King's Road was still open

1 MLR 1750/2/458–9.
2 MLR 1750/2/478–9.
3 MLR 1750/3/71–3.
4 KL, deed 37580.
5 KL, deed 35586.
6 KL, deed 25409.
7 KL, deed 25410.
8 Below, Artists and Chelsea.
9 MLR 1794/1/795; KL, deeds 35586, 25409.
10 MLR 1794/4/451.
11 CL, deed 3003.
12 Faulkner, *Chelsea*, I. 74–5.
13 Ibid., 74.
14 KL, deed 37614.
15 KL, deeds 40788–9.
16 Faulkner, *Chelsea*, I. 74.
17 KL, deeds 32644, 35581–3.
18 KL, deed 40235.
19 KL, deeds 37580, 37586.
20 KL, deed 35581.
21 Thompson, *Map* (1836).
22 CL, Tithe Map and Award, no. 15.
23 Stanford, *Map of London* (1862–5).

26. *World's End Passage looking south from Lacland Place, with houses of the 1840s*

land. Infilling continued east of World's End Passage. In 1849 John Johnson of Brompton, corn dealer, granted a 99-year building lease to Charles Greaves of Chelsea, builder, for four houses on the east side of Lacland Place, abutting onto the back gardens of houses in Riley Street.[1]

Between World's End Passage and Hob Lane George Norris junior had a house where he lived and three new cottages in 1827, replacing three former houses on a different site, near the river and adjoining Davis Place. Most of the land, however, was still used as garden ground, with some cottages, garden ground, and sheds, covering *c.*5 acres between the Thames and World's End Passage and Hob Lane on the west.[2]

In 1851 occupants of Davis Place included a boat-builder and several other craftsmen and labourers. There was a similar social mix in Jackson's Place and Lacland Place, which also however included a fundholder and an annuitant as well as James Trigg, a cowkeeper and farmer, and some other tradesmen. Bettsworth Cottages, Jackson's Buildings, and Baker's Buildings were occupied mainly by gardeners, labourers, and coalporters.[3]

In the late 1850s building leases were granted for houses at nos 353–7 (odd) King's Road, and nos 439–57 (odd) King's Road, known as Cambridge Terrace, and for houses at the northern end of World's End Passage, originally known as Heathfield Terrace.[4] By 1862 Jackson's Buildings and Foundry Place ran off World's End Passage as narrow alleys.[5]

FROM 1865 TO 1900

This section covers building in the whole parish from 1865 to the end of the century, covering improvements made by private landlords who built up Cremorne and World's End, by local authorities, and by philanthropic bodies, and the effect of the embankment and new building near the river, as well as the redevelopment of Hans Town and nearby open spaces. Between 1865 and the start of the 20th century nearly all of the remaining undeveloped land was covered by building, and some areas were rebuilt by private landlords, principally the Cadogan Estate.

1 CL, deed 3087.
2 KL, deeds 37580, 37584.
3 PRO, HO 107/1472/2/1/1.
4 KL, deeds 34558, 38525, 39016–17, 39020.
5 Stanford, *Map of London* (1862–5); KL, deeds 38061–5.

PRIVATE DEVELOPMENT

CREMORNE AND WORLD'S END

The largest area of land in Chelsea still unbuilt in 1865 formed most of the south-western corner of the parish, bounded by King's Road on the north, Chelsea Creek and the Thames on the west and south, and Blantyre Street on the east. The lessee of Cremorne Gardens, T.B. Simpson,[1] bought the freehold of the whole area stretching from Hob, or Cremorne, Lane to Chelsea Creek, except for the part of Lots meadow sold by the parish to the Kensington Canal Company *c.*1828.[2] He presumably bought the land with a view to building, which had already started by 1866 with three terraces of houses on the south side of Lots Road, with access left to the land behind stretching to the river.[3] By his death in 1872 Simpson had built 18 houses at a cost of £18,000, and paid £1,000 for embanking Poole's Lane, £2,000 for embanking the Cremorne frontage, £3,150 for sewers, £500 to the Thames Conservancy for the privilege of embanking, and another £1,500 for erecting two piers.[4] In 1876 his widow Jane sold land between Lots Road and the Thames to John Bennett Lee and George Hervey Chapman, London timber merchants, on which Cremorne wharf was built,[5] and part was sold to the vestry for a pumping station the following year.[6]

In 1870 the area between Poole's Lane and the canal comprised the large site (*c.*1 a.) at the north end by King's Road with buildings north and south of an open yard, let to Thomas Ferguson and including a house, mill, and iron foundry; the flour mill and stable let to James Edward Christie; a stone wharf, stable, and dwellings let to William Christie; and south of that an acre of open land described as 'wharves' and occupied by Simpson himself. One acre of land had been taken for new roads (Poole's Lane and Lots Road).[7] William Christie was among those involved in building new houses, taking a lease in 1869 for a newly-built house on the east side of Poole's Lane, one of at least six built on the south side of the junction with a new road.[8] In 1871 the MBW was considering applications to form new roads on the Ashburnham Estate,[9] and presumably the street plan for all Simpson's land was drawn up by the early 1870s.[10] Cremorne Road was extended from Cheyne Walk north-westwards to King's Road; the other streets ran north-south or east-west. The vestry stopped up Hob Lane and replaced it with a new street, Dartrey Road, a little to the west, completed in 1879.[11] Cremorne Gardens finally closed in 1877 when the site was required for building.[12]

By 1894 almost the entire area between Dartrey Road and the former Poole's Lane was built over with streets of small terraced houses, many having only small yards at the rear, and south and west of Lots Road adjoining the canal and the Thames were a string of wharves and other industrial and commercial premises. Much of the building was carried out in small lots and most of the known building leases were granted in the 1880s.[13] After open-air services, St John's CE iron church was built in 1873 at the apex of a triangular site between Tadema and Ashburnham roads, and the incumbent also started a mission church at the junction of Dartrey Road and Blantyre Street in 1880.[14] The Ashburnham board school opened in Upcerne Road in 1885.[15] In the 1890s the Ashburnham Park Nursery still fronted King's Road between Ashburnham Road and Edith Grove but was largely built with glasshouses: Wimsett & Company occupied the northern half, Bull & Son the southern.[16]

East of Dartrey Road the land belonging to George Norris was being built over in the 1860s to create Blantyre, Luna, and Seaton streets: most of Blantyre had been laid out by 1865 with 2- and 3-storeyed houses with area basements, and 3-storeyed houses with basements were built in Seaton[17] under leases granted in 1866–7, and in Luna Street under leases of 1868.[18] In 1870 the MBW renumbered World's End Passage, incorporating Heathfield Terrace, Cremorne Terrace, and Davis's Place in the numbering.[19]

On the west side of Milman's Street George Stephenson built Strewan Terrace in 1875, which included the corner house by the entrance to his builder's yard on part of the land,[20] and by 1878 Strewan Square had also been laid out behind with an entrance between nos 10 and 11 Strewan Terrace.[21] On the east side of Milman's Street, building had been extended

1 Below, Landownership, later ests (Chelsea Farm).
2 MLR 1866/18/637–43; Faulkner, *Chelsea*, I. 74.
3 MLR 1866/18/637; Old OS Map, London 87 (1865 edn). No bldg shown on *Stanford's Map of London* (1862).
4 CL, deed 43758.
5 KL, deed 34967.
6 KL, deed 34968.
7 CL, Tithe Map and Award, apport. no. 4, and map 41.
8 CL, deed 5453.
9 *The Times*, 18 Jan. 1871.
10 CL, deed 43755.
11 LMA, MJ/SBB 2485; MJ/SR 5564.
12 Below, Soc. Hist., social (Cremorne).
13 e.g. CL, deeds 5115, 5121, 5144, 5301, 5306, 5392, 5451, 5679, 43755; KL, deeds 34296, 34301–2, 34315–16, 34325–6, 34331, 34339, 34342, 34367, 34369, 34371, 35385, 38777, 40751, 40754, 40765–6, 40939.
14 Below, Rel. Hist., ch. extension; see Fig. 41.
15 Below, Soc. Hist., educ. (pub. schs).
16 Old OS Map, London 87 (1894 edn); Bacon, *Atlas of London* (1910).
17 Old OS Map, London 87 (1865 edn); CL, photographic survey, area 58 (1969); see Figs. 27, 28.
18 KL, deeds 34374, 35589–613; CL, deed 3192.
19 KL, deed 37585.
20 KL, deed 41485.
21 *Chelsea Dir.* (1878).

27. *Blantyre Street looking north from Cheyne Walk, showing houses of the early 1860s*

northwards to cover the nursery ground at the north-east corner with a terrace of houses and shops fronting Milman's Street and King's Road by 1894.[1] In Ann Place off the east side of Milman's Street, casual wards were built in 1893 with a small frontage onto Milman's Street.[2]

CHELSEA RIVERSIDE

The development around Cremorne followed a traditional pattern for mid Victorian London suburbs, but elsewhere in Chelsea the year 1874 marked the introduction of two new developments which changed Chelsea radically, both in its appearance and in its social structure: Chelsea Embankment, and the Hans Town improvements.

Before 1874 Chelsea's riverside was a collection of commercial wharves, public stairs, and various small houses and other premises.[3] The embankment constructed in Westminster in the 1850s stopped at the Royal Hospital, but after much campaigning it was extended westwards to Battersea Bridge in the 1870s.[4] Despite widespread support for the embankment, however, not all the changes it involved were welcomed. Although the inhabitants of Chelsea had often been hostile to the dirty conditions and other problems created by the wharves, they were reluctant to see the Cheyne Walk public draw dock closed,[5] but the MBW refused to provide a replacement behind the embanked roadway.[6] The parish then solicited a wharf west of Battersea Bridge,[7] and the matter was resolved by the vestry's acquisition of premises at the junction of Chelsea Creek with the Thames in 1876–7.[8] By 1894 the wharves built along the western end of Chelsea's riverside and along Chelsea Creek included Chelsea vestry wharf just east of the creek's mouth, and Kensington vestry wharf just west of Cheyne Walk; Lindsey wharf, west of Battersea Bridge, was an older wharf which survived construction of the embankment.[9]

The Impact of the Embankment

The creation of the embankment made a radical change to Chelsea, and especially to its picturesque riverside. As the vestry and improvement commissioners had hoped, it raised property values, or at least encouraged rebuilding or modernizing of older properties to provide the substantial middle-class houses that would bring in more affluent residents. In this period the more affluent wanted spacious modern houses which fronted major roads not side streets, and the embankment which replaced the old riverside road was a more appropriate setting for those houses. The old houses and wharves on the south side of Duke and Lombard streets abutting the river were swept away, land was reclaimed from the river to create Chelsea Embankment, and between the old church and the east end of Cheyne Walk strips of garden were laid out between the houses in Cheyne Walk and the roadway to provide some barrier from the increasing traffic there. Some small 18th-century houses formerly on the north side of Lombard Street and used as shops remained as Lombard Terrace between Danvers and Church streets, but by the 1890s the site at the eastern corner of Beaufort Street, built over since at least the late 16th century, had also been cleared between Beaufort and Danvers streets and rebuilt. Albert Bridge was built in 1873, displacing the Cadogan pier eastwards, and with the earlier Battersea (1771) and Chelsea (1858)

1 Old OS Map, London 87 (1894 edn).
2 Ibid.; below, Loc. Govt, loc. govt from 1837.
3 Above, 1680–1865 (Chelsea village).
4 Above, Intro., comms.
5 Improvement com. mins, 1845–6, 58–9, 62, 74, 78, 82–3, 97, 112, 137–8, 144, 146; Beaver, Memorials, 210.
6 MBW, *Mins*, July-Dec. 1871, 316.
7 Ibid., Jan.-June 1872, 448, 522.
8 *Vestry Supplemental rep. 1872–7*, 287–348; *Ann. Rep. of MBW* (Parl. Papers 1877 (225), LXXI), p. 60; PRO, BT 356/1122; KL, deed 34968.
9 Old OS Maps, London 87, 100 (1894 edns).

28. *Seaton Street looking south, with houses of the late 1860s*

bridges linked Chelsea more firmly with London on the south bank.

The desire to take advantage of an improved market after the creation of the embankment led to piecemeal rebuilding and improvement of older houses near the river, especially on the Cadogan Estate. In Cheyne Walk, no. 2 was refronted in 1879 from designs by S.B. Clark,[1] no. 1, at the corner of Flood Street, was rebuilt in 1887–8 from designs of Frederick Hemings,[2] and nos 7–12, were also rebuilt during the 1880s in Queen Anne style. Hemings also designed 4-storeyed mansion flats in or near Cheyne Walk in 1888.[3] The extended gardens behind the Cheyne Walk houses were replaced by Cheyne Gardens on the west side of Manor Street, a terraced row set back behind a strip of trees, and at about the same time the houses on the opposite side of Manor Street were rebuilt in a similar style and also renamed Cheyne Gardens. Near the old church the 6-storeyed Carlyle Mansions (1886 by W. Seckham Witherington)[4] and the Children's hospital (1888) were built either side of Lawrence Street, the latter replacing nos 59–61 Cheyne Walk.[5]

From the late 1870s most new buildings in Chelsea, like Cheyne Gardens, were built in the red brick and terracotta which were the preferred materials of the new Queen Anne style and for which the eastern part of Chelsea became famous. The new embankment led to an influx of the style, when sites for building on Chelsea Embankment between the eastern end of Cheyne Walk and the Royal Hospital, and in the newly-created Tite Street, were made available by the MBW from 1877. The houses on Chelsea Embankment were almost all built in the late 1870s, a collection of 18 individualistic and grand red-brick town houses in Queen Anne style, some of the first to break with the stucco of Belgravia and Kensington, and designed by some of the leading proponents of the style. The sites facing the river, large enough for substantial mansions, were quickly taken and architects engaged to work in the new style, mainly for 'rich people with artistic inclinations':[6] Richard Norman Shaw designed no. 8 (Clock House) 1878–80, nos 9–11 in 1878–9, no. 15 (Delahay, formerly Farnley, House) 1878–9, no. 17 (Swan House) 1875–7, and no. 18 (Cheyne House) 1875–7. E.W. Godwin designed nos 4–6 in 1877–8; Bodley & Garner, no. 3 (River House) 1876; I'Anson, no. 13 (Garden Corner) *c.*1878–80, refurbished inside by C.F.A. Voysey in 1906; R. Phené Spiers, no. 7 in 1878–9.[7]

The southern end of the gardens of Gordon House, part of land belonging to Chelsea Hospital, was taken for building in 1897. The score or two of lofty red-brick houses in Embankment Gardens and flats called Chelsea Court, designed by Delissa Joseph, dwarfed the Hospital, and aroused public fears that the government intended to build over the Hospital's grounds. Joseph had to respond that though the triangular site belonged to the Hospital, it had never been part of the grounds, and had been vacant since the site of the naval exhibition was held there in 1891.[8]

Changes Behind the River Frontage

By 1900 changes had also spread to areas behind the river frontage, with infilling on vacant sites and replacement of older houses with blocks of flats. Kings Mansions was built in Lawrence Street by 1894 and Tennyson Mansions nearby soon afterwards. The house and pottery occupied by William de Morgan from 1876 to 1882, at no. 36 Cheyne Row (Orange House) at the

1 *Survey of London*, II. 34.
2 Ibid., 31.
3 CL, Misc. 1998 (*Builder*, 11 Aug. 1888).
4 Ibid. (*Builder*, 30 Oct. 1886).
5 *Survey of London*, II. 84–6.
6 M. Girouard, *Sweetness and Light: the 'Queen Anne' Movement 1860–1900* (1977), 93.
7 Pevsner, *London NW.* 572–4; see Plate 2.
8 *The Times*, 21, 22 Apr. 1897.

northern end, was demolished and replaced in 1894 by the Holy Redeemer RC church.[1] Mansion flats called Carlyle Gardens were built on the west side at the corner of Lordship Place by 1902. Several ranges of mansion flats were also built between St Loo Avenue and the houses in Cheyne Walk, with St Loo Court on the north side and Rossetti Mansions on the south side of St Loo Avenue, both with frontages onto Flood Street,[2] and Rossetti Studios were built in 1894 further north in Flood Street.[3]

Building on the glebe estate continued from 1867 with leases granted for houses on the west side of Oakley Street (1867–8), houses and shops on the south side of King's Road and in Cook's Ground (1868–9), and 12 houses on the west side of Cook's Ground (1869–70), where a solid row of houses was built on the west side of the northern arm of the street; on the east side groups of larger houses with some open space, including Glebe Studios were built 1888–9.[4] Leases were granted 1868–9 for the east and west sides of Caledonian Terrace running north from Cook's Ground, and the 8 houses on each side of the road were extended northwards by another six on each side by 1878; by 1894 it was extended to join King's Road and renamed Bramerton Street.[5] By 1870 almost all the glebe had been leased and was in the process of being built over. The rectory stood in a heavily populated area and nearly surrounded by buildings; its grounds fronting King's Road were considered highly convenient for building, and an Act was obtained to allow the land to be leased for that purpose.[6]

The embankment also influenced new building north of Royal Hospital Road, in particular on the Cadogan Estate. In the 1870s the last of the nursery gardens in this area of Chelsea together with a detached mansion called Manor House in Smith Street and its grounds stretching westwards to Queen (later Flood) Street was laid out with Tedworth Square and Redesdale and Redburn streets; nos 38–50 Tedworth Square were built by Edward Wright under an agreement of 1876.[7] Lord Cadogan extended the line of Tite Street north of Royal Hospital road and leased land on the east side to Henry John Wright, builder, in 1883, who had built no. 25,[8] and made further attempts to upgrade existing parts of the estate, in 1886 agreeing to provide land to widen Flood Street and Queen's Road West (later Royal Hospital Road) if he was allowed to stop up George Place, a narrow cul-de-sac which ran northwards from Queen's Road close to the junction.[9]

HANS TOWN AND LENNOX GARDENS

The Queen Anne Style

Rebuilding in the Queen Anne style took place piecemeal over most of the Cadogan Estate after 1874, but in Hans Town the Estate engaged in wholesale rebuilding as well as developing the remaining open land, seeking a style and type of building which united the Hans Town area with the upper middle-class areas to the east, while much of the rest of Chelsea was to remain for some decades a fairly poor backwater of lower middle-class housing. The red-brick and terracotta Queen Anne was radically different from the existing stock brick and stucco in neo-classical or Italianate style that existed in Hans Town and neighbouring Belgravia.[10] Its use for individual houses had already started on Chelsea Embankment, but in Hans Town the style was used in a new form for mainly speculative building.

The Queen Anne style seemed to be an appropriate response to a demand for a new urban style. The version developed here, with forms and motifs borrowed from 17th-century Flemish town houses, emphasized the individuality of each house, stressed vertical rather than horizontal lines, and replaced 'the hated sham of stucco with the honesty of brick'. In planning, too, the new development broke new ground: houses had deep and ingenious plans, and on the south side of Cadogan Square J.J. Stevenson adopted almost standard plans with varied frontages, a novel idea for speculative development.[11] By adopting the new style the Cadogan Estate placed itself in the forefront of advanced taste, and no London estate in the later 19th century, except possibly Grosvenor, enjoyed a more favourable treatment by the architectural press. The new development, with a garden square named after the freeholder, was laid out along the usual lines, enforcing conformity with all houses faced with red brick, mainly enlivened by moulded brick and terracotta.[12] This startlingly different style eventually eliminated the use of the once ubiquitous Italianate, and its description by Sir Osbert Lancaster as 'Pont Street Dutch' made its association with the rebuilt Cadogan Estate even stronger.[13]

Pont Street, Cadogan Square, and Lennox Gardens

Between Marlborough Road (later Draycott Avenue) and the eastern boundary of the parish, only Prince's cricket ground, belonging to the Smith's Charity Estate, and the grounds and paddock of the Pavilion, belonging

1 *Survey of London*, IV. 61.
2 Old OS Map, London 87 (1894 edn); see Plate 10.
3 Plaque on bldg.
4 Below, artists and Chelsea.
5 Old OS Map, London 87 (1894 edn).
6 Chelsea Rectory Act 1870, 33 & 34 Vic. c. 1 (Private).
7 KL, deed 43307.
8 KL, deeds 36649–50.
9 LMA, MJ/SBB 2493.
10 D.J. Olsen, *Growth of Victorian London* (1976), 128.
11 Girouard, *Sweetness and Light*, 94, 111–12.
12 Olsen, *Victorian London*, 150.
13 Ibid., 147.

29. *No. 56 Cadogan Square (west side)*

to the Cadogan Estate, remained open land in 1865. In 1874 the Cadogan and Hans Place Improvements Act was passed,[1] which enabled the newly-formed Cadogan and Hans Place Estate Ltd, which carried out the development on the two estates, to extend Pont Street through the unbuilt area west of Sloane Street to Walton Street and to build other new streets. The chairman of the company, Col. W.T. Makins, already had some connection with John James Stevenson, one of the leading innovators in the Queen Anne movement, and its use for the company's buildings probably derived from Makins' taste.[2] The extended Pont Street ran west passing close to the southern end of Hans Place, and turned to meet Walton Street at right angles. South of the street, Henry Holland's Pavilion was demolished and Cadogan Square and adjacent streets were built over the site and the field behind on the Cadogan Estate, while Lennox Gardens, Lennox Gardens Mews, and Clabon Mews were laid out on the former cricket field belonging to Smith's. Building was under way in Pont Street in the late 1870s;[3] the houses built were mainly held on 99-year leases from 1874. The Cadogan and Hans Place Company by 1881 was responsible to Smith's for ground rents on eight houses at the west end of the new Pont Street, with part of Pont Street Mews behind. For this ground J.J. Stevenson designed nos 42–58 Pont Street, with angular bays and balconies supported on curving consoles, 1876–8, but building continued into the mid 1880s. No. 67 (Farm House) was built in 1884 for Sir Herbert Stewart to designs by C.W. Stephens, a red brick structure with tile-hanging to the upper storey and half-timbering in the gables.[4]

Cadogan Square was built between 1877 and 1888. The west side, of 1877–84, had the greatest variety of houses, all variations on the same Flemish-influenced theme; nos 54–8 were designed by William Young in 1877 for Lord Cadogan, and Stevenson was largely responsible for the south side, built 1879–85. The east

1 37 & 38 Vic. c. 82 (Local and Personal).
2 Girouard, *Sweetness and Light*, 93.
3 Walker and Jackson, *Kens. and Chelsea*, 175.
4 Stroud, *Smith's Char.* 46–7.

side was built 1879 by G.T. Robinson, with no. 61 an early example of high-class mansion flats, and no. 61a a studio-house for F.W. Lawson.[1]

The 54 houses in Lennox Gardens were under construction in 1882 and completed by 1886; in the centre just over an acre was laid out as a shrub and ornamental garden accessible to the householders. Lennox Gardens Mews, laid out on the west side of Lennox Gardens and running past St Saviour's school, which remained, and Clabon Mews were built in same period.[2] In 1882 the Smith's estate trustees granted a 99-year lease from 1874 of a plot in Pont Street near Walton Street for the Scottish Established Church; work began in 1883 on the new church, on the site which included some land from the Cadogan and Hans Place company.[3]

In 1890 the Cadogan and Hans Place Estate company was wound up, having built the streets and greatly improved the values on the estates; the capital was returned to the shareholders.[4] Successor companies were subsequently formed to carry out later phases of development.[5]

Southern Hans Town

The new streets laid across previously open ground caused only aesthetic alarm; the demolition of streets at the southern end of Hans Town caused social strife, as the Cadogan Estate decided in the 1880s to extend their successful Pont Street revolution into areas heavily populated by small shops and lower middle- and working-class inhabitants.

Lord Cadogan and the Chelsea vestry agreed in 1886 to reorganize the roads south of Sloane Square: Lower Sloane Street was widened, while Little George Street, Chelsea Market, Evans Cottages, Viner Place, George Place, and Woods Buildings, all east of Lower Sloane Street, were closed; Lower George Street was also closed and its upper end was replaced by the wider Sloane Gardens, linking into Lower Sloane Street. The straight Holbein Place replaced The Ditch, which had curved along the line of the Westbourne, and was linked to Lower Sloane Street by Holbein Mews.[6] All the houses in this area between Sloane Square and Pimlico Road were demolished, and the block formed by Holbein Place and Mews, Pimlico Road, and Lower Sloane Street was reserved for industrial dwellings in 1888,[7] presumably to rehouse some of the displaced working-class inhabitants.

The work of rebuilding was carried out by William Willett under an agreement made with Lord Cadogan in 1887.[8] He began in 1888 by forming the new roads and widening existing roads; he agreed with the vestry to pave on the south of side Sloane Square, east side of Lower Sloane Street, and west side of Lower George Street (Sloane Gardens).[9] By 1894 the area on the south side of Sloane Square was occupied by shops and flats and Willett had built substantial houses on the west side of Lower Sloane Street and both sides of Sloane Gardens. The two large blocks of working-class flats called Holbein Buildings had also been built behind the Baptist chapel of 1865 and the old, narrow 4-storeyed shops and houses fronting Lower Sloane Street and Pimlico Road, which had not been demolished.[10] Willett, who was also extensively concerned with development of the Holland estates in Kensington, opened one of his two principal estate offices in Sloane Square.[11]

Willett was also involved in improvements at the southern end of Marlborough Road, where Lord Cadogan had offered to improve some streets running between King's Road and Cadogan Street, if he was permitted to stop up some of the narrow cul-de-sacs north of King's Road near Blacklands House.[12] In 1890 the Cadogan Estate bought out the Blacklands lunatic asylum and gave one acre of Blacklands and Whitelands to the Guinness Trust for working-class housing.[13] Willett bought land nearby at the west end of Draycott Place including Blacklands and Whitelands from the Cadogan Estate, and built new houses there under leases dating from 1898–1900.[14] The part of the estate to the east was rebuilt under an agreement made between Cadogan and J.J. Wright in 1887, covering the area between Cadogan Terrace and King's Road, either side of Leete Street (renamed Cadogan Gardens) and including the east end of Draycott Place.[15]

Demolitions for higher-class modern houses involved sweeping away not only picturesque architecture and old memories, but also a large body of working-class inhabitants. In 1886 an open-air 'indignation meeting' was organized by working people to protest against Lord Cadogan's 'inhuman policy in breaking up workmen's homes to fill his own pockets', which would seriously affect them. Over 4,000 would be displaced by Cadogan's demolitions of cottage property, while the new model artisans' dwellings, separated from the better class by a mews, would only house 400. The displacement not only affected the residents but also the shop-

1 Pevsner, *London NW.* 579–80; see Fig. 29 and Plate 11.
2 Stroud, *Smith's Char.* 48–9, 74; *Rep. of Com. on London Sqs*, p. 65.
3 Stroud, *Smith's Char.* 41–3.
4 Cadogan and Hans Place Est. (Ltd) Act, 53 & 54 Vic. c. 49 (Local and Personal).
5 Below, twentieth cent.
6 LMA, MJ/SBB 2493
7 LMA, MJ/SR 5785.
8 Inf. from Mr S.A. Corbyn, Cadogan Estates Ltd.
9 KL, deed 35430.
10 KL, deed 35443; Old OS Map, London 88 (1894 edn); Clunn, *London Rebuilt*, 276.
11 F.M.L. Thompson, *Hampstead: building a borough, 1650–1964* [1974], 344.
12 LMA, MJ/SR 5732.
13 Below.
14 Guildhall MS 21058; Cadogan Est. Office, Agenda & min. bk 13, pp. 91, 121.
15 Cadogan Est. Office, Agenda & min. bk 13, p. 39, and inf. from Mr S.A. Corbyn.

keepers and tradesmen whose businesses depended on them. Evidence given to the Select Committee on Town Holdings in 1887 specifically criticized the fact that the Cadogan Estate's improvements schemes were called philanthropic, when instead of replacing working-class property with better houses for the working class, it was demolished to make room for residential property of a higher class.[1]

The north side of Sloane Square was also partially rebuilt soon afterwards. A building agreement was made in 1897 between Lord Cadogan and George Edward Wade to rebuild on the sites of no. 7 and parts of 6 and 8 Sloane Square, on the north side stretching back to Holy Trinity church and close to the junction with Upper George Street. Wade was to demolish the existing buildings, and by the end of the year build a house with a shop below, of grey stock brick with red brick on the frontage and Portland stone or terracotta dressings, in accordance with plans and elevations to be approved by Lord Cadogan or his surveyor; he would receive an 85-year lease running from 1895.[2] Wade had not finished the building nor received his lease by 1900, when he assigned his right to the lease to George Bernard and Amos Ballard, who built the Royal Court Hotel on that northern block of Sloane Square.[3]

The old-fashioned houses at the south-east corner of Sloane Square were replaced by a large block of shops and flats called Wellesley House, completed in 1906, and the houses adjoining the Royal Court Theatre on the east side were also replaced during the early years of the 20th century; only the west side retained the original houses of Sloane Square.[4] The original leases for the side streets east of Sloane Street between Cadogan Place and Sloane Square expired in 1887 and the Cadogan Estate then issued several short-term leases for houses in D'Oyley, Ellis and adjoining streets, possibly with future redevelopment in mind,[5] for which negotiations were underway in 1890.[6] The large mansion on the north side of Cadogan Place at the junction with Lowndes Street, no. 13 Cadogan Place, later no. 28 Lowndes Street, was acquired by Lord Cadogan in 1850 as his London residence and known as Chelsea House. In 1874 it was demolished and a new Chelsea House designed by William Young was built on the site, a ponderously eclectic stone-built house of 4 storeys with basement and attics, whose 21 rooms included a white marble hall and a large dining room on the ground floor, and an L-shaped drawing room cum ballroom on the first floor. It remained the Cadogans' London house until 1915, and was demolished in the 1930s.[7]

Though the social consequences of the estate's rebuilding policy engendered criticism, the aesthetic ones were on the whole greeted with pleasure and emulation: landlords of adjacent estates encouraged the new style, which spread through Chelsea and Kensington like a fiery rash, and was seen as a triumph of individualism. Some aesthetic criticism did emerge, however: crowded together the rows of tall red brick houses in Cadogan Square and Lennox Gardens ruined the effect of the architectural detail; there was too much 'cleverness' in picturesque planning, and too much confused variety of detail, far more than would ever have appeared in a genuine Queen Anne town (or country) house. There was also a fundamental incompatibility between the individualistic Queen Anne style and the traditional layout of the homogeneous urban square or terrace.

Whatever the aesthetic or social merits of the policy, it enhanced the residential character and social prestige of the estate.[8] The rebuilding and improvements which took place in eastern Chelsea in the last two decades of the 19th century were responsible for creating a handsome quarter of London out of what some observers had considered quite an unattractive place: Cadogan Square and Pont Street were constructed on a formerly 'poor neighbourhood', while Sloane Gardens had replaced the 'dismal rows' of 4-storeyed houses which had lined both sides of Lower Sloane Street, converting the neighbourhood from 'a poor quarter of London into an abode of the wealthy classes'.[9] A few remaining houses from the Holland period still stood in 2003 in Hans Place and Sloane Street,[10] and their slender elegance contrasted strongly with the larger and opulent late Victorian buildings. While in the early 21st century the houses of the late 18th seemed very attractive and desirable, to those living around 1900 the old houses, grubby from London's smog or poorly maintained, must indeed have seemed 'poor' and 'dismal'. However, it is hard to be sure whether the criticism was because of aesthetics or of class: if the houses were being criticized chiefly because they housed lower middle- and working-class inhabitants.

DEVELOPMENTS IN WESTERN CHELSEA

Chelsea Park

The 1870s also marked the end of open space and new building further west, mostly with large but austere terraced houses. Chelsea Park house was demolished in 1875 and its grounds of cedars, elms, and mulberries cut down:[11] Park Road was extended across the site to Park Place and the whole length renamed Elm Park Road,

1 Olsen, *Victorian London*, 151–2; *Mins of Sel. Cttee on Town Holdings* (Parl. Papers, 1887 (260), XIII), p. 259.
2 CL, deed 16867
3 CL, deed 16868. See Plate 15.
4 Clunn, *London Rebuilt*, 277.
5 e.g. KL, deeds 50268–9, 50279, 50289, 50310, 50331.
6 Cadogan Est. Office, Agenda & min. bk 13, p. 1.
7 Pearman, *Cadogan Est.* 89, 92–3, 107; Chelsea Misc. 1691–7; below, twentieth cent. (up to 2nd World War: private rebldg).
8 Olsen, *Victorian London*, 152, 154.
9 Clunn, *London Rebuilt*, 275–7.
10 See Fig. 19 for a survival.
11 *The Times*, 24 Nov. 1875.

where rows of houses were built from 1875 to 1882. The main part of the site of the house and grounds was laid out as Elm Park Gardens (1878–85), designed by George Godwin. The white brick houses formed three sides of a square open to Fulham Road, with two rows of houses on the east and west sides, and one row on the south facing north to the remaining open ground in the centre. In the centre of the Fulham Road frontage the small detached Park House, later called Elm Park House, was built in the same brick but in gothic style in 1884.[1] The building leases were granted 1878–83 to Alexander Thorn, builder, of Cremorne Wharf, Chelsea, whose family still held at least some of the leases in 1932.[2] Also built were Elm Park Terrace (1876–7); Elm Park Gardens Mews (1879–84) on the west side of the Gardens; and Henniker Street (1876–9), which continued from Park Road East to Fulham Road and was later renamed as a continuation of Beaufort Street; Henniker Mews (1886–8); and additional houses in Park Road West (1888–90) renamed Callow Street. New houses were also built on the south side of Fulham Road between Park Walk and the western side of Elm Park in 1869, 1879–80, and 1886–8.[3]

Fulham Road

Further west the south side of Fulham Road was dominated by St George's Workhouse, where after the creation of St George's union imposing additions designed by H. Saxon Snell were made 1876–8, including a large brick infirmary with seven blocks, each of 4 storeys, the north-western one fronting Fulham Road with a tower. Further additions to the south-west were made by E.T. Hall, 1899, including a nurses' home.[4] South and south-west of the workhouse the vacant land, just being laid out in the 1860s, was rapidly filled thereafter. The spacious villas of the earlier 19th century had not been continued over the southern part of the area; later building was in terraced rows of 3-storeyed Italianate houses with attics and basements, though the width of streets such as Langton, Shalcombe, Hobury, and Stanley Villas gave the area an open, gracious look.

By 1894 Veitch & Sons' Royal Exotic Nursery still stood on an expanded site stretching between Fulham and King's roads, but most of the area was glass-houses for delicate plants rather than open land, as was the other smaller nursery site on the east side of Gunter Grove, belonging to Bull's nursery. The original Stanley House, also known as Stanley Grove and now called St Mark's College, still had its grounds and ancillary buildings. Another Stanley House, belonging to the Veitch family, with substantial grounds stood next to it by 1894 on the King's Road end of the Royal Exotic Nursery.

PUBLIC IMPROVEMENTS

STREET IMPROVEMENTS

While striking changes were being made to Chelsea by private enterprise, the Chelsea vestry worked in more low-key ways to improve the now urbanized parish. With the increase in building and traffic much of their effort was concerned with roads, assisted by the MBW, which between 1864 and 1887 contributed to some 35 vestry street improvements, chiefly widening schemes, particularly along King's and Fulham roads and, in 1874, the extension of Beaufort Street to link Fulham Road with Battersea Bridge, which had been under consideration as early as 1860.[5] Another extension, of the new Oakley Street to link the proposed Albert Bridge and Fulham Road, was authorized in 1864 and still sought in 1873,[6] but was never made, and the route to Fulham Road ran indirectly via Sydney Street. Gates or rails across Upper (later Chelsea) Manor Street, Lincoln Street, Lowndes Square, and Lowndes Street survived until legislation of 1893 empowered the LCC to remove them.[7] By 1905 there were 33½ miles of highway in Chelsea.[8]

THE EFFECTS OF THE SANITARY ACT

More important, however, were the vestry's efforts to ameliorate housing problems in the parish. Chelsea was one of two London districts in which the overcrowding clauses of the Sanitary Act of 1866 were applied seriously, largely through the efforts of the medical officer, Dr Barclay, until his death in 1884. As the vestry had found house-to-house inspection effective during the cholera epidemic in 1866, they immediately obtained approval for bylaws which enabled their medical officer to inspect and register houses in multi-occupation, to limit the number of people to accord with the room sizes, and to have improvements made to water supplies, sanitation, and ventilation where necessary. In 1884 the parish was still applying the bylaws, and reported on the value of the system. Out of 11,000–12,000 houses in Chelsea, 1,700 houses in 100 streets were registered: this did not include all houses occupied by more than one family, but those the medical officer thought were the most important to cover, where a family with children

1 Pevsner, *London NW.* 586; *Chelsea Soc. Rep.* (1962), 15–19.
2 KL, deeds 27710, 27746.
3 KL, deeds 35374; 27417; 27440.
4 NMR, file 101096.
5 Edwards, *London Street Improvements*, 145, 269–87, 307; LMA, MBW 2460; MBW 2540.
6 LMA, MR/UP 724; 27 & 28 Vic. c. 235 (Local and Personal); Chelsea Misc. 1034.
7 LCC, *Ann. Rep.* (1894), 48–9.
8 LCC, *London Statistics*, XVI. 323.

occupied only one room, for instance, or where there were more than two families in a house, as opposed to single lodgers. By 1884 there were very few houses left where there were more than two adults of different sexes in one room. The houses registered were of all sizes, some two-roomed, but some very large, having been occupied by wealthier classes when Chelsea was a riverside pleasure town: a few were registered for occupancy by as many as 40 people. One year's typical activity by the sanitary inspector saw 300 houses wholly or partially cleaned under the regulations, 14 cases of overcrowding abated, 129 water supplies and 9 cases of ventilation improved, 37 cases where he prevented kitchens from being used as sleeping rooms, 146 cases of trapping sinks and drains, and 68 yards paved. He reported little opposition from property owners or others to the regulations, the only problem being the use of the term 'lodging-house' to describe houses with more than one family, as it was confused with the common lodging-houses registered by the police which in Chelsea were 'rather low places'.[1]

Although the early 1880s had seen a great deal of demolition and the building of better houses, Chelsea still had a large number of old houses and courts remaining, generally the very houses which required registration. Built originally for a wealthy family, they only had sanitation and water supplies suitable for one family, and when let out room by room there was an obvious lack of those facilities, especially for the occupants of the upper floors. The demolitions which took place in some parts of Chelsea did increase overcrowding in a few streets, but not, it was felt, in the whole parish.[2]

Chelsea was more fortunate than some inner London areas in that much of its 19th-century housing north of King's Road was two-storeyed: despite being prone to overcrowding it had none of the ventilation problems found in other areas. This part was occupied in 1884 chiefly by working people, with a considerable number of Irish in some streets, such as Oakham Street and Wickham Place: the latter was described as about the worse place in the parish.[3] No doubt Chelsea's accommodation problems were less severe than in areas close to the City of London, for example, but clearly the keenness of Dr Barclay in regulating overcrowding prevented Chelsea from developing the widespread crowded and unhealthy slums which bedevilled some other districts of inner London.

PRIVATE AND PHILANTHROPIC IMPROVEMENTS

Some efforts were apparently made to tackle the more blighted parts of Chelsea, occasionally by private companies. In 1869 the Belgrave Market Act was obtained to create a market in Chelsea for selling food and other commodities. The subscribers to the Belgrave Market Company were permitted to stop up the courts and alleys on the north side of Turk's Row, and with the permission of Lord Cadogan could take the part of the Cadogan estate bounded by White Lion Street, Franklin's Row, Turk's Row, and Queen's Road East. They could remove up to 15 working-class houses, and besides the market and market-house they were empowered to build dwelling-houses and shops, and to take tolls from shops, butchers' stalls, and vegetable and other stalls.[4] The Act was evidently an attempt to improve a decayed area of small alleys and slum houses, but there is no indication that the market was ever built. A second Act was obtained in 1873 to extend by two years the time allowed to purchase compulsorily the land and houses in the block,[5] but seemingly to little effect. In 1876 the Turk's Row block with 155 houses was referred by Chelsea's medical officer to the MBW for clearance under the Artizans' and Labourers' Dwellings Improvement Act of 1875: a scheme was under consideration in 1877, but seems to have been dropped by the Board by 1884.[6]

The six small houses built by the Chare family in Church Street south of the parsonage were by 1874 condemned by the sanitary authorities and partly demolished. The Church's surveyors recommended that the houses be bought to add to glebe: though they described the property in Church Street apart from the rectory itself as 'inferior' and the street narrow, they referred to a recent improvement in the value and character of property in district.[7] The houses, nos 50–60 (even) Church Street, had been demolished by 1888 when the site, measuring 110 ft along the street and 71 ft deep, was sold by Lord Cadogan to Queen Anne's Bounty to augment the rectory.[8]

Working-class housing was provided in Chelsea in the second half of the 19th century by philanthropic housing trusts and semi-philanthropic industrial dwellings companies. In the late 1860s, one of the first blocks built in London by the Peabody Trust was in Lawrence Street, in which tenancies began by 1870,[9] a densely-developed site using a block plan with staircases rather than

1 *Rep. Com. on Housing of the Working classes* (Parl. Papers 1884–5 (C.4402), XXX), pp. 402–4.

2 Ibid., p. 404.

3 Ibid., p. 405. Both on former Chelsea common.

4 Belgrave Market Act, 32 & 33 Vic. c. 157 (Local and Personal).

5 Belgrave Market (Extension of Time) Act, 36 & 37 Vic. c. 169 (Local and Personal).

6 *Returns under Artizans' & Labourers' Dwellings Acts* (Parl. Papers 1877 (230), LXVIII), p. 359; *Rep. Com. on Housing of the Working classes*, p. 405.

7 Guildhall MS 19224/367(1).

8 PRO, C 54/19295, m. 24.

9 LMA, Acc/3445/PT/07/013 (cal. of Peabody Recs).

corridors, which reduced the length of the block and made site planning more flexible.[1]

The industrial dwellings companies provided working-class housing in blocks of flats for a rent which allowed a return of five per cent to their shareholders. Octavia Hill was managing some working-class dwellings, producing a return on investment of 5 per cent, in Chelsea by the 1870s,[2] possibly Onslow Dwellings, built by 1862,[3] or the Gothic Hereford Buildings on the west side of Church Lane, designed by Elijah Hoole in 1878 for associates of Octavia Hill.[4] Other companies opened blocks later in the century. In 1885 the Chelsea Park Dwellings Company built an estate accommodating 60 families at the eastern corner of King's Road and Park Walk. Also designed by Elijah Hoole, it had three blocks on three sides of a courtyard garden, planted with trees to give a rural style. The north and south blocks were of four storeys with walkways facing the courtyard, and the 3rd linking block was two-storeyed. The more picturesque southern block had shops fronting King's Road, nos 374–84, and the flats were approached through a gateway between nos 378 and 380 King's Road.[5] The cottages in Bull's Gardens on the east side of Marlborough Road, with their gardens stretching east to Richards Place, were replaced by Marlborough Buildings, two blocks of 6 storeys housing 500 and facing across a courtyard with the principal entrance in Walton Street; they were built by the Improved Industrial Dwellings Company and opened in two phases in 1890.[6]

In 1890 the Cadogan Estate gave one acre of the grounds of Blacklands House and part of Whitelands, lying behind Marlborough Road and adjoining the burial ground of St Mary's RC church and St Joseph's convent, to the Guinness Trust to build working-class housing.[7] The Trust's Draycott Avenue estate of eight blocks was designed by Joseph & Smithem, and opened in 1892, one of the Trust's earliest schemes,[8] surrounded by housing on three sides and the burial ground on the fourth. Provision of social housing was not without a human cost however. In 1900 the medical officer of Chelsea estimated that since 1885 6–7,000 people had been displaced by private landlords and the industrial dwellings companies, and only 1,500 had been rehoused by their schemes.[9]

East and west of Marlborough Road (later Draycott Avenue) stood a variety of housing belonging to the Cadogan Estate and other freeholders, and some of it in a very bad state. In 1891 a notice was given by the vestry to Lord Cadogan that houses in Wickham Place and Oakham Street, on the former Common, were unfit for habitation, but the Estate was unable to act as they were held under a lease not expiring until 1908.[10] However, the likelihood of improvements taking place eventually on the Cadogan estate influenced some of this poorer property, well before leases had fallen in. The block on the east side of Marlborough Road stretching almost to the Metropolitan District railway, between Smith (later Ives) Street on north to Green (later Mossop) Street on the south was typical of the buildings in the area, with eight houses in 1899 fronting Marlborough Road including a public house and various shops: no. 86 was an entry leading back into a court with stabling for 27 horses and carriage houses occupied by several businesses, including a slaughter house and animal sheds approached by a private road from Green Street. The property was let partly at ground rents and partly at moderate rack rents and together with some houses on the north side of Smith Street the income amounted to £695 a year, but was valued at £1,525 a year if it was all rack rented. The leases were due to fall in *c.*1909, and when the freehold was put up for sale in 1899 it was suggested that the value was likely to increase considerably because of the great improvements which would probably have taken place on the adjoining Cadogan estate by then: the main lot between Ives and Green streets was advertised as a valuable building site for high-class shops and flats.[11]

SOCIAL CHARACTER OF CHELSEA *c.*1890

As elsewhere in London in this period, the rich and poor lived in close proximity: the rich occupied the houses lining the main streets and squares, while the smaller streets and mews behind were filled with a range of tradesmen and working-class residents. In 1887–9 a survey of Chelsea was made by School Board visitors to assess the need for public education, and comments made by them on the type of housing and occupations of residents were used by Charles Booth in his study of social and economic conditions in London in this period. His own survey of Chelsea, mentioned below, was carried out in 1899. Between Pont Street and Knightsbridge in the 1880s there were first-class shops in Sloane Street, and wealthy people living in Lowndes Square, Cadogan Place, Pont Street, and Hans Place; the remainder were smaller shopkeepers and assistants,

1 J.N. Tarn, *Five per cent Philanthropy* (1973), 46, 48.
2 *Rep. Sel. Cttee on Artizans' and Labourers' Dwellings* (Parl. Papers 1882 (235), VII), mins. q. 2978.
3 Above, 1680–1865 (Chelsea Pk to Blacklands).
4 Pevsner, *London NW.* 575.
5 Tarn, *Five per cent*, 96.
6 LMA, LMA/4013/01/01, f. 70; Old OS Map, London 74 (1894 edn).
7 PRO, C 54/19488, m. 2.
8 Tarn, *Five per cent*, 105; PRO, C 54/19859, m. 40; inf. from Guinness Trust, 27 Mar. 2003, via website (www.guinnesstrust.org.uk).
9 Wohl, *Eternal Slum*, 170.
10 KL, unmarked box – Cadogan.
11 KL, deeds 50208–9.

coachmen, mechanics, labourers, painters, and tailors, some rather poor but generally 'respectable'. From Little Cadogan Place on the eastern parish boundary to Marlborough Road, in the eastern part people were mainly far above the school board visitor's scheduling, except for coachmen, but the other part was thickly populated by artisans and labourers, many of whom let furnished lodgings. Between Cadogan Street/Whitehead's Grove and King's Road west to Markham Street, most people were of decent comfortable class; poorer houses were being demolished and mansions erected on the site; many coachmen and servants resided there and a fair number of lodging-house keepers. Between Sloane Square and the river most of the area was taken up by the Royal Hospital and Chelsea Barracks; the only signs of poverty were six common lodging houses in Turk's Row, used by a very rough class. South of King's Road between Smith and Flood streets there was very little poverty; the fairly well-to-do majority included artisans in regular work, policemen, and clerks. Houses were generally in fairly good repair, many of them being quite modern, with some very large mansions on the Embankment. Between Flood and Church streets some old cottage property was inhabited by poor, rough, labouring people, many in casual work, while mechanics, policemen, clerks, and agents were found in houses fronting the streets and in Peabody model dwellings; there were some small shops in Church, Manor, and Flood streets. North of King's Road between Markham Street and Marlborough Road across to Sydney Street, quiet streets, inhabited by decent artisans, clerks, and labourers, were mixed with a few busy streets with shops doing a fair business; there were many Irish in the poorer streets and some doubtful characters in Oakham Street. Between Sydney Street and Church Street there were no extremes of poverty nor wealth, but a gradient from decent regular labourers and artisans to comfortable middle-class people living either in good lodgings or owning houses above the School Board's schedules. Further west, between Fulham Road and King's Road west of Church Street, a district formerly bordering on Cremorne Gardens had been peopled by some 'very queer characters'. By 1887, however, it was much improved in tone, although perhaps poorer, with rough labourers in some of the streets. South of King's Road and west of Church Street the western half was newly built, partly on the Cremorne site, generally with 8-roomed houses occupied by decent mechanics, police, shop assistants, clerks, and labourers. Some poor people lived in the neighbourhood of World's End Passage, and Church Street was very mixed.[1]

Booth commented generally about the streets in the well-to-do parishes in Knightsbridge and Belgravia in 1899 including north-eastern Chelsea. Although there were some poor the number of them was rapidly decreasing: the back streets where they had lingered, such as Exeter Street, were being absorbed by great shops or used for flats and blocks of dwellings for the wealthy. Only near Marlborough Road did poverty remain, and it had increased as poor displaced by redevelopment elsewhere found homes there. The newly-built and smart region west of Sloane Street was only separated by a narrow borderland of respectable but shabby houses from a group of mean streets similar to the East End, though the poverty was described as of a respectable kind without the squalor and vice which was then establishing itself at World's End.[2] Chelsea Old Church district had mostly lost its poor near the river, and the late rector, incumbent for more than 39 years, had reported genuine improvement: there might be fewer rich and more crowding, but there was less distress, and people were individually better off.[3]

It was the western end of the parish which aroused most concern and analysis, though Booth's map of 1889 showed that most of the area had a reasonable level of comfort and earnings. The western arm of Lots Road adjoining the industrial premises, World's End Passage and Riley and Milman's streets had a mixed population, with some poor and some comfortably off, and a few groups of the poor lived in the alleys off World's End Passage. Nevertheless, the majority of the streets of the area were filled with people described as fairly comfortable with good ordinary earnings, while in the houses fronting King's Road, Cheyne Walk and Edith Grove the residents were described as well-to-do and middle class.[4]

Two districts at the western extremity of Chelsea were singled out as especially disreputable, compared to the rest of Chelsea: St John's, Tadema Road, and – especially after 1890 – St Luke's, West Brompton. In St John's the prostitutes were apparently a relic of the Cremorne Gardens. With the closure of the Gardens and new building they were displaced from the streets behind the gardens and moved more to the north; in doing so they had apparently become better behaved and fewer in number, notorious houses had been closed, and the women lived in private apartments and mainly pursued their trade elsewhere. However, some places in the poorer parts of the district had changed a good deal for the worse in the 1880s, as a result of demolitions elsewhere, partly on the Cadogan estate though the worst of the influx was connected with clearances made in Westminster and near the Strand, which in Booth's opinion had made those bits of Chelsea almost as bad as anything in London. The area he referred to covered World's End Passage and Davis Place, Riley and Milman's streets and the courts between. There was not apparently any extreme poverty; he thought that enough money was obtained, as the children looked fat and healthy, and the cats 'sleek', but there were many signs of low life and filthy habits: broken and patched windows, open doors,

1 Booth, *Life and Labour*, I(2), App. Table 1, pp. 5–6.
2 Ibid., III(3), 111.
3 Ibid., 116–17.
4 *Booth's Map* (1889).

drink-sodden women, and dirty children. The taint of poverty was merely carrying on an old tradition, but the advent of the rowdy semi-criminal, or quite criminal, element was new. Booth judged, however, that the affected areas were so small and the surrounding property so valuable, that landlords could, if supported and stimulated by public opinion and local administrative action, prevent this element from obtaining a permanent foothold. He believed that the decline of those streets was the direct result of the plan on which much of the land was laid out, with houses so crowded together and so high that the back windows were sunless, which had an immediate deleterious effect.[1]

Overcrowding in working-class areas which had increased in all central districts of London up to 1891, decreased thereafter in all the metropolitan boroughs including Chelsea. It continued to decrease there in the first decade of the 20th century in contrast to the general trend in the central area.[2] In 1891 only 5 per cent of Chelsea school board district was from the two lowest, very poor, categories, and of those only 0.3 per cent lived in philanthropic block dwellings.[3]

THE PERCEPTION OF CHELSEA

The creation of the embankment had swept away much of the remaining old Chelsea, and greatly diminished the charm of the riverside village. Whereas writers on Chelsea in the 18th and early 19th centuries could emphasize the distinguished people connected with houses still standing, the advantages in situation and the management of the parish, later writers emphasized the nostalgic element and dwelt on the Chelsea of the past. They had a catalogue of losses to record and were writing largely about buildings large and small which had disappeared. The principal writer on Chelsea from the earlier period, Thomas Faulkner, saw changes as an improvement and when he dedicated his two-volume history in 1829 to the Cadogan family, he praised the increase in buildings and population under their ownership, 'equal to a great city'.[4] The most detailed later account, by A. Beaver, *Memorials of Old Chelsea*, first published in 1892, started off by commenting on development which had led to the disappearance of the palaces, the squalid streets which had replaced open land around the village, and the present 'wave of destruction once more at the full'.[5]

Another topographical writer of London's suburbs in the 1890s a remarked on the 'grim old tower and church by the riverside' and the quaint effect of the monumental tablets encrusted onto the outside walls, but also the modern pseudo-Dutch mansions which lined Chelsea Embankment, remarkable for their variety of design, and thought that in 20–30 years when the trees are fully grown and the red brick had mellowed, they would add much to the picturesque attractions of that part of the river.[6] Cheyne Walk was said to have a charming old-fashioned air with its old red-brick houses, but the writer went on to recall the picturesque Cheyne Walk of 20 years before, when the old houses lined the riverbank with trees at the water's edge guarded by a white rail, while innumerable wherries and watermen were always clustered near, creating animation and bustle. Everything was trim and orderly but the writer was disheartened to read accounts of walks in the early 19th century and see how much had disappeared.[7]

Not all observers regretted the passing of picturesque Chelsea, however. Some praised the improvements which took place in Chelsea in the last 20 years of the 19th century, particularly the construction of Cadogan Square and Sloane Gardens, and felt that the Chelsea of *c.*1880 had been quite an unattractive place, apart from the Royal Hospital and the old residences in Cheyne Walk which had literary and artistic associations.[8]

TWENTIETH CENTURY

In the course of the 20th century, Chelsea underwent the most dramatic shift in its history, from an area which, apart from the neighbourhood of Knightsbridge and Cadogan Square, was a largely unfashionable lower middle- and working-class one with low demand, in which artists and others with low or irregular incomes could rent homes, to one where, after the property boom of the 1980s, was one of the most expensive and desirable places to live in London.

1 Booth, *Life and Labour*, III(3), 112–15.

2 A.S. Wohl, 'Housing of the Working Class in London 1815–1914', in *Hist. of Working-class Housing*, ed. S.D. Chapman (1971), 25.

3 R. Dennis, ' "Hard to Let" in Edwardian London', *Urban Studies*, XXVI (1989), 80.

4 Faulkner, *Chelsea*, I, p. iii.

5 Beaver, *Memorials*, 1–4.

6 P. Fitzgerald, *London City Suburbs as they are today* (1893), 225–6.

7 Ibid., 229–30.

8 Clunn, *London Rebuilt*, 276.

UP TO THE SECOND WORLD WAR

Three main strands of change affected Chelsea up to the Second World War: efforts by philanthropic societies, local groups, and the council to improve the most deprived areas; rebuilding by private landlords to improve their income from property; and the growth in organized opposition to rebuilding, especially in Chelsea village, and to the replacement of the older buildings and to 'improvement' for the sake of it.

In the first half of the 20th century large areas of Chelsea consisted of lower middle- and working-class residents whose housing was often poorly maintained and decaying, and included pockets of great poverty and deprivation, principally around World's End. The poverty was relative, however: the upper middle-class areas around Sloane Street, seen more as part of Knightsbridge, made the rest of Chelsea seem poor, but the areas of small houses, tradesmen, and shopkeepers were not necessarily slums, and compared with seriously deprived areas of London, such as Bethnal Green, Chelsea had only modest social problems. In 1902 only about a quarter of Chelsea's population were considered in poverty, and only about 14 per cent were assessed as overcrowded.[1] In 1921, 51 per cent of the dwellings in the borough were undivided houses, 39 per cent were flats and tenements, and 10 per cent were attached to shops, offices, and warehouses. Only 13.7 per cent of the population were living with more than 2 persons to a room,[2] and in 1936 only the equivalent of 6.6 per cent of the population of the borough, 749 families, were deemed overcrowded.[3]

Chelsea was prevented from falling into the worse type of multi-occupation by the control exercised by some ground landlords, whose leases prevented the lessees converted their houses into flats, but because demand for large houses had dwindled in most of London, such leasehold houses were standing empty, while the landowner received a good ground rent and the lessees had covenants to keep in repair. The lessees' plight was reported by a Chelsea householder who had a large house in a street of mostly very small houses, shops, and flats, and was subject to a high ground rent: no-one would take the house as a whole, and the leaseholder could not take in tenants, which meant there were 11 unused rooms.[4] Where there were no such restrictions many larger houses were converted into flats, such as no. 8 Chelsea Embankment (Clock House) and nos 9–10 (Turner's Reach House), both converted by 1927.[5]

Crosby Hall

While rebuilding generally meant the loss of older buildings and replacement by new, one particular rebuilding scheme brought Chelsea its oldest building. When efforts in 1907–8 to prevent the demolition of Crosby Hall, Bishopsgate (City of London) were unsuccessful, the owners of the building gave the fabric to the LCC for preservation for public benefit. University and City Association of London Limited put forward a scheme to re-erect the hall in connection with More House, Chelsea Embankment, a residential institution for university students. The LCC, which owned the freehold of the site of More House, agreed to the scheme on condition the freehold of the adjoining site was purchased and transferred to the Council, the whole used for academic purposes, and arrangements made for suitable public access to the hall. The buildings were to form the University Hall of Residence, Chelsea, recognized by the University of London. Crosby Hall was reassembled in 1909–10 along the south-western end of Danvers Street.[6] In 1922 the British Federation of University Women launched an appeal for funds for their scheme to build a new wing at Crosby Hall as an international residence for visiting women graduates. The new wing, at right-angles to the medieval hall and built of light red brick with stone dressings, was opened by Queen Mary in 1927.[7]

PHILANTHROPIC, PUBLIC, AND OTHER SOCIAL HOUSING BEFORE 1914

Working-class housing was provided by a number of agencies in the first half of the 20th century, with some receiving assistance from local landowners, particularly the Cadogan Estate. Though the Sutton Trust bought its site at market rate, the Lewis Trust and the borough council received land at low or even freely to provide such housing: the gifts of land were variously attributed to guilt over displacing so many people as leases fell in, or to the desire to remove poor housing encumbering the estates while retaining some necessary local labour in the vicinity.[8]

Before the First World War two large estates were built by philanthropic housing trusts in Chelsea. In 1908–10 the William Sutton Trust bought for £85,000 most of the triangular site at the west side of the former common, bounded by Leader Street (renamed Ixworth

1 A.S. Wohl, *The Eternal Slum* (1977), 312.
2 *Census* (1921).
3 LCC, *Overcrowding Survey* (1936), 3.
4 *The Times*, 31 Aug. 1923.
5 Chelsea Misc. 2336–42.
6 *Survey of London*, IV. 15; *Rep. of LCC for 1908–9*, 193–5; *1909–10*, 187. See Plate 12.
7 Chelsea Misc. 1860–1884.
8 Wohl, *Eternal Slum*, 276; P.L. Garside, *The Conduct of Philanthropy: William Sutton Trust 1900–2000* (2000), 120.

Place), Cale Street, and College Street (renamed Elystan Street), and including Marlborough Square. It covered 4.5 acres, and the Trust replaced the small crowded houses with the largest estate hitherto built by any of the four major housing trusts in London. The 14 red-brick blocks of model dwellings, designed by E.C.P. Monson, contained 674 dwellings and on completion in 1913 housed 2,200 people.[1] Rents on the estate were similar to elsewhere in London but for smaller flats: none had more than three rooms and two-thirds had only one or two. This benefitted very small households in Chelsea, who could get a Sutton tenancy at a relatively cheap rent, especially since cheap private rented accommodation was disappearing, and many of the beneficiaries of the Sutton flats were women in service jobs on low incomes.[2] Small houses and alleys were also cleared on the north side of Ixworth Place, where eight blocks of model dwellings were built in 1913 by the Samuel Lewis Housing Trust, completed after the First World War and housing 1,390 people.[3]

One industrial dwellings company continued to build in Chelsea around 1900. On the west side of Park Walk the 5-storeyed red-brick blocks of Elm Park Mansions were built *c.*1900 on the site of nos 26–60 Park Walk and Daltons stable, between Winterton Place and Chapel Place, by the Metropolitan Industrial Dwellings Company, to whom Major Sloane Stanley leased the site in 1900.[4] The company also bought land on the west side of Beaufort Street *c.*1902, and built red-brick terraces for better-off artisans.[5]

After 1900 the borough council also began taking a direct interest in housing working-class residents and improving some of the worse areas of Chelsea. Only a few borough councils built any public housing between 1890 and 1913, and then less than 2,000 dwellings in all. Of these, however, Chelsea was the most prolific.[6] The council bought and renovated the mid-Victorian tenements called Onslow Dwellings near Fulham Road, reopened by 1904 as 3 blocks with 108 flats,[7] and in 1905–6 they built Pond House in Pond Place nearby with 32 one- and two-roomed flats, designed by Joseph & Smithem.[8] The Cadogan Estate sold to the council 1.6 acres on the east side of Beaufort Street for just over half the market value on condition the site was used for working-class housing, and the council built the Thomas More estate, five 6-storeyed red-brick blocks with 262 self-contained flats, mostly with two or three rooms, designed by Joseph & Smithem, and opened in 1904 and 1905.[9] The council also applied successfully to the LCC Finance Committee in 1909 to borrow £18,000 to build 80 two-roomed and 40 one-roomed working-class dwellings in Grove Cottages, Manor Street; the half-acre site was given freely by Lord Cadogan on condition that the tenants had incomes of less than 25s. a week.[10] The council built 'associated' rather than self-contained flats, opened in four blocks as Grove Dwellings in 1910: the associated flats were provided with groups of 4 WCs to every 6 flats, and without bathrooms on the grounds that the municipal baths were only 200 yards away. The advantage was the cost, and meant that rents could be lower, especially for one- and two-roomed flats.[11] By 1914 the council had built 13 blocks on 4 estates with 522 flats containing 1,150 rooms.[12]

As in the previous century, clearance of the worst of working-class housing meant that not all displaced residents were rehoused. Between 1902 and 1913 3,467 rooms occupied by working-class residents were demolished, and of the sites only 763 rooms were replaced by working-class dwellings. Of the rest 953 sites remained vacant, 566 used for business premises, 522 for non working-class dwellings, 233 for public building, and 369 for street improvements.[13] By 1914 the council housed 1,580 people, and other model dwellings together housed about 5,290; it was estimated that 25 per cent of the working-class population of Chelsea lived in model or industrial dwellings in 1914.[14]

HOUSING IMPROVEMENT BETWEEN THE WARS

After the First World War both the council and voluntary organizations took steps to tackle the slums around World's End Passage, described as an area of 'sordid courts and alleys, where century-old worn-out cottages were crowded higgledy-piggledy together'.[15]

In July 1925 the Chelsea Housing Association held its first public meeting, expressing to the mayor and council its regret that no action had been taken under the recent Housing Acts, which had made local authorities responsible for addressing general housing need rather than just slum clearance, and which gave them state assistance. Later that year the Association put out a public statement of what they saw as the main requirements in the area: they wanted schemes for working-class housing providing *c.*100 flats, and intended to make housing the predominant issue in the forthcoming elections,

1 Garside, *Conduct of Philanthropy*, 15, 213 n5; Clunn, *London Rebuilt*, 281.
2 Garside, *Conduct of Philanthropy*, 120.
3 Wohl, *Eternal Slum*, 171; Pevsner, *London NW.* 588; see Plate 13.
4 KL, deed 35374.
5 Cadogan Est. Office, Agenda & min. bk 22, p. 70; Pevsner, *London NW.* 584.
6 A. Cox, *Public Housing* (1993), 8–9.
7 Wohl, *Eternal Slum*, 277; LCC, *London Statistics*, XVI (1905–6), 133.
8 Pevsner, *London NW.* 588.
9 Wohl, *Eternal Slum*, 276; LCC, *London Statistics*, XVI (1905–6), 133.
10 *The Times*, 3 Feb. 1909.
11 Wohl, *Eternal Slum*, 276, 366; Bacon, *Atlas of London* (1910).
12 Wohl, *Eternal Slum*, 366.
13 Ibid., 370.
14 Garside, *Conduct of Philanthropy*, 213 n5; Wohl, *Eternal Slum*, 171.
15 *The Times*, 17 Feb. 1931.

supporting candidates who pressed for building schemes. They also wanted the council to pursue the owners of unhealthy property and to make the office of medical officer full-time. A representative of one party on the council denied that their sanitary administration was not vigilant, and pointed out that there were 578 municipal flats in Chelsea. However, a report by the Association's surveyor stated that two-thirds of families lived in houses with between one and three rooms, and overcrowding was particularly acute in Church Ward, which included Cale Street, and in Stanley Ward, which included Slaidburn Street. 4,127 people lived in one-roomed dwellings, 11,261 in two-roomed, and 13,273 in 3 or more. Working-class inhabitants lived in tenements, small cottages, and the four estates of industrial dwellings in the borough, and the children had no parks or open spaces except the burial ground around St Luke's, Sydney Street. The surveyor also criticized the absence of town planning, and wanted wholesale clearance of areas such as World's End.[1]

Whether or not because of the Association's pressure on the council, by 1928 the Association could report some progress; the council's scheme for World's End (below), the lease by the council of a plot in King's Road to the Guinness Housing Trust, an increase in sanitary inspections, and support to tenants in conflict with landlords.[2] However, they were unhappy about the state of the central area near Cadogan Square, where the 'squalid condition of mean streets' needed attention; *c.*3000 people lived in the 13 acres of worn-out houses, which had been acquired for rebuilding before 1914 but could not now be dealt with because of rent restrictions. The Association wanted the council to take it in hand, but the very high value of land in Chelsea prevented municipal housing there.[3] In 1929 the Association again criticized the borough council for not taking advantage of state assistance under the Housing Acts to provide housing; not one of more than 7,000 people living in overcrowded conditions had been rehoused by the council, and their delay in building new houses had put pressure on tenants throughout the borough. At the same time 966 notices had been served on the Cadogan syndicate in connection with its property in the central area, and the Association felt there was a need for permanent reconstruction there and a private Act to deal with it.[4] In 1930 their aim was not to build directly but to bring pressure on the 'quite astonishingly supine borough council'. They thought there was now a great change in people's attitudes and an interest in building, and as Chelsea had very low rates it could afford more for building.[5]

The Housing Improvement Society and World's End

Meanwhile the Chelsea Housing Improvement Society Limited was established in 1926, with an office at no. 348 King's Road: its object was to buy, sell, let, or develop land, and provide and manage houses for working classes and others.[6] Like other such housing societies, it aimed to provide housing for the very poorest tenants, generally those formerly living in slum tenements,[7] and one of its main objectives was to deal with World's End Passage, where small 2-storeyed brick cottages opened directly onto the paved lane.[8] The borough council confirmed the World's End Passage Improvement Scheme in 1928 for 1½ a. covering 78 houses and tenements in World's End Passage, Davis Place, Riley Street, Foundry Place, Lacland Cottages, Lacland Place, and Jackson's Buildings, containing 379 people in 216 rooms: 340 people were to be rehoused in the area, 39 elsewhere. The site of nos 23–6 Riley Street had been rebuilt by April 1929,[9] and 89 of the 190 rooms in the scheme were completed by the end of 1930.[10] Part of the scheme was carried out by the Chelsea Housing Improvement Society, to whom the council leased the site for 99 years at a nominal rent, and the Society spent £6,000 on building Walter House, its first block of 12 flats, opened in 1929 for 24 adults and 42 children. It then appealed for funds to build three more blocks: the four-storeyed Follett House on the site adjoining World's End Passage followed in 1930 with 17 flats for 36 adults and 45 children, and Albert Gray House in 1931 for 42 adults and 65 children in 20 flats.[11]

The rising value of land in Chelsea, as elsewhere in London, made it difficult for the established housing organizations such as Guinness or Sutton, who had built in Chelsea before the First World War, to undertake new projects in the 1920s. The Guinness Trust built one new scheme in Chelsea under the 1919 Housing Act, made viable because the borough council offered the site to the Trust on a 999-year lease at a peppercorn rent.[12] This was the 2½-acre Wimsett Nursery site on the south side of King's Road, at the corner of Edith Grove, where the Guinness Trust built 4 five-storeyed blocks in 1929–30, designed by C.S. Joseph and containing 160 working-class flats, each with a bathroom/scullery; by agreement with the council only Chelsea residents were accepted.[13]

Chelsea Housing Association reported in 1930 and 1931 on the improvements carried out through the work of the Guinness Trust and the Chelsea Housing

1 Ibid., 14 July, 27 Oct. 1925.
2 Ibid., 14 Jan., 1 Feb. 1928.
3 Ibid., 17 Jan. 1928.
4 Ibid., 18 Feb. 1929.
5 Ibid., 6 Feb. 1930.
6 KL, deed 22085.
7 H. Quigley and I. Goldie, *Housing and Slum Clearance in London* (1934), 116.
8 Chelsea Misc. 2376; see Figs. 30, 31.
9 KL, deed 22086.
10 Chelsea Misc. 2334; LCC, *London Statistics*, XXXV (1930–1), 109.
11 *The Times*, 14 Feb. 1929; 22 Jan., 28 May 1930; 17 Feb. 1931. Fig. 40 shows the new bldg on E side of Passage.
12 P. Malpass, *Housing Associations and Housing Policy* (2000), 85; *The Times*, 22 Mar. 1929.
13 *The Times*, 22 Jan. 1930; P. Loobey, *Chelsea* (1999), 35; Chelsea Misc. 2247.

30. *World's End Passage, 1929, looking south from King's Road. The lamp has brush on top, indicating a chimney sweep's premises*

31. *World's End Passage, 1929, looking north from Riley Street. The same view in 1969 is shown in fig. 40*

Improvement Society, but still pressed for action over the area of *c.*10 acres near Marlborough Road, which, except where sold to smaller operators, continued to be unsatisfactory. The Association resolved to ask the borough council to acquire 2 acres of the site for working-class housing and 1 acre for recreational needs. They also reported that there were still some bad landlords who were covertly threatening tenants, and the medical officer of health had issued more than 1,000 orders to landlords to improve property.[1]

In 1933 a meeting of the Chelsea Housing Improvement Society was attended by two cabinet ministers, and Chelsea's MP, Sir Samuel Hoare, spoke about the great contrast 25 years ago between the upper class and working class parts of Chelsea. Feelings had been so bitter then that it had been impossible to hold meetings in some areas, but he believed that the two groups had come to know more of each other, and with the introduction of the housing subsidy and the current fall in building costs, clearance of slum areas should proceed faster.[2] Meanwhile the housing society felt it had been effective in fostering the growth of corporate feeling among tenants: a men's club was meeting in a workshop, and it was hoped soon to have a new club room and develop other clubs for women and girls; a children's library was well used. The years 1929–32 had seen the clearing and rehousing of World's End; in 1933 all the society's debts were paid off, and they were ready to help other schemes.[3]

Municipal Housing

Despite accusations of supineness, the council did try to prevent developments which would adversely affect working-class housing. In 1920 they sought to oppose the erection of a big motor works behind the Town Hall in the middle of a working-class residential area, but were powerless to prevent it despite the urgent need for more housing in the borough.[4] After facilitating rehousing at World's End, the council took a more active role in providing housing itself, putting forward a scheme in 1934 to demolish property in Wellington Street, behind the town hall, and housing 400 people

1 *The Times*, 16, 23 Feb. 1932.
2 Ibid., 22 March 1933.
3 Ibid., 5 Dec. 1933.
4 Ibid., 20 Feb. 1920.

instead of only the 260 already there.[1] The council also opened Chelsea Manor Buildings in 1939, designed by A.S. Soutar, and built on 1.6 a. with frontages to Chelsea Manor Street, Flood Street, and Alpha Place; it housed 422 people, mainly displaced by slum clearance, replacing old houses occupied by 81.[2] In 1939 the council also obtained a compulsory order to purchase a large area on the east side of Draycott Avenue between Orford and Denyer streets and including the tiny Cadogan Avenue.[3] They planned blocks of flats (Wiltshire Close) for working-class families, but building was delayed until after the Second World War.[4]

PRIVATE REBUILDING BEFORE THE FIRST WORLD WAR

The pace of wholesale rebuilding on private estates slowed in Chelsea in the decade before the First World War. Though the impetus for improvement which had begun in the last 20 years of the 19th century was sustained in eastern Chelsea, the difficulties of redeveloping estates to house affluent residents instead of the lower classes were becoming greater. Nevertheless, piecemeal rebuilding continued in areas of older settlement. By 1913 the houses of the 17th and 18th centuries which had once lined Church Street were rapidly being replaced by modern buildings rather out of keeping with the character of the street and in an indiscriminate motley of styles. Some older buildings did remain, however: eight on the west side still showed 18th or late 17th century features in 1913, and three on the east had features of the late 18th century. The early-18th century Petyt School had been rebuilt in 1890 on its original lines, though with the three arches of the cloister partly filled in.[5] In 1906 six of the row of ten houses of 1691 on the north side of Royal Hospital Road, formerly Paradise Row, nearest to Burton's Court were demolished and replaced with modern houses, despite appeals to Lord Cadogan by Lord Monkswell and several literary and artistic inhabitants.[6]

The south side of Chelsea Park still had some open ground at the beginning of the 20th century. The Vale, a small cul-de-sac entered from King's Road through a wooden gate and looking like a country lane, led to four isolated houses with spacious gardens, and the paddock behind. William and Evelyn de Morgan lived for 22 years at no. 1, a quaint rambling house with an ancient vine and fig tree, where old mulberry trees were cut down to make way for their studio, and other artists also sought accommodation there.[7] Vale Avenue, a new thoroughfare from King's Road to Elm Park Road, replaced The Vale in 1910.[8] Mulberry Walk and Mallord Street were added between 1910 and 1925 by Vale Estates Limited over the sites of Stanley Works, Camera Gardens, and the ground formerly belonging to Vale Grove house.[9] To the west, Veitch's nursery grounds had been considerably reduced when Hortensia Road was laid out across the site and several school buildings erected on the west side by 1907.[10]

At the beginning of the 20th century the Cadogan Estate, which by this date owned the freehold of more than half the area of the former common, considered how to rebuild the area between Marlborough Road and College Street, where most of the leases were due to expire in 1908–9. The houses, built about a hundred years previously, were described as of a very inferior character, inhabited by the lowest class of population: the best of the houses were in Whitehead's Grove; the remainder consisted of houses of less than 6 rooms, described as 'now unsuitable' for the locality, and hardly any were to be retained after the leases fell in. The Estate clearly wanted to redevelop the area with more upper middle-class housing, as had been done in Lower Sloane Street, instead of the modest artisan housing of the common area. However, there were now considerable obstacles. The scheme would have entailed the removal of around 700 dwellings, housing 5,700 people, including 100 in Beauclerc Buildings, a common lodging house in College Place, which would have caused the kind of uproar in the press which accompanied the clearances in Lower Sloane Street in 1888. Even if public opinion were to be ignored, the council's permission would have been required to alter the street layout, which was too narrow for the larger houses the Estate had in mind, and the council would also have required working-class dwellings to be included to accommodate the displaced population, thereby reducing the value of the property as a building estate. It had been intended to redevelop the area as an extension from the successful Cadogan Square, but this was difficult because of the intervening blocks of older housing belonging to other freeholders along the approach from that square, the very working-class public house, the Admiral Keppel, at the top of Marlborough Road, and the large board school half-way down.[11]

With all these factors in mind, in 1902 the Cadogan Estate conveyed the whole area of *c.*20 a., including the blocks on the east side of Marlborough Road between Green and Cadogan streets, to the Cadogan and Hans Place Estate (no. 3) company.[12] The company presented its plan in 1908 to rebuild the area, which as predicted provoked much comment in the press, who criticized the fact that over 20,000 working-class people were being driven from the borough as leases fell in, for the

1 *The Times*, 19 April 1934.
2 Ibid., 31 March 1939.
3 *Chelsea Soc. Rep.* (1939), 22.
4 Below.
5 *Survey of London*, IV. 51–3.
6 *N&Q*, 10th ser., V. 165, 272; *Home Counties Mag.* VIII (1906), 123.
7 Below, artists and Chelsea.
8 *Survey of London*, IV. 50; *Chelsea Soc. Rep.* (1958), 46–7; Walkley, *Artists' Hos in London*, 218; see Plate 11.
9 RBKC, *Chelsea Park – Carlyle, Conservation Area Proposals Statement*, p. 11.
10 Below, Soc. Hist., educ. (pub. schs).
11 Cadogan Est. Office, Agenda & min. bk 22, pp. 1–11.
12 Pearman, *Cadogan Est.* 113.

32. *Sloane Avenue Mansions 1934, corner of Sloane Avenue and Whitehead's Grove*

enrichment of Lord Cadogan and his family, and that the working class merely represented so much lost money to the earl.[1] A start was made on the roads: Keppel Street was widened and renamed Sloane Avenue, and Marlborough Road was renamed Draycott Avenue; a westward extension of Draycott Place was cut across both thoroughfares. Several high-class houses were built at the southern end of Sloane Avenue and in Draycott Place between 1902 and 1906, as well as Cadogan Court, a large block of private flats in Draycott Avenue, but several acres cleared of houses remained unsold: 'gaping and half-demolished slums' led out of Sloane Avenue, and Draycott Avenue remained unchanged.[2] Most of the streets in the area were renamed in this period, but nothing more was done until the late 1920s.[3]

At the north end of the area, however, the factory for Messrs Michelin, motor-tyre manufacturers, designed by François Espinasse, was built 1909–11 at no. 81 Fulham Road, with a service bay on the ground floor and offices above. The concrete structure was entirely concealed by ebullient and colourful decoration, mainly in tiles including 34 pictorial tiled panels of racing-car successes to advertize the virtues of Michelin tyres.[4] Also in Fulham Road Thurloe Court, a block of private flats, was built shortly before the First World War.[5]

REBUILDING BETWEEN THE WORLD WARS

In 1927 an observer of London's development commented that the embellishment of Chelsea, by which he meant rebuilding in a modern style, belonged almost entirely to the period before the Great War and he thought it was doubtful whether any other part of London had seen so few new buildings erected during the early post-War period.[6] However, replacements and small-scale rebuilding continued in the 1920s, mainly in the old village area, and in 1932 redevelopment took place on part of the Sloane Stanley estate, especially nos 1–5 Petyt Place and 68–70 Cheyne Walk near the church.[7] Sir Edwin Lutyens designed a large house at no. 42 Cheyne Walk in 1933, which was itself replaced in 1936 with a block of flats, more than 6 storeys and with a long row of garages behind abutting on the rear of houses in Cheyne Row.[8] The problem of filling large family houses was also being addressed in parts of Chelsea: in Elm Park Gardens the leaseholder was granted a licence to convert nos 99–101 on the corner of Fulham Road into five flats in 1932.[9]

In the 1930s large-scale building for middle-class residents began again after some 30 years, and because of the high cost of land it now mainly took the form of blocks

1 Chelsea Misc. 1594, 1627–8.
2 Clunn, *London Marches On*, 136–7.
3 Clunn, *London Rebuilt*, 279–81; below.
4 Pevsner, *London NW*. 588; see Plate 16.
5 Clunn, *London Rebuilt*, 281.
6 Ibid., 279.
7 *The Times*, 6 Jan. 1932.
8 Ibid., 12 May 1936.
9 KL, deed 27710.

33. *Chelsea Cloisters, Sloane Avenue*

of flats. By the end of the 1930s some parts of Chelsea had been radically transformed: the small terraced houses between Fulham and King's roads near Draycott Avenue were almost completely replaced by gigantic blocks of flats with underground garages, with a few streets of modern Tudor-style houses to the west.[1]

Draycott Avenue

On the partially demolished area between Draycott Avenue and Elystan Street, some vacant sites were used temporarily as motor works and garages,[2] but at the end of the 1920s building resumed. In 1929 the area still not redeveloped was sold to Sir John Ellerman, a shipping magnate, consisting of nearly 14 acres stretching from a narrow frontage on Fulham Road south to Elystan Place and from Elystan Street to Draycott Place with a block beyond reaching Rawlings Street. It included *c.*600 properties in 17 streets for which an improvement scheme was drawn up to clear away the existing houses and gardens, which did not reach modern standards, and develop it in a similar way to the adjoining Cadogan Estate, where at the end of the 1920s a good market for

1 Clunn, *London Marches On*, 7–8.

2 Clunn, *London Rebuilt*, 280–1.

34. *Mid 19th century houses on the east side of Trafalgar Square, rebuilt as Chelsea Square in 1938*

superior town houses had emerged. The estate agents described houses in Chelsea as generally of two types: the class of house for which Cadogan Square was noted; or the small early or mid Victorian house with no comforts or conveniences and desirable only for the site.[1]

Some houses were built on the west side of Sloane Avenue either side of the junction with Ixworth Place on 99-year leases from 1929 or 1930,[2] but predominantly the housing was in blocks of flats. By the end of the 1930s this district was filled with housing for the better off, 'a curious mixture of select, consciously picturesque low houses' and enormous and forbidding blocks of flats, either cautiously Art Deco or approximately neo-Georgian in style.[3] On the east side of Sloane Avenue several semi-detached houses were built and two immense ten-storeyed blocks of flats on either side of Whitehead's Grove with second frontages to Draycott Avenue: on the south corner Sloane Avenue Mansions was completed in 1933, and on north corner the larger Nell Gwynne House, faced with red brick and with a spacious open courtyard in the centre forming the main entrance, was finished in 1937. Both had parking space in the basements, and Nell Gwynne House had a restaurant open to non-residents. On the west side of Sloane Avenue Cranmer Court, one of the largest blocks of flats in London, was built 1934–5 covering most of the block bounded by Sloane Avenue, Whitehead's Grove, Elystan Street and Francis Street (later renamed Petyward), with its main frontage facing south in Whitehead's Grove with two open quadrangles. The buildings were nine storeys high with a row of shops on the Sloane Avenue side which extended through to the first quadrangle. Further north on the west side of Sloane Avenue another vast ten-storeyed block was built 1937–8 called Chelsea Cloisters. It too opened into a spacious courtyard and filled the block bounded by Sloane Avenue, Lucan Place, Makins Street, and Ixworth Place. On the south side of Whitehead's Grove, facing Cranmer Court a group of red brick Tudor style houses was built called The Gateways, which opened into courtyards extending through to Norman Street and was described as 'not unlike ancient almshouses'.[4]

The northern ends of both Sloane Avenue and Draycott Avenue next to Fulham Road were still bordered on the east side by poor-class shops and houses in the 1940s, considered out of keeping with the neighbouring redeveloped estate in Sloane Avenue, but in Fulham Road Pelham Court was built in 1933, a large block of shops and flats facing the gardens of Pelham Crescent.[5]

On the east side of Draycott Avenue the Cadogan Estate began to demolish houses between Green Street in the north and Orford Street in the south in 1930, partly for flats and partly for the Crown. More than 20 families were evicted, but many refused to move until offered suitable accommodation, and hundreds of men, many ex-servicemen, were reported to be armed with staves and prepared to resist the bailiffs.[6]

Chelsea Square

One major redevelopment in this period did not involve large blocks of flats, but again it was intended to attract middle-class residents. The early 19th-century Trafalgar

1 *The Times*, 26 Mar. 1929; *N&Q*, 13th ser., CLVI. 333.
2 Guildhall MS 21058.
3 Pevsner, *London NW.* 588.
4 Clunn, *London Marches On*, 137–8; Pevsner, *London NW.* 588.
5 Clunn, *London Marches On*, 138.
6 Chelsea Misc. 2246, 2248, 2295.

35. *Houses and garages at the south end of Chelsea Square*

Square had been built with nearly 2½ a. of open land in the centre laid out as a garden; by the time the lease for the square expired in 1928 it was sub-let to a tennis club. When the head lease fell in the Cadogan Estate decided to redevelop the area, demolishing the existing houses and building on their sites and on about a quarter of the open ground,[1] with a small mews at the north end and more substantial houses at the south. The rebuilding also meant the demolition of the early 19th-century villa called Catharine [sic] Lodge on the west side, deplored by many local residents. The original houses in the square, described by the Cadogan Estate as nondescript and unable to be adapted to modern use, were demolished from 1932.[2] The rebuilding scheme for the whole square involved new houses designed in early Georgian style by Darcy Braddell and Humphrey Deane, and built of pinkish stock brick, with bright red brick dressings and green-glazed tiles. In 1931 six houses on the south side were completed, fronting onto the central garden, and six on the east. The four centre houses were grouped in linked pairs, along one side of a mews with flats over garages.[3] At the south-west corner Catharine Lodge was replaced by neo-Regency villas in white stucco at nos 40–1, designed by Oliver Hill and built in 1930 and 1934 respectively.[4] By 1938 the rebuilding of Trafalgar Square, renamed Chelsea Square, with its 3-storeyed houses with garages was almost complete, and demolition started on the south side of South Parade and the east side of Old Church Street.[5]

Other Improvements

General improvements on a piecemeal scale continued to be carried out up to the Second World War. The borough council had widened the western end of King's Road up to Stanley bridge in 1908–9, important for local and through traffic,[6] and other improvements had gradually been made to King's Road since the beginning of the century, the building line set back and the road widened as leases fell in, especially west of Beaufort Street where the road made a sharp turn. The widening was accompanied by new building including the Chelsea Palace of Varieties between Beaufort Street and Chelsea Town Hall, but the widening was far from finished by the late 1920s.[7] On the north side houses between Cadogan and Anderson streets were rebuilt, and on the south side between Walpole Street and Royal Avenue the enormous 10-storeyed Whitelands House, a block of shops and flats, was completed in 1937. Further west near Chelsea Town Hall was Swan Court, another great block of flats with streamlined brick frontages to both Manor and Flood streets.[8]

The motor car was beginning to be an important factor in Chelsea's growth, as houses and flats were being built with garages or underground parking to meet the needs of middle-class residents. Attractive purpose-built garages and service stations also appeared, such as Carlyle Garages, no. 350 King's Road, originally called the Blue Bird Garage, designed by Robert Sharp in 1924 with capacity for 300 cars and segregated waiting rooms for chauffeurs, ladies, and owner-drivers,[9] which testifies to the growth of private motor transport and to the affluence of some Chelsea inhabitants. Smaller firms had showrooms and workshops, like Duff Morgan at the north end of Flood Street.[10] Other garages and petrol stations grew up on any vacant site, such as the razed streets of the Chelsea common area, left empty for some 25 years.[11]

Despite the amount of new private building in Chelsea in the 1930s, the outstanding examples of modernism were few. On the large site of Catharine Lodge and its grounds between Old Church Street and Trafalgar Square, divided into four, two houses fronting the square were built to neo-Regency designs by Oliver Hill,[12] but the two sites in Old Church Street received

1 *Rep. of Com. on London Sqs*, pp. 67–8.
2 Pearman, *Cadogan Est.* 114; see Fig. 34.
3 *The Times*, 31 July 1931; see Fig. 35.
4 Pevsner, *London NW.* 587.
5 *Chelsea Soc. Rep.* (1938), 18.
6 LMA, LCC/CL/IMP/1/22, LCC/CE/RB/3/4.
7 Clunn, *London Rebuilt*, 277–8.
8 Clunn, *London Marches On*, 136.
9 Pevsner, *London NW.* 584.
10 *PO Dir. London* (1934); Loobey, *Chelsea*, 63; see Fig. 36.
11 Above, private rebldg before 1st world war.
12 Above, Chelsea Sq.

36. *The Blue Bird Garage, no. 350 King's Road, in 1927*

different treatment. No. 64, designed in 1935–6 by Erich Mendelsohn and Serge Chermayeff for the émigré publisher Denis Cohen, and no. 66, by Walter Gropius and Maxwell Fry for the playwright Benn Levy, brought Continental standards of modernism to a conservative neighbourhood, and despite their uncompromising appearance were generally well received.[1]

Sloane Street and Square

The borough council *c.*1903 widened the north end of Sloane Street, a bottleneck where a third of the growing through traffic consisted of buses to other parts of the metropolis,[2] and the street underwent a transformation in the interwar years, being largely rebuilt after 1918 so that by the 1940s its northern end was altered almost out of recognition. On the east side a large annexe to Harvey Nichols' drapery store was built in 1923 at the Knightsbridge end, a 6-storeyed building faced with red brick and stone dressings. Next to it Richmond Court stretched nearly to Harriet Street, a towering block of shops and flats faced with yellow brick built in 1937–8, and behind it east of Harriet Mews were flats erected in Lowndes Square. The two buildings in Sloane Street replaced a long row of Georgian houses with high-class shops on the ground floor; by the 1940s only three of these remained, on the corner of Harriet Street, and between Harriet Street and Cadogan Place almost all the original houses had been replaced leaving only a few of the original buildings which once lined the east side of Sloane Street.[3]

Many buildings on the west side of Sloane Street had been erected not long before the First World War. Those built in the northern half between the world wars invariably combined flats or offices with ground floor shops and were reticent in design. They included Knightsbridge Court built 1926–7 to replace nos 9–16 Sloane Street, a 9-storeyed block faced with red brick, with the main entrance though a courtyard from Sloane Street and a second frontage onto Pavilion Road behind, a four-storeyed, stone-faced block at the north corner of Hans Crescent built in 1925, and beyond Hans Crescent and facing Cadogan Gardens another tall block built in 1935. At the south corner of Sloane and Pont streets stood the 19th-century Cadogan Hotel, enlarged by 1949.[4] Hugo House, built 1931 at nos 177–8 Sloane Street, provided 11 flats and 4 shops.[5]

Exclusively residential blocks were concentrated south of Pont Street among the remaining Holland houses, and included Dorchester Court, Cadogan House, and Sloane House, all facing Cadogan Place. While flats were popular, the older town houses such as those in Cadogan Square had remained empty for several years, but by the late 1940s were selling again and being renovated by new owners.[6] Cadogan Place also underwent changes. Some of the houses were divided into flats: no. 89, for example, was divided by 1928.[7] Chelsea House of 1874 at the corner of Lowndes Street and Cadogan Place was demolished in 1934 to make way for what is perhaps Chelsea's most stylish block of interwar flats and shops, designed by Thomas Tait, which made the junction into a local commercial focus.[8] By the 1940s the effect of the rebuilding since

1 Pevsner, *London NW.* 587; A. Powers, *Serge Chermayeff: Designer, Architect, Teacher* (2001), 86–8; R. Isaacs, *Gropius* (1983), 212.
2 LMA, LCC/CL/IMP/1/162.
3 Clunn, *London Marches On*, 133–4.
4 Ibid., 134.
5 Pearman, *Cadogan Est.* 114.
6 Clunn, *London Marches On*, 135.
7 KL, BRA 2641.
8 Pearman, *Cadogan Est.* 114; see Fig. 37.

37. *Chelsea House 1935, flats and shops built on the site of Lord Cadogan's Chelsea House*

1880 had transformed Sloane Street from a respectable commercial and residential street, bordered by the meaner streets of New, Exeter, and North streets, into a fashionable shopping centre which rivalled Bond Street, with opulent side streets in Basil Street and Hans Crescent.[1]

Sloane Square and the area to the south also saw further changes in the interwar years. In Sloane Square the crossroads was replaced in 1929 by a roundabout traffic system, making the centre of the square an island paved with flag-stones and planted with plane trees: in the 1930s it was often used as a meeting place by street orators.[2] On the west side of Sloane Square, the only side not rebuilt around the turn of the 20th century, the mid 19th-century buildings, one of which had been a public house, had become part of the Peter Jones department store. They were replaced 1935–7 when the whole shop was rebuilt with a 6-storeyed curtain wall of glass and steel, then unique in London, which was set back to King's Road to allow road widening.[3]

South of Sloane Square the 200-year-old Rose & Crown Tavern on corner of Lower Sloane Street and Turk's Row was pulled down and rebuilt in 1933 as a 5-storeyed block called Sloane Court, with flats above the tavern,[4] and in 1934 St Jude's church, opposite Sloane Court, was demolished and the site taken on a building lease for York House flats, designed by George Vernon.[5]

THE CHELSEA SOCIETY AND THE CONSERVATION MOVEMENT

Famous features of Chelsea, such as the grounds of the Royal Hospital, have always found vociferous public defence when they were threatened. When the temporary government buildings, which had been erected on Burton's Court in 1917 for the Ministry of Pensions, were still there and being increased early in 1919, blocking the view of Chelsea Hospital and destroying the playing field, many influential people protested about the threat to one of London's most beautiful and historic sites, and demanded that the government pledge to remove the buildings as soon as other accommodation was available. The campaign continued for several months, with approaches to leading government figures after the minister said that the buildings would remain for some years.[6] Lesser-known buildings and streetscapes, however, were constantly under threat, and without public pressure in their defence could disappear quite quickly.

In 1926 the imminent demolition of Lombard Terrace on the Sloane Stanley estate aroused local indignation, with a printed petition, and was commented on in the national press. This row of simple 3-storeyed 18th or early 19th century buildings with three or four old-fashioned shops, typical of its period, faced the river at the junction with Church Street, and was all that

1 Clunn, *London Marches On*, 134.

2 Ibid., 135–6; *The Times*, 30 Apr. 1929; Chelsea Misc. 2309; see Plate 15.

3 Clunn, *London Marches On*, 8, 136; see Fig. 58.

4 Clunn, *London Marches On*, 135. The original PH is shown in Fig. 63.

5 *The Times*, 13 Aug. 1934; below, Rel. Hist., dau. chs.

6 *The Times*, 10, 17, 18 Feb. 1919; passim, April, May, June 1919.

survived of Lombard Street after the creation of Chelsea Embankment, and almost all that remained of the old Chelsea riverside. One house incorporated the northern portion of the much older Arch House.[1] Chelsea residents petitioned against demolition but without success, and all disappeared but two, given temporary reprieve because the tenants were protected.[2] This and other losses in the recent past, with the threat to other parts of old Chelsea which had revived with renewed interest in redevelopment, led to the formation of the Chelsea Society in 1927, to protect and foster what were described as the amenities of Chelsea. It came into being at a meeting held at Wentworth House, Swan Walk, through the efforts of Reginald Blunt, who saw the need to co-ordinate local opinion before changes were forced through; the difficulties in saving buildings were exacerbated by the many residents whose stay in the area was only brief. The list of picturesque and historically important buildings already lost included Paradise Row, an 'exquisite old Queen Anne terrace', and the little old tavern opposite the Royal Hospital gates, Swift's lodging in Danvers Street, and Orange House in Cheyne Row. Local efforts had in the past saved the Physic Garden and Carlyle's house in Cheyne Row, but Blunt and the other founding members of the Society could see that the struggle to save other buildings and to resist schemes such as the westward embankment extension or building on the Duke of York's headquarters' site,[3] would continue relentlessly. They also thought it was important to ensure that any new buildings were good ones.[4] In June they held an exhibition in the Town Hall to make known their aims and purpose, exhibiting pictures of Chelsea from the late 18th and 19th centuries as well as photographs taken 1860–70 by J. Hedderley,[5] thus underlining the charm and character of Chelsea which they were seeking to preserve.

Thereafter the Society was a formidable watchdog where redevelopment was planned. Their annual reports and campaigns were always reported in the national press,[6] further galvanizing opposition to various threats. In the 1920 and 1930s they were concerned to keep the social mix of Chelsea and supported efforts to obtain better housing for working classes, such as at World's End.[7] From the 1970s on they fought even harder to prevent Chelsea becoming a rich ghetto.[8] The new society was quickly called into action when in 1927 the LCC wanted to demolish nos 16 and 18 Cheyne Row, the southernmost houses of the row of 1708 and still largely unaltered, to give a second access road to the land behind. Reginald Blunt wrote to *The Times* on behalf of Chelsea Society describing the houses and their history,[9] the works committee of the borough council voted to oppose the plan,[10] and eventually the houses were saved. The Society tried unsuccessfully in 1938 to prevent the demolition of the remaining two houses in Lombard Terrace, nos 64–5 Cheyne Walk, formerly a well-known artists' café. Change in legislation meant the tenants were no longer protected and had been given notice to quit by the owner, Major R.C.H. Sloane Stanley, who claimed he was bound by a verbal promise to demolish the houses when he could, to give a view of the river from no. 1 Petyt Place. The Chelsea Society, despairing at the attitude of an owner who thought the two unpretentious little Georgian houses were not worth preserving, sought the intervention of the LCC, but without success, because consent to develop the site had been given in 1926 in return for allowing widening of Old Church Street at the junction of Cheyne Walk, and the houses were not considered of sufficient architectural merit to warrant preservation.[11]

During the 1930s the Chelsea Society drew attention to the destruction of working-class housing and its replacement by monotonous blocks of middle-class flats. In 1936 the Society complained about the number of vast blocks of flats built the previous year, hoping that no more would be built as they meant the eviction of Chelsea's own working-class population who were replaced with less permanent residents, who contributed little to the communal and social life of the area. The high value of land in Chelsea meant that ordinary house building was not a commercial proposition.[12] In 1937 it was reported that under the Overcrowding Provisional Order there were an increasing number of evictions of old working-class inhabitants and replacement by others, and houses were about to be demolished in Burnsall, Blenheim, Britten and Cale streets, all working-class dwellings. Though the council expressed regret, it had no power to prevent their replacement by larger 3-storeyed houses and flats with garages for middle-class residents, and the Society suggested that the council should acquire sites for municipal dwellings.[13] The following year, however, while the rebuilding of Chelsea Square and its neighbourhood was being completed, work on yet another large block of flats, Nell Gwynne House, was beginning, and the Chelsea Society could only deplore the fact that the planning authority could not oppose an application for development on the grounds of the class built for, but only on construction and suitability.[14]

1 Chelsea Misc. 2375; *The Times*, 18 Nov. 1926 (with photo.).
2 *The Times*, 3 Jan., 15, 25 Feb. 1927; below.
3 *The Times*, 19, 21, 24 Feb., 2, 3, 8 Mar. 1927.
4 Ibid., 2 Apr. 1927; Borer, *Two Villages*, 259–60.
5 *The Times*, 10 June 1927.
6 Ibid., passim.
7 e.g. *The Times*, 12 May 1936.
8 Below.
9 *The Times*, 3 Dec. 1927.
10 Ibid., 9 Dec. 1927.
11 Ibid., 21 Oct., 14, 21 Dec. 1938.
12 Ibid., 12 May 1936.
13 *Chelsea Soc. Rep.* (1937), 34–5.
14 Ibid. (1938), 18, 20.

AFTER THE SECOND WORLD WAR

Bomb damage during the Second World War was comparatively heavy for such a small borough, probably because it lay close to Westminster and two power stations,[1] but being fairly random and spread out the damage had little effect on the overall appearance of Chelsea. The most serious single incident was the destruction of a wing of the Guinness Estate in West Chelsea, where 86 were killed and 111 injured in 1944; the estate was rebuilt in 1947–8.[2] Some serious historical losses were Chelsea Old Church, where virtually the whole building together with Petyt House was destroyed except for the More chapel, and Soane's stables, part of the infirmary at the Royal Hospital. The Old Church was rebuilt on the same plan, as was Petyt House next to it, conveyed to church authorities in 1959 to be rebuilt as the church hall.[3] Sloane Square underground station, only just rebuilt in 1940, was completely demolished in an air raid later that year. Other buildings damaged during the war were Thurloe Court, Fulham Road, and Cranmer Court, Sloane Avenue, in 1940, and Ashburnham Mansions, Ashburnham Road. Heavy damage occurred in Lower Sloane Street and Turk's Row in 1944, including parts of Sloane Court at corner of Lower Sloane Street on both sides of the Rose and Crown, which was, however, left unscathed.[4]

Although Chelsea was described as one of the areas of London which were 'neither blitzed nor blighted', and did not have the large expanse of slum, sub-standard housing, the overcrowding, nor industries intermingled with dwellings that affected some areas of inner London, it did have a small pocket of such housing at the World's End which required reconstruction, while the Lots Road power station with the 'depressed houses' under its shadow were seen as a blemish on the otherwise attractive borough.[5] A good deal of rebuilding and rehousing took place in the decade or so after the war by the council to rehouse people bombed out of their houses and to attempt to reduce poor housing at World's End, though it was some time before the housing problems of World's End were permanently solved. In 1957 Chelsea still had 77 'prefabs' erected by the council, of which 3 were dismantled during that year; the council also still had 396 requisitioned properties housing 1,150 families. By March 1957 post-war building in the borough totalled 1,065 including buildings rebuilt after war damage, 683 of them by the borough council, 33 by housing associations, and 349 privately. Proposals under the Housing Act 1954 for slum clearance had stated there were 15,924 houses in Chelsea of which only 72 were unfit for habitation.[6]

COUNCIL AND PUBLIC HOUSING

The council carried on with building postponed by the war, generally in a low-key manner that was often, because of external pressure, sympathetic to its surroundings. It began on the 3½-acre site on the east side of Draycott Avenue between Denyer and Orford (renamed Rosemoor) streets: work was underway there in 1946,[7] and in 1949 214 flats in 9 blocks housing *c.*1000 people were formally opened as Wiltshire Close.[8] During the Second World War the council had taken over half the houses in Elm Park Gardens, on the south side of Fulham Road in the former Chelsea Park, when they were mainly standing empty, under compulsory provision acts to rehouse those displaced by bombing, and by 1945 most of the requisitioned houses were occupied as flats. In 1946 the council, which had already converted 68 of the 108 houses in Elm Park Gardens into flats for 205 bombed-out families, sought to purchase compulsorily and convert the remaining buildings into flats, giving the existing tenants priority for rehousing. The owners argued unsuccessfully that the houses were unsuitable for conversion;[9] the council went ahead with the purchase in 1948,[10] and gradually bought up the leasehold interests over the next few years.[11] In 1953 they issued leases and tenancy agreements for the five flats at no. 1 Elm Park Gardens, originally two houses converted into flats in 1932;[12] a few other houses were occupied as flats in the 1950s. The earliest tenants included a schoolmaster and an art editor, and from the level of rent the housing was clearly not intended for working-class occupants: the ground floor flat at no. 1 Elm Park Gardens was leased for 21 years at £100 a year.[13] The need for smaller dwellings led to proposals in the 1960s to replace the houses by new blocks of flats: some of the houses had new additions at the rear overlooking the gardens, others were completely rebuilt as modern flats. Some tenancies dated from 1968, but most from the 1970s. The council also demolished the detached Elm Park House which stood in the middle of the open space at Elm Park Gardens, and replaced it with Elm Park House containing 34 bed-sitting-room flats, 20 one-bedroom and 6 two-bedroom flats, and an underground garage. All the blocks were planned to respect

1 Borer, *Two Villages*, 237.
2 Loobey, *Chelsea*, 35.
3 *Chelsea Soc. Rep.* (1959), 11–13.
4 Clunn, *London Marches On*, 135, 137–8.
5 J.H. Forshaw & P. Abercrombie, *County of London Plan* (1943), 20, 28.
6 LCC, *London Statistics*, NS, III (1947–56), 106–7, 110.
7 *The Times*, 8 Aug. 1946.
8 Ibid., 4 May 1949; Clunn, *London Marches On*, 137–8.
9 *The Times*, 25 Sept. 1946.
10 KL, deed 27746.
11 e.g. KL, deeds 27530, 27726–36, 28091–113, 29128–223.
12 KL, deed 27710.
13 KL, deeds 41719–25.

38. *Cheyne Walk west from Beaufort Street, threatened by the West Chelsea housing scheme in 1949, with Lindsey House* (right)

their 19th-century context and the gardens were preserved, protected under the London Squares Act of 1931.[1]

The first of three phases of the council's estate of 45 flats in Lucan Place was completed in 1953 with artists' studios at the top of the building, the first of *c.*30 studios the council planned to incorporate into its new buildings throughout Chelsea. Those included 250 flats and 6 studios in brick-faced slab blocks on the Cremorne estate, a block of more than 40 flats and 10 studios in Dovehouse Street, and smaller building schemes in Hortensia Road, and in Limerston Street,[2] where the scheme of 1954–8 was designed to fit in with the existing villas, some of which were reconstructed as flats with eight studios.[3]

After its union with Kensington in 1965, Chelsea was drawn into the controversy about the contrast between the southern part of Kensington and Chelsea with the very run-down and immigrant-filled North Kensington,[4] and pressure groups continually agitated for the introduction of measures to halt the polarization in the royal borough between very rich transients and subsidized council tenants, with the middle class and single driven out. In 1978 the Empty Homes Group demanded a public inquiry into the housing policies of RBKC, claiming that the council had sufficient empty houses to house 10,000 families, but was spending £5,000 a week on bed and breakfast accommodation for homeless families, and had a housing waiting list of more than 7,500 families.[5] Another solution put forward was a co-ownership housing scheme, a partnership between a housing association and the council whereby the association acquired and converted suitable property and the council put up the money. The members of the association would get cheaper than normal flats and 100 per cent mortgages; council would get new young, middle-income residents.[6]

West Chelsea (Cremorne Estate)

Various schemes temporary and permanent were carried out for the area west of Beaufort Street and south of King's Road. Some late 19th-century houses at the south-east junction of Dartrey and Cremorne roads were sold to the council in 1949 under a compulsory purchase order as the site for the erection of 'Model Residences',[7] and also the freehold of land at the north-west corner of Ashburnham and Stadium roads in 1950 for a temporary housing estate.[8]

The council drew up the West Chelsea housing scheme in 1949 to redevelop the area west of Beaufort Street. In 1946 surveyors commenting on decayed buildings at no. 105 Cheyne Walk, near the corner with Milman's Street, described the area as socially the 'wrong' end of Chelsea,[9] and were presumably advising against investing there. The council's scheme involved sweeping away nos 105–19 Cheyne Walk, two rows of 18th- and 19th-century houses containing 239 occupants on the edge of the site stretching westwards from Milman's Street, which would be replaced by two blocks of flats. Both the Chelsea Society and the Georgian Group pressed to retain the houses, which had 18th- and early 19th-century interiors: no. 119 was the house where Turner had lived and died, and others were mid Victorian stuccoed houses, where artists like Dame Ethel Walker still lived, which were by no means slums. The LCC decided to rebuild Turner's house, badly damaged in the war though some interior panelling survived, and rebuilt it to look as before, while an alternative scheme was adopted for the site of nos

1 *Chelsea Soc. Rep.* (1962), 15–19.
2 *The Times*, 8 Dec. 1952; below, artists and Chelsea.
3 Pevsner, *London NW.* 586.
4 e.g. *The Times*, 28, 30 March 1972.
5 Ibid., 26 April 1978.
6 *Sunday Times*, 9 July 1978.
7 KL, deeds 34784, 34786.
8 CL, deeds 18514, 18518.
9 Guildhall MS 16806.

39. *Brunel Flats, Cheyne Walk, built 1955 as part of the Cremorne Estate*

105–6, a house of 1878 and bombed open space used as a garage and petrol station.[1] The council's Cremorne Estate, completed in 1956, covered 9.5 acres which stretched westward from the rear of houses in Beaufort Street across Milman's Street to Riley Street.[2] It left untouched all the houses fronting Cheyne Walk except nos 105–6, which were replaced by a four-storeyed block of flats called Brunel House, designed by Frederick MacManus of Armstrong and MacManus on a scale and appearance to harmonize with the adjoining 18th-century houses;[3] it opened in 1955 and was let by the council at unsubsidized rents to tenants in slightly higher income groups. However, the extended scheme, which would have included World's End, lapsed owing to high land costs and re-housing problems.[4]

The council also planned to rebuild the river wall at the west end of Cheyne Walk between Battersea Bridge and the Old Ferry Wharf, reclaiming land from the foreshore and routing the road a little further from the houses, but met with opposition from the Chelsea Society and the London Society, who wanted the wall rebuilt in the same position, because the new scheme would sweep away 'the picturesque scene, the marine character of the little harbour and the friendly river folk'.[5] The road and river wall remained unchanged, but decades later the increasingly heavy road traffic probably made that decision a source of regret to the inhabitants of Lindsey House and its neighbours as well as to pedestrians along the river bank.

World's End Estate[6]

In 1961 the council began to look again at the scheme for World's End, partly because of new pressures on housing caused by the surrender of wartime requisitioned property, and the fact that this was the last major housing site which would be available for some time.[7] There followed an eight-year battle to get the LCC to accept a higher density of people per acre (ppa) than the county plan allowed. Cremorne had been built at the prescribed density of 136 ppa, but using this density at World's End would not allow all the displaced people to be rehoused. By 1962 central government was accepting the need for densities over 200 ppa; the LCC opposed this fearing they would end up with the social problems of Victorian tenements,[8] but were willing to consider a density of 170 taking the new World's End and the Cremorne estates together and including suitable open

40. *World's End Passage 1969. The right-hand side had been rebuilt in the 1930s: its earlier buildings are shown in fig. 31*

1 *The Times*, 12, 15, 19, 25 Feb., 7 March 1949; 28 June 1958.

2 S.L. Elkin, *Politics and Land Use Planning: the London Experience* (1974), 33.

3 *Chelsea Soc. Rep.* (1955), 32–4.

4 Elkin, *Politics and Land Use Planning*, 33.

5 *The Times*, 1 Nov. 1951.

6 Section based on Elkin, *Politics and Land Use Planning*, Chap. 3, World's End.

7 Elkin, *Politics and Land Use Planning*, 35.

8 Ibid., 32.

41. *King's Road at World's End and the junction with Blantyre and Seaton streets, with public house* (left)*, the Salvation Army hall* (adjoining)*, and St John's mission church* (far right)

space. Misunderstandings about density in the course of meetings between the borough and the LCC led eventually to a scheme which the LCC turned down at the end of 1962, not only on the grounds of population density, but also the lack of architectural merit and the appearance that the height and mass of buildings would have along the river. A new scheme was then drawn up by Eric Lyons, architect, and E.G. Goldring of the Chelsea borough engineers, which included 8 tower blocks grouped around podiums, all interconnected around gardens; the area, stretching to Edith Grove, would be traffic-free with cars put underground.[1] The LCC town planning committee recommended rejection, because it would result in a density of 232 ppa (excluding a one-acre school site), while the LCC wanted no more than 150.[2] After an inquiry held in 1965 the Minister of Housing turned down the borough's plan while accepting the need for higher densities in specific cases, and was prepared to treat Chelsea's application as exceptional because of the high standard of layout and design, which might permit the high density of the revised scheme.[3] The borough was able to adapt their plan to meet the recommendations of the planning inspector, and the revised scheme, for 765 flats in blocks of 5 to 14 storeys forming three irregular squares, with two level walk-ways, and including underground parking, shopping centre, church, public house, and community centre, with a school on an adjoining site, received ministerial approval in 1967. Building finally started in 1969, and the first families moved in by early 1975.[4] The estate was completed in 1977 and its six towers of stacked polygons, a Brutalist aesthetic softened by brownish red brick facing, immediately became a new riverside landmark.

A building next to the World's End estate, Moravian Tower, no. 355 King's Road, designed in 1969 and completed in 1971 to house 50 families, was a less successful council venture. In 1983 the council-owned block, once hailed as an 'architectural achievement', faced demolition: the core of the building was rotting, brickwork was falling apart, and sulphates were eating away the mortar. From the beginning there had been a problem with damp and leaks, and in 1975 a High Court action had been brought by the council against the architects, Chamberlin Powell & Bon, and the builders.[5] It was not demolished, however, but sold by the council

1 *The Times*, 10 Oct. 1963.
2 Ibid., 2 Oct. 1964.
3 Ibid., 18 Aug. 1965.
4 CL, Chelsea cuttings: World's End Housing scheme 1963–7 (*Daily Telegraph*, 22 May 1967); World's End, Misc. (*Chelsea Post* 25 April 1969; *Chelsea News* 13 Sep. 1974); see Plate 1.
5 *The Times*, 5 April 1983.

and revamped in 1988 by Fitch & Company as private flats, with custard-coloured cladding to hide the problematic brickwork, and a new top floor.[1]

Housing Society

With working-class housing being provided on a large scale by the borough council, the Chelsea Housing Improvement Society turned to different provision after the Second World War. Between 1949 and 1952 they converted seven unmodernized houses in Danvers Street into flats for the elderly: the first five houses were acquired from the council and converted with a bed-sitting room and a sitting room-kitchen for each of 18 elderly people and a matron by 1950, when they appealed for funds for further conversions. By 1960 the society had bought the leases of two more houses there to convert into eight flats for the elderly and were again appealing for funds. In 1950 they also converted 49 Elm Park Gardens into flats.[2]

Providers of social housing in Chelsea earlier in the century still maintained their estates in 2003. The Guinness Trust managed 384 homes in 3 estates in the London borough, including Draycott Avenue and Edith Grove. The William Sutton Trust's largest estate was at Cale Street in Chelsea, where they had 637 homes, mainly one- and two-bedroom flats. The Peabody Trust managed 103 flats in Chelsea Manor Street, and 37 in Lawrence Street.[3]

PRIVATE BUILDING

In the 1950s private development got off to a slow start, but even piecemeal development could threaten the character of Chelsea, and some architecturally important buildings had been neglected. Norman Shaw's Swan House, Chelsea Embankment, empty since 1931 and decaying, aroused the concern of the Chelsea Society who were pressing for its preservation;[4] in 1954 permission was given to convert it into offices, which at least preserved it from destruction.[5] The demolition of Markham Square congregational church and sale of the site for six houses in 1953 removed an attractive landmark, and in 1955 the entrance and west window of Markham House, at the corner of King's Road and Markham Square, was demolished and replaced by a shop front. Built in the early 19th century as a dwelling, the house had a central entrance looking down Smith Street and the change spoiled the vista; it was felt that a house facing onto King's Road could have been used unchanged as offices. A licence had been granted for a coffee bar in the basement, though refused for a night club.[6] The adaptation of this particular old building for modern uses was seminal, however, as Mary Quant opened Chelsea's first boutique here in 1955 and her husband Alexander Plunket Greene a restaurant in the basement.[7]

Housing Problems for Private Tenants

The main threats to the character of Chelsea after the Second World War came from two sources, local government and the property market. While the borough council's plans were acceptable once older buildings, such as those in Cheyne Walk, were preserved, the LCC's plans for public buildings in place of houses aroused great opposition. In 1959 the borough council, local householders, the Chelsea Society, and the local MP opposed the LCC's scheme to extend the London Oratory voluntary-aided secondary school, which would involve demolition of 77 houses in Sydney Street, Fulham Road, Stewart's Grove, Cale Street, and Guthrie Street, and the eviction of 300 people; the opposition was successful in getting the scheme removed from the 5-year plan.[8] The threat was always there, however. Chelsea was over-endowed with institutions in relation to its size, and their needs were continually pushing out residents. Several hospitals, the college, the fire brigade, and the old people's home all needed more space, which threatened the older buildings, especially homes. The accompanying reduction in affordable accommodation also meant that the artists who had given Chelsea much of its character were leaving the borough because of the high cost of living and the scarcity of cheap studio accommodation, and the Chelsea Society feared that soaring property values would destroy the 'left-bank' quality of Chelsea.[9]

Resurgence in the property market after the Second World War led to many problems in Chelsea, a desirable area with a lot of privately rented flats and houses. One was the threat to existing private tenants, faced with either enormous rent rises or eviction as property owners sought to take advantage of new markets. In 1946 it was reported that the 75 tenants of flats and one-room flatlets at Pelham Court, Fulham Road (rents £100–180 a year) had been given notice to quit by the management company on behalf of the owners, Joseph Constantine Steamship Line.[10] The borough council then considered requisitioning Pelham Court, as it would not tolerate actions which would make 80 families homeless at a time of very complicated housing need, and required the owners to withdraw the notices.[11] In 1960 the tenants of King's Court North and South, 2

1 Pevsner, *London NW.* 584.
2 KL, deeds 26375–6; *The Times*, 2 May 1952, 31 March 1960.
3 Inf. via websites from Guinness Trust (www.guinnesstrust.org.uk); William Sutton Trust, (www.williamsutton.org.uk); Peabody trust (www.peabody.org.uk).
4 *Chelsea Soc. Rep.* (1952), 18.
5 Ibid. (1954), 17.
6 Ibid. (1953), 25–6; (1955), 21–2.
7 Below (Chelsea and fashion).
8 *The Times*, 7 Dec. 1959; *Chelsea Soc. Rep.* (1959), 20–1, 31, 35–40.
9 *Chelsea Soc. Rep.* (1959), 64; (1960), 18–19.
10 *The Times*, 26 March 1946.
11 Ibid., 3 April 1946.

blocks of flats in Chelsea Manor Gardens, asked the council to make a compulsory purchase, as the landlords, Town and Commercial Properties, were demanding rent increases of 58–117 per cent and had refused to negotiate after the tenants had offered 25 per cent.[1] Also in 1960 the Chelsea housing committee reported that the terms offered to tenants of Alexandra Mansions, 26 flats in King's Road (rent £150), were exorbitant: the tenants had been asked to buy 14-year leases at £3,500 each. On the committee's recommendation the council decided to purchase the flats from the owners, Thorney Court Ltd, but withdrew in 1961 after the owners offered to let at new rents of £255–325, rather than the £500 a year which they had sought.[2] In 1962 the tenants of Dorchester Court, Sloane Street, requested the council to buy their flats compulsorily following their dispute with the landlords, Peachey Property Corporation Ltd, who wanted to charge market rents, claiming rents there had never been subject to any form of control.[3] The council decided to purchase Beaufort House flats, a Victorian block of 12 flats in Beaufort Street with 28-year leases, in 1964 to protect the tenants. The owners, S.P. Mercantile, had bought the block 14 months previously but denied making a great profit from the sale to the council, having spent a lot on improvements.[4]

Tenants in less desirable property were also at risk. In 1964 private landlords served notices to quit on the tenants of 17 decontrolled flats at nos 16–46 Lots Road, almost against the wall of the power station, which housed families who had lived in Chelsea for generations. The landlords, a property firm, said that the property had to be modernized, but a tenants' association had been formed and asked Chelsea council to buy compulsorily. The council's housing committee decided to rescue the tenants threatened with eviction and negotiated to buy 28 houses: those in Lots Road and 11 in Stadium Street, where residents of four of them were told to pay double the rent or leave.[5] The fear of redevelopment and eviction was present when any sale came up, as in 1964 when the tenants of 27 properties in St Luke's and Britten streets protested against the decision to sell by the freeholders, United Westminster Schools foundation, an educational trust. The trust had property at nos 2–24 St Luke's Street and 14–20 (even) Britten Street, mostly small early 19th century terraced houses with 2 small shops.[6]

A contrast was emerging between the older Chelsea and a new more highly priced Chelsea as it moved into the property boom of the 1980s. Houseboats moored in Chelsea Reach at Chelsea Yacht & Boat Club provided an alternative to high-priced houses and flats: in the 1940s they had been owned by artists and theatre people, but in the 1970s the *c.*50 boats had a varied population including journalists, architects, editors, and students. There were still *c.*100 artists living in Chelsea but the number was falling.[7]

One of the most highly publicized controversies, perhaps because its size affected so many tenants, concerned the massive 10-storeyed Chelsea Cloisters, which consisted of over 800 small flats, many let to elderly residents on fixed incomes, with *c.*50 porters and other staff. Most of it was let unfurnished, and it also contained a restaurant, snack and cocktail bars, squash court, library, and hairdresser. It was acquired with other property in 1968 by Freshwater Corporation, who sold a 99-year lease of the block in 1970 to a company which turned the 4th and 5th floors into a hotel, providing under contract 260 rooms for Pan American air crews. Tenants complained that part had also been used as a tourist hotel. The borough council opposed change of use because of the loss of residential accommodation and the increase in traffic and noise a hotel would bring, and in 1971 a planning inquiry was held; the residents' association of 375 members held a meeting at the House of Commons to present a petition against the proposed changes. The company's request to use a third of the block as a hotel was turned down by the secretary of state for the environment.[8] The lease was sold on, but the block was not returned to its former use, and in 1973 the council were considering compulsorily purchasing the block, then consisting of 796 furnished and unfurnished flats with a mixture of long and short-term leases, called one of London's largest and most luxurious blocks of flats. It was claimed that Freshwater had transformed it into luxurious pied-a-terre for business executives, doctors, actors, and successful journalists, offering luxury services; the number of unfurnished flats had declined to 300, and short-term tenants in furnished flats increased to 212. The rest were being converted and notice given. Older residents had regulated rents but were still afraid they would be greatly increased.[9] In the event neither the council nor the GLC, which had been hoping to buy the block in 1974 to house public service workers, bought the block,[10] and in 1984 Chelsea Cloisters, one of the largest blocks of flats in London, was put up for sale, with 747 flats, garage, petrol-filling station, restaurant, and coffee shop.[11] In 1986 it was reported that £7.5 million was being spent on refurbishing it, and prices ranged from £55,000 for a studio to £125,000 for a 2-bedroom flat on a 125-year lease; it was aimed to attract businessmen, particularly international executives, wanting a base in London, providing

1 *The Times*, 20 Sep. 1960.
2 Ibid., 12, 15 Dec. 1960, 28 Sep. 1961.
3 Ibid., 4 Aug. 1962.
4 Ibid., 13, 14 July 1964.
5 Ibid., 30 Sep., 10 Oct. 1964.
6 Ibid., 1 Feb. 1964.
7 Borer, *Two Villages*, 258.
8 *The Times*, 2 Aug. 1968, 23 March, 26 May, 9 Nov. 1971.
9 Ibid., 10 Aug. 1972, 5, 6 April 1973.
10 Ibid., 1 May 1974.
11 Ibid., 7 June 1984.

switchboard, laundry, secretaries, boardrooms, and word processors.[1] In 2003 luxury furnished apartments were available to rent there,[2] alongside privately-owned leasehold flats.

Development Problems

More difficult to deal with were the larger redevelopments proposed by ground landlords: they sought to replace the mainly 19th-century streets and houses, which seemed to them outmoded and incapable of modernization, and were often in an indifferent condition, with modern and often high-rise replacements, trying to maximize return in a popular residential area. The rediscovery of urban living among middle-class professionals, which was gentrifying some parts of inner London for the first time, also had some effect on Chelsea despite the higher socio-economic level at which it began. As the 1960s and 70s introduced a new fashionable dimension to Chelsea's appeal, the consequent rise in prices put further pressure on the balance in Chelsea between the older communities, still mainly middle-class, and the drive to bring in newer, often transient, residents as well as the very well off. The Chelsea Society had to continue its vigilant campaigning against the destruction of the small scale which contributed to the charm of Chelsea and what they saw as inappropriate new developments.

Though the LCC aroused opposition with its plans for institutions in the borough, on the whole it opposed the destruction of older, attractive buildings. In 1961 a public inquiry was held by the Ministry of Housing and Local Government on an appeal by the Sloane Stanley estate against the LCC's preservation order on Paultons Square and houses in Stanley Terrace, which formed a corner of the square and along King's Road. The estate wanted to demolish Stanley Terrace, built in 1840, and build shops with flats over them, but it was felt that if the terrace disappeared it would affect the appearance of the square, described as one of the best surviving squares in West London, with elegant brick houses and wrought-iron balconies.[3] The minister confirmed the preservation order on both the houses in the square and the terrace on the grounds that the buildings were an integral part of an unspoilt architectural composition.[4]

In 1973 Chelsea was described as the centre of the tourist industry, deeply affected by the great rise in property prices and by speculation. Under pressure from amenity societies the council had fought back, and about half the borough had become a conservation area. Kensington & Chelsea Corporation Act was passed to stop any more conversion of houses to hotels. Other trends were the conversion of top-class property into embassies and headquarters for big international companies. While Chelsea's remaining working class had an increasing pool of council and housing trust accommodation, the middle class were being pushed out of the area with very high rises in rents used by ruthless landlords who wanted to let for short stays.[5]

In 1973 Chelsea still had many 18th-century houses in streets behind the south side of King's Road; St Leonard's Terrace, Cheltenham Terrace, Royal Avenue, and Wellington Square were renovated, as were smaller houses to the west between King's Road, Royal Hospital Road, and Cheyne Walk. Many Regency houses still stood to the north between King's and Fulham roads, and as houses became vacant or leases expired their value soared. There were still islands of dilapidated housing, however, especially in mid and west Chelsea, with houses divided into flats or occupied in single rooms. In the 1940s and 1950s artists had returned to Chelsea because of the studios there, but left because of rising prices in 1960s and 1970s.[6]

Cadogan Estate Redevelopment

Proposals for redeveloping part of the Cadogan Estate were included in the London Development Plan, published in 1955, incorporating 8-storeyed terraced flats, and buildings of 35 and 26 storeys in Sloane Gardens and Pont Street, with rezoning of Sloane Street on the west side of Cadogan Place for expensive shops. Georgian houses on the north side of Cadogan Place, still largely residential, were in the course of being replaced by the 18-storeyed Carlton Tower Hotel, but the rest of that area was still largely residential. The Chelsea Society opposed the plans, fearing that 'thinking people' would be replaced by a continuous stream of American tourists and provincial tycoons, and that the new proposals would lead to demolition of all remaining buildings around Cadogan Place and their replacement by 8-storeyed flats.[7]

Though the tower blocks in Sloane Gardens and Pont Street did not go ahead, the development of Sloane Street as an important commercial area began to take shape. The Carlton Tower Hotel of 1961 was a large building complex, including an 18-storeyed stone-faced tower, on a one-acre site at the north end of Cadogan Place, and the west side of the site provided a 2-storeyed block combining shops fronting Sloane Street with Coutts Bank on its original site. It was designed by Michael Rosenauer, and the interior included glass murals by Feliks Topolski.[8] Also in 1961 Liscartan House was built at nos 127–131 Sloane Street, a 7-storeyed building by J. Douglass Mathews and Partners, with shops on the ground floor and offices above; behind it, in Pavilion Road, the site included two mews flats over four garages.[9]

1 *Sunday Times*, 13 April 1986; see Fig. 33.
2 Notice at Chelsea Cloisters.
3 *The Times*, 25, 31 May 1961.
4 Ibid., 2 Oct. 1961.
5 Borer, *Two Villages*, p. x.
6 Ibid., 244–5.
7 *Chelsea Soc. Rep.* (1959), 14–20.
8 Ibid. (1960), 45–9; Pevsner, *London NW.* 582; see Fig. 42.
9 Pearman, *Cadogan Est.* 117.

42. *Carlton Tower Hotel, Cadogan Place*

In 1962 the Cadogan Estate put forward a bold development plan for the Sloane Street area, to be carried out over 40 years. It involved bridging Sloane Street south of Cadogan Gardens and just north of Carlton Tower hotel, building flats on the bridges, and enclosing the gardens in Cadogan Place as a residential precinct. A 26-storeyed block of flats was proposed for Pont Street; the Willet building in Sloane Square was to be brought into the traffic circulation; a two-storeyed shopping block and a 26-storeyed residential block were to be built, and the sides of the square linked by pedestrian bridges. Lower Sloane Street was to be widened to provide another residential square with a 30-storeyed tower block. The Estate aimed to keep the area south of Sloane Square predominantly residential and were asking the LCC to prevent more offices being built, confining them to northern part of Sloane Street and Sloane Square. However, the scheme was similar to the earlier one, and like it received an unfavourable response from the planning authorities and was dropped.[1]

The Estate took majority shareholdings in 1962 in companies formed to build specific properties on the estate: Fordie House and Oakley House in Sloane Street, Clunie House in Hans Place, and a commercial building at nos 190–2 Sloane Street.[2] Also in 1962 the Estate proposed redevelopment for residential purposes of *c.*4½ acres around Walton Street, including First, Hasker, and Ovington streets. The plan included two blocks of flats *c.*110 ft high, but was mostly for several terraces of family houses with 4–6 bedrooms each and garages and gardens, with a new little square.[3] The scheme did not go ahead, however, although town houses were built at nos 64–112 Walton Street. The Estate built other small-scale residential and commercial buildings in keeping with the existing building stock: 13 houses, 7 studio flats, and 15 garages in Manresa Road and Dovehouse Street; town houses in Astell and Cale streets; a block of shops, offices, and flats at nos 155–67 Fulham Road.[4]

Also in 1962 the Cadogan Estate sold the freehold of land at the corner of Oakley Street and Cheyne Walk to Wates Ltd for £265,000 at auction, including 12 houses in Oakley Street, the Pier Hotel, shops, residential and workshop premises at nos 32–3 Cheyne Walk, and 3

1 *The Times*, 26 Jan 1962; Pearman, *Cadogan Est.* 117.
2 Pearman, *Cadogan Est.* 118–19.
3 *The Times*, 13 Sep. 1962.
4 Pearman, *Cadogan Est.* 118–19.

shops and living accommodation at nos 34–6 Cheyne Walk, all let on leases expiring in 1963 or 1965.[1] Wates put forward a scheme in 1965 to redevelop the site with 6-storeyed blocks,[2] and despite protests the Pier Hotel of 1844, the Blue Cockatoo restaurant, favoured by artists from the 1930s to 1950s, and Thurston's billiard factory were all demolished in 1968 to make way for Pier House Flats.[3]

Although large-scale commercial and residential schemes in Sloane Street got approval, attempts to redevelop elsewhere with tower blocks brought out opposition in force. In 1965 the Estate unveiled proposals for 9½ acres near the river stretching from Flood Street to Smith Street and including Shawfield Street, Redesdale Street, Radnor Walk, Tedworth Gardens and Square, Redburn Street, Tite Street, and Christchurch Street and Terrace; it included 634 flats and houses, mostly built *c.*1820 onwards, and 1,229 residents. The existing property was held on leases expiring in 1965 or 1972–3, and the scheme, by Chapman, Taylor and Partners, was to be carried out to coincide with those dates. It would include two tower blocks of 33 storeys, 159 houses, and a 3-storeyed garage for 294 cars, giving 385 flats in all; the tower blocks would be built first to take up displaced people and facilitate the remainder of the scheme. Low-rental housing would be provided for poorer tenants, subsidized by higher-value properties, to retain the existing mixed economy of the area; the existing density of 112 an acre would be increased to 150. Strong opposition came both from local conservationists and residents, and from the town planners of GLC, who objected to the tower blocks, which they wanted reduced to 125 feet. The Estate saw the towers as essential to the scheme and planning permission was refused, a decision upheld by a public inquiry in 1967.[4] In the meantime the introduction of the Leasehold Reform Act, 1967, which allowed certain lessees to buy the freehold of their premises, also helped to undermine the Estate's plans. The freehold of the north side of Tedworth Square and the southern end of St Leonard's Terrace was eventually sold and redeveloped by an outside company.[5] However, the Estate did receive planning permission in 1971–2 to redevelop the Christchurch Street and Tedworth Square area, and in 1974 began demolishing houses there, but were stopped by preservation orders on listed buildings at nos 26–52 and 60–76 Christchurch Street. The Estate and local residents were deeply divided over the need for redevelopment: the Estate thought the houses incapable of being brought up to modern standards at economic cost, and wanted to replace them with luxury modern town houses; in the House of Lords Lord Cadogan described the terrace as 'nasty cheap little houses that were built a long time ago'. Conservationists, however, claimed that the Georgian terrace in Christchurch Street was the only example of that particular type left in London.[6]

Two public inquiries were needed over a plan to build a car park under the north garden of Cadogan Place, which was eventually built in 1968 for 349 cars. In the early 1970s two major buildings went up on the Estate in Sloane Street: the Danish Embassy at no. 55, by Arne Jacobsen, 1972–7, and the Chelsea Hotel, in 1974, but the property market crash halted any further major development for a number of years, efforts being confined to converting and updating old buildings, particularly in Culford Gardens, Lower Sloane Street, and Sloane Gardens where the late Victorian leases were expiring.[7]

With the slump in the property market in the mid 1970s, another problem arose as rebuilding stalled and landmark buildings became neglected. In 1976 the 6-year campaign to save from dereliction the Pheasantry in King's Road, once patronized as an arts club by Augustus John and Annigoni, reached a peak. The leaseholder (Devereaux Land (King's Road) Ltd) promised they would restore the listed building the following year after finishing the redevelopment programme around it. A campaign was mounted by the Friends of the Pheasantry, under the patronage of Sir John Betjeman, who wanted the building restored with residential studios, an art gallery, and exhibition space; the surrounding site had been demolished *c.*2 years before, and the Friends wanted the whole area as a garden.[8] They were not successful in preventing the adjoining development, but the front and gateway of the Pheasantry survived, heavily restored, as part of the rebuilding of 1971–81, forming a restaurant hemmed in by shops and offices.[9]

The issue of large public buildings in Chelsea was also one which surfaced again in the 1970s. Opposition had prevented the destruction of much of Sydney Street for a school in the 1950s, but was unable to prevent the expansion of what became the Royal Brompton hospital. In 1979 the GLC's historic buildings committee expressed regret at the proposed demolition of six houses in Sydney Street for a scheme for the National Heart and Chest hospital, which it felt was out of scale with the early Victorian houses.[10] At St Stephen's hospital in Fulham Road, the buildings of the former St George's Union workhouse were replaced by a three-storeyed out-patient department in 1965, but St Stephen's subsequently closed and was demolished to make way for a new building uniting four other hospitals as the Chelsea and Westminster hospital in 1993.[11] By 2000 the hospital buildings had expanded to include the east side of Netherton Grove.

1 *The Times*, 25 July 1962.
2 Ibid., 18 June 1965 (photo).
3 Bignell, *Chelsea 1860–1980*, 57; Loobey, *Chelsea*, 27.
4 *The Times*, 12 March 1965; Pearman, *Cadogan Est.* 119–22.
5 Pearman, *Cadogan Est.* 121–2.
6 *The Times*, 24, 25, 31 July 1974.
7 Pevsner, *London NW.* 581; Pearman, *Cadogan Est.* 122.
8 *The Times*, 17 Jan. 1974 (photo.).
9 Pevsner, *London NW.* 583.
10 *Daily Telegraph*, 28 Sep. 1979; similar to hos in Fig. 22.
11 Below, Loc. Govt, pub. svces (medical).

Development from the 1980s

In the early 1980s the redevelopment increased again, with completion of the Pheasantry site in King's Road, Anchor House in Britten Street providing offices, and the Waitrose supermarket in King's Road.[1] Redevelopment of residential flats for the first of the Holland houses in the southern terrace of Cadogan Place was pending in 1986, retaining the original façades.[2] The pressure to rebuild was constantly being felt as leases fell in. In 1989 great opposition was aroused to plans to redevelop a block of assorted Victorian buildings at nos 242–77 King's Road, facing the open south side of Carlyle Square, and viewed as typical old Chelsea. The landlords, the Church Commissioners, originally owned most of area, formerly part of the glebe, and over the years had sold off houses in the side streets, but had granted leases in this block to end in 1990, which would allow redevelopment of whole site extending up to Old Church Street. It was intended to replace the buildings with shops onto King's Road, a covered market at the back, a pedestrianized area, and a terrace of town houses at the rear overlooking the old rectory garden, in a style described as 'objector-proof banal'. The successful opposition was led by Old Chelsea Residents Committee, which expressed deep anger because of the threat to old shops which were part of Chelsea life, including the artists' materials shop of Green & Stone at no. 259, founded in 1927.[3]

In the late 1980s the property market in Chelsea saw a demand for high-quality modernized properties; whereas five years previously Chelsea still had some scruffy streets, prices were now booming to reflect the depth of the facelift, and exceeded a million pounds for exceptional examples: Chelsea Park Gardens (£1M), Upper Cheyne Row (£1.75M), and Cheyne Walk, a house of 1711 (*c.* £1.8M). Infilling took place in former commercial yards and other spaces: in Charles II Place off King's Road between Radnor Walk and Smith Street, a developer built 52 new town houses around a courtyard in 1989.[4] In 1985 the plans were announced for a residential, commercial, and leisure development on derelict land on the west side of Chelsea Creek.[5] Though in Fulham, the choice of Chelsea Harbour as its name was obviously intended to link it with the more fashionable and expensive area to the east.

Another sharp increase in house prices from the late 1990s again encouraged developers to squeeze more properties into Chelsea: in 2001 Ranelagh House in Elystan Place was extended to add 11 modern flats on a slim triangle of land, the cheapest one-bedroom flat selling for £450,000.[6] Those who wanted modern minimalism in the historic listed buildings of Chelsea had to seek a more radical approach. The owner of the listed no. 11 Cheyne Walk, rebuilt in the 1880s but in a badly neglected state in 1999, after buying the leasehold also bought the freehold from the Cadogan Estate. The exterior was repaired and the interior was designed by Ivana Porfiri, who managed to retain the period fittings – cornices, arches and staircase – by building inside the original building: suspended false ceilings and new walls could be removed in days if necessary. The bathrooms in opaque ultra-white glass and stainless steel were allowed by English Heritage as a mark of their time; the work took 3 years to complete. As the owner was then moving abroad the house was on the market in 2002 at £9.5M.[7] The rise in property value had its benefits for old Chelsea too, however. The Old Church's vicarage and Petyt Hall were rebuilt *c.*2002 to designs by John Simpson to include space for a fine neo 18th-century town house, the sale of which paid for the rebuilding.

CONSERVATION AREAS

By the early 1970s the new borough council had created a number of conservation areas under the Civic Amenities Act of 1967, which allowed planning departments to consider the townscapes when developments were proposed, and gave local groups a positive role in changes. Between 1969 and 1971 eight areas were designated, covering about half of Chelsea, extended and redefined during the next two decades, so much was there worthy of preservation. By the mid 1980s the areas were Cheyne; Hans Town; Chelsea, which included three of the original areas and some additional streets; Chelsea Park/Carlyle, which included Elm Park; Sloane Square; Royal Hospital; and Thames, an area designated in 1981 to cover the whole river frontage and features such as the houseboats at the western end.[8]

CHELSEA AND FASHION

After the Second World War a small social group known as the Chelsea Set filled the gossip-columns with their parties and other doings: socially well-connected but willing to include talented middle- and working-class members, they included writers and artists, and apparently had a penchant for opening little restaurants with 'an ambiance of that particular cosy if slightly self-congratulatory intimacy'. In 1955 two of them, Mary Quant and her husband Alexander Plunket Greene, with their partner Archie McNair opened a boutique at the corner of Markham Square called Bazaar with a restaurant below called Alexander's, where Quant sold clothes which expressed rebellion against the adult establishment as well as membership of a social élite, and 'allowed girls to stop dressing like their mothers', a major contribution to the youth culture which emerged

1 Pearman, *Cadogan Est.* 122.
2 Ibid., 123.
3 *Sunday Times Mag.* 9 April 1989.
4 *The Times*, 7 June 1989.
5 Ibid., 16 Aug. 1985.
6 *Financial Times*, 28 April 2001.
7 Ibid., 27/28 April 2002.
8 RBKC, *Conservation Area Proposals Statements* for *Cheyne* [1983]; *Thames* [1983]; *Royal Hospital* [1984]; *Chelsea* [1986]; *Sloane Square* (1991); *Chelsea Park/Carlyle* (1992).

43. *Mary Quant's boutique Bazaar, no. 138A King's Road*

in the 1960s.[1] Quant's popularization of a fashion which depended solely on being different from the older generation, rather than being very expensive, allowed the increasing numbers of young working people with disposable income to participate and to generate a demand for shops to meet their needs. King's Road naturally became a focus for the new boutiques which sprang up everywhere, and also became a centre for socializing and leisure among the young and fashion-conscious. By the early 1970s King's Road was a mix of old and new shops, some good, some tatty, antique shops and junk shops, and many cafés, bistros, coffee houses, steakhouses, restaurants of many nationalities, and delicatessens; crowds promenaded along King's Road, some wearing outrageous costumes, to see and be seen. It brought an increase in crime, drunkenness, and drug addiction, with vandalism by hooligans on Saturday nights.[2]

Chelsea Drug Store, on the corner of Royal Avenue, was one of the leading venues in King's Road, with a bar, restaurant, discotheque, and boutiques, attracting young people from all over London. Residents of Royal Avenue formed an association to protest at 'rubbish, noise, and hippies' and eventually Royal Avenue was closed at the King's Road end:[3] led by the film director, Joseph Losey, they demanded that the council improve amenities for Royal Avenue or they would withhold rates. They complained that people were sleeping on benches under the trees or eating and sleeping in a mini-bus parked on the pavement 24 hours a day; and that commercial interests had turned the avenue into a 'hippies' haven'.[4]

Chelsea continued to enjoy its split personality, however. Though the King's Road brought fame and fashion, it was fashion in its popular sense. The eastern fringe of Chelsea between Knightsbridge and Sloane Square continued to be a centre for more conservative wealth. In the course of the 1970s the term 'Sloane Ranger' was coined to characterize a type of upper-class, fashionable but conservative young woman in London, and was subsequently extended elliptically as 'Sloane' to men, inanimate objects, and a life-style.[5]

Ultimately it was the old-fashioned type of fashion which survived in Chelsea. As fashion and retailing changed towards the end of the 20th century, Chelsea lost its place at the cutting edge of youthful fashion, and instead provided fashionable clothes and furnishings for the well off.[6] Chelsea still attracted many visitors, often nostalgically in search of the scenes of the Sixties or of its older artistic connections, but both its pop and its bohemian pasts had been largely smartened away.

1 G. Melly, *Revolt into Style* (1989 edn), 163–5; K. McIntyre, 'The Most "In" Shops for Gear', in *Twentieth Century Architecture 6: The Sixties*, ed. E. Harwood and A. Powell (2002), 38; below, Econ., trade (retail); Fig. 43.

2 Borer, *Two Villages*, 253–4.

3 Ibid., 251–2.

4 *The Times*, 7 Nov. 1969.

5 *OED*.

6 Below, Econ. Hist., trade (retail).

ARTISTS AND CHELSEA

The presence in Chelsea of many leading artists during much of the 19th and 20th centuries made up a large part of Chelsea's renown beyond its borders and its reputation as an artistic and bohemian colony. While artists in previous centuries were attracted to Chelsea to paint its riverside and houses, its artistic reputation was created through its position as one of a handful of places which saw a concentration of artists' studios when, in the 60 years prior to the First World War, over 1,300 domestic artists' studios were erected in London as a whole. Chelsea was favoured because at the time when the fashion for large and luxuriously fitted studios flourished, prompted by the rise of professionalism among artists, it had sites available for building at reasonable cost, while still being close to the West End and the picture-buying public.[1]

TURNER AND THE RIVERSIDE

Chelsea, like other villages around London, always had its share of artists living there, attracted by its charm and its cheapness compared with more fashionable areas near central London. The most famous of these was Joseph Mallord William Turner (1775–1851), but the fame he brought to Chelsea was posthumous, since hardly anyone knew he was living there. He kept his house and gallery in Queen Anne Street (St Marylebone), where he had lived since the end of the 18th century, but when his companion, Mrs Sophia Booth, moved to London in 1846, they looked for a house by the river and took a 21-year lease of no. 6 Davis's Place, at the western end of Chelsea's riverside. Turner spent most of his time there, concealing his private life from his friends and acquaintances; he was known in the neighbourhood as Mr or Admiral Booth. The house, 3-storeyed but only one bay wide, was one of a row of seven small cottages which stretched westwards from the King Arms public house. It had a small garden in front bounded by a low wooden fence, and Turner had the roof flattened and added a railing to make a balcony from which he could observe the river.[2] Their neighbours included a boat builder and shops selling beer, wine, and ginger beer, and across the road were steps down to the Thames foreshore. Turner died at this house in December 1851; it was later incorporated with its eastern neighbour into a larger house, now nos 118–119 Cheyne Walk.[3]

PRE-RAPHAELITES AND OTHERS, 1850–1880

While Joseph Turner was dying in 1851 in secrecy in a nondescript row at the west end of Cheyne Walk, a younger generation of artists was finding accommodation farther east. The 22-year-old William Holman Hunt (1827–1910), one of the Pre-Raphaelite Brotherhood, was living in 1851 at no. 5 Prospect Place, at the corner of Lawrence Street,[4] where he painted 'Light of the World' in 1854 in his 1st-floor studio facing the river.[5] Other artists along Chelsea's riverside in the 1850s and 60s included John Martin, the historical painter, at no. 4 Lindsey Row (part of Lindsey House)[6] from 1849 to 1853, while a better-known occupant of Lindsey House was James McNeill Whistler, who lived at no. 101 Cheyne Walk in 1863 and at no. 96 (no. 2 Lindsey Row), also part of Lindsey House, from 1866 to 1878.[7] At the eastern end of Cheyne Walk, William Dyce, RA, lived briefly at no. 4 Cheyne Walk 1846–7, succeeded later by Daniel Maclise, RA, from *c.*1861 until his death in 1870.[8] Dante Gabriel Rossetti bought the lease of no. 16, Tudor or Queen's House, in 1862, giving him a dozen bedrooms and an acre of garden. He invited several relatives and friends to join him, some of whom accepted, and for a while his household included his brother William, and Algernon Swinburne.[9] Some friends of Rossetti sought their own accommodation in Chelsea, among them George Pryce Boyce (d. 1896), painter of topographical watercolours, who could afford to commission Philip Webb to design a house for him: West House was built 1869–70 on the south-east corner of the rectory grounds at the angle of Glebe Place, with a view down Cheyne Row to the river, and had an extended first floor with a studio; the dining room bay was added in 1876. After Boyce's death the house was tenanted by James Guthrie and E.A. Walton. Some garden-studios were also beginning to appear in Glebe Place: the sculptor Giovanni Fontana built one in 1865 on the east side of Glebe Place, behind King's Road, like Boyce an early vanguard of the main settlement. On the whole, artists were drawn to the older and more picturesque Chelsea village and riverside, but Sloane Street also had a number of artists and sculptors at work during this period, and in 1863 John Birnie Philip occupied the kitchen wing of Henry Holland's former mansion, The

1 Walkley, *Artists' Hos in London*, p. xxiii.
2 Painting by J.W. Archer in 1852, reprod. in A. Bailey, *Standing in the Sun: Life of J.M.W. Turner* (1997).
3 Bailey, *Standing in the Sun*, 367–9, 397, 416; see Fig. 38.
4 PRO, HO 107/1472/2/1/5, p. 28.
5 *Survey of London*, II. 86.
6 PRO, HO 107/1472/2/1/2, p. 34.
7 *Survey of London*, IV. 7, 40.
8 Ibid., II. 40.
9 Ibid., 59.

Pavilion, to sculpt the 99 figures for the Albert Memorial. In 1870 Birnie Philip moved his workshop to a villa in Manresa Road, and artists were also starting to move into Upper Church Street: Robert Hannah, the Scots historical painter, made large additions to no. 153.[1]

STUDIOS IN TITE STREET AND ELSEWHERE

The main period in the building of studio-houses, their styles as idiosyncratic and artistic as their occupants, began at the end of the 1870s, when sites for building along the newly-created Chelsea Embankment and Tite Street became available.[2] The riverfront property was too expensive for artists, though no. 7 was designed for the judge and amateur painter Sir Robert Collier, later 1st Baron Monkswell, by R. Phené Spiers, architectural master at the Royal Academy, and also included a flat with a proper studio for Collier's son John and his wife Marion Huxley, both professional painters.[3]

Around the corner in Tite Street, however, artists dominated. Having had some professional success, in 1877 Whistler took a site in Tite Street, later no. 35, backing onto the Royal Hospital's grounds, and asked E.W. Godwin to design a house which included a teaching atelier. The White House had the teaching studio within the huge Japanese-inspired gambrel roof, taller than the stark and asymmetrically composed façade, and a personal studio in one of the two floors below. The design proved quite unacceptable to the MBW, who threatened to withhold the lease unless changes were made. Parapets were raised, Queen Anne details in moulded brick added, and approval was obtained, but financial problems soon led Whistler to sell the house in 1879.[4]

Whistler's influence led several of his friends and admirers to move to Tite Street,[5] and many also commissioned Godwin despite the difficulty Whistler had had in getting the designs accepted. In 1878 Godwin designed Chelsea Lodge for the Hon. Archibald Stuart-Wortley, on a double site on the west side of Tite Street at the corner of Dilke Street, with two sets of principal rooms and studios so that Stuart-Wortley could share the house with his friend Carlo Pellegrini, a successful cartoonist who used the sobriquet Ape. The arrangement soon broke down and Chelsea Lodge was sold in 1879, to the Hon. Slingsby Bethell, an amateur painter who retained one of the studios. Edwin Abbey, RA, who owned the house from 1899 until his death in 1911, may have reunited the studios and added an extra window;[6] at a sale of the house in 1937 it had 2 large studios.[7] Frank Miles commissioned Godwin to design Keats House at no. 44, completed in 1880 after the designs of 1878, considered to be 30 years ahead of their time, were again unsurprisingly rejected by the MBW, and had to have additional Queen Anne-style decoration added. Miles moved there with his friend Oscar Wilde.[8]

After selling Chelsea Lodge, Stuart-Wortley had a second house built 1879–80 at no. 29 Tite Street, called Canwell House, in Queen Anne style with red and yellow brick; when he left in 1885 the house passed to Mary Grant, the sculptress, but was later sold to the adjacent Victoria Hospital. Between White and Canwell houses were two plots, nos 31–33: in 1880 a studio-house was built at no. 31 for Frank Dicey, and a block of studio-flats at no. 33,[9] both designed by Robert Edis. John Singer Sargent bought no. 31 in 1901, having lived in the ground floor flat at no. 33 since *c.*1886, and he knocked through to connect up no. 31 and the flat. Plots opposite at nos 50 and 52 were bought by Mrs Anna Lea Merritt and John and Marion Collier: Mrs Merritt was an widowed American figure painter acquainted with the Colliers, and they asked Marion's brother-in-law Frederick Waller to design a pair of studio-houses in 1881–2. Mrs Merritt occupied no. 50 which she called The Cottage; no. 52 was called More House.[10]

A few studio-houses were built away from the main concentration. R. Norman Shaw designed a studio-house 1882–4 for an irregular site at the corner of Walton Street and Lennox Gardens Mews for Edward and Florence Sherard Kennedy, 'Sunday painters' with private incomes. Called Walton House, it had separate studios for the couple, and also the Victorian arrangement which allowed models to reach separate changing rooms unseen. In 1883 J.P. Seddon designed a studio-house at no. 76 Elm Park Road for Paul Naftel and his wife and her family, several of whom were painters of some repute, and nos 74 and 78, also built *c.*1884, were occupied by landscape painters.[11] In 1879 William Burges designed a pair of garden studios behind no. 28 Beaufort Street for Louise and Joe Jopling, both painters. After Joe died suddenly in 1884 Louise let one studio to Maria Zambaco, sculptress; the studios were later converted into a Roman Catholic chapel.[12] In 1892 Mortimer Menpes, Australian-born painter and etcher, engaged Arthur Mackmurdo to design a five-storeyed studio-house for him on a site at no. 25 Cadogan Gardens, for which Menpes obtained a vast quantity of interior fittings from Japan,[13] installed by 70 Japanese craftsmen.[14]

1 Para. based on Walkley, *Artists' Hos in London*, 78–82.
2 Above, 1865–1900 (Chelsea riverside).
3 Walkley, *Artists' Hos in London*, 82–3.
4 Pevsner, *London NW.* 574; Walkley, *Artists' Hos in London*, 84–6; *E. Godwin: Aesthetic Movement Architect and Designer*, ed. S.W. Soros (2000), 165–8.
5 Girouard, *Sweetness and Light*, 177.
6 Walkley, *Artists' Hos in London*, 86–9.
7 *The Times*, 2 March 1937.
8 Walkley, *Artists' Hos in London*, 89; Pevsner, *London NW.* 574.
9 Below, mass-produced studios.
10 Walkley, *Artists' Hos in London*, 91–3.
11 Ibid., 95–7.
12 Ibid., 94–5; below, Rel. Hist., rom. cathm (Brotherhood of Expiation).
13 Walkley, *Artists' Hos in London*, 214.
14 Denny, *Chelsea Past*, 100.

44. *No. 127 Old Church Street, adapted for William and Evelyn de Morgan*

45. *Mallord House, no. 1 Mallord Street, at corner of Upper Church Street*

ARTISTS AT THE VALE AND UPPER CHURCH STREET

Individual artists' houses continued to be built on the remains of Chelsea Park, the last open ground in Chelsea to be built over, and the adjoining parts of Upper Church Street before and after the First World War. Until it was extended The Vale was a shady lane bordered by three or four houses. Whistler took no. 2 in 1886, where Messrs Ricketts and Shannon later started the Vale Press. No. 1 was acquired at same time by William and Evelyn de Morgan after their marriage, and when on trips abroad they let the cottage with its painting and craft room to Walter Sickert and his Chelsea Life School. Sculptor Thomas Stirling Lee built a studio for himself in the new Vale Avenue in 1910.

In the 1890s several artists also moved into Upper Church Street. No. 123 on the corner of Elm Park Road was built in 1894 for Felix Moscheles, and by 1901 the Chelsea Arts Club had moved into two old villas at nos 143–5. Evelyn and William de Morgan moved to nos 125–7 (nos 8–9 Bolton Place), Upper Church Street, where two terraced houses were adapted for them in 1909–10. Augustus John occupied Robert Hannah's at no. 153, until he moved to Mallord Street (below).[1]

The Vale was extended northwards *c.*1909, with picturesquely grouped neo-Georgian houses along the west side. Mallord and Mulberry streets were added to link it with Upper Church Street, and several studios were built in this group of streets before and after the First World War. In Mallord Street no. 28 was designed 1913–14 like a Dutch cottage by Robert van t'Hoff for Augustus John, and Mallord House, designed by Ralph Knott, was built at the north-east corner in 1911 for Cecil Hunt. No. 22 Mulberry Walk and no. 113 Old Church Street were built as a double house with two studios for John DaCosta, children's portraitist. No. 117 Upper Church Street was designed by Halsey Ricardo in 1914–15, as a wedding present for his daughter Anna and her husband Charles Maresco Pearce, the painter of architectural subjects.[2]

At Little Chelsea an area on both sides of Fulham Road also developed an artistic element near the end of the 19th century. On the Chelsea side, a life class in Limerston Street had attracted 300 students within 4 years of its establishment in 1872, and later in the 1880s individuals began seeking artistic provision on the Gunter estates. Fred Brown, founder of the New English Art Club[3] and later Slade Professor, led several artists from Bolton Studios in Brompton (Kens.) to Netherton Grove. In due course the fashion for garden-studios affected the surrounding streets, Gunter Grove in particular. Following the lead of sculptor Alfred Drury, nearly every other property along its west side had a studio unit by end of the century.[4]

1 Pevsner, *London NW.* 586–7; Walkley, *Artists' Hos in London*, 218–19, 256–7; see Fig. 44.
2 Walkley, *Artists' Hos in London*, 220; Pevsner, *London NW.* 586–7; see Fig. 45 and Plate 14.
3 Below, Soc. Hist., social.
4 Walkley, *Artists' Hos in London*, 203.

In the early 20th century a small group of studio-houses (destroyed in the Second World War) were designed by C.R. Ashbee in Cheyne Walk, in which he recreated the serendipitous atmosphere of the lost Chelsea riverside. He designed no. 37 Cheyne Walk for himself, his mother and sisters in 1893–4, nos 72–4 Cheyne Walk in 1896–8, nos 72–3 for two clients, and no. 74, a studio-house as a speculation which he and his bride moved into. Ashbee also restored and added a studio to nos 118–19 (no. 119 being Turner's house) for Max Balfour, and designed studio projects at no. 38 Cheyne Walk in 1898 for the still life painter, Miss Clara Christian, which had 3 studios in the house and the entrance to a 4th in the back garden, and no. 39 as a free-hold family house speculation. For a few years before her death in 1906 Miss Christian was joined by (Dame) Ethel Walker, with whom she had shared studios in Pembroke Gardens and Tite Street. He also designed no. 75 in 1901–2 for Mrs William Hunt, an art collector, and no. 71 in 1912–13 for Mrs Adeline Trier, a flower painter.[1]

MASS-PRODUCED STUDIOS

More interesting socially than individual studio-houses were the mass produced studios, usually multiple units, often of several storeys and built to let. They occurred in London where the building of individual studio-houses drew newer or less successful artists to live nearby, so demand was strong in Chelsea, and by making studios available to artists of a wider income range it gave Chelsea the mass of artists that created its artistic profile. A three-tier, 15-unit block called Trafalgar Studios was the first of such multiple studios, built in 1878 in Manresa Road. E.W. Godwin drew up a proposal the same year for 30 studio-flats for an unspecified site, but did not find a backer, and for another multi-level scheme next to the White House in Tite Street, but the site was sold to Jackson & Graham, furnishers of Oxford Street, who in 1880 commissioned Robert Edis to design The Studios at no. 33 Tite Street, which had annual rents of *c.*£100. Whistler lived there 1881–5, John Singer Sargent, Charles Furse, and, later, Augustus John. Godwin also designed a tower of studio-flats in 1867, with 4 double-height floors with mezzanines, and a communal kitchen in the basement, but eventually sold the site and drawings to Denton, Son & North, who adapted and built it as Tower House, no. 46 Tite Street, in 1884–5.[2]

A number of small studio groups also sprang up just off King's Road, most probably prompted by the success of Trafalgar Studios: the builder there converted his own neighbouring villa into another set, Wentworth Studios (1885). Later activity remained localized, with the Manresa Road-Glebe Place area the prime location in Chelsea. In Glebe Place Conrad Dressler, sculptor, built the glass shacks of Cedar Studios (1885–6), and three more groups were built in Glebe Place, at nos 60–1, nos 64–5, and nos 52–9. Nos 60–1, known as Glebe Studios, were developed 1888–9 by the rector, who gave his son one of the first tenancies. This interesting development attracted Walter Sickert, William Rothenstein, and Ernest Shepard amongst others.[3] It was during the 1880s and 1890s that Chelsea secured its international name as the art centre of London. The presence of artists' studios led naturally to the teaching of art in Chelsea: although Whistler did not apparently have much success in Tite Street,[4] the Life classes held in Limerston Street and by Sickert encouraged others hold formal classes in Chelsea, and Chelsea School of Art, part of the poly-technic, opened in 1895.[5]

Multiple studios continued to be built there into the early 20th century, notably the Rossetti (1894) and King's House (1911) groups, but suitable sites were becoming scarcer and development more costly.[6] Nevertheless, in 1921 Chelsea's profile as the artists' centre in London was confirmed when the population census noted especially that Chelsea MB had the greatest concentration of male artists, at 9 per 1000 men; the next highest was Hampstead with 6 per 1000.[7] However, just as artistic endeavour was spreading from experts to beginners, Chelsea's position as the centre of artistic life in London was starting to be threatened. At the beginning of the 20th century many artists' studios were gradually acquired for other purposes, and artists were starting to find it hard to compete financially for property in Chelsea, a situation which became critical in the second half of the century, as studios were lost to developers and the artists left the area.[8]

In 1948 the Royal Academy presented a fountain placed in Sloane Square as a tribute to the great contribution of Chelsea to the artistic life of London.[9] In the same year the borough council asked the LCC to promote legislation enabling it to provide studios for artists, a unique inclusion in their Act. In 1939 there were 316 known studios in use, designed and built for the purpose: of those 47 had been destroyed and 42 made unfit for occupation, and by 1948 many others were used as private residences; only 76 were in reasonably good repair and used by working artists.[10] The LCC's General Powers Act of 1949 specifically conferred on Chelsea MB powers to build new studios and equip old ones. By 1953 the first municipal studios were completed, on the top storey of the Lucan estate in Lucan Place; they also planned 6 on the Cremorne Estate at World's End and others in Hortensia Road (3), Limerston Street (6), and Dovehouse Street (10).

1 Walkley, *Artists' Hos in London*, 214–15; A. Crawford, *C.R. Ashbee: Architect, Designer and Romantic Socialist* (1985), 240–59.
2 Walkley, *Artists' Hos in London*, 151–3.
3 Pevsner, *London NW.* 576.
4 Walkley, *Artists' Hos in London*, 86.
5 Below, Soc. Hist., educ. (adult).
6 Walkley, *Artists' Hos in London*, 154–5.
7 *Census*, 1921.
8 *Chelsea Soc. Rep.* (1959), 68–9; (1961), 33.
9 *The Times*, 30 April 1948; see Plate 15.
10 *The Times*, 23 March 1948.

Studios were to be offered to those at head of the council's list of 180 artists needing accommodation. The recent migration of artists away from Chelsea, mostly priced out, was of serious local concern, and artists wrote to *The Times* urging other councils to follow the borough's example.[1]

In 1960 the council's finance committee urged the council to become modern patrons of the arts, because private patrons were disappearing. Although the council had built studios, they had not given much practical encouragement to artists, as they did not offer subsidies or reduced rents for the studios; the committee urged them to introduce an annual subsidy of £500 to be split between successful applicants.[2] Despite all attempts, however, Chelsea continued to lose its artistic element. A brief resurge in the early 1960s, when several of the newly fashionable photographers worked in Chelsea, continued to keep its bohemian reputation alive, but by the end of the 20th century young artists were congregating east and north-east of the City of London, where cheap warehouse accommodation was still available. Few of Chelsea's studio-houses were still inhabited by artists in 2003, when the Chelsea College of Art and Design was also about to leave the borough.[3]

1 *Chelsea Soc. Rep.* (1952), 17; *The Times*, 8, 19 Dec. 1952.
2 *The Times*, 24 May 1960.
3 *Evening Standard Mag.* 30 May 2003.

LANDOWNERSHIP

ALTHOUGH Chelsea manor was only assessed at 2 hides in 1086, perhaps as a royal concession to the holder, the number of ploughs suggests that the manor did cover the whole of the 780-acre parish.[1] The demesne of the manor probably accounted for less than half the acreage, and several medieval freeholds included lands in Chelsea as well as Kensington, Westminster, Brompton, Knightsbridge, or Eye (Ebury) in various combinations. The detached part of the parish of Kensington lying by Chelsea's riverside, which belonged in the 16th–17th centuries to the manor of Earl's Court, as well as the land in Chelsea detached, may be the remnants of a landholding interdependence between Chelsea and Kensington.

By the 15th century the only tenants of the manor of Chelsea in the records were freeholders paying a small assized rent or quitrent to the manor, of whom there are a few lists from 1453 and the 16th century.[2] The lack of correlation between the amounts due in 1453 and later suggests much amalgamation and splitting of holdings took place; the extant feet of fines also indicate an active market in land. Unfortunately the changes in holdings has helped obscure any link between medieval estates and those in the 16th century, and not enough evidence for location survives to make firm connections between holdings.

Among local families owning an unknown quantity of land were the Wests (1269–1389),[3] the Ests (1279–1408),[4] and the Stokets (1333–1405).[5] Many large land transactions involving several parishes do not indicate how much land lay in each parish. In 1332, for example, Adam de Bedyk and his wife Sibyl conveyed 250 a. and 2s. ¼d. rent in Kensington, Chelsea, and Fulham to Robert of Wodehouse, archdeacon of Richmond:[6] there had been disputes in 1301 and 1311 between the Bedyks and the prioress of Kilburn over 20 acres in Chelsea,[7] and possibly at least part of the estate lay in Chelsea detached and involved Malories manor.[8] A large estate belonging to John Convers and his wife Joan in 1309[9] was eventually acquired between 1350 and 1354 by Westminster abbey, when it consisted of three houses, 91 acres, and 10s. 2d. rent in Knightsbridge, Kensington, Chelsea, and Eye.[10] Again, the acreage that lay in Chelsea is unknown: a John Convers acquired 1 a. in Chelsea from Roger and Christine West in 1274,[11] and probably *c.*1300 he or his son John and his wife Joan acquired at least 10 a. and the reversion to a house in Chelsea with rent in Westminster from John Wolward.[12] Wolward's father Richard had been in contention with William West over rent in Chelsea in 1285,[13] and it is possible that the property in John Wolward's grant had been part of the West estate in 1273.[14]

London merchants were increasingly involved in land in Chelsea. In 1371, for example, John Fish, citizen of London, conveyed a house, 36 a. arable, 1½ a. meadow, and 5s. rent in Chelsea to William Hunt and William Multon.[15] In 1403 John Hunt conveyed 4 marks rent from the same property to Thomas Garlethorp (Garthorp), citizen and fishmonger of London,[16] who before 1405 acquired the Stoket estate,[17] and left instructions in his will of 1412 that his estate was to be sold for an obit after the death of his wife, Margaret.[18] Some brief accounts of medieval estates and small freeholdings are given below.

By the late 16th century, Chelsea had three principal freehold estates: the manorial demesne, increased by the purchase of two freeholds by Henry VIII; More's estate; and Hungerford's estate. The last two were formed from several smaller freeholdings of the 15th century but when this happened is not certain: More seems to have built up his estate, as at least three purchases by him are known. Both estates also included a large quantity of land in Kensington. By the 17th century, however, the process was in reverse and several separate freehold estates were formed from the two estates. The continuing formation of new estates is apparent in the sometimes complicated descents given in the individual accounts below: this is especially true of the offshoots from Hungerford's estate, belonging to the Young, Blake, Arnold, Mart, and Greene families, where the complexities so obscured the original estate that much of the land has hitherto been claimed as part of More's property. The manorial estate also lost

1 Below, Econ., agric.
2 WAM 4804; BL, Lansd. MS 2, f. 11; Harl. Roll L.26.
3 PRO, CP 25/1/147/23, no. 467; WAM 4810, m. 2.
4 PRO, CP 40/31, rot. 25; Guildhall MS 9171/2, f. 114.
5 PRO, CP 25/1/150/56, no. 93; *Cal. Close*, 1405–9, 71; Guildhall MS 9171/1, f. 429.
6 PRO, CP 25/1/150/55, no. 69.
7 *Year Bk.* 4 Edw. II (Selden Soc. XLII), 45–7.
8 *VCH Middx*, VII. 214–15; *Cal. Inq. p.m.* (Rec. Com.), II. 122.
9 PRO, CP 25/1/149/39, no. 16.
10 WAM 16209–10, 16270; PRO, CP 25/1/150/64, no. 288; B. Harvey, *Westminster Abbey and its Estates in the Middle Ages* (1977), 419.
11 PRO, CP 25/1/148/25, no. 17.
12 WAM 17547.
13 PRO, CP 40/60, rot. 4.
14 Ibid., 40/2A, rot. 15.
15 PRO, CP 25/1/151/72, no. 487.
16 PRO, CP 25/1/151/82, no. 18.
17 *Cal. Close*, 1405–9, 71.
18 Guildhall MS 9171/2, ff. 220v.–221v.

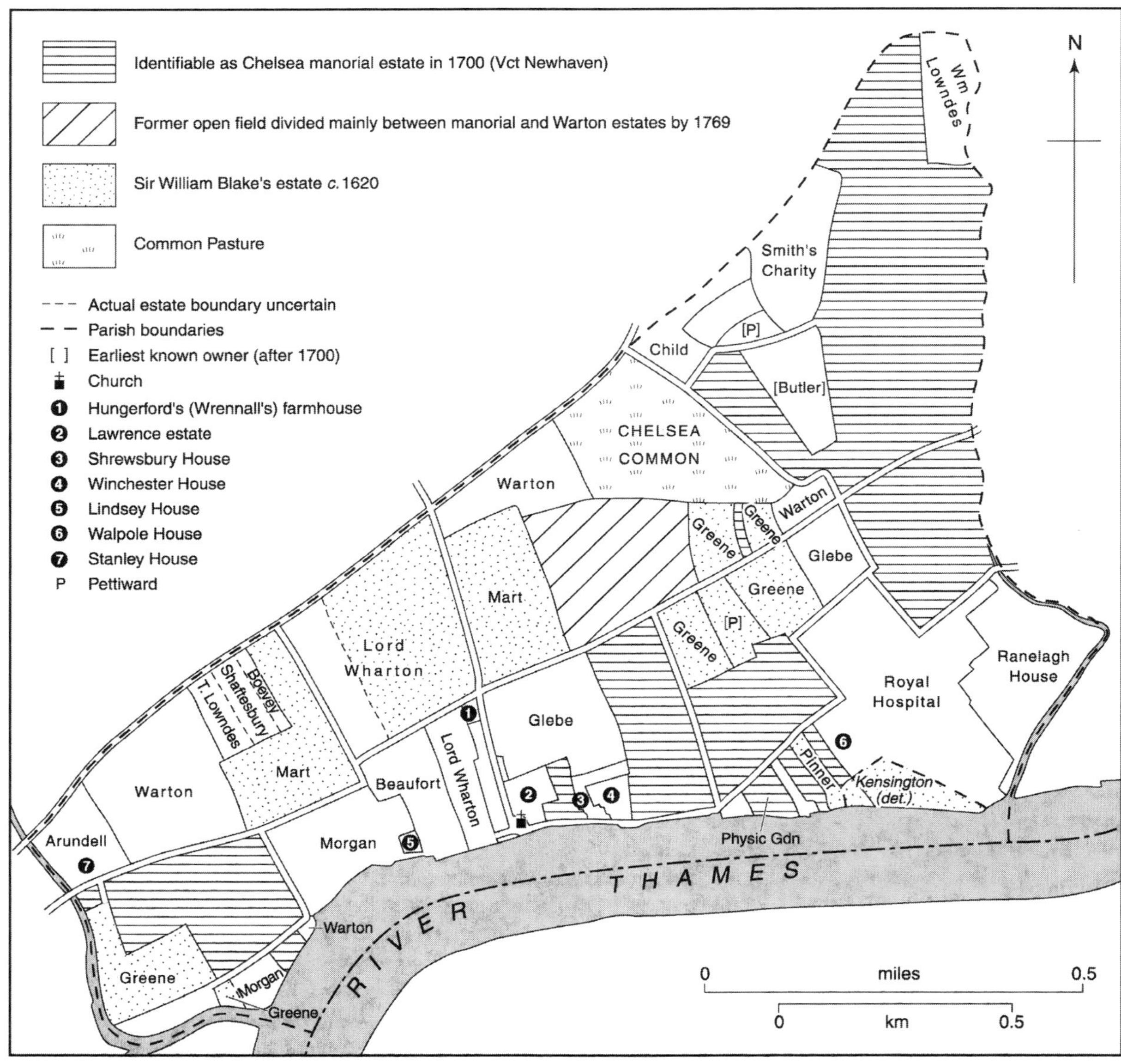

46. *Chelsea's principal estates in 1700*

portions of demesne to create separate freeholdings, but as Chelsea manor its identity was not lost.

The accounts of the estates are divided into the principal estates: the manorial estate, More's, and Hungerford's; the medieval and small freeholdings; and later estates presented in alphabetical order.

CHELSEA MANOR

Before 1066 the manor of Chelsea, worth £9, was held with estates in Hertfordshire and Buckinghamshire by Wlwen, a woman, though described in Domesday Book as the man (*homo*) of King Edward the Confessor. She had the right to dispose of the manor to whom she pleased, and by 1086 had been succeeded in Chelsea, as elsewhere, by Edward of Salisbury, sheriff of Wiltshire. The estate, which was assessed at 2 hides, was still valued at £9 in 1086.[1]

Within 30 years Chelsea had passed to Westminster Abbey. There is no charter recording the grant, probably because of confusion by Norman scribes between Chelsea (*Chealhythe*) and Chalkhill (*Cealchylle*) near Edgware, corrected in the 15th century.[2] Between 1115

1 *VCH Middx*, I. 103, 129; *VCH Herts.* I. 329–30; *VCH Bucks.* III. 337.

2 F.E. Harmer, *Anglo-Saxon Writs*, 114, 496–9; Westm. Abbey, Mun. Bk. II, f. 114v. Chalkhill is in Kingsbury: *VCH Middx*, V. 61.

and 1117 Abbot Gilbert Crispin granted Chelsea to William of Buckland to hold for life for £4 a year, the manor reverting to the abbey after his death.[1] The 12th-century Middlesex Hidage also listed Chelsea as two hides belonging to the abbey.[2]

Gervase of Blois, abbot *c.*1138–*c.*1157, illegitimate son of King Stephen, granted the manor of Chelsea to his mother Dameta to hold for £4 a year, but instead of the manor reverting to the abbey at her death, the grant was made to her and her heirs to hold in fee and heredity, an alienation for which Gervase was later criticized. As an entry fine Dameta paid £2 and a pall worth £5.[3] Although the pope, in a bull addressed to Gervase in 1157, confirmed the abbey's possessions including Chelsea,[4] the abbey apparently never recovered full possession apart from a temporary escheat in the 1450s;[5] its title henceforth was to the £4 annual rent,[6] and to a common fine or cert of 3s. at the view of frankpledge.[7]

William 'de Sefuntaine' witnessed a charter as lord of Chelsea in 1244,[8] but the *de Septem Fontibus* or Setfountain family may have held Chelsea manor from the beginning of that century or even earlier. Ralph de Setfountain was a witness to Abbot Gervase's charters before 1157,[9] and in 1197 he or another Ralph bought a virgate in Chelsea.[10] Ralph (d. 1211) was succeeded by his son William,[11] who in 1214 acknowledged a tenant who held in villeinage from him in Chelsea.[12] By *c.*1254 William had been succeeded by his son Ralph.[13]

In 1274 Ralph was coroner of Middlesex and described as of Chelsea,[14] but in 1281 he granted the manor of Chelsea to Laurence de Septem Fontibus, presumably a relative, for the duration of Ralph's life at £7 a year.[15] Ralph, still alive in 1286, was succeeded in Essex by his son Thomas, who died *c.*1297 leaving his sisters, Cecily and Isabel, as heirs. There was a formal partition of the family estates in 1315 in which the manor of Chelsea was allotted to Cecily, wife of Richard de Heyle,[16] but she was already apparently in possession of the manor, since as a widow she had granted the manor to her son Richard and received it back for life from him in 1314.[17] In the 1316 assessment the vill of Chelsea was said to be held by 'the heirs of Bartholomew de Septem Fontibus', not otherwise known.[18] Richard de Heyle was lord of Chelsea in 1339,[19] and in 1349 settled the manor on himself for life, with successive remainders to his children, Nicholas, Margaret, and Elizabeth, and then to John Bray of Chiswick and his wife Joan, and then to William and Robert, sons of William atte Water of Ware (Herts.).[20] It seems probable that all Richard de Heyle's children died during his lifetime: in 1367 in return for a corrody he leased the manor of Chelsea together with its feudal rights to Westminster abbey for his lifetime for £20 a year, a discharge of his £4 annual rent, and an undertaking not to farm out the manor.[21]

After Heyle's death, probably in 1370, the manor reverted to his heirs,[22] and was held by William son of William atte Water of Ware in 1370; by 1383 it had descended to William's daughter Helen and her husband John Shoreditch the younger of Hackney. In that year Shoreditch leased out most of the dwelling house in Chelsea which had been William atte Water's, probably meaning the manor house.[23] Shoreditch, described as lord of the manor in 1394,[24] died in 1407 leaving instructions for burial in Chelsea church in his chapel on the north side of the chancel, where his wife Helen was buried.[25] He was succeeded by his son John, who in 1412 was said to hold the manor of Chelsea worth £10.[26]

John's title to the manor was challenged *c.*1445 by William Heyle, descended from another branch of the family,[27] but Shoreditch must have successfully defended his title since he subsequently enfeoffed Thomas Burgoyne and others, probably on the marriage of his son Robert to Margaret Tanfield.[28] John died in 1452, and though his widow Maud held his other property, Chelsea apparently escheated to Westminster Abbey as chief lord of the fee, since it was administered for the abbey from 1453 to 1455 by a farmer and rent-collector, William Young.[29] John Shoreditch's son Robert brought a suit in Chancery for the Chelsea and Hackney estates in 1452–3,[30] which was presumably settled in his favour by 1455, and he was described as

1 *Westm. Abbey Charters c.1066–1214*, ed. E. Mason (London Rec. Soc. XXV), no. 242.
2 M. Weinbaum, *London unter Ed. I und II*, II. 85–6.
3 *Westm. Abbey Charters*, no. 262; *Flete's History of Westm. Abbey*, ed. J.A. Robinson (1909), 89; B. Harvey, 'Abbot Gervase and the Fee Farms of Westm. Abbey', *Bull. Inst. Hist. Research*, XL (1967), 127–9, 137.
4 Westm. Dom., f. 3b.
5 Below.
6 Listed under fee farms: Westm. Dom., f. 129.
7 WAM 4816; *Valor Eccl.* (Rec. Com.), I. 417.
8 WAM 17371, dated from fine: PRO, CP 25/1/147/13, no. 218.
9 *Early Med. Misc. for D.M. Stenton* (PRS, NS, XXXVI), 103.
10 PRO, CP 25/1/146/1, no. 161.
11 *Pipe R.* 1211 (PRS, NS, XXVIII), 120, 123, 247.
12 *Cur. Reg. R.* VII. 12–3.
13 *VCH Essex*, VII. 111; *Trans. of Essex Archaeol. Soc.* NS, XVIII. 18.
14 *Cal. Pat.* 1272–81, 61.
15 PRO, CP 25/1/148/29, no. 104.
16 PRO, CP 40/352, m. 558; *VCH Essex*, VII. 111,115; Lysons, *Environs*, IV. 619–20.
17 PRO, CP 25/1/149/45, no. 159.
18 *Feudal Aids*, III. 374.
19 *Cal. Close*, 1339–41, 85.
20 WAM 16366*. Possibly Joan Bray and the wife of Wm atte Water were also daughters of Heyle.
21 WAM 4799; *Cal. Close*, 1364–8, 385–6; B. Harvey, *Living and Dying in England, 1100–1540* (1993), 246.
22 WAM 4808, 19863, 19864A, 19865.
23 *Cal. Close*, 1381–5, 387; WAM 16355.
24 WAM 4809.
25 Guildhall MS 9171/2, f. 109v.
26 *Feudal Aids*, VI. 489.
27 WAM 16355.
28 PRO, C 1/22/105.
29 WAM 4804.
30 PRO, C 1/22/105; *VCH Middx*, X. 82.

'late of Chelsea' in 1478 at the marriage of his son George.[1] In 1485 Robert, his wife Margaret, and his son George sold Chelsea manor for £300 to Sir Reginald Bray, royal official and administrator under Henry VII, acknowledging the abbot of Westminster as chief lord of the fee.[2]

Sir Reginald by will proved 1503 instructed his feoffees to allow his wife Katharine to receive the profits from Chelsea for life, and after her death to make an estate in the manor to the sons of his younger brother John, provided they married his wards, Agnes and Elizabeth Lovell, his wife's nieces.[3] Katharine received £46 17s. 4d. in rent from the manor in 1505–6,[4] but had died by February 1508.[5] The provisions of Sir Reginald's will were not carried out, possibly because the elder of John Bray's sons, Edmund, had not fulfilled the marriage conditions. There was also a prolonged dispute over Sir Reginald's estates between Edmund Bray, claiming as his eldest surviving male relative, and Margery, wife of Sir William Sandys, who was the daughter of Sir Reginald's older half-brother, also called John:[6] her claim was based on an earlier will of 1497. The dispute was settled in 1510 by a partition of all Sir Reginald's estates between the claimants, under which Chelsea was allotted to Margery and Sir William Sandys and their issue, with a remainder to Bray.[7]

Sandys, a royal official and courtier created Baron Sandys in 1523,[8] conveyed the manor of Chelsea to Henry VIII in May 1536 as part of an exchange, and the king acquired Westminster Abbey's rent-charge and overlordship with property in Westminster as part of another exchange that year, giving the Crown absolute title to Chelsea manor.[9] Chelsea was granted to Queen Catherine Parr for life in 1544 as part of her jointure.[10] After Henry's death she married her former suitor, Sir Thomas Seymour, the Lord Admiral and Baron Seymour of Sudeley, but died after childbirth in 1548; Seymour was executed for treason in 1549 and Chelsea reverted to the Crown.[11]

Edward VI granted Chelsea manor, valued at £30 3s. 1½d. a year, to John Dudley, earl of Warwick and later duke of Northumberland, in 1551 as part of an exchange to hold in chief for 1/40th knight's fee.[12] Northumberland surrendered the manor to the king early in 1552,[13] though he apparently continued to be resident in Chelsea,[14] and in 1553 he with his wife Jane were again granted Chelsea for service of a knight's fee and rent of £3 16s. 10¼d.[15] Shortly afterwards the property was confiscated by the Crown on Northumberland's attainder and execution, but in 1554 his widow successfully petitioned for a grant of Chelsea to her for life,[16] and she died at the manor house in 1555.[17] Between grants the manor was managed by bailiffs and keepers of the manor house appointed by the Crown.[18]

From 1560 to 1638 the Crown leased out the manor for lives or terms of years. In 1560 Queen Elizabeth granted the manor for life to Anne Seymour, duchess of Somerset and widow of Protector Somerset, for £13 6s. 8d. a year and payment of the bailiff's and steward's wages.[19] In 1570 Anne and her second husband, Francis Newdigate, were successfully prosecuted for failing to pay any rent for 10 years.[20] Anne died in 1587,[21] and in 1588 a grant was made on identical terms to her nephew, John Stanhope (d. 1621), gentleman of the Privy Chamber, who already subleased demesne land under the duchess.[22] He presumably surrendered his grant, as in 1591 a similar grant for life was made to Lady Catherine Howard (d. 1603),[23] first wife of Charles Howard, Lord Howard of Effingham and later earl of Nottingham, and in 1604 to his second wife Margaret (d. 1639).[24] The lease to Margaret was repeated in 1606,[25] and in 1609 James I granted a reversion of the lease for 40 years after Margaret's death to her son James, at a rent of £45 15s. 7d. a year, which reverted to the countess when James died in 1610.[26] After the earl of Nottingham's death in 1624, Margaret married Sir William Monson, later Viscount Monson of Castlemaine,[27] and in 1628 the Monsons conveyed the 40-year reversionary lease in Chelsea Place to Sir John Monson and Robert Goodwyn, probably as mortgagees.[28]

In 1638 James Hamilton, marquess, and from 1643 duke, of Hamilton, bought the life lease from Monson and his wife and the 40-year reversion,[29] and Charles I

1 LMA, H1/ST/E65/c/1/1/27.

2 PRO, CP 25/1/152/100, 1 Hen VII Trin.; BL, Add. Ch. 70849. Reginald had no known connection with John Bray of Chiswick. Also acquired adjoining manor of Kensington: Lysons, *Environs*, III. 173.

3 N.H. Nicolas, *Testamenta Vetusta*, II. 446–7; *VCH Sussex*, IV. 15.

4 PRO, SC 6/Hen.VII/1843.

5 Nicolas, *Test. Vet.* II. 488.

6 'The Brays of Shere', *The Ancestor*, VI (1903), 2–3

7 PRO, C 54/378, no. 30; CP 25/2/51/358/2HENVIIIMICH.

8 *Complete Peerage*, XI. 441.

9 PRO, SC 6/HENVIII/2101, m. 4; *L&P Hen. VIII*, XI, p. 84–5, no. 202(4), p. 87, no. 202 (29).

10 *L&P Hen. VIII*, XIX(1), p. 644.

11 James, *Kateryn Parr*, 331–2, 339. Their dau. Mary died mid 1550.

12 *Cal. Pat.* 1550–3, 127.

13 Ibid., 117.

14 Beaver, *Memorials*, 180.

15 *Cal. Pat.* 1553, 179.

16 Ibid., 1553–4, 129.

17 *Complete Peerage*, IX. 726.

18 e.g. in 1551: PRO, E 318/38/2050; Geo. Brise (Brice) bailiff in 1555, had been keeper of the ho. in 1551: *Cal. Pat.* 1554–5, 46, 283.

19 *Cal. Pat.* 1558–60, 420.

20 PRO, E 368/382, rot. 53.

21 BL, Harl. Roll L.26.

22 Ibid.; PRO, C 66/1315, m. 10; *Complete Peerage*, XII(1), 239.

23 PRO, C 66/1366, m. 29.

24 *Cal. SP Dom.* 1603–10, 119; *Complete Peerage*, IX. 782.

25 PRO, C 66/1696; NRA(S) 332, L2/103 (12/5/5).

26 *Cal. SP Dom.* 1603–10, 560; NRA(S) 332, L2/103 (12/5/1).

27 *Complete Peerage*, IX. 67, 782.

28 Faulkner, *Chelsea*, I. 325.

29 NRA(S) 332, L2/103 (12/5/1); PRO, CP 25/2/458/14CARIMICH.

47. *A depiction of the north* (rear) *side of the Tudor manor house, showing the 17th-century addition* (right)

granted the manor to him to hold in socage for a fee farm of £10 a year.[1] The fee farm rent was still payable to the Crown in the reign of Charles II,[2] when it was sold by the Crown, probably to Sir John Bennet (d. 1695), 1st Lord Ossulston, whose son Charles (d. 1722), 1st earl of Tankerville, held the right to the £10 in the early 18th century.[3] William Lord Cheyne settled the Feathers Inn and a small adjoining house on Robert Butler and William Clarkson in 1709, in trust to pay the £10 annually,[4] but in 1725 Charles Bennet, 2nd earl of Tankerville, sold the fee farm to Sir Hans Sloane,[5] who merged it into the freehold.

Although Hamilton could only pay £2,000 of the £8,000 required by Monson for the leases, he embarked on extensive building at Chelsea and by 1641 had accumulated debts of £22,800.[6] As part of the financial transactions he conveyed the main house, Chelsea Place, in 1638 to his brother-in-law, Sir John Hamilton,[7] and in 1640 his trustee mortgaged the 40-year term of the rest to Monson's trustee.[8] The duke fought for the king in the civil war, was imprisoned from 1644 to 1646, and was executed for treason in 1649. He left his estates by will to his brother William, who succeeded him as second duke but died of wounds received at the battle of Worcester in 1651.

All the Hamilton estates were confiscated under the Act for the sale of estates forfeited for treason.[9] The duke's property in Chelsea, said to be worth £500 a year, was sequestered in 1649 on the grounds of his delinquency,[10] and in 1651 Chelsea Place was leased for seven years by the Commissioners for Compounding to William Heveningham and John Goodwin.[11] Meanwhile Monson, whose first wife Margaret had died in 1639, had married Frances Alston in 1646,[12] and as part of the marriage settlement his trustee conveyed the 40-year term to Frances's brothers, Sir Thomas, John, and Edward Alston in trust for Monson and his wife.[13] Monson had difficulty is getting the rents paid to him by 1646, and this was still a problem in 1651,[14] when he was in possession of the manor for payment of his mortgage debt and was said to be receiving *c.* £400 a year from the manor.[15] In 1652, when Monson and the Alstons were negotiating with the commissioners for the purchase of Chelsea manor (excluding Chelsea Place), they found that at least five undertenants had purchased their farms, which prevented the commissioners making a contract with Monson.[16] Monson succeeded in getting at least some of the sales reversed on the grounds of his rights in the manor,[17] but his efforts to buy the manor were eventually defeated because of the prior grant in 1638 to Sir John Hamilton, Lord Belhaven from 1647,[18] to pay Hamilton's debts. Belhaven assigned all his interest in the manor to Andrew Cole, the duke's agent, in trust to sell to pay off the creditors, beginning with Monson's mortgage.[19] Cole and Robert Austin, one of the principal creditors, contracted to purchase the forfeited manor, with the exception of Chelsea Place and some farmland,[20] supported in 1654 by a petition from the other creditors to the parliamentary trustees.[21] The trustees had simultaneously been negotiating to sell to Monson,

1 *Cal. SP Dom.* 1637–8, 526–7; NRA(S) 332, L2/103 (12/5/5).

2 PRO, E 351/1502, m. 4.

3 C. Jones, 'The London Life of a Peer in the Reign of Anne: A Case Study from Lord Ossulston's Diary', *London Jnl*, XVI (1991), 140; *Complete Peerage*, X. 189–91; XII(1), 633.

4 CL, deed 3033.

5 MLR 1725/1/2.

6 NRA(S) 332, L2/110 (ES 15/6/3); below (Tudor man. ho.).

7 NRA(S) 332, L1/191; L2/110 (ES 15/6/23). Sir John's wife was illeg. dau. of Hamilton's father: *Complete Peerage*, II. 93.

8 NRA(S) 332, L2/103 (12/5/1); C 6/15/67.

9 R. Marshall, *The Days of Duchess Anne. Life in the household of the Duchess of Hamilton, 1656–1716* (1973), 12; NRA(S) 332, L2/103 (12/5/1).

10 *Cal. Cttee Money*, II. 948.

11 NRA(S) 332, L2/103 (12/5/3);

12 *Complete Peerage*, IX. 67.

13 NRA(S) 332, L2/103 (12/5/1).

14 PRO, C 5/6/55; C 7/88/111; C 7/15/82; NRA(S) 332, F1/174.

15 *Cal. Cttee Money*, II. 948.

16 NRA(S) 332, L2/103 (12/5/1).

17 NRA(S) 332, L1/194 (9/5).

18 *Complete Peerage*, ii. 93.

19 NRA(S) 332, L1/191.

20 NRA(S) 332, L1/194 (9/5).

21 Ibid. (9/9).

but he was unable to raise the sum required until 1655.[1] In April 1654 all claims on Chelsea manor were examined and the parliamentary trustees conveyed the manor and Chelsea Place to a group of Hamilton's creditors.[2] William Heveningham and John Goodwin, lessees since 1651 of Chelsea Place, protested at being ejected from the house, having spent more than £1,000 making it habitable after the depredations by billeted soldiers; the creditors agreed to pay them £800 but their ejection was confirmed.[3] Monson's final attempt to purchase the manor in 1655 came too late,[4] but the mortgage debt owed to him was eventually repaid.

From 1655 rents were paid to Andrew Cole for the creditors and Chelsea Place itself was leased in two separate parts, to Charles Cheyne and Sir Henry Herbert.[5] Negotiations began in 1657 for the sale of both the manor and Chelsea Place to Charles Cheyne,[6] a Buckinghamshire gentleman who had acquired considerable wealth through his marriage in 1654 to Jane daughter of William Cavendish, duke of Newcastle.[7] Cheyne seems to have begun paying for the house in 1657 (£1,900), paying in instalments until the final payment for whole estate in 1661; the total cost was £13,626.[8] By that time Monson's mortgage (in the name of the Alston brothers) was finally paid off,[9] and a conveyance of the manor and Chelsea Place was made to Cheyne by Hamilton's heirs.[10]

Charles Cheyne (d. 1698), Viscount Newhaven from 1681,[11] by will proved 1699 bequeathed to his second wife Isabella, countess of Radnor, for life all his arable lands in Eastfield with any buildings thereon, and any houses in Chelsea 'town' not mentioned in the 1675 marriage settlement of Charles's son William and his first wife, Elizabeth Thomas (d. 1677).[12] He left Blacklands, apparently not included in the 1675 settlement, and all other lands to William, requesting that he allow Isabella to have one of his mansion houses in Chelsea or Buckinghamshire.[13] Isabella continued to live in Chelsea, but in Radnor House, Paradise Row. William, Viscount Newhaven, does not appear to have lived at Chelsea after his father's death: his interest in Chelsea was financial, raising several mortgages on the estate and granting building leases.[14] In 1712–13 Newhaven sold the manor, the advowson of Chelsea church, and the manor house and demesne to Dr Hans Sloane, created baronet in 1716;[15] Isabella, countess of Radnor, and the trustees under the settlement of 1675 also conveyed all their interests to Sloane,[16] who apparently paid £17,800.[17]

Sloane continued Cheyne's interest in building on the estate, but in 1742 he retired to the manor house, which housed his collections. On his death in 1753 he left the manor jointly to his daughters, Sarah widow of Sir George Stanley of Paultons (Hants.), and Elizabeth wife of Charles Cadogan, 2nd Lord Cadogan.[18] Sarah's undivided moiety of the manor was inherited by her son Hans Stanley, who died unmarried in 1780: under his will and a subsequent settlement the Stanley moiety of Chelsea manor passed to his sisters, Anne (d. 1804), wife of Wellbore Ellis, Lord Mendip, and Sarah (d. 1821), wife of Christopher D'Oyley, for their lives and then to their issue,[19] but both died childless, and in 1821 the estate was reunited in the Cadogan family.[20] Elizabeth Cadogan (d. 1768) and her husband Charles (d. 1776) were succeeded by their son, Charles Sloane (d. 1807), Earl Cadogan from 1800, and his son Charles Henry Sloane (d. 1833). The latter was insane for more than 25 years, during which time the Cadogan estates were administered by trustees called committees. He was succeeded by his half-brother George (d. 1864), and the estate thenceforth passed in the direct male line with the earldom to Henry Charles (d. 1873), George Henry (d. 1915), Gerald Oakley (d. 1933), William Gerald Charles (d. 1997), and Charles Gerald John.[21]

By the late 19th century the estate was settled and the earl held as a tenant for life;[22] the Cadogan Estate Office was established to run the estate in 1890.[23] Heavy death duties led to a substantial mortgage to preserve the Chelsea estate in 1934,[24] and to avoid further death duties Cadogan Estates Ltd was created *c.*1961 to hold most of the estate, a small portion being left in the personal ownership of Earl Cadogan and his son, Viscount Chelsea.[25]

1 NRA(S) 332, L2/103 (12/5/1).
2 Lysons, *Environs*, II. 76, quoting Cadogan title deeds since lost.
3 NRA(S) 332, L2/103 (12/5/3–4); *Cal. SP Dom.* 1655–6, 128.
4 NRA(S) 332, L2/103 (12/5/1).
5 NRA(S) 332, F1/182; below (Tudor man. ho.).
6 NRA(S) 332, L2/103 (12/5/6).
7 *Complete Peerage*, IX. 539; *VCH Bucks.* III. 219.
8 NRA(S) 332, L2/110 (ES 15/6/16).
9 NRA(S) 332, F1/182; L2/110 (ES 15/6/20).
10 PRO, CP 25/2/689/13CHASIITRIN; NRA(S) 332, L1/194/9/6.
11 *Complete Peerage*, IX. 539.
12 i.e. Chelsea Place, 6 other hos., manorial quitrents of £7 a year, and *c.*158 a.: MLR 1714/6/33–4; CL, deed 2997.
13 PRO, PROB 11/449, f. 155v.
14 MLR 1711/1/130–1; 1711/4/166; 1709/2/270–1; above, Settlement, 1680–1865 (Chelsea village).
15 MLR 1712/4/50–1; MLR 1713/4/2; *Complete Baronetage*, V. 32.
16 CL, deeds 2996–7; MLR 1714/6/33.
17 Cadogan Est. Office, indenture 21 Mar 1712/13; PRO, CP 43/520, rot. carte 5 seqq.
18 Lysons, *Environs*, II. 135–6; CL, deed 3016; *Complete Peerage*, II. 461.
19 PRO, PROB 11/1063, ff. 102v.–3.
20 Act 6 Geo. IV, c. 16 (Private); *Burke's Landed Gentry* (1952), 2388–9. Sloane Stanley cousins also acted as trustees for Chas. Hen. Cadogan.
21 *Complete Peerage*, II. 460–5; Pearman, *Cadogan Est.* 83; *Who's Who* (2001).
22 Cadogan Est. Office, Agenda & min. bk 22, pp. 1 seqq.
23 Ibid., p. 66.
24 Pearman, *Cadogan Est.* 109; Cadogan Group Ltd, *Cadogan* [brochure *c.*1998].
25 Pearman, *Cadogan Est.* 119.

THE DEMESNE

The original manorial demesne probably comprised about 200–250 acres in the Middle Ages. It was at least 173 acres in 1454,[1] and the more accurate and detailed assessments in the 16th century suggest it was as much as 242 acres.[2] By 1519 some 5 acres had been used for site of the new Tudor manor house.[3] In addition Henry VIII added two freeholdings of the manor to the demesne by exchange: Thomas Keyle's tenement and close, later called the Pye or Magpie, in 1538,[4] and Robert White's 2 tenements, 40 a. arable, and 7 lots of meadow in Chelsea with the manor of Notting Barns (Kens.) in 1542.[5] In 1557 the medieval manor house with 4 acres adjoining was granted away.[6] Over 228 a. and 10 houses were described in 1639,[7] and 233 a. in 1664.[8] From the late 17th century there was steady building of new houses on parcels of the demesne, which were let on building leases. In 1713 the demesne conveyed to Sir Hans Sloane included 11 houses, an unknown number of tenements, and 166 a.,[9] but by that date more demesne had been granted away: 27 a. to King James's College in 1610; *c.*2½ a. with Winchester House in 1664; sales to the Royal Hospital of 21 a. in 1682, 6 a. (Sweed Court) in 1686, 13 a. (Burton's Court) in 1687; 3½ a. to Gough House *c.*1706; and 3½ a. to the Apothecaries' Company for their physic garden in 1722.[10]

MANORIAL ESTATE FROM THE 18TH CENTURY

A steady stream of additions were made to the manorial estate as sizeable blocks of land came up for sale. Sir Hans Sloane bought the Beaufort House estate of *c.*7 a. in 1737.[11] In 1794 Charles, Lord Cadogan, purchased 8½ a. comprising the farmhouse with barn, garden, and meadow at Sandy End from the trustees of Edward Burnaby Greene's estate;[12] and in 1821 trustees for Lord Cadogan purchased the Winchester House estate of 2½ a.[13] Garden ground on the west side of Milman's Street, formerly part of the Gorges House estate, and Ashburnham Cottage with 4 a. had been purchased by 1847.[14]

Sir Hans Sloane and his successors also made gifts of parts of the estate for parish and church purposes,[15] and from the 19th century some of the building development on the estate involved selling parcels of freehold, such as 5½ a. in Lower Sloane Street to William Willett, and *c.*4 a. north of Hans Place in 1889.[16] Larger sales were made of areas which the Cadogan Estate did not wish to develop itself, such as 44½ a. in the south-western corner of the parish including the Cremorne and Ashburnham estates in 1866,[17] and 20 a. near Draycott Avenue in 1902.[18] In the later 20th century sales increased, partly because of the right to buy the freehold given to leaseholders, but more recently as part of Cadogan Estate's deliberate policy of selling residential property to concentrate on commercial holdings. By *c.*1998 the estate covered approximately 90 a.[19]

MEDIEVAL MANOR HOUSE

The medieval manor house and its gardens and outbuildings lay to the east of Church Lane, encircling the north and east sides of the parish church. It was probably the house let for 5 years by John Shoreditch to John Bacun, clerk, in 1383, when Shoreditch reserved the solar and chimney of the new chamber to himself but Bacun was to have the chamber under the solar; the lessee could also buy hay, litter, doves and other things from the manor, and could use the little grange for his hay if he did so.[20] The house with its gardens and a 4-acre close was leased out in 1519 by the lord, William Sandys,[21] and in 1557 the Crown granted away the site of the medieval manor house with gardens, a dovecote, and 4-acre close, to John Caryll to hold in free socage of the manor of East Greenwich.[22] Its later history is recorded below under the Lawrence estate.[23]

TUDOR MANOR HOUSE (CHELSEA PLACE)

The new manor house, usually called Chelsea Place, was built about a fifth of a mile to the east of the medieval house, fronting the riverside. Since the early 17th century it has been claimed that Chelsea Place was built by Henry VIII, but there is no contemporary evidence for this, nor did the king show any particular interest in Chelsea.[24] Chelsea Place was probably built either by Sir Reginald Bray or William Sandys, and presumably by 1519 when Sandys let the old manor house. Some improvements and repairs are recorded: in 1536 or 1537 framed timber was carried from Whitehall to Chelsea for the king's and queen's new closets there, and there are various accounts

1 WAM 4804.
2 BL, Harl. Roll L 26; PRO, SC 6/HENVIII/2101, m. 4 seqq; CP 43/520, carte rot. 5; below, Econ., agric., for location.
3 Faulkner, *Chelsea*, I. 328.
4 PRO, E 326/12183.
5 PRO, E 326/12775; E 305/5/C54.
6 Below, later ests (Lawrence).
7 NRA(S) 332, E1/7; L2/110 (ES 15/6/11).
8 NRA(S) 332, L2/110 (ES 15/6/16).
9 Mostly in Eastfield but including 70 a. of Blacklands: MLR 1713/4/2.
10 Below.
11 MLR 1737/2/587–8; below, later ests (Beaufort).
12 Act 6 Geo. IV, c. 16 (Private).
13 Below.
14 CL, Tithe Map and Award.
15 e.g. burial ground and workho. in 1733: below, Loc. Govt, poor relief to 1837; ibid., pub. svces.
16 Cadogan Est. Office, Agenda & min. bk 22, p. 1 seqq.; bk 11, p. 193.
17 Below, later ests (Chelsea Farm).
18 Above, Settlement, twentieth cent.
19 Cadogan Group Ltd, *Cadogan* [brochure *c.*1998].
20 *Cal. Close* 1381–5, 387.
21 Below, later ests (Lawrence).
22 *Cal. Pat.* 1555–7, 464.
23 Below, later ests (Lawrence).
24 Above, Settlement, to 1680.

for repairs in the 1540s.[1] In November 1538 suitable plants such as bay and rosemary were sent from the Charterhouse to the king's gardener for his garden at Chelsea.[2] The house had gardens on the north side and, by the mid 16th century, a walled 'great garden' on the east side. Only one of the garden accounts that survive for Chelsea is dated: in 1545–6 Queen Catherine Parr's gardener, John Colman, was paid 8d. a day and two women weeders 4d. a day, and he was also paid for seeds to be sown.[3] Another refers to the making of the privy garden, and payments for five women weeders for 32 days and someone to mow the alleys;[4] a Westminster gardener sent two banks of rosemary and six borders of lavender;[5] and in one year 29 gardeners and 6 women weeders were employed, and 29 cherry, 5 filbert, 5 damson, and 2 peach trees were ordered, as well as 200 damask roses, 11,000 sets of whitethorn and 64,000 of privet for hedges.[6]

Queen Catherine Parr spent much time at Chelsea Place after Henry VIII's death and her marriage to Sir Thomas Seymour, until her own death in 1548.[7] John Dudley, duke of Northumberland, lived in Chelsea occasionally while he held the manor from 1551 to 1553,[8] and his widow Jane lived there from 1554 until her death at Chelsea Place in 1555.[9] Anne of Cleves died at the house in 1557.[10] James, marquess of Hamilton, began extensive building when he acquired the manor in 1638, repairing the Tudor house but also building a slightly larger west extension.[11] The resulting mansion, considered fitting for a man known for being 'very sumptuous and magnificent in his way of living', was only occupied by the Hamiltons until the early 1640s.[12] The property was later used for billeting soldiers until it was let in 1651.[13]

From 1655 the Tudor and Stuart parts of Chelsea Place formed separate dwellings divided between Charles Cheyne and Sir Henry Herbert;[14] the latter probably occupied the newer part, which was sold in 1664 to the bishop of Winchester and became known as Winchester House.[15]

Charles Cheyne bought the manor and continued to live in the Tudor Chelsea Place; he was the occupier in 1674.[16] Later in the century Henry Winstanley designed some 'ingenious water-works' in the gardens which John Evelyn viewed in 1696. Though Sir Hans Sloane had an interest in plant-collecting and supported the Physic Garden, he did not maintain the manor house's gardens,

48. *Winchester House* c.*1800, originally the 17th-century addition to the Tudor manor house*

surrendering the great garden to the building of Cheyne Walk, and laying out a strip of garden, probably that lying along the north side of the former great garden, which was described disparagingly by Edmund Howard, who worked in it.[17] Sloane retired to Chelsea Place in 1742, and the house became a library and museum for his collections, described in 1748 as a square of over 100 ft on each side enclosing a courtyard with a gallery the length of one side. At his death in 1753 Sloane directed his trustees to preserve the house as a repository for his collections, which he offered to the nation. However, Montague House in Bloomsbury was purchased instead and the collection was moved there in 1759 to form the nucleus of the later British Museum.[18] Chelsea Place was demolished and the site covered by the houses and gardens of nos 19–26 Cheyne Walk between 1759 and 1765.[19]

Winchester House

An Act had been passed in 1663 to enable the bishop of Winchester to dispose of the old Winchester palace in Southwark, which had been destroyed during the Civil War, and to purchase another suitable house in or near London. In 1664 he bought from Cheyne the 17th-century part of Chelsea Place: the new house, which became known as Winchester House, thereafter belonged to the bishopric of Winchester and was exempted from the jurisdiction of the bishop of London and considered as in the Winchester diocese.[20] During the next 20 years the bishops spent considerable sums on alterations, mostly in wainscotting and building a chapel.[21] Winchester House was described in the early 18th century as 'a noble seat' with 'a good front and

1 *Hist. King's Works*, IV. 64–5; PRO, E 101/459/19, 21.
2 *L&P Hen. VIII*, XIII(2), p. 374.
3 PRO, E 314/22, file 27, no. 43.
4 PRO, E 101/459/20.
5 *Hist. King's Works*, IV. 64.
6 BL, Royal Roll 14B.iv.a.
7 James, *Kateryn Parr*, 145.
8 Beaver, *Memorials*, 180.
9 *Complete Peerage*, IX. 726.
10 Lysons, *Environs*, II. 75; Beaver, *Memorials*, 181.
11 Shown on the plan of 1706 reprod. in Hunting, *Manor Ho. to Mus.* 16–17.
12 Marshall, *Days of Duchess Anne*, 20.
13 NRA(S) 332, L2/103 (12/5/3–4); *Cal. SP Dom.* 1655–6, 128.
14 NRA(S) 332, F1/182.
15 Hunting, *Manor Ho. to Mus.* 12–13; below.
16 PRO, E 179/143/370, m. 5.
17 Hunting, *Manor Ho. to Mus.* 15, 18, 20.
18 Ibid., 21–2.
19 Above, Settlement, 1680–1865 (Chelsea village). Cadogan fam. later had residences in Chelsea: above, Settlement, 1680–1865 (SE Chelsea); 1865–1900.
20 Dr King's MS, pp. 109, 113.
21 BL, Stowe MS 541, f. 139.

noble staircase',[1] and *c.*1781 as 'a most incomparable mansion',[2] but change of taste meant that by the 19th century it was no longer appreciated.[3] The house was dilapidated by 1821 when Bishop Tomline applied for an Act enabling him to sell it.[4] The house and its grounds of 2½ a. was bought by trustees for Earl Cadogan in 1823 and added to the manorial estate; in 1825 the house was demolished and Oakley Street was later built through the site.[5] In 1962 the Cadogan Estate sold 1 a. of the site to Wates Ltd,[6] and the freehold of the whole site had been sold by 1998.[7]

Manor House: The Buildings

Since the Tudor house was demolished as late as the 1750s, it is surprising that there are no known authentic images of that house. The drawing first published by Faulkner, the basis of all subsequent known pictures, was said to come from an 'old roll' and is rather dubious.[8] It seems to show only the rear or north side, and the 17th-century extension to the west. The Tudor front appears from this to have been two-storeyed, with a battlemented parapet and bold chimneystacks as regular punctuation to five unequal bays. A plan of Chelsea village drawn in 1706 to show the water supply gives more information, showing a courtyard-plan house with external stacks on the north and south fronts. At that date there was an entrance court on the river front.[9] Though the houses later built on the site in Cheyne Walk were 200 ft wide and were thought to cover the house site exactly,[10] the 1706 plan shows a house between 100 and 150 feet wide with space on the east for access to the gardens.

The marquess of Hamilton's new range adjoined the west side of the manor house. Early 19th-century drawings show an externally plain house of brick with Artisan mannerist details. It appears to have been of nine (south) by ten bays (west) entered from the south, and retaining many of its mullioned and transomed cross windows. Part of the house seems to have been three storeyed, and part two, plus garrets with dormers. Hamilton seems also to have remodelled the Tudor house, giving it new windows.[11]

The enlarged manor house was described in 1653 as consisting of 3 cellars on the first level, 20 rooms with a large staircase on the first storey, and 24 rooms on the next floor with garrets over part of them, and summer rooms with a bedroom; in 1674, when it was two houses, the Tudor part was assessed at 23 hearths and the new part at 33.[12] In 1653 there was a garden and orchard on the north side of the house, and a courtyard on the south side. The premises also included a stable and coachhouse, three little gardens, a parcel of ground enclosed with a brick wall formerly called the Great Orchard which had been ploughed up, and part of Coney close and the conduit head in 'Chelsey field' (part of the glebe). The house with its gardens and courts was estimated to contain 5 a. 20 p.[13]

When the ownership of the two parts of the house was divided, Winchester House received a share of the front courtyard, with stables and coachhouse on the west, and gardens on the north and west.[14] At its sale in 1823 Winchester House, still a courtyard house, had its principal entrance on the south. On the ground floor was a great hall and chapel, connected by a grand staircase to three grand drawing rooms with stucco ceilings and coloured Italian marble chimney-pieces on the first floor. There were two libraries in the north wing and in the east a great gallery containing many fine antiquities, including murals from Herculaneum which the bishop had collected in 1791.[15] By 1791 too, sashes had been fitted into the upper windows on its south front.[16]

MORE'S ESTATE

Sir Thomas More, lawyer and king's secretary, built up an important estate in Chelsea as his career at court developed.[17] In 1524 he acquired a house, garden, 7 a. arable and ½ a. meadow in Chelsea and Kensington from Andrew and Joan Hickes and John and Margaret Fletcher, and 24 a. arable and 3 a. meadow in Chelsea from John and Lettice Greenfield.[18] At about the same time he purchased a house with a wharf and little close adjoining, and Butts close of *c.*2½ from Thomas Keyle, citizen and mercer of London,[19] and evidently made other acquisitions, as his estate in 1538 consisted of the mansion and grounds where he lived, a messuage called the Farm with 77 a. arable and 12½ a. meadow, a substantial messuage in Brompton, another 28 a. 3 r. of

1 Bowack, *Antiquities*, 15. 2 HMC, *15th Rep.* pt. 6, p. 512.
3 J.N. Brewer, *Beauties of Eng. & Wales*, X (1816), 50; J. Dugdale, *New Brit. Traveller* (1819), III. 476.
4 Act 1 & 2 Geo. IV, c. 5 (Private); Faulkner, *Chelsea*, I. 293–6.
5 Act 6 Geo. IV, c. 17 (Private); above, Settlement, 1680–1865 (Chelsea village).
6 *Chelsea Soc. Rep.* (1962), 36–8.
7 Cadogan Group Ltd, *Cadogan* [brochure *c.*1998], map.
8 *Survey of London*, II. 65–7.
9 Hunting, *Manor Ho. to Mus.* 16–17.
10 *Survey of London*, II. 67.
11 Ibid., 65–6; Hunting, *Manor Ho. to Mus.* 16–17.
12 PRO, E 179/143/370, m. 5.
13 Deed quoted in Faulkner, *Chelsea*, I. 327–8.
14 R.K. Marshall, 'The House of Hamilton in its Anglo-Scottish setting in the 17th cent.' (Edinburgh Univ. Ph.D. thesis, 1970), 10–12; Hunting, *Manor Ho. to Mus.* 12, 15 (plan).
15 *Gent. Mag.* 1822, pt. 1, pp. 506–9.
16 Wash and ink drawing of Winchester House, 1791, in Guildhall Lib., prints and maps; and see Fig. 48.
17 *DNB.*
18 PRO, CP 25/2/27/179/16HENVIIITRIN, nos 51, 53.
19 PRO, C 1/540/78.

arable in Chelsea, and 7 other messuages in Chelsea;[1] this excluded a house and Butts close given to William and Margaret Roper in 1534.[2] More was evidently living in Chelsea by the beginning of 1525 when he was appointed to search for suspected persons in the area, presumably as a justice of the peace.[3] There has always been considerable doubt about the exact location of More's house, and of the new building which he built containing his chapel, library and gallery,[4] as extensive building by his successor in the property, William Paulet, marquess of Winchester, has obscured the location of the house and the layout of More's property. It seems most likely that More's mansion was a medieval house close to the riverside, and that it was More's new building in the grounds behind which formed the site of the mansion known later as Beaufort House.[5] He also built a tomb for himself and his wives in the parish church.[6] He farmed directly at least some of his land, as a fire destroyed his corn-filled barns *c.*1529;[7] the previous year he had reported under the commission on corn that he had wheat, barley, and oats of his own to supply his daily household of 100.[8]

More became lord chancellor in 1529, and conducted some state business at his Chelsea house, including hearing petitions and examining heretics. In 1532 he resigned the chancellorship as he could not support the king's policy regarding the Church, and retired to Chelsea.[9] According to William Roper, More made a settlement of his estates on himself for life with remainders of part to his wife, part as a jointure for his daughter-in-law, and part to his daughter Margaret and her husband William Roper, but shortly afterwards More reinforced this settlement by an outright grant in possession to the Ropers.[10] Before being committed to the Tower in 1534, More granted all his estates in Chelsea to feoffees for uses he had previously indicated, but on his attainder all his estates were taken into the king's hands except for the portion given to the Ropers.[11] More's deed of feoffment was annulled by an Act in 1536,[12] following More's execution in 1535. However, although the king granted More's chief house to Sir William Paulet to hold at the king's will,[13] contrary to tradition More's family retained life interests in some of the Chelsea estate much in accordance with More's settlement, and were assessed for taxation under Chelsea from 1535–6 until 1547.[14] In 1540–1, for example, Sir Thomas's widow Alice was assessed in Chelsea at £50 for lands and fees held for life, his son John at £60 for lands held in his wife's right for life, presumably her jointure, and William Roper at £10 for lands, office, and fees for life.[15] Roper was listed as a free tenant of the manor in 1543,[16] and in 1547 he was said to hold for life a house and close called Butts close, with houses built there, a barn, and garden rent-free by gift of Sir Thomas More. The property was supposed to revert to the main estate after Roper's death,[17] but did not apparently do so, and it remained a separate estate. Its later history is traced below under the Earl of Lincoln's other estate and Sloane Stanley.[18]

In 1547 Edward VI granted More's estate with other lands in fee to Sir William Paulet, Lord St John and later marquess of Winchester, Lord Treasurer from 1550; the estate was as described in 1538 (above) plus Roper's property.[19] In 1566 Winchester enlarged the estate when he acquired the parsonage and 14 a. adjoining it, which lay on the west side of his lands and farm, and 3 a. in Eastfield, by an exchange in which he gave the rector a newly-built house and 18 a. on the east side of Church Lane;[20] there is an indication that this land may have been granted to Winchester from the manorial demesne.[21] In 1567 he leased most of the estate to Nicholas Holborne and his wife Catherine for 50 years at £13 6s. 8d. a year, including the farmhouse in Chelsea, which lay on the south-west side of Winchester's grounds, a quill of water to the farmhouse, 130 a. of land in Chelsea and Kensington, and the mansion formerly called the parsonage with its land.[22] Winchester evidently put up new buildings at his Chelsea estate before he died in 1572, as that year the property was described as his 'new buildings, chief mansion, capital messuage and manor house' in Chelsea,[23] and that, the case brought by his grandson indicating heavy expenditure,[24] and the design of the house itself are a good indications that the house shown in the Cecil survey plan of *c.*1595, and later known as Beaufort House, was built by Winchester and not by Sir Thomas More.[25]

The estate passed to Winchester's son John (d. 1576), 2nd marquess, who sold the whole estate, described in the fine as 20 messuages, 20 cottages, 10 gardens, 10 orchards, 40 a. land, 40 a. meadow, 200 a. pasture, 40 a. wood, and 200 a. waste and briar in Chelsea and

1 PRO, SC 6/HENVIII/7247.
2 Below, later ests (Sloane Stanley).
3 *L&P Hen. VIII*, Add. I(1), p. 140.
4 W. Roper, *The Life of Sir Thos Moore, Kt.*, ed. E.V. Hitchcock (E.E.T.S. 197, 1935), 26.
5 Discussed above, Settlement, to 1680. Subsequent hist. of Beaufort Ho. is discussed below.
6 *Sir Thos More: Selected Letters*, ed. E.F. Rogers (1961), 179–83.
7 Ibid., 170–1.
8 PRO, E 36/257, f. 44.
9 *DNB.*
10 Roper, *Life of Moore*, 79; BL, *Facsimiles*, Suppl. I (k), f. 46.
11 Roper, *Life of Moore*, 79–80.
12 27 Hen. VIII, c. 58; PRO, E 315/2, f. 20v.
13 *L&P Hen. VIII*, X, p. 328.
14 PRO, E 179/141/122, m. 2; 141/131; 141/138; 141/160, m. 15; 141/154.
15 PRO, E 179/141/131.
16 PRO, SC 2/188/42–3.
17 PRO, C 66/801, m. 38.
18 Below, later ests (Earl of Lincoln; Sloane Stanley).
19 PRO, C 66/801, m. 38; *Complete Peerage*, XII(2), 757.
20 PRO, E 371/433, rot. 107; BL, Add. MS 15609, f. 2.
21 *Cal. Pat.* 1557–8, 26.
22 Lease quoted in Faulkner, *Chelsea*, I. 120.
23 BL, Add. Ch. 16153.
24 Below.
25 Above, Settlement, to 1680 (Sir Thos More's Ho.).

Kensington, to his wife's daughter, Anne Sackville, and her husband Gregory Fiennes, Lord Dacre, in 1575,[1] leading his son William, 3rd marquess, to accuse his father's widow of selling the house at Chelsea, costing £14,000, with its lands worth another £1,400, to the Dacres for barely a fifth of its value.[2]

Dacre was listed among the free tenants of Chelsea in 1587 for a capital messuage, various cottages and 119 acres, for which he paid the lord of the manor 4s. a year.[3] He died in 1594 and his wife, who died a few months later, by will proved 1595 bequeathed the estate to William Cecil (d. 1598), Lord Burghley, for life, with remainder to his son Sir Robert and the latter's wife Elizabeth, 'my dear friend'.[4] Sir Robert Cecil had plans drawn up to enlarge the main house,[5] and was having building done there by 1597,[6] though apparently the extant plans, of a significantly different character to that shown in the survey plan, were not carried out. The house was remodelled into a broadened version of an **H**-type with short wings, of which the plan drawn by John Thorpe *c.*1620 seems to be an accurate record.[7] The description of the house in 1652 gives some indication of its character.[8] However, the cost and the burden of Cecil's other houses, as well as the death of his wife in 1597, may have led to his decision to sell the estate, and in 1599 for £6,000 he conveyed it to Henry Clinton *alias* Fiennes, 2nd earl of Lincoln (d. 1616), and Sir Arthur Gorges with a settlement on Lincoln for life, then successive remainders to Gorges and his wife Elizabeth, Lincoln's daughter, for their lives, their children, and in default of issue to Elizabeth Gorges's heirs, or to Edward Fiennes, Lincoln's 2nd son.[9] The purchase may have been part of a dowry for Elizabeth: when Lincoln tried to change the settlement Gorges accused him of meanness towards his only daughter. The same settlement was expressed in the licence to alienate granted to Cecil when he sold to them the Kensington land included in the estate.[10]

Lincoln was notorious for his miserliness and bad behaviour towards his second wife, his son, his brother, his tenants, and his neighbours, as well as towards his sovereign.[11] Despite having paid £500 down for the estate, he threatened not to go ahead with the purchase, claiming it would cost him £100 more a year than he would make out of it, and insisting on the inclusion of various furnishings: the table, carpet, curtains, and hangings in the great chamber, and the chair canopy and cushions in the withdrawing chamber.[12] He had severe financial problems and his attitude may have stemmed from a discovery too late that all the property except the house and grounds and a couple of dwellings was let to Holborne until 1617 and could not be exploited financially: he apparently carried out a campaign of harassment against Holborne and his subtenants,[13] perhaps hoping they would surrender the lease. In addition, he was prevented from selling any of the property by the settlement on Arthur and Elizabeth Gorges, who refused to release their interests, and Lincoln later brought an unsuccessful case in Chancery *c.*1609 against Gorges to try to get the estate resettled.[14]

On Lincoln's death in 1616 the estate duly passed to Sir Arthur and Lady Elizabeth Gorges, and in 1617 they presumably also took possession of the farmhouse, former parsonage, and land leased to Holborne; it was most likely at this time that Sir Arthur built Gorges House just south of the stables of the main house.[15] In 1618 they began negotiations to sell some of the estate, to provide dowries for their daughters,[16] and in the course of the next 50 years the whole estate was divided up or sold by Sir Arthur and Lady Elizabeth or their heirs.[17] In 1619 the marriage settlement between the Gorges's eldest daughter, Dudley, and Sir Robert Lane involved the 'great and fair house' at Chelsea which Lady Elizabeth intended to sell towards her daughters' portions,[18] presumably referring to the principal mansion, which with its grounds, Dovehouse Close (5 a.), and Brickbarn Close (10 a.), was sold in 1620 to Lionel Cranfield. Its later history is covered below under Beaufort House. In 1622 Sir Arthur and Lady Elizabeth Gorges settled four houses and other property to give two of their daughters life interests: one was the Farmhouse, with a wharf and common of pasture, held for life by Edward Cecil and his wife, which was settled after their deaths on Gorges's daughter Frances, or Gorges's heirs; the other houses were settled on their daughter Elizabeth.[19] Frances seems to have died before her father, as she is not mentioned in his will,[20] and the Farmhouse, later the site of Lindsey House, was apparently conveyed in fee in 1638 to Sir Theodore de Mayerne; its later history is covered below under Lindsey House. The

1 PRO, C 260/169, no. 10; *Complete Peerage*, IV. 10.
2 PRO, SP 12/110, no. 30.
3 BL, Harl. Roll L.26.
4 PRO, PROB 11/86, f. 17.
5 In Hatfield Ho. MSS, reprod. in *Survey of London*, IV. 20–4.
6 Dr King said that the date 1597 and initials of Rob. and Eliz. Cecil were still visible on pipes in his day (*c.*1700): BL, Add. MS 4455, f. 15v.
7 J. Summerson, *Architecture in Britain, 1530–1830* (9th edn, 1993), 81; *Walpole Soc.* XL (1964–6), 63, plate 30; *Survey of London*, IV. 25.
8 Below, later ests (Beaufort).
9 PRO, C 54/1634.
10 PRO, C 66/1510, m. 20.
11 *Complete Peerage*, VII. 694n–95n; C.J. Sisson, *Thos Lodge and Other Elizabethans* (1933), 264–7; L. Stone, *Crisis of the Aristocracy: 1558–1641* (1965), 215, 224–5, 330, 454.
12 *Cal. SP Dom.* 1598–1601, 166–7.
13 Sissons, *Thos Lodge*, 264–7.
14 PRO, C 78/136, m. 23 (no. 4); *Cal. SP Dom.* 1598–1601, 166–7, 169.
15 Below, later ests (Gorges).
16 M. Prestwich, *Cranfield: Politics and Profits under the early Stuarts* (1966), 266–7.
17 Below, later ests (Beaufort; Gorges; Lindsey; Sloane Stanley; Stanley Ho.; Warton).
18 PRO, C 8/20/82.
19 PRO, C 66/2268, no. 24.
20 PRO, PROB 11/147, f. 324v.

other property seems to have remained with Gorges House.

Sir Arthur died in 1625 and the Chelsea estate passed to his widow, Lady Elizabeth, who also received Gorges House for life under Sir Arthur's will.[1] By 1630 Dudley Lane, now a widow, had bought from her mother a little house called the Brickills with 6 a., and held other land in Westfield; the house was later the property of another daughter, Elizabeth, widow of Sir Robert Stanley.[2] In 1630 Sir Arthur Gorges of Surrey, son and heir of Sir Arthur and Lady Elizabeth, and his wife Elizabeth settled lands in Chelsea and Kensington on themselves for life and then to each of their sons in tail.[3] In her will, which was proved in July 1643 but not registered,[4] his mother Lady Elizabeth gave several houses in Chelsea to Sir Arthur's four children for their lives, with remainder to Sir Arthur, on condition he did not try to claim Brickills from Elizabeth Stanley.[5] On the death of his mother Sir Arthur's property at Chelsea was sequestered and he compounded for it. It then comprised a life interest in 133 acres in Chelsea and Kensington, in the house where he lived and in 6 tenements in Chelsea, and the freehold of the 13 houses in Chelsea given to his children for life by his mother. Apparently built along Duke Street near the river, the last produced an annual rent of £43 8s.[6]

In 1646 Sir Arthur leased a house and lands in Chelsea and Kensington for 21 years as security for debts, which seem to have caused increasing difficulties.[7] The same year he, his wife, and their son Arthur, to whom the estate would eventually pass, joined in leasing a brick barn and ground, possibly the site of the former parsonage, to William Cox to rebuild as dwelling houses.[8] In 1647, probably to settle some of their more pressing debts, they joined in a sale of 4 a. in Eastfield, by the river, to Edward Cheyne, merchant taylor of London.[9] In 1649 they mortgaged and then in 1650 sold 11½ a. by Fulham Road called the Flatts to Henry White of Putney.[10] In 1650 they also disposed of a house in Little Chelsea together with barns and stables, 9 a. arable in Westfield and ½ a. meadow near Hobgate,[11] and another house, together with barn and stable, 14 a. in Kensington, and *c.*31 a. of meadow in Chelsea,[12] 9 a. of Parsonage Close and 3 a. of meadow in Westfield.[13] In 1651 the Gorges family, Henry White, and the mortgagees conveyed the 2 messuages, the 11½ a., and all the mortgaged land, except the 12 a. in Parsonage Close and Westfield, to Sir Michael Warton of Beverley (Yorks.).[14]

From 1657 to 1662 several creditors brought suits to get their debts settled out of the estate: at least two of the houses left by Lady Elizabeth were resettled and sold, then another five, the rest being settled on Elizabeth Gorges, Lady Elizabeth's granddaughter.[15] Sir Arthur Gorges died in 1661, shortly after his wife, and the remainder of the Chelsea estate, consisting of Gorges House and grounds, Parsonage Close, and 3 a. meadow in Westfield passed to his eldest son Arthur. The latter sold all the remaining property to Thomas Pritchard and Richard Spoure in 1664.[16]

HUNGERFORD'S ESTATE

John Barnard (d. 1537), citizen and mercer, chamberlain of the City of London, and his wife Alice had property in Chelsea, described as 3 messuages, 6 cottages, 100 a. land, 10 a. meadow, and 10 a. pasture, with property in Kent, which they settled in 1528 on themselves for life and then on their son James and his heirs.[17] Barnard owed 54s. 6½d. quitrent to the manor of Chelsea,[18] and at least three of the houses which can be traced later had commoning rights,[19] suggesting that the estate had been built up from a number of medieval freeholdings. James (d. 1540) left his mansion house at Chelsea and all his lands to his widow Ursula for life on condition that if she married again she should support his children until they came of age. The lands were then to pass to his son Richard,[20] who seems to have died without issue, as James's heir in 1582 was his daughter's son.[21]

By 1543 Ursula had married Thomas Hungerford (d. 1581), courtier and gentleman pensioner, who in 1544 acknowledged that he held in his wife's right seven cottages and 100 a. freely from the manor for 54s. 6½d. rent and suit of court.[22] He was presented for overstocking on the common with his cattle in 1543, and his property in 1566 included a messuage on the south side of the new parsonage house in Church Lane and land in

1 PRO, PROB 11/147, f. 324v.
2 Below, later ests (Stanley Ho.).
3 PRO, CP 43/317, carte rot. 1.
4 *Abstracts of Probate Acts in PCC*, 1640–4, p. 221.
5 PRO, C 9/6/89.
6 PRO, SP 23/202, p. 432; SP 19/150, p. 45.
7 PRO, SP 23/202, p. 415.
8 PRO, C 8/331/196.
9 PRO, C 54/3382, no. 5.
10 LMA, BRA 203/152–3
11 Ibid., 203/160–1.
12 Ibid., 203/157–8.
13 Ibid., 203/159.
14 Ibid., 203/154–6,162–6; below, later ests (Warton).
15 PRO, C 7/428/42; C 8/331/196; C 6/46/67; C 7/456/40; C 8/220/43.
16 Below, later ests (Gorges).
17 PRO, CP 25/2/51/366/19HENVIIIEASTER; C 1/1298/23–6.
18 BL, Lansd. MS 2, f. 11.
19 i.e. Wrennall's farm; Powell; Chare.
20 PRO, PROB 11/28 (PCC 13 Alenger).
21 *Index to Remembrancia of City of London, 1579–1664* (1878), 310.
22 PRO, SC 2/205/40.

Eastfield.[1] He also received 2 messuages and 2 gardens in 1569 from Adam Powell and his wife Alice, William Dabourne and his wife Anne, and William Beane.[2] Alice, Anne, and William were the children of Thomas Beane (d. 1549): he left his house called the Great Rose next to the church to his son William, two houses to Alice and another to Agnes,[3] and the property conveyed to Hungerford may have included the Great Rose, which stood on the corner of Church Lane opposite the church, since a house on that site was later said to have belonged to Hungerford.[4]

Ursula Hungerford died in 1583 leaving her leases to her son Edmund Hungerford, and bequests of 12 pictures, including portraits of all the Tudor sovereigns which hung in the parlour and the great chamber of her house in Chelsea.[5] The property which had belonged to Hungerford had been divided by 1587: the smaller part passed to Edmund Hungerford,[6] while the Barnard freeholding, known as Hungerford's farm, was held in 1587 by Thomas Young for 54s. 6½d. In 1595 Young conveyed to John Shuckburgh (Shugborow, Shuckborough) of Warwickshire a messuage or farm and land in Chelsea, possibly as a settlement on the marriage of Young's daughter Christian with John's brother Henry; whatever the case, in 1599 Henry Shuckburgh conveyed the property to another brother Francis.[7] Young seems to have been the man of that name who had a prebendal lease in Willesden, and may have died *c.*1604: a Thomas Young, Yeoman of the Guard, gave to the each of the parishes of Chelsea, Kensington, and Willesden 20s. a year for use of the poor.[8] The grant of the Chelsea farm was confirmed to Francis Shuckburgh in 1606 by Henry and his wife and Young's widow Elizabeth,[9] and in 1607 Francis sold to William Blake for £1,100 the farmhouse, 74 a., and 11 lots of meadow in the tenure of William Wrennall and another acre in West meadow. The land included 32 a. called Sandhills,[10] which Blake later sold to Sir Lionel Cranfield and which formed part of Chelsea Park.[11]

Elizabeth Young still held other land once belonging her husband, and in 1607 settled all her property in Kensington, Chelsea, and Fulham for the use of herself for life, then for her daughter Christian Shuckburgh and her issue. The property consisted of a mansion called Brompton Hall in Kensington with its outhouses and grounds, and all the land belonging to it in Kensington, Chelsea, and Fulham; the Catherine Wheel in Kensington; a messuage and buildings in Chelsea in the tenure of William Gawnte; the messuage called the Blackhouse in Chelsea where Elizabeth lived, with outbuildings, dovehouse, grounds, 2½ a. in Eastfield, and two closes lying together next to Chelsea Heath containing 6 a.; a messuage in the tenure of Thomas Creake with one orchard or garden and all buildings belonging to it in Chelsea; houses occupied by 10 tenants; meadow in Fulham; and 4 lots in the western common mead of Chelsea. The conveyance included the right of revocation by Elizabeth, which she exercised in 1611,[12] just prior to selling the Catherine Wheel in Kensington to Robert Chare, citizen and fletcher of London, and at her instruction Thomas Baldwin sold to Chare two messuages lying together on the east side of Church Lane and south of the parsonage, which were the Hungerford tenement of 1566.[13]

Elizabeth Young died between 1611 and 1615 and was succeeded by her daughter Christian, who was estranged from her husband.[14] In 1626 Christian wife of Henry Shuckburgh was assessed at £2 in lands in the subsidy,[15] and in 1645, then a widow, was assessed at £200, but in 1646 was successful in getting that reduced to the £35 which she claimed was a fifth of her revenue.[16] Christian's son John died by 1647, leaving a will in which he devised his land in Chelsea and Brompton to his son Thomas, with payments to his other children, Henry and Frances, and called upon his mother to confirm that she and his grandmother had both promised he should have the land.[17] In 1648 Christian and her grandson Henry Shuckburgh, both of Chelsea, conveyed to her eldest grandson Thomas for payments under will of Christian's husband, Brompton Hall and 6 acres, the houses once occupied by William Gawnte, Elizabeth Young, and Thomas Creake, and houses occupied by 6 tenants.[18] She probably occupied her mother's house, the Blackhouse, and was succeeded there by Thomas Shuckburgh, who died in 1670.

Later history of the remaining estate is uncertain. By 1706 the Blackhouse alias the Whitehouse, formerly held by Elizabeth Young, Christian Shuckburgh, and Thomas Shuckburgh, had passed to Edward Harris of Aldenham (Herts.), together with the messuage called the Dog tavern, formerly held by Thomas Creake, with an orchard and garden and all other premises belonging to the two houses; 5 houses purchased from Thomas Crompton by Thomas and Henry Shuckburgh; and 6 cottages built on part of the orchard and ground belonging to the Blackhouse and the Dog. Harris's property was inherited by his daughter Elizabeth, wife of William Grove, and then passed to their daughter

1 PRO, E 371/433, rot. 107.
2 PRO, CP 25/2/171/11ELIZTRIN.
3 Below, other medieval ests.
4 Below; above, Settlement, to 1680.
5 PRO, PROB 11/66, f. 42.
6 Below.
7 PRO, C 54/2445, no. 1.
8 *VCH Middx*, VII. 209, 254; Faulkner, *Chelsea*, II. 105–6, who recorded it as £20.
9 PRO, C 54/2445, no. 1.
10 PRO, CP 43/99, carte rot. 41v.–43v.
11 PRO, C 54/2445, no. 1; below, later ests (Beaufort).
12 PRO, C 54/2095, no. 56.
13 PRO, C 54/2107, nos. 4–5; CL, Ar.4/76/2.
14 PRO, C 8/66/75; *VCH Middx*, VII. 209.
15 PRO, E 179/142/284.
16 *Cal. Cttee Money*, II. 607.
17 PRO, PROB 11/200, f. 305.
18 CL, Ar.4/76/2.

Elizabeth and her husband Edward Peacock, goldsmith, who were holding it in 1718. By then the Blackhouse and the Dog had each been divided into two dwellings occupied by tenants, with 6 cottages in Waterman's Court, and 6 houses in or near Church Lane with their outhouses and gardens.[1] The Blackhouse apparently lay on the west side of the four houses making up Arch House and the White Horse, and the Dog lay on the west side of the Blackhouse. In 1739 the property was conveyed to Grove Peacock of St Martin-in-the-Fields, coachmaker, son of Edward and Elizabeth.[2] The estate has not been traced further.

EDMUND HUNGERFORD'S HOLDING AND ARCH HOUSE

In 1587 Edmund Hungerford held freely 2 tenements once Cleybrooke's for 7½d.,[3] possibly the 2 messuages and 2 gardens conveyed to Thomas Hungerford in 1569.[4] A conveyance in 1584 by Anthony Hungerford to John Wall and John Towgood of a messuage, wharf, garden, and orchard in Chelsea[5] may be a resettlement or a sale of part of Thomas Hungerford's property.

Edmund Hungerford sold to Michael Forth of Enfield waste ground between a messuage and the river near Danvers House which by 1624 had houses on it when it was sold to Sir John Danvers.[6] Though Thomas Hungerford is said to have sold property to Richard Fletcher, bishop of London,[7] it seems more likely that it was sold to the bishop after Hungerford's death. This was a capital messuage and other buildings where the bishop was living by 1592, and formed the basis of the property later known as Arch House. In 1594 Bishop Fletcher married as his second wife Mary the widow of Sir Richard Baker, and died in 1596 leaving large debts to the queen for First Fruits of his various ecclesiastical preferments, and only his house in Chelsea, plate, and some other goods to provide for his children.[8] His Chelsea house was presumably sold: it was said to have belonged to Robert Cecil, earl of Salisbury,[9] perhaps on behalf of the Crown, and was probably the messuages, two gardens, and one wharf conveyed in 1610 by Sir William Selby and Talbot Bowes and his wife Agnes to Sir Thomas Baker, Mary Fletcher's stepson.[10] Sir Thomas died in 1625 leaving his house and garden in Chelsea to his wife Constance for life, with permission to sell it for the benefit of his children. In 1625 Constance conveyed the house and other houses which had been converted into one dwelling, with its barns, stables, wharf, and landing places to Sir Edward Powell, Bt, Master of Requests, and his wife Mary for £600.[11] In the 1650s it was claimed that Mary Powell's mother Jacoba, widow of Sir Peter Vanlore, had provided the money for the purchase and intended the house to be conveyed to her trustees. Jacoba was said to have lived in the house until her death in 1636 when she left it to Thomas Crompton, her steward, and Lady Powell seems to have lived there from about 1636, when she separated from her husband, until her death in 1651.[12] The Powells had a substantial mansion there, having incorporated into it another messuage in Church Lane and a little cottage adjoining, and in 1646 Sir Edward bought the freehold of the additional houses from Thomas Fisher for £150.[13] Sir Edward was listed as owner of rights of common for 'cottages'.[14]

Sir Edward Powell died in 1653 without heirs, devising his lands to his sister's son, William Hinson, who added the name Powell and was granted a baronetcy in 1661.[15] In 1679 Sir William was presented at the court leet for encroaching on Church Lane opposite the church by erecting 3 stacks of chimneys each jetting 10 inches.[16] He died in 1680, devising the rents from the mansion, stables, barns, and coachhouses in Chelsea, then in possession of William Dyer, to his wife Mary for life, and then to his only child Mary (d. 1723), wife of Sir John Williams, Bt, and her issue.[17] By 1685 the house was standing empty and in need of repair, and was leased by Sir John and Mary Williams to Charles Stanton of London, carpenter.[18]

Lady Williams's property was inherited by her four daughters as coheirs, and in 1733 they conveyed to Richard Coope of London four houses in Chelsea which had formerly been one, with 4 stables and 3 gardens, one called the White Horse inn, abutting the Thames on the south and Church Lane on the east, purchased from Lady Baker and Thomas Fisher and occupied by tenants, together with pews in the churches of Fulham or Chelsea.[19] In 1743 a 61-year lease of tofts and parcels of buildings running from 1684 and made by Mary Williams in 1686 to Stanton was assigned to Richard Coope, citizen and salter.[20] The four houses occupied the site of nos 64–7 Cheyne Walk. No. 67 was Arch House, so-called because it was extended southward to the riverside wharf, leaving an archway over the public highway along the riverside. It is not known when this extension

1 MLR 1718/6/223–5; 1739/2/294.
2 MLR 1739/2/293.
3 BL, Harl. Roll L.26.
4 PRO, CP 25/2/171/11ELIZTRIN; above.
5 PRO, CP 25/2/172/26ELIZHIL.
6 CL, deed 2989.
7 PRO, C 54/2634, no. 21.
8 *DNB*.
9 PRO, C 54/2634, no. 21.
10 PRO, CP 25/2/323/8JASIMIC.
11 PRO, C 142/420/107; C 54/2634, no. 21.
12 PRO, C 7/397/61; C 7/402/135; *Cal. SP Dom.* 1654, 129–30; HMC, *7th Rep.*, p. 110.
13 PRO, C 54/3340, no. 37.
14 Faulkner, *Chelsea*, II. 50.
15 GEC, *Baronetage*, I. 188; III. 154.
16 Quoted by Faulkner, *Chelsea*, II. 156.
17 *Baronetage*, III. 154; PRO, C 7/257/56.
18 PRO, C 8/523/14.
19 CL, Ar.4/76/12.
20 Ibid., /15.

was built, though it is shown in illustrations of Chelsea in the mid 18th century. The southern wing was demolished when the embankment was created *c.*1870; nos 64–6, which had been rebuilt in the early 19th century, and no. 67 were then renamed Lombard Terrace. They were all demolished in the 20th century.[1]

OTHER MEDIEVAL ESTATES AND FREEHOLDINGS

HASELEY AND WAVER

In 1433 a messuage fronting the highway by the Thames was conveyed to Thomas Haseley, esquire, Alice Haseley, widow, and two others and their heirs, with 3 roods of arable in Westfield apparently near the messuage.[2] In 1448 Sir Thomas Haseley and his wife Agnes had a house in Chelsea which included a chapel.[3] In 1449 the house, arable, and meadow in Chelsea were settled on Sir Thomas Haseley (d. *c.*1450), then under-marshal of England and Chancery Clerk of the Crown, his wife Agnes, and Agnes's heirs, together with lands in Fulham, Chiswick, and Kingsbury.[4] In 1451 Agnes Haseley, widow, settled her estates including the house and land in Chelsea on herself for life with remainder to Henry Waver, citizen and draper, and his wife Christine or Christian, probably Agnes's daughter.[5] In 1453 Agnes headed the list of assized rents owed to Chelsea manor with 30s. 4d.[6]

By 1465 Henry Waver was in possession of property in Chelsea and he and Christine granted to Master Robert Kirkham, Keeper of the Chancery Rolls, John Catesby, sergeant-at-law, and William Morland, clerk, two messuages in Chelsea, one newly-built with an enclosed garden, and the other adjoining in which Peter Carpenter lived, rendering 4d. a year to Waver, and with a warranty against Christine's heirs. It was quitclaimed to the three and to the heirs of Kirkham by two Londoners, probably feoffees.[7] In 1466 Sir Henry Waver and the two Londoners granted a 20-year lease to Kirkham of 1 a. ½ r. of arable on the north side of Kirkham's wall for 3s. 4d. a year. Waver still retained other land in the parish.[8] Sir Henry Waver, alderman of London, died in 1470 leaving all his lands and tenements in the towns and parishes of Chelsea, Fulham, Kingsbury, Hendon, and Willesden to his wife Christine and her heirs, and made her one of his executors.[9] By 1472 Christine had married Thomas Cooke of Chelsea and they and another of Waver's executors gave a bond in connection with Waver's estate.[10] In 1472 Thomas and Christine conveyed to William Essex, John Young, and Thomas Wylkyns eight messuages, five gardens, 60 a. land, 1 a. meadow, and 16d. rent in Chelsea, with a warranty against the heirs of Christine to the heirs of Essex.[11]

William Essex also acquired property from John Drayton of London (d. 1467). Drayton's will instructed the feoffees of his lands and tenements in Chelsea to grant the property with the profits to his wife Christine for life, and if she married then to convey it to William Essex.[12] In 1476 Christine, now the wife of John Rolle, claimed that Essex had purchased from Drayton a messuage called a brewhouse, two cottages, 60 a. land, 6 a. meadow, and 12 a. pasture in Chelsea for £53 6s. 8d., of which he still owed part.[13] William Essex, under treasurer of England, and described as of Walham Green (Fulham), died 1480 holding the manor of West Town in Kensington with lands in Kensington, Brompton, Chelsea, Tyburn, and Westbourne, acquired in 1454, Wanden manor in Fulham, and land in Knightsbridge. His heir was his son Thomas.[14] The descent of his land in Chelsea has not been traced further.

FRENSHE

John Frenshe, citizen and goldsmith of London, held land in Chelsea in 1447 which was used as security for a sale by Frenshe of an inn in Fleet Street.[15] In 1453 Frenshe was paying an assized rent of 12s. 10d. to the manor of Chelsea,[16] and in 1457 he joined with Robert Beaufitz and his wife Joan to convey to Ralph Botiller and others, probably feoffees, a messuage, two tofts, a dovecote, 46 a. land, and 2 a. meadow in Chelsea.[17] By 1464 Frenshe's former tenement belonged to Richard Beauchamp, bishop of Salisbury (d. 1481), and lay fronting the riverside.[18] In 1484 Elizabeth Mowbray (d. by May 1510), the widowed duchess of Norfolk, was granted for life the tenement, houses, and land in Chelsea which had belonged to the bishop.[19] The holding has not been reliably traced thereafter.

CROKE

In his will of 1477 proved in 1481, John Croke, citizen and skinner, alderman of London, left all his messuage or place in Chelsea to his wife Margaret for life, and then

1 *Survey of London*, IV. 3–6; above, Settlement, twentieth cent.; see Fig. 75.
2 PRO, C 54/284, m. 22d.; above, Settlement, to 1680.
3 PRO, C 1/20/13.
4 *Cal. Close*, 1447–54, 134–5.
5 Ibid., 285–6; *VCH Middx*, V. 59.
6 WAM 4804.
7 PRO, CP 25/1/152/96, no. 16; C 54/317, mm. 21d., 25d.
8 PRO, C 54/317, m. 7d.
9 PRO, PROB 11/5, f. 245.
10 *Cal. Close*, 1468–71, 327.
11 PRO, CP 25/1/152/97, no. 41.
12 Guildhall MS 9171/6, f. 2v.
13 PRO, C 1/49/47.
14 PRO, C 140/77/80.
15 *Cal. Close*, 1447–54, 32.
16 WAM 4804.
17 PRO, CP 25/1/152/95, no. 181.
18 *Cal. Close*, 1461–8, 246.
19 *Cal. Pat.* 1476–85, 503.

to his daughter Margaret, wife of Sir William Stokker, draper, and her heirs.[1] In his will of 1485 Sir William Stokker, mayor of London, left to Chelsea church 20s. and a torch, and his wife Margaret received the residue of his goods and his livelihoods in London, Deptford, and Bedfordshire for life. All his lands were to go to his daughter Margaret and her issue, or in default to John Stokker of Willesden.[2] His property has not been traced further.

FENROTHER

Robert Fenrother, alderman and goldsmith of London, in 1525 left to his wife Julian his manor of Notting Barns and lands in Westbourne (Paddington) and Chelsea for life, thereafter to remain to Henry White and his wife Audrey, Fenrother's daughter.[3] He headed the list of assized rents owed to Chelsea manor *c.*1536 with 14s. 3d.[4] In 1536 Julian Fenrother leased to John Pattenson of Chelsea, husbandman, for 20 years the Chelsea property consisting of a brewhouse with various vessels and utensils used for brewing, a tenement on the east side of the brewhouse with 40 a. of arable belonging to it, and 7 lots of meadow in Westfield.[5] In 1542 Robert White, presumably the son of Henry and Audrey, sold to Henry VIII in an exchange the two tenements, 40 a. arable, and 7 lots in Westfield, the manor of Notting Barns in Kensington, a messuage at Westbourne, and other property in Kensington, Paddington, and Chelsea; the fine was made in 1544.[6] Thereafter the Chelsea property became part of the demesne of Chelsea manor. As a freehold of the manor it had had grazing rights belonging to it, which suggests that the brewhouse may have been at the Feathers, which like the Magpie (below) was a demesne property with freeholders' rights.

THE ROSE

In 1503 Thomas Whitehead and his wife Emmota conveyed to William Birrell, his wife Joan, and William Champion and William Babeham grocers, a messuage, a garden, and one virgate and 2 acres in Chelsea.[7] In the 1540s William Birrell paid 4d. assized rent for his freeholding, described as a tenement and half an acre of garden. Birrell died before April 1547, and the heir to his freeholding was his daughter Lettice, wife of Robert King of Essex. In 1547 they conveyed to Thomas Beane junior and his wife Katharine 9 messuages or tenements with gardens, one called the Rose, and 6 others occupied by tenants including Thomas Saunders.[8] Some of Beane's estate including the Rose was later acquired by Thomas Hungerford.[9]

WYLKYNS

John Wylkyns, yeoman, of Chelsea was a witness in 1463 to a grant in Knightsbridge.[10] In 1464 Agnes Wylkyns, widow of John Wylkyns senior of Chelsea who died after 1461, conveyed to William Rous and Henry Carpenter, clerks, John Bedford, and her son Thomas Wylkyns and Wylkyns's heirs the cottage and adjoining curtilage in Chelsea, which she and husband had been granted by Lora widow of William Laurens of Chelsea, baker, and which lay next to the house of John Frenshe. Agnes also granted to Thomas Wylkyns and John Lynde of Chelsea all her goods there and debts owing.[11] Thomas Wylkyns, formerly a clerk to William Rous, Chancery clerk of the Crown *c.*1452, in 1465–7 or 1476–80 brought a suit to recover deeds against John Lynde who had acted as arbiter in a dispute between Wylkyns and his tenant, Thomas Mytton, over a messuage in Chelsea let for £4 a year.[12]

Thomas's property may be part of that held by William Wylkyns in the 1540s, when he owed an assized rent to Chelsea manor of 19s. 1d.[13] In 1545–6 he and his wife Alice conveyed to John Bowyer two messuages, a barn, garden, orchard, 40 a. land, 20 a. meadow, 20 a. pasture, 5 a. wood, 10 a. marsh, 10 a. waste, and 5s. rent in Chelsea and Fulham.[14] They also owned Chelsea ferry and its landing place in 1550 and 1564.[15]

THOMAS KEYLE

Maud, widow of Richard Est, held for life a freehold messuage and barn with one rood of land adjoining it and another 2 acres in the fields of Chelsea, which was to remain to her son John Est. John was succeeded by his daughter Katharine who married William Hunteley and had a son Thomas. William Hunteley was a freehold tenant of the manor, paying 8s. assized rent in 1453, and also leased 3 acres demesne that year;[16] in 1464 his tenement lay next door but one to that of John Frenshe. Thomas Hunteley, who leased the property in 1493 to John Lamprey for 14 years, died when his daughter and heir Jane was 6 months old. The lease was sold successively to John Morecote, John Whitehead, and William Birrell of London. Birrell was succeeded by his son John, who took possession of the property and would not acknowledge Jane's right. In Henry VIII's reign, probably *c.*1520, Jane and her husband John Kyngton brought a suit against John Birrell for the property, to which they claimed Jane was entitled as Thomas Hunteley's daughter under an entail.[17] The outcome is unknown, but in 1522 John and Joan (*sic*) Kyngton

1 PRO, PROB 11/7, ff. 26–8.
2 Ibid., f. 198–v.
3 *Cal. of Husting Wills, London 1258–1688*, II(2), 630.
4 BL, Lansd. MS 2, f. 11.
5 PRO, E 312/12, no. 57.
6 PRO, E 305/5/C54; E 326/12775.
7 PRO, CP 25/1/152/101.
8 BL, Lansd. MS 2, f. 11; PRO, SC 2/188/43.
9 Above.
10 *Cal. Close*, 1468–76, 72.
11 Ibid., 1461–8, 246.
12 PRO, C 1/32/154.
13 BL, Lansd. MS 2, f. 11.
14 PRO, CP 25/2/27/186/37HENVIIIEASTER.
15 PRO, CP 25/2/61/474/4EDWVIMICH; CP 25/2/171/6ELIZIHIL; above, Intro., comms.
16 WAM 4804.
17 PRO, REQ 2/4/11.

conveyed to Thomas Keyle and others a messuage, 8 a. land, and 2 a. pasture in Chelsea, which may have been Jane's inheritance.[1] In 1538 Keyle sold to Henry VIII a tenement with a barn, stable, and buildings, and a close of land, which had once belonged to Kyngton and his wife and lay next to a messuage called the Lord Sandys place,[2] the Tudor manor house. In 1538–9 40s. was due as the rent of a tenement and parcel of land next to the king's manor and acquired from Thomas Keyle of London. The property was later called the Pye or Magpie, and was part of the manorial demesne estate thereafter, though as a former freeholding it retained its commoning rights. Courts were sometimes held there, and one tenant, James Leverett, gardener, who had been granted the property with its outbuildings and a garden, 6 roods by 3½ roods, in 1642 on unknown terms, left £4 a year to be spent on 4 dinners a year at the Magpie for the parochial officers.[3]

Thomas Keyle also acquired other land in Chelsea: in 1526 a fine was levied by John Greenfield and his wife Lettice to Keyle and others for the manor of Brompton Hall, which included 2 messuages, one tenement, 20 a. land, 4 a. meadow, 22 a. pasture, and 4 a. wood;[4] within three years Keyle brought a suit against them for detention of the deeds to this property, which included land in Kensington, Chelsea, and Fulham.[5] Both the Greenfields and Keyle also sold property to Sir Thomas More:[6] Keyle's property in Chelsea included Butts close of 2½ a. and a house, wharf, and adjoining close, which Sir Thomas More bought from Keyle.[7] Keyle was also lessee of the medieval manor house in 1519.[8]

LATER ESTATES

ARNOLD – GREENE

William Arnold of Fulham, yeoman, held land in Chelsea in the early 17th century which included 10 acres in Westfield bordering Fulham Road, later the site of houses and gardens enclosed out of the field by 1618.[9] In 1607 he sold to William Blake of the City of London, scrivener, for £400 14½ a. in Westfield lying on the south side of the 10 acres, 6½ a. in Westfield on the north side of the Lots meadow, and 3 a. in Eastfield between Chelsea common and King's Road.[10] The 14½ a. had been sold on to the earl of Lincoln by 1618, when Lincoln sold it to William Blake of Kensington.[11] Arnold also sublet from Nicholas Holborne a close called the Nine Acres adjoining the Thames near the earl of Lincoln's house in 1611, possibly Parsonage Close.[12] He and William Blake, probably the scrivener, were trustees for Arnold's brother John (d. *c.*1619), also of Fulham, and the latter's two daughters, Elizabeth, who inherited John's freehold, and Catherine, who inherited the copyhold land.[13] The Arnold family were long-established in the area, with branches in Fulham and Kensington: William Arnold (d. 1638) seems to have moved to Kensington by 1625, and his son William, who married John Arnold's daughter Elizabeth, lived in Kensington and was usually described as of Earl's Court.[14]

In 1634 William Arnold junior of Kensington, bought from Ralph Massie for £1,660 a farmhouse in Chelsea with 43 a. in Eastfield in the tenure of William Wrennall, 3 a. arable and 10 a. meadow in Eastfield, the latter lying between Chelsea College and the Thames in Kensington detached, 16 lots and 1 a. of meadow and 9½ a. arable, all in Westfield, and 1½ a. meadow in Fulham.[15] In 1652 William and his wife Elizabeth made a settlement with John Saunders, who married their daughter Dorothy, of a messuage, malthouse, and 3 a., which was sold by the latter's son John Saunders to William Mart in 1677. In 1668 Arnold sold to Anne Bennett 17 a. in Chelsea, which also passed to Mart,[16] possibly part of the 43 a. land belonging to Wrennall's farm, which was in separate ownership from the farmhouse *c.*1700.[17] The main farmhouse, occupied by William Wrennall in the early 17th century and then James Leake (d. *c.*1653),[18] lay with its barn, yards, and garden on the west side of Church Lane at the corner of King's Road, and stretching back to the land of the duke of Buckingham (Beaufort House). It was still known as 'Reynolds's farm' in 1663, with right of commoning 6 cows and 3 heifers, and in 1647 as 'James Luke's house in Church Lane'. Before his death (before 1685) William Arnold built four new brick houses with gardens by the farmhouse, and it was all described in 1676 as part of the great farm.[19] The farmhouse and new houses, right of commoning, and possibly the land belonging to the farm as well, belonged to Mr Bennet by 1674,[20] and the farmhouse and houses were leased by James Bennet of Westminster, tanner, to

1 PRO, CP 25/2/27/179/32.
2 PRO, E 326/12183.
3 PRO, C 10/416/5; PROB 11/310, f. 11.
4 PRO, CP 25/2/27/180/17HENVIIITRIN.
5 PRO, C 1/533/18.
6 Above, More.
7 PRO, C 1/540/78.
8 Below, later ests (Lawrence).
9 Below, Blake; Boevey.
10 PRO, C 54/1884.
11 Below, Blake.
12 PRO, STAC 8/91/25.
13 PRO, PROB 11/134, f. 274.
14 *Par. Reg. of Kensington 1539–1675*, ed. F.N. Macnamara and A. Story-Maskelyne (Harl. Soc. Reg. XVI, 1890).
15 PRO, C 54/3026, no. 24.
16 PRO, C 10/266/37.
17 Dr King's MS, p. 38; below, Blake.
18 PRO, PROB 6/28, f. 80.
19 CL, deed 3009; Faulkner, *Chelsea*, II. 50.
20 Faulkner, *Chelsea*, II. 50.

John Greene of St Margaret Westminster, brewer, in 1676 for 1,000 years, presumably as a mortgage. In 1685 James Bennet and Arnold's son, William Arnold of Kensington, sold the houses to Henry Newdick, poulterer of London, for £780, and John Greene's widow Elizabeth assigned the lease to Newdick.[1] A query arose *c.*1700 over who had the rights of common attached to the farm lately held by Mr Bennet, as the farmhouse belonged to Newdick and the land to Mart.[2] This suggests that the 21 a. on the east side of Upper Church Lane was formerly part of Wrennall's farm as it seems to have belonged to William Mart *c.*1700, with a house marked as his in the south-west corner.[3]

Greene Estate

William Arnold was said to have sold lands in Chelsea *c.*1670 to John Greene, who had married Elizabeth daughter of John Arnold of Kensington:[4] Greene certainly held extensive property in Chelsea, which his wife controlled after his death and nearly all of which can be identified with Arnold's property, including *c.*18 a. in Eastfield in about 6 parcels lying south of King's Road and on the opposite side near Chelsea common, and *c.*15 a. arable and meadow in Westfield.[5] Greene also had extensive estates in Westminster and Kensington, as well as a major brewery near Tothill Fields, later known as the Stag brewery. He sold 1½ a. arable and just under half an acre of the meadow adjoining it, all near Chelsea College, to Mary Pinner before 1683.[6] Under his will his houses and land were divided between his three sons, John, William, and Thomas, with remainders to each other: all the property in Chelsea and the 10 a. in Kensington detached by the Thames went to William when 22 or married, and in default of heirs to his brother John.[7] In 1685 William Greene sold to the Crown the 10 a. of meadow near Chelsea College (less the plot sold to Pinner) for £550 to form part of the grounds of the Royal Hospital.[8] John and William brought a suit in 1688 against William Arnold junior and a creditor of his father to take possession of the property their father had bought,[9] apparently with success.

John's widow Elizabeth (d. *c.*1716) left her lands in Chelsea to trustees who were pay the profits to her son William for life and then to his issue or in default to her other son Thomas and his heirs.[10] William Greene, brewer, of Westminster, apparently died without children and the Chelsea property passed to Thomas Greene (d. 1740) of St Margaret Westminster. Thomas died leaving one child, Elizabeth, wife of Edward Burnaby (d. 1759), a Clerk of the Treasury, and his personal estate was left to his sister Mary Greene, Charles Lord Cadogan, and Justinian Ekins as trustees for his daughter and his second wife Frances. The trustees also held his real estate for his daughter, which was to pass to her eldest son, Edward, for whom an Act was obtained permitting him, as a minor, to adopt the surname Greene in addition to Burnaby.[11] Mary Greene also apparently died in 1740, at which a fortune of £4,000 a year was said to have passed to Elizabeth Burnaby (d. 1754). Edward Burnaby Greene (d. 1788), poet and translator, also inherited the brewing business, but by 1779 was so deeply in debt that all his property had to be sold.[12] His only son, Pitt Burnaby Greene, joined with trustees and creditors in sales of the Chelsea estate in 1793.[13]

The Greene estate in Chelsea included 6 a. in Eastfield adjoining the south side of King's Road, leased by William and Thomas Greene to Robert Walpole in 1736,[14] and sold to Thomas Smith of Chelsea, vintner, in 1793;[15] further west near Robinson's Lane a close of 3¾ a. leased to Thomas Richardson of Chelsea, surveyor, in 1778,[16] and a strip of land next to it adjoining King's Road, both sold to Richardson in 1793 and 1795;[17] 2¼ a. with five houses built on the south side, forming Green's Row, sold individually in 1793–4;[18] 6½ a. in two separate parcels on the north side of King's Road, adjoining Chelsea common, with two houses, barn, and garden, and two other houses and gardens, all sold in 1793 to Matthew Markham of St Martin-in-the-Fields, coachmaker;[19] a house and 3 a. in Westfield with an acre of lammas meadow south of Lots Lane, occupied before 1748 by Robert Cook, and sold to Lady Mary Coke in 1793;[20] and a house and 8 a. in Westfield by Chelsea Creek, occupied for many years by the Burchett family, and sold to Lord Cadogan in 1794.[21]

ASHBURNHAM HOUSE AND COTTAGE

Dr Benjamin Hoadley, a fashionable physician, took 61-year leases from Chelsea manor in 1747 of two parcels of garden ground in Westfield lying on the west side of Chelsea Farm (Cremorne);[22] he let 4 acres of it to a gardener until 1754.[23] He also took a 21-year lease in 1748 from the trustees of the Greene estate of a house and 3 acres, lying on the west side of his leaseholds, and another acre of meadow south of Lots Lane.[24] Freehold osier ground of *c.*3 acres south of Lots Lane, formerly

1 CL, deeds 3012, 3029.
2 Dr King's MS, p. 38.
3 Ibid., p. 35.
4 PRO, C 6/262/123; *Par. Reg. of Kens.*
5 Below.
6 Hutt, *Royal Hosp.* 137.
7 PRO, PROB 11/373, ff. 34–6v.
8 Hutt, *Royal Hosp.* 137–9.
9 PRO, C 6/262/123.
10 PRO, PROB 11/552, ff.234–5v.
11 Ibid. 11/704, ff. 179–84; Act 14 Geo. II, c. 16 (Private).
12 *Gent. Mag.* XI (1741), 50; *DNB* s.v. Greene, Edw. B.
13 Below.
14 MLR 1725/1/224.
15 MLR 1793/6/733.
16 MLR 1779/1/294.
17 MLR 1794/1/161; 1795/5/75.
18 MLR 1794/1/216, 274, 556, 558; 1794/2/550.
19 MLR 1793/6/339.
20 Below, Ashburnham.
21 Faulkner, *Chelsea*, I. 55.
22 MLR 1747/1/83; 1747/2/359.
23 CL, deed 3269.
24 CL, deed 3271; above, Arnold.

49. *Ashburnham House*

part of the Gorges House estate and sold in 1750,[1] was also acquired by him. Hoadley is said to have built a mansion, later called Ashburnham House, at the southern end of the land leased from the manor, fronting Lots Lane.[2] In 1758 Hoadley's widow Anna sold the residue of the three leaseholds and the freehold ground to Sir Richard Glyn, Bt, alderman of London, who in 1767 sold them all to John Ashburnham, 2nd earl of Ashburnham.[3] Ashburnham presumably renewed the lease from the Greene trustees, as the premises were still part of the estate when he sold it. In 1781 Ashburnham held leases of 11¾ a. of manorial demesne forming a rectangular estate next to Chelsea Farm and stretching from King's Road to Lots Lane, including his house and gardens, all in his own occupation; the Greene property consisted of a house and 3 a. on the south-west side of his property and an acre of meadow on the south side of Lots Lane opposite his mansion.[4] In 1786 he sold the whole leasehold and freehold estate to Lady Mary Coke, widow,[5] who in 1793 purchased the freehold of the Greene property, described as a house at Sandy End near Chelsea Creek, 3 a. land, and a piece of Lammas meadow ground opposite her dwelling.[6] In 1807 Lady Mary sold her interests in the two manorial leases to Joseph Brown, who had agreed with the owners of the manor to take a new lease of the Ashburnham House property for 41 years from 1808, and she also sold to him the freeholds of the former Greene property and the 3 a. by the Thames.[7] By 1825 the lease of the Ashburnham estate had been assigned to a Mr Stephens, but a house and 1¾ a. bordering King's Road had been surrendered and let by the owners of the manor in 1820 to another tenant.[8] By 1845 Ashburnham House was leased to Col. Leicester Stanhope, who succeeded as 5th earl of Harrington in 1851;[9] in 1847 the estate was described as 11¾ a., once more including the 1¾ a. of garden ground by King's Road.[10]

By 1847 the freehold of the former Greene property of 7 a. bought by Lady Mary Coke and now known as Ashburnham Cottage, the remaining Greene freehold between the manorial leaseholds and Chelsea Creek, and the meadow south of Lots Lane had all been purchased by the owners of the manor and belonged to Lord Cadogan, except for Lots meadow belonging to the Kensington Canal Company; some of the new acquisitions, if not all, belonged to Cadogan by 1825. Ashburnham Cottage was leased to General Sir S.S. Barnes by 1847.[11] In 1859 Lord Cadogan leased Ashburnham House and Cottage to Thomas Bartlett Simpson, lessee of Chelsea Farm, who wanted to expand the popular Cremorne Gardens westwards.[12]

BEAUFORT HOUSE

In 1620 Sir Arthur and Lady Elizabeth Gorges sold to Lionel Cranfield, later lord treasurer and earl of Middlesex, for £4,300 the chief mansion on their estate, described in the deed as 'the greatest (i.e. largest) house in Chelsea', which formed a substantial part of the property formerly belonging to Sir Thomas More.[13] Its grounds consisted of two forecourts, a wharf with brick towers at east and west ends, a high water tower on the west corner of the wharf, a watercourse, garden, terrace with a banqueting house at the eastern end, the great garden, orchard, a house with courtyard in front and garden behind lying on the south side of the orchard and leased to Edward Smith for 99 years, Dovecote Close (5 a.) at the north-eastern end, a kitchen garden and, on the north side of the gardens, Brickbarn Close (10 a.),[14] originally part of Westfield, which had been enclosed by the earl of Lincoln.[15] In 1620 Cranfield bought 32 a. in five closes called Sandhills east of Brickbarn Close from William Blake,[16] and having commissioned Inigo Jones in 1621 to design a gate to lead northwards from his gardens, in 1625 he enclosed the whole 42 acres to create Chelsea Park.[17] By 1652 it was enclosed with a brick wall and had brick buildings at south-east and south-west corners, by which time it was divided from the gardens by King's Road. Cranfield spent lavishly on the house, which he valued in 1624 at £8,000, and lived there very grandly, entertaining both Court and City guests, as he

1 MLR 1750/2/585; below, Gorges.
2 Faulkner, *Chelsea*, I. 72.
3 CL, deeds 3270–1; MLR 1767/4/283–5.
4 MLR 1835/4/726; 1808/5/357 (plan); see Fig. 49.
5 MLR 1787/3/322–3; CL, deed 3000.
6 MLR 1794/1/757.
7 CL, deed 3272; MLR 1808/5/357; 1808/7/166.
8 Act 6 Geo. IV, c. 16.
9 Beaver, *Memorials*, 160–1; *DNB* s.v. Stanhope, Leicester. Stanhope's son was born at Ashburnham Ho. in 1845: *Complete Peerage*, VI. 328.
10 CL, Tithe Map and Award, nos. 4–5.
11 CL, Tithe Map and Award; Act 6 Geo. IV, c. 16 (schedule).
12 CL, deed 43773; below, Soc. Hist., social (Cremorne); for later history, below, this section, Chelsea Farm.
13 Above, More.
14 PRO, C 54/2440, no. 38; see Fig. 11. Key to Kip's View is given in *Survey of London*, IV. 26.
15 PRO, C 2/JasI/G2/16.
16 Below, Blake. Once part of Hungerford's est.
17 Summerson, *Architecture in Britain, 1530–1830* (1993), 531; Davies, *Greatest Ho.* 141–3.

evolved from a City merchant to a great minister and courtier.[1]

In 1625 Cranfield, convicted of malfeasance as lord treasurer, offered the Chelsea estate to George Villiers, duke of Buckingham, as part of his efforts to clear his fine, which stood at £20,000. The transaction was negotiated by his intermediary with Buckingham's wife and mother, on whose rapacity he later blamed the loss of Chelsea even more than on the animosity of Buckingham.[2] In 1627 Charles I granted the estate to Buckingham for a fee farm of £1 a year.[3] Known as Buckingham House, the mansion was used by the duke until his assassination in 1628 and then by his widow Catherine. The estates of the duchess, who had married Randall, earl of Antrim, were sequestered in 1644; on her death in 1649 the property would have passed to her son George, 2nd duke of Buckingham,[4] but he had fought for Prince Charles in 1648 and escaped abroad, forfeiting his estates.[5] In 1649 the 54-acre estate, consisting of the house, grounds and park, was leased to Bulstrode Whitelocke and John Lisle, commissioners for the Great Seal: the rent on the 21-year lease was set at £40, as soldiers quartered in the house had pulled down the walls and wainscot, broken the glass in the windows, destroyed the gardens, and 'much defaced the whole house'.[6] In 1652 the trustees for sale of confiscated estates sold the estate to Whitelock and Lisle for £920. Buckingham House was described as built of brick and roofed partly with tiles and partly with lead; it had five cellars on the lowest floor, 20 rooms including two halls and nine kitchens, butteries, and larders, and a large staircase on the ground floor, and 21 rooms on the next floor including two dining rooms, a gallery, and 11 chambers, with garrets above most of those. Outside there was a little yard at the west end of the house with a brick building used as a dairy and wash house, and part as a coachhouse; another yard on the north side of the house with seven stables; three gardens containing another brick building, an orchard, and two courts on the south side. A brick building at the west corner next to the Thames was used as a lodge, and one on the east corner with a rod of land adjoining was let. The mansion and its grounds and outhouses enclosed with a brick wall contained 10 a. 1 r.; Dovecote close, also enclosed with brick, contained 4 a.; and the park, again enclosed with brick, 39½ a.[7]

The 2nd duke regained his estates at the Restoration in 1660,[8] but possibly to pay off debts he conveyed the Chelsea property in 1664 to John Godden (d. by 1668), Richard Blake, and several other London tradesmen for £12,000;[9] between 1668 and 1672 the land and house were sold off separately.[10] The house, by far the largest in Chelsea, was empty when it was assessed for 58 hearths in 1666 and 61 in 1674.[11] With 15 a. of grounds it passed to James Plumer, one of Buckingham's main creditors, who in turn sold it in 1674 to trustees for George Digby, earl of Bristol; Bristol is said to have paid £7,000.[12] The earl, by will proved 1677, left the house to his widow Anne,[13] who in 1681 sold it for £5,000 or £5,500 to Henry Somerset (d. 1699), marquess of Worcester.[14]

John Evelyn described the house in 1679 as 'large, but ill contrived', despite the money which Lord Bristol had spent on it, though he thought its grounds and situation were spacious and excellent, and Lady Bristol gave him some of her rare collection of orange trees.[15] Another contemporary, Lord Ossery, noted that the estate consisted of 16 a. including walled gardens planted 'with the choicest fruit' and that the house had been 'altered according to the mode'.[16] Lord Worcester, created duke of Beaufort in 1682,[17] spent £5,180 on improvements to the house, eventually reconciling his wife Mary to the purchase: she, like others, had thought that the house was too old to be fitted out with modern comforts, while Henry had emphasized the excellent air of Chelsea, and the good offices and plentiful water piped from Kensington. The architect Robert Warren was employed to modernize the house, and he extended the garden parterres down to the Thames. Grinling Gibbons was commissioned to make ornamental carvings. The house, known as Beaufort House, became a show place where the duke and duchess entertained their friends, neighbours, and the king,[18] although when Evelyn visited it in 1683 he was still critical, thinking that the duke might have built a better house with the materials and money employed.[19]

In 1705 Bowack exaggerated the size of the house as 200–300 feet long – it cannot have been more than 150 feet on that site – but described its 'stately ancient front to the river', two spacious courtyards and fine gardens behind. He also noted that for some years the 2nd duke (a minor) had spent most of his time at Badminton (Glos.).[20] The dowager duchess was forced to leave Badminton after a disagreement with her grandson over the 1st duke's personal estate, and she moved to Chelsea in 1709 where she lived until her death in 1715. Mary was an ardent botanist with one of the most important

1 M. Prestwich, *Cranfield: Politics and Profits under the Early Stuarts* (1966), 266, 383, 420, 423.
2 Ibid., 474–5.
3 PRO, C 66/244, m. 22; E 318/50/12. Conveyance repeated descriptions in 1619 conveyance, i.e. excluding Sandhills.
4 *Cal. Cttee Comp.* I. 254.
5 *DNB.*
6 *Cal. Cttee Money*, I. 528–30.
7 PRO, C 54/3676, no. 12.
8 Guildhall MS 15613.
9 PRO, C 8/601/13; CL, deed 2990.
10 Below, Sloane Stanley.
11 PRO, E 179/252/32/40, f. 24; E 179/143/370, m. 5.
12 PRO, C 8/601/13.
13 PRO, PROB 11/353, f. 301v.
14 PRO, C 8/601/13; M. McClain, *Beaufort: the Duke and his Duchess* (2001), 103.
15 *Diary of John Evelyn*, ed. E.S. de Beer, IV. 161–2.
16 Quoted in Davies, *Greatest Ho.* 197.
17 *Complete Peerage*, II. 51–4.
18 McClain, *Beaufort*, 103, 203.
19 *Diary of John Evelyn*, 335.
20 Bowack, *Antiquities*, 14.

collections of exotic plants in Europe and her greenhouses at Badminton and Chelsea surpassed even those built by William and Mary at Hampton Court. She was assisted in her collecting by her friend Sir Hans Sloane, and her catalogue of plants filled 12 volumes.[1] The 2nd duke, who had died shortly before his grandmother, left the house by will to trustees to sell to raise money towards his third marriage settlement,[2] but it remained empty until *c.*1724 when it was acquired by Samuel Travers with the idea, which failed, of opening it as a school.[3] In 1737 Travers's executors sold it to Sir Hans Sloane, owner of Chelsea manor,[4] and the freehold descended thereafter with the manor. Sloane placed the house, which had been empty for nearly 20 years, in the care of his gardener and factotum, Edmund Howard, with instructions to pull it down, which was done in 1740.[5] In 1750 Sloane leased out the whole estate, known as Beaufort Ground and stretching from King's Road to open ground called Beaufort green by the Thames, for 91 years to trustees for the *Unitas Fratrum* or Moravian congregation, who had bought the adjoining Lindsey House.[6] They laid out a burial ground on the stable yard with a chapel on the north side, reached by a passage from the rear of Lindsey House. It was intended to build a settlement called Sharon on the rest of the site, but after the leader of the *Unitas Fratrum*, Count Zinzendorf, returned permanently to the Continent in 1755, financial difficulties prevented the settlement being built. Apart from the Moravian burial ground, which continued in use by the congregation,[7] Beaufort Ground was leased as building plots by 1770, and eventually Beaufort Street was laid through the site.[8] In 1781 the Beaufort estate consisted of over 7 a. land, 19 houses, and wharves.[9]

BLAKE ESTATE

William Blake (d. 1630), citizen and vintner of London, was resident in Kensington by 1606 and built up a large estate in Kensington, Knightsbridge, Westminster, and Chelsea: despite sales before his death, he still left *c.*370 a. to his heirs.[10] He was knighted in 1627. William Blake, scrivener of London, was also involved in land sales in Chelsea in the same period,[11] but has no known relationship to Sir William.

In 1607 Blake purchased from Francis Shuckburgh for £1,100 a farmhouse with 32 a. in five closes called Sandhills, 42 a. arable in Eastfield, and 1 a. and 11 lots of meadow in West meadow, all occupied by William Wrennall and formerly part of Hungerford's estate.[12] Blake also made two purchases in 1618 from Thomas Fiennes, 3rd earl of Lincoln. One, for £200, was of 14 a. inclosed in Westfield and in the tenure of Wrennall, which lay on the north side of King's Road, and another close of 5 a. between the 14 a. and Fulham Road with a house built on it and once part of the lands of William Arnold of Fulham; Richard Stocke held a lease of *c.*31 years granted by Lincoln of the 5 a. and the house, which he had probably built.[13] The other purchase was of 9 a. meadow in Thamesmead in the tenure of the countess of Nottingham, 30 a. close called Coleherne in Kensington, and the rights Lincoln held in the Chelsea ferry:[14] the meadow seems to be the so-called 10 a. in Eastfield between Chelsea College and the river which became part of the Royal Hospital's grounds.[15]

William Blake sold the 32 acres called Sandhills in 1620 to Sir Lionel Cranfield, owner of the house later called Beaufort House, who used the land to create Chelsea Park.[16] In 1623 Blake sold the ferry to Oliver St John, 1st Viscount Grandison,[17] and in 1630 sold probably all his remaining property in Chelsea to Ralph Massie (or Massey) of London, vintner, consisting of the farmhouse held by Wrennall, the house formerly held by Stocke, 75 a. arable, 11 a. and 16 lots of meadow, all in Chelsea, and 1½ a. in Fulham.[18]

In 1634 Ralph Massie sold to William Arnold junior, of Kensington, for £1,660 all the land he had bought from Blake except for the 5-acre close and house at Little Chelsea and the adjoining 14 acres in Westfield.[19] Massie died soon afterwards and the property he had retained passed to his son William, who in 1650 conveyed it to trustees for Ralph's widow, Isabella Lusher.[20] In 1682 Massie conveyed the property, which now consisted of two houses and 18 acres of land, to William Mart, citizen and vintner of London, and Isabella surrendered her right in that property in 1683.[21]

Prior to this purchase Mart bought a house, malthouse, and 3 a. in Eastfield in 1677 from John Saunders, who had acquired it as part of the settlement on his marriage with William Arnold's daughter, Dorothy, and in 1678 Mart bought 17 a. from Anne Bennett, who had bought it from Arnold in 1668.[22] The main house bought from Massie, and probably the newer house as well, fronted Fulham Road at Little Chelsea. According to Bowack, Mart built there a

1 McClain, *Beaufort*, 206, 210–12, 215.
2 PRO, C 78/1438/465; *Complete Peerage*, II. 51–4.
3 Beaver, *Memorials*, 139.
4 MLR 1737/2/587–8.
5 Davies, *Greatest Ho.* 230–2.
6 MLR 1750/1/487; below, Lindsey.
7 Below, Rel. Hist., prot. nonconf. (Moravians).
8 *Fetter Lane Moravian Congregation London, 1742–1992*, ed. C. Podmore (1992), 23; above, Settlement, 1680–1865 (Chelsea village).
9 MLR 1835/4/726.
10 *Survey of London*, XLI. 58; PRO, WARDS 5/30/433.
11 Above, Arnold.
12 PRO, C 54/2445, no. 1; above, Hungerford.
13 PRO, C 54/2376, no. 5.
14 PRO, C 66/2193, no. 78.
15 G. Hutt, *Royal Hosp.* 138.
16 PRO, C 54/2445, no. 1; above, Beaufort.
17 Above, Intro., comms.
18 PRO, C 9/15/92. For details of the land, below, Econ., agric.
19 PRO, C 54/3026, no. 24; above, Arnold.
20 PRO, C 9/15/92–3.
21 PRO, C 10/266/37.
22 PRO, C 6/184/92; C 10/266/37.

'regular, handsome house with a noble courtyard and good gardens', where Sir John Cope, Bt (d. 1721), lived when he retired from active public life.[1] In 1704 Sir John was occupying the house with its garden, stable and coachhouse, while the other house, described in 1715 as lately built, was occupied by Christopher Grimstead with the 18 a.,[2] which stretched to King's Road.[3] Cope's house was later occupied as Duffield's private madhouse, and then demolished to form the site of Odell's Place;[4] it therefore lay east of Shaftesbury House.[5]

At his death in 1704 Mart also owned a principal messuage with garden, malthouse, barns, stable, and coachhouses, occupied in 1705 by John Lefevre, schoolmaster, a house and 43 a. held by Nathaniel Terrett, and a house and 3 a. occupied by Mr Stubbington, all freehold in Chelsea and Kensington, as well as copyhold in Fulham and property in the cities of London and Westminster. Mart's widow Jane unsuccessfully claimed the estate, which passed to Mart's nephew, William Mart of Addiscombe (Surrey).[6] In 1719 Mart sold to Sir John Cope's son, Sir John Cope, Kt, the house still occupied by Cope senior and the other house and 18 a.[7] In 1721 after his father's death, Sir John conveyed the two houses and 18 a. to Sir Hans Sloane, who in 1733 conveyed them to his nephew, William Sloane; thereafter they passed as part of the Sloane Stanley estate.[8] The remaining parts of Mart's estate have not been traced.

BOEVEY ESTATE AND SHAFTESBURY HOUSE

William Arnold of Fulham held a 10-acre close on the south side of Fulham Road in 1607, of which 5 a. had a house and land held by Richard Stocke when it was sold in 1618 to William Blake. The remaining 5 a. on the west side were described as Stocke's orchard in 1618, but the property's location indicates that it became the site of the houses fronting Fulham Road in Little Chelsea with gardens of 2 a. and 3 a. respectively which Thomas Wood, citizen and merchant taylor of London, sold in 1634 to Johanna, widow of Andries Boeve (Andrew Boevey), a Huguenot merchant of London, for £1,090.[9] Johanna may have carried out some improvements to the property, which once had a datestone of 1635 on one of the houses.[10] She married as her second husband John Abell, but under their marriage settlement Abell was to have no claim to the property, which Johanna (d. 1644) conveyed to trustees in 1642 for the uses of her will. The Chelsea property was left in her will to her four daughters, Johanna, widow of Abraham Clarke, Mary Boevey, Elizabeth Lemott, widow, later wife of John Beex, and Ann, wife of David Bonnell.[11] Mary died unmarried. Elizabeth Beex mortgaged her share to Johanna Clarke *c.*1656, and Johanna was said to have spent £4,000 in building work there by 1658, when she and the Bonnells sold the whole property, described in the fine as 4 messuages, 2 barns, 3 gardens, and 7 a., for £1,231 to William Boevey (d. 1661), the son of Andrew Boevey by his first wife and one of the trustees. William left it to his wife Anne for life and then to their son John, and in 1663 Anne married Sir James Smith (d. 1681).

The sale to William Boevey led to a series of law suits and appeals until the end of the 17th century by James son of Andrew and Johanna Boevey, excluded from the Chelsea property and notorious for his law-suits,[12] and by Elizabeth Beex (d. *c.*1683) and her daughter Elizabeth and the latter's husband Thomas Lowndes, on the grounds that they still held the equity of redemption of two thirds of the property.[13] By 1687 the estate consisted of the principal house and garden of 3 acres occupied by Lady Smith, which had been assessed to Sir James Smith in 1666 and 1674 for 18 hearths,[14] flanked on one side by a house and garden of 2 acres occupied by Sir Robert Wiseman, and on the other by a house with a little garden plot of a quarter of an acre, which had been occupied by Elizabeth Beex,[15] neither of which can be identified with certainty in the hearth tax. Elizabeth Beex was awarded the redemption of the two thirds after the balance of the mortgage had been repaid, and her interest passed to her daughter. Anne Smith (d. 1698) and her son John Boevey were allotted the house and grounds she occupied, although it was noted that they were worth more than a third of the estate. The rest was allotted to Thomas and Elizabeth Lowndes on payment of £750. In 1687 the Lowndes brought another case against Anne and her son, alleging that they had entered the disputed premises, while the defendants countered that they had not been paid the £750. The estate was eventually divided by commissioners in 1698: Margaret the widow of James Boevey (d. 1696) and his heirs received a fifth of the estate consisting of the house and a garden 521 ft deep on the east side of Sir James Smith's former house; John Boevey was awarded the latter in the centre; and the house on the west side went to Thomas Lowndes.[16]

Shaftesbury House

The central house, Sir James Smith's, was sold to Anthony Ashley Cooper, 3rd earl of Shaftesbury, who

1 Bowack, *Antiquities*, 15.
2 MLR 1715/2/60.
3 CL, maps drawer 1, no. 5, Survey of King's Rd.
4 Faulkner, *Chelsea*, I. 142.
5 Thompson, *Map* (1836).
6 PRO, C 10/266/37.
7 MLR 1719/2/203–5.
8 MLR 1721/1/67–8; 1721/3/284; 1733/1/210–11; below, Sloane Stanley.
9 PRO, C 6/62/16; *Brief Lives by John Aubrey*, ed. A. Clark (1898), I. 112–13.
10 Croker, *Walk from London to Fulham*, 119.
11 PRO, C 6/62/16.
12 *Aubrey's Brief Lives*, 113.
13 PRO, C 5/143/48; C 5/148/126; C 6/62/16; C 6/282/53; C 10/354/32; HMC, *MSS of HL*, IV. 275–8.
14 PRO, E 179/252/32/40, f. 25v.; E 179/143/370, m. 5.
15 PRO, C 6/282/53.
16 Davies, *Chelsea Old Ch.* 200–2.

was in Chelsea by 1700.[1] According to Bowack, Shaftesbury built 'a very neat seat' there and *c.*1705 was 'planting gardens'. He wanted the Chelsea house as a residence during parliamentary sittings,[2] but moved away in 1706 because smoke gave him asthma attacks,[3] and in 1710 he sold the house with garden plot, court-yard, great and little gardens, totalling 3 acres, newly-erected building and barns, stables, and outhouses, to Narcissus Luttrell (d. 1732).[4] It passed to Luttrell's second son Francis (d. 1740),[5] and then to his nephew, William Wynne, serjeant-at-law (d. 1765). Wynne was succeeded by his sons, Edward (d. 1784), a barrister, and the Revd Luttrell Wynne, who sold it in 1786 to William Virtue. Virtue sold it the same year to the parish of St George, Hanover Square, for use as a workhouse.[6]

The fine classical-looking building of four storeys and basement, with its pediment and flight of steps added by Shaftesbury, was demolished in 1856 and replaced by new workhouse buildings.[7]

Lowndes

The Lowndes's portion of the Boevey estate, on the west side of Shaftesbury House, consisted of at least two houses and a cottage by 1700.[8] The large house was occupied by Sir Robert Wiseman (d. 1684), dean of the Arches and Vicar General,[9] then Lady Wiseman,[10] followed by Thomas Lowndes himself, though the rector commented *c.*1700 that the house was 'seldom inhabited'.[11] After Lowndes's death his only daughter and heir, Mary, conveyed the estate in 1710 to William Burchett of Fulham, whose widowed mother Elizabeth lived at Little Chelsea,[12] and whose family owned and leased several holdings in Chelsea and farmed there.[13] In 1721 Burchett leased the large house to Ralph Verney, 2nd Viscount Fermanagh (d. 1752), who was there until at least 1735,[14] and both he and his wife Catherine (d. 1748) died at Little Chelsea,[15] though they did not necessarily still occupy that house. It seems to have been occupied by the Revd Dr Doyley in 1750. Burchett himself occupied the second of the houses.[16]

CHELSEA FARM (CREMORNE HOUSE)

In 1745 Theophilus Hastings, 9th earl of Huntingdon, leased from Sir Hans Sloane a house and garden of 2 a. in Westfield, 1 a. meadow south of Lots Lane, and 60 rods

50. *Chelsea Farm or Cremorne House from the south-west, with Battersea Bridge and the Old Church in the background*

on the east side of a newly-erected building belonging to Huntingdon, for 61 years at £33 a year.[17] He built a villa called Chelsea Farm at the southern end by Lots Lane, and after his death in 1746 his widow Selina, the Methodist enthusiast, lived there until 1750, when she sold the lease to Richard Wingfield, Viscount Powerscourt.[18] In 1751 Powerscourt obtained a new lease for 71 years from Sloane of the original property, together with another house, farm buildings, and 8 a. of farm and garden ground. Powerscourt died that year and in 1760 his widow Dorothy assigned the 71-year lease to Brownlow Cecil, earl of Exeter, who in 1761 obtained a 61-year lease from the heirs of the Warton estate of a rood of meadow in the angle by the Thames south of Hobgate.[19] This created a compact, rectangular estate stretching from the King's Road to the river, bounded on the east by Hob Lane and on the west by Ashburnham House estate. The revised and doubtless more accurate description in 1781 was of 9¼ acres of manorial demesne and a rood of Warton land.[20]

Exeter assigned both leases in 1765 to Sir Richard Lyttelton (d. 1770), and after the death of Lyttelton's widow Rachel in 1777 the leases passed to Rachel's son, Francis Egerton, duke of Bridgewater, who sold them in 1778 to Thomas Dawson, Lord Dartrey, later Viscount Cremorne.[21] In 1781 the owners of the manor granted a reversionary lease to Dartrey, to run for 29 years from

1 Dr King's MS, p. 11.
2 Bowack, *Antiquities*, 14.
3 *DNB*.
4 MLR 1709/3/35–6.
5 Poor rate bk, 1728–42, f. 388; Croker, *Walk from London to Fulham*, 129.
6 Beaver, *Memorials*, 330.
7 Croker, *Walk from London to Fulham*, 117–19. Probably the large ho. shown in top left of Fig. 11.
8 PRO, C 10/369/11.
9 PRO, PROB 11/377, f. 71v.
10 Poor rate bk, 1662–1718, f. 21v.
11 Dr King's MS, p. 15.
12 MLR 1709/1/148; MLR 1709/1/174; 1709/2/147.
13 BL, Sloane MS 2938, f. 2.
14 *Verney Letters of the Eighteenth Century*, ed. Margt Maria, Lady Verney (1930), II. 80, 85, 88, 93; Poor rate bks, 1716–27, p. 355; 1728–42, f. 388.
15 *Complete Peerage*, V. 295.
16 Poor rate bks, 1716–27, p. 355; 1728–42, f. 388; MLR 1750/1/122.
17 MLR 1745/2/218.
18 Beaver, *Memorials*, 156–7; *Complete Peerage*, VI. 660–2; MLR 1750/2/30.
19 MLR 1778/4/462; *Complete Peerage*, V. 220–1; X. 637; below, Warton.
20 CL, deed 43743, plan; MLR 1825/4/726.
21 MLR 1778/4/462; *Complete Peerage*, II. 313–14.

1822.[1] In 1785 he purchased the freehold of the rood from Warton's heirs, and also leased 13½ a. of the Sloane Stanley estate north of King's Road for 66 years.[2] Soon afterwards he employed James Wyatt to enlarge the house into a rambling rather than picturesquely planned building, subsequently called Cremorne House.[3] Lord Cremorne (d. 1813) left the estate to his American widow Philadelphia Hannah, friend of Queen Charlotte and local benefactor. On her death in 1826 the estate passed under her will to her cousin, Granville Penn, who after several unsuccessful attempts eventually sold it in 1830 to Henry Philip Hope for £2,990. It then consisted of the freehold rood and the residuary terms of leases of 29 years (from 1822), 40 years (from 1851), and 66 years (from 1785).[4]

In 1834 Henry Philip Hope sold the estate to John Raphael as trustee for Charles Random, self-styled Baron de Berenger, who ran the estate as a sports club: de Berenger was to have the rents and profits for life but subject to Beatrix Crowder receiving rents during her lifetime.[5] By 1840 de Berenger (d. 1845) was in debt, and he directed that the property was to be held in trust for Beatrix.[6] In 1845 Beatrix Crowder, of Cremorne House, and Robert Russell, one of de Berenger's creditors, granted an under-lease of the estate to John Wolsey,[7] who shortly afterwards assigned it to Thomas Bartlett Simpson, hotelkeeper,[8] and under the latter the Cremorne pleasure gardens were opened in the grounds.[9] In 1859 Simpson obtained leases of the neighbouring Ashburnham House and Ashburnham Cottage,[10] for expansion of the Gardens.

Simpson purchased the freehold of the Cremorne and Ashburnham estates from Lord Cadogan in 1866, together with the remaining Cadogan freehold as far as Chelsea Creek, consisting of land south of Lots Road, 24½ a. of garden ground, another acre of garden ground between Poole's Lane and the canal, and the site of the mills and other buildings in Poole's Lane, giving him an estate of *c.*45 a. covering the whole of south-west Chelsea except for Lots meadow; it was clearly with a view to build, as part of the Ashburnham estate south of Lots Road was already divided into plots.[11] After Simpson's death in 1872 his widow Jane, who inherited under his will, increased the rate of building, selling some land, but mostly granting building leases to cover the whole area.[12] Cremorne Gardens, already in financial difficulties, had to close anyway in 1877 when Jane Simpson refused to renew the manager's tenancy, having decided to lay out the site for building.[13] Jane (d. 1893) bequeathed all her property by will to her sons as trustees to sell for the benefit of her seven daughters, but they retained the freehold, distributing the rental income instead. In 1915 the freehold was divided between the six surviving daughters, who had all died by 1956. The inheritance apparently passed out of the hands of the Simpson family in 1975 on the death of Thomas Bartlett Simpson's granddaughter.[14]

EARL OF LINCOLN'S OTHER LAND

Henry Fiennes, 2nd earl of Lincoln, or his son Thomas, 3rd earl, acquired several pieces of property in Chelsea in addition to the former estate of Thomas More, which was settled on the 2nd earl and Sir Arthur and Lady Elizabeth Gorges,[15] and those other properties passed instead to the 3rd and 4th earls. The 2nd earl bought Morehouse from the Roper family, which was the former Butts close with houses, barns, and garden which had been given to William Roper by Sir Thomas More. The Ropers assigned leases to Lincoln, and the freehold was probably obtained from the Crown.[16]

Thomas, 3rd earl of Lincoln, made two sales of property in Chelsea acquired either by himself or his father to Sir William Blake in 1618.[17] The first was of a close of 14 acres in Westfield, and another close of 5 acres with a house built on it in the tenure of Richard Stocke, which had once belonged to William Arnold of Fulham; the release from any claims under the late earl or Thomas's brothers suggest that the property had been bought by Henry, 2nd earl.[18] The other sale followed the grant of a licence to the 3rd earl, John Eldred, and Robert Henley allowing them to sell Chelsea ferry and landing place, 47 a. in Kensington, and Thamesmead in Chelsea containing 9 a., all held of the king in chief, which they then sold to Blake.[19] The ferry and Thamesmead had both been part of the manor of Chelsea and were probably granted by James I to the 3rd earl or his father, but the actual grants by the Crown, or by the Ropers to the Fiennes, have not been traced, and may been conducted through agents.

GORGES HOUSE AND PARSONAGE CLOSE

Gorges House, standing just west of Beaufort House, and close to its stables, is unlikely to have been built before 1617, as the site was part of the farm leased to Nicholas Holborne until that date. Sir Arthur is recorded as presenting the queen with a jewel in 1599 as she

1 CL, deed 43743.
2 CL, deeds 3047, 43744; MLR 1786/2/50.
3 Faulkner, *Chelsea*, I. 65; LMA, Acc.2079/D3/9/1–2 (bldg accts 1788–90); see Fig. 50.
4 CL, deed 43746; Beaver, *Memorials*, 158–9.
5 CL, deeds 43734–5.
6 CL, deeds 43737, 43774.
7 CL, deed 43738.
8 CL, deed 43767.
9 Above, Soc. Hist., social (Cremorne).
10 CL, deed 43773; above, Arnold; Ashburnham.
11 MLR 1866/18/637–43; CL, deeds 5679, 43758.
12 CL, deed 43758; KL, deed 34967; MLR 1866/18/637.
13 LMA, MR/LMD 20/13.
14 CL, deeds 5301, 5360, 43796; KL, deeds 28819, 34788, 35915.
15 Above, More.
16 Below, Sloane Stanley.
17 Above, Blake.
18 PRO, C 54/2376, no. 5.
19 PRO, C 66/2193, no. 78; above, Intro., comms (ferry).

passed by 'the fair new building' on her way to the manor house,[1] but there is no indication which new building that might be, and the later Gorges House would not in any case have been on the queen's likely route. The house is depicted on the drawing by Kip *c.*1700 as a half **H**-plan building facing west and with each range, apparently built of brick, crowned by rows of shaped gables.[2] By that date it fronted a lane leading from the Thames to the king's road, probably the way first mentioned in 1622 giving access to the coachhouse there.[3] Gorges House has also been suggested as the site of the medieval parsonage, but again it seems an unlikely and inconvenient place for the parsonage since there was no highway past it.[4]

When Sir Arthur sold the principal mansion on More's estate in 1620, he retained the right to burial in More's chapel, which thereafter passed with Gorges House.[5] Sir Arthur (d. 1625) was succeeded by his son Arthur (d. 1661), and grandson Arthur (d. 1668), who in 1664 sold Gorges House and its gardens, orchard, and small adjoining close, and the 9-acre field called Parsonage Close which stretched from King's Road to the Thames, and all the remaining Gorges property there including the land and four houses and gardens at the southern end of the later Milman's Street held by Thomas Rosse, and 3 acres of meadow in Westfield, to Thomas Pritchard and Richard Spoure who conveyed it all, initially in a mortgage in 1666 and then in a sale in 1670, to William Morgan, chancery clerk.[6] The house was occupied as a boarding school by 1676, run by Josias Priest from 1680 to *c.*1711.[7] William Morgan's son or grandson Richard sold the house and gardens before 1714 to Sir William Milman, and the grandson Richard sold Parsonage Close, the small close and other property in 1718 to Samuel Strode of London, barber surgeon.[8]

Milman left his property by will proved 1714 to his nieces, Elizabeth Palmer, and Diana, Robella, and Mary Milman. In 1726 the nieces and their husbands made an agreement for the building of houses called Millman Row, and granted building leases the following year for the individual houses, which stood on the site of Gorges House, presumably demolished by that date.[9]

Strode died *c.*1720, and in 1747 his sons William and Samuel surrendered their interest to their mother Anne, who conveyed the estate to Charles Simes and Samuel Meredith;[10] the latter divided up and sold off all the property in 1750. They sold 4½ a. with 23 houses, including the World's End and King's Arms public houses, to Richard Davis (or Davies) of Chelsea, shoemaker, which represented about half of Parsonage Close.[11] Richard Davis (d. *c.*1769) left his estate to his wife Sarah for life and then to trustees for his grand-niece, Mary Ann Jones, who in 1785 married Stephen Riley. Riley, by will proved 1816, left the estate to trustees including his widow; it was sold by auction in lots in 1823.[12] The other half of Parsonage Close, 5½ a. with four houses south of World's End Passage, was conveyed to George Norris (d. 1805), gardener, at the same time. Norris's estate was still in the hands of his son, George, also a gardener, in 1827.[13] They also sold to Norris a brick house with a courtyard and garden standing at the south-east corner of Milman's Street, and a wharf on the Thames opposite the Hole in the Wall public house.[14] The Hole in the Wall, by Milman's Street and facing the river, was conveyed to Charles Munden,[15] as well as two houses and gardens on the opposite side of Milman's Street.[16] The 3 acres in Westfield lying south of Lots Lane, used as osier ground in 1747,[17] was also sold in 1750 and passed to Benjamin Hoadley.[18]

GOUGH HOUSE

John Vaughan, 3rd earl of Carbery, had bought 3½ acres of manorial demesne from Viscount Newhaven called Little Sweed Court by 1707, the year a conveyance to Carbery of just under half an acre of manorial demesne was confirmed by Act, part of a rationalization of boundaries connected with larger sales to the Royal Hospital.[19] The rector referred *c.*1704 to the land as 'lately-purchased', and to Carbery's newly-built house, which lay west of the later Walpole House estate.[20] Lord Newhaven also granted to Carbery in 1707 a passage and new gate into the garden ground which was part of the premises. The half **H**-plan red brick house, of two storeys above a tall basement, had a grand river front with giant pilasters, a central pediment and hipped roof with grouped chimneystacks; it resembled the main front of Ranelagh House.[21] A pedimented door led through the garden, laid out in broad terraces, to a gate in the riverside wall, to which was attached a summerhouse as at the neighbouring Walpole House. The north façade was much plainer.

Carbery died in 1713 and his only child Ann married

1 *Sidney Papers*, I. 141: presentation probably part of campaign to get Sir Rob. Sidney, with whom Gorges had served, recalled from Ireland.
2 See Fig. 11.
3 PRO, C 66/2268, no. 24.
4 Above, Settlement, to 1680.
5 Davies, *Chelsea Old Church*, 128.
6 CL, deed 37614; PRO, C 6/201/55; LMA, BRA 203/159; Beaver, *Memorials*, 149.
7 Below, Soc. Hist., educ. (private schs).
8 MLR 1718/4/206–9; KL, deed 37614.
9 CL, Ar4/76/7–8; MLR 1750/3/749; 1750/2/391; Davies, *Chelsea Old Church*, 135; above, Settlement, 1680–1865 (Lt. Chelsea).
10 MLR 1747/3/41–4.
11 MLR 1750/2/458.
12 KL, deeds 32644, 35486, 37613–14.
13 MLR 1750/3/71–2; KL, deeds 37580, 37584.
14 MLR 1750/3/71–3.
15 MLR 1750/2/478–9.
16 Ibid., /481–3.
17 CL, deed 3268.
18 MLR 1750/2/584–5; above, Ashburnham.
19 Hutt, *Royal Hosp.* 221–3.
20 Dr King's MS, pp. 16, 42–3.
21 Illus. in Beaver, *Memorials*, 245.

Charles Powlett, marquis of Bolton,[1] who in 1714 sold the estate with its recently-built mansion house to Richard Gough, a London merchant knighted by 1716.[2] Gough also leased the adjoining Walpole House estate in 1714, where he built stables by the highway,[3] and enlarged his estate in 1716 by purchasing from the sister and heir of Mary Pinner 1½ a. on the west side,[4] which Mary had bought from John Greene.[5]

Sir Richard Gough (d. 1728) was succeeded by his son, Sir Henry, Bt (d. 1774), whose son Henry (d. 1798) took the name Gough-Calthorpe in 1788 when he inherited the estates of his maternal uncle; he was created Baron Calthorpe in 1796.[6] Gough House was occupied by 1780, and possibly 1777, by the Pemberton family,[7] and in 1790 the widow of Thomas Pemberton opened a girls' school there.[8] Lord Calthorpe was leasing land on the west side of the house and garden for building by 1792,[9] and by 1846 his property included Druces' wharf by the Thames.[10] Gough House remained largely unaltered until it was acquired by the MBW as part of the Embankment scheme and converted into the Victoria Hospital for Children in 1866; the house continued to exist among additional hospital buildings.[11] The MBW used some of the riverside land for the Embankment, and the southern part of Tite Street was constructed over much of the rest.[12]

HENRY SMITH CHARITY ESTATE

Henry Smith (d. 1628) of Wandsworth, salter, left £2,000 to trustees for the benefit of captives and his relatives. His trustees, who included Sir William Blake, purchased a small farm in the parishes of Kensington, Chelsea, and St Margaret Westminster, which in 1664 included a close called Quailfield of *c.*14 a. lying partly in Kensington and partly in north-east Chelsea.[13] In 1772 the trustees for the charity obtained an Act enabling them to grant building leases of the estate.[14] Building on the Chelsea portion began in the late 1830s with St Saviour's church and Walton Place. Walton Street was built across the northern part of Quailfield *c.*1847, but most of the close remained open land until the 1880s. The land was let to Mr Cattleugh in 1836 as nursery ground, and in 1874 was assigned to Mr Prince who used it as a playing field for his adjoining cricket club, but shortly afterwards Pont Street was extended across the field, and during the 1880s Lennox Gardens and adjoining mews were built.[15] In 1995 the Charity sold the whole estate to the Wellcome Trust.[16]

LAWRENCE ESTATE

The medieval manor house,[17] which lay on the east side of Church Lane next to the parish church, with its gardens, orchards, and pasture enclosed by a pale, was leased in 1519 by William Lord Sandys and his feoffees to Thomas Keyle, citizen and mercer of London, for 40 years at £1 6s. 8d. a year, but excluding the barns and granary, commons, and the great court and all buildings of the manor outside the wall; Keyle later assigned the lease to another mercer, Richard Jervis (Gervoise, Jervoise) (d. 1556).[18] In 1557 the Crown granted the freehold of the house with its gardens, a dovecote, and adjoining 4-acre close to John Caryll to hold in free socage of the manor of East Greenwich.[19] Caryll sold the property in the same year to James Basset, whose widow Maria sold it for £120 in 1559 to Thomas Parrys, another London mercer.[20] It passed to Robert Chamberleyn and William Mounsey, both London ironmongers, who sold it in 1583–4 to Thomas Lawrence (d. 1593), citizen and goldsmith of London.[21] He devised his house at Chelsea with its grounds and gardens and an estate at Iver (Bucks.) to his wife Martha for life, and then to his son Thomas in tail with remainders to his other son John and to his daughters.[22] By 1621 the Chelsea property with 2 gardens, orchard, dovecote, and close of 4 acres, was in the possession of his son John (d. 1638), baronet from 1628.[23] He left it to his widow Grissell (d. 1675) until it had provided enough to pay portions to his younger children,[24] after which it passed with the baronetcy to Sir John's eldest son John (d. between 1680 and 1682), and grandson Thomas (d. 1714).[25]

The main house was occupied by Grissell until her death, and was also for a while occupied by the Dutch ambassador, who paid £60 a year for the house, gardens, and 2 acres. He built a stable, coachhouse, hayloft, and 'a very fair lodging chamber and a little closet', which afterwards burnt down. By 1665 the property consisted of the old manor house, described as a timber house 'of great

1 *Complete Peerage*, III. 7–8.
2 MLR 1714/2/87–90; Faulkner, *Chelsea*, I. 193.
3 MLR 1714/2/86; below, Royal Hosp. (Walpole Ho.).
4 MLR 1715/4/166; Dr King's MS, pp. 42–3.
5 Hutt, *Royal Hosp.* 137–9; above, Arnold.
6 *Complete Peerage*, II. 490; Beaver, *Memorials*, 246.
7 CL, deeds 17752, p. 34; 17553, p. 46; LMA, MR/PLT 4598.
8 *Chelsea Soc. Rep.* (1988), 41–5; below, Soc. Hist., educ. (private schs).
9 Above, Settlement, 1680–1865 (SE Chelsea).
10 Act 9 & 10 Vic. c. 39, schedule.
11 *Chelsea Soc. Rep.* (1963), 9–10; below, Loc. Govt, pub. svces (hosps).
12 *Chelsea Soc. Rep.* (1988), 41–2.
13 Inf. from Henry Smith Charity via web site (www.henrysmithcharity.org.uk), 7 Dec. 2002; Stroud, *Smith's Char.* 13–14.
14 Stroud, *Smith's Char.* 16.
15 Ibid., 25–8, 46–7; PRO, C 54/15791, m. 43; C 54/20299, m. 15; above, Settlement, 1865–1900.
16 Inf. from Hen. Smith Char.; *Guide to the Major Trusts: 2001/2002 edn*, vol. 1, 284–5.
17 Above, Chelsea man. (medieval man. ho.).
18 BL, Lansd. MS 2, f. 11; Davies, *Chelsea Old Ch.* 221.
19 *Cal. Pat.* 1555–7, 464.
20 CL, deed 3265.
21 Ibid., 3266.
22 PRO, PROB 11/82, f. 243.
23 PRO, C 142/574/89; Davies, *Chelsea Old Ch.* 162.
24 PRO, C 10/87/21.
25 Davies, *Chelsea Old Ch.* 167–78.

antiquity and much wanting repair',[1] and in 1666 and 1674 the house, assessed at 13 hearths, was occupied by Lady Grissell Lawrence. The next property in the assessment for hearth tax had 19 hearths and was occupied by George Wilcocks in 1666 and Mr Blameber or Bomflur in 1674:[2] it suggests that the old manor house may have been divided, as there is no evidence that a new, larger house had been built on or near the estate, and it was probably that part which had been occupied by the Dutch ambassador. The estate also included three adjoining cottages on the north side of Lordship Yard, built on the close, and probably eight on the east side of Church Lane.[3] It is likely that Dame Grissell's daughter and executrix, Frances Lawrence, continued to live in the house until her death in 1685.[4] In 1687 Sir Thomas made a building agreement for the whole four-acre site, and the house was probably demolished about that time.[5]

Sir Thomas and his wife Anne petitioned the king in 1687 for letters under the privy seal, authorizing the justices of common pleas to allow the Lawrences' under-age son and heir John to suffer a common recovery, in order for them to make a long lease of their old and decayed messuage and a close adjoining in Chelsea; it was granted on condition that all consented and the uses were limited.[6] The estate was conveyed to trustees that year for the purpose of making building leases and giving Sir Thomas a life estate,[7] though a later settlement seems to have been made to give John a life estate with remainder in default of male heirs to his father. In 1705 Sir Thomas relinquished this right in the property by a sale to his son John for £200,[8] and the following year John sold three cottages and gardens on the north side of Lordship Yard to William Cheyne, Lord Newhaven.[9] John's wife had died in 1701, and he had apparently died without issue by 1710 when Margaret Lawrence, spinster, sold or mortgaged three houses in Lawrence Street, two facing the Thames, and seven in Church Lane, with ground used as a garden by Sir John Munden, who occupied one of the latter houses, before her marriage that year to Crew Offley, MP, of Wychnor (Staffs.); she is assumed to be the only surviving child of Sir Thomas and Anne Lawrence and was presumably her brother's heir.[10] In 1712 Crew and Margaret settled the estate consisting of 33 newly-erected houses, land not yet built on, and the lord's chapel in the parish church.[11] In 1717 Crew sold three new houses at the upper end of Church Lane to Adrian Westerband, bricklayer, who occupied one of them.[12] Crew (d. 1739) left the estate to his son John for three years, after which it was to pass to another son, Lawrence, and his heirs, with remainder to John. John inherited after Lawrence's death in 1749,[13] and in 1750–1 sold many of the houses, usually to the occupants, including all nine in Church Lane between Justice Walk and the church, others north of Justice Walk, the Cross Keys tavern in Lawrence Street with its garden which had become a yard with stable and coachhouses in Lawrence Street and Church Lane, and the five houses of Church Row.[14]

John Offley, MP, who still owned seven houses and the lord's chapel in 1780,[15] was a well-known gamester who died unmarried in 1784, devising all his remaining property to a cousin, Lieut.-Col. Francis Needham, to pay legacies to other relatives and annuities to his servants.[16] Needham sold the chapel and some houses to Henry Lewer,[17] whose descendant, Henry Furnival Lewer, conveyed the chapel in 1894 to the rector and other church trustees.[18] The land which formed Justice Walk and other property in Lawrence Street was sold *c.*1788 to John Gregory of Westminster, builder.[19]

LINDSEY HOUSE

The principal farmhouse on More's estate, which lay south-west of the chief mansion in 1567,[20] has been identified with both the later Gorges House[21] and Lindsey House,[22] but the latter is more likely as it was called the 'Farmhouse' in 1618 when Sir Arthur and Lady Elizabeth Gorges settled it with its outbuildings, garden, orchard, wharf, and a lane on Sir Edward Cecil (d. 1638), Viscount Wimbledon from 1626, and his wife Diana for their lives and that of their daughter Anne, and then on the Gorges and their male heirs.[23] In 1622 the Gorges received a licence to make another settlement of the house, with its gardens, stables, yards, and coachhouses, all enclosed with a wall, with access for coaches to the house on the west side of the coachhouse, the wharf lying between the south side of the house and the Thames, and common of pasture, by conveying it to

1 PRO, C 10/87/21.

2 PRO, E 179/252/32, no. 40, f. 23; E 179/143/370, m. 5.

3 PRO, C 10/87/21.

4 CL, deed 2994. Frances was buried at Chelsea: *Herald and Genealogist*, IV. 543.

5 PRO, C 10/511/74; above, Settlement, 1680–1865 (Chelsea village).

6 *Cal. SP Dom.* 1687–9, 55, 71–2, 138–9.

7 PRO, C 7/330/22.

8 MLR 1715/6/13; Guildhall MS 1809; CL, deed 2994.

9 CL, deeds 3031, 3015.

10 MLR 1709/2/85; *Par. Regs of St Stephen Walbrook and St Benet Sherehog* (Harl. Soc.), I. 73; *Hist. of Parl. Commons, 1715–54*, II. 304.

11 LMA, AC.79.55; MLR 1712/2/148.

12 MLR 1717/4/174–5.

13 MLR 1750/1/124; Davies, *Chelsea Old Ch.* 181.

14 LMA, AC.79.55; MLR 1750/1/66–7, 125, 160–6, 349, 532–3, 540; 1750/2/201–2.

15 LMA, MR/PLT 4598.

16 *Hist. Parl. Commons 1754–90*, III. 223; S. Shaw, *Hist. and Antiquities of Staffs.* (1798), 124; PRO, C 54/12850, m. 26.

17 J.N. Brewer, *Beauties of Eng. & Wales*, X (1816), 63.

18 PRO, C 54/19894, m. 34.

19 MLR 1788/6/392; Vestry orders, 1771–90, f. 163v.

20 Lease quoted in Faulkner, *Chelsea*, I. 120.

21 Beaver, *Memorials*, 146.

22 Davies, *Chelsea Old Ch.* 153, followed by *Survey of London*, IV. 37 seqq, favour Lindsey Ho., citing its possession of a stint, which Gorges Ho. did not have.

23 PRO, C 66/2195, no. 57; *Complete Peerage*, XII(2), 740.

51. *Lindsey House, Cheyne Walk with* (right) *Belle Vue House and Belle Vue Lodge, showing junction with Beaufort Street before the embankment was built*

Griffin Robinson and Thomas Brooke in trust for their daughter Frances after the deaths of Edward and Diana Cecil.[1]

In 1638, however, Sir Francis Swift, perhaps another trustee, conveyed the property, described as a messuage, two barns, two stables, a wharf, two gardens, and two orchards, with common of pasture, to Sir Theodore Turquet de Mayerne, Baron of Albin, an eminent physician who attended the royal family from 1611, and his wife Isabella, apparently in fee.[2] Mayerne died in 1655, and his widow shortly afterwards; by will proved in 1655 she left the estate to trustees for their daughter Adriana.[3] In 1659, when Adriana married Armand de Coumonde, marquis de Montpolion,[4] she granted the capital mansion where she lived, still called the 'Farmhouse in Chelsea', to Peter Rousseau, a Frenchman, and Josiah Cuper to hold as trustees. Cuper died in 1660 and Adriana in 1661, and her husband's attempts to seize the property were challenged by Mayerne's relatives. In 1671 Rousseau's conveyance to John Snell and Richard Newman was opposed on the grounds that Rousseau was an alien; the grant, however, was confirmed by letters patent.[5]

Snell and Newman may have been acting as trustees for Robert Bertie, 3rd earl of Lindsey and Lord Great Chamberlain (d. 1701), who was in possession of the Farmhouse, wharf, and common of pasture in 1671 when he mortgaged it with a 200-year term. He settled the house at Chelsea and his personal estate *c.*1687, probably on his 3rd wife Elizabeth and his youngest son Charles, who were also executors of his will:[6] they reassigned the mortgage in 1716.[7] By 1727 the estate was described as a messuage, courtyard, 3 gardens, wharf, one acre, and common of pasture.[8] Under his will proved 1730 Charles Bertie left the Chelsea house and contents to his trustees and executors to sell to pay debts with the residue going to his trust,[9] but instead they included the house with his other lands which they were holding for the minority of his nephew, Lord Albemarle Bertie, second son of the duke of Ancaster, to whom he had devised his real estate. In 1750–1 the trustees and Lord Albemarle conveyed the house, by then called Lindsey House, to trustees for Nikolaus Ludwig, count of Zinzendorf, patron of the Society of *Unitas Fratrum* or the Moravian Church.[10] Zinzendorf, who also took a 91-year lease of the Beaufort House estate from Sir Hans Sloane,[11] bought the property to make it the headquarters of the Moravian Church, and lived there, making considerable alterations especially to the roof,[12] but after he returned to the Continent in 1755 the projected plans for a Moravian settlement failed. Lindsey House was sold in 1774 to Charles Cole, carpenter, Thomas Bannister, bricklayer, and Thomas Skinner, auctioneer,[13] who divided the house into five, subsequently seven, dwellings and made other alterations; the house was then known as Lindsey Row.[14] Some houses were sold,[15] but Skinner and Bannister were still owners of four, one occupied by Lady Hamilton, in 1780,[16] and Bannister still had a house, coachhouse, stables and 'field behind' in 1795.[17]

1 PRO, C 66/2268, no. 24; CP 25/2/324/20JASIEASTER.
2 PRO, CP 25/2/458/14CHASITRIN; C 66/3126, no. 17; *DNB.*
3 PRO, PROB 11/250, f. 299.
4 Lysons, *Environs*, II. 127.
5 *Cal. SP Dom.* 1671, 187; *Cal. Treas. Bks*, III(2), 799; PRO, C 66/3126, no. 17; C 10/92/81.
6 PRO, PROB 11/463, f. 191.
7 MLR 1717/4/24.
8 PRO, CP 25/2/1037/13GEOIHIL.
9 PRO, PROB 11/636, f. 296v.
10 CL, deed 3155; *Fetter Lane Moravian Cong.* 23.
11 MLR 1750/1/487; above, Beaufort.
12 *Survey of London*, IV. 36.
13 CL, deed 3155; *Fetter Lane Moravian Cong.* 23.
14 *Survey of London*, IV. 36–7, 40.
15 CL, deeds 3154–6.
16 LMA, MR/PLT 4598.
17 CL, deed 17552, p. 11.

The House

The old house itself, to which pasturage rights for two cows and a heifer were attached, may have been pulled down by 1664: a transcription from court books of 1663–4 gives a rather ambiguous reference to a house losing its right of common when demolished until a new one is built, which may refer to Sir Theodore Mayerne's but in any case does not definitely say the old house had been demolished before that date.[1] It also leaves open the question of whether Lindsey's house was an entirely new structure or incorporated any part of the earlier building, occupied by Sir Theodore Mayerne 1639–55: some sources also suggest that Sir Theodore rebuilt the house. It is thought, perhaps based on a datestone of 1674, re-cut or copied and inserted over no. 100 Cheyne Walk, that the later Lindsey House was rebuilt in its present external form by the 3rd earl of Lindsey in 1674.[2] However, Lord Lindsey's mortgage deed of 1671 suggests that a house was standing on the site by that date, and probably a new one, so that Lindsey House would be the house of 26 hearths for which Lord Lindsey was assessed in 1674, and Lord Robartes in 1666.[3] The thickness of some walls and general plan arrangement suggest that the existing house might incorporate the form of an early-17th century house, but there is no fabric of that date.[4] By *c.*1700 Lindsey House had the character of a magnificent town mansion on a relatively restricted site. In 1705 the house, then occupied by the countess dowager of Plymouth and her son Lord Windsor, was described as a 'fair handsome house . . . built in the modern manner' with a good frontage to the river.[5] By 1718 it was occupied by Francis, Lord Conway (d. 1732), *c.*1727 by the duchess of Rutland, a niece of the countess of Lindsey,[6] and in 1735 by 'Lady Fitzwater'.[7] Although altered in the 1750s and 1770s and divided into separate dwellings, and altered again in the 19th century, it still survived in 2003, as nos 95–100 Cheyne Walk.[8]

LOWNDES ESTATE

Two parcels of meadow lying either side of the Westbourne, formerly attached to the lazar house in Knightsbridge and probably belonging to Westminster Abbey before the Dissolution, were leased by the Crown in the late 16th century to Thomas Poultney (or Pulteney), lessee of other lands in Westminster.[9] The parcels were included in a further Crown lease granted to Michael Poultney by 1619, and described in 1650 as Great Spittle Meadow in the parish of Chelsea, containing 11 a. 2 r., and Little Spittle Meadow containing 8 a. 2 r., in the parish of St Martin-in-the-Fields adjoining the former on the south-east.[10] They were confirmed in the possession of Sir William Poultney (d. 1691) in 1660,[11] and in 1668 Sir William was granted a reversionary lease for 34 years of his land in St James, Westminster, and the Spittlefields in return for surrendering land in Westminster for Green Park.[12]

In 1692 Sir William's executors sold the lease to William Lowndes, financier and politician, who became Secretary to the Treasury in 1695. By that date the Spittlefields also included a house built by Henry Swindell, to whom the property was leased for £30 a year. In 1693 Lowndes petitioned for a further lease of the property including the Spittlefields, and was granted a 99-year lease from 1723 at 13s. 4d. a year.[13] He petitioned in 1723 to purchase from the Crown the reversionary freehold of the property, and the Act was passed permitting this sale by the Crown.[14]

William died in 1724 and the Knightsbridge property passed to his 3rd surviving son Charles (d. 1783), and to the latter's son William (d. 1808), but from 1805 was tied up in a trust after the threatened bankruptcy of William's son William (d. 1831).[15] Building on the estate was planned in 1826 but the land in Chelsea was only finally built over, with Lowndes Square, in the 1830s and 1840s.[16]

PHYSIC GARDEN

The Society or Company of Apothecaries, which became an independent society in 1607, leased for 61 years 3½ acres in Eastfield belonging to the manorial demesne and lying between the highway to Westminster and the Thames, initially to build a barge-house for the company's state barge.[17] The Society built three barge-houses in the south-east corner of the site by 1675, the easternmost housing the Society's state barge; the other two, which formed a double house separate from the first, were leased to various City companies.[18] The remaining land was used by the members who were the proprietors of the Laboratory stock, to grow medicinal herbs, and plants were transferred there from the Society's garden at Westminster. A wall was built around the Chelsea Garden in 1674 at the expense of 14 of the Society's members plus £50 from the proprietors of the

1 Ct Baron, 25 Feb. 1663/4, quoted in Dr King's MS, p. 59.

2 Faulkner, *Chelsea*, I. 77; *Survey of London*, IV. 39.

3 PRO, E 179/143/370, m. 5; E 179/252/32; below, Sloane Stanley.

4 *Survey of London*, IV. 35–7.

5 Bowack, *Antiquities*, 14.

6 *Survey of London*, IV. 39.

7 Poor rate bk, 1728–42, f. 388.

8 *Survey of London*, IV. 35–7, for this bldg hist.; see Fig. 51.

9 *Survey of London*, XXXI. 176–7; XLV. 19; BL, Lansd. MS 71, no. 22.

10 PRO, E 317/Middx/39, f. 5.

11 *Cal. Treas. Bks*, 1660–67, 10.

12 *Cal. SP Dom.* 1667, 265; 1667–8, 514.

13 *Cal. Treas. Bks*, 1693–6, 30, 69–71; *Survey of London*, XLV. 31.

14 *Survey of London*, XXXI. 190; *CJ*, XX. 93, 127, 177.

15 Centre for Bucks. Studies, cal. of Lowndes of Chesham MSS.

16 Above, Settlement, 1680–1865 (Hans Town).

17 C. Welch, 'Hist. & Antiquities of Worshipful Soc. of Apothecaries', *TLMAS*, NS, I(7), 438–50; CL, deed 2997; P.É.F. Perrédès, *London Botanic Gardens* [1905–6], 53.

18 Guildhall MSS 8268 (Apothecaries' Soc. Recs), plan; leases 1738–1818; 17954.

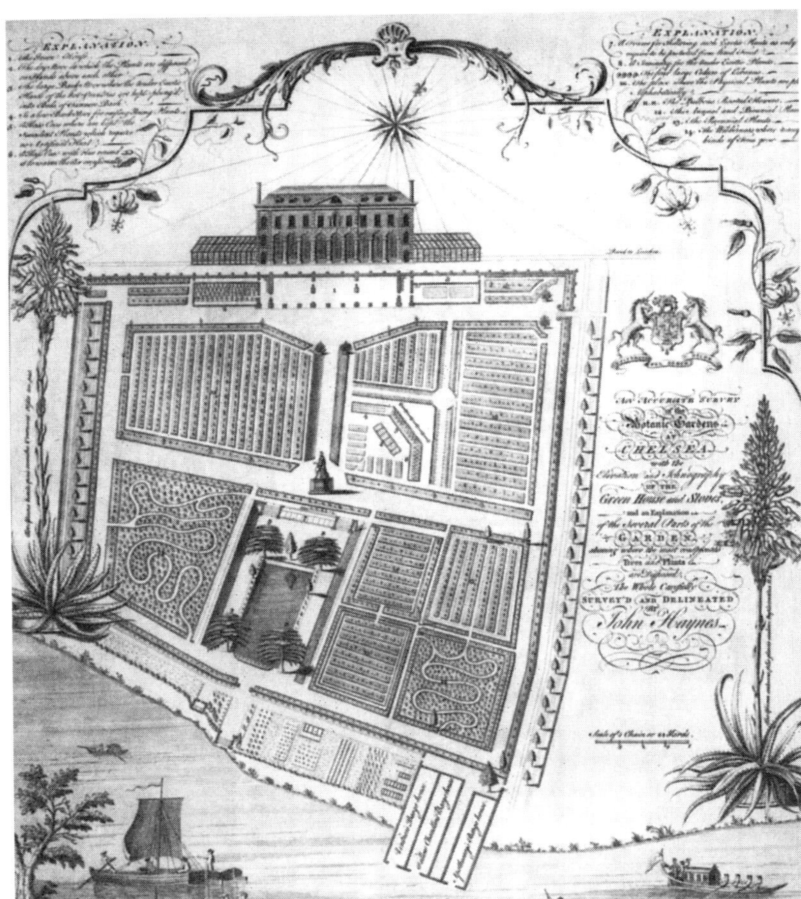

52. *Plan of the layout of the Physic Garden in 1751, showing the Greenhouse and stoves and location of principal trees and plants*

Laboratory stock in return for the privilege of growing herbs for their own use in the garden.[1] The garden soon became well known, visited by Paul Hermann, professor of Botany at Leiden University in 1683, John Evelyn, who described its heated conservatory in 1685, and Linnaeus in 1733.[2]

In 1722 Sir Hans Sloane conveyed the freehold to the Society in return for an annual rent charge of £5 and on certain conditions, chiefly the presentation of 50 different plants annually to the Royal Society until it had 2,000; in case of default Sloane's heirs were to hold the garden in trust for the Royal Society or Royal College of Physicians on similar terms. The rent charge does not appear to have been collected by Sloane or his successors, but by 1794 at least 2,550 specimen plants had been delivered.[3]

Under the Thames Embankment (Chelsea) Act of 1868, the Society of Apothecaries lost its river frontage to the new embankment but gained an additional 3,400 sq. ft of reclaimed land.[4] The physic garden remained the private research garden of the Apothecaries until the end of the 19th century, but because of financial difficulties the society contemplated giving it up. A local pressure group ensured the garden's survival and in 1899 its administration was transferred under a Charity Commission Scheme to the City Parochial Foundation, which ran it as a botanical research resource for various London colleges. In 1981 control passed to a newly-constituted independent charity which ran it as a research and educational resource, financing it by opening the gardens to the public, by letting part of the premises, and by using the gardens to house various public and private events.[5]

RANELAGH ESTATE

The Ranelagh estate, created out of land purchased for the Royal Hospital, in the early 18th century contained one of the most significant mansions in Chelsea. Richard Jones, 3rd Viscount Ranelagh, 1st earl of Ranelagh from 1677, was Paymaster-General of the Army and Treasurer of the Hospital from 1685 to 1702, responsible for the building and running of the Royal Hospital.[6] He designed a house for the Treasurer, which was built 1688–91 to the south-east of the Hospital buildings,[7]

1 Perrédès, *London Botanic Gardens*, 53.

2 A.P. Paterson, 'Chelsea Physic Gdn', *Chelsea Soc. Rep.* (1977), 63–9; see Fig. 52.

3 Perrédès, *London Botanic Gardens*, 56–7; LMA, MDR/MB/287; Lysons, *Environs*, II. 166.

4 Guildhall MS 9270.

5 *Chelsea Soc. Reps.* (1977), 63–9; (1993), 43–6.

6 Dean, *Royal Hosp.* 95. For his career see *Hist. of Parl. Commons, 1660–1690*, II. 661–3; *1690–1715*, IV. 520–7.

7 Bowack, *Antiquities*, 14; C.G.T. Dean, 'Lord Ranelagh's House in Chelsea', *TLMAS*, NS, VII(13), 210–1.

and was already planting orchards and walling gardens in 1690 when he obtained a lease of 7½ acres of the Hospital's lands for 61 years at £15 7s. 6d. a year to the Hospital.[1] In 1693 he leased another 15 acres for 58 years at £30 4s. 6d.,[2] and in 1696 he obtained a 99-year lease of the total 22½ acres for £5 a year.[3] Pleading the loss of his Irish property in the late Irish war, he successfully petitioned for the freehold of his Chelsea estate so that he could make a family settlement,[4] and in 1698 the Crown granted to Ranelagh's trustees the freehold of the leased 22½ acres and an additional 5 acres of Crown land, called St James's Acres, adjoining it on the east side of the Westbourne in the parish of St Martin-in-the-Fields, all held of the manor of East Greenwich in free socage on payment of £5 a year to the Royal Hospital.[5] The grounds, converted to orchards and formal tree-lined and walled gardens, formed the setting for the house, a substantial brick building of two storeys and attics with a pedimented centre, entered from the garden by stone steps. Inside it had a painted staircase and wainscotting of Norway oak.[6] In 1710 a visitor considered the estate, with its views over the Thames and towards London, to be 'one of the most costly and elegant in all England'.[7]

In 1695 Ranelagh made a settlement for the benefit of his two daughters, with the residue left as a charity for the Royal Hospital.[8] However, in 1702 the commissioners of accounts found his accounts as Paymaster-General were about 10 years in arrears; this together with large sums of money issued throughout the war led to rumours of embezzlement running into millions of pounds. He was expelled from the House of Commons and forced to resign his post on the grounds of misapplying public money, mainly as part of an attack by the Tories against the previous administration: no real evidence of misappropriation or embezzlement was put forward then or in a second report in 1704. He spent the rest of his life trying to settle his accounts, and died in 1712 leaving the large debt to the Exchequer hanging over his estate;[9] his attempts to sell Chelsea and his other property to pay off his debts were unsuccessful because of the fear that the Crown would seize them for the debt.[10] His daughter Catherine (d. 1740) continued to live in the house, but his debts were such that there was an unsuccessful attempt in 1717 to pass a bill to sell the estates.[11] Eventually in 1730 trustees for the Chelsea estate were appointed by Parliament, and the estate was sold in ten lots in 1733.[12] The largest section, 12¾ acres including Ranelagh House and the Avenue from the house to the highway at Ebury, was bought by Benjamin Timbrell, master builder, and James Swift,[13] partly as building land, but most of it, including the house, was leased out to create Ranelagh pleasure gardens, which opened in 1742.[14] In 1742 the Royal Hospital used Ranelagh's legacy to purchase 4 acres of his former estate, which became the Governor's Meadow.[15]

Subscriptions were raised to finance the pleasure gardens, and after the bankruptcy of the remaining lessee of the grounds, 36 shares in the property were issued to the proprietors.[16] Sir Thomas Robinson (d. 1777), a wealthy London merchant who was instrumental in promoting the gardens, held several of the shares, and by 1767 had built a large house called Prospect Place to his own design to the east of the rotunda.[17] After his death his house and shares were bought by the proprietors, and by 1793 the freehold of almost all the pleasure gardens was vested in Tompkins Dew and Albany Wallis as trustees for the proprietors.[18] Ranelagh Gardens closed in 1803 and Ranelagh House and rotunda were demolished in 1805.[19] The Royal Hospital purchased another 6¾ acres of the Ranelagh estate, including the site of the 'place of amusement', from G.W. Bulkley in 1826.[20]

The Wilford/Brett Estate

One of the 36 proprietors of the Ranelagh estate in 1777 was Edward Wilford, who held a parcel of the former Ranelagh estate next to that of Robinson, as well as land adjoining Ranelagh on the east side of the parish boundary.[21] In 1788 Wilford conveyed his share of the Ranelagh estate to his son Richard,[22] who as General Richard Wilford purchased most of the remainder of the Ranelagh estate, demolished Prospect Place, and built another house for himself, three-storeyed with a 100-ft frontage, parapet roof, and cupola, on an adjacent site. The estate was broken up after his death in 1822, but part including his house passed to the Brett family, who may have been related.[23] The Revd Joseph George Brett (d. 1852) owned 10 acres on the eastern border of the Ranelagh estate in 1847.[24] Wilford's house was demolished to make way for Chelsea Bridge Road in 1854,[25]

1 *Cal. Treas. Bks*, 1689–92, 541, 553; Dean, *Royal Hosp.* 154.
2 *Cal. Treas. Bks*, 1693–6, 215, 227; PRO, E 371/950, rot. 14.
3 PRO, E 371/953, rot. 58. Ranelagh Ho. is shown at top left of Hosp. in Fig. 16.
4 *Cal. Treas. Bks*, 1697–1702, 37.
5 PRO, C 66/3398, no. 18.
6 Dean, *Royal Hosp.* 153–4, illus. p. 145; *Survey of London*, XI, plate 8.
7 Quoted in Dean, *Royal Hosp.* 158.
8 PRO, C 7/290/40.
9 *Hist. of Parl. 1690–1715, Commons*, IV. 525–7.
10 Dean, *Royal Hosp.* 164.
11 Ibid., 224; *MSS of HL*, XII. 431; *LJ*, XX. 597.
12 Dean, *Royal Hosp.* 224; LMA, MDR/MB/1734/1/145–6, 179, 208–9, 276–7; ibid., /4/122–3, 332–3; ibid., /5/344–5.
13 LMA, MDR/MB/1734/1/145–6.
14 Below, Soc. Hist., social (Ranelagh).
15 Hutt, *Royal Hosp.* 96, 327, 1859 map.
16 Lysons, *Environs*, II. 174; MLR 1778/4/325; 1788/8/260.
17 Dean, *Royal Hosp.* 226–7; MLR 1767/4/385–7.
18 Lysons, *Environs*, II. 174.
19 Dean, *Royal Hosp.* 227.
20 Hutt, *Royal Hosp.* 328, 1859 map.
21 CL, deed 17553; Dean, *Royal Hosp.*, 1777 plan opp. p. 145.
22 MLR 1788/8/260.
23 Dean, *Royal Hosp.* 227, 282.
24 CL, Tithe Map and Award.
25 Dean, *Royal Hosp.* 227.

and in 1857 Brett's son, Wilford George Brett, and other trustees sold to the Royal Hospital 3 acres forming a strip along the south-west side of Chelsea Bridge Road, which was inclosed into the Hospital's grounds.[1]

Chelsea Barracks The War Office, which originally planned Chelsea Barracks to face the river at what is now the lower end of Ranelagh Gardens, built them instead in 1860–2 on the eastern section of the Brett estate, east of Chelsea Bridge Road.[2] In 1959–60 the barracks were demolished and replaced in 1962 with new accommodation, including a 700-ft long building for other ranks, and two 14-storeyed blocks of flats for married quarters, designed by Tripe and Wakeham under the direction of Sir Donald Gibson.[3]

THE ROYAL HOSPITAL ESTATE

King James's Theological College

A college of divinity to defend the protestant religion was promoted by Dr Matthew Sutcliffe, Dean of Exeter, and supported by James I, who laid the foundation stone of the college building in Chelsea in 1609, and granted a charter of incorporation in 1610. The king also endowed the college with the reversion of 27 acres of Chelsea manorial demesne in the south-east of the parish, consisting of Stonybridge Close (4 a. meadow), Thamesshot (20 a. arable), and 3 a. arable in Eastfield on the west side of Thamesshot, stretching westward from the Westbourne and lying on the south side of the road from Westminster to Chelsea.[4] The earl and countess of Nottingham, who then held the manor for the life of the countess and for a 40-year term after her death, surrendered their interest in the 27 acres in return for £7 10s. a year to the Crown as holder of Chelsea manor.[5] By the 1630s the college was being treated as one manorial lease among many, the provost paying £7 10s. a year for the college buildings and 6 acres around them, while the rest of the land was leased out to other farmers,[6] and the college and its lands were included in the conveyance of the lease for life and 40-year term of the manor by Monson and his wife to James, marquess of Hamilton, to whom the freehold of the manor was granted by the Crown in 1638.[7] In 1647, by which time it was claimed that no such college at Chelsea had been created,[8] there was a case in Chancery over title between Monson and his second wife and the provost, Samuel Wilkinson.[9] In 1651, when the Commonwealth authorities were considering using the college buildings to house prisoners, they conceded Wilkinson's claim,[10] but when the estate was surveyed the next year, the buildings and the 27 acres were deemed to be in the possession of the Commonwealth because the college was discontinued.[11] Only one wing of the proposed college buildings had ever been built, measuring 130 ft by 33 ft in 1652.[12]

At the Restoration the college's farmland was listed by the Hamilton estate as part of the property from which payment of Monson's mortgage was taken. The college itself, described as a large house, and its 6-acre grounds were in hand, valued at £1,000.[13] Among various claimants to the buildings was John Sutcliffe, nephew of the first provost, who was granted the property, with power to sell, in 1664,[14] but the grant was stopped when the Royal Society petitioned for the college.[15] The grant to the Royal Society of the lands granted by James I to the College was authorized in 1666, and passed in 1668, to be held in socage of the manor of East Greenwich.[16] Hamilton's heirs in 1667 assigned their rights in the lease of Chelsea College and 5 acres for the residue of the 40-year lease and all other claims to their agent, Andrew Cole, who in 1668 assigned all interests to the Royal Society.[17] The royal grant was formally confirmed in March 1669, with the proviso that the Society should not sell or alienate the lands.[18]

The Royal Hospital

In 1682 the Royal Society sold the estate back to the king for his new Royal Hospital.[19] The Hospital was planned on a much more lavish scale than the college, however, with a building 240 feet long being built by early 1683,[20] and more land was needed, especially to give a frontage to the river. Several purchases of manorial demesne were made from Charles Cheyne: 21 a., probably Thamesmead, between the original 27 a. and the river in 1682;[21] 6 a. known as Sweed or Swede Court on the west side of the college site in 1686;[22] 13 a. of Eastfield on the north side of the Hospital, which formed Burton's Court, in

1 MLR 1857/13/452; PRO, C 54/7411, m. 38; Hutt, *Royal Hosp.* 97, 329.

2 Dean, *Royal Hosp.* 285.

3 *The Times*, 19 Mar. 1959; Chelsea cuttings: Chelsea Barracks.

4 BL, Add. Ch. 18205; Add. MS 15609, f. 18; PRO, E 317/MIDDX/8; *Survey of London*, XI. 1.

5 Hutt, *Royal Hosp.* 90.

6 Thamesshot, then 17½ a., was leased from 1632 to Pet. and Rob. Sewell, and Stonybridge Close from 1637 to Hen. Ashton: NRA(S) 332, E1/7–8.

7 Hutt, *Royal Hosp.* 122; above, Chelsea man.

8 *Acts & Ordinances of the Interregnum*, ed. C.H. Firth and R.S. Rait, I. 915.

9 Hutt, *Royal Hosp.* 91–2.

10 With the proviso 'unless the law orders otherwise': *Cal. SP Dom.* 1651, 453, 463.

11 PRO, E 317/MIDDX/8; S.J. Madge, 'Rural Middx under the Commonwealth', *TLMAS*, NS, IV(10), 427–8.

12 PRO, E 317/MIDDX/8; above, Settlement, to 1680.

13 NRA(S) 332, L2/110 (ES 15/6/16).

14 *Cal. SP Dom.* 1663–4, 384, 485; 1665–6, 163.

15 Ibid., 1663–4, 610.

16 Ibid., 1666–7, 247; 1667–8, 227.

17 Hutt, *Royal Hosp.* 122.

18 *Cal. SP Dom.* 1668–9, 258.

19 *Cal. Treas. Bks*, 1681–5, 383.

20 Ibid., 790.

21 Ibid. 1685–9, 1350; Hutt, *Royal Hosp.* 131.

22 Hutt, *Royal Hosp.* 95, 221–3, 327. Old red brick wall between Gt and Lt. Sweed Cts became Hosp. boundary, still existing in 1950: Dean, *Royal Hosp.* 113.

1687.[1] The Crown also bought 10 a. which formed the detached triangle of Kensington parish by the Thames from William Greene of Westminster in 1685:[2] 1 r. 26 p. of that was conveyed to Cheyne to tidy up the boundaries.[3] In 1687 a two- or three-acre parcel of meadow belonging to the manor of Ebury (Westm.) was purchased from Sir Thomas Grosvenor, Bt,[4] and a small piece of glebe was leased to the Hospital, probably by 1692, for the Royal Avenue.[5] Charles Cheyne died before a proper conveyance was made, but an Act of 1707 confirmed the purchases and authorized final payment to William Cheyne, making some boundary adjustments in which just under half an acre was transferred to the earl of Carbery.[6]

The Crown granted leases in 1690 of parts of the Hospital's estate not required for the building and grounds. On the west side 4½ a. were leased for the house and grounds which became Walpole House, while on the south-east side 7½ a. were leased for Ranelagh House, to which another 15 a. was added in 1693. The Walpole House land was returned to the uses of the Hospital in 1808 and 1889, but the freehold of the Ranelagh land was granted away in 1698.[7] In 1742 the Commissioners of the Hospital repurchased 4 a. of the Ranelagh land, lying between the Hospital and the river and known as Governor's Meadow,[8] another 6¾ a., including the site of the rotunda, in 1826, and 3 a. adjoining Chelsea Bridge Road in 1857.[9] Some 4¾ a. east of the parish boundary in the parish of St George's Hanover Square, were purchased for the Hospital from the Grand Waterworks Company in 1843, and another 3 a. from the Royal Commissioners of Works and Buildings in 1858, including land reclaimed from the river during the building of the Embankment.[10]

Initially the Royal Hospital was managed by commissioners who included the Paymaster-General, and from 1702 an independent Board of Commissioners was appointed by letters patent, who managed not only the Hospital but all army pensions.[11] Management of the Hospital property passed on the abolition of the office of Clerk of Works in 1837 to the Office of Works,[12] and then by 1847 to the Commissioners of the Queen's Woods, Forests and Land Revenues, whence it was transferred by Act in 1875 to the Commissioners of Chelsea Hospital.[13] By 1872 the Royal Hospital estate totalled 61¼ a., including 3½ a. leased for Gordon House, 1½ a. outside the parish boundary also leased out, and 6¾ a. outside the parish boundary which formed the south-east corner of the estate in the angle formed by Chelsea Bridge Road and Chelsea Embankment.[14] In 1947 the Hospital bought the freehold of the small piece of glebe at Royal Avenue.[15]

Walpole House

In 1690 the Crown granted to William Jephson, Secretary to the Treasury, a 61-year lease of 4½ a. of Great Sweed Court, on the west side of the Hospital's outbuildings, containing an old brick tenement which Jephson intended demolishing and replacing with a house and garden.[16] He died the following year before he could build, and left the estate to his widow Mary, who in 1696 with her second husband Sir John Awbrey, Bt, assigned the residue of the lease to Charles Hopson, Deputy Clerk of Works. Hopson may have been acting on behalf of Edward Russell, earl of Orford, as he assigned the lease to him, and Orford's ownership was later confirmed by an Act of 1708.[17] When Orford acquired the estate there was no house on it, and he requested permission *c.*1696 to occupy Hopson's rooms in the south-west corner of the stables, which bordered the Jephson lease. He enlarged the accommodation at the Hospital's expense, with additional rooms, garrets, coachhouses, and basement, and laid out a garden on the 4½ a. with a gazebo on the riverbank.[18] In 1703 the lodgings which Orford had adapted were given to the new Treasurer of the Hospital, the previous Treasurer's house having been retained by Lord Ranelagh. Orford tried to regain them with a lease in 1708, claiming that the land he had acquired from Jephson's executors was too small for a house, but the Board refused, and the house, now known as the Treasurer's Lodgings, passed to Robert Walpole in 1714 on his appointment as Paymaster-General. Walpole began making improvements, designed by Sir John Vanbrugh, building new coachhouses and stables and enlarging the small walled garden.[19]

Having failed to get his lodgings back, in 1714 Orford granted the remaining years he held in the Jephson lease to Richard Gough,[20] who had just acquired the mansion and grounds adjoining to the west,[21] and who paid the rent to the Hospital until 1719.[22] Walpole, having

1 Hutt, *Royal Hosp.* 95, 221–3, 327.
2 Ibid., 137–9; above, Arnold.
3 Hutt, *Royal Hosp.* 327; *Cal. Treas. Bks*, 1685–9, 818; see Fig. 16.
4 Hutt, *Royal Hosp.* 327.
5 Hosp. pd £3 p.a. rent to the rector: Guildhall MS 9628/5/3; Dr King's MS, pp. 37, 40; Hutt, *Royal Hosp.* 94–5.
6 Act 5 & 6 Anne c. 60; *MSS of HL*, VII. 83–4; Hutt, *Royal Hosp.* 221–3; above, Gough.
7 Below, (Walpole Ho.; Gordon Ho.); above, Ranelagh.
8 Hutt, *Royal Hosp.* 327, 1859 map.
9 Ibid., 328–9, 1859 map; Dean, *Royal Hosp.* 285; Act 5 Geo. IV, c. 107; below, (Wilford/Brett).
10 Hutt, *Royal Hosp.* 328–9, 1859 map; Dean, *Royal Hosp.* 284–5.
11 Hutt, *Royal Hosp.* 103.
12 Dean, *Royal Hosp.* 283.
13 38 & 39 Vic. c. 118 (Local).
14 Hutt, *Royal Hosp.* 329 and 1872 map.
15 C.G.T. Dean, 'The Royal Avenue', *Chelsea Soc. Rep.* (1959), 54–5.
16 *Cal. Treas. Bks*, 1689–92, 620, 685.
17 Hutt, *Royal Hosp.* 221–3; Act 6 & 7 Anne c. 24 (Private).
18 Dean, *Royal Hosp.* 116.
19 Ibid., 201–2.
20 MLR 1714/2/86.
21 Above, Gough Ho.
22 Hutt, *Royal Hosp.* 310–1.

obtained a lease of the Treasurer's Lodgings, is said to have persuaded Gough to join with him in getting Orford to assign the Crown lease to them both, with Walpole taking possession of most of the 4½ a., leaving to Gough some stables he had built near the highway and Lord Orford's gazebo near the river.[1] Walpole obtained a further Crown lease of the estate and of the Treasurer's lodgings for 29 years after the expiry, in 1751, of the original term, as well as leases of some of the Hospital's outbuildings in the stable yard.[2] The latter were necessary to allow major extensions to be made to the Treasurer's Lodgings 1720–3, with a new wing making the whole building **Z**-shaped, and it was subsequently known as Walpole House. Walpole again employed Vanbrugh for the alterations and to design garden buildings, including an octagon where Walpole entertained royalty in 1729.[3] Walpole also leased 16 a. on the south side of King's Road 1724–5,[4] abutting west on Robinson's Lane (Flood Street).

In 1742 Walpole (d. 1745) was created earl of Orford and retired to Houghton (Norf.);[5] the Chelsea house was occupied by the duke of Newcastle. In 1749 Walpole House estate was leased by the Crown for 50 years to John Murray, earl of Dunmore (d. 1752), at the nomination of Robert Walpole, 3rd earl of Orford;[6] there was an adjustment of boundaries with the Royal Hospital at the same time. After Dunmore's death his executors let the house to Viscount Palmerston from 1754 to 1757, and to the duke of Norfolk in 1758. In 1759 they sold the leasehold estate for £2,700 to George Aufrere, a London merchant and art connoisseur, who in 1760 obtained from the Crown an additional 10-year lease to run from 1799, and another in 1776 for 15 years from 1810;[7] he also leased 16½ a. of manorial demesne.[8] In 1796 he assigned the leases of Walpole House to his son-in-law, Charles Anderson-Pelham, Lord Yarborough, who granted Aufrere and his wife a life interest.[9] In 1808 Yarborough sold the outstanding leases back to the Crown so that the Hospital could be given full possession.[10]

The Royal Hospital retained the northern part of the estate, which was used for additional buildings including a new infirmary, built 1808–12 by Sir John Soane, Clerk of Works, and incorporating part of Walpole House. The building was extended in 1868–9, and only that later part survived bombing in 1941; by 1980 it was the site of the National Army Museum.[11]

Gordon House

Soane's original plans for the infirmary incorporated the whole of the 4½ a. of Walpole House, but had to be altered when in 1810 a Crown lease was granted of 3½ a. at the southern end of the estate to Lieut.-Col. James Willoughby Gordon, who had already commissioned Thomas Leverton to build Gordon House there: the yellow-brick house was used for the entertainment of grandees, including the Tsar of Russia, in 1814, and additions were made in 1825 and in 1931–2.[12] The lease lapsed in 1889, and *c.*1893 the house became a home for the Hospital's infirmary nurses.[13]

SHREWSBURY OR ALSTON HOUSE

Shrewsbury House, a courtyard building with 1½ acres of grounds, may have been built well before the 16th century: illustrations of the house made shortly before its demolition suggest an earlier building, perhaps timber framed, which was faced with brick in the 16th century and had subsequent alterations.[14] The owners were freeholders of Chelsea manor in the 16th century and had commoning rights, suggesting a medieval origin for the holding.[15] In the early 16th century the house belonged to George Talbot, 4th earl of Shrewsbury (d. 1538), steward of the household of Henry VIII, and he occasionally resided there; his son Richard was born in Chelsea in 1519.[16] George was succeeded by his son, Francis (d. 1560), 5th earl, who was listed among the freeholders of Chelsea in 1543,[17] and his entry into Chelsea accompanied by 140 horse was described in 1551.[18] His son George (d. 1590), 6th earl, dated letters from Chelsea in the 1580s which refer to his longing to be in the country, and make it clear he was only in Chelsea because of his duties at court.[19] Under a settlement the house passed at his death to his formidable widow Elizabeth (Bess of Hardwick),[20] and when she died in 1608 it passed under her will to her son William Cavendish (d. 1626), created earl of Devonshire in 1618.[21] His wife Elizabeth wrote to Lionel Cranfield in 1624 of her affection for the friends she had in Chelsea,[22] and she lived there after her husband's death until her own in 1643.[23]

1 Dean, *Royal Hosp.* 203.
2 PRO, E 367/4730; 367/7127; Dean, *Royal Hosp.* 204; *Cal. Treas. Bks*, 1742–4, 108.
3 Holme, *Chelsea*, 88–9.
4 MLR 1725/1/222–4.
5 *Complete Peerage*, X. 77–81; *DNB.*
6 PRO, E 367/7415; *Complete Peerage*, IV. 543.
7 PRO, E 367/7219, /7415; Hutt, *Royal Hosp.* 310–1.
8 MLR 1835/4/726.
9 MLR 1796/2/732–3; *Complete Peerage*, XII(2), 884.
10 PRO, E 367/6452.
11 D. Stroud, 'Sir John Soane and the Royal Hosp.', *Chelsea Soc. Rep.* (1980), 45–7; M. Richardson, 'Soane in Chelsea', *Chelsea Soc. Rep.* (1992), 45–51.
12 Dean, *Royal Hosp.* 256–8; PRO, E 367/6452; *CJ*, LXIV. 229, 284, 301.
13 Dean, *Royal Hosp.* 287.
14 See Fig. 7.
15 PRO, SC 2/188/42; Dr King's MS, pp. 58–9.
16 Lysons, *Environs*, II. 78–9.
17 PRO, SC 2/188/42.
18 *Diary of Hen. Machyn 1550–63*, ed. J.G. Nicholas (Camden Soc. XLII), 6.
19 HMC, *12th Rep.* pt. 4, pp. 171, 173, 175, 195, 199, 201, 213.
20 PRO, C 142/231/106.
21 *DNB* s.v. Eliz. Talbot; *Complete Peerage*, IV. 339.
22 Davies, *Greatest Ho.* 149–50.
23 Faulkner, *Chelsea*, I. 282.

The house was acquired by a London merchant, Joseph Alston, presumably by 1659 when the family is mentioned in the parish registers;[1] it is not known whether there was a connection with the Alstons who were trustees of the manor in the 1640s.[2] When Joseph's son Joseph married in 1662 the Chelsea property was described in the settlement as the mansion house where the elder Joseph lived and three other houses near it,[3] and Alston was assessed in 1666 for 21 hearths and as the owner of an empty house of 6 hearths.[4] He had pasturage rights in 1664 and 1674.[5] By 1674 the house was apparently divided, with Alston and 'Esquire Maynard' next to him assessed at 16 hearths each in addition to the smaller house, now 8 hearths.[6] In 1684 Alston House, as it was now usually called, was still occupied as two dwellings, with part still the residence of the Alstons and the other part, in which Lady Bateman had once lived, occupied by Banaster Maynard for a rent of £100 a year. Sir Joseph, granted a baronetcy in 1681, by will proved 1688 left his 'great house at Chelsea' to his son Joseph on condition he allow Sir Joseph's second wife Anne to continue living there, with the use of a stable, hayloft, and coachhouse: his wife received 2 coaches and 2 horses as well as use of Alston's plate.[7] Anne (d. 1696) was very highly assessed on her personal estate in Chelsea in 1694,[8] where she was resident when she wrote her will.[9]

The property was in the possession of William Wollaston, clerk, *c.*1700 who with Anthony Roch conveyed it to Robert Butler.[10] Butler by will proved 1712 left it to his wife Martha (d. 1739) for life, and then to his son Edward.[11] Edward Butler, president of Magdalen College Oxford, in 1739 leased the whole building to two men, one of whom was occupying part, for 7 years with covenants to make substantial repairs to brickwork, tiled floors, and window frames. A plan of the 1½-acre estate shows the buildings on three sides of the courtyard, with the gateway, a butcher's shop, and slaughter house on the south side facing the river; on the north side of the house were gardens stretching north to the glebe, and a long narrow garden stretched eastwards from the northern end of the garden, behind the house and garden of the bishop of Winchester.[12] On Butler's death in 1745 the property passed to his daughter and heir Mary, who in 1747 married Philip Herbert (d. 1749), MP. In 1765 she married her first cousin Benjamin Tate,[13] who was taxed in 1780 for four properties in Chelsea, one of them large.[14] Mary died in 1798 without children, and the Chelsea estate together with the Tate estates she had inherited through her mother, Mary Tate (d. 1730), passed to George Tate, Benjamin's son by his first marriage. George died in 1822 devising his property in Chelsea and Brompton, including 9 acres near Blacklands, to his only child Mary for life, and then to his stepson Richard Moore and his children, the Revd John FitzMoore Halsey, Mary Bridget Moore, Charlotte Selina Hobart, Mary Jane Moore, and Edward FitzMoore. Mary Tate assigned her life interest to the Moore family in 1829.[15]

From the late 17th century the house had a variety of occupants, and was apparently divided into two dwellings by 1674. After Lady Alston's death it was apparently no longer occupied by its owners. From 1695 to 1713 it was occupied as a school run by Robert Woodcock (d. 1710) and his wife Deborah,[16] who were probably in residence in part of the house before Lady Alston died, as Robert was a witness to her will in April 1694.[17] In 1771 it was converted into a distillery,[18] and later housed a paper factory.[19] The house was pulled down and the materials sold in 1813 by the 'speculating builder' to whom George Tate presumably sold it.[20] The house was described *c.*1810 as an irregular brick building surrounding three sides of a quadrangle, with one room 120 ft long, carved oak wainscotting, panels painted with portraits, and a room which had been an oratory.[21] Remnants of Jacobean panelling supposedly belonging to the west wing of the house survived until 1934, embedded in nos 43–45 Cheyne Walk including Terrey's shop, which were either built on the site of a wing of the mansion, or possibly incorporated the original walls of the wing.[22] Later building revealed old brickwork, including splayed window surrounds and Tudor boundary walls.[23]

SLOANE STANLEY ESTATE

William Roper, listed as a free tenant of the manor in 1543,[24] in 1547 was said to hold for life a house and close called Butts close, with houses built there, a barn, and garden, rent-free by gift of his father-in-law Sir Thomas More. The property, called the Morehouse in 1617, was supposed to revert to More's main estate after Roper's

1 Davies, *Chelsea Old Ch.* 273.
2 Above, Chelsea man.
3 LMA, Q/HAL/19.
4 PRO, E 179/252/32/40, f. 23.
5 Dr King's MS, pp. 58–9.
6 LMA, MR/TH 45.
7 PRO, PROB 11/291, f. 232v.; *Burke's Extinct and Dormant Baronetcies* (1838), 6.
8 Corp. of London RO, Assessments Box 43, MS 20.
9 PRO, PROB 11/432, f. 162.
10 Dr King's MS, p. 38; PRO, CP 25/2/946/7ANNEEASTER.
11 Davies, *Chelsea Old Ch.* 273.
12 CL, deed 2900.
13 Inf. on Tate fam. from Burke, *Hist. of the Commoners*, ii. 491–2.
14 LMA, MR/PLT 4598.
15 CL, deed 2897.
16 *Survey of London*, II. 80; below, Soc. Hist., educ. (private schs).
17 PRO, PROB 11/432, f. 162.
18 Beaver, *Memorials*, 199.
19 Lysons, *Environs*, II. 79.
20 Faulkner, *Chelsea*, I. 282.
21 Ibid., 277.
22 *Chelsea Soc. Reps.* (1928), 131; (1933), 19; (1934), 13–14.
23 *Survey of London*, II. 76; *Chelsea Soc. Reps.* (1937), 16; (1957), 43, 45.
24 PRO, SC 2/188/42–3.

death,[1] in 1578, but it was not specified in the grant by Cecil to Henry Fiennes, 2nd earl of Lincoln, in 1599. The Roper family seem to have continued to have at least a leasehold interest in it: Lord Lincoln was said to have bought it from 'Mr Roper',[2] and Anthony and Henry Roper, presumably descendants of William and Margaret, assigned leases to the earl. It passed with Lincoln's principal estates to his heir Thomas, 3rd earl (d. 1619), who in 1617 sold the Morehouse to Sir John Danvers, to whom the Roper leases were also assigned. The estate comprised the house and a two-acre close of pasture with barns, stables, and other buildings.[3] Some difficulty ensued between Danvers, Sir Arthur Gorges, and Lincoln's heirs over a garden plot occupied with Danvers House, which Danvers subsequently found belonged to Gorges as part of More's estate;[4] in 1623 Theophilus, 4th earl of Lincoln, confirmed the sale to Danvers but minus the garden plot.[5]

According to Aubrey, Danvers 'had a very fine fancy, which lay (chiefly) for gardens and architecture': he had travelled in Italy and was credited with introducing Italian-style gardens to England.[6] John Thorpe produced drawings of a house on the property, which he probably designed.[7] Danvers House was a compact villa in Italian mannerist style, planned on an axis of hall and staircase; its deep cellars were uncovered when Crosby Hall was transferred to the site in 1909. The English sculptor, Nicholas Stone, was working on statues for the garden in 1622.[8] Pepys, who visited in 1661, described Danvers House as 'the prettiest contrived house that ever I saw in my life'.[9]

In 1652 Danvers, who had been deeply in debt for many years, settled some lands on trustees to pay his debts and the rest on his son Henry, and died in 1655 leaving his personal estate to his wife and infant son John. Henry, who was heir to his uncle, the earl of Danby, died before his father, in November 1654,[10] and left both the lands settled on him and those to which he was heir to his sister Anne and her heirs, and also appointed her as executrix.[11] After Sir John's death, however, there may have been a further settlement of lands, though Anne still received the Chelsea estate.[12] Anne died in 1659 a few months after her husband, Sir Henry Lee, Bt, leaving her lands and leases to trustees, and her two infant children, Eleanor and Anne, and her goods to the care of her mother-in-law Anne, countess of Rochester.[13] In 1661 the estate, described as the house where Danvers had lived, then occupied by John Robartes, Lord Robartes and later earl of Radnor (d. 1685), and another house held by Richard Gilford and then Francis Gilford,[14] was forfeited to the Crown because Danvers had been a regicide.[15] The estates were still held by the Crown in 1670,[16] but seem to have been restored to the Lee heiresses by 1675.[17] In 1666 Lord Robartes occupied a house of 26 hearths in Chelsea, but its location in the tax assessment between Buckingham (Beaufort) House and Gorges House makes that more likely to have been Lindsey House.[18] However, the location in the list of the 48-hearth house occupied in 1666 by Charles Rich, 4th earl of Warwick, former brother-in-law and cousin by marriage of Robartes, and in 1674 by the Lord Chancellor (Sir Heneage Finch), makes that more likely to be Danvers House; it was the second largest house in Chelsea.[19] Lord Robartes continued to be named as in possession of the house,[20] and held a lease of the property, which was referred to as Lord Robartes' house in the 1670s, but he was not necessarily the occupant during that period. In 1673 the king and court were entertained there by the duke of Monmouth, and by the French ambassador.[21]

In 1668 the trustees for Anne Lee's daughters acquired 5 acres of the Buckingham House estate called Dovehouse or Dovecote Close, which lay north of Danvers House and gardens, and in 1670 they also bought the 40-acre Chelsea Park.[22] In 1672 Eleanor (d. 1691) married James Bertie, Lord Norreys or Norris, younger son of the earl of Lindsey and created earl of Abingdon in 1682, and in 1673 Anne (d. 1685) married Thomas Wharton (d. 1715), Lord Wharton, created earl of Wharton in 1706 and marquess of Wharton in 1715.[23] In 1681 the sisters and their husbands agreed to the equal partition of all their inherited estates and in 1685 the Chelsea property, consisting of Danvers House, Dovehouse Close, and Chelsea Park, was allotted to Anne Wharton for life with remainder to her husband.[24] Danvers House was later demolished and Wharton granted building leases for the site on which the southern end of Danvers Street was begun in 1696.[25] In

1 PRO, C 66/801, m. 38.
2 PRO, SP 14/97, f. 299.
3 CL, deed 2988. Wm and Marg. had 2 sons, Thos (d. 1598) and Anthony: *DNB* s.v. Roper.
4 PRO, C 78/224, no. 13; C 2/Jas.I/G3/12; C 3/306/31.
5 PRO, C 54/2558, no. 5.
6 *Aubrey's Brief Lives* (Penguin edn), 240.
7 *Walpole Soc.* XL (1964–6), 24, 48, plate 8.
8 *Survey of London*, IV. 11–12. Foundation walls, a large bath, and fragments of columns and capitals were found in 1822: Beaver, *Memorials*, 163.
9 *Diary of Sam. Pepys*, ed. R. Latham and W. Matthews, II. 187–8.
10 *Cal. Cttee Money*, I. 459–65; II. 1330; PROB 11/248, f. 2; *DNB*, s.v. Sir John Danvers.
11 PRO, PROB 11/246, f. 224v.
12 PRO, C 78/719, m. 38.
13 PRO, PROB 11/246, ff. 253–4.
14 PRO, E 178/6326.
15 PRO, C 78/719, m. 38; PROB 11/248, f. 2.
16 PRO, C 78/719, m. 38.
17 LMA, Q/HAL/20.
18 PRO, E 179/252/32/40, f. 24.
19 Ibid., f. 23 and v.; E 179/143/370, m. 5.
20 PRO, C 5/637/73.
21 *Complete Peerage*, IX. 713n.
22 CL, deed 2990; MLR 1737/2/587.
23 Davies, *Chelsea Old Church*, 136, 144, 188; *Complete Peerage*, I. 45; XII(2), 607.
24 PRO, C 5/637/73.
25 CL, deed 2991; above, Settlement, 1680–1865 (Chelsea village).

Chelsea from the Thames

1 *The World's End estate's towers among a variety of housing at the west end of the parish. Cheyne Walk (right) is lined with 19th-century houses, Brunel House flats, and Lindsey House (extreme right); the Moravian Tower lies behind*

2 *Nos 4–12 Chelsea Embankment, individual town houses built in the 1870s at the eastern end of the parish*

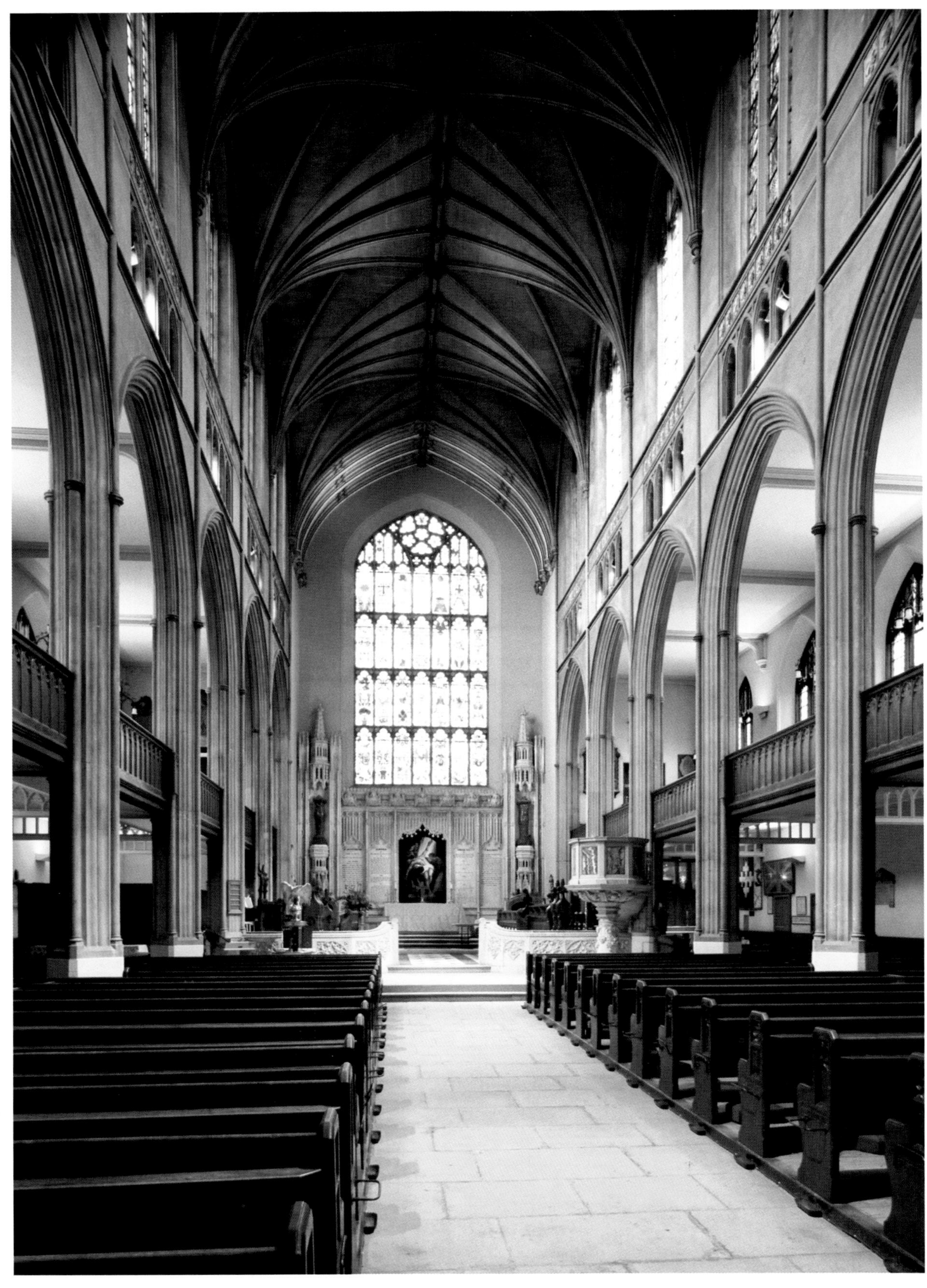

3 St Luke's parish church, Sydney Street, built 1820–4 to designs by James Savage, for its date an unusually ambitious example of the Gothic revival. The stone-vaulted nave looking east to the painting of 'The Entombment of Christ' (1823) by James Northcote, and the east window by Hugh Easton, installed in 1959

4 St Saviour's church (1839–40) set among the Italianate terraces of Walton Place and Street, built in the 1840s. Polychrome brick façade added in 1890

5 Holy Trinity church, Sloane Street, begun in 1888 and popularly known as the 'Cathedral of the Arts and Crafts Movement'; the nave looking north-east

6 *Gertrude Street, formerly Stanley Villas, looking east with villas (left) and later terraced houses (right). One of a group of unusually wide streets with a relaxed and spacious atmosphere*

7 *Carlyle Square (formerly Oakley Square), mid-19th century Italianate villas on the north side*

8 First Street viewed from the south: modest houses built in twos and threes by different lessees

9 Cheyne Row, nos 16–24, from the south, built 1708 but altered in the mid 19th-century with Italianate stucco and porticoes. No. 24, sixth from the south end, was the home of Thomas and Jane Carlyle

10 St Loo Mansions, on the north side of St Loo Avenue, one of the many blocks of mansion flats built in Chelsea from the late 19th century

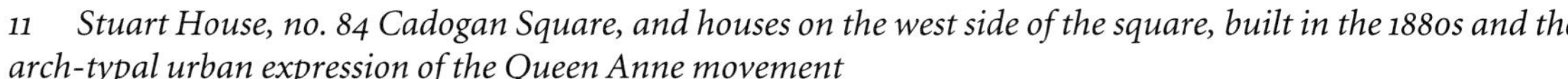

11 Stuart House, no. 84 Cadogan Square, and houses on the west side of the square, built in the 1880s and the arch-typal urban expression of the Queen Anne movement

12 Crosby Hall, Danvers Street, a 15th-century merchant's house moved from Bishopsgate, 1909, incorporated after 1988 into a re-creation of a Tudor courtyard house facing Cheyne Walk

13 Samuel Lewis Trust Dwellings, built from 1913 for working-class residents on a triangular site fronting Ixworth Place and Pond Street, formerly part of Chelsea common

14 The Vale, west side, individual houses built 1912–13 as a single picturesque composition

15 Sloane Square with the Royal Court Theatre (east), former Royal Court Hotel (north) and the tower of the First Church of Christ, Scientist, at the head of Sedding Street

16 Michelin House, no. 81 Fulham Road, garage and offices of the Michelin Tyre Company converted into restaurant, oyster bar, and shop in the 1980s. The Michelin man, Bibendum, figures here as it does in all the company's promotions

1717 the devisees of Thomas, marquess of Wharton, and Montagu Bertie, earl of Abingdon, the heirs of the Lee sisters, conveyed their interests in the Danvers estate to Sir Hans Sloane; the estate was described as the site of the mansion, its gardens, the site of former stables and coachway from Church Lane, houses held by Francis Gilford and Thomas Gilbanck or others, waste 60 ft by 40 ft enclosed by a brick wall and adjoining the Thames between the horseferry and the above houses, 11 brick houses in the tenure of Benjamin Stallwood in Danvers Street and facing the river, the 5-acre Dovehouse Close and the 40-acre Park both enclosed with brick walls.[1] The estate included pews in the parish church in 1719.[2]

A series of conveyances of the estate were made from 1719 between Sir Hans and his nephew, William Sloane junior (d. 1767),[3] who had bought up the building leases on the property.[4] Sir Hans settled it in 1726 to give his brother, William Sloane senior, the right to charge the lands with portions for his younger children, but in 1733 it was resettled on William Sloane junior, reserving the 11s. quitrent owing to Sir Hans as owner of Chelsea manor. In 1721 William Sloane or Sir Hans Sloane bought 2 houses at Little Chelsea and 18 a. stretching southwards to King's Road from Sir John Cope,[5] and they were also settled in 1733 on William Sloane.[6] William Sloane's estate passed to his son Hans (d. 1827), who added the name Stanley in 1821 after the death of Sarah D'Oyley, when he inherited Paultons (Hants.) and other property under the will of Hans Stanley (d. 1780).[7] The Sloane Stanley estates descended in direct male line to William (d. 1870), William Hans (d. 1879), Hans (d. 1888), and Roger Cyril Hans (d. 1944), who was succeeded by his daughters, Lavender Elizabeth, wife of John Everett, and Diana, wife of Elwyn Villiers Rhys.[8]

STANLEY HOUSE OR GROVE

Dudley, widow of Sir Robert Lane, by 1630 had bought from her mother, Lady Elizabeth Gorges, a little house called the Brickills with 6 acres, of which 4 acres had been inclosed from Westfield and were subject to lammas grazing rights; in 1630 Lady Lane agreed to give a rent of 20s. a year forever to the poor if she was permitted by the freeholders of Chelsea to enclose 3 acres of the lammas lands. She and her mother were presented to the Privy Council for inclosing the ground, which had been converted to gardens, but were supported by the inhabitants of Chelsea. Lady Lane also held another 11 a. inclosed from Westfield.[9] The property was the site of the later Stanley House, standing just north of King's Road at the western end of the parish. Later in 1630 Lady Lane sold to her mother a small house and half an acre adjoining it where pits had been dug, and one acre of pasture on the south side of Fulham Road, with access through Lady Lane's land from King's Road to the premises; and in 1631 she sold to her 220 rods of land recently converted into an orchard, also lying on the south side of Fulham Road and next to Lady Elizabeth's land;[10] both transactions are probably of parts of the Brickills property.

Lady Lane may have sold all of the Brickills back to her mother, as in 1637 Lady Elizabeth Gorges leased the Brickills and 5 acres to another daughter, Elizabeth widow of Sir Robert Stanley, for 31 years for payment of £20 a year to James Stanley, Elizabeth's second son.[11] Lady Stanley may have bought the freehold from her mother before 1643, when she was assessed in Chelsea for £60.[12] Lady Elizabeth Gorges, by will dated 1643, left her other property in Chelsea for the benefit of the children of her eldest son Arthur, on condition he did not try to claim the Brickills.[13] By 1646 Lady Stanley (d. 1675) had married her cousin Theophilus Fiennes, 4th earl of Lincoln (d. 1667),[14] and as Lady Lincoln she was assessed for 11 hearths in 1666,[15] being listed just before houses at Little Chelsea; she presumably lived in the house on the Brickills. The estate was inherited by her son, Sir Charles Stanley (d. 1676), and then successively by his sons Clinton (d. 1682) and William (d. 1691).[16]

The estate was described in the 1690s as a capital messuage and 7 acres with barns, stables, gardens and orchards. At the request of William Stanley, Thomas Panton had spent £2,000 by 1683 in rebuilding the house, later known as Stanley House, which was unfinished at William Stanley's death. Stanley married Panton's sister Dorothy, but she was presumably dead by 1691 when he made his will leaving the estate to his sister-in-law, Elizabeth Panton (d. 1700), who married Henry Arundell (d. 1726), 5th Lord Arundell of Wardour.[17] From 1703 to 1726 the house was occupied by Joseph Collins,[18] and from 1727 to 1751 by Thomas Arundell, a younger son of Lord Arundell, who seems to have been the owner.[19] The subsequent rate-payers for the house, John Jackson 1754–72, Mrs Frances Southwell 1773–5, and Miss Mary Southwell 1777, were probably also the owners.[20] Miss Southwell sold Stanley

1 MLR 1717/4/130; 1717/5/104–6; 1717/6/151.
2 MLR 1719/3/20.
3 Ibid., /23.
4 Above, Settlement, 1680–1865 (Chelsea village).
5 Above, Blake.
6 MLR 1733/1/364–6.
7 PRO, PROB 11/1063, ff. 102v.–3; above, Chelsea man.
8 *Burke's Landed Gentry* (1952 edn), 2388–9; KL, deed 35376.
9 PRO, SP 16/193, f. 101v.; rec. quoted by Faulkner, *Chelsea*, II. 106–7.
10 PRO, C 54/2845, no. 13; C 54/2852, no. 21.
11 Lease quoted by Faulkner, *Chelsea*, I. 57.
12 *Cal. Cttee Money*, I. 230.
13 Rec. quoted by Faulkner, *Chelsea*, I. 57; PRO, C 9/6/89.
14 *Complete Peerage*, VII. 690.
15 PRO, E 179/252/32/40, f. 25.
16 Stanley family tree in Davies, *Chelsea Old Ch.* 131.
17 PRO, C 8/531/65; C 10/243/62; C 10/289/4; *Complete Peerage*, I. 265–6.
18 BL, Add. MS 2934; Poor rate bks, 1707–16, pp. 2–12; 1716–27, p. 335; *Survey of London*, IV. 44.
19 Poor rate bks, 1728–42, f. 488; 1748–51, s.v. 22 Feb. 1750; MLR 1727/4/337–8; *Survey of London*, IV. 44.
20 *Survey of London*, IV. 44.

53. *Stanley House or Grove in the 1820s*

House in 1777 to the countess of Strathmore (d. 1800), an enthusiastic botanist who added conservatories to the house and raised exotics which were destroyed by her barbaric husband Andrew Robinson Bowes. After the marriage broke up the countess sold Stanley Grove in 1780 to Lewis Lochie or Lochée, founder of a military academy at Little Chelsea and a military adventurer who was executed by the Austrians in 1791.[1]

The estate was acquired *c.*1815 by William Hamilton, the English envoy at Naples, who had accompanied Lord Elgin to Greece and who built a large hall on the east side of the house to accommodate his antique casts, mentioned by Fanny Burney, who visited in 1821. In 1841 Hamilton sold the estate to the National Society, which built St Mark's College in the grounds and used Stanley House as the principal's residence.[2] When the college moved to Plymouth in 1973 the GLC purchased the estate, which was subsequently sold to Chelsea College.[3] After that college left, the buildings were threatened with demolition, but from *c.*1999 the college buildings were converted into residential accommodation, called Kings Chelsea, with the grove on the east side being kept for public access.[4]

Stanley House, 'in excellent condition and but little altered' *c.*1892,[5] had been considerably altered and was in a poor state of repair by 1991 when it was under threat of conversion to commercial offices. The square house, with characteristics of the 1680s when it was rebuilt, had two principal floors of equal grandeur linked by a spacious staircase, a hipped roof and dormer windows, surmounted by a leaded flat roof with a balustrade and cupola, and early 18th-century internal panelling.[6] It was exhaustively renovated by the developers of the estate *c.*2000, but no plans for its use were available in 2002.

WARTON ESTATE

In 1650 and 1651 Sir Michael Warton of Beverley (Yorks.) bought a considerable part of the Gorges estate in Chelsea and Kensington,[7] including in Chelsea 53½ a. arable and 3½ a. and 28 lots (*c.*7 a.) of meadow, mostly in Little Chelsea, Westfield, and Eastfield near Chelsea common; it was occupied by five lessees, two of whom had farmhouses in Little Chelsea.[8] After Sir Michael's death in 1655 his estates passed to his son Michael (d. 1688), and then to the latter's son Sir Michael (d. 1725). Sir Michael left his estates to his heirs, his three sisters Elizabeth (d. 1726), wife of Charles Pelham, Mary (d. *c.*1727), wife of Sir James Pennyman, Bt, and Susannah (d. 1737), wife of Sir John Newton, Bt; he appointed his nephew Michael Newton as his executor.[9] In 1775 an Act was passed for the partition of the Warton estates in Yorkshire, Lincolnshire, Middlesex and the City of London among the grandsons of the sisters, Charles Anderson-Pelham (d. 1823), later Lord Yarborough, Sir James Pennyman, Bt (d. 1808), and Michael Newton.[10]

Newton's portion included the 3½-acre close called Queen's Elm Field, at the junction of Upper Church Lane and Fulham Road, occupied by John Rubergall, gardener, and sold for building in 1792; the western portion became the Jews' burial ground.[11] Pennyman's portion, including property in Fulham, Kensington, and Holborn, with 1½ a. meadow by the Thames in Chelsea, was sold by auction in 1780.[12] The Kensington property

1 Faulkner, *Chelsea*, I. 59; *Chelsea Soc. Rep.* (1956), 24–35; below, Soc. Hist., educ. (private schs). Lysons quotes 'title deeds in possession of Mrs Lochée' which suggests that their title was to the freehold: *Environs*, II. 125.

2 Beaver, *Memorials*, 153–5; PRO, C 54/12709, m. 9; below, Soc. Hist., educ. (adult).

3 *Chelsea Soc. Rep.* (1981), 29–32.

4 *Concept*, Issue 4, Spring 2000 (brochure of developers European Land and Northacre).

5 Beaver, *Memorials*, 155; see Fig. 53.

6 *Chelsea Soc. Rep.* (1991), 24–7, argue for late 17th-cent. date on architectural grounds against *Survey of London*, IV. 43–4, which thought it Georgian.

7 LMA, BRA 203/152–68; *Survey of London*, XLI. 163; above, Gorges.

8 Pet. Sewell and John Burchard. At least 18½ a. of the Kensington land also lay in Little Chelsea, N. of Fulham Rd.

9 Faulkner, *Chelsea*, II. 158; *VCH Yorks. E. Riding*, VI. 210; LMA, O/217/1; PRO, PROB 11/602, ff. 221v.–222v.

10 LMA, O/217/1; PRO, C 54/9678.

11 LMA, BRA 641/1/15; above, Settlement, 1680–1865 (Chelsea Pk to Blacklands).

12 LMA, O/217/1.

was acquired in 1812 by James Gunter (d. 1819), confectioner of Berkeley Square,[1] who had made a fortune as a fashionable pastrycook in Mayfair. He built up a substantial estate at Earl's Court (Kens.), where he lived and which was the centre of his family's successful market gardening business.[2] In 1817 he also acquired the Warton land which lay between Stanley House and Little Chelsea and stretched from Fulham Road to King's Road.[3] The estate, entailed under his will, passed to his son Robert (d. 1852), who in 1847 had 19 acres of unbuilt land at Little Chelsea.[4] He was succeeded by his son Robert, later Sir Robert Gunter, Bt (d. 1905), the latter's son Sir Robert Benyon Nevill Gunter, Bt (d. 1917), and his son Sir Ronald Vernon Gunter, Bt.[5] The estate was sold off gradually: land forming the eastern part of St Mark's College chapel was sold to the National Society in 1854,[6] many houses and parcels of land were sold by auction in 1857, including nos 429–35 Fulham Road (formerly nos 1–4 Hollywood Place), and Week's Nursery in King's Road,[7] and part of Fernshaw Road (formerly Maude Grove) in 1918.[8]

1 *Survey of London*, XLI. 163, 195, 198.
2 Ibid., XLII. 200–3.
3 KL, deed 19549.
4 CL, Tithe Map and Award, nos 28–31.
5 KL, deeds 29592, 29603–4.
6 PRO, C 54/14719, m. 4.
7 KL, deed 19549; CL, deed 5820.
8 KL, deeds 29591–2, 29600.

ECONOMIC HISTORY

AGRICULTURE

In 1066 the two-hide manor of Chelsea was valued at £9, considerably more than the much larger manor of Kensington at £6, and had land for five ploughs. The five ploughs are appropriate for the 780 acres of the parish and suggest that the manor and parish were roughly coterminous, but the assessment of the Domesday manor at 2 hides seems low, perhaps the result of a concession to a pre-Conquest holder by the king.[1] The value remained the same in 1086. The demesne was assessed at one hide and had two ploughs, while the remaining hide with one plough was shared between six villeins, three serfs, and three bordars, with land available for two more ploughs. There was enough meadow and pasture for the cattle of the vill, and woodland worth 52d. a year; there were also 60 pigs kept on the manor.[2] As there is no trace of woodland in later records for the main parish, the Domesday woodland may have been in Chelsea detached, sometimes called Kingsholt, which means king's wood. Another possibility is the area in the north-east corner of the parish, known from the Middle Ages as Blacklands, which was not part of the open field system and may therefore have been cleared from woodland before the earliest extant records.

THE MANOR AND ITS TENANTS

In 1214 a tenant acknowledged he held 20 acres in villeinage of the lord of Chelsea,[3] and heriot is mentioned in 1350 and 1367,[4] but by the later 14th century the surviving manorial court records show no trace of villein or copyhold tenure in Chelsea. According to 16th-century records, the manorial tenants held freely for a fixed money payment (assized rent), suit of court held every 3 weeks, and relief.[5] In 1453 there were 20 tenants paying the assized rents; in 1536 there were 13, and the changes in the rent suggest that division and amalgamation of holdings frequently took place. Four of the holdings were cottages in Fulham, some or all at Wanden (Walham) Green. It seems likely that the 11 properties which had commoning rights on Chelsea common in the 17th century were successors to the freeholdings: some can certainly be traced from estates paying assized rents in the 16th century.

DEMESNE AGRICULTURE IN THE MIDDLE AGES

In 1453 the manorial demesne comprised 173 a. plus three unspecified closes in Landmedes. By far the greater part, 160 a., was arable, of which 28 a. lay in Westfield, 24 a. in Blacklands, 20 a. in Landmedes, and the rest in Eastfield: 38 a. in Gospelshot, 24 a. in Medshot, 16 a. in Crosshot, and 10 a. next to the manor close. Of the meadow, 1 a. and 3 lots lay in Westfield, and 12 a. lay in three pieces in Eastmead.[6] By 1587 some demesne had been taken to form the new manor house and its gardens, as well as the sites for other buildings, and many closes mentioned have unspecified areas: nevertheless, taking quantities given in later sources, the demesne included 242 a., excluding additional land bought by Henry VIII.[7]

In the mid 14th century nearly all the manorial demesne was apparently managed directly by the lord of the manor. A note of the income from Chelsea manor shows that only a few small parcels were let: a pightle, or small field, at Sandfordbridge (Stamford Bridge) was leased for 6s.; 1 a. 3 r. and a little garden were leased to Robert Shepherd for 4s. 4d.; two other small parcels were let at 2s. and 3s. 4d.; and Richard Est held some meadow valued at 13s. 6d. Other income from the manor consisted of the rents of assize totalling £7 6s. 6d. and from cottages £2 7s. 6d.; profits from customary works were valued at 8s.; profits from the courts 10s.; 2 mowings of the meadow were valued at £8; a close of pasture was valued at 26s. 8d., a croft at 8d., and pasture opposite the manor 6s. 8d.[8] However, no accounts survive for the medieval manor except for two brief periods when Westminster Abbey administered it. The first of these was 1367–70, when the lord of the manor, Richard de Heyle, granted it to the abbey for his lifetime on condition that they did not farm it out. The four surviving accounts show the abbey, which lay only a couple of miles from Chelsea, setting up a short-term farming system, presumably mainly for their domestic needs at Westminster in conjunction with one or two of their other manors in the region, principally Battersea. Nevertheless, the abbey apparently carried on much the

1 Inf. from Dr C.P. Lewis.
2 *VCH Middx*, I. 129.
3 *Cur. Reg. R.* VII. 152–3.
4 *Cal. Close*, 1349–54, 264; WAM 4813.
5 PRO, SC 2/205/40. Similar to situation in man. of Westm., also originally a Westm. Abbey man.
6 WAM 4804. For location of fields, above, Settlement, to 1680.
7 BL, Harl. Roll L 26; PRO, CP 43/520, carte rot. 5.
8 WAM 4797.

same agriculture as that under the lay lord. When their occupation began in July 1367, the monks bought from Heyle for £38 10s. all the corn growing on the demesne – wheat, rye, barley, dredge, and oats – and all the stock: farm horses, bulls, cows, boars, sheep and ewes, young sheep and lambs. Further stock costing £21 was bought by Michaelmas: 2 carthorses, 6 farm horses (*affri*), 9 oxen including 4 from Heyle, and 11 cows in addition to 11 cows and a bull bought 'in the manor'. Another bull, an ox, and 3 bullocks were received from another manor, and a pig as a heriot.[1] More stock was bought in the following 12 months: a boar, sow, 14 piglets, a ram, 39 young sheep, 58 ewes and their lambs, 21 young ewes, an ox, and 14 calves. The sergeant also bought hay for the horses and additional grain to top up the manor's needs: wheat and rye mainly to pay to servants, dredge (barley and oats) for the pigs.[2]

About 145 a. of arable were sown each year, and an unknown acreage lay fallow annually.[3] Over half the acreage in 1367–8 was sown with barley (78 a.), about 27 a. with rye, and 21 a. with wheat. The remainder consisted of oats (11 a.), a little vetch, and mixed crops such as maslin (wheat and rye), and haras (oats and vetch). The following year barley was still the largest crop but only 53 a. was sown, while 16 a. of dredge was added. A high proportion of the grain produced each year was used for next year's sowing: nearly two-fifths of the barley, most of the wheat and maslin, and half the oats. Of the remainder of the harvest, three-fifths of the barley, some of the wheat, and all the dredge were sent to the Westminster granary or to Battersea. Small quantities of barley were used for brewing for the harvest or fed to the pigs; a little wheat was used for harvest expenses; the oats were used to feed servants, or the oxen and horses. Over three-quarters of the rye was used within the manor as payment to the servants and for bread for tenants doing customary work.

The manor was worked by a combination of servants, customary or boon work by manorial tenants, and paid piece work. The sergeant, who kept the manor's accounts, a carter, roofer, reaper, two herdsmen, a shepherd, dairymaid, and swineherd all received money wages, as did a named individual for carrying dung with his cart. A servant was also employed to cart dung and cultivate at sowing time. Food and dues were also paid at Christmas and Easter to eight servants, and food was paid during the year to a carter, two ploughmen, the shepherd, the farmer of the cows, and a reaper. The sergeant received a bushel of wheat each week, and oats were used for flour and pottage for the servants. In addition, all those working in the harvest received their food and drink, as did manorial tenants. The lord benefited from several customary works by the tenants. At least 12 boon ploughmen worked and received wheat and rye bread for customary ploughing; the manor provided 4 ploughs, made or repaired, but customary work in winter and at Lent involved 11 ploughs. The 24 men and 12 ploughmen who ploughed for winter sowing received wheaten bread. The manor had the use of customary work to reap and lift 14 a. of hay but two or more extra mowers had to be brought in to assist; customary mowers received rye bread and drink. The second hay crop was cut by paid labour for 6 days. During the harvest 69 men and 5 servants of the manor were used for 1 day each to reap and bind. It is not clear how many of the 69 were doing customary work and how many were employed at piece rate: only 18–20 a. were reaped by customary work; the remaining 125 a. were reaped by paid labour, at 1s. an acre. The customary tenants received bread and cheese during the day and ale and meat for supper. The servants, carters, two loaders, a binder, and a reaper received money payment for 4 weeks and 2 days work, as well as bread and ale. The manor also employed 2 carters and 4 other men at piece work during the harvest, plus a cook to provide for them. Most of the crops were threshed in the manor by named grangers, paid at piece work plus a bushel or two of wheat or maslin. Other work carried out concerned the manorial buildings: the sergeant paid for removing and stacking straw from the grange and cleaning it out as well as re-roofing it over 3 weeks. Roofing of buildings was a regular expense; the sheephouse was walled, and the piggery mended.

The main produce exported from the manor was wool and barley, and neither were valued in the accounts. In the first full year 116 fleeces were produced and 135 in the second; after a tenth had been given to the rector the rest were sent to Westminster. Nearly three-quarters of the barley crop was sent to Westminster, and a quarter of the wheat was sold, to the manor of Battersea. Sales of grain accounted for were small, and probably all at the barn door in the manor; a small quantity of straw and a larger amount of hay were also sold. Similarly, a few sales of surplus or unproductive animals were made each year, including 12 hens out of 18 obtained as rent at Christmas. Dairying was also a main source of income but was farmed: the manor received £6 13s. 4d. a year for dairy produce and calves from 20 cows, paid by the farmer of the cows at 6s. 8d. a head. In the final year of the abbey's possession, 1370–1, most of the barley, maslin, rye, wheat, vetch, dredge, and oats produced was removed from the manor and was either sent to Westminster or to other Westminster manors such as Battersea, Finchley, or Hendon; some oats and rye were sold.

In the mid 15th century, when Westminster again had temporary possession, the manor was farmed out in several parcels: some of the parcels are described as short leases for that year, but it seems likely that most of the manor was already farmed out before Westminster

1 WAM 4813; 19861; 30014.
2 WAM 4807.
3 Foll. 3 paras based on surviving accounts: WAM 4806–8, 4813.

took possession for the years 1453–55. Assized rents were £9 1s. 6d., but neither cottage rents nor customary works were mentioned: the latter had probably been commuted when the demesne was farmed out. The site of the manor with 54 a. arable, and 4 a. and 3 lots of meadow were let to Simon Bayley, who also leased 3 a. next to the close of the manor and two other small parcels out of the remaining 15 parcels of the demesne land; the total rental for the demesne was £15 17s. 8d. in 1454 and £16 7s. 7d. in 1455. The lord also received 60s. a year from Richard Hurlock, the farmer at 'Westbourne', presumably Chelsea detached. A stipend of 20s. a year was paid to the collector of the rents and farms of the manor; other annual payments included the £4 chief rent to Westminster Abbey and 7s. 10d. to the manor of Knightsbridge for the Westbourne land. In 1455 nearly £36 was paid for 'repairs to the manor', presumably the manor house or manorial buildings. Overall, in the two and a half years the manor was held by Westminster the income of £71 was exceeded by expenses of £75.[1]

THE TENANTS AND THEIR HUSBANDRY

There were about 60 men listed in the tithing in 1389.[2] The chief pledges of the manor in the late 14th century included William Cotes, John Stoket, William Est, John Passour, William of Chikewell (Chigwell) and Richard Est, and tithing-men included Thomas Partrich, John Carter, Richard North junior, Richard Titegrove, John Couper, John Partrich, Edward Smith, and William Helder. John atte Water, John Stoket, Richard North and Thomas Churchman were presented for ploughing up markers or highways, and other tenants for encroaching on highways with dung heaps, straw stacks, and pigsties. Chief pledges in 1396 were Stephen Wilkyn, Richard Est, John Est, Hugh Hunt, Thomas Churchman, and John Partrich. Several women were presented for illegally mowing the meadow of other tenants or taking sheaves of corn.[3]

In 1340 the rector's tithes of corn, wool, and lambs produced within the parish was valued at £6 13s. 4d.: 40s. had been deducted because 30 a. arable and 2 a. meadow belonged to the rectory. There were 30 a. of titheable meadow; 100 a. lay fallow or waste.[4] Little detail is available concerning the type of farming by Chelsea's inhabitants, but the animals who died of murrain in 1369 – a cart-horse, 3 cows, 3 young ewes, and 10 lambs – suggest the range of animal husbandry was similar to the demesne, as do the strays found within the manor between 1369 and 1399: horses, steers, a boar, wethers, piglets, chickens, and geese.[5]

FIELD SYSTEM AND INCLOSURE

Inclosure and Common Rights

Although Blacklands and Landmedes were in closes by the 15th century,[6] and possibly always had been, land in the two large arable fields of Eastfield and Westfield was in open parcels, confirmed by the fines for ploughing over the markers of the strips and field paths.[7] By the 15th century there is some indication of piecemeal inclosure of parts of Eastfield: although listed in four pieces, 24 a. of Medshot was farmed out as pasture by 1453.[8] Any inclosure took place slowly, however, and on a piecemeal basis, with some parts, such as on the south side of Chelsea common, remaining open until built on. Despite this, however, there are no indications of a common agricultural system, such as organized rotations, nor of common management of the fields except for the Lammas rights.[9] This may partly be because few court proceedings survive, but equally the lack of court rolls, even when Westminster Abbey managed the manor, suggests that there was no need of such records because any common management had long since disappeared.

Lammas rights became a source of conflict between landowners and parishioners by the late 16th century with the gradual enclosure of parts of the open fields, particularly Westfield. The freeholders and tenants of the manor of Chelsea had the right to graze the open arable fields with any stock except temporary sheep flocks between Lammas day (1 August) and Candlemas (2 February), and were prevented from doing so on about 50 a. in Westfield belonging to the earl of Lincoln when he inclosed it *c.*1607. Lincoln's successor, Sir Arthur Gorges, opened up most of the land by 1619, but was challenged by inhabitants over Brickbarn close, which he claimed had never been open. The commoners maintained that the close had formerly had one side left open until the earl had inclosed it; after a suit in 1612 he had left a gate into the close open for the exercise of common rights, but the gate was kept closed after the earl's death (in 1616).[10]

In 1631 a report was made for the Privy Council after complaints about inclosure in Chelsea. In Eastfield an inclosure near Stonebridge had been reversed, and *c.*20 a. of Sir William Blake's estate had been inclosed and partially hedged, but was still laid open at Lammas. The meadow in the detached part of Kensington by the Thames which was ditched and banked had also usually been commoned at Lammas over the bank. In Westfield, however, inclosures seem to have become permanent. The five acres on which Richard Stocke's house and

1 WAM 4804.
2 WAM 4805.
3 WAM 4805, 4809–12, 4814–17.
4 *Inq. Non.* (Rec. Com.), 197.
5 WAM 4805, 4809–12, 4814–17.
6 Above, Settlement, to 1680.
7 e.g. WAM 4817.
8 WAM 4804.
9 Below.
10 PRO, STAC 8/160/18; C 2/JASI/G2/16.

garden had been built by 1619, and 14 a. adjoining it behind the houses at Little Chelsea was inclosed, with another 31 a. in Westfield belonging to Lady Elizabeth Gorges, probably including the grounds of Stanley House, and 3 a. meadow of Lady Elizabeth's in the open field had also been ditched and common rights prevented.[1] Prior to that Lady Elizabeth and her daughter Lady Lane had been allowed to inclose 4 acres in return for a payment to the parish poor.[2]

Lammas rights presumably became less of an issue as Chelsea's agriculture changed, but even in 1834 the parish officers and inhabitants repossessed the Lots meadow after the bankruptcy of the Kensington Canal Company on the grounds that it was Lammas lands on which they had a right to put their cattle, with Lord Cadogan having the right to let it for the other six months.[3] However the status of the Lots is unclear. It was divided into portions called lots, about a quarter of an acre each, and in extant sources individual lots were held in severalty and passed with other land holdings. However, the name suggests that the strips of meadow had once been apportioned annually to manorial tenants, though no hint of this survives in the medieval court rolls or accounts. The Lots meadow was still called Lammas land in the Chelsea Improvement Act of 1845, when it was owned by Lord Cadogan, the West London Railway, the Kensington Canal Company, and Chelsea parishioners.[4]

Chelsea Common

Chelsea common or heath was referred to in 1373,[5] and in 1386 a tenant was presented for illegally digging there.[6] By the 1540s manorial freeholders were presented for grazing too many cattle and sheep.[7] The right to graze the common was limited by the 17th century to 40 cows and 20 heifers divided in the proportion of one heifer to every two cows between 11 named properties, apparently successors of houses or holdings belonging to the manorial freeholders.[8] By the late 17th century the commoners were the leading landowners in the parish, and in 1674 they agreed to allow the common, computed at just over 37 a., to be inclosed temporarily and leased for 21 years to pay for rebuilding the parish church. In 1707 the vestry decided to approach the commoners about using the grazing rights to support the parish charity school, but apparently without success. In 1713, because of carting and illegal pasturing, the commoners let their rights to John Huggett for 3 years for proportionate payments to each commoner of 18s. for each cow or heifer they were entitled to graze. Huggett was also to inclose the common with a ditch and bank at his own expense. The lease was renewed in 1716 for 20s. an animal and continued until Huggett withdrew from the agreement in 1723; the commoners then proposed to seek another tenant.[9] They also had problems with the Kensington turnpike trust, who tried to dig gravel on the common in 1726 and 1736, but were prevented when it was shown that the common was not a public waste belonging to the parish but a private stinted common belonging to the proprietors.[10] Some encroachments were made: by 1674 there were 4 small houses, presumably the 'poor houses' mentioned in Hamilton's survey, and a pond or water-place made for rotting dung which was ordered to be filled.[11] The common disappeared *c.*1810 when it was laid out for building.[12]

FARMING AND TENANTS FROM THE 16TH CENTURY

In the 16th and 17th centuries the manorial demesne continued to be leased out in parcels, as were the manorial farm buildings, but after the original manor house was replaced by a Tudor building, the latter and its immediate gardens and closes were usually occupied by the Crown lessee or later by the owner of the manor.[13] Sir Thomas More's estate was partly farmed by himself and partly let. In 1528 he had enough barley and oats to feed his daily household of 100, and was able to sell 20 quarters of barley and 24 quarters of oats; he also had enough wheat until midsummer, after which he would have to buy it. The only other resident listed with corn available to sell was William Chamberlain, with a household of 8, who could sell 20 quarters of barley and 4 of rye. About 16 households in the parish had no corn at all.[14] By 1537 all More's estate apart from his mansion and grounds was let, the farmhouse in Chelsea with *c.*90 a. to Thomas Beane junior, and the remaining land and houses in Chelsea and Kensington to 11 other tenants.[15] In 1567 the owner, Lord Winchester, let the farmhouse and all the land, perhaps 130 a., to Nicholas Holborne, of Lincoln's Inn, for 50 years. Holborne also leased part of the manorial demesne and in 1587 was holding from year to year 5 bays of the great barn, the longhouse next to the barn, the granary, 12 a. in the common fields, and 1 a. called Wiffes acre.[16] After the death of Nicholas and his wife Catherine, the leasehold passed to his son Nicholas, who let parts of the Winchester estate: a close called Nine Acres near the mansion, to William Arnold of Fulham,[17] and the Farmhouse and 3 a. to tenants including Lodowick Briskett and Sir Robert Stapleton.[18]

1 PRO, SP 16/193, f. 101 and v.
2 Faulkner, *Chelsea*, II. 106–7.
3 *Chelsea Soc. Rep.* (1955), 42.
4 8 & 9 Vic. c. 143 (Local and Personal).
5 WAM 4811.
6 WAM 4814.
7 PRO, SC 2/188/42–3.
8 Dr King's MS, p. 38; Faulkner, *Chelsea*, II. 50.
9 Faulkner, *Chelsea*, II. 51–2, 55–7.
10 Ibid., 58–60.
11 Ibid., 60–1.
12 Above, Settlement, 1680–1865 (Chelsea Pk).
13 Above, Landownership, Chelsea man.
14 PRO, E 36/257, f. 44.
15 PRO, SC 6/HENVIII/7247.
16 BL, Harl. Roll L.26.
17 PRO, STAC 8/91/25.
18 Below.

Most of the third large estate in Chelsea, Hungerford's, was also let in one large farm, to William Wrennall.[1] In 1607 it consisted of a messuage or farmhouse, which stood in Church Lane opposite the rectory, 4 closes of arable or pasture called Sandhills (32 a.), 21 a. arable in two parcels in Eastfield adjoining Upper Church Lane, 9 a. arable on the south side of King's Road, 6 a. arable in Eastfield in same area, two parcels of 2 a. each on the north side of King's Road, parcels of 1½ a. and ½ a. arable in Eastfield between the road to Westminster and the Thames. In the West meadow he had two separate parcels containing 11 lots in all, 7 long and 4 short, and another 1 a. None of the arable is described as being in closes, and its description suggests it was still in open parcels in Eastfield and Westfield.[2] From the deeds, reference to Wrennall's crops in Sandhills, and from Wrennall's involvement with Lammas rights, it seems likely that Wrennall was farming his leasehold himself, together with land he rented from others. This included 6½ a. described as arable, meadow or pasture in Westfield on the north side of the Lots, and 14½ a. arable in Westfield on the north side of the King's Road, all leased from William Arnold of Fulham.[3] In 1630, when Sir William Blake sold Wrennall's farm to Massie, it consisted of the farmhouse in Chelsea and 7 parcels of arable in Eastfield totalling 43 a. all occupied by Wrennall, another 3 a. arable and 10 a. meadow in Eastfield, 11 lots and 1 a. of meadow, 21 a. arable, three 1 a. parcels of arable, a close of 5 a. all in Westfield, 2 parcels in Westfield called the two long lots (½ a.), and 3 roods called three lots in Westfield, a messuage or tenement in the tenure of Nicholas Harman (or Herne), and 1½ a. meadow in Fulham.[4]

Like the neighbouring parishes of Kensington and Fulham, agriculture in Chelsea was transformed during the 17th century as land was increasingly turned over to growing vegetables for the London market, and where traditional arable crops were still grown it was apparently in conjunction with vegetables.[5] The other influence on Chelsea's agriculture from the 17th century was the growth of residences for gentlemen and noblemen, with substantial parts of the open fields being inclosed to create pleasure gardens and parkland. Ten acres of Westfield, which had been enclosed in 1605 by the earl of Lincoln to make Brickbarn close, was with the adjoining 32 acres called Sandhills turned into Chelsea Park attached to Sir Lionel Cranfield's great house *c.*1620, and other parts of Westfield were inclosed for gardens to the houses at Little Chelsea by 1631:[6] William Arnold's 10 a. arable, which had been partially inclosed and built on by 1618,[7] was apparently all inclosed by 1631 as gardens for houses along Fulham Road.[8] In the south-east corner of the parish some demesne farmland was taken for the site of Chelsea College, and later much more was taken for the Royal Hospital. Although part remained farmland until required for building, by 1700 land not used for the Hospital and its grounds had been leased to create Ranelagh House and gardens and Walpole House. The remaining strips between the highway and the Thames were soon afterwards being used for non-agricultural purposes and the Apothecaries' Physic Garden.

Pastoral farming in the form of grazing animals and making hay was also limited, though in 1800 substantial areas of enclosed meadow or pasture were dotted around the parish, generally as closes attached to the larger houses.[9] Some grazing was used for dairy cattle, though increasingly during the 19th century cowkeepers kept their animals in sheds and did not have any land. By 1851 there were at least 25 registered cowkeepers in the parish, as well as those in related occupations, such as dairymen.[10] In 1867 the parish recorded 17 farmers who kept 308 cows and heifers for milking; as only one of the farmers had any land, with 6 a. of grass,[11] most of the cattle were being kept in sheds by cowkeepers. In 1877 18 cowkeepers kept 382 cows in sheds,[12] in 1882 20 had stock but no land with 340 cows in milk or in calf,[13] and in 1885 14 had stock only with 327 cows in milk, 3 horses were kept for agriculture or market gardening, 4 unbroken horses, and 44 hens.[14] As late as the 1890s cows were kept in premises on King's Road.[15] Chelsea still had 1 cow shed just before the First World War, but by 1918 there were none.[16]

FARM-GARDENING AND MARKET GARDENING

Chelsea participated in the great expansion of market gardening around London between the 17th and 19th centuries, supplying the growing London market. By 1600 garden crops formerly imported into London from East Anglia were being grown closer to the city, particularly in the south-western parishes of Middlesex, where the easily-cultivated gravels together with use of dung from London made intensive commercial cultivation of

1 Above, Landownership, Hungerford.
2 PRO, CP 43/99, carte rott. 41v.–43v.
3 PRO, C 54/1884 (not numbered).
4 PRO, C 9/15/92; above, Landownership, other ests (Blake).
5 Below, farm-gardening.
6 *Cal. SP Dom.* 1631–3, 73.
7 PRO, C 54/2376, no. 5.
8 Above, Settlement, to 1680.
9 *Thos Milne's Land Use Map of London and Environs in 1800* (LTS 118–119, 1975–6).
10 PRO, HO 107/1472/2/1.
11 PRO, MAF 68/136.
12 Ibid., 68/535.
13 Ibid., 68/820
14 Ibid., 68/991.
15 *Chelsea Soc. Rep.* (1958), 56–61.
16 LCC, *London Statistics*, XXVI (1915–20), 90.

vegetable crops possible. In 1607 the neighbouring parish of Fulham was mentioned as a carrot-growing area,[1] and as early as 1605 the Gardeners' Company of London had been founded to regulate market gardening.[2] Initially, the company was concerned with the activities of husbandmen in London itself, but by the reign of Charles I the company was also attempting to regulate those husbandmen in Kensington and Chelsea. From the mid 17th century intensive horticulture near London was also stimulated by a new fashion among the rich for a wide range of vegetables in their diet, which was then imitated by the middle classes.[3]

From at least the early 17th century many husbandmen in Chelsea included the intensive spade cultivation of roots and other garden crops in rotation with traditional arable crops such as wheat and barley,[4] which not only meant the survival of some corn-growing in Chelsea into the 19th century, but also ensured that Chelsea's open fields survived far longer than those in some other parishes around London, where land was used almost entirely for pasturing animals and for hay. Despite a penalty of £3 for ploughing it up, pasture in two of Blacklands closes next to the Westbourne was ploughed up each year between 1729 and 1734 by the tenant, Henry Linford, a gardener of Kensington, who leased 5 closes of Blacklands for 33 years from 1714;[5] the penalty was possibly because they were originally meadow and worth much more than ordinary pasture or arable, but it is likely that Linford was using them for market gardening.

Farmer-gardeners grew corn and vegetables without a fallow, a system made possible by heavily manuring the land with dung and night soil from London, and in Chelsea and Fulham they occupied much of the agricultural land from the early 17th century to the middle of the 19th. Their methods were so original that agricultural writers frequently drew attention to them and the lessons they could give to husbandmen elsewhere. Root vegetables were a particular speciality in Chelsea, with two or three crops taken each year, and often grown in rotation with corn or barley in Chelsea's open fields.[6]

The earliest indications of the practice in Chelsea concern the use of dung: William Arnold of Fulham, subtenant of part of the earl of Lincoln's estate in 1611, was manuring heavily a close near the Thames, buying dung brought by boat from London by the dung farmers or scavengers there.[7] Nicholas Holborne senior, lessee of the Farmhouse and land of Lincoln's estate, grew early peas on land by the Thames *c.*1575 or later.[8] The house and a small close were later leased to Lodowick Briskett 1603–4, and although he was unlikely to have been seriously growing vegetables commercially, Briskett dug the ground at the back of his house and set part with cabbage plants and part with barley in order to experiment how yields might be increased.[9] William Wrennall, lessee of Hungerford's farm, was growing carrots and garden roots in addition to corn on the 32 a. called Sandhills in 1620.[10]

An increasing number of Chelsea residents were designated as gardeners in the 17th century, meaning in this period market gardeners, and included some of the leading inhabitants: James Leverett (d. 1662–3), gardener, was lessee of the Magpie inn and also had property in Lambeth.[11] Several gardeners in the late 17th century had only small acreages. Curtis Akers (d. 1686), who held land along the southern end of Chelsea creek in 1673 and was described as yeoman,[12] had 1½ a. of 'herbs and sparrow grass', 1 a. of carrots and parsnips, 1 a. of peas, 2 a. of beans, and 1½ a. of grass valued in April at his death.[13] Richard Samm (d. 1673) had ½ a. parsnips, 6 a. turnips and 2½ a. of wheat sown or planted by November.[14] The crops grown by Robert Hopperton (d. 1686), valued at £10, were not specified, but he also had 'glasses' valued at £2 10s. in his ground, which were bell glasses used for protecting early crops.[15] John Harvest in 1681 had 150 glasses valued at £4; a lease with about 14 years to come, of 6½ yards of land with a house and seeds sown, was valued at £50.[16] Not all the growers were small husbandmen however. Thomas Franklin, who leased a large acreage from the Greene family in the vicinity of the Royal Hospital, received compensation *c.*1682 for his crop of turnips on ground taken for the Hospital.[17] Because of the large amount of turnips, carrots, beans, peas, and other similar crops 'with which the fields are for the most part sowed', the rector found it more convenient after 1670 to farm the tithes rather than collecting them in kind, and from 1694 individual farmers and gardeners compounded for their own tithes.[18]

When Pehr Kalm visited Chelsea in 1748, he observed that on all sides there was scarcely anything to be seen except orchards or vegetable market gardens. In the open fields were beans and cabbages, sometimes with the latter planted between the rows of beans, and asparagus, which grew up through the necks of broken bottles used for forcing. There were also numerous orchards with apples, pears, plums, and cherries.[19]

1 M. Thick, *Neat House Gardens: Early Market Gardening around London* (1998), 22–4.
2 L.G. Bennett, *Horticultural Industry of Middx* (1952), 8.
3 Thick, *Neat Ho. Gardens*, 23, 25–9.
4 G.B.G. Bull, 'The Changing Landscape of Rural Middx 1500–1850' (Unpubl. Ph.D. thesis, London, 1958), 201.
5 PRO, E 13/901, mm. 5–6.
6 Thick, *Neat Ho. Gardens*, 47, 53, 65, 75, 86, 101–2.
7 PRO, STAC 8/91/25.
8 PRO, C 24/319, no. 18.
9 PRO, C 24/318, no. 30.
10 PRO, C 54/2445, no. 1.
11 CL, deed 18629.
12 LMA, WCS 332/99.
13 LMA, AM/PI/1/1686/36.
14 LMA, AM/PI/1/1673/72.
15 LMA, AM/PI/1/1686/46; Thick, *Neat Ho. Gardens*, 104–5.
16 LMA, AM/PI/1/1681/11.
17 *Cal. Treas. Bks*, VIII(3), 1350.
18 Dr King's MS, pp. 7–9, 11.
19 *Kalm's Visit*, 90–1.

The value of market gardening both to owners and to occupiers was evident. By the 1690s the rector had let several small parcels of glebe near the rectory house to 'French gardeners', apparently Huguenots, who had thereby greatly improved his income from the rectory.[1] Owners of the manorial estate, William Cheyne, Lord Newhaven, and his successor Sir Hans Sloane, also leased land for garden use. Before 1713 Cheyne had leased 3 a. in Gospelshot by the highway to Westminster as garden ground to David Morgan,[2] who also leased 6 a. of glebe between King's Road and Burton's Court for the same purpose in 1717.[3] Cheyne had also leased a considerable acreage in Westfield to gardeners during the previous decade. Some of those leases were for land already in use for market gardening, such as the 3 a. held by George Burr or the 9 a. held by John Bartholomew, both in Westfield. Some leases, however, were for land in the process of conversion, such as the house and 5 a. converted to garden ground in Westfield, or the 4 a. 'latterly converted' held by John Wivell, again in Westfield.[4] A close called the Eighteen Acres near Little Chelsea belonging to William Mart and then Sir John Cope was converted to garden ground by 1733.[5] Landowners in Chelsea obtained much higher rents for garden ground. The 4 a. held by John Wivell, though only recently converted, still yielded over £3 an acre in rent, far higher than a similar area used for grain crops. Even higher rents could be charged for land which had been used for market gardening for some time and was therefore well manured: George Burr's 3 acres in Westfield were leased for £10 an acre, while the glebe land let to two other early market gardeners, Francis Duneau and John Narbonne, both fetched rents of about £15 an acre.[6] Similarly for the producer, though admittedly the labour of digging an acre by spade was far greater than ploughing, the return on the vegetable crops was even greater: in 1673 Richard Samm's 2½ a. of wheat was valued at £10, or £4 an acre, but ½ a. of parsnips at £4 (£8 an acre).[7] This may be on the high side, though, as Curtis Akers's vegetable crops in 1686 are all valued at £3 an acre.[8]

John Rubergall, who with his family occupied many parcels of land in Chelsea in the mid to late 18th century as well as in Brompton (Kens.), was a Frenchman said to have been the first person to grow lettuce successfully in England.[9] By the end of the 18th century, however, market gardening began to contract, as the value of land in Chelsea for building purposes started to outstrip its value as garden ground: between 1664 and 1795 the acreage of land cultivated as arable for the market was said to have fallen from 334 a. to 170 a., of which no more than 12 a. was used for corn. Pasture or meadow accounted for another 130 a., and about 12 a. was occupied by nurseries and florists.[10]

In 1800 most of the market garden ground lay in the west between the Ashburnham estate and Chelsea Creek, and between Little Chelsea and Stanley House. There were other smaller areas throughout the parish: Parsonage Close, the Eighteen Acres along the east side of Upper Church Lane, Dovehouse Close and part of Danvers House site, the unbuilt land behind the rectory and two fields across to Flood Street bordering King's Road, another small patch behind a house in King's Road half way between Flood and Smith streets, and the ground of the Royal Hospital south of the burial ground and north of Ranelagh rotunda. Land on the north side of King's Road east of Eighteen Acres was common garden field with the land in open parcels.[11] Some land was marked as nursery ground: Prince's field, Bull's small area, Colvill's and the next plot on the west. The remaining undeveloped land was marked as paddocks or closes attached to large houses, or as meadow or pasture. The north part of the common was marked as meadow or pasture, the southern part as common land.

Arable accounted for 267 a. in 1801, possibly indicating under-accounting in 1795, but equally there may have been an increase in acreage because of war with the French.[12] Farmer-gardeners were still growing 37 a. of wheat, 24 a. of barley, and 16 a. of oats in Chelsea, although overshadowed by 140 a. of vegetables. Potatoes were the largest crop, with 43 a.; turnips (possibly including rape) remained a staple of Chelsea market gardening with 39 a., peas covered 30 a., and beans 28 a.[13] In neighbouring Fulham it was commented that peas, beans, and turnips were all grown for Covent Garden market, and were intermixed with other crops obscuring the true acreage of vegetables grown; corn land was sown with cabbages after harvest.[14] The same was doubtless true for Chelsea as well.

By the early 19th century, agriculture, presumably including market gardening, accounted for a very small proportion of the population of Chelsea. Only 183 out of 11,604 inhabitants were employed in farming in 1801, and the number employed in agriculture continued to decline, despite a threefold increase in the population of the parish, to only 87 people, mostly cowkeepers, out of 32,371 in 1831.[15]

Profitable though market gardening was, from the middle of the 19th century onwards it could not keep pace with the escalating value of land for building, as

1 Dr King's MS, p. 24.
2 MLR 1719/6/276.
3 MLR 1725/1/244.
4 CL, deed 3014; MLR 1712/4/50.
5 MLR 1733/1/365.
6 Dr King's MS, pp. 13, 24.
7 LMA, AM/PI/1/1673/72.
8 LMA, AM/PI/1/1686/36.
9 E.J. Willson, *West London Nursery Gardens* (1982), 81–2.
10 Lysons, *Environs*, II. 71.
11 *Thos Milne's Land Use Map of London and Environs in 1800* (LTS 118–119, 1975–6).
12 Bull, 'Changing Landscape of Rural Middx', 204.
13 '1801 Crop Returns for England', ed. M. Turner (TS 1978, in IHR), p. 331.
14 '1801 Crop Returns', p. 333.
15 Vestry mins, 1822–33.

suburban London continued to expand westwards. In some cases, gardeners themselves were actively involved in the shift from gardening to building, as was the case at Bull's Gardens. This four-acre holding on the north side of Green Lettuce Lane was converted to a market garden before 1817, when it was sublet to John Bull, gardener, who was granted a new head lease for 52 years from 1825. The lease passed to John Bull of Birmingham, inspector of mail coaches, who in 1839 granted a lease for the remainder of the term to to the then occupier, William Davis or Davies, market gardener, together with fruit and other trees, a recently-built house, packing house, stable and outbuildings, and also the 22 small houses or cottages called Bull's Gardens, recently built on the land and presumably by one of the Bull family. In 1845 Davis took a building lease from Lord Cadogan of part of the property for additional speculative building.[1]

NURSERY GARDENING

Alongside commercial market gardening, Chelsea also became noted for its nursery gardens, which like market gardening was stimulated by a fashionable taste which developed for exotic plants and trees. The early growth in the industry is obscure: John Burton (d. *c.*1680) of Little Chelsea, who leased 3 a. of garden ground and left a share in the flowers growing on half an acre to his younger daughter,[2] may be an early harbinger of the trade. In 1712 Narcissus Luttrell bought 25 varieties of pear from nurserymen near Little Chelsea, some of whom may have been in Chelsea parish,[3] and Kalm commented in 1748 that many gardeners had nurseries from which they sold plants to the gentry.[4] An observer in 1798 remarked on Chelsea as one of the select parishes east and west of London where much ground was occupied by nurserymen 'who spare no expense in collecting the choicest sort, and greatest variety of fruit trees, and ornamental shrubs and flowers, from every quarter of the globe', all cultivated to a high degree of perfection. Many of their plants were exported annually to Europe and Russia, but still more were sold in England.[5]

Although early details of the industry are unclear, several nurserymen became extremely well known, as did the businesses they founded; Bull's, Weeks's, Davey's, and Colvill's nurseries were household names in England, and Veitch's was internationally famous.[6] While market gardening quickly shrank before the expansion of building in Chelsea in the 19th century, nurseries were less affected. Partly this was because they needed much less open space in Chelsea itself, sometimes only keeping their retail outlet there while using cheaper land in the Home Counties to grow their stock for sale, but also because nurserymen could for a while afford ever-increasing rents, with the fashion for rare and unusual plants and trees.[7] From the 18th century the main premises of many of Chelsea's leading nurseries were situated in King's Road, which was very much the fashionable hub of nursery gardening in West London and south-west Middlesex, and nurserymen from neighbouring Kensington and Brompton also had showrooms there. Between the 1750s and 1916 25 nursery-gardening firms are known to have had premises in King's Road; nurserymen with their main grounds in Battersea, Hackney, Sunbury, and elsewhere also had show nurseries in King's Road.[8]

Eventually nurseries, too, began to be swallowed by the westward expansion of suburban London, and though the larger firms of Veitch, Wimsett, and Bull all survived into the 20th century, Veitch and Wimsett had closed by the First World War and Bull soon after it.[9] By the end of the 20th century the once-famous trade was represented by local garden centres at World's End and in Sydney Street.

Leading Nurseries and Nurserymen

James Colvill (King's Road Nursery). A nurseryman and florist (*c.*1746–1822), he raised a number of new roses and was involved in the early development of the China roses. He had a remarkable collection of plants, many of which were the subjects of plates and descriptions by Robert Sweet, who was employed by Colvill and his son James from 1819 to 1831: the best-known of his publications was *The British Flower Garden* (1838), with 712 coloured plates.[10] In 1795 Colvill was singled out in Chelsea as carrying on a very extensive business in the sale of scarce exotic plants, the culture of which had 'been brought to very great perfection'.[11] It was also notable for the quality of its geraniums.[12] Colvill senior founded his King's Road nursery *c.*1783 on 2½ a. of the Warton estate on the north side of the highway near the junction with Blacklands Lane. It was known as Colvill & Buchanan in 1790, and Colvill & Son by 1807; James junior (1777–1832) carried on after his father's death. The nursery was distinguished for the first real display of the garden chrysanthemum in Britain in 1795, and later for hybridization of pelargoniums, gladioli, and hippeastrums; by 1811 it specialized in rare exotics and forced flowers, having between 30,000 and 40,000 sq. ft under glass. Colvill's occupied a second nursery at Roehampton by 1827. From 1834 to 1840 the nursery was occupied by Adams & Durban.[13]

1 KL, deeds 22293–5; above, Settlement, 1680–1865 (Chelsea Pk).
2 PRO, C 7/327/73.
3 Croker, *Walk from London to Fulham*, 125.
4 *Kalm's Visit*, 90.
5 Middleton, *View*, 269.
6 Below.
7 Bull, 'Changing Landscape of Rural Middx', 227.
8 Willson, *W. London Nursery Gdns*, 93.
9 Bull, 'Changing Landscape of Rural Middx', 228; below.
10 M. Hadfield, *Hist. of British Gardening* (1979 edn), 292.
11 Lysons, *Environs*, II. 71n.
12 Bull, 'Changing Landscape of Rural Middx', 223.
13 J.H. Harvey, 'The Nurseries on Milne's Land-Use Map', *TLMAS*, XXIV (1973), 181–2.

William Salisbury (Cadogan Gardens). A gardener and botanist (d. 1823), in 1792 he became a pupil and partner of William Curtis of Pond Place, Chelsea, whose nursery was on the north side of Fulham Road at Queen's Elm, Brompton (Kens.). In 1807 Salisbury sold his ground at Queen's Elm and acquired 6 acres on the east side of Sloane Street forming the south end of the gardens in Cadogan Place and opened the London Botanic Garden, an example of the nursery garden as entertainment, since he intended to hold lectures and concerts there. He wrote books on botanic subjects but the garden was not a success and was taken over by James Charles Tate in 1822. Tate renamed it the Nursery and Botanic Garden and was more successful, possibly because he concentrated on the selling and nursery side rather than the botanic and educational. He imported plants from Mexico, South America, and China. In 1842 it was taken over by James Hunter Tuck, who had moved from Eaton Square (St George, Hanover Sq.) and it continued until 1876.[1]

Thomas Davey (King's Road). A florist (1758–1833), he moved from Camberwell to a half-acre site on the west side of Colvill's by 1798, and was nationally famous for Florists' Flowers, especially carnations, pinks, and tulips, and for pelargoniums; he imported tulips from France and camellias from China. Part of his ground was given up to Downing's floorcloth factory prior to 1828, and his nursery closed with his death.[2]

Little's Botanic Nursery, King's Road. Thomas Little established a nursery in Upper Gloucester Place in King's Road by 1821, and by 1832 the nursery was listed as that of Henry and Thomas Little, and called Little's Botanic Nursery in 1836. Some land was given up for building in 1844 and again in 1850, when the proprietor was Henry Little, Florist, Nursery and Seedsman to the Queen, who was selling off fruit trees and shrubs. By 1854 the proprietor was Henry Thomas Little,[3] whose premises were at nos 99 & 101 King's Road in 1878.[4] It was said to have closed *c.*1892.[5]

Joseph Knight (King's Road). A nurseryman (*c.*1781–1855), he had been gardener to a wealthy plant collector in Clapham and eventually acquired the collection and brought it to Chelsea, where in 1808 he opened his Exotic Nursery at Stanley Place, between King's and Fulham roads, just east of Stanley House.[6] By 1829 he had erected a large Conservatory and several other buildings, housing camellias, orange trees, evergreen exotic shrubs, acacias, rhododendrons, and many plants from southern Africa and elsewhere. The collection was said to have become 'so much increased, that it is now one of the most respectable in the vicinity of London'. It included alpine plants, hardy herbaceous plants in open borders, many rare shrubs, and fruit trees, and there was heating for tropical plants.[7] Pineapples and fuchsias were also among early specialities; conifers later became prominent in his collection, of which he published a catalogue in 1840 with 140 species and varieties. By 1850 he had been joined in the business by Thomas Perry; the catalogue they published showed the King's Road premises with an awning over the footpath to protect their patrons when they alighted from their carriages. Their stock included hardy ornamental trees and shrubs, many personally acquired abroad; beautiful and fashionable American plants, rhododendrons and azaleas; fruit trees supplied from their nursery at Battersea; hot-house plants, including Indian azaleas and camellias; seeds and bulbs; standard bay trees in tubs. The firm could also supply trained gardeners.[8] The business was bought in 1853 by James Veitch & Sons.

James Veitch & Sons (King's Road). In 1853 the Exeter firm of James Veitch & Sons bought Knight's nursery business and leased the site, developing the nursery so that within a few years it had become internationally famous and the most important in England. In 1863 the London business, known by 1878 as the Royal Exotic Nursery,[9] under James Veitch the younger was separated from the Exeter firm, and three additional nurseries were developed in the Home Counties where trees, shrubs, and plants were grown.

James's eldest son, John Gould Veitch, was a well-known plant collector in Japan, and his second son, Harry James (1840–1924), took over running the business on his father's death in 1869. Harry was a powerful personality with commercial acumen and imagination which brought a new standard to the nursery trade, and he was one of the few horticulturalists to be knighted, in 1912. From the 1880s to 1914 Veitch's dominated the nurserymen's world. The firm's scientific outlook ensured that their collectors contributed much information to scientific institutions: they were instructed to collect information and specimens wherever possible of all kinds of natural objects likely to be of value to learned institutions. The company's outstanding achievement was probably to promote the first journey into western China, which eventually resulted in some of the best-known garden plants reaching England. In addition to bringing in new plants, the firm also produced many hybrids, employing some of the greatest plant hybridizers of the day, including John Dominy (1816–91), successful with orchids and fuchsias, and John Seden,

1 Willson, *W. London Nursery Gdns*, 82–3.
2 Ibid., 103; Harvey, 'Nurseries on Milne's Map', 182; J.H. Harvey, 'Mid-Georgian Nurseries of the London Region', *TLMAS*, XXVI (1975), 296; below, Trade.
3 Willson, *W. London Nursery Gdns*, 100.
4 *Chelsea Dir.* (1878).
5 Beaver, *Memorials*, 320.
6 Willson, *W. London Nursery Gdns*, 48; Croker, *Walk from London to Fulham*, 155.
7 Faulkner, *Chelsea*, I. 61–2.
8 Hadfield, *Hist. British Gardening*, 338–9.
9 *Chelsea Dir.* (1878).

who worked for Veitch's from 1861 and during his career produced 490 hybrid plants thought worthy of sale to the public. Harry Veitch retired in 1912, but the nephew who succeeded him did not have his ability, and Sir Harry closed the nursery in 1914, selling off the stock but not the name. Kew Gardens acquired some of Veitch's rare trees and shrubs. The 2½ a. site at Chelsea was sold.[1]

John Weeks (King's Road). By 1816 Edward Weeks had established a nursery in King's Road, but sometime before 1836 he had turned to developing the design and heating of horticultural buildings. His son John Weeks, described as Horticultural Builder and Hotwater Apparatus Manufacturer, carried on his business as J. Weeks & Company on the north side of King's Road between nos 124 and 126, midway between Keppel and Bywater streets,[2] held under a lease of 76 years from 1842 from George Downing and formerly the site of John More's nursery, 1822–7.[3] In 1857 the national press covered the opening of the 'magnificent winter garden' of Weeks & Company, described as horticultural architects, in their King's Road premises. The large conservatory included bays, orange trees, myrtles, fancy geraniums, azaleas, and many varieties of camellias, and mentioned one of the partners, Charles Gruneberg, son of a German nurseryman, who had been in England for 25 years.[4]

In 1855 Weeks also leased one acre further west along the north side of King's Road, between Gunter Grove and Maud Grove, from James Gunter, and purchased the freehold from Robert Gunter in 1857.[5] On the northern part adjoining Edith Road stood a groom's cottage, stables, coachhouse, workshops, and a covered yard used by Weeks's business; the larger part to the south was leased to William Bull for 28 years in 1863 with a house, outbuildings and forcing houses, conservatories, greenhouses, and seed houses, at £300 a year. When he retired in 1869 John Weeks vested his business in Alfred G.W. Weeks, George Deal, George Lillywhite, and Alexander Saunders, all horticultural builders. The groom's cottage, coachhouse, and stables were reserved to Weeks and his wife Lucy for life, and Alfred Weeks and the others were to pay annuities to John and his wife. Articles of partnership between Alfred Weeks and the others were drawn up in 1869. In 1874 Weeks contracted to sell to Bull the freehold of the latter's leasehold, then known as Bull's Establishment for New and Rare Plants, for which Bull would pay to Weeks (d. *c.*1879) and his wife £500 annually during their lives. The company continued to be called J. Weeks & Company, Horticultural Builders, becoming a registered company limited by shares in 1897, to which the two surviving partners, Alfred Weeks and Alexander Saunders, assigned and conveyed the leasehold and freehold premises. The firm seems to have ceased business *c.*1908. The remaining freehold adjoining Bull's nursery, then fronting Fernshaw Road, was sold to Messrs Derry & Toms in 1910, and in 1925 was sold by their successor, John Barker & Company, to Watney, Combe, Reid & Company.

William Bull (King's Road). A market gardener called John Bull had premises at Green lettuce Lane near the top of Blacklands Lane by 1817, giving his name to Bull's Gardens, but had apparently left the area by 1839;[6] any relationship to William Bull, who was born in Winchester in 1818, is unknown. William Bull apparently acquired the nursery of John Weeks in 1861,[7] and in 1863 took a 28-year lease from Weeks of part of the nursery at no. 536 King's Road, at the corner of Gunter Grove (above). Bull purchased the nursery outright in 1874, changing the name to Bull's Establishment for New and Rare Plants.[8] In 1878 he was called a new plant merchant.[9] He specialized in greenhouse plants and in pelargoniums, fuchsias, and verbenas; Chelsea Gem, a pelargonium he introduced in 1880, is still grown. He later specialized in orchids and became one of the three great orchid growers of the period: his annual orchid exhibition, which started in 1883, became one of the sights of the London season.[10] Bull also acquired nursery ground on the south side of Wimsett's nursery in Ashburnham Road, and when he died *c.*1902 he had just over 3 acres with glasshouses.[11] He left his business to his sons William and Edward: William junior died in 1913 but Edward continued to develop the orchid business, producing large numbers of hybrid plants and opening up new markets by bringing down the price. In 1916 he retired as a nurseryman and devoted his time to the nursery's two specialities, Bull's Plant Food and Bull's Fumigating Compound, at no. 536.[12] By 1920 the business had ceased and Edward sold the site for £19,500.[13]

James William Wimsett (Ashburnham Park Nursery, King's Road). Wimsett's nursery was founded in 1859, and by 1861 employed six men; it was enlarged after Cremorne Gardens were closed in 1877. Its proximity to the more famous nurseries of Veitch and Bull may have helped its business. After James Wimsett retired in 1904 the site of over 2 acres was offered for sale for building; the nursery continued under Wimsett's son Henry until 1907 when the site was used for a school.[14]

1 Hadfield, *Hist. British Gardening*, 338–41, 388–91; Willson, *W. London Nursery Gdns*, 50–7.
2 *Chelsea Dir.* (1878).
3 CL, deed 5825; Willson, *W. London Nursery Gdns*, 107.
4 *The Times*, 25 April 1857.
5 Para. based on CL, deeds 5816–21, 5825, 5830, 5832, 5834.
6 Above, farm-gardening.
7 Willson, *W. London Nursery Gdns*, 99.
8 CL, deeds 5816, 5819, 5827.
9 *Chelsea Dir.* (1878).
10 Willson, *W. London Nursery Gdns*, 99.
11 CL, deed 5827.
12 Willson, *W. London Nursery Gdns*, 101.
13 CL, deeds 5827, 5833.
14 Willson, *W. London Nursery Gdns*, 102–3; Chelsea Misc. 1812.

TRADE AND INDUSTRY

Early commercial activity included the brewing and selling of ale, and gravel extraction (below). A degree of industrial activity is indicated from the late 16th century. In 1594, for example, Ursula Smith was paid £49 10s. for two and a quarter years' rent of her house in Chelsea, which had been used for making the queen's 'engines',[1] possibly for use in warfare. From 1639 to 1642, a Mr Fletcher and others conducted experiments at Chelsea in dyeing wool, calico, and silk with various substances.[2]

Industrial premises are recorded from the later 17th century. In 1672 John Baker leased from Charles Cheyne two brick messuages near Chelsea College, one of them called Sweed Court, and two adjoining plots of land, one enclosed with a wall, which stretched from the highway to the Thames. He put up several buildings for a glass-making factory: two glasshouses, an ashhouse, pot chamber, sandroom and rooms for fetting and mettle, a long large warehouse and an accounting house nearly 100 ft long, a mill house, a kilnhouse with several kilns, a smith's shop, several warehouses, and 2 furnaces. By 1681 he had made some improvements and purchased much equipment, but Cheyne had seized back the property for rent arrears, and refused to complete the lease to Baker.[3]

Other industrial premises were also built between the Westminster highway and the Thames, including William Kemp's brewery near the Physic Garden in 1686,[4] the wharf and premises called the Swan belonging to Francis and Samuel Smith in 1664,[5] the Clarkson family's timber wharf, and Richard Wayte's dyehouse and wharf nearby prior to 1722.[6] Chelsea's riverside location made it a prime site for industry which required large quantities of water, either as an ingredient, such as brewing, or where river transport was necessary for raw materials and finished goods, which seems to be why Thurston's (below) moved there in 1857. There were wharves at Davis Place, Lombard Street, and Swan Walk and by 1829 considerable quantities of coal and timber were handled.[7] Though the creation of the embankment ended many of Chelsea's wharves and their trade, a considerable variety of business was still handled by the remaining wharves concentrated west of Battersea Bridge along Lots Road and Chelsea Creek. In addition to the Chelsea and Kensington municipal wharves, Lots Road had wharves of timber, slate, hay, lime, malt, stone, brick, and tile merchants in 1902.[8] Some wharves on Chelsea Creek were used for boat hire and repair as late as the 1930s.[9] Chelsea Yachts' boatyard was based near Lots Road power station in the 1930s, and during the war carried out a considerable amount of contract work for the Admiralty. After 1945 the firm expanded to workshops in Lacland Place: it was here that one of Donald Campbell's record-breaking speedboats was built. The company also diversified their activities away from purely maritime concerns, building parts for pre-fabricated housing.[10] After the Second World War Chelsea and Kensington borough wharves also served refuse barges, to which there was considerable opposition.[11] The new Cremorne Gardens used the site of Durham and Kensington wharves, and two jetties once used for transferring refuse survived in 2001. To the west the borough council still used Cremorne Wharf for waste management in 2001, and former wharves west of Lots Road were used as depots.

Several industries in Chelsea from the later 18th century were also associated with the growing demand created by the constant expansion of urban and suburban housing in London, such paper-stainers, Downing's floorcloth factory, and Thomas Crapper's sanitary fittings,[12] and others met the demands of the growing number of well-off consumers. These included several coach builders, such James Stocken, carriage builder, who had a workshop at no. 10 Upper George Street on the corner of Sloane Terrace by 1888, when he also took an underlease of part of Downing's factory at the northern end of no. 120 King's Road. There he had a coachhouse and took an addition lease in 1896 giving him access into College Place.[13] Hoopers, coach builders, had works in Smith Street, originally building horse-drawn coaches, but later becoming coach builders for the motor car manufacturer Daimler.[14] Another business serving middle-class consumers was Joubert's, fashionable cabinet makers and decorators, who in 1881 opened a workshop and showroom at no. 152 King's Road, known popularly as the Pheasantry. The last of the family to work there, Felix Joubert, made miniature furniture and other items for Queen Mary's dolls' house, and also designed the cinema next door at nos 148–50 called the Electric Theatre in 1912.[15] The showroom had closed by 1914 when only the basement was kept as workshops, and the rest let as studios, and Felix Joubert retired in 1932.[16]

1 *Cal. SP Dom.* 1591–4, 503.
2 BL, Sloane MS 3423.
3 PRO, C 8/249/81.
4 PRO, C 8/410/12.
5 PRO, C 10/488/248.
6 MLR 1722/4/271.
7 CL, deeds 3156, 17552; PRO, HO 107/1472/2/1/1; Faulkner, *Chelsea*, II. 172–3, 189.
8 *PO Dir. London* (1902); see Fig. 54.
9 Chelsea MB, *Official Guide* [1937], 79.
10 Denny, *Chelsea Past*, 53.
11 PRO, MT 39/349; *Chelsea Soc. Rep.* (1955), 43–6.
12 Below.
13 PRO, C 54/19359, m. 8, CL, deeds 19357, 19409.
14 H. Marsden-Smedley, 'Fifty years of the King's Road', *Chelsea Soc. Rep.* (1977), 56–62.
15 Above, Soc. Hist., social (theatres).
16 Denny, *Chelsea Past*, 38.

54. *Boatyards and wharves at Cheyne Walk and Lots Road 1956, with Chelsea Flour Mills (later Chelsea Wharf) and Lots Road power station*

A wide variety of occupations and trades were practised by Chelsea's inhabitants by the 19th century. In 1845 those qualified to serve as jurors included victuallers, brewers, maltsters, paper-stainers, coach builders, silk weavers, drapers, cordwainers, and coal dealers.[1] In 1831, 3,544 of Chelsea's inhabitants were employed in the retail trade, as shopworkers, apprentices and journeymen, 1,224 men were employed in professional positions, 1,445 worked on the river, the canals or on the roads, and over 20,000 were employed in domestic service. Those engaged in trade or the professions performed a wide variety of jobs and included 13 gun-makers, one pipe-maker, 16 hucksters, one calico-printer, six toymen, three wine-dealers, and one cork-cutter.[2] In 1938, the number of Chelsea's inhabitants employed in manufacturing had declined as a proportion of the parish population as a whole, and especially in relation to those employed in retail. In 1938 the borough had 370 factories employing 5,459 people, of whom the majority worked for clothing manufacturers, engineering firms and boatyards, and for furniture makers.[3]

PRINCIPAL INDUSTRIES AND FIRMS

Extractive Industries

Gravel was being dug in Chelsea manor in 1399, and earlier references to 'digging' probably also concerned gravel.[4] Gravel was also dug from Chelsea common.[5] Brickills, the name in the 1630s for the house later known as Stanley House, may indicate brick making or perhaps the digging of clay; some pits had been dug by 1630 on land associated with the property.[6] Sir Richard Manningham was granted a lease of Chelsea Park in 1724 which allowed him to dig and carry away gravel.[7] The nursery ground at the north-west corner of King's Road and Park Walk was being dug for clay and gravel in 1785.[8] The brick kiln in 'Chelsea fields' in 1613 was probably not in Chelsea parish but at Ebury (Westm.), near the later Chelsea Bun house, where many bricks were made in the 18th and 19th centuries.[9]

1 LMA, MR/FR 1845/J54.
2 Vestry mins, 1822–33.
3 J.H. Forshaw and P. Abercrombie, *County of London Plan* (1943), 88–9.
4 WAM 4805, 4810.
5 Above, Settlement, 1680–1865 (Chelsea Pk).
6 PRO, C 54/2845, no. 13.
7 CL, deed 3006.
8 CL, deed 3047.
9 *Middx Sess. Rec.* NS, I. 150–1; *Chelsea Soc. Rep.* (1971), 26–31; Denny, *Chelsea Past*, 38.

Brewing

Extant views of frankpledge between 1369 and 1399 show that many tenants of the manor were brewing and selling ale, in their houses and outside: between 10 and 25 men and women were presented at each view for breaking the assize of ale and other infringements, such as regrating, selling before the aletasters had been summoned, not using cups with the stamped measure, and not posting the customary sign.[1] William Nicoll and William Halle of Chelsea were described as brewers *c.*1425,[2] and premises which included brewhouses are recorded from the late 15th century, such as that owned by John Drayton prior to 1476 and John Young prior to 1524.[3] In 1536 Julian Fenrother of London leased property to John Pattenson of Chelsea which included her brewhouse in Chelsea with brewing vessels and utensils, furnace, 2 barrels, malt mill, and all equipment except for the horse and harness.[4] The property was added to the manorial demesne, and may have been the Feathers which stood by the riverside near Lordship Yard.[5]

A number of brewers and maltsters are recorded in the parish during the 17th century, and breweries and malt houses were recorded in Chelsea in 1648, 1658, 1677, and 1708.[6] William Kemp had a brewery near the Physic Garden in 1686,[7] and near it were the wharf and premises called the Swan belonging to Francis and Samuel Smith in 1664,[8] which included two malt houses and continued in use as a brewery until the formation of the embankment in the 1870s.[9] Thomas Harris leased a malt house with kiln and granaries near Lordship Yard from the manor in 1725.[10] The Two Brewers in King's Road, leased to Joseph Aldridge of Chelsea, brewer, had a brewhouse, yard, malthouse, and stabling for 6 horses in 1734.[11] There continued to be a number of breweries and brewhouses in Chelsea well into the 20th century. The Archer brewery had premises on the corner of Church Yard and Russell Street in the late 19th century;[12] there was a brewery tap at no. 22 Queen Street, and the Hans Town Brewhouse in George Street.[13]

By 1729 William Green of Fulham, brewer, had built a brewhouse and other buildings on 2 acres which lay on the south side of King's Road at Stanley Bridge.[14] In 1747 the lease and buildings of Green's brewery were assigned to John Poole of Strand (Westm.), staymaker, together with the utensils and goods including a malt mill, liquor engine and stand pipes, 2 coppers with ironwork and copper backs, 2 mashing tuns, and other items used in the brewery.[15] Thereafter it was known as Poole's brewery, and the family were still there in 1785,[16] but there was no longer a brewery there by the mid 19th century.[17]

Silk Production

In 1718 John Appletree of Worcester took out a royal patent for a way of raising silk in Great Britain, and established the Raw Silk Company to produce silk in Chelsea.[18] Appletree, Richard Musgrave, and others took a 61-year lease from William Sloane of the 40-acre Chelsea Park in 1718 at £200 for the use of the members of a joint-stock company who had a patent for silk production and intended growing mulberry trees for silkworms.[19] The park had been recommended to them as suitable for growing the trees and about 2,000 were planted. A large house with heating was built 'for nursing silkworms'.[20] In 1723 satin was made for the Princess of Wales from the English silkworms, but by the following year the enterprise was in financial difficulties, possibly because the import tax on raw silk had been removed in 1721 and other economic conditions at the time, and seems to have ceased operations. In 1724 the park was leased to Sir Richard Manningham, a member of the silk company, for building, subject to the lease of the silk producers' house and ground during the term of their patent; if their lease was not renewed, Manningham was permitted to sell the mulberry trees growing there.[21] Christopher Le Blon, a Flemish engraver, set up a factory in the park, fronting King's Road near the south-west corner of the park, to weave tapestries of Raphael's Cartoons 1732–4, but this also failed,[22] and his 3 workshops were empty in 1735.[23]

Chelsea Porcelain

The industry most closely associated with Chelsea, even two hundred years after it ceased to be a part of the economic life of the parish, was porcelain manufacture. A Huguenot silversmith, Nicholas Sprimont (d. 1771), then living in Soho, rented a house on the east side of Church Lane, later nos 26 and 28, in 1744 and began making fine hard-paste porcelain in the style pioneered

1 WAM 4805, 4809–12, 4814–17.
2 PRO, C 1/26/604.
3 PRO, C 1/49/47; REQ 2/3/41.
4 PRO, E 312/12, no. 57.
5 Above, Settlement, to 1680.
6 PRO, CP 25/2/575/1658MICH; CP 25/2/691/29CHASIIMICH; CP 25/2/946/7ANNEEASTER; C 6/184/93; C 8/410/12; *Cal. SP Dom.* 1655–6, 34; HMC, *7th Rep.* 158.
7 PRO, C 8/410/12.
8 PRO, C 10/488/248.
9 Denny, *Chelsea Past*, 126–7.
10 CL, deed 3040.
11 MLR 1734/5/116.
12 PRO, C 54/15239, m.7.
13 PRO, HO 107/1472/2/1/9–19; CL, deed 5360.
14 MLR 1730/2/261.
15 MLR 1747/3/54.
16 MLR 1785/2/186.
17 *PO Dir. London* (1845); PRO, HO 107/1472/2/1/1.
18 B. Smith, 'An Attempt to Grow Raw Silk in Chelsea in 18th Cent.' *Chelsea Soc. Rep.* (1971), 17–21; *Chelsea Soc. Rep.* (1962), 16.
19 MLR 1718/4/89; Beaver, *Memorials*, 143–6; above, Landownership, later ests (Sloane Stanley).
20 MLR 1732/3/68.
21 CL, deed 3006.
22 Beaver, *Memorials*, 144.
23 Poor rate bk, 1728–42, f. 388.

at the Meissen workshops in Germany.[1] He himself moved to Chelsea *c.*1748. A factory showroom was opened by 1747 in the double house forming the eastern half of the Monmouth House group at the top of Lawrence Street, and by 1749 the business was so successful that it expanded into the neighbouring property in Church Lane (later nos 32–6 even), and in 1750 into a purpose-built factory behind fronting Lawrence Street, on an empty site north of the house at the corner of Justice Walk. Sprimont seems to have had financial backers, who may have included Charles Gouyn up to *c.*1749, and Sir Everard Fawkener and his brother William, Governor of the Bank of England, from 1746, who probably paid for the new factory buildings in Lawrence Street. Sir Everard also helped get Meissen models for Chelsea to copy, and encouraged royal and noble patronage. Henry Porter, who bought the Church Lane premises when the freehold was sold by John Offley in 1751, was also involved in the business, especially in marketing the porcelain. Chelsea porcelain quickly established a reputation for high quality: in 1762–3 the factory produced the famous Mecklenburg-Strelitz service given by George III and Queen Charlotte to the queen's brother. The factory was at its height in the 1750s, producing some of its best work with much of the decoration inspired by plants and flowers from the nearby Physic Garden.[2] Sprimont also founded a training school of 30 boys taken from the parish and charity schools, training them as modellers and painters, who were among the *c.*100 workers at Chelsea in the early 1750s. From 1756 Sprimont was afflicted by ill-health, which led to a gradual decline in output, and in 1763 he held his last public sale. In 1765 the warehouse in the eastern half of Monmouth House was given up, and Sprimont's own residence in the western part was also used as a warehouse until it and the factory closed in 1768. The factory with its equipment, remaining stock, and leases was put up for sale in 1769, and sold to James Cox, jeweller, who in turn sold the failing factory in 1770 to William Duesbury, a ceramics decorator, and his partner John Heath, who together had opened a porcelain factory at Derby in 1756. The purchase of the Chelsea factory enabled them to found a branch of the Derby business in London and acquire Chelsea's rich and fashionable clientele, as well as to make use of the expertise and technical knowledge of the Chelsea artists and workers. However, production at the factory was greatly reduced from Sprimont's time, with no more than a dozen people employed. Duesbury renewed the ground lease until 1784, when the final sale to include Chelsea was held and the factory buildings in Lawrence Street were demolished.

Other China Workshops

Between 1769 and 1773, Thomas Bentley, a partner of Josiah Wedgwood of Burslem, had a workshop in Chelsea, located in Glebe Place and Upper Cheyne Row, for the purposes of enamelling and glazing.[3] It is possible that the large dinner service made by Wedgwood for the Empress Catherine was decorated and finished in Chelsea.[4] Wedgwood's workshop closed in 1774, but in the same year W. Ruhl established a pottery in Little Cheyne Row.[5] In 1790 the lease expired on this property and the factory moved to the King's Road. Nearly a century later, William de Morgan, an associate of William Morris, moved his pottery workshop from Fitzroy Square to Cheyne Row in 1872, where a kiln was built and pottery sold through Morris. The factory moved from Chelsea in 1882 and the firm established by de Morgan closed in 1907.[6]

More recently, the Chelsea Pottery was founded in 1952 by David and Mary Rawnsley at no. 13 Radnor Walk, formerly used for many years by Buchanan, coachbuilders. As an 'open' studio, any potter could come and work there, and lessons were also given to amateurs. In 1959 the Rawnsleys left the pottery in the hands of Brian Hubbard, who went on to run it for nearly forty years. In 1961 it was threatened with closure when the lease expired, because of the high property prices in Chelsea: a committee of artists and residents called on the borough council to use compulsory purchase powers to preserve the pottery, but eventually private individuals raised £26,000 to buy the premises. Redevelopment of Radnor Walk eventually forced the pottery to move to Ebury Mews, Belgravia, in 1994, and when the lease on the new premises expired, the Chelsea Pottery closed in 1997. The pottery produced a wide range of hand-made ceramics, using sgraffito technique, and was best known for its highly decorated earthenware, the colour of the pieces being achieved by the use of painting and coloured glazes, a technique that has been referred to as 'inlay and overlay'.[7]

Metalwork

A major foundry was established in World's End Passage by the bell founder Thomas Janaway, possibly the same premises as the New Foundry whose newly invented cannon was proved on Hampstead Heath in 1750 with great success. Thomas Janaway is thought to have learned bell-founding from Thomas Lester at the Whitechapel Foundry, and had set up at Chelsea by 1759, when he recast Chelsea's bells; peals for Kensington and St Martin-in-the-Fields were also cast there, but most of his work was for churches in Sussex, Surrey, and Kent.

1 Account based on E. Adams, *Chelsea Porcelain* (1987), passim.
2 *Chelsea Soc. Rep.* (1962), 46; *The Times*, 25 June 1936.
3 *DNB* s.v. Bentley.
4 Borer, *Two Villages*, 129.
5 Beaver, *Memorials*, 220.
6 Borer, *Two Villages*, 202.
7 Inf. from Studio Pottery web site (www.studiopottery.com/potteries/chelseapottery.html), 21 July 2003; *Chelsea Soc. Rep.* (1952), 41; Denny, *Chelsea Past*, 39–40; *The Times*, 21, 24 June, 3 July 1961.

He died in 1788, his tools and stamps being purchased by William Mears at Whitechapel. The foundry may have carried on working after his death, but had closed by 1824 when the site was sold for building.[1]

In 1809 James Pilton's Manufactory in King's Road advertised its fences, verandahs, and other ornamental metalwork.[2] Weaponsmiths Wilkinson Sword had workshops in Chelsea in the later 19th century: their Oakley works were located on the north side of King's Road between Sydney Street and Manor Street.[3] Thomas Ferguson had a mill and an iron foundry on land leased from the Cremorne estate,[4] possibly the same site as the Cadogan ironworks, which had a foundry on Lots Road in the early years of the 20th century.[5] George Glover & Company, patent dry gas meter manufacturers, who operated from the Ranelagh Works in Ranelagh Road, Pimlico (Westm.) in 1869 and 1878,[6] leased Downing's factory at nos 120–2 King's Road in 1878 and apparently moved their works there, as it was later referred to as Ranelagh Works.[7]

Downing's Floorcloth Factory

Floorcloth manufacture involved coating canvas in several thick layers of paint and then applying a pattern using wooden blocks, apparently carried out in summer to ensure drying, which provided a popular and inexpensive floor covering. The oil-cloth was also used for awnings, tents, and garden buildings.[8] A large floorcloth factory was established *c.*1750 on the south side of the Knightsbridge road, just outside the Chelsea boundary, and in the later 1780s it was let to Thomas Morley, who acquired the head lease in 1791.[9] In 1796 Thomas Smith sold to John Morley of Chelsea, floorcloth manufacturer, and William Frogatt a large plot of land on the south side of King's Road behind the new houses on the east side of Smith Street and south of a house already leased to Morley;[10] Morley was rated in 1795 for a factory in King's Road.[11] By 1813 two large factory buildings had been erected there,[12] and Morley is said to have opened the Chelsea factory in 1794. In 1799 Morley's business was taken over by Thomas Downing, who carried on making floorcloth at the Knightsbridge factory until it was demolished in 1823 to make way for Lowndes Terrace.[13]

In 1825 Thomas Downing acquired a 99-year lease of part of the ground of Thomas Davey's nursery on the north side of King's Road, opposite the Royal Avenue, with buildings he had erected on it,[14] and the premises were conveyed to Thomas and his sons Charles and George as partners in his business. The partnership was dissolved in 1832 and Thomas (d. 1834) made over the property to his sons. Charles died in 1833 and in 1835 his widow and sons sold their share to George Downing.[15] The factory on the south side of King's Road had been demolished by 1836 and became the site of Wellington Square.[16] George Downing let land fronting College Place for 5 houses and a Wesleyan chapel in 1838,[17] and a small parcel at the south-west corner was let to J. Weeks & Company, horticultural builders.[18] George (d. 1859) was succeeded in the business by his only son George Francis Downing.[19] The factory was destroyed by fire in 1873 and the business closed.[20] In 1878 G.F. Downing let the factory, at nos 120–2 King's Road, to George Glover & Company for 45 years, on which they opened a gas meter works; part of the site was sublet to Russell Depository and James Stocken, carriage builder.[21] In 1922 Thomas Crapper & Company bought part of the site, no. 120 King's Road.[22]

Paper-Stainers

Paper-staining, the creation of wallpaper, was another industry which benefitted from the expansion of house-building in London, and Chelsea had several firms in the 18th and 19th centuries, one of them quite long-lived. James Woodmason of Chelsea, paper-stainer, is said to have established a stained-paper factory in 1786 in Whitelands House, at the southern end of Marlborough Road, in partnership with the Dutch Eckhardt brothers,[23] but this is not substantiated by the existing evidence. Woodmason was in business at an unknown location in Chelsea in 1787, but sold his factory to Peter Bowers and William Harwood in 1789,[24] and the business was carried on under the name Messrs Harwood & Company, still trading in 1820.[25] Antoine George Eckhardt and his brother Frans Frederick are also said to have established their own new factory at Whitelands or Blacklands House in 1791, producing painted silk, varnished linen, cloth, and paper for furnishing rooms. The linen was painted by hand, by 40 girls at a time, aged 8 to 14 years.[26] The Eckhardt brothers went bankrupt in 1796,[27] and the stained-paper factory at Whitelands was run by Messrs Hinchliffe and

1 Faulkner, *Chelsea*, I. 74, reciting *Gent. Mag.*
2 Chelsea Misc. 468, 1103.
3 Bignell, *Chelsea 1860–1980*, 36.
4 CL, Chelsea Maps 41, altered tithe apportionment no. 4, 1863, Cremorne.
5 CL, deed 5360.
6 Old OS Map, London 88 (1869); *Chelsea Dir.* (1878).
7 CL, deeds 19402; 19369; 19415–6.
8 *Survey of London*, XLV. 31, 105.
9 Ibid., 31.
10 CL, deed 19418.
11 CL, deed 17552, p. 55.
12 *Regency A to Z.*
13 *Survey of London*, XLV. 31.
14 CL, deeds 19369, 19371.
15 CL, deed 19415.
16 Thompson, *Map* (1836).
17 CL, deed 19374.
18 CL, deed 19402.
19 CL, deed 19415.
20 *Survey of London*, XLV. 30.
21 CL, deeds 19345, 19349, 19357, 19402, 19404
22 CL, deed 19417; above. For hist. of site, below, retail trade.
23 Faulkner, *Chelsea*, II. 337.
24 LMA, O/81/1–2.
25 *Ambulator* (1820), 54–5.
26 Faulkner, *Chelsea*, II. 337.
27 Exeter Working Papers in British Book Trade History 10, at www.devon.gov.uk/library/locstudy/bookhist/e.html, 19 Feb. 2003.

Company in 1829.[1] In 1878 Scott, Cuthbertson & Company occupied Whitelands making, and hanging, wallpaper.[2] Timothy Wilsher, who had been apprenticed to Woodmason in 1787, built up his own business as a paper stainer, including a contract to supply and hang the paper for several new houses in and around College Street.[3] William Plees of Chelsea took out a patent for the manufacture of veined or mottled paper and making imitation leather by treating paper, in 1802.[4] John Goodson had a paper-staining factory in Ann Place in 1851.[5]

Crapper & Company

Thomas Crapper (1836–1910), notable as a manufacturer and supplier of sanitary goods and improver of the syphons used in flushing toilets, came to Chelsea from Yorkshire *c.*1850 as an apprentice to a master plumber.[6] In 1861 he set up Thomas Crapper & Company in Robert Street, and in 1866 moved to the larger premises called Marlborough Works,[7] nos 50 & 52 Marlborough Road (later Draycott Avenue). He took a partner, Robert Marr Wharam, whose financial skills added to Crapper's enterprise built up a successful firm. Described, as many plumbers were, as lead merchants in 1878,[8] the works had 'manufacturing sanitary engineers' emblazoned across the building by 1892. Part of Crapper's success was due to his promotion of the use of plumbed-in bathroom fittings and his introduction of the concept of a showroom. Sanitary fittings, especially WCs, were subject to enormous prudery and whispered consultations with architects; Crapper installed plate-glass windows at the front of the Marlborough Works with toilet pans prominently displayed to a shocked public, who claimed that ladies would faint at the sight. His firm was also successful because of the quality of its manufactures and its service in fitting them using the best engineers. In the 1880s the firm was invited to supply and install new fittings for the bathrooms and cloakrooms at Sandringham and all the plumbing and drainage work involved, the first of a succession of royal warrants. Thomas Crapper retired in 1904, and was succeeded by his partner Robert Wharam and his nephew George Crapper. The comprehensive nature of the work they undertook can be gauged by a description of the business in 1905: brass founders and engineers; manufacturers of sanitary appliances, heating apparatus, electrical, hydraulic, steam and gas fittings; and lead, zinc, glass, colour, and varnish merchants.[9] In 1905 the firm negotiated for a site at nos 111–15 (odd) Fulham Road, near the corner of College Street, on which they were going to build a new showroom and warehouse, possibly to replace the Marlborough Works, but the agreement was cancelled in 1907,[10] and later that year they acquired no. 120 King's Road, a large house in the south-east corner of George Glover & Company's Ranelagh Works, part of Downing's factory site. This attractive 3-storeyed house with its substantial portico became their showroom, and the Marlborough Works were retained for the manufacturing side. The company purchased the freehold in 1922 with some additional property behind,[11] and extensions were made to give more showroom and storage space. All operations were based at King's Road by the late 1950s, the Marlborough Works having been sold, and the company was run by Wharam's son, Robert G. Wharam. On his retirement he sold the firm in 1966 to nearby rivals John Bolding & Sons, who closed the showroom at no. 120, sold off the property, and moved Crapper & Company to their own premises in Davies Street (Westm.). Thomas Crapper & Company was later revived as an independent firm, and in 2003 was manufacturing high-quality period bathroom fittings from its base at Stratford-upon-Avon (Warws.).

Thurston & Company

John Thurston founded Thurston & Company, billiard table and cabinet makers, in Newcastle Street (St Clement Danes) in 1799,[12] and is credited as the creator of the modern billiard table, introducing innovations such as the slate-bed table and rubber cushions. In 1857 Thurston's obtained a 99-year lease of no. 33 Cheyne Walk, initially using the premises for a warehouse in conjunction with the adjoining riverside wharf. Although it continued to maintain a central London office, the factory was moved in 1872 to the Cheyne Walk site. It remained there until 1962, moving out of Chelsea when the land was sold for redevelopment.

RETAIL TRADE

The shops which served Chelsea's residents expanded as the built-up area increased. Originally the old village had the main concentration of local shops, in Church Lane and along the riverside, but after King's Road became public in 1830 more shops were built along its length, and other concentrations developed along Marlborough Road (renamed Draycott Avenue in 1907)[13] and at the Knightsbridge end of Sloane Street. Until the second half of the 20th century, Chelsea's shops were mainly local, supplying food, drink, and basic commodities, such as ironmongery and haberdashery, to local residents. King's Road also had a concentration of retail outlets for

1 Faulkner, *Chelsea*, II. 337.
2 *Chelsea Dir.* (1878)
3 LMA, O/81/3–4.
4 CL, deed 3048.
5 PRO, HO 107/1472/2/1/1.
6 Acct based on inf. from Thos Crapper & Co. via website, www.thomas-crapper.com, 18 Feb. 2003.
7 Or Marlboro', as engraved across front of bldg.
8 *Chelsea Dir.* (1878).
9 KL, deed 12113.
10 KL, deeds 12113–16.
11 CL, deed 19417.
12 Acct based on H. Reid, 'Thurston's Billiard Table Factory', *Chelsea Soc. Rep.* (1957), 43–9; (1962), 36–8; inf. from co. 29 Mar. 2003, via website (www.thurston-games.co.uk).
13 LCC, *Names of Streets* (1929 edn).

55. *Sloane Street looking north to Knightsbridge in the early 20th century*

nursery gardeners from the late 18th century,[1] and later some light industrial and manufacturing premises. The changing use of King's Road is encapsulated by the history of nos 120 and 122, the site of several well-known firms mentioned above. They were the premises of a well-known nursery gardener and florist, Thomas Davey, by 1798,[2] Thomas Downing's floorcloth factory from 1825,[3] with a small parcel at the south-west corner let to J. Weeks & Company, horticultural builders,[4] and up to 1878 the house at no. 120 was let to Dr F. Palmer, surgeon.[5] Downing's factory closed in 1873,[6] and in 1878 the site was leased to George Glover for his gas meter works. Part of the site was sub-let to the Russell Depository company, which was followed by the Army and Navy Depository, and part at the northern end with the access into College Place was let to James Stocken, carriage builder. In 1903 part was leased to Joshua Binns, timber merchants. Glover's, which had bought the freehold of the site, sold no. 120 King's Road, an attractive mid-Victorian villa, in 1922 to the sanitary engineers, Thomas Crapper and Company, who opened a showroom there;[7] they remained until 1966.[8] The whole site was soon afterwards rebuilt, and in 2003 the street front of nos 120 and 122 were occupied by a women's fashion boutique and a branch of a well-known fashion chain.

Marlborough Road/Draycott Avenue was until the 1930s a busy local shopping centre. In 1855 the southern end of the road had a cowkeeper, Charles Wray, in John's Place, and a number of tradesmen connected with building trades, as well as shopkeepers.[9] In 1878 it had numerous small tradesmen and services, including newsagent, bootmaker, furniture dealer, hairdresser, baker, dairy, pork butcher, fried fish dealer, coffee room, gas fitter, beer retailer, zinc worker. Some larger premises were also dotted along the street, such as Crapper's works,[10] the National Penny Bank, a board school, the Free Registry Office for Young Servants, the Aerated Bread Company, and London Parcels Delivery Company. There were also some private residents, mainly at the southern end.[11] In the 1870s the street was also something of a centre for drapery. In 1871 Peter Jones started his drapers' shop in two buildings in Marlborough Road, moving to King's Road in 1877. In 1877 Joseph Cox at nos 163–5 described himself as 'the People's Draper' and invited ladies to recommend his business to their servants, being the cheapest house in the neighbourhood for drapery, hosiery, haberdashery, flannels, and blankets. Marlborough Road was referred to as in Brompton, which was much nearer than Chelsea, still associated with the village near the river.[12] In 1902 Cox's premises had become the drapers' shop of Jones Brothers, who by 1934 were called fancy drapers and occupied nos 159–65.[13]

Occupation of Marlborough Road remained substantially the same in 1902, but by 1934 the redevelopment of the street and adjoining areas had brought many changes. Blocks of flats and houses for middle-class residents had been built at the southern end, and the block between Green and Ives streets now contained a telephone exchange. Some smaller premises north of the council school had been replaced by Harrods' 5-storeyed depository building of 1911, and Jones Brothers covered three shops near the Fulham Road end. By 1942 nearly all the east side had been cleared of smaller premises, except for the D'Oyley Arms public house; the block between Denyer and Mossop was

1 Above, farm-gardening.
2 Ibid.
3 CL, deeds 19369, 19371, 19415; *Chelsea Soc. Rep.* (1991), 52.
4 CL, deed 19402.
5 *Chelsea Dir.* (1878).
6 CL, deed 19415; above, Downing's.
7 CL, deeds 19343, 19349, 19357, 19360, 19402, 19404, 19409, 19412, 19416–17.
8 Above, Thos Crapper.
9 *PO Dir. London* (1855).
10 Above, Thos Crapper.
11 *Chelsea Dir.* (1878).
12 A. Adburgham, *Shopping in Style: London from the Restoration to Edwardian Elegance* (1979), 132, 134; *Chelsea Dir.* (1878).
13 *PO Dir. London* (1902, 1934).

occupied by a new service building for John Lewis and Peter Jones department store, with a building for the Inland Revenue north of Mossop Street. On the west side smaller local shops were limited to the part of the street north of Ixworth Place.[1]

Sloane Street in 1855 was little different from the other retail areas of Chelsea, with shops providing a range of goods and services for local inhabitants, several private residents, some lodging-houses, and a range of other occupants such as the Cadogan Hotel at no. 75, Hans Town School of Industry, Cadogan baths, and some private schools.[2] By 1902, however, although it still had a few food shops, Sloane Street now had a more distinctive profile. Between Knightsbridge and Pont Street the most dominant group of occupants were dressmakers, furriers, milliners, and ladies' tailors, an extension of the shopping area of Knightsbridge. South of Pont Street, with Cadogan Gardens on the east side, there was a high proportion of private residents, many titled, and professional men such as surgeons and dentists.[3] This profile was altered a little by 1934 by the erection of several large blocks of flats, though most at the northern end of the street had shops on the ground floor.[4]

56. *United Dairies, no. 46 Old Church Street, in 1951; a private house in 2003*

Later 20th Century

A wide variety of shops still existed in the borough of Chelsea in 1947, when there were 52 dairies, 32 street traders, 71 public houses, 29 butchers, 18 bakers, 13 fishmongers, 44 grocers, 46 confectioners, 37 greengrocers, and 23 canteens and clubs. However, the broader social dimension can be seen in the large number, 198, of restaurants and clubs in the borough.[5]

In the 1960s, however, the King's Road led a new retail movement with the arrival of the fashion boutique, and Chelsea became the epicentre of a great cultural change in Britain, usually referred to as the 'Swinging Sixties'. Although Mary Quant's first boutique, Bazaar, opened at no. 138A King's Road in 1955 and led a trend for those aware of her clothes, it was the mass-production of youthful fashion by Quant's Ginger Group and other innovative young designers in the early 1960s which led to the flood of boutiques opening in King's Road together with coffee bars and cafés providing for the new, young market.[6] Although Bazaar closed in 1968,[7] Quant made the new styles – the mini-skirt, hot pants, tights – available for the mass market by introducing the Chelsea Girl boutiques across the country, but King's Road remained the mecca for the young and style conscious in the 60s and 70s.[8] Boutiques sprang up, and property prices, especially at the east end of the road, soared: a shoe shop worth £4,500 in 1950, was worth £30,000 in 1967, and £45,000 in 1969.[9] A traders' association was formed for King's Road in 1970, describing itself as 'London's newest and most exciting'; its members claimed to form the élite of British fashion in clothing, restaurants, and antiques. One of its objects, however, was protection against crime: fashionableness had brought a lot of shop-lifting and bad cheques, and the association was considering having its own security guards.[10] By the early 1970s, planning applications for shops had reached 250 a year and it was noted that the character of King's Road had changed dramatically over the previous thirty years from 'daily shops to an almost unbroken series of so-called boutiques'; over the same period the number of restaurants and clubs had also increased dramatically.[11] The old-established traders disappeared, replaced by supermarkets, large stores, dress shops and boutiques, which served not local people but the whole of London as well as foreign visitors.[12] Chelsea also became the focus for other innovative shops, such as Habitat, which Terence Conran first opened at no. 77 Fulham Road, between the northern end of Draycott and Sloane avenues in 1964, moving to the former Gaumont cinema at no. 206 King's Road in 1973.[13] By the 1980s, art galleries had also become a regular feature of King's Road and Sloane Square, forced out of central London locations by rising property prices.[14]

1 Ibid. (1902; 1934; 1942).
2 Ibid. (1855).
3 Ibid. (1902); see Fig. 55.
4 *PO Dir. London* (1934).
5 LCC, *London Statistics*, NS, III (1947–56), 146–7; see Fig. 56.
6 Above, Settlement, twentieth cent. (Chelsea and fashion).
7 K. McIntyre, 'The Most 'In' Shops for Gear', in *Twentieth Century Architecture 6: The Sixties*, ed. E. Harwood and A. Powell (2002), 38.
8 *Chelsea Soc. Rep.* (1972), 20–1.
9 Borer, *Two Villages*, 248–51.
10 *The Times*, 13 May 1970.
11 *Chelsea Soc. Rep.* (1972), 20–1.
12 Borer, *Two Villages*, 248–51.
13 McIntyre, 'Most 'In' Shops', 41; inf. from Habitat via website (www.habitat.co.uk), 30 June 2003.
14 D. Farr, 'London as an Art Centre', *Illus. London News*, 274(1), no. 7054 (1986), 58–9.

57. *Duke of York Square, on part of the Royal Military Asylum site, opened in 2003*

King's Road's fashionableness accelerated locally a national trend which was changing the way people shopped and reducing the viability of small local shops and thereby their range and number. The demand for sites in and around King's Road quickly pushed up prices beyond the reach of ordinary local shops, as Chelsea became an increasingly fashionable and socially exclusive area in which to live and to shop. By the end of the 20th century the era of individualistic but cheap fashion had gone, and in King's Road quirky boutiques had been largely replaced by retail outlets for designers, and branches of leading fashion chains, together with the ubiquitous coffee bars and well-known high-street names. A few individual, but expensive, fashion shops remained, such as the unprepossessing shoe shop of Manolo Blahnik just off King's Road in Church Street, and other shops selling antiques, furnishings, and, at the World's End, bric-a-brac. The independent shops and restaurants which remained were constantly under pressure, however. In 2003 the individualism which had marked out Chelsea, especially King's Road, since the 1960s was said to be in its 'death throes' as the few remaining independent boutiques, restaurants, and specialist shops were threatened again by rent rises which only large chains would be able to afford.[1]

The pressure to move retailing upmarket had also effected Draycott Avenue. By the end of the 20th century the shops at the northern end, like the adjoining parts of Fulham Road and Walton Street, served a well-off and fashionable clientele with the remaining older houses converted into shops for leading designers, antiques, and expensive furnishings, and into restaurants and cafés. Peter Jones's warehouse had been converted into an offshoot of its department store as PJ2, housing its furnishing and interior design departments; the Harrods depository of 1911 had been converted into shops and a café. The Michelin building, no. 81 Fulham Road, refurbished and restored in 1985–6 by Conran Roche and YRM, housed a restaurant, the Conran shop, and offices.[2] In Sloane Street, already a concentration of expensive fashion shops, the late 20th century brought fewer changes but a greater number of designer shops. Retail outlets were grouped at the northern and southern ends of the street, and were mainly occupied by top designers and expensive interior furnishers. The demand for smart and attractive shopping facilities was also being met at the beginning of the 21st century by the redevelopment of the former Duke of York's Headquarters (the Royal Military Asylum). The boys had moved out of the Asylum in 1909 and the buildings and grounds had been used by territorial army units;[3] the grounds had also provided playing fields for a variety of clubs, schools, and army sports teams.[4] The Ministry of Defence sold the site to Cadogan Estates *c.*2000, and the part between the original Asylum buildings and shops in King's Road was redeveloped with a new shopping area called Sloane Place, whose occupants included several leading fashion names, and west of that a public paved area laid open to King's Road with fountains and a café, called Duke of York Square, all opened in 2003.[5]

Peter Jones

Peter Jones was the one major department store entirely within Chelsea's boundary.[6] Peter Jones opened his own draper's shop in 1871 in two shops in Marlborough Road (Draycott Avenue), possibly nos 163 and 165. In 1877 he moved his shop to nos 4 and 6 King's Road, on

1 *Evening Standard Mag.* 30 May 2003.
2 Pevsner, *London NW.* 588–9; see Plate 16.
3 *Survey of London*, IV. 91.
4 Denny, *Chelsea Past* (1996), 67.
5 Cadogan Estates, *Duke of York's News*, July 1999; *Sloane Square* (magazine, issue 9, June 2003); see Fig. 57.
6 Based on Adburgham, *Shopping in Style*, 134–5; M. Effendowicz, 'The Shop on the Corner', *Chelsea Soc. Rep.* (1987), 22–5.

58. *Shops in King's Road in 1970, looking towards the curving façade of Peter Jones*

the north side near Sloane Square and by 1878 occupied nos 2, 4, and 6.[1] This strategic position allowed him to attract custom from Hans Town and Belgravia, and by 1884 his drapery had expanded to absorb two neighbouring shops, and by the end of the 1880s he had acquired a further ten premises on the Kings Road and Symons Street. The miscellaneous collection of buildings was replaced in 1889 by a five-storeyed building of red Mansfield stone and red Fareham brick with a green slate roof and a corner turret; it was the first such store to be lit by electricity. The grand rebuilding of what had once been a draper's reflected the changing clientele of the shop and its area: Jones's earliest customers had been largely from Chelsea's artisan population, but by 1890 the area near Sloane Square was filled by upper- and middle-class residents, for whom the rebuilt store was designed.[2] Jones died in 1905, and the store was sold in 1906 to another draper, John Lewis, who handed it over to his son, Spedan Lewis, in 1914. As chairman of Peter Jones, Spedan put into practice his democratic ideas including staff involvement and profit sharing, which became the foundation of the John Lewis Partnership. By the 1930s the store also occupied the public house and other buildings facing Sloane Square and in 1932 a new building was designed by J.A. Slater & A.H. Moberly and William Crabtree with C.H. Reilly as consultant to replace the 1889 building. It was built 1935–7, one of the first examples of the use of the curtain wall in England and one of the most elegant, with a continuous run of glass curving along the King's Road façade. An extension of 1937 linked the King's Road section with the Cadogan Gardens section, enlarged at the back in 1965.[3] In 2000 a £100M redevelopment of the Grade II*-listed building was begun, under the design of J. McAslan & Partners. Some departments were moved to the shop's warehouse in Draycott Avenue, called PJ2, to facilitate the work, during which the store remained open. The centre of the site was demolished and replaced by a large central window-lit atrium with escalators linking all the floors, which opened in 2002; the entire work was scheduled for completion at the end of 2004.[4]

1 *Chelsea Dir.* (1878).
2 *Chelsea Soc. Rep.* (1987), 23.
3 Pevsner, *London NW.* 581; see Fig. 58.
4 Inf. from Peter Jones via web site (www.peterjones.co.uk), 31 Mar. 2003.

SOCIAL HISTORY

SOCIAL AND CULTURAL ACTIVITIES

INNS, TAVERNS, AND COFFEE HOUSES

Chelsea's importance as a pleasure resort near London from the 17th century was reflected in its large number of places of refreshment. The earliest recorded alehouse in Chelsea may have been the Rose, which stood on the corner of Church Lane opposite the parish church in 1538 and in which an assize of ale was held in 1547.[1] The Pye or Magpie, so-named by 1587,[2] fronted the riverside road on the east side of Shrewsbury House; courts leet were occasionally held there.[3] It was known as New Pier House, Cheyne Walk, in the 1840s but renamed the Magpie and Stump by 1855. In 1886 it was destroyed by fire in 1807 and replaced by a private house, and its early 19th-century skittle alley was converted into a garden studio.[4] From the early 17th century, references to alehouses and coffee houses are frequent. The Dog, under Richard Eeds, was recorded in 1636 by John Taylor the water-poet,[5] and renamed the Rising Sun in 1670, while the Feathers, later on the corner of Cheyne Row, was first recorded in 1666.[6] Samuel Pepys tried to visit the Swan east of Cheyne Walk with friends in 1666.[7] The village, particularly the riverside, had the largest concentration of better-known inns, such as the Cricketers, the King's Head, the Magpie, Saltero's Coffee House, the Thames Coffee House, the Yorkshire Grey, the Feathers, and the Cross Keys.[8] At the corner of Church Lane and Cheyne Walk stood the White Horse by 1694,[9] the stopping place for coaches in the 18th century. By the end of the 17th century several inns had bowling greens, such as the one behind the Three Tuns by the river, another attached to an inn by the river west of Lindsey House, and Ninepin Place on the glebe next to College Walk in 1717.[10] Victuallers, recorded in Chelsea from the middle of the 17th century,[11] were licensed in increasing numbers during the 18th century, from 31 in 1716, 52 in 1728, and 68 a century later.[12] They were also prominent amongst tradesmen licensed to serve as jurors, making up over two thirds of those qualified in 1845.[13] Peter Newhall's coffee house in Chelsea, licensed in 1730 but whose location is unknown, was a meeting-place for a society of gardeners *c.*1725: 20 working nurserymen met monthly to discuss specimen plants and new varieties shown by their growers. The members included Thomas Fairfax, author of *The City Gardener* (1722).[14]

One of the better known of Chelsea's resorts in the 18th century was Don Saltero's Coffee House.[15] Saltero, more correctly James Salter, had formerly been a barber and a valet to Sir Hans Sloane, before opening a coffee house at no. 59 Cheyne Walk, at the corner of Lawrence Street, by 1697. By 1715 he had moved his coffee house to the west side of Danvers Street, and then to its final location at the newly-built no. 18 Cheyne Walk by 1718. Saltero's soon became frequented by the wealthy and fashionable of Chelsea, being noticed by *Tatler* in 1709. Part of the attraction was the large collection of unusual objects and curiosities collected by Saltero, including, reputedly, a hat which had belonged to the sister of Pontius Pilate's wife's chambermaid. Items were donated by Sir Hans Sloane, Rear Admiral Sir John Munden, and other Chelsea residents, and so extensive was the collection that a catalogue was printed. Saltero died in 1728, and his daughter and her husband, Christopher Hall, ran the premises as a tavern until 1758. It continued to attract considerable custom, largely because of the collection of curiosities, but in 1799 the collection was sold and dispersed.[16] By the middle of the 19th century, the coffee house was described as a 'quiet tavern', and in 1867 no. 18 was converted into a private residence.

Some other pleasure resorts popular in the 18th century were thought of as being in Chelsea as they stood near to the Royal Hospital, but were in fact at Ebury or Pimlico in Westminster: these included Stromboli House and Gardens, Star and Garter Tavern in Five Fields, and Jenny's Whim.[17] The most famous, however, was probably the Chelsea Bun House in Grosvenor Row,

1 PRO, SC 2/186/43; SC 6/HenVIII/2103, m.3d.

2 BL, Harl. Roll L.26.

3 W. Gaunt, *Chelsea* (1954), 69; Beaver, *Memorials*, 202.

4 Chelsea Misc. 13(1); *PO Dir. London* (1844–1855 edns).

5 *Middx & Herts. N&Q*, IV. 78.

6 Beaver, *Memorials*, 163, 218; Davies, *Chelsea Old Ch.* 75.

7 *Diary of Sam. Pepys*, ed. R. Latham and W. Matthews, VII. 94.

8 Beaver, *Memorials*, 201–2, 218; Davies, *Chelsea Old Ch.* 41; Bignell, *Chelsea 1860–1980*, 28, 120; LMA, MR LV3/95; LV5/23; LV8/29.

9 PRO, C 5/619/126.

10 Dr King's MS, pp 47, 49, 64.

11 Cal. Middx Sess. Bks, 1638/9–44, 148; PRO, C 6/230/53; C 7/341/47.

12 LMA, MR/LV 3/4, 3/95, 20/5.

13 LMA, MR/FR 1845/J54.

14 Lillywhite, *London Coffee Hos*, 679; LMA, MR/LV 5/23.

15 Para. based on *Survey of London*, II. 61–3; B. Lillywhite, *London Coffee Houses* (1963), 194–5; E.B. Chancellor, *The Pleasure Haunts of London* (1925), 272–5.

16 *Gent. Mag.* LXIX(1), 160.

17 W. Wroth, *London Pleasure Gardens of the 18th Cent.* (1896), 219–24.

which was flourishing by the early years of the 18th century, and also housed a museum of curiosities and antiquities. In addition to having royal patronage, it reportedly sold 240,000 buns on Good Friday 1829, but this could not prevent it from being closed and demolished in 1839 and its collection of curiosities sold at auction.[1]

In the course of the 18th century taverns and tea gardens opened up away from the river. The Marlborough Tavern, halfway along Blacklands Lane, had a garden attached by 1794.[2] The Cow and Calf stood on the eastern edge of Chelsea common in Blacklands Lane where it joined Fulham Road by 1764 when it was licensed to Richard Shelmandine or Shelmerdine; he held it by lease from the owners of the manor by 1781.[3] It was said to have been rebuilt and renamed the Admiral Keppel in 1790, but William Sandeford received a victuallers' licence for the latter in 1780.[4] Admiral Keppel public house, later no. 77 Fulham Road, was in use between 1790 and 1856 with a music and dancing licence; the building was demolished and replaced in 1856.[5]

A detached house called Manor House in King's Road between Little's Nursery and Shawfield Street was turned into a tea and recreation garden by Richard Smith *c.*1836. Commercial Tavern was later built there and Manor House became the Chelsea Literary and Scientific Institution.[6] The Six Bells, no. 197 King's Road, dated at least to 1722 when John Westerbone was licensed.[7] In 1810 it was licensed to William Bray, who with his brother John ran a tea garden there in the 1820s. In 1895 it still had a bowling green with arbours or little summer-houses in style of an old-fashioned tea garden, and had a flourishing bowling club with 65 members. The inn was rebuilt in Tudor style in 1900.[8]

Several of Chelsea's picturesque 18th-century inns survived into the later 19th century but were gradually picked off by redevelopment, especially along the river. They were replaced by pubs and restaurants concentrated in and around the King's Road as the commercial and social heart of Chelsea, where venues like the Markham Arms and the Chelsea Potter became famous in the 1960s and 70s.

RANELAGH GARDENS

When the Ranelagh House estate was sold in 1735, the largest section, 12¾ acres including Ranelagh House and the Avenue, a coachway made by the earl of Ranelagh from the house to the London road at Ebury (Westm.), was bought by Benjamin Timbrell, master builder or carpenter, and James Swift,[9] partly as building land and

59. *The Chelsea Potter Public House, no. 119 King's Road*

partly to lease out. They are said to have leased part to James Lacey, patentee of Drury Lane Theatre, and Solomon Rietti, for creation of Ranelagh pleasure gardens,[10] but Lacey and Rietti do not appear in the extant papers regarding the creation of the gardens. In 1741 Timbrell and Swift leased to William Crispe and James Myonet the mansion and gardens for 21 years at £130, and the Avenue or walk, paved and planted with a row of lime trees and hedges on both sides, for 4 years at a peppercorn rent. Under an agreement drawn up with John David Barbutt and James Myonet just before the lease, Timbrell and John Spencer, carpenter, were to erect a building in the gardens according to an agreed design at a cost of £300: this may be the Rotunda, said to have been built by Timbrell in 1741, possibly to a design by William Jones, architect to the East India Company.[11] The Rotunda was 555 ft in circumference and 150 ft in internal diameter. It had four Doric porticoes marking its entrances. On the exterior was an arcade encircling the building above which was a gallery reached by steps at the porticoes. In the interior was a circle of 52 boxes separated by wainscotting, each of which could accommodate 7–8 people and their refreshments. Above the boxes was a gallery with a similar range of boxes entered from the outside gallery. The Rotunda was lit by 60 windows and chiefly built of wood. From the ceiling hung numerous chandeliers. The roof was supported by a square erection in the centre of the building made up of decorated pillars and arches, which included a fireplace with a chimney and open fire. Originally this structure

1 Chancellor, *Pleasure Haunts of London*, 279–81; Gaunt, *Chelsea*, 73.
2 Horwood, *Plan* (1792–5).
3 LMA, MR/LV 8/29; MLR 1835/4/726.
4 LMA, MR/LV 9/94
5 D. Howard, *London Theatres and Music Halls 1850–1950* (1970), 3.
6 *Chelsea Soc. Rep.* (1991), 45–8.
7 LMA, MR/LV 3/95.
8 *Survey of London*, IV. 86; *Chelsea Soc. Rep.* (1992), 52.
9 Above, Landownership, later ests (Ranelagh); LMA, MDR/MB/1734/1/145.
10 Lysons, *Environs*, II. 173; Dean, *Royal Hosp.* 225; *TLMAS*, NS, vii(13), 216–17.
11 Wroth, *London Pleasure Gdns*, 199–218; see Fig. 60.

60. *Interior of the Rotunda at Ranelagh Gardens, during a breakfast*

had contained the orchestra but after a few years the latter was moved to the side for acoustic reasons. Behind the orchestra an organ was set up by Byfield in 1746.

Also in 1741 Crispe and Myonet made an agreement with Michael Christian Festing, who was to make contracts with performers for musical entertainments, with Crispe and Myonet paying the salaries of Festing and the entertainers; they also arranged to pay for slating work on the new building. To raise sufficient capital Crispe and Myonet, who were erecting a 'grand amphitheatrical structure' for entertainment of the public by 'musick ridottos', had borrowed money from two bankers who would raise £5,000 from subscribers, each paying 25 guineas and receiving a free ticket for two people to each evening's entertainment, up to 6 a year. To secure this capital Crispe and Myonet conveyed the house, garden, and avenue for 8 years to trustees for themselves, Barbutt, and the rest of the subscribers.[1] Capital for the undertaking was also said to have been raised by issuing 36 shares of £1,000 each, perhaps later on when it became clear that more capital was required. The principal shareholder and manager was Sir Thomas Robinson, Bt, MP, who built a house, Prospect Place in the grounds.[2]

The Rotunda and gardens opened in 1742 with a public breakfast, and Ranelagh quickly became one of the most fashionable resorts around London.[3] Horace Walpole wrote about it a couple of weeks after it opened, breakfasting there and describing the immense amphitheatre with balconies full of little ale-houses. In the 1740s he like many others went constantly to Ranelagh, getting held up in traffic jams of coaches trying to get there. In the early days admission was sometimes 1s. sometimes 2s., including the breakfast and morning concert. On special nights with firework displays the price was 3s. or more. Tickets costing from a half to two guineas (10s. 6d.–42s.) were issued for masquerades. Later on the usual admission charge was 2s. 6d., which included the refreshments of tea, coffee, and bread and butter. It was usually open on three days in the week. The regular season for evening concerts and garden-promenade began at Easter, but the Rotunda was often open in February or earlier for dances. In its early days the public breakfastings and morning concerts were a constant feature, but in 1754 the proprietors were refused a license for music, and only breakfasts were held; thereafter the breakfasts and concerts were apparently abandoned.

Between the acts of the evening concerts visitors walked in the gardens to the sound of music, and a garden-orchestra was erected *c.*1767. The fairly formal gardens had several gravel walks shaded by elms and yews, a flower-garden, and an octagon grass plot. The principal walk led from the south end of Ranelagh House to the bottom of the gardens, where there was a circular Temple of Pan, and the walks were lit at night with lamps in the trees. There was also a canal with a structure called the Chinese House or the Venetian Temple.

The chief diversion at Ranelagh, mentioned frequently and critically, was the promenade in the Rotunda, with the company walking round and round inside the building in a quiet and orderly fashion, rarely disturbed by the unseemly behaviour found at Vauxhall and elsewhere. The company was fairly mixed, and the nobility complained about the number of tradesmen, but it seems to have been more exclusive than Vauxhall. By 1774 it was usual for the fashionable to arrive at 11 p.m. after the concerts had ended.

For the first 30 years or so Ranelagh was highly fashionable and had attractive entertainments. The concerts featured many fine singers and instrumentalists of the day, and performances of choruses from oratorios and operas; Mozart performed there in 1764. Also popular were the masquerades at which the company wore masks, which included tents in the garden, maypole and rustic dancing, a gondola and a sea-horse lit with lamps on the canal, shops attended by masked shopkeepers, booths for tea and wine, and gaming-tables and dancing in the Rotunda. Later in the 18th century, in addition to the concerts in the Rotunda there were garden concerts, fireworks, and transparent pictures in a building in the grounds.

By the late 1770s, however, Ranelagh began to lose its fashionable cachet, and by 1788 its shares had fallen 10 per cent in value; it was described as a bore and its distance from Town told against it. Efforts to revive its popularity had some success, such as masquerades lasting till day break *c.*1791, and firework displays. In 1792 the exhibition called Mount Etna was introduced and remained popular for several years, held in a special building in the gardens: it showed the Cyclops forging the armour of Mars amid smoke and explosions. By the late 1790s the directors offered prizes for regattas and shooting-matches, and several spectacles were presented to the public to try to regain support, but without success. In

1 PRO, C 105/37, no. 32.
2 Above, Landownership, later ests (Ranelagh).
3 Rest of section based on Wroth, *London Pleasure Gdns.* 199–218; see Fig. 61.

61. *A masquerade at Ranelagh, showing the canal, Chinese building, and Rotunda*

July 1803 the Rotunda opened for the last time, and in the autumn of 1805 the proprietors ordered the demolition of Ranelagh House and the Rotunda; the furniture was sold by auction, and the organ was sold to Tetbury church (Glos.). By 1826 much of Ranelagh's gardens had become part of the Royal Hospital's grounds (below).

CREMORNE GARDENS

Cremorne House was first opened to the public in 1831 as a sports stadium or club by Charles Random, self-styled Baron de Berenger, a firearms specialist, who taught shooting in butts erected there.[1] In 1845 the lessee, Beatrix Crowder,[2] and Robert Russell, probably one of de Berenger's creditors, granted an under-lease of the estate to John Wolsey, to run both Cremorne House and a nearby house, the Canteen, as taverns,[3] but the same year Wolsey assigned the under-lease to Thomas Bartlett Simpson, hotelkeeper of the North and South American Coffee house in Threadneedle Street.[4] Simpson sublet the Cremorne estate to James Ellis, confectioner, in 1846 for 20 years to run the two buildings and grounds as taverns and a place of amusement,[5] and Ellis laid it out as a typical London pleasure garden, but went bankrupt and surrendered the lease back to Simpson in 1850.[6] Simpson took over management of the gardens, and although he may not have initiated the opening as pleasure grounds, he seems to have been the one responsible for their success.

Cremorne Gardens was opened to the public in 1846 and within a few years became established as a popular feature of London's summer season, its annual programme of events being welcomed by the press each May. It took advantage of the greater number of people with leisure in the mid 19th century: its admission remained 1s. to enter the grounds, making it relatively affordable not only for the middle class but for the growing class of office workers in the expanding metropolis. It could be easily reached by cab or bus from Charing Cross, or by river steamer to Cremorne pier, yet still seemed far enough from the noise and dirt of London to be a rural retreat. The grounds offered several attractions and side-shows: the Crystal Grotto, Marionette Theatre, Hermit's Cave, American Bowling Saloon, a circus, a fireworks temple, and a theatre for musical and dramatic performances. Probably the most popular attraction was the orchestra and dancing-platform, surrounded by tables among the trees and overlooked by tiers of supper-boxes. As well as the regular facilities, there were also spectacles and novelties, some of which exceeded the bounds of good taste and possibly legality in an effort to keep the crowds coming in. To maximise income the management had to appeal to a broad public and to attract customers from mid afternoon to after midnight, and because of this Cremorne developed a dual personality. By day it had attractive lawns, trees, and flower-beds, with balloon ascents and marionette shows, to appeal to the family outing and respectable women; at night it had dazzling,

1 Beaver, *Memorials*, 159–60.
2 Above, Landownership, later ests (Chelsea Farm).
3 CL, deed 43738.
4 CL, deeds 43767, 43774; MLR 1846/9/191.
5 MLR 1846/9/173, 192.
6 CL, deed 43790; E. Croft Murray, 'Cremorne Gdns', *Chelsea Soc. Rep.* (1974), 31.

62. *A poster for Cremorne Gardens' attractions, including the American bowling alley, Fireworks Temple, Crystal Grotto, theatre, and promenade*

gaslit music and dancing and refreshments enjoyed by a wide range of society including loungers and prostitutes. The gas lights gave Cremorne much of its appeal, strung out along the walks and in the trees, and blazing around the sites of the main attractions.[1]

In the 1850s Simpson was able to secure court and aristocratic patronage, but by the 1860s Cremorne was attracting criticism. It was distinctive among places of entertainment in the wide range of social groups who came together there, but this social promiscuity, and the sexual promiscuity which the Gardens drew into its vicinity, led to sustained attacks from the Chelsea vestry, local residents, and moralists from a wider area.[2] In 1861 Simpson retired from active management and assigned the leases to Edward Tyrrell Smith of the Theatre Royal, Drury Lane.[3] Under Smith Cremorne entered its most popular and commercially successful period,[4] and writers emphasized the economics of Cremorne as a business, which helped to deflect criticisms made on social and moral grounds: the Gardens required 15 gardeners during the summer season, 20 carpenters, 6 scene-painters, and 5 house-painters out of season, 12 gasmen, 8 bill-posters, and gave custom to a variety of performers, fireworks manufacturers, and security guards.[5] Smith remained in control until 1867, when Simpson agreed to lease the Gardens to William Watling for three years,[6] and then granted a 21-year lease in 1870 to John Baum, the last manager of the Gardens, who spent more than £10,000 on the gardens and premises,[7] and provided a variety of entertainments which became increasingly rowdy and provoked annual opposition to the renewal of his music and dancing licence. Baum was refused a renewal of his licence in 1871,[8] though it was subsequently renewed, but ultimately it was the value of the land for building which finally closed the Gardens in 1877, when the freeholder decided to lay out the area for houses.[9]

OTHER PARKS AND OPEN SPACES

In 1929 Chelsea had only 13 acres of public open space, one of the smallest proportions in London at just two per cent of its area. It had 3 acres of private playing fields,[10] and other private open spaces included the Physic Garden and the borough's garden squares. Before *c.*1815 the extensive grounds of the Royal Hospital, which included Burton's Court on the north side and gardens by the river, were apparently generally accessible, but access was then restricted, to local discontent. In 1845 the vestry petitioned that the 'comparatively useless' grounds be opened to benefit the populous neighbourhood,[11] and in 1846 the improvement commissioners petitioned for Burton's Court, on the north side of the Hospital, to be opened to the public.[12] In 1850 the

1 L. Nead, *Victorian Babylon: People, Streets and Images in Nineteenth-Century London* (2000), 109–11, 114–15, 117; see Fig. 62.
2 Nead, *Victorian Babylon*, 131, 135.
3 CL, deeds 43777–81.
4 Nead, *Victorian Babylon*, 109.
5 Ibid., 112.
6 CL, deeds 43764, 43784.
7 CL, deed 43754.
8 CL, deed 43753.
9 Above, Landownership, later ests (Chelsea Farm).
10 LCC, *Survey of Open Spaces* (1929), 2, 5, 7.
11 *2nd Rep. Com. Met. Improvements*, pp. lxv–lxvi, 11–12, 36–40; Vestry mins, 1843–56, pp. 35–6.
12 Improvement com. mins, 1845–6, p. 309.

Hospital did open its gardens to the public on Sundays and at certain times of the year, and later daily all year round, especially the centre walk and terraces next to the river,[1] but *c.*1887 use of Burton's Court was again restricted, to military personnel.[2] The grounds were increased when part of the former Ranelagh estate was added: as Ranelagh Garden it provided 14 of the Hospital's 60 acres. The area was used as in-pensioners' allotments from 1832, and a summerhouse attributed to Sir John Soane survived in 2000, its thatch replaced with tiles, but the gardens were laid out afresh under John Gibson's scheme of 1859–66. The northern part remained private, with the river end (and the Hospital's South Grounds) publicly accessible, until in 1912 access was allowed throughout. From 1947 Chelsea MB rented the South Grounds as sports grounds,[3] which continued to be used by the RBKC, though inhabitants relied largely on facilities outside the borough.[4] The Hospital's grounds became perhaps best known in the 20th century as the site of the Chelsea Flower Show: the Royal Horticultural Society first held its summer show at the Royal Hospital in 1913, and subsequently the show became an annual event of international renown.[5]

Other open spaces in Chelsea comprised former burial grounds and small public gardens. After Chelsea Embankment was created in 1874 the MBW laid out surplus ground on the north side of the carriageway as ornamental gardens extending from Old Church Street to Flood Street; smaller gardens flanked Albert Bridge. Ground at the northern end of Chelsea Bridge was laid out in 1884. The gardens, maintained by the MBW and then by the LCC, totalled one acre,[6] but were badly affected by traffic in 2002. In 1887 the vestry created a public garden out of the disused burial ground around St Luke's church, the MBW contributing half of the cost.[7] The design, by G.R. Strachan, the vestry surveyor, involved moving most of the stones;[8] a few altar tombs remained. Its 4 acres passed to Chelsea borough council.[9] There were no facilities for children's games there in 1929,[10] and in 1934 conversion of the northern side to a children's recreation ground was authorized, although sports were forbidden.[11] The western part was subsequently tarmacked for a sports area, with a children's playground adjacent.

By the 1880s the poor condition of the King's Road burial ground caused controversy. A mortuary was constructed there in 1882, and the remaining ground was reserved for the recreation of workhouse residents. After war damage a scheme of 1947–50 to develop the garden, with a small part opened to the public, removed most of the stones and demolished the mortuary. In order to improve its condition and make the whole area publicly accessible the Chelsea Society and the RBKC re-modelled the garden in 1977, retaining mature trees and the remaining monuments; it was named Dovehouse Green.[12]

Roper's Garden, north of the Embankment between the old church and Danvers Street, was so-named because it lies partly on the site of property given by Sir Thomas More to William and Margaret Roper in 1534.[13] The buildings which stood on the site were destroyed in 1941, and from 1948 volunteers and the Chelsea Gardens Guild created gardens there. A public garden on the site, designed by Bridgwater, Shepheard, & Epstein, was opened in 1964.[14]

The public Cremorne Gardens, at the west end of Cheyne Walk, were opened in 1982 by RBKC on the south-eastern extremity of the site of the former Cremorne pleasure gardens and Cremorne pier,[15] and replaced wharves. The 1¼-acre park included gates which had apparently stood at the King's Road entrance to the earlier gardens.[16]

THEATRES

Chelsea Palace Theatre

It opened as a music hall called Chelsea Palace of Varieties in 1903 at nos 232–42 King's Road, a music hall designed by Oswald Wylson and Charles Long in baroque style with a capacity of 2,524 in stalls, circle and boxes, and gallery. Standing on the corner of Sydney Street with its striking orange-red terracotta dome it was an important feature of King's Road. It also housed straight plays, ballet, and in 1923 was used for films, but by 1952 was almost exclusively a music hall again. In March 1957 it closed temporarily because of financial difficulties, but reopened when Jack Hylton took a short lease for the English Stage Company's production of *The Country Wife* by Wycherley, transferred from the Adelphi Theatre. After that short season it closed for good in 1957.[17] It was bought by Granada and used as television studios until it was demolished in the 1960s,[18] and replaced with a shop and a 9-storeyed block of flats; the shop was occupied by Heal's in 2003.

1 *The Times*, 2 April 1850.
2 Dean, *Royal Hosp.* 283; *Builder*, 2 Nov. 1901, p. 384.
3 Faulkner, *Chelsea*, II. 315; *Chelsea Soc. Rep.* (1986), 47–9; Dean, *Royal Hosp.* 286–7; TS account on display in summerho.
4 Chelsea MB, *Official Guide* [1937], 83; *The Times*, 21 Aug. 1983.
5 *Chelsea Soc. Rep.* (1976), 67.
6 *Ann. Rep. of MBW* (Parl. Papers, 1875 (246), LXIV), pp. 16, 19, 24, 71; ibid. (Parl. Papers, 1877 (225), LXXI), pp. 13, 71; ibid. (Parl. Papers, 1884–5 (186), LXVII), p. 22; J.J. Sexby, *Municipal Parks* (1898), 626.
7 Blunt, *Chelsea*, 23; *Builder*, 2 Nov. 1901, p. 382.
8 CL, Roll 4: plans, 1887.
9 LCC, *London Statistics*, XXVI. 160.
10 PRO, WORK 14/1184.
11 Chelsea Misc. 2307; *St Luke's vestry mins. 1934–5*, 151, 221–2, 256–7.
12 *Chelsea Soc. Rep.* (1977), 52, 54–5; ibid. (1978), 42–3; *Vestry rep. 1882–3*, 6.
13 Above, Landownership, More.
14 Plaque on S. wall; Bignell, *Chelsea 1860–1980*, 69; *Chelsea Soc. Rep.* (1954), 7–8.
15 Above.
16 Beaver, *Memorials*, 160; Chelsea cuttings: Cremorne Gdns (*Chelsea News*, 2 April 1982).
17 Howard, *London Theatres and Music Halls*, 44; I. Mackintosh and M. Sell (eds), *Curtains !!! Or a new life for old theatres* (1982), 222; *The Times*, 21 Oct. 1952, 12 March, 5 April 1957.
18 Bignell, *Chelsea 1860–1980*, 133.

Court Theatre

The Court Theatre, Lower George Street, off Sloane Square, opened in 1870 as the New Chelsea Theatre in the former Ranelagh Chapel. In 1871 its interior was altered by Walter Emden and it was renamed the Belgravia Theatre. Further alterations were made in 1882 by Alexander Peebles, after which its capacity was 728, distributed between stalls and boxes, dress circle and balcony, amphitheatre, and gallery, and it was presumably renamed Court Theatre at this time. It was closed in 1887 and demolished,[1] being replaced by the Royal Court Theatre on another site.

Royal Court Theatre

The Royal Court Theatre was built on the east side of Sloane Square and opened in 1888, designed by Walter Emden and Bertie (W.R.) Crewe to replace the earlier Court Theatre (above). Built of fine red brick, moulded brick, and a stone façade in free Italianate style, it had a capacity of 841 in stalls, dress circle, amphitheatre, and gallery. It ceased to be used as a theatre in 1932,[2] but was used as a cinema 1935–40 until bomb damage closed it. The interior was reconstructed by Robert Cromie and the theatre reopened in 1952; further alterations were made in 1956 and 1980, retaining the façade largely unaltered. The capacity in 1982 was 442.[3] George Devine became artistic director and opened the English Stage Company at the Royal Court in 1956 as a subsidised theatre producing new British plays, international plays, and some classical revivals.[4] Devine aimed to create a writers' theatre, where the play was more important than the actors, director, or designer, and to discover writers whose plays were stimulating, provocative and exciting: the Royal Court production of John Osborne's *Look Back in Anger* in May 1956 was later seen as the decisive starting point of modern British drama, and Devine's policy created a new generation of British playwrights: John Osborne, Arnold Wesker, John Arden, Ann Jellicoe, N.F. Simpson, and Edward Bond. Early seasons included new international plays by Bertolt Brecht, Eugene Ionesco, Samuel Beckett, Jean-Paul Sartre, and Marguerite Duras.

The theatre started with the 400-seat proscenium arch Theatre Downstairs, and then in 1969 opened a second theatre, the 60-seat studio Theatre Upstairs. Though the quality of the auditorium and the façade were greatly appreciated by audiences, the remainder of the building had little merit, providing poor facilities for both audience and performers. By the early 1990s the theatre was becoming dangerous, particularly in its electricity circuits, and was threatened with closure in 1995. The theatre also backed onto the Westbourne (Ranelagh) sewer, possibly why the drains caused flooding in the stalls and understage throughout the 20th century. The Royal Court received a grant of £16.2 million from the National Lottery and the Arts Council for redevelopment, which began in 1996. The structure was completely rebuilt, but the façade and the intimate auditorium were preserved; facilities for performers and theatre-goers were improved, and additional office and dressing-room space was provided by building a new annex over the Ranelagh sewer. The refurbished theatre, supported by the Jerwood Foundation, reopened in 2000 with the 330-seat Jerwood Theatre Downstairs, and also maintained a studio theatre, the Jerwood Theatre Upstairs. In 2003 the Royal Court remained influential in world theatre, producing new plays of high quality, encouraging writers from across society, and developing connections abroad.

The Man in the Moon theatre in the public house at the corner of King's Road and Park Walk was one of London's fringe theatres for about 20 years, before closing in 2002.

CINEMAS

By 1912 Chelsea had six cinemas or theatres which also showed films. Chelsea Electric Palace, nos 180–2 King's Road, seating 400, was used for films and variety shows. Those showing films only were Cremorne Cinema, World's End, King's Road, seating 240; Electric Theatre, nos 148–50 King's Road; King's Picture Playhouse, Church Street; Royal Electric Theatre, Draycott Avenue, seating 300. The Palace of Varieties (above), King's Road, was the 6th.[5]

In 1910 the Palaseum, designed by A.W. Hudson for 960, was opened at no. 279 King's Road, on the corner of Church Street. In 1911 it was renamed King's, and is presumably the King's Picture Playhouse, Church Street, mentioned in 1912 with a capacity of 1,200. It became the Ritz in 1943, and the Essoldo in 1949 after remodelling by C. Edmund Wilford.[6] The Essoldo was noted as an 'enterprising cinema' in 1969 showing both general entertainment and films reflecting modern society.[7] It was modernized in 1968 with 432 seats, and became the Curzon in 1972, but closed in 1973. The building reopened as King's Road Theatre for live performances, closing again in 1979. It then reopened in 1980 as the Classic with four screens, seating 245, 277, 161, and 153 respectively. Screen 4 was renamed The Arts in 1984, and the whole complex was renamed Cannon in 1986.[8] It was still open in 2003 as UGC Chelsea, seating 220, 238, 122, and 111 for the four screens.

The Picture House at no. 148 King's Road, between Markham Street and the Pheasantry, was the site of the Electric Theatre, nos 148–50, in 1912, designed by Felix

1 Howard, *London Theatres*, 54.
2 Ibid., 202.
3 Mackintosh and Sell, *Curtains!!!*, 155. See Plate 15.
4 Rest of acct based on inf. from Royal Court Theatre web site, www.royalcourttheatre.com, 17 Dec. 2002.
5 *The Bioscope Annual and Trades Dir.* (1912), 42.
6 M. Webb, *The Amber Valley Gazetteer of Gtr. London's Suburban Cinemas, 1946–86* (1986), 18, 95.
7 *The Times*, 8 Jan. 1969.
8 Webb, *Amber Valley Gaz. of Cinemas*, 18, 95.

Joubert with a capacity of 394. Known as the Classic by 1972,[1] it closed in 1973 and reopened with live shows, but was demolished in 1978 and replaced by shops and flats.[2]

In 1934 the Gaumont Palace opened at no. 206 King's Road, designed by W.E. Trent and E.F. Tulley with a capacity of 2,502. It became the Gaumont by 1946, and the Odeon in 1963. It closed in 1972 and was converted into a department store for Habitat, which incorporated in the complex a new Odeon seating 739 which opened in 1973. It closed in 1981 and reopened 1983 as the Chelsea Cinema,[3] and was still open in 2003 as an independent cinema.

SPORTS

Prince's Club, an exclusive sports club with socially restricted membership, was opened in 1870 by George and James Prince. The club houses were built on the grounds of Holland's Pavilion, and the club used former nursery land adjoining as a cricket ground. In addition to cricket there were facilities for tennis, badminton, and, later, skating. The ground was being built on in 1879, and the club finally closed in 1885 when its lease expired, moving to W. Kensington where it operated as the Queen's Club.[4]

Chelsea had two other skating rinks, at Royal Avenue from 1875, and at the Glaciarium in Milman's Street from 1876.[5] Catharine Lodge, in south-west corner of Trafalgar Square, became a cycling club for society people *c.*1896.[6] The area in the centre of Trafalgar Square was sub-let to the Chelsea Lawn Tennis Club by lease expiring in 1928;[7] occupied the centre of Trafalgar Square from before First World War until the square was redeveloped in 1928.[8]

Chelsea Football Club

Chelsea Football Club was founded in 1905 to play in a sports ground at Stamford Bridge bought by H.A.(Gus) Mears and his brother, Mr J.T. Mears, after Fulham FC turned down the ground.[9] Gus Mears had his team officially recognised by the Football League and it played its first match in 1905, against West Bromwich Albion. A match later that year had 60,000 spectators, and by 1906/7 Chelsea had reached the First Division.[10] Chelsea were winners of the League Division One in 1955, and of the F.A. Cup in 1970, 1997, and 2000; they were runners up 4 times, semi-finalists 8 times. They were particularly successful, both at home and in Europe, in the 1950s and 60s, and in the 1990s.[11] The main history of the development of the ground, Stamford Bridge stadium, is reserved for treatment under Fulham.

63. *The Rose and Crown Public House, Lower Sloane Street, meeting place of local friendly societies*

FRIENDLY SOCIETIES AND SAVINGS CLUBS

A number of friendly, loan, and building societies met in Chelsea, mainly in public houses.[12] Among early ones, the Freedom and Friendship with Hope Society, which met in the King's Arms, was registered from 1794 to 1816, the Friendly Assistants' Society was registered at the Cricketer's Inn in 1799, the Brotherly Society of Bricklayers at the Coach & Horses inn in Marlborough Street in 1803, the Chelsea Female Union Society at the Magpie and Stump in 1804, and the Chelsea Union Friendly Society at the Duke of Wellington inn, South Street, Sloane Square, in 1823. By the 1840s societies not meeting at pubs included the Chelsea Independent Total Abstinence Society, which met at the Tee Total Coffee House, Exeter Street, and the Temperance Provident Society which met at the Mechanics' Institution in King's Road. Burial societies included the Catholic Burial Society of St Joseph and St Patrick, at the Coach & Horses inn, Marlborough Street, registered from 1839 to 1861, and the West London Philanthropic Burial Society, registered from 1849 to 1859 which met first at the Rose & Crown, Lower Sloane Street, and then at the Queen's Head, Keppel Street. Loan societies included the Chelsea & General Joint Stock Loan Society, at the Prince of Wales in Exeter Street, and the Chelsea New Loan Society at no. 24 George Street, near Sloane Square. The Chelsea Building Society was registered at no. 7 Sloane Terrace in 1842.

1 *PO Dir. London* (1972).
2 Webb, *Amber Valley Gaz. of Cinemas*, 18; *Chelsea Soc. Rep.* (1979), 71.
3 Webb, *Amber Valley Gaz. of Cinemas*, 18; *PO Dir. London* (1975).
4 Walker and Jackson, *Kens. and Chelsea*, 175; Denny, *Chelsea Past*, 136, 138; Stroud, *Smith's Charity*, 46–7.
5 Denny, *Chelsea Past*, 138.
6 *The Times*, 18 Aug. 1939.
7 *Rep. of Com. on London Sqs*, p. 67.
8 *Chelsea Soc. Rep.* (1966), 16.
9 Inf. from Chelsea Football Club via website www.chelseafc.co.uk, 14 Dec. 2002.
10 Bignell, *Chelsea 1860–1980*, 100.
11 Inf. from Chelsea FC web site.
12 Para. based on PRO, FS 2/7; LMA MC/R/1.

Chelsea Savings Bank was founded in 1819 under the patronage of the duke of York and duke of Wellington. In 1861 Chelsea Savings Bank reported it had over 10,000 contributors, and included 53 charitable societies and 25 friendly societies.[1]

Chelsea Temperance Society was founded in 1837, and had a hall in Pond Place (later Street). In 1908 it built Sydney Hall in Pond Street near its old hall, which had served for many years.[2]

The Chelsea Permanent Building Society, later Chelsea Building Society, was founded in 1875 in London.[3] In 1934 new offices on 3 floors of a corner site in King's Road were opened for it,[4] presumably that still in use in 2003.

PHILANTHROPIC SOCIETIES

Chelsea Benevolent Society was founded in 1838 to alleviate individuals' distress, its members being entitled to refunds if they had given up to 2s. 6d. for immediate relief in the most deserving cases. It had relieved 2,502 cases by 1856, 141 in that year, and 5,892 by 1873, when the funds totalled £3,370. Gifts from Earl Cadogan and Leedham White brought the total to £6,482 and permitted the relief of 469 in 1885. Meetings were held at the Commercial Hall, King's Road, until 1855, at the Pier Hotel, Cheyne Walk, until 1869, and thereafter at the White Hart, King's Road. They were not recorded after 1885, although it was not until 1918 that amalgamation with Chelsea Relief Society created Chelsea Benevolent and Relief Society. The society was amalgamated with Kensington and Chelsea Benevolent Society in 1933, and was wound up *c.*1961.[5]

Chelsea Relief Society, founded in 1861 and with volunteer visitors, from 1871 defined its aim as the discouragement of indiscriminate almsgiving by distributing the largest amount of relief for the smallest cost of management. In 1875 *c.*1,300 tickets for bread, meat, and coals at Christmas were issued, and in 1896 230 persons or families received sums of 5s. to £2, at a total cost of £119. Unrecorded after 1896, the society was amalgamated with Chelsea Benevolent Society (above) in 1918.[6]

World's End Boys' Club was founded 1934 at no. 1a Lacland Place to help local boys aged 14–18 to make good use of their leisure. It provided physical training, boxing, rowing and other sport, handicrafts, a reading and games room and a canteen, and a summer camp.[7] Funds were raised through balls and other functions held in Chelsea.[8] In 1940, though younger boys had been evacuated, it still had an average nightly attendance of 85–90,[9] and was considering expanding into a neighbouring house 1942: it had *c.*100 members, 60 of them under 16.[10] In 1947 it received a council grant,[11] and was still there in 1953 at the top of Lacland Place opposite the mission hall,[12] but presumably closed soon afterwards for development of the Cremorne Estate. A West Chelsea Girls' Club was started in 1917 with headquarters at no. 484 King's Road; it was still operating in 1938.[13]

Chelsea Central Club started in 1941 at St Luke's schools, remaining there until 1945 when it moved to no. 30 Chelsea Square. It was apparently originally for boys, and had 80–90 members in 1947, providing sport, a library, and discussions. A mixed club started in 1947 with 60 members, with opportunities for carpentry, boot repairing, badminton, acting, and dancing.[14] Balls were held at the Town Hall in aid of the clubs in 1952 and 1962.[15]

CULTURAL ORGANIZATIONS

In 1851 there was a Library Institution in King's Rd between nos 102 and 105; the secretary was William Hill.[16]

Chelsea had several music societies in the 20th century. The Chelsea Music Club was founded in 1922 by Lady Piggott, and apart from the Second World War, provided Chelsea with a regular programme of chamber music in spring and autumn concerts, and included many well-known artists. Its first concert was held in 1923, conducted by Eugene Goossens at the Town Hall; in 1955 it gave its 200th concert.[17] Also in the 1920s a group of madrigal singers called the Chelsea Singers was founded, and gave their first concert in 1926.[18] The Chelsea Opera Group was formed in 1950 from a group of amateurs and students, many living in Chelsea, giving concert performances of operas under the conductorship of Colin Davis. Performances were given in Oxford and Cambridge as well as London, including a concert performance at Festival Hall.[19] In 1957 as their annual spring performance they performed the *Merry Wives of Windsor* under Colin Davis, who brought his own Chelsea Opera Group Orchestra, at Peter Jones department store in conjunction with the music society of the John Lewis Partnership. In 1957 the Chelsea Chamber Orchestra was giving performances at the Town Hall, and in 1958 performed with the Goossens

1 CL, deed 18642; *The Times*, 25 March 1861.
2 *The Times*, 5 June 1908; datestone.
3 Inf. via web site www.thechelsea.co.uk.
4 *The Times*, 26 Oct. 1934.
5 Chelsea Benevolent Soc. *13th to 47th Ann. Reps* (1850–85), in CL (deeds 17831–91).
6 Chelsea Relief Soc. *1st to 35th Ann. Reps* (1861–96), in CL.
7 *Chelsea Soc. Rep.* (1936), 12; (1942), 23–4.
8 *The Times*, 19 June 1935.
9 *Chelsea Soc. Rep.* (1940), 16.
10 Ibid. (1942), 23–4.
11 Ibid. (1947), 46–7.
12 KL, deed 37062.
13 *The Times*, 3 March 1938.
14 *Chelsea Soc. Rep.* (1947), 45–6.
15 *The Times*, 13 Feb. 1952; 14 March 1962.
16 PRO, HO 107/1472/2/1/14.
17 *The Times*, 16 Dec. 1955; *Chelsea Soc. Rep.* (1947), 32.
18 *The Times*, 8 Nov. 1926.
19 Ibid., 3, 6 Jan. 1958.

family, the well-known instrumentalists.[1] The Chelsea College Orchestra was founded by Nicholas Dodd with 10 students at Chelsea College where he taught. It changed its name *c.*1980 to Chelsea Symphony Orchestra and by 1986 was one of the country's leading amateur orchestras, giving about eight concerts a year and the occasional overseas performance. Its main base was Chelsea Old Town Hall, King's Road, where it gave many of its performances.[2]

Chelsea Book Club, at no. 65 Cheyne Walk (Lombard Terrace), like an 18th-century bookshop held exhibitions and lectures as well as selling books. In 1920 it held an exhibition of sculpture from Ivory Coast and Congo; it was the first to stock Joyce's *Ulysses* in 1922. In 1928 it was sold because of financial problems, and became the Lombard Restaurant.

The Chelsea Festival was started *c.*1992 and referred to as Chelsea Week in 1993, when it was intended to be a festival of all local activities: it included a fashion show, a range of musical and theatrical performances, and an exhibition involving the Chelsea Society, Chelsea Arts Society, and Chelsea Arts College.[3] It was still being held in 2003 when it lasted for three weeks from the middle of June.

Chelsea Arts Club

The Chelsea Arts Club was founded in 1891 by Whistler and his contemporaries in rooms at no. 181 King's Road. In 1902 it moved to larger premises at no. 143 Old Church Street. In 1933 the club's premises, which had an acre of garden, were remodelled. From 1908 to 1958 the club held a series of public fancy dress balls at the Albert Hall, latterly on New Year's eve, which raised funds for artists' charities,[4] but they ceased owing to their notoriety and rowdiness, and private functions were held at the club instead.[5] In 1966 the club was redecorated, a new bar was opened, and membership was opened to women artists as well.[6] The club had 700 members *c.*1973 and was open to all in professions associated with arts: writers, dress designers, antique dealers, and theatre.[7] In 2003 it had 1,600 painters, sculptors, architects, designers, photographers, and filmmakers, and 800 writers, dancers, musicians, and other kinds of artists as its members. The club's facilities included a dining room, billiards room, garden, and 13 simple bedrooms for members.[8]

New English Art Club

Cliques of painters who were not part of the more established schools of painting of the 1880s, and who therefore found it difficult to get exhibition space, formed their own clubs. The New English Art Club was one such, formed in 1886 following meetings in Luke Fildes' house and at the Wentworth Studios, Chelsea. The NEAC had no formal HQ, as most of its leading members also belonged to the Chelsea Arts Club.[9] In 2003 the NEAC, which had about 70 members, continued to support contemporary British figurative artists, especially through exhibitions, and also held drawing classes and other events.[10]

POLITICAL CLUBS

In 1792 there was a political discussion club called the Free and Easy or Arthurian Society, which met at the Star & Garter in Sloane Square, and which, because of the mood of the time and based on an anonymous warning, was suspected of plotting to start a riot, arming its members with bludgeons and intending to kill anyone they came across. Hand bills alerting the populace were posted up in parts of Chelsea, Kensington, and Knightsbridge, and brought out the Chelsea Association to keep the peace and prevent trouble, and this was thought to have deterred the rioters.[11]

A Chelsea Liberal Association existed by 1877; it adopted the Birmingham system of party organization in 1878.[12] By then there was also a Conservative Association, which dined in the Vestry Hall.[13] Both main parties' associations remained active in the 1880s.[14] A Conservative Club in the King's Road was begun in 1887;[15] in 1910 one for Stanley ward alone was begun, with provision for shooting, smoking, and gambling.[16] In 1879 it was claimed that a great proportion of the Chelsea working class was Radical, whereas their opposite numbers in Kensington were Conservative.[17]

Systematic political activity by Radical clubs began in Chelsea in the mid-1870s, where the Eleusis, which evolved from a branch of the Reform League, promoted working-class electoral registration, and with the three other components of the parish's combined political committee of Radical Clubs, the Cobden, Progressive, and Hammersmith clubs, had involved itself in the selection of parliamentary candidates.[18] The committee was

1 *The Times*, 2–3 April 1957, 4 Feb. 1958.
2 *Chelsea Soc. Rep.* (1983), 26–8; *The Times*, 12 Nov. 1986.
3 *Chelsea Soc. Rep.* (1992), 19; (1993), 24–5.
4 *The Times*, 28 July 1910.
5 Ibid., 23 June 1973.
6 Ibid., 5 Dec. 1966.
7 Borer, *Two Villages*, 261.
8 Inf. from club via web site (www.arts.co.uk), 31 March 2003.
9 Walkley, *Artists' Hos in London*, 199–200.
10 Inf. from NEAC, www.newenglishartclub.co.uk, 19 Feb. 2003.
11 PRO, TS 11/1118, no. 5748.
12 *The Times*, 5 Sept. 1877, 26 Feb. 1878.
13 Ibid., 17 May 1878.
14 Ibid., 27 Sept. 1880, 23 Jan., 13 March 1884, 13 Jan., 27 June 1885.
15 Ibid., 19 May 1887.
16 Ibid., 23 May 1910.
17 *Dickens's Dict. of London* (1879), pp. 48–9.
18 J. Davis, 'Radical Clubs and London Politics 1870–1900' in *Metropolis London*, ed. D. Feldman and G.S. Jones (1989), 105–6; *The Times*, 13 Jan. 1879.

often represented at radical demonstrations, and was enlisted to support the local Liberal candidate, Charles Dilke. There was also a Chelsea Labour Association, a weekly meeting of Dilke's trade unionist supporters.[1] The Eleusis club had a lease of nos 180 and 182 King's Road, expiring in 1902.[2] The radical committee was still active in 1898,[3] but the Independent Labour Party in Chelsea disintegrated after 1895 when the Fabians, including presumably the Webbs, seceded.[4] By 1898 working-class support in the main part of the parish had been weakened by the Cadogan estate's gentrifying rebuilding. In 1914 Chelsea was one of six metropolitan boroughs with no Labour party, and in 1918 the exclusion of Kensal Town crushed the anti-Conservative elements. G.B. Shaw remarked that in Chelsea 'no progressive has a dog's chance. . . . lord Cadogan rebuilt it fashionably and drove all the Radicals across the Bridge to Battersea'.[5]

NEWSPAPERS

Chelsea was served by three long-lived titles.[6] The *Chelsea Mail* began in 1856 as the *West Middlesex Advertiser and Family Journal*, changing its name in 1897 to the *Chelsea Mail and West Middlesex Advertiser*, which it retained until it ceased publication in 1913, apart from 1905 to 1908 when the title was reversed. The *Chelsea News and General Advertiser* began publication in the early 1860s, changing its name to *The Westminster and Chelsea News* in 1879, and the *West London Press, Westminster and Chelsea News* in 1855. From 1962 it was published as the *Chelsea News, West London Press and Westminster & Pimlico News*, and from 1972 as the *Chelsea News*. In 1920 the *Chelsea Courier and Kensington Gazette* began publication, changing it name to *Chelsea Gazette* in 1923 and the *Chelsea & West London Gazette* in 1927, but the *West London and Chelsea Gazette* from 1929 until it was discontinued in 1971.

There were a number of other short-lived titles, especially in the second half of the 19th century, several of them political newspapers including the *Battersea and Chelsea News*, published between January 1866 and July 1869, and the *Independence*, covering Chelsea, Knightsbridge, Fulham, Wandsworth and Battersea, between January 1862 and March 1863.[7]

EDUCATION

In 1583, when Thomas Browne was rector, his assistant John James was described as curate and schoolmaster (*ludimagister*).[8] A house for the parish clerk and a schoolhouse were built by Richard Ward, rector 1585–1615, at his own expense and with a donation by Richard Fletcher, bishop of London (d. 1596), who lived nearby.[9] 'Our poor schoolmaster' was buried in 1608 and a schoolmaster was also recorded in 1656.[10] The churchwardens provided clothing and schooling for a boy from 1686 until 1688 and similarly for a girl in 1691–2; presumably both pupils were orphans, paid for separately as extra charges on the parish school.[11] 'Bell, the schoolmaster' paid poor rates in 1695.[12] The writer Edward Chamberlaine (d. 1703) was said to have paid £5 a year to apprentice one Chelsea boy to a waterman and to have intended to settle that sum. His son John accordingly settled a £10 rent charge on a house in Church Lane, half to the master of the charity school to teach five boys and half to apprentice one every year.[13] The same schoolhouse presumably remained in use until replaced by one built by William Petyt, keeper of records in the Tower, in 1706.[14]

Petyt's or the boys' charity school offered parishioners the only free education until the foundation of a girls' charity school by the rector Sloane Elsmere in 1740,[15] although a school for the daughters of in-pensioners at the Royal Hospital was founded in 1729 by the authoress Mary Astell (d. 1731) and others.[16] Both the boys' charity school and the Hospital school benefited from church collections until Elsmere, seeing the pensioners as a national responsibility, decided that their share should go to the girls' charity school.[17] Many bequests were made to the boys' and girls' schools, although often without effect. Voluntary contributions provided most of the funds in 1786, augmented by Chamberlaine's rent charge and the income from stock worth £455 8s. 4d. representing seven charities; £200 had come from Stephen Fox in 1772 and £115 8s. 4d. from Sloane Elsmere.[18]

A charity school adjoining Knightsbridge's Holy

1 P. Thompson, *Socialists, Liberals and Labour: the Struggle for London 1885–1914* (1967), 92.
2 Cadogan Est. Office, Agenda min. bk 22, p. 61.
3 *The Times*, 20, 26 April 1898.
4 Thompson, *Socialists, Liberals and Labour*, 92, 164.
5 Ibid., 239; H. Pelling, *Social Geog. of British Elections 1885–1910* (1967), 31; *Vestry Rep. 1899–1900*, 44–5; *Chelsea Soc. Rep.* (1997), 32.
6 Section based on BL, newspaper lib. cat.
7 J. Davis, *Reforming London: The Local Govt Problem 1855–1900* (1988), 6 n.24.
8 Guildhall MS 9537/5, f. 13.
9 *Survey of London*, IV. 53.
10 Beaver, *Memorials*, 106.
11 Vestry orders, 1662–1718, ff. 43, 47, 48, 55-v.
12 Poor rate bk, 1695–1705, f. 5.
13 Beaver, *Memorials*, 108; *Chelsea Chars 1862*, 37. 1694 may have been the date of Edw.'s gift rather than of his son's settlement, as in *Endowed Chars London* (1897), 2.
14 Below, pub. schs; see Fig. 64.
15 Faulkner, *Chelsea*, II. 93; BL, Sloane MS 4034, f. 67; below, pub. schs.
16 Dean, *Royal Hosp.* 195; *DNB*.
17 Faulkner, *Chelsea*, II. 93–4; below, pub. schs (Petyt's).
18 *Chelsea Chars 1862*, 37, 203.

64. *Petyt School, Church Street, built in 1708 next to the parish church*

Trinity chapel from *c.*1785 may have taken some Chelsea children, since the hamlet of Knightsbridge lay partly in Chelsea and was included with it in returns of 1819.[1] Sunday schools were established in 1787 and later consolidated with a 'knitting school' opened in the same year.[2] Schoolrooms were added to the workhouse, for boys in 1792 and for girls in 1822.[3] The Royal Military Asylum school, opened in 1803 and included in many returns, was not parochial. A day school, later known as Ranelagh Lancasterian or British, existed from 1802, a Roman Catholic charity school probably from 1811, and a new British school from *c.*1812. The first National school, Park chapel, originated in a Sunday school of 1814.[4] The poor of Chelsea and Knightsbridge were said not to be without the means of education in 1819, when Petyt's school had 105 pupils, two National schools (presumably Park chapel boys' and girls') together had 150–200, and numerous unspecified dissenting schools over 400; small day and evening schools were 'numberless'.[5]

By 1833 Chelsea had ten day schools that were free or partly free,[6] including a School of Discipline[7] founded in 1825 and the Hospital's, the Asylum's, the workhouses', and industrial schools. Thirty-one day schools charged fees; at least 15 had been founded in or since 1820 and probably none had more than 30 pupils.[8] Another 12 private schools were partly boarding and included seven which had been founded in or since 1825. In addition, St Luke's parochial schools had been opened in 1824 superseding Petyt's and the girls' charity schools. Together with another Anglican (Holy Trinity) and two Roman Catholic schools, they were classified separately as being both day and Sunday schools. There were also eight Sunday schools, two of them Anglican, and 19 private schools, presumably small, whose owners refused to answer 'inquisitorial' questions.

Schools were founded for the new Anglican churches:[9] for St Jude's in 1837, Christ Church in 1843, St Saviour's in 1847, and St Simon's in 1852. The first two were among those by 1847 in union with the National Society, which also noted a girls' and infants' school in the Rectory garden and stressed the need to serve the poorest boys in the neighbourhood.[10] The opening in 1841 of St Mark's and Whitelands teacher training colleges was followed by that of their practising schools, which, too, were National. Both a day and an evening ragged school existed by 1849. Chelsea poor law union was annexed to North Surrey school district in 1849 and pauper children were sent to Anerley in Upper Norwood from 1850 until Chelsea joined Kensington in 1876 in a new district, for which cottage homes were built at Banstead (Surrey).[11] Roman Catholic expansion included the foundation of Brompton Oratory school, in Chelsea from 1856, and was cited as a danger by Anglican clergy in 1845 and 1863.[12] In 1861 Chelsea union was said to have 46 public day schools with 6,215 pupils, and 91 private day schools with 2,224, besides an unknown number of Roman Catholic schools. Ten evening schools had a total of 515 pupils and 37 Sunday schools had 5,361.[13]

Parliamentary grants were paid to Holy Trinity, St Jude's, and Christ Church schools by 1846 and to St Luke's parochial and St Mark's practising schools by 1850. In 1859–60 grants were also paid to St Saviour's, to the School of Discipline, to a female home, and to three Roman Catholic Schools.[14] By 1868 the most recent National school, St Simon's, had been added to the list, although Roman Catholics had removed St Joseph's from inspection.[15] In 1871 the four wards of Chelsea together had 11,530 school places, 9,110 pupils enrolled, and an average attendance of 6,919; in addition night schools had 561 enrolled and an average attendance of 275. The total of 26 public schools receiving government grants was reached by counting separate departments[16] and by including St John's, Kensal Green, in Chelsea detached, besides three non-parochial military schools (those of the Royal Military Asylum and, at Chelsea barracks, for the Coldstream and Scots Fusilier Guards).[17] A further 13 schools ranked as private, including industrial and

1 Lysons, *Environs*, II. 180–1; *Educ. of Poor Digest*, 548.
2 Below, pub. schs.
3 Clayton, 'Poor Law Relief', 2; below, Loc. Govt.
4 Below, pub. schs.
5 *Educ. of Poor Digest*, 548.
6 Para. based on *Educ. Enquiry Abs.* 556–7.
7 Below, pub. schs.
8 e.g. four schs, founded in 1825, together held 92 girls.
9 Para. based on accounts of individual schs, below.
10 Nat. Soc. *Inquiry, 1846–7*, Middx, 203.
11 LMA, TS notes to CLSD.
12 Nat. Soc. files (St Jude; St Luke, Onslow Dwellings).
13 *Rep. Com. Popular Educ.* (Parl. Papers, 1861 [2794-I], XXI(3)), p. 327.
14 *Mins. of Educ. Cttee of Council, 1846* (Parl. Papers, 1847 [787], XLV), p. 152; *1850–1* (Parl. Papers, 1850–1 [1357], XLIV(1)), pp. clxix, 44–5, 57; *1859–60* (Parl. Papers, 1860 [2681], LIV), pp. 684–5.
15 *Rep. of Educ. Cttee of Council, 1868–9* (Parl. Papers, 1868–9 [4139], XX), pp. 568–9.
16 LMA, SBL 1518, pp. 13–18.
17 Ibid., pp. 13–14; *VCH Middx*, IX. 267.

ragged schools offering a free education, and 30 as small (private) adventure schools.[1]

Under the Education Act, 1870, the London school board's Chelsea division included the detached part of the parish besides Kensington, Hammersmith, and Fulham. The division, with offices in Kensington and later in Hammersmith,[2] returned four members of the board until 1882 and five thereafter.[3] In 1872 it was suggested that Chelsea needed 4,900 new places, partly because general use could not be made of the unfilled accommodation at the military schools.[4] The divisional board had hired nine temporary premises and closed eight of them by 1885, six of them being in the recently developed Chelsea detached.[5] The main part of the parish, already comparatively well supplied, was given only four permanent board schools.[6] Chelsea detached by *c.*1890 had three new board schools, Kensington ten, chiefly in the northern part, Hammersmith 11, and Fulham 20.[7] Some children from the workhouse, presumably temporary inmates, were educated locally: in 1884 the board threatened to exclude them from Park Walk school unless the guardians paid the fees.[8] A Scheme of 1888 allowed the apprenticing part of Chamberlaine's charity to be spent on the technical education in Westminster of boys from Chelsea's elementary schools.[9]

By 1903, when the school population of Chelsea MB was 12,716, the board schools had accommodation for 6,077 and a total average attendance of 4,719. Three of the permanent schools had separate departments for boys, girls, and infants. A fourth school, the more recently founded Ashburnham, had two departments and was higher grade. In addition there was a temporary single department school in Walton Street. Although most of the small private establishments had closed, denominational education still flourished. St Saviour's had made way for Walton Street board school, but there remained 15 Anglican or Roman Catholic schools, four of them being branches of the Oratory. Together the non-provided schools could accommodate 4,631 and had an average attendance of 3,499.[10]

The LCC's education committee, which succeeded the school board in 1904,[11] opened a temporary school in Hortensia Road in 1907, replaced by one in Tadema Road in 1913.[12] The borough council vainly protested at the choice of Hortensia Road, claiming that many children from Fulham and Kensington were already accommodated in Chelsea, notably at the nearby Ashburnham.[13] Also in Hortensia Road were secondary schools for girls and boys respectively (later Carlyle and Sloane schools), originating in a day school at the South-West London (later Chelsea) polytechnic but transferred to the LCC. Although the LCC had opened 17 secondary schools by 1908, its Hortensia Road girls' school was the first to be built for the purpose.[14]

Apart from Carlyle and Sloane, which were often listed separately, there were by 1919 six county schools, including Tadema Road and counting the Ashburnham as separate all-age and central schools; six schools were Roman Catholic, including the Oratory's four (two of them central), and four were Anglican. All, except Tadema Road, survived in 1938,[15] although provision was reduced in line with the population. The council's elementary schools had accommodation for 5,525 in 1920 and 4,913 in 1937, non-provided schools for 3,342 in 1920 and 2,936 in 1937. For secondary education the number of places was raised slightly to 830 (536 of them free) by the enlargement of Carlyle school in 1937.[16]

The Second World War brought the closure of St Luke's parochial schools.[17] In 1947 there were six county and eight voluntary schools, including the Servites' which shared LCC premises and was soon to move to the Kensington side of Fulham Road.[18] The assets of the former Anglican schools of St Jude, St Luke, and St Simon were vested in the London Diocesan Board of Education in 1948 for disposal, as in 1968 were those of St Saviour's, which had been retained for educational purposes after its closure.[19] Public primary education was provided by three county and five voluntary schools in 1952 and 1958, while secondary education was provided by four of each class in 1952 and three in 1958. The Oratory's continuance as four separate establishments perhaps exaggerated the role of the Roman Catholics, although the departure of St Mark's practising school for Fulham left them with all three of the voluntary schools.[20]

The London Government Act, 1963, united Kensington and Chelsea with Hammersmith (later

1 LMA, SBL 1518, pp. 13–18, 29–30.

2 *PO Dir. London* (1879, 1902); *Kelly's Dir. Chelsea* (1881).

3 S. Maclure, *One Hundred Years of London Educ.* (1970), 15–16.

4 LMA, SBL 1329, pp. xii–xiii.

5 LMA, SBL 1527 (list of temp. schs 1885).

6 Stanford, *Sch. Bd Map of London*; *Rep. of Educ. Cttee of Council, 1890–1* (Parl. Papers, 1890–1 [C.6438-I], XXVII), p. 634.

7 Stanford, *Sch. Bd Map of London.* For schs in Chelsea detached which later lay within Paddington (Queen's Pk), *VCH Middx*, IX. 266–7; those later within Kens. (Kensal New Town) will be treated under Kens.

8 LMA, SBL 649, p. 38.

9 *Endowed Chars London* (1897), 10. Apprenticeship indentures of 1868 and 1872 are in LMA, O/443/1–2.

10 LMA, SBL 1527 (return of elem. schs 1903). Roughly similar figures were supplied for 1905: LCC, *London Statistics*, XVI. 266.

11 Education (London) Act, 3 Edw. VII, c. 14.

12 Below.

13 Chelsea BC, *Mins*, 29 June, 13 July 1904.

14 M. Seaborne, *The English Sch. 1870–1970* (1977), 102; *The Cheynean*, summer 1970, 5 (copy in CL).

15 *Bd of Educ., List 21, 1919*; ibid. *1938*.

16 LCC, *London Statistics*, XXVII. 174, 193; XLI. 258, 273.

17 For individual schs, below.

18 *PO Dir. London* (1947).

19 Nat. Soc. files (St Luke).

20 *PO Dir. London* (1952); Chelsea MB, *Official Guide* (1957–8); Chelsea cuttings: schs.

Hammersmith and Fulham) to form division 1 of the new ILEA.[1] Reorganization on comprehensive lines with the availability of larger sites outside the old parish further reduced the number of Chelsea's schools. Primary education was still provided by three county and four voluntary schools, the Oratory junior and infants' schools having united, but by 1975 amalgamations had left only one ILEA secondary school, Chelsea, and the departure of the Oratory senior schools had left one voluntary secondary, St Thomas More.[2]

Under the Education Reform Act, 1988, the ILEA was superseded by Kensington and Chelsea LB. In 1991 the new education authority's Chelsea district, corresponding with the old parish, contained 1,307 of the borough's 6,531 primary pupils.[3] In 1995 it still had three county and four voluntary primary schools, two being Roman Catholic and two Church of England. There was an open-air nursery school in Glebe Place, in addition to nursery classes at all the county and one of the Roman Catholic schools. St Thomas More remained the sole secondary school.[4]

PUBLICLY FUNDED SCHOOLS

Except where otherwise stated, basic historical information and figures of accommodation and average attendance have been taken from: files on Church of England schools at the National Society; PRO, ED 7/74, 80; *Mins of Educ. Cttee of Council, 1846* (Parl. Papers, 1847 [787], XLV); *1850–1* (Parl. Papers, 1850–1 [1357], XLIV(1)); *1859–60* (Parl. Papers, 1860 [2681], LIV); *Rep. of Educ. Cttee Of Council, 1865–6* (Parl. Papers, 1866 [3666], XXVIII); *1868–9* (Parl. Papers, 1868–9 [4139], XX); *1869–70* (Parl. Papers, 1870 [C.165], XXII); *1870–1* (Parl. Papers, 1871 [C.406], XXII); *1880–1* (Parl. Papers, 1881 [C.2948–I], XXXII); *1888–9* (Parl. Papers, 1889 [C.5804], XXIX); *1890–1* (Parl. Papers, 1890–1 [C.6438–I], XXVII); *Return of Elem. Schs 1893* (Parl. Papers, 1894 [C.7529], LXV); *1899* (Parl. Papers, 1900 [Cd.315], LXV(2)); *Return of Non-Provided Schs* (Parl. Papers, 1906 (178–XXXIII), LXXXVIII); *Pub. Elem. Schs 1906* (Parl. Papers, 1907 [Cd.3510], LXIII); LCC, *London Statistics*; *Bd of Educ., List 21, 1919–38* (HMSO); LCC (ILEA from 1965), *Educ. Svce Inf.* (1951 and later edns). Inf. on Church of England schs 1846 is from National Society, *Inquiry, 1846–7*, Middx. Roll and attendance figures for 1871 are from LMA, SBL 1518, for 1872 from SBL 1329, and for 1903 from SBL 1527. School rolls for 1989 are from *RBKC Schs Statistics Rep. 1990–1*, and for 1995 have been supplied by the principal schools officer, RBKC directorate of education and libraries.

The following abbreviations are used in addition to those in the index: a.a., average attendance; accn, accommodation; amalg., amalgamated; asst, assistant; B, boy, boys; bd, board; C, County; CE, Church of England; Cong., Congregationalist; demol., demolished; dept, department; G, girl, girls; I, infant, infants; J, JB, JG, JM, junior, junior boys, girls, mixed; M, mixed; Meth., Methodist; Nat., National; parl., parliamentary; perm., permanent; RC, Roman Catholic; reorg., reorganized; roll, numbers on roll; S, SB, SG, SM, senior, senior boys, girls, mixed; SBL, School Board for London; sec., secondary; Sun., Sunday; temp., temporary; vol., voluntary; Wes., Wesleyan. The word 'school' is to be understood after each named entry. Separate departments are indicated by commas: B, G, I; JM, I.

Arthur Street Nat. See St Luke, Arthur Street.

Ashburnham, The, Upcerne Rd. Opened 1885 as the Ashburnham bd for 1,197 MI. Accn 1899: 1,474; a.a. 1,342. Higher grade dept opened 1903. Accn 1906: 300 SM, 821 M, 533 I. S dept called the Ashburnham central (q.v.) by 1919. Other depts accn 1919: 821 M, 453 I; reorg. between 1927 and 1932 for 521 JM, 363 I. As Ashburnham primary (below), moved from Upcerne Rd when threatened by proposed West Cross route 1972. Premises let by ILEA for community use 1974 and housed Heatherley Sch. of Fine Art from 1979.[5]

Ashburnham Central, The, Upcerne Rd.[6] Opened 1903 as higher grade dept of the Ashburnham (q.v.). Accn 1919, 1927: 370 SM; 1932, 1938: 480 SM. Called Chelsea central 1946, when about to move to Townmead Rd, Fulham. B moved 1968 to join Kingsley (formerly Cook's Ground qq.v.) as Chelsea sch. (q.v.) and G to Hurlingham Rd, Fulham.

Ashburnham Primary, Blantyre St. Moved 1972 from Upcerne Rd. to single-storeyed brown brick bldgs designed by Eric Lyons for 280 JMI in new World's End est.[7] Roll 1989: 149; 1995: 186.

Brompton Oratory. See London Oratory.

Cale Street Nat. See St Luke, Cale Street.

Camera Street Ragged. Recorded only 1849 in Camera (later Beaufort) St, with thrice weekly evg classes for 48 B, 38 G, under 13 vol. teachers.[8]

Carlyle, Hortensia Rd. Opened 1908 for G from South-West London Polytechnic sch. (q.v.) as LCC sec. sch. in 4-storeyed bldg designed by T.J. Bailey. Accn

1 *Ann. Abstract of Gtr London Statistics* (1967), 119.
2 *PO Dir. London* (1975); below.
3 RBKC, *Schs Statistics Rep.* 1990–1, 9, 183, maps.
4 Inf. from RBKC, principal schs officer.
5 Chelsea cuttings: Ashburnham; ILEA, *Educ. Cttee Mins*, 30 Oct. 1973; below, private schs.
6 Additional inf. from *'The Ashburnham' Higher Grade Sch. Mag.* (1908–13) in CL.
7 Chelsea Cuttings: Ashburnham; ILEA, *Educ. Cttee Mins*, 31 March 1971.
8 *Ragged Sch. Union Mag.* I. 135.

65. *Hortensia Road school, later Carlyle school and Chelsea secondary, part of the Kensington and Chelsea College in 2003*

1908 said to be for 510 SG[1] but 1937, before enlargement, for only 256. Accn 1937: 320, inc. 226 free places.[2] Adjoined Sloane sch. (q.v.) from 1919 but given separate governing body 1961.[3] Moved with Sloane to new Pimlico sch., Westm., 1970.[4] Premises occupied briefly by Harwood primary sch., from Fulham, and then Chelsea sec. sch. 1971.[5]

Chelsea Baptist Chapel, Lower Sloane St. Opened by 1869 as day sch. for GI in room where Sun. sch. held beneath chapel built 1865.[6] Accn 1871: 511; roll: 90; a.a. 90. Day sch. probably soon closed.

Chelsea British, King's Rd. Opened for G by 1814.[7] Chelsea and Borough Rd, Southwark, schs the only ones wholly maintained by Brit. and Foreign Sch. Soc. According to its treasurer 1816.[8] Not recorded later unless identifiable with Chelsea Wes. sch. (q.v.).

Chelsea Central. See Ashburnham central.

Chelsea Charity. See Petyt's.

Chelsea Secondary, Hortensia Rd. Opened 1968 as SB comprehensive in Glebe Place on amalg. of Chelsea central with Kingsley (formerly Cook's Ground, q.v.) sch. Moved to premises of former Carlyle and Sloane schs 1971.[9] Accn 1973: 550 SB, soon to be raised to 750. 'Non-authoritarian'[10] and praised by ILEA inspectors.[11] Closed 1980. Premises used by Kensington and Chelsea College from 1990.[12]

Chelsea Wes., Sloane Terr. Associated with Sloane Terr. Wes. chapel by 1844 until *c.*1856. Always listed as for B, although mistress employed with master from 1850.[13]

Cheyne Walk RC. Inc. in list of schs which had received parl. grant between 1833 and 1859. Not listed in dir. of 1858 or 1863.

Christ Church CE Primary, Robinson St. Opened 1839 at ch. as Sun. sch. for B, 1840 for G. Day sch. opened 1840 for B at 2d. a week in Flood St.[14] BG sch. opened 1843 at S corner of Christchurch and Robinson streets, where site given by Earl Cadogan, whereupon I sch. opened in former B sch.[15] 122 B, 79 G on weekdays and Sun. by 1846 in partitioned schoolroom under mistress and 23 vol. teachers; 85 I in 2 schoolrooms under master and mistress; both depts with £150 grant from Nat. Soc. Parl. grants from 1843; income from subscriptions, collections, and sch. pence 1848; £200 left by Ann Hill 1881.[16] Site for I sch. on N corner of Robinson St given by Earl Cadogan 1851; additional land for playground given 1869.[17] Rolls 1871: 152 B, 143 G, 188 I; a.a. 121 B, 110 G, 144 I. G sch. enlarged 1872.[18] a.a. 1906: 331 BG, 124 I. Accn reduced 1907. Falling roll led to reorg. as M sch. 1925. Roll 1927: 230 M, 130 I; a.a. 196 M, 107 I. I sch. amalg. with M 1937.[19] Roll 1938: 360 MI; a.a. 165 MI. Two-storeyed Tudor style bldgs in use 1995. Roll 1995: 181 JMI.

Church Street Ragged. See Old Church Ragged.

Cook's Ground, Glebe Place. Opened 1874 as bd sch. for B,G,I. Accn 1880: 840; 1890: 1,345; 1919: 1,122 but a.a. only 729. Reorg. between 1927 and 1932 for 360 SG, 360 JM, 312 I. Reorg. by 1936 for 360 SG, 416 JM & I. SG by 1948, when amalg. with SB from Marlborough sch. (q.v.) in Cook's Ground bldgs, renamed Kingsley

1 *The Cheynean*, summer 1970, 5, in CL; *The Times*, 23 Nov. 1908; Seaborne, *Eng. Sch. 1870–1970*, 102–3.
2 Chelsea MB, *Official Guide* [1937]; LCC, *London Statistics*, XL. 273.
3 LCC, *Educ. Cttee Mins*, 11 July 1961.
4 ILEA, *Mins* (1964–9), 466.
5 CL, cuttings from *Chelsea News*, 31 Oct. 1969, 2 Feb. 1970, 19 Feb., 4 June 1971.
6 Bryan, *Chelsea*, 208.
7 *Rep. Brit. and Foreign Sch. Soc.* (1815), pp. ix–x; V. Moger, *The Favour of Your Company* (1980), 18.
8 *Rep. Sel. Cttee on Educ. of Lower Orders in Metropolis* (Parl. Papers, 1816 (469), IV), pp. 117, 119.
9 CL, cuttings (*Chelsea News*, 31 Oct. 1969, 2 Feb. 1970, 4 June 1971); see Fig. 65.
10 CL, cuttings (*Chelsea Post*, 30 Nov. 1973).
11 Ibid. (*Chelsea News*, 26 Nov. 1976, 20 June 1980).
12 Below, adult educ.
13 *PO Dir. London* (1844, 1850, 1855, 1857).
14 *Christ Ch., Chelsea. Brief Hist.* (pamphlet *c.*1990); Reid, *Hundred Years in Chelsea Par.* 38; Nat. Soc. Files (*First Ann. Rep. of Christ Ch. Schs*).
15 PRO, C 54/13089, m. 39.
16 *Vestry rep. 1881–2*, 33.
17 PRO, C 54/14199, m. 24; C 54/16987, m. 39.
18 Inscription on bldg.
19 Reid, *Hundred Years in Chelsea Par.* 47.

sch. 1949.[1] Kingsley absorbed SB from Parsons Green sec. (Fulham) 1963[2] and amalg. with former Chelsea central sch. to form Chelsea sec. (q.v.) 1968, moving to former Carlyle and Sloane premises 1971.[3] Cook's Ground site bought by Libyan govt for Jamahariya sch. 1979.[4]

Denyer Street Temp. Bd. Opened 1878 in rented schoolroom for GI. Closed 1878. Pupils transferred to Marlborough sch. (q.v.).

Discipline. See Reformatory Sch. of Discipline.

Exeter Buildings Ragged, Exeter St (later Hans Crescent). Founded by Lady Charlotte Gordon in support of London City Mission by 1845, with attendance of 70 besides Sun. sch. and adults' classes.[5] Attendance 1849: 56 B, 55 G, 45 I, also Sun. sch. and evg classes for 30 B, with 4 paid and 7 vol. teachers.[6] Industrial classes daily for 50 G and twice weekly for 8 B by 1851. Small sum raised from sale of articles 1862, when many refused admission to night sch.[7] Rolls 1871: 74 B, 73 G, 72 I, 45 night sch.; a.a. 45 B, 47 G, 64 I. Closed as day sch. 1876, when children transferred to Queen's Gdns (q.v.).[8]

Fulham Road Servite. See Servite RC.

Gunter Grove Temp. Bd. Opened in 1878 in rented schoolroom for B, as feeder for projected perm. sch. (possibly Ashburnham). Closed by 1880.

Hans Town School of Industry, Sloane St.[9] Opened *c.*1804 when ladies took lease of ho. near Hans Pl. where 6 G were trained for domestic svce. 50 G given elem. educ. and training by 1833, financed by subscriptions, needlework, and 1 guinea a quarter from parents.[10] No. 103 Sloane St leased to new cttee 1849 and bought 1850, when subscribers of £50 a year could keep one G at sch. for additional £7 10s. Matron, asst, and mistress employed for 57 G aged 8–16 in 1851.[11] Accn 1871: 64; roll: 52. Closed 1886 under Order for proceeds of sale to finance inmates' instruction elsewhere and to endow cot at Nat. Orphan Home, Ham Common (Surrey). Chelsea vestry's request for endowment of scholarships at polytechnic rejected by Char. Com. 1894, as trust had not been exclusively intended for or financed by parishioners.

Holy Trinity CE Primary, Sedding (formerly Upper George) St. Opened 1831 as Trinity I sch.; 160 I, paying sch. pence, under master and mistress 1833. G sch. at E. end of ch., B sch. along S. side of ch.[12] Site for Upper Chelsea Nat. sch. on E. side of Sloane St S. of ch. given by Earl Cadogan 1835.[13] 222 B, 116 G on weekdays, with smaller Sun. attendance, by 1846 in 2 schoolrooms under master, mistress, 2 assts, and 47 vol. teachers shared with I; 210 I in one schoolroom under master and 2 asst mistresses. Parl. grants from 1837. 'Excellent' BG sch. supplied many pupil teachers for other schs. 1846. Site on W. side of Upper George St given by Ch. Bldg Commrs 1847; site with new bldgs on E. side given by Earl Cadogan 1889.[14] Rolls 1871: 245 B, 135 G, 148 I; a.a. 221 B, 108 G, 107 I. BG in Sloane St, I in Upper George St in 1871; BG in Upper George St, I in Cadogan Gdns (formerly Draycott St) at corner of Pavilion Rd 1903. a.a. 1906: 405 B, 130 G. Accn reduced 1907. Roll 1919: 278 B, 138 G, 140 I; a.a. 211 B, 225 G & I. JMI in 3-storeyed Sedding St bldg dated 1888 and in 19th-cent. bldg in Cadogan Gdns by 1958. Roll 1995: 145 JMI.

Home for Destitute and Friendless Girls, Cheyne Walk. One schoolroom at no. 46 for 33 G. Roll 1872; 40. Bldg later taken for Cheyne Hosp. for Sick Children.[15]

Hortensia Road Girls' Sec. See Carlyle.

Hortensia Road Temp. C. Opened 1907 in 3 iron bldgs for 240 JM, 120 I on closure of Park Chapel (q.v.).[16] Closed 1913 on opening of Tadema Rd sch. (q.v.).

Industrial School for Girls, Sloane St. Opened by 1858 at no. 125 as Industrial Home for G.[17] Cert. as industrial sch. by educ. cttee of Council 1859.[18] Accn 1871: 74; roll: 50. Closed after 1895.[19]

Industry, schs of. See Hans Town; Industrial Sch. for Girls; St Jude.

Ives Street Ragged. See Shaftesbury.

Ives Street Temp. Bd. Opened 1877 in rented schoolroom and classroom for BGI. Closed 1878; reopened for 6 months in 1879. Accn 1880 recorded as 462. Pupils on both occasions transferred to Marlborough sch. (q.v.).

1 LCC, *Educ. Cttee Mins,* 30 June 1948, 23 Feb. 1949.
2 Ibid., 11 May 1960.
3 CL, cuttings (*Chelsea News,* 31 Oct. 1969, 2 Feb. 1970).
4 Below, private schs.
5 *Ragged Sch. Union Mag.* XII. 15; *London City Mission Mag.* X. 237.
6 *Ragged Sch. Union Mag.* I. 135.
7 Ibid., III. 207; XIV. 120.
8 *Vestry rep. 1877–8,* 276–7.
9 Based on *Vestry mins, 1894–5,* 186.
10 *Educ. Enquiry Abs.* 556.
11 PRO, HO 107/1474/2/3/9, ff. 343 seqq.
12 Lambeth Pal. Lib., Fulham Papers, Creighton 2, *passim.*
13 PRO, C 54/11425, m. 2; Spicer, *Holy Trinity Ch.* 15.
14 PRO, C 54/13487, m. 3; C 54/20003, m. 27.
15 Below, Loc. Govt, pub. svces (medical).
16 LMA, SBL 648, p. 402.
17 *PO Dir. London* (1857, 1858).
18 *London Gaz.* 5 April 1859, p. 1415.
19 *Kelly's Dir. Chelsea* (1895).

Kingsley. See Cook's Ground.

London Oratory, Stewart's Grove.[1] Opened 1852 for B by Fathers of London Oratory on acquisition of site which inc. former Blemell Ho. sch., Brompton Rd, Kensington.[2] Moved 1856,[3] as Brompton Oratory RC Free sch., to leased ho. in Marlborough Sq. with 3 schoolrooms, classroom, and master's residence, financed by vol. contributions and sch. pence (1d. from 40 B). GI Free sch., opened 1857, in new bldg of 1860 in Bond (later Cale) St between Bury St (later Bury Walk) and Sydney St; similarly financed. New B sch. built 1863–4 immediately to E. GI sch. in Stewart's Grove, next to St Wilfrid's convent and staffed by Daughters of the Cross, opened 1870. B 1871: roll 132, a.a. 110; GI 1871: roll 198, a.a. 218. Often listed as Brompton Oratory schs.[4] Brompton and Chelsea Middle sch. for B opened 1881 in part of B Bury St premises. Middle sch. for GI by 1904. Classified by LCC as 2 schs (B and GI) until managers secured recognition as 4 separate institutions named Oratory B Free, Oratory B Middle, Oratory G and I, and Oratory G and I Middle 1905.[5] Accn 1904–5: B Free 188, B Middle 188, GI Free 350, GI Middle 330.

Middle schs renamed Oratory B and Oratory G central schs 1921, when fee paying ceased. Free schs renamed Oratory B and Oratory G and I RC schs by 1927. Accn 1932: 300 SB, 320 SG, 170 B, 314 GI. Central schs renamed London Oratory RC sec. schs. for B and for G 1949, when Oratory B and Oratory G and I were reorg. as Oratory JM and I and renamed Oratory primary (q.v.).[6] London Oratory sec. schs, in Stewart's Grove, vol. aided from 1951.[7] Rolls 1958: 355 B; 335 G.[8] Sec. schs amalg. 1959, when residents began successful opposition to plans for expansion in Sydney St.[9] G phased out, Daughters of the Cross being withdrawn 1962 and sch. classified as B grammar 1963. Moved to Seagrave Rd, Fulham, as B comprehensive with G in sixth form, 1970, when Chelsea site passed to Royal Marsden hosp. Grant maintained from 1989. Roll 1996: 1,280.

Manor Street Temp. Bd. Opened 1872 in rented assembly rooms in Manor (later Chelsea Manor) St. Closed 1874. Pupils transferred to Cook's Ground (q.v.).

Markham Street Nat. See St Luke Parochial.

Marlborough Primary, Draycott Ave. Opened 1878 as Marlborough Rd bd sch. for BGI. Accn 1880: 762; 1890: 1,215; 1907: 512 SM, 510 JM, 551 I. Called Marlborough sch. after name of rd changed to Draycott Ave. Reorg. 1917 for 494 B, 494 G, 521 I. Accn 1936: 400 B, 393 G, 320 I. Primary and sec. schs 1952, when St Thos More sch. (q.v.) also occupied premises. Primary alone by 1955. JM,I by 1958. Roll 1989: 132; 1995: 163.

Old Church Ragged, Church St. Former Petyt's sch. (q.v.) repaired with help from Ragged Sch. Union to make 3 classrooms by 1869.[10] Roll 1871: 202; a.a. 93 B, 78 G. Transferred 1871 to SBL,[11] which used premises rent free until opening of Cook's Ground (q.v.).[12]

Onslow Dwellings Nat. See St Luke, Onslow Dwellings.

Oratory Central. See London Oratory.

Oratory Free. See London Oratory.

Oratory RC Primary, Bury Walk, Cale St. Renamed from Oratory JM and I schs 1949. JM in Bury Walk and I in Stewart's Grove by 1952 until 1964 or later. I presumably moved 1970 when London Oratory (q.v.) left Stewart's Grove for Fulham. Single vol. aided primary sch. in Bury Walk by 1975. Roll 1995: 208 JMI.

Paradise Chapel Ragged, Queen's Rd West. Sch. held in chapel 1869 by cong. which had moved to Chelsea Bapt. chapel, Lower Sloane St.[13]

Park Chapel Nat., Park Walk and Millman Row (later Milman's St). Originated in 1814 as Sun. sch. for B in Robinson's Lane (later Flood St). Moved to Church St, where day sch. for BG opened 1816 in hired rooms, with rector as patron. Allotted seats in Park chapel, Park Walk, then in Ebury chapel and finally in old sch. Moved to rear of Millman Row 1817 and behind Park chapel 1820, where new schoolrooms for B and for G were built 1827. Associated with chapel and sometimes called Chelsea Nat. schs. because the first in neighbourhood to adopt system. 120 B and 75 G, inc. 24 clothed, in 1829, when supported by vol. contributions, sermons, fees of 3d. a week, and annual subscribers whose nominees were taught free.[14] The 'Clockhouse sch.', established 1831 and with 55 B and 55 G in 1833, was presumably in former stabling at N. end of Moravians' burial ground

1 Additional inf. from *London Oratory Sch. Prospectus* (1996) and the headmaster.

2 *London Oratory, Centenary 1884–1984*, ed. M. Napier and A. Laing, 12; *Survey of London*, XLI. 50.

3 Normally taken as foundation date for B sch., e.g. *Return of Non-Provided Schs* (1906).

4 e.g. *PO Dir. London* (1879, 1902).

5 LCC, *Educ. Cttee Mins*, 1 Feb., 5 April 1905.

6 Ibid., 4 May 1949.

7 Ibid., 10 Oct. 1951.

8 Ibid., 19 Feb. 1958.

9 RBKC, *Chelsea Conservation Area Proposals Statement*, 10.

10 Bryan, *Chelsea*, 24.

11 *Return of Schs transferred to Sch. Bds* (Parl. Papers, 1875 (253), LVIII), p. 16; SBL, *Mins of Procs.* 2 Aug., 11 Oct. 1871.

12 SBL, *Mins of Procs.* 13 Nov. 1872, 11 Feb. 1874.

13 Bryan, *Chelsea*, 208; above, Chelsea Bapt. chapel sch.

14 Above based on Faulkner, *Chelsea*, II. 338–9.

off Millman Row; leased by them for Park chapel B.[1] 92 B, 71 G on weekdays and Sun. by 1846 in 2 schoolrooms under master and mistress; 113 I weekdays in schoolroom under mistress, 100 on Sun. when aided by 25 vol. teachers. B at Clockhouse and in former Moravian chapel by 1869, when GI in Park Walk.[2] Rolls 1871: 242 B, 109 G, 158 I. Rolls 1903, at same sites: 210 B,[3] 329 GI. Bldgs condemned by LCC 1905;[4] closed 1906.

Park Walk Primary. Opened 1881 for BGI as special bd sch. Accn 1899: 1,204 BGI, inc. defectives' class; a.a. 1,042. Accn 1927: 350 B, 350 G, 347 I. Reorg. by 1932 for 350 SB, 350 JM, 368 I. Primary by 1952; JM, I by 1958. Roll 1989: 98; 1995: 154.

Petyt's or Chelsea Charity, Church (later Old Church) St.[5] Parochial sch., recorded in 1583, held in part of clerk's ho. built on N. side of churchyard by Ric. Ward, rector 1585–1615. Replaced 1706 at expense of antiquary Wm Petyt (d. 1707),[6] a resident of Church St, who built vestry room and schoolroom, with upper rooms for master, on same site slightly enlarged by parish. Vestry, which paid for some fittings,[7] undertook to make repairs and pay master; also to appoint master after deaths of Petyt and John Chamberlaine. B to be taught free, apart from five supported by Chamberlaine's gift (above). Inclosure of commons sought to provide funds for clothing and teaching 1707, but apparently without success. Called 'the Grey Coat sch.' in will of Thos Bromwich, proved 1710, whose rent charge of 20s. a year was in arrears by 1749.[8] Trustees, inc. rector and churchwardens, were chosen yearly by vestry, which formally approved appointments of master,[9] inc. John Bellas 1746 and his son Rob. Bellas 1771.[10] G char. sch., Lordship Place, founded 1740 by rector Sloane Elsmere, with same trustees. B additionally supported by one third of collections at Sacrament 1740, when G to receive another third besides proceeds from sermon previously for daughters of pensioners at Royal Hosp. and from volume of sermons left by Elsmere (d. 1766). Gift of stationery for B in 1754.[11] Rector subscribed 2 gns a year and 33 other trustees, inc. ladies, 1 gn. 1792.[12] 70 pupils, inc. 50 clothed, in 1816; 120, all clothed, by 1823, after treasurer Luke Flood had increased vol. contributions, improved salaries, and secured partial introduction of Dr Bell's system. B transferred to new St Luke's Parochial sch. (q.v.) 1826, G to Petyt's bldg before joining B. Petyt's bldg, brick, of three bays and two storeys beneath a dentil cornice and dormers and with a ground floor arcade,[13] was used for fire engines, then repaired by incumbent of old ch. with grants from vestry 1867 and Ragged Sch. Union by 1869 and later served as mission hall and Sun. sch. until found unsafe 1887. Vested in Char. Com. and leased for 80 years from 1890 to incumbent, who rebuilt it in facsimile as Sun. sch.[14]

Queen's Gardens Bd. Opened 1876 for M on Kensington side of boundary S. of Brompton Rd. Fees reduced to 1d. for sake of children from Exeter Bldgs (q.v.) 1877.[15] Enlargement to take 180 B, 60 G approved 1879. Amalg. 1886 to form Queen's Gdns and Walton St sch., with G and I at Queen's Gdns and B at Walton St.[16] Queen's Gdns premises bought by Harrods 1897 and closed on reorg. of Walton St and Marlborough Rd (q.v.) 1902.[17]

Ragged schs. See Camera St; Exeter Bldgs; Old Church; Paradise chapel; St Jude; Shaftesbury.

Ranelagh Lancasterian, Lower George St. Opened *c.*1802 for poor children in room in Ranelagh Ho. Schoolrooms for nearly 300 attached to new Ranelagh chapel 1818.[18] 160 B, 140 G under master and mistress in 1833, when connected with Calvinistic Meths. and supported by vol. contributions.[19] 'Subterraneous' accn for 300 in 1845, when a.a. said by CE curate to be 90 B, 60 G.[20] Survived as Ranelagh British sch. 1855 and listed among Brit. schs until 1863 or later, although renamed Chelsea Commercial sch. by 1857, when probably taken over as private sch. by Alf. Bonifacio.[21]

Rectory Garden Nat., Church (later Old Church) St. Opened by 1846 in 2 schoolrooms at S. end of Rectory garden presumably by Revd Chas Kingsley or his wife, who was an active supporter.[22] 200 G on weekdays and Sun. by 1846 under mistress and asst; 55 I under mistress and 27 vol. teachers. Replaced by G of St Luke's Parochial schs (q.v.) in 1861.[23] Bequest of £200 from Laetitia Rawlings transferred to St Luke's schs.[24]

1 Blunt, *Chelsea*, 66, 157; below, Rel. Hist., foreign chs (Moravians).
2 Bryan, *Chelsea*, 48, 71.
3 Address by 1879 normally listed as no. 381 King's Rd.
4 LMA, P74/AND/31.
5 Additional inf. from *Survey of London*, IV. 53–4; Faulkner, *Chelsea*, I. 255–8, II. 92–6; Beaver, *Memorials*, 105–9, 115; *Endowed Chars London* (1897), 2, 10–19; see Fig. 64.
6 *DNB*.
7 Vestry orders, 1662–1718, f. 144v. Detailed regulations in BL, Add. MS 15609, f. 6.
8 Vestry orders, 1745–71, p. 56; Dr King's MS, p. 117.
9 Vestry orders, 1745–71, pp. 12–15, 46, 96, 98, 166.
10 Ibid., pp. 15, 350.
11 BL, Sloane MS 4034, f. 67; Vestry orders, 1745–71, p. 156.
12 Vestry orders, 1790–1809, p. 24.
13 *Images of Chelsea*, nos 19–20; Chelsea Misc. 10.
14 Appeal leaflet, 1890, in Chelsea Misc. 11.
15 *Vestry rep. 1877–8*, 276–7.
16 LMA, SBL 649, pp. 131, 133, 139–40.
17 *Survey of London*, XLI. 18; LMA, SBL 648, p. 241.
18 Faulkner, *Chelsea*, II. 316; *Chelsea Soc. Rep.* (1956), 7–8.
19 *Educ. Enquiry Abstract*, 557.
20 Nat. Soc. files (St Jude).
21 *PO Dir. London* (1855, 1857, 1863); below, private schs.
22 Old OS Map, London 87 (1865 edn); Bryan, *Chelsea*, 140.
23 Rectory Gdns sch. listed 1890 was presumably a Sun. sch., later St Luke's institute: *Kelly's Dir. Chelsea* (1890, 1891).
24 *Vestry rep. 1867–8*, 309.

Reformatory Sch. of Discipline, Queen's Rd West.[1] Opened 1825 by Eliz. Fry as first reformatory for G in London. Known also as Ho. of Discipline or Sch. of Reform. Soon moved to larger Ormonde Ho., Paradise Row (no. 2 Queen's Rd W., from 1902 Royal Hospital Rd). 33 G taught in 1833, financed by subscribers and parents. Cert. as reformatory sch. by Home Office 1856 but as industrial sch. by educ. cttee of Council 1859,[2] when G under detention were discharged or transferred.[3] Parl. grant 1859 but not thereafter. Received G at risk, committed by magistrates and some paid for by Home Office. Roll 1871: 42. Closed after *c*.1890, when bldg taken over by Middx Cyclist Volunteer Corps.[4]

St Anne's Home RC, Stewart's Grove. Orphanage built 1857 for Servite Sisters taken over by Daughters of the Cross (St Wilfrid's Convent) 1869.[5] Recorded as sch. with 2 rooms 1871–2: accn 133 G; a.a. 37.

St Joseph RC Primary, Cadogan St (formerly Cadogan Terr.). Opened 1844 for B in schoolroom and 2 classrooms and 1845 for GI in 2 schoolrooms paid for by Jos. Knight and on part of site given by him in 1842 for St Joseph's convent.[6] Managed by clergy of RC (St Mary's) mission and financed by vol. contributions. Parl. grant by 1859 but removed from inspection by 1867. Irish Christian Brothers taught B until replaced by laymen 1880.[7] Rolls 1871: 180 B, 156 GI; a.a. 145 B, 92 GI. Accn 1880: 303 BGI; 1890: 633; 1893: 712. Reduced by 1919 to 418 and by 1932 to 234. Vol. aided from 1951; primary by 1952. Roll 1995: 204 JMI.

St Jude Industrial, Franklin's Row. 'Knitting sch.' opened 1787 under Mrs Keyt in Lawrence St as sequel to opening of Sun. schs. 36 G clothed by Lord and Lady Cremorne 1788.[8] As sch. of industry, it had been 'long consolidated' with Sun. schs by 1811, when Lord Cremorne helped to clothe 30 G paid for by vol. contributions.[9] 50 G by 1819. Listed separately as St Jude's industrial sch., Franklin's Row, 1871: roll and a.a. 50 G. Probably closed with home *c*.1880.[10]

St Jude Nat., Turk's Row. Opened 1846 with Nat. Soc. and parl. grants on site N. of new ch. given by Ch. Bldg Commrs 1845.[11] 88 B, 110 G on weekdays, fewer on Sun., in partitioned schoolroom[12] under master, mistress, and 14 vol. teachers shared with I; 102 I under mistress. Financed by vol. contributions and sch. pence 1852. Roll 1871: 77 B, 99 G or GI. Nearby bldg taken on lease for additional St Jude's Lower I sch. 1872, replaced by new rooms over sch. 1873. Accn 1880: 507 BGI, a.a. 294. Pence (1d.–2d.) paid 1881, when sch. in debt to vicar. I sch. only by 1883, Sun. sch. only by 1894.[13]

St Jude Ragged, Turk's Row. Opened 1837. Said to be in union with Nat. Soc. as Turk's Row dist. sch., in one overcrowded schoolroom for 80 BG, 1845.[14] New schoolroom for BG 1863, owned by adjoining Industrial Home (above, St Jude industrial) in Franklin's Row but with its own entrance from Turk's Row. Roll 1871: 211 in two schoolrooms. Financed by parl. grant, vol. contributions, and sch. pence (1d.) 1875. Probably closed by 1880, when no parl. grant recorded, but listed until 1887.[15]

St Luke, Arthur Street, Nat.[16] Opened in Arthur (later Dovehouse) St by 1869, when a.a. 73. Accn 1872, when at nos 55 and 57: 126; a.a. 56 B, 78 G. Accn 1890: 162; a.a. 156. Probably closed by 1893.

St Luke, Cale Street, Nat. Opened 1874 for I in new bldg at corner of Robert (later Sydney) St leased to rector, with schoolroom, classroom, and ho. for mistress. Accn 1880: 151; a.a. 150. Same accn but no a.a. recorded 1890, when presumably closed.

St Luke, Onslow Dwellings, Nat., off Pond Place. Opened 1864 by asst curate in brick hall of 1862 leased by C.J. Freake, with 2 schoolrooms and 2 classrooms for GI. Intended for poor moving into Freake's model dwellings.[17] Parl. grant by 1865, when a.a. 136. Roll 1871: 200 M; a.a. 51 B, 116 G. Open in 1880, probably closed by 1881;[18] used as Sun. sch. 1894.[19]

St Luke Parochial, King (later St Luke's) St.[20] Opened 1826 as Nat. sch. for B formerly at Petyt's sch. (q.v.) on site acquired 1824 E. of new par. ch. I sch. built 1827–8 on E side of Markham St. G probably moved to King St by 1846 but again at Petyt's sch. in 1861, when moved to former Rectory Garden (q.v.). 164 B, 70 G on weekdays and Sun. by 1846 in 2 schoolrooms under master, mistress, and asst master, with £100 grant from Nat.

1 Additional inf. from Blunt, *Chelsea*, 105; ibid. *Paradise Row*, 108; Bryan, *Chelsea*, 185.
2 *London Gaz.* 26 Aug. 1856, p. 2917; 14 June 1859, p. 2322.
3 *3rd Rep. Inspectors of Reformatory Schs* (Parl. Papers, 1860 [2688], XXXV), p. 7.
4 *Kelly's Dir. Chelsea* (1890, 1891).
5 Chelsea cuttings: St Wilfrid's; *Cath. Dir.* (1870); below, Rel. Hist., rom. cathm.
6 PRO, C 54/15672, m. 55; *The Times*, 3 April 1845; below, Rel. Hist., rom. cathm.
7 *PO Dir. London* (1879); W.J. Anderson, *Hist. of Cath. Par. of St Mary's, Chelsea* (1938), 50.
8 BL, Add. MS 21252, ff. 17v., 28; below, St Luke's Sun. schs.
9 Lysons, *Environs*, Suppl. 113.
10 *PO Dir. London* (1879).
11 PRO, C 54/13256, m. 25.
12 LMA, Y/SP/74/3/A–C.
13 Old OS Map, London 88 (1894 edn).
14 Nat. Soc. files.
15 *Kelly's Dir. Chelsea* (1887, 1890).
16 So described in parliamentary reps, but listed only as Arthur Street Nat. by SBL.
17 Nat. Soc. files.
18 *Kelly's Dir. Chelsea* (1881).
19 Old OS Map, London 87 (1894 edn).
20 Additional inf. from *Endowed Chars London* (1897), 24–5, 32, 48–9; Bryan, *Chelsea*, 139, 150.

Soc.; 110 I in one schoolroom under mistress and asst. Parl. grant by 1859. Bequests, in addition to those to charity schs (above), inc. £2 2s. a year from Eliz. Smith's charity by will proved 1828, £100 from William Gibbs by will proved 1833,[1] stock bought by Earl Cadogan to clothe and educate 10 B and 10 G 1835, three-fifths of income from £2,500 left by Luke Flood for apprenticing 1 B and 1 G or clothing 2 B and 2 G and for prizes for catechism 1849, income from £200 given by Laetitia Rawlings for prizes 1867, and £200 left by Ann Hill 1881.[2] Elizabeth Smith's Educational foundation established under Bd of Educ. Act, 1899, by Char. Com. Order 1906.[3] Parochial schs regarded as separate from St Luke, Onslow Dwellings, sch. (q.v.), established in 1864. Rolls 1871: 508 B, 188 G, 272 I; a.a. 400 B, 164 G, 217 I. New lease of improved Markham St premises secured 1890; I had moved to King St and G to Markham St by 1896, leaving Rectory Garden as boys' institute. a.a. 1906: 334 BI, 206 G. Rebuilt G sch., LCC having threatened closure, opened 1909.[4] Rolls 1919: 271 B, 233 G; a.a. 256 B, 225 G. Rolls 1938: 235 B & I, 223 G & I; a.a. 144, 121. Closed after evacuation 1939.[5] Bldg on W side of King St by Jas Savage 1824–6: Gothic style, matching that of St Luke's ch., with 'original plan' or single-storeyed battlemented wings N and S of centre containing tall gateway between accn for master and mistress. Survived 1952 and later replaced by neo-Georgian nos 23–9 St Luke's St and church hall.[6]

St Luke Sun. schs.[7] 2 each for 25 B and 1 for 25 G, opened 1787 under cttee which inc. rector and Revd Mr Butler,[8] with Lord and Lady Cremorne among many prominent subscribers. Classes for 51 B and 71 G held in 1788 at schs of Mrs Fryer, Mrs Liddel, Mrs Winterbottom, Mr Keyt, and Mr Lomax. B sch., diminished by employment at paper factory, temp. suspended by 1799. Same benefactors in 1787 had opened 'knitting sch.' under Mrs Keyt, with which Sun. sch. had been 'long consolidated' by 1811.[9]

St Mark's College Nat., Fulham Rd. Normal and model sch. for B planned in 1842 as part of St Mark's training college for teachers[10] established in Stanley Grove[11] by Nat. Soc. 1841. New octagonal bldg, paid for by parl. grant,[12] used by junior pupils 1843. Cottage acquired for upper sch. 1845; second storey added to octagon 1848; 6 rooms added 1865.[13] a.a. 1865: 185; 1867: 395. Mat. Arnold arranged visit by Leo Tolstoy 1861.[14] Usually described as St Mark's Practising schs. Lower sch. 1871: accn 205, roll 168; Middle sch. 1871: accn 333, roll 212. Middle sch. alone by 1890: accn 488. Reduced to 260 B in 1907 after opening of JM dept 1905. JM closed by 1919. Accn 1922: 300 B; 1932: 328 B. Vol. aided from 1949. Renamed St Mark's CE 1951, when about to move to Bishop's Ave, Fulham. Two-storeyed octagon of stock brick in Byzantine style, with 4 main teaching areas and central position for supervisor, by E. Blore 1843, 1848, converted into lib. for college by Seely & Paget 1953 after removal of extensions.[15] Bldg housed Octagon sch. 1995.[16]

66. *The octagon school at St Mark's college, used as a library in 1966*

St Mary RC Charity, Cadogan Terr. Opened probably with St Mary's chapel of 1811, perhaps at first only for G, in Symons St. Increase from 80 pupils by 1824[17] to 150 BG, of whom 60 B and 40 G were clothed, by 1829,[18] presumably following bldg of two schoolhos by Abbé Voyaux de Franous under lease of 1825 from Lady Charlotte Denys,[19] who had leased site for chapel. Described as two schs, clothing 75 B and 60 G, in 1833, when vol. contributions needed supplementation by chaplain. *c.*250 BG by 1838.[20] Superseded by St Joseph's schs (q.v.), although Sisters of Mercy at St Joseph's convent

1 *Chelsea Chars 1862*, 37.
2 *Vestry rep. 1881–2*, 32.
3 62 & 63 Vic. c. 33; Char. Com. files.
4 *The Times*, 31 July 1908; Chelsea cuttings: St Luke's; Nat. Soc. files.
5 Chelsea cuttings: St Luke's.
6 *Gent. Mag.* XCVI(1), 205; Pevsner, *London*, II. 93; *Images of Chelsea*, no. 421; RBKC, *Chelsea Conservation Area Proposals Statement*, 19; Chelsea cuttings: St Luke's sch.
7 Based on BL, Add. MS 21252, *passim.*
8 Presumably Weeden Butler: below, private schs.
9 Lysons, *Environs*, Suppl. 113; above, St Jude.
10 Below, adult educ.
11 Below, private schs.
12 PRO, C 54/12709, m. 9; see Fig. 66.
13 M. Roberts, *Coll. of St Mark and St John, 1840–65* (1946), 31.
14 R.G. Clark, *Chelsea Today* (1991), 52–4.
15 Pevsner, *London*, II. 93; ibid. *London NW.* 567; Seaborne, *Eng. Sch. 1870–1970*, 205–6.
16 Below, private schs.
17 Anderson, *Hist. St Mary's*, 34; below, Rel. Hist., rom. cathm.
18 Faulkner, *Chelsea*, II. 345.
19 PRO, C 54/15672, m. 51.
20 *Cath. Dir.* (1838).

conducted a poor sch. for G until 1865 or later.[1] St Mary's I sch. opened in 1857 in accn rented annually. Managed by missionary rector of St Mary's and supported in 1858 by vol. contributions and sch. pence. Parl. grant from 1859. Last listed 1870, when a.a. 92.

St Philip, Charlotte Street, RC, Pavilion Rd. Opened by 1868 for GI in rented schoolroom over stable connected to landlord's ho. in Exeter St. Managed by Fathers of London Oratory, to whose schs most pupils proceeded, and financed in 1868 by vol. contributions and sch. pence (1d.). Accn 1871: 61; roll 106; a.a. 79. One schoolroom and one classroom 1872, when enlargement planned. Accn 1888: 219; a.a. 91. Not in receipt of parl. grant but survived until after 1895, when G were at no. 45 Pavilion Rd and I nearby in Charlotte St.

St Saviour Nat., Walton St. Opened 1846 with Nat. Soc. grant in temp. bldg in Exeter Place. 110 B, 117G on weekdays and Sun. 1846 in 2 schoolrooms under master, mistress, and 16 vol. teachers shared with I; 65 I in one schoolroom under asst mistress. Parl. grants from 1847. Site on S side of Walton St E of Stanley (later Ovington) St acquired from trustees of Hen. Smith's char. 1862.[2] Rolls 1871: 213 B, 180 G in Walton St, 155 I in Exeter Place; a.a. 160 B, 143 G, 118 I. Freehold, with reservations on use by trustees, conveyed to SBL 1879, when taken for Walton St temp. bd sch. (q.v.).

St Simon Nat., Moore St. Opened 1852 as I sch. by incumbent of St Simon's. In one schoolroom in iron bldg next to ch. 1861.[3] Financed by vol. contributions and sch. pence (2d.). Parl. grant by 1868, when a.a. 122. New Nat. sch. built 1871 with schoolroom and classroom for B and schoolroom and classroom for I. Rolls 1871: 37 B, 172 I.[4] B sch. closed before schoolroom and classroom for G added 1877.[5] Accn 1893: 258 MI; a.a. 136. GI by 1899. Premises declared unsuitable and closed 1905.[6]

St Thomas More RC Sec., Cadogan St.[7] Opened 1948 as SM sch. Vol. aided from 1951. Occupied 4 classrooms and specialist accn in Marlborough primary sch., Draycott Ave, and from 1952 9 classrooms in St Joseph's convent, Cadogan St.[8] Classrooms and from 1954 rest of convent adapted with help from LCC. Retained annexe at Draycott Ave 1958. New assembly hall block, reputedly first bldg in London designed in metric dimensions, 1970. Sch. oversubscribed in 1984, when cramped site gave rise to Westm. diocese schs cttee's controversial proposal for amalg. with St Edmund's, Fulham. Further controversy over need for repairs at Cadogan St and proposed move to adult educ. centre (formerly Carlyle and Sloane schs) in Hortensia Rd 1991.[9] Sole maintained sec. sch. in Chelsea 1995, when part of sch. in Hortensia Rd and rebuilding under way in Cadogan St. Roll 1995: 600 SM.

Servite RC Primary, Fulham Rd. Opened 1868 for GI as Mount Senario or Senaris Gardens[10] sch., no. 379 Fulham Rd, leased to and managed by Revd Phil. Bosio. Started with 2 unpaid lay teachers, succeeded by Sisters of the Precious Blood.[11] New bldg on same site, with 2 classrooms, 1869. Managed by Bosio and financed by £50 p.a. from Archbishop Manning, vol. contributions, and sch. pence 1872, when mistress uncertificated and a.a. 25 G, 68 I. Reorg. for BGI 1872. New site in Winterton Pl., W side of Park Walk off Fulham Rd, leased from 1874.[12] Parl. grant by 1880. Accn 1880: 395 BGI; a.a. 195. Taken over by Servite Sisters 1882.[13] Accn 1903: 357; a.a. 422. Accn 407 by 1905, reduced to 380 in 1907 and to 250 between 1927 and 1932. Primary sch. from 1946, vol. aided *c.*1948. Moved from Park Walk to no. 252 Fulham Rd, on Kensington side, 1950.[14] Roll 1995: 194 JMI.

Shaftesbury Ragged, Ives St. Opened 1859. In rented schoolroom for BGI 1871, with certificated master and mistress and 4 paid monitors.[15] Roll 1871: 190; a.a. 67 B, 93 G. Transferred to SBL by 1877[16] and reopened as Ives Street temp. (q.v.).

Sloane, Hortensia Rd. SB at South-West London Polytechnic sch. (q.v.) renamed Sloane sch. by 1914, when LCC planned move. Opened 1919 in new bldg N. of Carlyle sch. (q.v.).[17] Accn 1919, 1937: 510 SB.[18] 310 free places by 1937. Given joint governing body with Kingsley (formerly Cook's Ground) sch. 1961.[19] Moved with Carlyle to Pimlico sch., Westm., 1970. Premises occupied by Chelsea sec. sch. (q.v.) 1971.[20]

South-West London (later South-Western) Polytechnic Day, Manresa Rd.[21] Opened 1895 by polytechnic for BG from age *c.*13 who had passed 5th standard of elem.

1 *Cath. Dir.* (1853 and later edns). For the Sisters' ladies sch., below, private schs.
2 Stroud, *Smith's Char.* 39; PRO, C 54/15971, m. 43.
3 Both 1852 and 1861 are given as foundation dates in PRO, ED 7/80.
4 I nos recorded only as 83 B, 89 G.
5 SBL, *Mins of Procs*, 9 May 1877.
6 LCC, *Educ. Cttee Mins*, 12 April, 19 July 1905.
7 Based on sch. prospectus and inf. from head teacher.
8 LCC, *Educ. Cttee Mins*, 12 Oct. 1955, 18 April 1956.
9 Chelsea cuttings, St Thos More sch.
10 Below, Rel. Hist., rom. cathm.
11 Corr, *Servites*, 36.
12 PRO, C 54/18337, m. 43.
13 Inf. from headmistress.
14 Inf. from headmistress.
15 *Shaftesbury Ragged Sch. 10th Ann. Rep. 1870*, attached to PRO, ED 7/80.
16 *Vestry rep. 1877–8*, 276–7.
17 *The Cheynean*, summer 1970, 5.
18 Chelsea MB, *Official Guide* [1937]; LCC, *London Statistics*, XLI. 273.
19 LCC, *Educ. Cttee Mins*, 11 July 1961.
20 CL, cuttings from *Chelsea News*, 2 Feb. 1970, 4 June 1971.
21 Based on *Endowed Chars London* (1904), 127–8; *The Cheynean*, summer 1970, 5.

code or gained entrance scholarship from elem. sch. Roll 1902–3, when higher classes charged for scientific and commercial courses: 260–70 BG; 1908: *c.*400 BG. Staff from polytechnic's Chelsea pupil teachers' centre.[1] G moved to Carlyle sch. (q.v.) 1908 and B, after delay caused by war, to Sloane sch. (q.v.) 1919.

Tadema Road Temp. C. Opened 1913 for MI on closure of Hortensia Rd sch. (q.v.). M dept closed 1915. Accn 1919: 144 I. Closed 1921.

Walton Street Temp. Bd. Opened 1879 in former St Saviour Nat. sch. (q.v.). Amalg. with Queen's Gdns (q.v.) 1886. Accn 1890: 1,019 BM; a.a. 631. Reorg. as single dept for MI 1902.[2] Accn 1906: 224 JM, 220 I. Sch. for physically defective from 1909.[3]

Whitelands College Nat., King's Rd.[4] Sch. for G opened 1842 in part of college established at Whitelands Lodge[5] to train women teachers 1841 and taken over by Nat. Soc. 1849.[6] Bldg at E. corner of Walpole St extended and partly rebuilt by Nat. Soc. with parl. grant 1851.[7] Three Whitelands schs 1846: Middle, 72 G; Practising, 128 G; Infants, 134 BG; all taught free by students at college, apart from paid mistress for I. Rooms designed for National, Practising, and I schs in same bldg 1850, 1855.[8] Three schs 1871: Practising Mixed, accn 156, roll 115; Practising (Girls'), accn 262, roll 142; Model (Infants'), accn 152, roll 104. Pupils, who shared chapel with college students, mainly daughters of local professional men or shopkeepers *c.*1900. Closed when college extended premises 1917.

Special Schools

Cook's Ground.[9] Classroom on ground floor of I dept in use for partially blind 1922, when accn 20.[10] Second classroom increased accn to 45 from 1924. Sometimes called Cook's Ground Myope sch., pupils spending half or two-thirds of time there and rest at elem. sch. Closed 1933 on transfer of 34 children to enlarged Kingwood Rd sch., Fulham.

Park Walk Bd. From 1887 had deaf and dumb centre, where spare room was opened 1893 for mentally defective.[11] Accn 1903: 24; roll: 45.[12] More places for mentally defective 1904, when rest of deaf and dumb centre was adapted as laundry centre.[13] Certified under Elem. Educ. (Defective and Epileptic Children) Act, 1899, in 1906,[14] when accn 100; roll: 82; a.a. 71. Accn 1926–7: 100; a.a. 32.[15] Not listed after 1927–8.

Walton Street.[16] Temp. bd sch. opened 1903 for mentally defective and certified under Act of 1899 in 1906.[17] Children transferred to Park Walk 1907.[18] Ground-floor rooms recognized as temp. sch. for physically defective M 1909; first-floor rooms, in exception to general rule, recognized 1914. Accn 1911–12: 60; 1918–19: 112.[19] Overcrowded and unsuitable 1922; improved by LCC, in absence of alternative site, 1923–4. Accn 1925–6: 132; a.a. 85;[20] children stayed until aged 16. Closed 1937 on opening of Gideon Rd sch., Battersea. Later a probation svce centre and juvenile court.[21]

The borough maintained a few pupils with emotional difficulties at Oak Hall school, Heathfield (East Sussex) in 1990–1, and a few with learning difficulties at Parkwood Hall school, Swanley (Kent) then and in 1995.[22]

ADULT AND TECHNICAL EDUCATION

Adults' evening classes at Christ Church school in 1848 had increased its expenses[23] and may not have lasted. Evening classes at Exeter Buildings ragged school in 1845 were for adults, although those at ragged schools from 1849 were apparently for children,[24] but adults may have attended the Oratory school in 1857, when a teacher, with volunteer assistants, was paid 1s. for two hours a night from Monday to Friday.[25] The composition of the 515 evening pupils recorded in 1861 or of the 561 enrolled in 1871 is uncertain.[26] Night schools existed in 1871 at Holy Trinity, Park Chapel (boys' and girls'), St Saviour's, and Exeter Buildings schools and in 1872 at St Luke's in both King Street and Arthur Street. The largest roll in 1871 was 130 for Park Chapel (boys'), where the average attendance was 54.[27]

The school board enrolled 149 males for evening classes at Marlborough Road school for 1882–3; 116 were aged from 14 to 21, 8 were younger, and 25 were

1 *The Times*, 23 Nov. 1908.
2 LMA, SBL 648, p. 301.
3 Below, special schs.
4 Based on TS notes at CL.
5 Below, private schs.
6 Below, adult educ.
7 PRO, C 54/13872, m. 45; C 54/14326, m. 10.
8 LMA, Y/SP/7/6/A–N.
9 Based on PRO, ED 32/520.
10 LCC, *London Statistics*, XXVIII. 196.
11 LMA, SBL 649, pp. 40–1, 43; *Return of Elem. Schs 1899*, 552.
12 LMA, SBL 1527, p. 5.
13 LMA, SBL 648, p. 225.
14 62 & 63 Vic. c. 32; LCC, *Educ. Cttee Mins*, 25 April 1906.
15 LCC, *London Statistics*, XVI. 287; XXXII. 219; XXXIII. 222.
16 Based on PRO, ED 32/521. Log bks 1909–37 in LMA.
17 LCC, *Educ. Cttee Mins*, 9 May 1906.
18 LMA, SBL 648, p. 301.
19 LCC, *London Statistics*, XXII. 354; XXVI. 249.
20 Ibid., XXXI. 204.
21 Stroud, *Smith's Char.* 39; *PO Dir. London* (1968).
22 RBKC, *Schs Statistics Rep.* 1990–1, 180–1.
23 PRO, ED 7/74.
24 *London City Mission Mag.* X. 237; *Ragged Sch. Union Mag.* I. 135; III. 207.
25 PRO, ED 7/74.
26 *Rep. Com. Popular Educ.* (Parl. Papers, 1861 [2794-I], XXI(3)), p. 327; LMA, SBL 1518.
27 LMA, SBL 1518; ibid. 1329. Night schs also existed at St John's, Kensal Green, in Chelsea detached.

older. Females in 1882–3 attended Queen's Gardens school, Brompton, which was superseded by Park Walk school for 1883–4, when there were 51 enrolments there and 87 at Marlborough Road. The most popular advanced classes at Marlborough Road were for the civil service, with an average attendance of 18, followed by those for shorthand, with 10, and for drawing, with 9. Cook's Ground school was opened as Chelsea's third centre for 1885–6 and the Ashburnham as a fourth for 1890–1, by which time enrolments totalled 647. Both sexes could attend Marlborough Road from 1889.[1] The first cookery centre, one of three in the Chelsea division, was opened at Marlborough Road in 1882.[2] Under an Order of 1888 the apprenticing half of Chamberlaine's charity might be spent on the technical education in Westminster of boys from schools in Chelsea. Apprenticing later became more popular, however, and still accounted for payments, made by Chelsea MB, in 1930.[3]

Evening classes continued at the four board schools after the opening of a polytechnic (below). A total of 786 attenders received a grant for 1905–6 and evening institutes offered junior commercial and technical subjects at Park Walk and general subjects at Marlborough in 1918–19, when classes were also held at Chelsea branch post office.[4] There were classes at the Ashburnham, Marlborough, and Park Walk in 1937 and at Kingsley school, for women, and Marlborough and Park Walk in 1957.[5] They survived as part of the ILEA's Chelsea–Westminster adult education institute at Marlborough and Park Walk in 1980 and at Chelsea secondary and Marlborough schools in 1987, before forming part of Kensington and Chelsea College (below).[6]

Onslow College of Science and Technology was leased no. 183 King's Road for 80 years from 1880. Subject to a trust for educating children and adults in the arts or in sciences applicable to industry, it secured a grant from the committee set up to establish a polytechnic. The college nonetheless went bankrupt and its premises were sold under an Order of 1898, leaving *c.*300 students to form the nucleus of the polytechnic's student body.[7]

The South-West London Polytechnic Institute[8] originated in an offer of £50,000 made in 1888 by the City Parochial Foundation under the City of London Parochial Charities Act, 1883, in a Charity Commissioners' Scheme providing for annual grants, and in the establishment in 1891 of a governing body to build and maintain a polytechnic serving Chelsea, south Kensington, and neighbouring parishes. A matching sum was eventually raised locally and the freehold of a site in Manresa Road, of which the leasehold had to be bought, was given by Earl Cadogan. As the sole vestry to offer an annual grant, Chelsea was allowed to appoint a governor from 1894. Classes started in 1895 and a full range was provided from 1896, when over 1,500 students had enrolled. By 1902–3 there were day colleges for men and women aged 16 or more, schools of art and domestic economy, miscellaneous lectures, and evening classes, besides a mixed secondary school[9] and many societies.

Early expansion, like the delayed foundation, was affected by strained relations with the City Parochial Foundation, which felt that a relatively prosperous area should do more to help itself. The polytechnic's recreational side allowed it to remain with the Charity Commissioners after many endowments had been transferred under an Act of 1899, although supplementary grants were soon made both by the LCC's technical education board and by the Board of Education. Criticism *c.*1930 that most students had already attended elementary school, suggesting neglect of the working class, brought a slight reduction in the Charity Commissioners' grant, but it was only under an order of 1949 that control passed to the Ministry of Education. National status followed, with designation as a college of advanced technology from 1957,[10] when the school of art was to become separate.[11] Escaping the threat of removal to Hertfordshire in 1965 but failing to gain full independence,[12] the college was admitted as a school of London University in 1966. The name changed from South-West London Polytechnic Institute in 1895 to South-Western Polytechnic in 1898, Chelsea Polytechnic in 1922, Chelsea College of Science and Technology in 1957, and Chelsea College on the final reception of its charter in 1971.[13] After merging with King's College London in 1985, the premises formed part of that college's Chelsea campus.[14]

The main building of 1891–5 was designed by J.M. Brydon in an ornate Georgian style, of red brick with bold Bath stone dressings. Two- or three-storeyed and over a semi-basement, it had north and south wings and included a swimming bath, gymnasium, and hall for

1 LMA, SBL 1456 (1st to 21st *Ann. Reps of Special Cttee on Evg Classes*).

2 LMA, SBL 691, pp. 353, 366.

3 *Endowed Chars London* (1901), 231; Char. Com. files; Wheeler, *Chelsea Chars.*

4 LCC, *London Statistics*, XVI. 266; XXVI. 274–5.

5 Chelsea MB, *Official Guide* [1937]; ibid. *1957–8*.

6 *Phone Bk 1987*; *Kensington and Chelsea Coll. Ann. Rep. 1994–5*.

7 *Endowed Chars London* (1904), 122; Chelsea Misc. 474; *Brit. Jnl of Educ. Studies*, XVII(3), 263; S.J. Teague and others, *Chelsea College – A Hist.* (1977), 18.

8 Para. based on *Endowed Chars London* (1904), 121–8; *Brit. Jnl of Educ. Studies*, XVII(3), 262–6; Teague, *Chelsea Coll.* 17; *The Times*, 24 July 1891.

9 Above, pub. schs (South-West London Polytechnic).

10 V. Belcher, *The City Parochial Foundation, 1891–1991* (1991), 3, 120–1, 132, 140, 151, 263, 265.

11 Chelsea MB, *Official Guide 1957–8*; below.

12 *The Times*, 6 July 1965; 2 May 1966.

13 BL catalogue; Teague, *Chelsea Coll.* 36, 56, 77, 81; Maclure, *One Hundred Years of London Educ.* 186.

14 *Univ. of London Calendar, 1993–4*, 52. King's Coll. also took over St Mark's (below).

700.[1] First and second extensions were built in 1899–1900 was a west wing and as additions to the south, and a third was finished in 1904 at the west end.[2] Additional buildings were opened in 1932[3] and more, designed by the LCC's architect Hubert Bennett, were provided with the new art school opened in 1965.[4] They included a communal block and the 11-storeyed Lightfoot Hall on the west side of Manresa Road and a chemistry block on the east side. In 1980 the college acquired the former public library in Manresa Road, which it linked to the main building by a bridge, and the site of St Mark's College, where an accommodation block was renamed Ingram Court.[5] The Chelsea campus in 1994 could house 197 residents in Lightfoot Hall and 233 in Ingram Court at no. 552 King's Road.[6]

Chelsea School of Art,[7] which evolved into one of the two main sections of Chelsea Polytechnic and published its own prospectus from the 1930s, closed in the Second World War and afterwards temporarily moved to St Martin's School of Art in Westminster.[8] In 1957 it was decided to separate Chelsea's art school from the newly designated college of advanced technology by uniting it with the Polytechnic Art School, which was part of Regent Street Polytechnic. Separation took place in 1964, despite protests at a threatened reduction in student places to 250 and in teaching posts, since Regent Street relied on full-time staff while Chelsea drew more heavily on instruction from practising artists, including Henry Moore and Graham Sutherland.[9] A site was provided by the LCC on the east side of Manresa Road for buildings which would include an art school, to be built between 1961 and 1963. A four-storeyed building faced with white mosaic and with single-storeyed wings, designed by Bennett and set back from the road,[10] it was officially opened in 1965. The art department of Hammersmith College of Art and Building was taken over in 1975.[11] As part of the London Institute, which was established in 1986 and left the ILEA in 1989, Chelsea College of Art and Design in 1992 contained schools of both fine art and design at degree and post-graduate levels, besides offering part-time A-level study.[12] It temporarily occupied former school premises in Hortensia Road in the 1980s and had sites in Fulham and Hammersmith in 1996, when the Chelsea site had 354 full-time and 130 part-time students.

Kensington and Chelsea College was formed by the new education directorate in 1990, replacing the ILEA's Chelsea–Westminster adult education institute, whose Chelsea premises became its Hortensia (formerly Chelsea secondary school) and Marlborough centres. In 1996 it also had a third, smaller, centre in Park Walk, housing sculpture studios, besides three centres in Kensington. The college was incorporated in 1993 and drew 58 per cent of its income form the Further Education Funding Council and 154 per cent from the royal borough in 1994–5, when four faculties offered both certificated and personal interest courses to nearly 17,000 students, over 6,000 of whom were part-time.[13]

Two training colleges, maintained by the National Society and situated in Chelsea, contributed to local public education both by supplying teachers and by the use of a practising school attended by local children. Stanley Grove, which once had housed Lochée's military academy, was bought in 1840[14] to house St Mark's College, for men. Whitelands Lodge, once the Misses Babington's school,[15] was bought in 1841 to house Whitelands College, for women.

St Mark's College, aided by a parliamentary grant, opened in 1841 and was so named from 1843, when the chapel was consecrated. The principal until 1864 was the Revd Derwent Coleridge (d. 1883), who earned it a high reputation and was visited by Macaulay, Charles Kingsley, and the French statesman François Guizot.[16] In 1870 there were 104 students, admitted when aged 18–21 and mostly former pupil teachers, who paid nothing beyond a £10 entrance fee for two years' residence; in 1890 there were 115.[17] Accommodation was increased after amalgamation with St John's, Battersea, in 1923 and again in the 1960s, when numbers rose from 230 to 700, Except during the Second World War, the College of St Mark and St John remained in Chelsea until it moved to Plymouth in 1973. The 7-acre site, thought to be needed for the West Cross route, was compulsorily purchased in 1975 by the GLC, which after much controversy sold it in 1980 to Chelsea College, itself soon taken over by King's College London (above).[18]

The buildings of St Mark's[19] in 1997 included Stanley House or Grove, dating from the early 1690s and with a sculpture gallery added in the early 19th century by William Hamilton (d. 1859). As Stanley House, approached from King's Road, it had been the principal's residence and at first had also housed the students

1 Pevsner, *London* II. 93; *Brit. Jnl of Educ. Studies*, XVII(3), 263; Plans in Chelsea Misc. 186–7.

2 *Endowed Chars London* (1904), 122.

3 *The Times*, 5 Nov. 1932.

4 Ibid., 2 Oct. 1959; below.

5 Chelsea cuttings: Chelsea Coll.

6 *King's Coll. London Undergraduate Prospectus, 1994.*

7 Para. based on inf. from head of learning resources.

8 Chelsea, *Official Guide, 1957–8*; Teague, *Chelsea Coll.* 47.

9 *The Times*, 30 Dec. 1957; 1, 3 Jan. 1958 et seq.

10 Ibid., 23 Jan., 17 April 1958; 2 Oct. 1959.

11 ILEA, *Educ. Cttee Mins*, 25 June, 29 Oct. 1974.

12 *RBKC 1992* [guide].

13 *Kensington and Chelsea Coll. Ann. Rep. 1994–5*; *Rep. from Inspectorate, April 1996*; *Prospectus 1996–7*; see Fig. 65.

14 Below, private schs.

15 Ibid.

16 M. Roberts, *Coll. of St Mark and St John, 1840–65* (1946), 6–9, 35. For the practising sch., above, pub. schs (St Mark's).

17 *Rep. of Educ. Cttee of Council, 1870–1*, 173; ibid. *1890–1*, 445; F.S. de Carteret-Bisson, *Our Schs and Colleges* (1872), 293.

18 Roberts, *Coll. of St Mark*, 44; *Chelsea Soc. Rep.* (1942–3), 21–2; ibid. (1980), 16; ibid. (1981), 29, 32; inf. from college sec., King's Coll. London.

19 Para. based on Pevsner, *London*, II. 93; *Chelsea Soc. Rep.* (1981), 31–2; Chelsea cuttings: St Mark and St John; see Fig. 53, Stanley Ho.

until the opening of a block at its west end, designed by Edward Blore and built around a quadrangle in a mixed Byzantine and Italianate style. To the north, along Fulham Road, were Blore's stock-brick Romanesque chapel and the practising school to the west,[1] both of 1841–7. His King's Road block had been replaced in 1923 by a larger building, itself later extended farther west. The GLC had used the former students' accommodation as a hostel and it had been only after local resistance and government intervention that it had sold what was known as the Marjon site to Chelsea College, which had not been the highest bidder. King's College London renovated many buildings as a campus but provoked further controversy in 1989 by proposing to sell the whole site for development.[2] A sale was still intended in 1997, when planning consent had been obtained for offices at Stanley House and for commercial use of the Octagon.[3]

Whitelands College[4] opened in 1841 with 12 students, soon increased to 40. On a site leased from the glebe, it received no parliamentary grant and in 1849 was taken over by the National Society. Later benefactors included Angela Burdett-Coutts, who from 1854 encouraged practical domestic training, and John Ruskin, who instituted a May Day festival.[5] Over 100 students, aged 18–25, attended by 1869.[6] The 18th-century Whitelands Lodge, of three storeys and five bays, in 1890–1 made way for a larger block, in alignment with extensions which had been built closer to King's Road. Henry Clutton, who designed additions for the training school in 1850 and 1855,[7] also designed a chapel, with glass by Burne-Jones and a reredos by Morris, which was built in 1881; in 1900 *c.*200 staff and students attended the chapel daily and St Luke's church on Sunday morning.[8] The College left in 1930 for new premises in Putney, where fittings from the chapel and the iron gates to Whitelands Lodge were installed. It was replaced by the flats and shops of Whitelands House, next to no. 33 King's Road.

PRIVATE SCHOOLS

King James's Theological College or Chelsea College, incorporated in 1610 and intended as a polemical centre for the defence of the Church of England, was national rather than parochial. So too was the Museum Minervae, a courtly academy which Sir Francis Kynaston (d. 1642) proposed to move from his London house into the half-built college during the plague of 1636 before the college's resistance forced him to go to Little Chelsea. Although neither institution survived the collapse of royal patronage, the college's site eventually being taken for the Royal Hospital,[9] their presence suggests Chelsea's early attraction for those engaged in private education. In 1650 Henry Bull, late of Chelsea, was said to have taken a house there as a school *c.*1644 but to have been distrained for not paying the rent.[10] Masques at a Chelsea school in 1656 or 1657 were recalled in 1663 by Elizabeth Pepys's paid companion Mary Ashwell, who still assisted with small children there.[11] Possibly it was the good school which had been within convenient distance of a house leased to William Lawrence in 1652 and 1662.[12]

The Restoration brought the fruitless publication of a pamphlet aimed at reviving Chelsea College.[13] The lexicographer Adam Littleton (d. 1694) opened a school in Chelsea where he practised a new way 'of learning the Latin tongue by the English', presumably before becoming rector in 1670.[14] One lessee of a large house in 1675 sued another for not having opened it, as promised, as a school for young gentlemen.[15] The boarding schools of Mrs Priest (at Gorges House, below) and Mr Woodcock (below) were advertised in 1694 and 1695.[16]

Music and dancing were the subjects most notably associated with a new girls' boarding school at Gorges House under Jeffrey Banister and James Hart, whose scholars in 1676 presented the masque *Beauties Triumph*, written by Thomas Duffet and with music by John Banister, a presumed relation of Jeffrey.[17] In 1680 Josias (also recorded as Jonas, Joseph and Josiah) Priest,[18] a dancing master, and his wife took over the school, where in 1682 Sir Edmund Verney's 8-year old daughter learnt japanning and distinguished herself at a ball.[19] Priest persuaded Henry Purcell, with Nahum Tate as librettist, to compose *Dido and Aeneas*, 'the first true English opera', which was performed there *c.*1689 or 1690,[20] on one occasion with an epilogue written by

1 Above, pub. schs (St Mark's); below, private schs (Octagon). Proposed plans by Hen. Clutton are in Chelsea Misc. 243–56; see Fig. 66.

1 *Chelsea Soc. Rep.* (1989), 16; ibid. (1991), 17, 27; ibid. (1993), 16.

3 Inf. from college sec., King's Coll. London; above, Settlement, twentieth cent.

4 Para. based on *Survey of London*, IV. 90; *Chelsea Soc. Rep.* (1994), 50–1; LMA, A/WSO/29, 31. For the practising sch., above, pub. schs (Whitelands).

5 Blunt, *Chelsea*, 18; E. Healey, *Lady Unknown* (1984), 130; A. Burdett-Coutts, *Summary Account of Prizes for Common Things* [1857], 65, 1205; Chelsea Misc. 258–9, 1053.

6 Bryan, *Chelsea*, 176.

7 LMA, Y/SP/7/6/A–N.

8 Lambeth Pal. Lib., Fulham Papers, Creighton 2/12.

9 *Survey of London*, XI. 104; Lysons, *Environs*, II.149–54; *VCH Middx*, I. 242.

10 PRO, C 8/93/15.

11 *Diary of Sam. Pepys*, ed. Latham, IV. 41–2, 45, 72, 82.

12 PRO, C 8/223/8; C 8/329/161.

13 *Survey of London*, XI. 1.

14 *VCH Middx*, I. 245; *DNB*; below, Rel. Hist., par. ch.

15 PRO, C 8/331/60.

16 J. Houghton, *Colln for Improvement of Husbandry and Trade* [weekly newsheet'], V, nos 100, 104. Schs were not listed after vol. VIII, no. 169 (25 Oct. 1695).

17 E.W. White, *Rise of Eng. Opera* (1951), 41–2; *New Grove Dict. of Music and Musicians*, II (1980), 117; *DNB* s.v. Duffet.

18 Vestry orders, 1662–1718, *passim.*

19 Beaver, *Memorials*, 150; F.P. and M. Verney, *Memoirs of Verney Fam.* II (1925), 312, 371.

20 White, *Eng. Opera*, 42–3, 216.

Thomas D'Urfey and spoken by the earl of Clanricarde's daughter Lady Dorothy Burke. D'Urfey's caustic comedy *Love for Money, or the Boarding School* of 1691 probably derived material from Priest's school,[1] which may have continued until 1710–11, the last year for which Priest paid rates.[2]

Another girls' school at Chelsea was that kept by William Dyer, who in 1683 moved to Kensington where he took over an established dancing school.[3] Mr Woodcock who advertised in 1694 was presumably Robert Woodcock (d. 1710), who kept at school at Shrewsbury House from 1694; it was continued by his widow Deborah until she moved the school in 1713 to Manor House, as a tenant of Sir Hans Sloane, where she continued until 1728, and was probably succeeded by Mrs Edwards.[4] Bowack in 1705 cited the great number of boarding schools, especially girls', as an instance of Chelsea's growing prosperity.[5] Among them was Blacklands House, a French boarding school, which may have survived for a century.[6] Priest, Woodcock, Webster, and Lefevre were all named as schoolmasters.[7] John King, rector 1694–1732, likewise noted the leasing of several large houses as schools.[8] The wife of a papist, Thomas Humphreys, kept a small school in 1706.[9]

Sir Robert Walpole's two daughters attended the expensive Blacklands school *c.*1715[10] when it was kept by Mme Judith Nezerauw or Nazareau, who paid rates from 1702;[11] Charles Nezerauw paid in 1728.[12] Mrs Woodcock's school at Manor House was continued by Mrs Edwards from 1729 until 1741.[13] At Turret House, Paradise Row,[14] the parish lecturer William Rothery taught boarders and day boys including the botanist Thomas Martyn (1735–1825), who attended for ten years and remembered him as an excellent master but one who had died in 1759 'lost in drink'. Rothery offered a comprehensive education,[15] as did an advertisement for a school 'at the Five Houses in Chelsea Park', probably of 1729.[16]

Mid 18th-century schools, otherwise unrecorded, included Mr and Mrs Phillips's girls' boarding school in Lawrence Street in 1750,[17] Mr Glover's school for deportment and dancing, praised by the master of Tonbridge school in 1751,[18] and probably a house leased to Mrs Jeuslin for boarders in Millman Row. Mrs Sarah Bellie, 'governess of an eminent boarding school in Cheyne Row', died in 1766,[19] as did a servant of Mrs Aylworth, keeper of a boarding school near Chelsea Common.[20] Mary Robinson, the actress 'Perdita' (b. 1758) recalled a seminary of 5 or 6 girls which she had attended from 1768 under Meribah Lorrington, the most accomplished woman known to her. After its closure in 1770 due to the intoxication of Mrs Lorrington, who died in Chelsea workhouse, Mary briefly went to Battersea, leaving her brother under the Revd Mr Gore at Chelsea, until in 1773 her own mother Mrs Darby opened a short-lived school at Little Chelsea, where Mary taught English to 10 or 12 boarders.[21] Whitelands House or Lodge in King's Road was a girls' school in 1772, when the Revd John Jenkins gave a lecture there on women's education. Formerly under Mrs Grignon in 1791, it continued as a school, where in 1797 the music master complained of his treatment.[22] The author Elizabeth Montagu was pleased at the progress of her favourite niece at a Chelsea boarding school in 1772.[23]

David Williams (d. 1816), founder of the Royal Literary Fund, began his radical career by moving to Lawrence Street, where in 1774 he opened a school which charged high fees but soon had *c.*20 boys. It closed on his wife's death in 1775, despite its success based on the preference for scientific training expressed in his *Treatise on Education* (1774), and has since been seen as a unique attempt to put into practice the educational principles of Rousseau.[24] The Revd Weeden Butler (d. 1823), miscellaneous writer, kept a classical school at no. 4 and then no. 6 Cheyne Walk from the early 1770s, retiring after more than 40 years in 1814.[25] His son the Revd Weeden Butler (d. 1831), author, succeeded him and died at Cheyne Walk, apparently having closed or handed over the school.[26] The historian Robert Bissett

1 *DNB*; D. Gardiner, *Eng. Girlhood at Sch.* (1929), 215–16, 220.

2 Vestry orders, 1662–1718, ff. 168, 179.

3 Gardiner, *Eng. Girlhood*, 216.

4 Houghton, *Colln*, V, nos 100, 104; *Survey of London*, II. 73, 80; Faulkner, *Chelsea*, II. 133.

5 Bowack, *Antiquities*, 13.

6 Faulkner, *Chelsea*, II. 134; Beaver, *Memorials*, 49, 343. Miss Fearnside, a pupil and later mistress of Blacklands sch., died aged 54 in 1811: *Gent. Mag.* LXXXI(1), 684.

7 Bowack, *Antiquities*, 15.

8 Dr King's MS, p. 154.

9 Guildhall MS 9800/2.

10 *Studies in Social Hist., Tribute to G.M. Trevelyan*, ed. J.H. Plumb (1955), 203. Walpole's daus were born in 1703 and 1705.

11 Vestry orders, 1662–1718, f. 103; poor rate bk, 1695–1705, *passim.*

12 Poor rate bk, 1728–42, f. 53; inf. from par. records supplied by J.J. Tobin.

13 *Survey of London*, II. 73–4.

14 Illus. in H. Phillips, *The Thames c.1750* (1951), 216.

15 *Chelsea Soc. Rep.* (1947), 37–8; C. Blunt, *Paradise Row* (1906), 175; Beaver, *Memorials*, 247–8; G.C. Gorham, *Memoirs of John Martyn and Thos Martyn* (1830), 85; *DNB.*

16 Chelsea cuttings: schs.

17 N. Hans, *New Trends in Educ. in 18th Cent.* (1951), 250.

18 Beaver, *Memorials*, 49.

19 Chelsea cuttings: schs.

20 *Chelsea Settlement Examinations 1733–66*, no. 461.

21 Hans, *New Trends*, 197; *Memoirs of Mary Robinson*, ed. J. Fitzgerald Molloy (1895), 21–8; *DNB.*

22 *Survey of London*, IV. 90; Chelsea Misc. 1101.

23 Gardiner, *Eng. Girlhood*, 340; E. Doran, *A Lady of the Last Cent.* (1873), 170; *DNB.*

24 Hans, *New Trends*, 164; *DNB*; W.A.C. Stewart and W.P. McCann, *The Educational Innovators, 1750–1880* (1967), 35–52.

25 *Survey of London*, II. 40, 48; *Gent. Mag.* XCIII(2), 182–3; *DNB.*

26 *Gent. Mag.* CI(2), 186; *DNB.* The yr Weeden's bro. Geo. was headmaster of Harrow sch.

(d. 1805) kept an academy in Sloane Street, perhaps only briefly.[1]

More specialized schools, although still offering some general education, included that of the mathematician Samuel Dunn (d. 1794), who apparently taught astronomy and navigation with commercial subjects from 1758 until 1763 at Ormonde House (below), where there was an observatory.[2] 'The English Grammar School' opened in King's Road in 1766 under the Revd William Williams and Jacob Desmoulins, a writing master, both as a preparatory school and for foreigners, where it was recognized that some boys would not need Latin.[3] The Revd Mr Porter, who had included naval and military subjects at his London school, offered them together with the classics when advertizing for boarders at Tobias Smollett's former house in Lawrence Street *c.*1766.[4]

Greater success attended a military academy at Little Chelsea from *c.*1770 under Louis Lochée and a maritime school at Ormonde House, acquired in 1777, opened in 1779, and later under John Bettesworth.[5] Lochée wrote several works on fortifications and provided examples at his academy, which he publicized as a 'military republic' in 1773. The scene of an attempt at military ballooning in 1784, it won royal patronage and offered a course without holidays, for which cadets paid £50 a year and provided their own uniforms.[6] Although it occupied a large building on the Kensington side of Fulham Road, which was extended in 1776, Lochée also acquired Stanley House and other property on the Chelsea side in 1780–1. The school probably closed in 1788 or 1789, before his execution at Lille in 1791 as a supporter of Belgian independence.[7] The maritime school was founded by subscribers and with the philanthropist Jonas Hanaway (d. 1786) as treasurer, to train 25 boys who would become midshipmen in the Royal Navy; the course was normally 2 years and 13 boys were on the foundation. The drawing master was John Thomas Serres (d. 1825)[8] and the mathematical master from 1777 until 1782 was Bettesworth. The governors in 1785 transferred control to Isaac Dalby and Henry Fox, the mathematical and French masters,[9] and the school closed in 1787, to be reopened as a 'naval and commercial' academy under Bettesworth, who offered a more general education in partnership with Fox. Both partners wrote on education. A fully rigged ship had been 'lately erected' in 1782 in the playground. The school was under William Goddard, another naval author, in 1802 and its 'recent extinction' led James Simpson to seek more pupils for his own naval and commercial academy in Wilderness Row *c.*1805.[10] Presumably only the naval side had ended, as a school known as Ormonde House continued under Edward Francis in 1827 and 1828 and was replaced by Elizabeth Fry's School of Discipline in 1830.[11] Distinguished sailors who had been pupils included the master's son George Bettesworth (1780–1808)[12] and Hans Hastings, later earl of Huntingdon (1779–1828).[13]

A French boarding school in Sloane Street was advertised by Mrs Chassaing in 1797.[14] Nearby at no. 22 Hans Place was a superior school kept from 1796 or 1797 by Dominique de Saint-Quentin, an emigré who had married Miss Pitts and taken over her Abbey House school at Reading. Saint-Quentin was among subscribers to a fund for poor relief in Chelsea in 1795, 1809, and 1814. At Hans Place, which offered Greek and Latin, the chief mistress was apparently Frances Rowden, who as a parlour boarder at Abbey House had met the writer Mary Martha Sherwood (1775–1851). Miss (styled Mrs) Rowden was herself a writer and an enthusiast for the theatre and, as a former governess, was probably responsible for the attendance of Lady Caroline Ponsonby (later Lamb).[15] After moving to Paris with the Saint-Quentins, Miss Rowden kept a small school connected with theirs, her pupils in the early 1820s including the actress Frances (Fanny) Kemble (1809–93), and later married Saint-Quentin. Among their Chelsea pupils were the novelist Mary Russell Mitford (1787–1855) from 1798 until 1802, the poet Letitia Elizabeth Landon (1802–38), who was born at no. 25 Hans Place, and the writers Emma Roberts (1794?–1840) and Anna Maria Hall (1800–81).[16] The education of young ladies by French nuns of the Visitation, presumably at Queen's Elm, was to be continued by a Miss Berthe in 1808.[17]

Another Frenchman, J. Ouiseau, by 1801[18] had opened a preparatory school at Durham House which was continued from 1808 by Hector Clement and from

1 Hans, *New Trends*, 112; Faulkner, *Chelsea*, II. 138; *DNB*.
2 Hans, *New Trends*, 106; Faulkner, *Chelsea*, II. 211; *DNB*.
3 Chelsea cuttings: Eng. Grammar Sch.; *VCH Middx*, I. 247.
4 Chelsea cuttings: Porter's acad.
5 Para. based on Hans, *New Trends*, 101–5; Faulkner, *Chelsea*, I. 59, 139–40; II. 210–11; Beaver, *Memorials*, 240–1, 334–5; Chelsea cuttings: Bettesworth; Chelsea Misc. 1605 (cutting from *Jnl of Soc. for Nautical Research*).
6 Chelsea Misc. 1097 (adverts.).
7 *Survey of London*, XLI. 181–2.
8 *Chelsea Soc. Rep.* (1987), 26–8; *DNB*.
9 Chelsea Misc. 2052 (booklet, *Plan* for sch.).
10 Chelsea Misc. 1102.
11 *Pigot's Comm. Dir.* (1826–7); *Boarding Sch. and London Masters' Dir.* (1828). It later housed the Reformatory Sch. of Discipline: above, pub. schs.
12 *DNB*.
13 Ibid.
14 Chelsea cuttings: Sloane Ho.
15 Hans, *New Trends*, 198–9; F.J. Harvey Darton, *Life and Times of Mrs Sherwood* (1910), 123–6, 128, 131–2, 142, 183; Chelsea cuttings: St Quentin; E. Jenkins, *Lady Caroline Lamb* (1932), 23.
16 Darton, *Mrs Sherwood*, 450; F.A. Kemble, *Record of a Girlhood* (1878), i. 73–4, 78, 84, 99, 109; *Letters of Mary Russell Mitford*, ed. H. Chorley (1872), I. 6; L. Blanchard, *Life and Literary Remains of L.E.L.* (1841), 7; Beaver, *Memorials*, 49, 346–7; *DNB*.
17 Anderson, *St Mary's*, 16; below, Rel. Hist., rom. cathm.
18 Established for 24 years according to Faulkner in 1829 but recorded as sch., total household 17, in Pop. bk (1801), p. 61.

1826 until 1834 or later by Dr Bonaventure Granet; it had 40–50 boys 'nearly related to the nobility' by 1829[1] and perhaps *c.*100 in the late 1830s.[24] Durham House school was long lived, as it was under Henry Hofland in 1842 and 1855 and perhaps was still maintained by the Revd Dr J. Wilson in 1863.[3] The premises were leased to the Girls' Public Day School Trust in 1873.[4] Another well reputed boys' academy was that kept at Cheyne House, Upper Cheyne Row, in 1801 by Thomas Edwards, tenant since 1795. It was a 'finishing school' under the Revd Dr David Felix, brother of Chelsea's assistant curate Peter Felix, in 1828 and probably survived in 1836.[5]

In 1801 there were at least 25 private schools, although not all were described as such, their existence being implied by the size of the household: Dominique de Saint-Quentin's totalled 23 and Weeden Butler's 27. Largest of all was Thomas Pemberton's girls' school at Gough House, Paradise Row, with 72 residents.[6] Sarah Fernside's predominantly female household in Garden Row numbered 62 and Thomas Whiting's predominantly male household at Chelsea Common 58. After Pemberton's, the largest to be called a school was Thomas Edwards's, with 53.[7] Eight of presumed schools were in Sloane Street, all save one being for girls and the largest being Ann Babbington's, with a household of 44.[8]

Short lived schools included one near Oakley Square under the poet and novelist Isabella Kelly (d. 1857)[9] and Albion school in Paradise Row, which presented its second public examination in 1812.[10] Pemberton's school[11] was continued at Gough House by his widow Maria in 1826 and later probably by his daughter; it was a 'finishing establishment, very select'.[12] A boys' school was kept there by the Revd Dr Richard Wilson in 1845 and 1861.[13] Thomas Pilsbury's girls' school at Monmouth House, Lawrence Street, in 1801 was continued by his widow in 1815.[14] Few other schools of 1801, apart from Ormonde House, Durham House, and Cheyne House, survived in 1828. Catherine Elmes, who had kept a school in Smith Street, had been reduced to poverty at the time of her murder in 1833.[15] Thomas Bilby, author of several books on infants' instruction from 1828, taught briefly at an unidentified Chelsea school.[16]

At least 28 gentlemen's academies and 46 ladies', both day and boarding, existed in or on the borders of Chelsea in 1834. Another estimate gave Chelsea at least 95 private schools and Kensington 75. Masters included Richard Bailey of no. 10 Manor Terrace, King's Road,[17] who was presumably the man of that name at no. 9 Adam's Place, King's Road, in 1838, where John Paxton Hall had succeeded him by 1844.[18] Hall's day preparatory school by 1861 was called Oxford House, no. 185 King's Road, and by 1863 was under Charles Henry Lake, a founder of the Teachers' Guild, who taught 120 boys with 10 masters.[19] It was under Alfred Bonifacio, whose Chelsea Commercial School had replaced Ranelagh British school, by 1879 and closed between 1881 and 1885.[20]

The Roman Catholic Manor House boarding school for boys was kept from 1834 or earlier until 1851 by William Frederick Mylius at no. 7 Cheyne Walk, which in 1828 had accommodated boarders under the Revd H. Blunt. Mylius, who had moved from Carshalton (Surrey) was said in 1852 to have conducted it for upwards of 50 years. His sons Charles and John offered a wide curriculum but failed to maintain the school after 1853.[21] Roman Catholic girls could board from 1834 or earlier at no. 1 College Street under Mrs Lloyd and Miss Little. In 1846 Miss Little's seminary, established upwards of 20 years, was at College House, Rayner Place (later St Leonard's Terrace), and from 1847 to 1849 at no. 6 Paradise Row. Roman Catholic support was also sought by the Misses Keats at no. 46 Paradise Row in 1838 and by Mr De Wuits at Cam House, College Street, in 1846–7.[22] Such establishments may not have been able to compete in the 1850s with the London Oratory school[23] or with St Mary's day school for young ladies, recently opened in 1860 in Halsey Terrace (later Cadogan Street) by the Sisters of Mercy in addition to their charity school.[24] St Mary's took boarders by 1865 and proved to be Chelsea's most enduring private school, being described as a girls' boarding school in 1935 but receiving small boys in

1 Faulkner, *Chelsea*, II. 215; *Pigot's London & Provincial Dir.* (1834); Chelsea cuttings: Durham Ho. (letters from librarian).
2 J.B. Ellenor, *Rambling Recollections of Chelsea* [1901], 19.
3 PRO, C 54/12850, m. 26; *PO Dir. London* (1855); *Simpson's Dir.* (1863).
4 Below.
5 Pop. bk (1801), p. 43; *Survey of London*, IV. 72; Faulkner, *Chelsea*, I. 261; ibid. II. 88; *Alum. Cantab. 1752–1900*, 475.
6 Pop. bk (1801), pp. 47, 53, 116.
7 Ibid., pp. 43, 66, 77.
8 Ibid., pp. 79–81, 85–7.
9 Bryan, *Chelsea*, 166; *DNB*, Missing Persons.
10 Chelsea cuttings: Albion sch.
11 Established by Pemberton's widow according to Blunt, *Paradise Row*, 167, and *Survey of London*, II. 9, but recorded as sch. in Pop. bk (1801), p. 61.
12 *Pigot's Comm. Dir.* (1826–7); Ellenor, *Rambling Recollections*, 17; *Boarding Sch. and London Masters' Dir.* (1828).
13 *PO Dir. London* (1845); *Crockford's Scholastic Dir.* (1861).
14 Pop. bk (1801), p. 39; Beaver, *Memorials*, 92.
15 *The Times*, 6, 8 May 1833.
16 [B.I. Buchanan,] *Buchanan Family Rec.* (1923), 9; T. Bilby, *Course of Lessons for Infant Instruction* (3rd edn 1836); *Infant Teacher's Assistant* (4th edn 1835).
17 *Pigot's London & Provincial Dir.* (1834); *VCH Middx*, I. 255.
18 *Pigot's London Dir.* (1838); *PO Dir. London* (1844).
19 *Crockford's Scholastic Dir.* (1861); *PO Dir. London* (1863); *VCH Middx*, I. 279.
20 *Crockford's Scholastic Dir.* (1861); *Kelly's Dir. Chelsea* (1881, 1885).
21 *Laity's Dir.* (1835); *Cath. Dir.* (1838–53); *Boarding Sch. and London Masters' Dir.* (1828); *Pigot's London & Provincial Dir.* (1834); *PO Dir. London* (1844 s.v. court, 1850 s.v. trades).
22 *Cath. Dir.* (1838–49).
23 Above, pub. schs.
24 *Cath. Dir.* (1860); above, pub. schs.

1938. It had 148 mixed pupils, aged 5–11, on the eve of its closure in 1954.[1]

Other comparatively long lived mid 19th-century schools included that of William Webbe, probably at no. 32 Paradise Row by 1834 and at no. 9 Lower Sloane Street by 1838, at no. 18 Sloane Terrace in 1848, and at no. 17 in 1850. Webbe was styled principal of Sloane Terrace Academy in 1872 and remained at no. 17, as a 'private teacher', in 1881.[2] Frances and Elizabeth Faulkner, daughters of the local historian, taught 11 young boys at their father's house, no. 27 Smith Street, in 1851, when Mary Ann Faulkner taught girls at no. 24, Waldegrave House.[3] The first advertised their preparatory school as Cadogan House and had moved it to no. 1 Markham Square by 1863 but Waldegrave House remained a ladies' school, under Mrs Frances Clarke, in the 1870s.[4] Catharine or Katharine Lodge, Trafalgar Square, was so named from 1850 when Mrs Julia Field and Miss Lowman renamed Bath lodge and opened a girls' school there, which passed to Miss Catherine Hall and closed probably in 1895.[5]

Of 29 private schools advertised in 1861, 11 were solely for boys. Only four masters were associated with the College of Preceptors: J.P. Hall and Dr Richard Wilson, who were fellows, Bonifacio, and J. D'Arnaud in Whitehead's Grove. Among the ladies, only Miss A. Ward in Markham Square was an associate of the college.[6] Many more schools existed, since in 1871 13 were classed as private and 30 as 'adventure'. Most, however, with attendances of under 30, can have occupied no more than one room and did not survive the opening of board schools.[7] St Leonard's Terrace provided instances of short lived enterprises, with schools kept by Mrs Mary Little at no. 18 (then Rayner Place) in 1845, by Mrs Caroline Smart at no. 9 in 1850 and at no. 13, with Robert Smart and apparently as two schools, in 1855, by Mrs Burnett next door until 1869, and by Henry and Clara Durant at no. 23 in 1872, where they were followed by Mrs Ann Harrison and in 1879 by Misses Mary and Jane Moore.[8]

Chelsea Grammar School, for 35 boys including boarders, was opened by the Revd J.E. Wilson in 1870 and survived in 1879. Other apparently new and short lived preparatory schools in 1872 were F.J. Weightman's Hollywood and the Revd W. Harris's school at no. 10 Walton Place, Hans Place.[9] The Girls' Public Day School Trust in 1873 was leased Durham House for its first school, from which it moved in 1879 to Cromwell Road, Kensington.[10] The Daughters of the Cross at St Wilfred's convent, besides briefly conducting an orphanage school, from 1870 taught young lady boarders.[11] The Daughters later also taught at the Oratory middle school.[12] Advertising a commercial class in 1920 and a high school in 1935, they apparently still took boarders in 1938 but after the Second World War may have provided merely a hostel.[13] Chelsea High School for girls, under Miss Hitchcock in 1884 and under Miss Hart at no. 10 Durham Place in 1891, had closed by 1894.[14]

In 1902 only two preparatory schools were listed, both presumably for boys, at no. 103A Fulham Road and at no. 37 Sloane Street.[15] In 1924 there was a girls' school at no. 131 Sloane Street and a boys' at no. 134.[16] The first survived under Miss D.M. Birtwhistle in 1938; the second had opened by 1918 under Charles Herbert Gibbs, a 'pioneer of pre-preparatory schools', and was still at no. 134, under C.H. Taylor and W.W.M. Holding, in 1938.[17]

Several schools flourished from the 1950s, most of them in the area of Sloane Street. Hill House, opened by Lt-Col. H.S. Townsend in Switzerland in 1948 and at no. 17 Hans Place in 1951, was the first school attended by Prince Charles (later Prince of Wales), in 1957. Described as pre-preparatory in 1958 and as Hill House International Junior School by 1970, it had five premises around Knightsbridge and over 1,000 boys and girls aged 4 to 13 in 1999, when it was managed by the founder.[18] Garden House was opened by Margery de Brissac-Bernard, originally a ballet teacher,[19] at no. 53 Sloane Gardens in 1951. It had 347 pupils in 1997, when the school office was at no. 53 and girls aged 3–11 were at nos. 28, 49, and 51 Sloane Gardens and boys aged 5–8 were in new premises at nos 26 and 28 Pont Street.[20] Sussex House was opened in 1952 by V.W. Davies of Davies's (Tutors) at no. 68 Cadogan Square, where he had taken tutorial pupils since 1950. Named after an earlier tutorial establishment in Holland Park

1 *Cath. Dir.* (1861 and later edns); *Dir. of Cath. Schs. in Gt Britain* (1935); *Cath. Schs in Eng. and Wales* (Cath. Educ. Council, 1954); *St Thos More Sch. Prospectus* (1996).

2 *Pigot's London & Provincial Dir.* (1834); *Pigot's London Dir.* (1838); *PO Dir. London* (1844 and later edns).

3 PRO, H 107/1472/2/1/13, ff. 323 sqq.

4 Chelsea cuttings: Cadogan Ho.; *PO Dir. London* (1857 and later edns).

5 P.R.O., H 107/1473/2/2/5, ff. 99 seqq.; *Survey of London*, IV. 77; Blunt, *Chelsea*, 153; Chelsea cuttings: Katharine Lodge; *Kelly's Dir. Chelsea* (1894, 1895); Chelsea Misc. 313 (1891 sch. mag. *Katharine Wheel*).

6 *Crockford's Scholastic Dir.* (1861).

7 LMA, SBL 1518.

8 *Chelsea Soc. Rep.* (1958), 32.

9 F.S. de Carteret-Bisson, *Our Schs and Colleges* (1872), 289, 291, 517; ibid. I [boys] (1879), 745.

10 L. Magnus, *Jubilee Bk of G.P.D.S. 1873–1923* (1923), 26, 54–6.

11 Above, pub. schs (St Anne's); *Cath. Dir.* (1870).

12 *Cath. Dir.* (1890); above, pub. schs (London Oratory).

13 *Cath. Dir.* (1900, 1920, 1938, 1976); *Dir. of Cath. Schs in Gt Britain* (1935); Chelsea cuttings: St Wilfred's.

14 Bisson, *Schs and Colleges*, II [girls] (1884), 660; *Kelly's Dir. Chelsea* (1885–6, 1891, 1894).

15 *PO Dir. London* (1902).

16 Truman & Knightley, *Schs* (1924).

17 *PO Dir. London* (1918, 1938); Chelsea cuttings: Gibbs.

18 R.G. Clark, *Chelsea Today* (1991), 112; Chelsea cuttings: schs; *PO Dir. London* (1960 and later edns); *The Oldie*, Feb. 1996; *Daily Telegraph*, 28 April 1999.

19 *The Times*, 14 June 1994.

20 Prospectus and inf. from sch. sec.

(Kensington) and a sister of Lyndhurst House (Hampstead), Sussex House was managed by Davies's Educational Services Ltd from 1974 and by an independent trust from 1994. In 1958 it bought premises which it had shared at no. 67 Cadogan Street, formerly a Sunday school of Westminster's Belgrave Presbyterian chapel, and which it converted in 1977 into the Nicholl hall. Sussex House had 175 boys aged 8–13 in 1997.[1] Bridge House, no. 2 Cadogan Gardens, existed in 1958 but perhaps only briefly.[2] A house in the Vale was used as a day school without planning permission from 1958 and had 107 pupils in 1963, when the LCC ordered its closure.[3] Cameron House, founded in 1980 as a co-educational preparatory school called Cameron Learning Tree, moved in 1986 from St Luke's church to no. 4 The Vale, where it had 100 pupils aged 4–11 in 1997.[4]

The Octagon school took its name from the former St Mark's Practising School, which was equipped as a library when the neighbouring science block was opened as a co-educational nursery and preparatory school in 1994. Although fashionable and soon with 210 pupils, it only had a short lease which had been granted to an American businessman, Ed Loyd, by King's College. Friction over plans for expansion and arrears of rent led to the school's abrupt closure in 1996.[5]

Jamahariya school opened in 1982 in the former Kingsley (originally Cook's Ground) school in Glebe Place which had been sold by the ILEA to the Libyan People's Bureau in 1979. The sale caused alarm, bringing assurances from the United Kingdom and Libyan governments that the school was solely to provide an Islamic education. It was expensively refurbished for *c.*300 children, mainly of diplomats and aged 5–17, and was still open in 1995.[6]

Private institutions for older pupils[7] included the Automobile Engineering Training College, found in 1924 to train for the car industry and including aeronautics from 1931. Its war-damaged premises at no. 102 Sydney Street were largely rebuilt in 1950, when the college had 350 students and was about to offer agricultural engineering. It had ceased to be independent by 1989.[8] The London Academy, residential and 'run on university lines', offered a general education and a course for continental students at no. 15 Cadogan Gardens in 1958[9] and until 1975 or later. The Heatherley School of Fine Art, originating in a secession from the government's School of Design in 1845, moved from Warwick Square, Westminster, in 1978. It used part of the former college of St Mark and St John until the ILEA helped to install it in 1979 in the former Ashburnham school, whose east wing was bought by the Heatherley charity in 1988. The school had 50 full-time and 120 part-time students in 1997, besides 160 at its 'open studio' which retained the traditional atelier system.[10]

The many nursery schools since 1945 have included the Violet Melchett Training College at no. 43 Chelsea Manor Street, which offered a 20 months' course at its own residential and day nursery in 1958.[11]

CHARITIES FOR THE POOR

For a small and relatively rural parish Chelsea received many charitable donations at an early period, 11 charities being endowed between 1590 and 1660 and a further four before 1700, compared with nine in the 18th century. The greatest flow of new endowed charities followed urbanization, with 30 new gifts in the 19th century and five more in the 20th.[12]

Nevertheless, as in many other parishes, gifts for the poor were not well managed. Accounts were ill kept, gifts sometimes did not reach the intended trustees, and the trustees themselves failed to distribute as stipulated or at all. In the 18th and early 19th centuries most charities were distributed by the churchwardens, sometimes with the rector or overseers; confusion over the charities contrasted with the parish's usually conscientious management of public poor relief.[13] The loss to Chelsea was perhaps more severe than elsewhere. By 1862 all but one charity founded before 1660, and six others founded before 1800, had been lost. Besides the national returns of 1786–8[14] and the early 19th-century investigations of the charity commissioners, who included Chelsea in their 1825 report, the commissioners' inspector Walter Skirrow made a special report on Chelsea's charities in 1858, having in 1857 reported specifically on Lady Dacre's charity. Local efforts had been made to keep track of charities. The vestry minute book recorded donations from 1707. The vestry also kept a book entitled 'Account of Public Charities', beginning in 1739

1 *VCH Middx*, I. 288; ibid. IX. 166; *The Cadogan* [Sussex Ho. sch. mag.], no. 6 (1992), pp. 7–25; inf. from headmaster.

2 Chelsea cuttings: schs.

3 *The Times*, 19 Feb. 1963.

4 Prospectus and inf. from headmistress.

5 *Sun. Telegraph*, 27 Oct. 1995; *Daily Telegraph Mag.* 3 Nov. 1996.

6 *Chelsea Soc. Rep.* (1980), 52–4; Chelsea cuttings: Kingsley sch.; *Phone Bk* (1995).

7 Based on *PO Dir. London* (1927 and later edns).

8 *The Times*, 1 April 1950; *The Times Educ. Suppl.* 17 Feb. 1989.

9 Chelsea MB, *Official Guide* (1958).

10 Prospectus and inf. from principal.

11 Chelsea MB, *Official Guide* (1958).

12 Section based on Char. Com. files; *14th Rep. Com. Char.* (Parl. Papers, 1826 (382), XII), pp. 2194–8; *Chelsea Chars 1862*; *Endowed Chars London* (1901).

13 Above, Loc. Govt, poor relief to 1837.

14 *Abstract of Ret. of Char. Donations for Poor, 1786–8*, (Parl. Papers, 1816 (511), XVI).

and continued by the rector's churchwarden, John Fielder (d. 1859).[1] The report of the metropolitan vestry for the year ended 25 March 1859, based on Fielder's records, listed 20 charities.[2]

In 1860, after the late rector had failed to put matters to rights, the vestry was urged to issue an annual report on all charity affairs, it being not a question of dishonesty but of disorder. The vestry accordingly set up a committee to inquire into the parochial charities, their property, and the application of their proceeds.[3] Its report in 1862 showed that the total principal was £32,000 with an income of £448 17s. 7d. excluding Lady Dacre's charity. It contained a short account of the charities, intended to replace the list made in 1858–9. A recommendation that all the surviving funds be vested in the Official Trustee for Charity Funds was carried out within a few years; the capital of most later gifts was similarly transferred. Finding that many practices did not accord with the donor's instructions, the report declared that trustees should meet only in public and on dates notified in advance. Despite those precautions, several more charitable funds had disappeared by 2000.

As Chelsea developed, new ecclesiastical parishes were established both in Chelsea detached (Kensal Green) and in Upper Chelsea.[4] In 1864 the incumbent of Holy Trinity applied to the Charity Commissioners for an apportionment of the income between the (old) parish of St Luke and Upper Chelsea, which was poorer and whose population entitled it to a third. The trustees resisted the proposal as all parts of the parish were equally entitled. An informal arrangement in 1866 recognized that four twelfths should go to Upper Chelsea and one twelfth to Christ Church on the basis of population. In 1896 all distributions were found to have been made for the benefit of all the inhabitants of Chelsea, including Kensal Green, unless the donor otherwise stipulated.

Charities whose income was to be distributed as coal or bread came to be administered through a Bread and Coal fund. In 1936 a Charity Commission Scheme embraced 28 charities as the Non-Ecclesiastical charities of Chelsea. Six other charities became the Ecclesiastical charities, four of them having been divided from a Non-Ecclesiastical gift.[5] All the capital was then held in low-interest stock.

In 1996 the Chelsea Non-Ecclesiastical charities held securities with a value of £51,286 giving 4.5 per cent interest. There were 7 pensioners, the eldest being 101 years old, each receiving £160 a year besides a £25 Christmas bonus, and donations totalled £700.

ALMSHOUSE CHARITY

Anne, Lady Dacre, by will dated 1594 made a gift to establish Emanuel Hospital, almshouses near Tothill Fields (Westm.) for 20 poor people, 3 of them from Chelsea.[6] Unless the inhabitants of Chelsea maintained the tomb of Lord and Lady Dacre[7] the right to nominate two people would be given to Westminster. In 1892 the trustees of Emanuel Hospital sold the building, a Scheme to use the proceeds was approved in 1894, whereby 20 men and 20 women as 'Lady Dacre's pensioners' were each to receive under certain conditions £25 a year; four were to be elected from Chelsea, subject to the vestry keeping in repair the chapel in the Old Church containing the Dacres' tomb.[8] The first four pensioners were approved by the vestry in 1894. By 1898 the tomb had been renovated.[9] By 1930 there was provision for only 12 pensioners, 6 men and 6 women, each receiving £25 a year, and one minor pension for a man of £12 a year, subject to maintaining the tomb. The incumbent of the Old Church *c.*1925 raised a fund of £300 which was settled in trust to maintain the Dacre tomb, thus preserving the benefits of the charity for Chelsea.[10]

The Scheme of 1894 was varied in 1911, 1953, 1959, 1969, 1977, and 1992. The original areas from which pensioners were to be drawn were the parishes of St Luke, Chelsea, Hayes (Middx), and of the city and liberties of Westminster. The Scheme of 1992 expanded those areas to cover the whole area of the relevant local authority. Thereafter the number of applicants increased and grants were made for durable goods and respite care: in 1995–6 the total number of pensioners for all three areas was 127. In 1994–5 Lady Dacre's pensioners received £33,289 and there were grants to pensioners, including for convalescence and holidays, of £14,894. By a deed of 1926 the fund for the Dacre tomb became part of the Ecclesiastical charities of Chelsea, confirmed by the Scheme of 1936.[11]

DISTRIBUTIVE CHARITIES INCLUDED IN BREAD AND COAL FUND

The following charities were gathered together as the Bread and Coal Fund (below). Unless otherwise stated, charities named in the Scheme of 1936 thereafter formed part of the Non-Ecclesiastical charities.

Edward Cheyne, by will proved 1663, bequeathed to overseers of Chelsea rent charge of 6s. a year for distribution of bread, from land identified in 1862 as Cox's Close at west end of Paradise Row, the site of George Place. Sir Hans Sloane apparently paid 14 years' arrears

1 'Accts of Pub. Chars' (in CL).
2 *Vestry rep. 1858–9*, 69–75.
3 *Vestry rep. 1860–1*, 20–1.
4 Below, Rel. Hist., ch. extension.
5 Ibid., par. ch.
6 Almshos reserved for treatment under Westm.
7 Below, Rel. Hist., par. ch.
8 *Vestry rep. 1892–3*, 27, 92–3.
9 Ibid., *1897–8*, 22.
10 J.H.W. Wheeler, *The Chelsea Chars* (based on vestry rep. 1890 and revised to Dec. 1930).
11 Below, Rel. Hist., par. ch.

in 1752, and Earl Cadogan in 1825 paid 82 years' arrears from 1753.[1] By 1862 the capital together with the Gibbs bequest of £630 had been invested in £656 13s. 9d. stock, the annual income of 6s. being spent on bread. In 1862 the churchwardens bought 35½ loaves for £1 2s. (6s. from Cheyne bequest and 16s. interest on lump sum paid by Earl Cadogan). By Order of 1889 the rent charge was redeemed for £12 by Earl Cadogan. Income was carried to Bread and Coal fund by 1901, and charity was included in Scheme of 1936 (item 1), represented by £26 13s. 9d. stock.

James Leverett by will proved 1663 bequeathed a yearly rent of £14 from the Magpie in Great Chelsea to be distributed by his widow and thereafter by the churchwardens and overseers: £10 was to be distributed among widows of the parish, each to receive 2s. 6d., and £4 was to provide dinner at the Magpie for the churchwardens, overseers, constables, parish clerk, and occupier of the Magpie. In 1858 charity was being applied as directed, though recipients described as housekeepers rather than widows in 1862. In 1861 the house was called the Magpie and Stump, no. 34 Cheyne Walk.[2] It was burned down in 1886 and rebuilt with a house of the same name designed by and for C.R. Ashbee; in 1901 rent charge was paid regularly by Elizabeth Ashbee and applied in 2s. 6d. tickets for poor residents. The balance of £4 was applied towards the dinner, in 1902 still held at the town hall shortly before Easter, the additional expense being met by the churchwardens.[3] Charity was included in Scheme of 1936 (item 2), represented by £560 stock.

Richard Gilford by will proved 1680 bequeathed yearly rent of £10 charged on property in London to his brother and thereafter to Chelsea for 16 poor people, 8 of them women, each to receive 10s. on 5 December.[4] In 1781 there had been difficulties in collecting from the owner, Sir John Mordaunt, Bt, but solicitors secured regular payments from 1785. In practice a balanced distribution was not maintained. In 1739 there were 15 women and one man and for many years women, principally widows, predominated. In 1808 there were 6 men and 6 women. In 1858 there were 12 payments, 6 to women, 3 to men, 3 unidentified. In 1862 it was recommended that distribution should be annual in December, half to men and half to women. Income still derived from rent charge in 1862, but by 1936, when charity was included in Scheme (item 3), it had been redeemed for stock then worth £275 13s. 4d.

Judith Cale by will proved 1717 left £100 to purchase land, the income to be distributed among 6 poor widows in Chelsea. Following action by the rector and vestry against her executors and a Chancery order of 1737,[5] the £100 plus £80 interest was paid and charity was applied from 1739, when £5 distributed. In 1825 ordered that £20 be added to the capital of £180 and whole was invested in £230 stock. Interest was applied, usually annually, between 1739 and 1824, and by 1862 income of £6 18s. was distributed as directed; stock then held as part of Bread and Coal fund.[6] By 1901 income £6 6s. 4d., still applied as directed, and in 1930 was £5 15s. Charity was included in Scheme of 1936 (item 4), being represented by £230 stock.

John Franklin by will proved 1790 gave £10 to both boys' and girls' charity schools, and £100 stock from which interest was to be spent by churchwardens and overseers on bread for poor every December and January. In 1822 £3 was carried to Bread and Coal fund (below), and in 1858 dividends were distributed thus. In 1861 one churchwarden spent £1 on 30 loaves and 10s. on coal, while the other spent £1 10s. on coal. In 1901 annual income was £2 15s., and £2 10s. in 1930. Charity included in Scheme of 1936 (item 6), represented by £100 stock.

Samuel Hunton by will proved 1798 gave £100 to be invested in government stock, the interest to provide bread and coal in week before Christmas for neediest widows with large families. By 1823 £167 stock purchased, yielding £5 5s. 6d. a year, transferred in 1833 to Bread and Coal fund (below). Income £4 16s. 8d. in 1901. Hunton's preference for widows with large families not specifically observed. Income £4 8s. in 1930, and charity included in Scheme of 1936 (item 7), represented by £176 stock.

Martha Burnsall by will proved 1805 gave leasehold property in South Street (St George Hanover Square) to be sold, the proceeds to be invested in government stock for relief of decayed householders who had not been public beggars or chargeable on the parish. Net proceeds of sale, £250, with bequest of additional £50 invested to produce £15 a year. By 1862 the capital amounted to £315 stock. In 1858 income was distributed in sums of 10s. 'amongst the second class of poor designated by the trust', but in 1861 part was distributed to women in cash, part in bread, and part withheld. In 1901 income was £8 13s., distributed in cash to nine poor male householders. Charity included in Scheme of 1936 (item 8), represented by £315 stock.

Henry Hailstone by will proved 1812 gave 50s. a year for 21 years to be distributed to poor in bread on Christmas day. Payments were noted from 1822, into Bread and Coal fund, and continued until the 21 years had expired in 1833.

John Gregory by will proved 1813 gave £21 to St Luke's, the interest to provide bread for the poor yearly. The churchwardens added £2 14s. 6d. from unknown source and purchased stock, which in 1811 produced 15s. 8d. a year. In 1861 28 loaves were distributed costing 18s. 9d., the churchwardens apparently having

1 Vestry mins, 1833–9, p. 84.
2 Above, social (inns).
3 Menu cards of 1890s: Chelsea Misc. 342–6.
4 PRO, PROB 11/364, f. 318.
5 CL, deed 18628.
6 Below, bread and coal fund.

made up the difference. In 1896 annual dividend of 14s. 4d. was carried to Bread and Coal fund. Gift was included in Scheme of 1936 (item 10), represented by £26 5s. stock.

Mary Norman by will proved 1827 left £100, the income to purchase coal yearly for poor residents. The legacy was invested in stock providing £3 7s. 2d. a year, added to the Bread and Coal fund. No separate returns apparently made by overseers. Income £3 1s. 8d. in 1896 and £2 16s. in 1930. Gift included in Scheme of 1936 (item 13), represented by £112 4s. stock.

The Bread and Coal Fund

In 1822 the income from John Franklin's charity had been carried to a general Bread and Coal fund, which then received £13 16s. 6d. a year, made up of £3 from Franklin, who had directed only purchase of bread, 18s. from Judith Cale, £1 from Christopher Plucknett, £5 5s. 6d. from Samuel Hunton, £2 10s. from Henry Hailstone, and £1 3s. from John Gregory. In 1833 the rector J.W. Lockwood, the minister of the old church, the parish treasurer, and a churchwarden were entrusted with stock worth £718 4s., representing the charities of Mary Norman, Thomas Stewart, Franklin, Cale, and Hunton; only 18s. from Cale's charity went into the fund. The stock for Stewart's charity, although intended for a sermon,[1] was held with that of the others, for all of which separate accounts were kept in 1862. Later only George Wood's charity was administered separately, but no bread and coal fund was referred to as such. The fund for 1895–6 apparently consisted of 12 charities together yielding £36 17s. 9d., of which £19 14s. 7d. was spent on bread and £17 3s. on coal. Distribution was by tickets issued about a week before Christmas. The 12 charities, augmented by a further 13, formed the subject of the Scheme of 1936, by which time the relationship to the Bread and Coal fund had been lost.

OTHER DISTRIBUTIVE CHARITIES[2]

Margery Whitworth by will proved 1767 left £100 stock, the income to be spent on poor people attending the Scottish church in Swallow Street (Westm.). Congregation moved to St Columba's church in Pont Street, Chelsea, *c.*1884 and capital transferred to Official Trustee 1885, with additional £42 17s. 3d. from accumulated dividends in 1886. Scheme of 1885 authorized minister and elders of St Columba's to apply income in gifts of money or in kind to poor. Income in 1896 was £3 18s. 4d., paid quarterly in grants of £1 10s. or less.

Catherine Abbott by will proved 1810 gave income from £200 to be distributed by churchwardens equally among 6 decayed women of the parish, preferably former householders. Capital was invested in stock producing £8 3s. 3d. a year, first distributed in 1812. Three years' income was distributed to 17 women and one man in 1832–3; thereafter charity apparently applied as directed. In 1896 the income was £7 9s. 8d. and, with 4d. added by rector's churchwarden, provided six gifts of £1 5s. to women, mainly elderly. By 1930 annual income had dropped to £6 16s. Gift was included in Scheme of 1936 (item 9), represented by £272 4s. 3d. stock.

John Long by will proved 1822 gave £100, the income to provide bread for poor 'not wholly supported' by St Luke's parish. Gift invested in stock and yielded £3 11s. 4d. a year, first clearly recorded in 1829–30. Income £3 5s. 4d. in 1896 and £2 19s. 4d. in 1930. Gift included in Scheme of 1936 (item 11), represented by £118 17s. 5d. stock.

Elizabeth Dennis Denyer, Chelsea's most substantial benefactor, by will proved 1824 gave directions concerning £7,000 in 3 per cent consols. Christ's Hospital having declined a legacy on the trusts, a Chancery decree of 1829 vested the fund in the rector and three other trustees. In 1832 they presented a memorial to the Treasury stating that the testatrix and her parents had lived and were buried in St Luke's, a parish with many poor and many of the peculiar objects of her bounty, namely aged and deserving spinsters; they sought directions to enable them to pay permanent annuities of £10. A royal warrant of 1833 settled the fund subject to annuities specified in the will, the capital thereafter to be added to the trust: only one annuitant survived in 1862 for whom £1,000 was set aside, and this was added to the stock held for the charity in 1878 after his death.[3] In 1862 17 elderly spinsters benefited annually, in amounts from £7 to £11 2s. 7d. Income of £210 4s. a year was distributed in 1896 to 15 women in sums of £7 to £17 10s. Normally vacancies among recipients of the larger pensions were filled by those receiving the smaller amount; pensioners were rarely chosen from outside Chelsea. Any balance of income was normally applied in doles or bread. Part of the original gift should have fallen to the Crown and was known as the King's Bounty, and from that fund were paid 4 pensions of £12 10s. In 1930 annual income remained the same, and gift was included in Scheme of 1936 (item 12), represented by £7,023 11s. 11d. stock.

Elizabeth Smith[4] by will proved 1828 left £800 consols, reduced by codicil to £500 stock. Income, after payments for sermon[5] and to charity schools,[6] was to provide bread for poor. Net legacy bought £450 stock yielding £13 10s. a year. Income £12 7s. 4d. in 1896, of which £7 2s. 4d. went for bread. Separate Educational foundation established by Order of 1906. Under Scheme of 1936 Elizabeth Smith's Educational and Eleemosynary charity (item 14) was divided, £240 out of its £366 stock becoming part of Non-Ecclesiastical charities.

Anne Sammon by will proved 1832 left £210 stock, to

1 Below, Rel. Hist., par. ch. (ch. life).

2 Unless otherwise stated, chars named in the Scheme of 1936 thereafter formed part of the Non-Ecclesiastical chars.

3 *Vestry rep. 1878–9*, 24.

4 Memorial on S wall of St Luke's.

5 Below, Rel. Hist., par. ch.

6 Above, educ. (pub. schs, St Luke's par.).

provide a yearly distribution in bread and coal to the poor of the parish 'not receiving alms'. The interest was progressively reduced from 4 per cent to 3 per cent by 1861, when £6 6s. was spent on bread and coal. Income £5 15s. in 1895 and £5 5s. in 1930. Gift included in Scheme of 1936 (item 15), represented by £210 stock.

William Gibbs by will proved 1833 left £700 stock to support 18 poor men and 18 poor women aged over 60 who had not been maintained in the workhouse. After legacy duty, 9s. was given to each of 17 men and 19 women in 1835 and the £2 14s. balance of the dividend was distributed in 1836. In 1862 18 men and 18 women each received 10s. 6d. In 1896 the dividend of £17 6s. 4d., with 13s. 4d. added by one of the churchwardens, was paid as 10s. each to 18 old men and 18 widows. Usually fresh recipients chosen each year. Income £15 15s. in 1930. Gift included in Scheme of 1936 (item 16), represented by £630 stock.

Charles Hatchett by will proved 1847 left £100, the income to be paid half yearly to buy bread in January for deserving poor parishioners of St Luke's. Gift was invested in stock which yielded £3 7s. 4d. a year, but £3 1s. 8d. in 1896, and £2 16s. in 1930. Included in Scheme of 1936 (item 17), represented by £112 7s. 2s. stock.

Luke Thomas Flood by deed poll of 1849 gave £1,500 to the parochial charity schools and £1,000 to trustees appointed under Act of 1819 for building a new church. The first sum was to provide for a catechism on 13 January, a concert, and apprenticing, any residue to provide bread for poor attending the catechism examination and then to apprentice and clothe any children.[1] The second was to provide payments to one man and one woman, not being husband and wife, aged at least 60 and once householders of the parish, who attended the examination. The legacies were reinvested in stock under Order of 1888 and out of income of £76 14s. 4d., £30 19s. 9d. went to the trust for deserving persons. In 1986 the church trustees divided £30 between a man and women chosen from 8 applicants. A further charity was established in 1856 by the church trustees' purchase of £400 to provide two dinners, one for themselves and subscribers to the schools and one, more modest, for officials involved in the examination. The meals were held at Bailey's Hotel, South Kensington, in 1896, when among other items £30 was spent on a man and a woman, £39 9s. on payments specified by Flood, and £10 14s. 8d. on bread. The income of £92 3s. 4d. was unchanged in 1930. Scheme of 1936 divided the charity of 1856 (item 19), when £8 6s. 8d. stock became the Ecclesiastical charity of Thomas Flood.[2] The rest, £44 15s. stock, with the charity of 1849 (item 18) represented by £1,299 4s. 2d. stock, became part of Non-Ecclesiastical charities.

Washington Cornelius Ashfield, otherwise Winter, by will proved 1850 left £1,000 stock, the income to be distributed on St Thomas's day equally among 30 poor widows of St Luke's parish who had been householders there for at least ten years. Annual dividend was £30, and in 1861 the rector and the two churchwardens each nominated 10 beneficiaries. In 1896 income was £27 10s., with 27 widows receiving £1 each and one 10s., all housekeepers as stipulated by the donor, and all but one over 60. In 1930 income was £25. The gift was included in Scheme of 1936 (item 20), represented by £1,000 stock.

Sophia Forbes by will proved 1857 left £200 to maintain her vault in the parish church, any surplus to be distributed by rector at his sole discretion among poor of parish not receiving parochial relief. Legacy invested in stock, held by trustees who by Order of 1862 were thereafter to pay the income, then £6 4s. 4d., to rector. Income £5 14s. in 1896, when most recipients lived in district still attached to parish church. Income £5 3s. 6d. in 1930. Gift formed part of Scheme of 1936 (item 21), represented by £207 5s. 1d. stock.

Frances Elizabeth Eggleton by will proved 1861 left £200 stock after death of her sister Christian Mary (d. 1867), to provide on Christmas Eve a shoulder of mutton and 4 lb bread to persons recommended by respectable householders, including tenants occupying nos 2–6 Lordship Place and nos 1–7 Waterloo Place, whether married and having families or not; any surplus to be spent on wine for the distributors. As further directed, a board was put up in the vestry room in 1862. The houses were pulled down shortly before 1896, when annual income of £5 10s. purchased 20 shoulders of mutton and 20 loaves, distributed by tickets; the 10s. used for bread was carried to Bread and Coal fund (above) which supplied the loaves. Gift formed part of Scheme of 1936 (item 22), represented by £200 stock.

Charles Rawlings by deed dated 1862 gave income from £400 stock to 4 poor householders or former householders of the parish, male or female, no one to benefit in two consecutive years. Annual income was then £20 and £14 13s. 4d. in 1896, when 4 beneficiaries, all over 60, each received £3 13s. 4d. In 1930 income was £14 13s. 8d. Gift formed part of Scheme of 1936 (item 23), represented by £419 7s. 4d. stock.

Mary Rogers by will proved 1863 left £300, income to provide blankets and coals for aged poor of St Luke's parish. In 1896 income, from stock, was £7 19s. Pairs of blankets were distributed around Christmas, and any residue carried to Bread and Coal fund (above). In 1930 income was £7 5s. Gift formed part of Scheme of 1936 (item 24), represented by £290 6s. 5d. stock.

George Wood by will proved 1877 left £1,000 free of duty to be invested, interest to be distributed half yearly among poor of Chelsea 'utterly irrespective of clime or creed'. Legacy was invested in stock. The oldest applicants were usually preferred and no one could benefit more

1 Ibid.

2 Below, Rel. Hist., par. ch.

than once in two years.[1] In 1896, out of 25 applicants with an average age of 70, 4 men and 3 women were chosen, six receiving £2 10s. each and one 16s. 8d. The whole income of £31 13s. 4d. was distributed annually in two tranches. It was unchanged and still distributed half yearly in 1930. Whole gift formed part of Scheme of 1936 (item 25), represented by £1,055 16s. 4d. stock.

Alfred Haines by will proved 1878 left £500 free of duty, income to be divided among widows and other poor of district of Kensal Green at Christmas. Gift was invested in £514 16s. stock. Sole ecclesiastical parish in Kensal Green at time of bequest was St John's, whose vicar and churchwardens became trustees. In 1895 dividend after income tax amounted to £13 3s. 8d. and, with 2s. 6d. added by vicar, was spent on coal, meat, and groceries, distributed by tickets to residents in ecclesiastical parish of St John. Charity was registered in 1963. In 1998–9 the income and expenditure were £121; possibly capital was being spent, as in 2000–1 income was too small to be recorded.[2]

Ann Hill by will proved 1881 left £1,000, income to be divided equally amongst 3 widows and 3 spinsters, parishioners of St Luke's, aged 50 or more. Invested in stock, and in 1896 income was £24 15s.: six recipients each received £4 2s. 6d. In 1930 income was £22 10s. Gift formed part of Scheme of 1936 (item 26), represented by £900 stock.

John Henry Brass by a declaration of trust dated 1892 gave £100, income to be paid to a poor single, widowed, or deserted woman, irrespective of faith, resident in St Luke's parish and over 60. He asked that the gift be called Brass's charity. Gift invested in stock, yielding £2 17s. 4d. In 1890s there was a fresh recipient every year. In 1930 annual income was £2 12s. Gift formed part of Scheme of 1936 (item 27), represented by £104 11s. 5d. stock.

Catherine Henrietta Penn by will proved 1893 left to incumbent of the old church £500 free of duty, to be spent at his discretion on poor of Chelsea. Gift invested in stock, yielding £15 a year. Incumbent informally divided income equally between vicars of St Luke's and St John's and minister of Park chapel; distribution was in money or food. Gift formed part of Scheme of 1936 (item 28), represented by £500 stock.

Isaac Stroulger by will proved 1904 left £200 to Chelsea MB, subject to his wife Jane's life interest, income to be applied by council annually on his birthday (3 January) equally between one poor man and one poor woman resident in Chelsea and aged over 60, regardless of faith or marital status. Gift formed part of Scheme of 1936 (item 30), when Jane Stroulger was still alive.

The Chelsea Relief of Hardship Fund[3] was created out of the Chelsea Community Centre for Unemployed Men by Scheme of 1957 to relieve the poorer inhabitants of the MB, in particular the unemployed. Its assets then were £300 stock and £81 2s. 7d. cash. A grant of £10 for clothing was recorded in 1968 but there had been no expenditure for at least five years in 1992, when assets of £1,142.39 consisted of £451.09 stock, money on deposit, and interest. The stock presumably had been sold by March 1995, when current and deposit accounts amounted to £387.87 and £418.18. The balance brought forward, with earlier interest totalling £522.72, apparently had been spent by 1996, leaving £284.75 on deposit; the expenditure was unexplained.

LOST DISTRIBUTIVE CHARITIES

Edward Page (d. 1597) by will gave £10 for poor of Chelsea.[4] Money apparently used by rector Richard Ward in 1603 to build Church House, on which was secured annual rent charge variously stated to be 16s. 4d. and 26s. 8d. The Church Place pulled down to make way for Paulton Street may have been Church House. Charity not mentioned in 1786 or 1825 and definitely lost by 1862.

Lady Anne Harrington *c.*1600 gave £20, income to be distributed to poor. Gift not mentioned in her will proved 1620. Although noted earlier in 19th century,[5] it could not be traced in 1862.

John Powell of Fulham by will dated 1606 left rent from Westminster to poor of St Margaret Westminster, Chelsea, and Kensington. His heirs were ordered to pay £1 a year in 1612, but nothing further recorded.[6]

Thomas Young, a Yeoman of the Guard, in 1604 gave to the parishes of Chelsea, Kensington, and Willesden 20s. apiece yearly for the poor. Whereas Kensington and Willesden's shares were secured by rent charges, Chelsea's had been lost by 1862.

Lady Lane was permitted to inclose 3 a. of Lammas land near her house called Brickills *c.*1630, and in return agreed to pay 20s. a year for poor of Chelsea 'until the world's end'. No record of its payment or application.

Lady Stonor by will allegedly proved 1645 left 20s. to be given annually in bread. Although gift was listed 1804, it was reported in 1862 as never paid.

Henry Ashton by will proved 1657 left 40s. to be lent to eight poor tradesmen without interest. By 1862 it had been lost.

Christopher Plucknett by will dated 1681 gave £1 yearly for bread. Money not paid until after 1787. In 1815 eight years' arrears were paid, and in 1825 gift was charged on Hanger and Town Mead in Fulham, occupied by Mr Bolton from whom rent was received annually. Money spent on bread distributed in January. Payments were received in 1820s and 1830s, but in 1858 the owner refused to pay, and in 1862, as no

1 *Vestry rep. 1877–8*, 88, 320; *1878–9*, 24.

2 Char. Com. no. 212857 (formerly 32806).

3 Char. Com. no. 233326 (formerly 136812). For earlier Benevolent and Relief socs, above, social activities.

4 Davies, *Chelsea Old Ch.* 296.

5 By Faulkner, by Skirrow, and in a pamphlet by Fred. Gaskell (1849) cited in *Chelsea Chars 1862*.

6 PRO, C 93/5/1, no. 18.

payment had been made for over 20 years, the claim was barred.

Thomas Morrison by will proved 1827 left fund to meet annuities and provide £20 a year for poor of Chelsea, but as gift could only bind his personal effects, worth less than £20, the charity lapsed.

Sabina Stirling Burgess by will proved 1856 left £100 stock free of duty to Holy Trinity parish, income to purchase bread for distribution on 6 March. In 1896, when number of poor had fallen, income of £2 15s. was distributed as 50 bread tickets worth 1s. Charity not mentioned in 1930 or in Scheme of 1936.

Henry Comyn by will proved 1866 provided that the residue of his estate was to be invested if his wife and two sons should die without issue, and income was to provide annual sums of £10 to poor widows in reduced circumstances. After his surviving heir's death in 1895, Chancery in 1896 held that the charitable gift had failed.

Mrs Rebecca Vandervell by deed of 1867 gave money to buy £107 4s. 9d. stock in trust to provide yearly distribution to at least six unrelieved poor of district of Kensal Green. In 1896 income was £2 19s., which with 1s. from private funds provided 5s. gifts to 12 poor of Kensal Green district. Charity registered in 1963 but deregistered in 1997 as not operating.[1]

Sarah Styles by will proved 1875 gave £150 to be invested for poor of St Jude's parish to receive half crowns annually on New Year's Day. Gift invested in stock, which in 1896 yielded £3 18s. 8d., distributed in money. Charity not mentioned in 1930 or in Scheme of 1936.

Margaret Morris[2] by will proved 1910 left £500 free of duty to parish of Kensal Green upon trust, the income to be applied for the benefit of the poor subject to maintenance of a certain grave in All Saints' cemetery, Kensal Green. In case of default the gift with the same condition was made to St Thomas's, Kensal Town. By Order of 1910 capital was invested in stock. In 1996 the trustees, empowered to spend the capital,[3] reported that the capital, amounting to £102.43, had been given to charity of Emily Josephine Gunning for poor of parish of St Andrew, North Kensington.[4]

Sarah Campbell left one half of residue of her estate, subject to a life interest, to churchwardens of Chelsea parish for bread and coal for the aged poor annually on 21 December. To be called the Sarah Campbell gift, it was subject to maintaining the tomb of her husband in Kensal Green cemetery. Trustees under her will made their first payment, of £94 1s. 9d., to the churchwardens in 1929.[5] Chelsea's share was excluded from Scheme of 1936 and came to be applied to ecclesiastical purposes, the life interest expiring in 1945.

Mary Clare by will proved 1914 left £200 to be invested, income to be used by incumbent of St John's, Kensal Green, for poor of that parish. Gift was subject to his maintaining and personally visiting every year the grave of Stephen McDonnell Clare, where she wished to be buried, for which he was to receive 10s. In case of default, the £200 was to go to St Mary's hospital absolutely. Charity was voluntarily registered in 1963, in 1964 stock was worth £204 16s., yielding £7 3s. 4d. Charity had lapsed by 2000 and was deregistered.[6]

1 Char. Com. no. 220658.
2 Para. based on Char. Com. no. 220656 (formerly 89419).
3 Under the Charities Act, 1993, c. 10.
4 Char. Com. no. 248382.
5 Wheeler, *Chelsea Chars*, 22.
6 Char. Com. no. 220657.

LOCAL GOVERNMENT

MANORIAL GOVERNMENT

Westminster Abbey, as overlord of the manor, was holding view of frankpledge in Chelsea by 1367, and between then and 1399 views took place normally once a year on Whit Monday. Presentments were of the usual transgressions: failure to do suit of court or to join the tithing, the drawing of blood, brewing, stray animals, obstructions of and encroachments on highways and watercourses, and minor nuisances. Officers were occasionally presented for failure to perform their duties.[1] As lessee of the manor the Abbey held a court baron about once a year between 1367 and 1370; no record of its business survives.[2] Chelsea manor courts leet and baron were being held for the Crown in the late 1530s, in 1543, in or after 1548, and in 1555, and for Queen Catherine in 1544 and 1547. Leet business was little changed, but there was probably little business overall since perquisites were less than in the 14th century. The courts were held once or twice a year and in some years were omitted, as in 1552.[3] The Magpie inn in the later Cheyne Walk was the venue for courts in the 1650s,[4] and housed joint courts leet and baron in 1679 and 1682 and probably the intervening years. Then and in the early 18th century business included presentments of obstructions, encroachments, and nuisances. In 1705 and 1706 several inhabitants were presented for harbouring lodgers, and three signposts for business premises erected on the highways or waste were presented in 1706.[5] The leet still functioned in the late 18th and earlier 19th century. In 1794 it recommended making a small sewer in Turk's Row to clear mud.[6] In 1819 it presented the defective footpath at Hospital Row: perhaps then, as certainly in 1833, the court was held in the Row either at the Royal Hospital or an inn of that name. It still appointed constables and headboroughs.[7] Court rolls survive for 1543–4 and 1547, and a roll of presentments for 1555.[8] All other court rolls were apparently lost in a disastrous fire when the Cadogan estate archives were being moved in the early 1890s.[9]

MANORIAL OFFICERS

In the late 14th century the leet elected two constables, two headboroughs, and two aletasters, and there was a hayward in 1378. The bailiff was mentioned in 1379[10] and the predecessors of George Bryce, regranted the office in 1555, had been active,[11] but in the late 16th century the office may have lapsed.[12] The leet in the 1540s still chose two headboroughs and two aletasters, but only one constable.[13] Constables and headboroughs were occasionally mentioned in the 17th century,[14] and an aleconner occurred in 1616.[15] In 1612 the justices forbade a drunken constable to serve again or keep a tavern,[16] and in 1732 fined another for not producing accounts and for contempt of court.[17] Constables and headboroughs were reprimanded in 1692 for failure to keep sufficient watch and ward, allowing a spate of robberies and burglaries.[18] There may have been only one headborough in 1748 and 1762, but from 1769 there were again sometimes two.[19] In 1796 the constable's obligation to raise a special levy for riot compensation, directed by quarter sessions, was instead met by the vestry out of the poor rate.[20] By 1800 there were several constables.[21] In 1822 the vestry proposed to select an extra constable for approval by the magistrates and court leet.[22] In 1824 the parochial committee resolved that a compensation be allowed the five constables belonging to the parish instead of charges; it was not to exceed £52

1 WAM 4805–6, 4809–12, 4815–16 (no recs. for 1370, 1375, 1377, 1380); below, man. officers.
2 WAM 4806–7, 4813.
3 PRO, SC 2/188/42–3; SC 2/191/73; SC 2/205/40; SC 6/HENVIII/2101; ibid. /2103, m. 31; ibid. /6661; ibid. /EDWVI/299, mm. 40 and d., 44; ibid/PHIL&MARY/187 m. 3 and d; BL, Lansd. MS 2, f. 11.
4 NRA(S) 332, F1/182.
5 Faulkner, *Chelsea*, II. 156–61.
6 Vestry orders, 1790–1809, pp. 61–2.
7 *Rep. Sel. Cttee on Police of Metropolis* (Parl. Papers, 1828 (533), VI), p. 350; E. Ffooks, 'Kens. Turnpike Trust' (TS in Kens. Lib.), 40; Chelsea Scraps, 385; Vestry mins 1822–33, p. 55.
8 PRO, SC 2/188/42–3; SC 2/205/40; SC 2/191/73.
9 Pearman, *Cadogan Est.* 11.
10 WAM 4805, mm. 1–2; 4809, m. 1 and d.; 4811, m. 2; 4815, m. 2; 4816, m. 2 and d.
11 *Cal. Pat.* 1554–5, 46; BL, Lansd. MS 2, ff. 11, 15; BL, Harl. Roll N 30; PRO, SC 2/188/42; SC 2/205/40, m. 4; SC 6/EDWVI/299, m. 44.
12 BL, Harl Roll L 26.
13 PRO, SC 2/188/42; SC 2/188/43; SC 2/205/40.
14 *Middx Sess. Rec.* NS, I. 250, 444; II. 95, 209, 288; III. 59, 231, 339; IV. 24, 193, 200, 220, 279, 331; Cal. Middx Sess. Rec. 1611, pt. 2, 90–1; BL, Add. MS 11056, ff. 284, 289, 295; PRO, PROB 11/272, f. 47 (will of Hen. Ashton); PROB 11/310, f. 11 (will of Jas Leverett); CL , deed 18629; Vestry orders, 1662–1718, f. 9.
15 *Middx Sess. Rec.* NS, III. 253.
16 Cal. Middx Sess. Rec. 1612, pt. 2, 25.
17 Cal. Middx Sess. Bk July 1732–Dec. 1735, p. 10.
18 *Middx County Rec. Sess. Bks 1689–1709*, 87.
19 Vestry orders, 1745–71, pp. 48, 259, 330.
20 Vestry orders, 1790–1809, p. 106.
21 Ibid., p. 218.
22 Vestry mins 1822–33, p. 55.

a year. The constable who attended the billetting of any soldiers quartered in the parish, and the one who attended the magistrate at petty sessions, each received £14; each of the others £8.[1] By 1828 there were 15 constables and 4 headboroughs.[2] Parish constables were still being appointed in 1852.[3]

Instruments of punishment were still a manorial responsibility in 1705.[4] The 'old pound' in 1694 lay at the east end of Cheyne Walk,[5] but it is not clear where the pound mentioned in 1749 lay.[6]

PARISH GOVERNMENT TO 1837

The parish vestry met in the later 17th and early 18th centuries to appoint officers, approve accounts, and order rates, as well as for exceptional purposes,[7] but it is not clear how often it met each year. The parish built a meeting room for it in 1706 in Church Street, as part of Petyt's school gift,[8] perhaps the same vestry room being used in 1837.[9] In the mid and late 18th century the vestry was meeting at irregular intervals between 8 and 17 times a year.[10] In the 1800s meetings were scarcely less frequent.[11] In 1662 James Leverett bequeathed a rent charge for the poor which included £4 a year for fours dinners a year at the Magpie for the churchwardens, overseers, parish clerk and constables, and the master of the Magpie.[12]

The vestry remained open. By the early 18th century those attending apparently included a varying core of parish officers, ex-officers, and substantial householders who signed resolutions. In 1713 the churchwardens' accounts were passed by 12 signatories, in 1715 by 22.[13] In the 1740s and 1750s typically from 5 to 35 people, on one occasion 84, signed.[14] The range was similar in 1810.[15] A much larger fringe of parishioners, up to 120 in the mid 18th century and up to 1,600 by the 1830s,[16] voted at disputed elections of parish officials and may have attended other meetings without signing, even though the resolution was formally unanimous. Votes on specific issues were restricted to landholders in 1783, to ratepayers in 1786, to £10 ratepayers in 1795, to £8 ratepayers in 1798 and 1805, and to paid-up ratepayers from 1809 to 1825.[17] In 1751, though 77 people voted on a disputed resolution, only 18 and 27 respectively signed the opposing versions.[18] Sometimes differing numbers of people signed different resolutions at the same meeting.[19] Women sometimes voted, as in 1759[20] and especially between 1775 and 1809.[21]

Decisions of the vestry were normally unanimous or by informal majority. Polls were usually restricted to elections of officers, although formal votes on motions were recorded in 1751 and from 1835 to 1837.[22] Occasionally a vestry meeting rescinded a decision of a recent predecessor. Sometimes this seems to have been because of a change in circumstances,[23] sometimes because of a genuine change of view, such as over the best way of maintaining streets in Hans Town in 1790 or repairing the church in 1815.[24] Sometimes rescinding resulted from a legal challenge to a decision made without sufficient notice, or resistance to a salary increase.[25] In 1788 resident JPs claimed that a vestry order rescinding a motion about highway widening was not complete; the vestry responded by a unanimous rebuttal.[26] Increasing, though intermittent, controversy over management of rates and the workhouse from 1809 led to the rescinding of a scheme of 1809 to manage workhouse contracts[27] and of a proposal for a local Act in 1811–12.[28]

VESTRY COMMITTEES

Like open vestries in other populous parishes[29] Chelsea made extensive use of committees, an approach which

1 LMA, P74/LUK/27, p. 155. For the cttee, below, poor relief to 1837.

2 *Rep. Sel. Cttee on Police of Metropolis* (Parl. Papers, 1828 (533), VI), p. 350. Lewis, *Topog. Dict. Eng.* (1831), A–C, 416, states that the court appointed 4 headboroughs and 9 constables.

3 CL, deed 18631.

4 Faulkner, *Chelsea*, II. 160. For the instruments, below, pub. svces (pub. order).

5 Dr King's MS, p. 5.

6 Cal. Middx Sess. Bk Jan. 1747/8–Dec. 1751, p. 69.

7 Vestry orders, 1662–1718, ff. 57v., 77, 103, 118, 219v., 229.

8 Faulkner, *Chelsea*, I. 255; below, Soc. Hist., educ. (pub. schs, Petyt's).

9 Vestry mins, 1833–9, p. 171; cf. Vestry mins, 1839–43, p. 94; below, metropolitan vestry.

10 Vestry orders, 1745–71, 1771–90.

11 Ibid., 1790–1809.

12 PRO, PROB 11/310, f.11; CL, deed 18629.

13 Vestry orders, 1662–1718, ff. 219v., 240v.

14 Ibid., 1745–71, pp. 9, 104, 167–8, 170.

15 Ibid., 1809–22, pp. 24, 26–7, 29, 31–2, 34, 37–8, 40, 46.

16 Ibid., 1745–71, pp. 190–4; Vestry mins, 1833–9, pp. 17–18.

17 Vestry orders, 1771–90, ff. 105, 127v.; 1790–1809, pp. 80, 154, 315; 1809–22, pp. 11, 229, 402; Vestry mins, 1822–33, pp. 74, 141.

18 Vestry orders, 1745–71, pp. 110–11.

19 Ibid., pp. 95–6, 119–20, 154–6, 185–6, 189, 194.

20 Ibid., pp. 203–12.

21 Ibid., 1771–90, ff. 23–5, 43v.–45v., 54v.–57, 128–133v.; 1790–1809, pp. 81–6, 316–28; 1809–22, pp. 12–16.

22 Ibid., 1745–71, pp. 110–11; Vestry mins, 1833–9, pp. 88, 154, 173.

23 Vestry orders, 1771–90, ff. 157v., 159, 160v.

24 Ibid., 1790–1809, p. 4; 1809–22, p. 167.

25 Ibid., 1790–1809, p. 253; Vestry mins, 1822–33, pp. 62–3, 94; 1833–9, pp. 153–4.

26 Vestry orders, 1771–90, f. 160v.

27 Below, poor relief to 1837 (workho.); Vestry orders, 1790–1809, pp. 394–407.

28 Below, poor relief to 1837 (workho.).

29 S. and B. Webb, *Eng. Local Govt* [I]: *The Par. and the County*, 130–4.

probably helped to facilitate a high standard of day-to-day administration, at least in the mid 18th century.[1] Besides a standing committee to manage the workhouse from 1735[2] and a regular committee from 1825 to examine the surveyors' accounts,[3] ad hoc committees for particular purposes were often appointed in the mid 18th century, and again, after an apparent gap between 1765 and 1780, in the late 18th and earlier 19th centuries. Besides workhouse matters[4] and church affairs,[5] they considered or managed almost all types of business: boundary disputes in 1753,[6] procedures for rating the Royal Hospital or negotiating with its commissioners in 1747, 1780, 1781, and 1795,[7] for rating St George Hanover Square's proposed parish workhouse in Little Chelsea in 1787[8] and meeting costs of Trinity chapel, Sloane Street, in 1831,[9] the walling, maintenance, or replacement of burial grounds in 1789, 1799, 1807, and 1810,[10] Chamberlaine's bequests in 1827,[11] paving of Sloane Street in 1790,[12] surveying drains in Riley Street in 1800,[13] rebuilding the embankment at Millman Row in 1815,[14] investigating parish lighting in 1832,[15] managing a corps of volunteer infantry in 1803[16] and an association against felons in 1811,[17] and organizing special collections for the poor in 1809 for George III's jubilee and again in 1820.[18] Until the 1820s,[19] financial committees were only set up at moments of special concern to examine recent accounts: of the officers in 1751, the churchwardens in 1765, the overseers in 1782.[20]

Committees were used to lobby or petition parliament, in 1753 with neighbouring parishes to get an Act to reform the highway rate,[21] and in 1800 to confer with them about a proposed Paddington to Harrow turnpike Act;[22] in 1797 to lobby against increased general taxation,[23] and to monitor a poor-law bill and seek relief from supporting the Royal Hospital's poor,[24] and in 1812 to resist a new bill for the metropolitan night watch,[25] as well as to prepare Chelsea's own rates Bills in 1811 and 1820.[26] Committees to lobby parliament were again set up in 1833 and 1835.[27] The ad hoc committees usually included officers, but varied in size from 5 to 57; the usual number seems to have been between 10 and 20. In 1832 the lighting committee explicitly included the parish magistrates. A quorum was usually specified, often a much smaller number than the total: thus in 1806 a committee of 50 had a quorum of 11.[28]

PARISH OFFICERS

Two churchwardens were mentioned from 1552.[29] In 1693 and again in 1702 the justices were ordered to examine a churchwarden's accounts,[30] and in 1695 the churchwardens were ordered to be reimbursed for costs defending a parish suit.[31] By 1746 they were chosen at the Easter Tuesday vestry.[32] As was quite common one churchwarden was nominated by the rector and the other by the parish, and the parish warden's post was sometimes disputed,[33] though more often he was nominated by an outgoing warden unopposed. Between 1785 and 1825 there seems to have been no disputed election,[34] but from 1826 to 1830 numbers voting rose from 190 apparently to 999. The 1830 election may have been disorderly and no other was disputed until 1841.[35] There were sidesmen by 1672, when they collected church rates and gifts to the poor and distributed the latter.[36] Two were appointed yearly from 1826, when the election was disputed, as in 1827.[37]

Though two witnesses in 1552 may not have been

1 *Chelsea Settlement Examinations 1733–66*, pp. xiv, xvii.
2 Below, poor relief to 1837 (workho.)
3 Vestry mins, 1822–33, pp. [1]55–6, 230–1, 251–3, 294, 312; 1833–9, p. 113.
4 Below, poor relief to 1837.
5 Vestry orders, 1745–71, pp. 66, 68, 102, 104, 255, 294; 1771–90, ff. 135 and v., 145; 1790–1809, pp. 265–6, 346–7; 1809–22, pp. 135–6, 288–9, 310–11; Vestry mins, 1822–33, pp. 90, 124.
6 Vestry orders, 1745–71, pp. 136–7.
7 Ibid., pp. 31–2; 1771–90, ff. 52, 62; 1790–1809, pp. 115–16.
8 Ibid., 1771–90, f. 148.
9 Vestry mins, 1822–33, pp. 280–1.
10 Vestry orders, 1771–90, ff. 169v.–170; 1790–1809, pp. 194, 365; 1809–22, p. 23.
11 Vestry mins, 1822–33, pp. 190, 198.
12 Vestry orders, 1771–90, f. 173v.
13 Vestry orders, 1790–1809, p. 199.
14 Ibid., 1809–22, pp. 133–4.
15 Vestry mins, 1822–33, pp. 316–17.
16 Vestry orders, 1790–1809, pp. 283–4.
17 Ibid., 1809–22, p. 67.
18 Ibid., pp. 18–19, 356–9.
19 Below, poor relief to 1837 (local Act and par. cttee).
20 Vestry orders, 1745–71, pp. 98–9, 296; 1771–90, ff. 76–77v.
21 Ibid., 1745–71, pp. 147–9.
22 Ibid., 1790–1809, pp. 215–16.
23 Ibid., p. 140.
24 Ibid., pp. 115–17.
25 Ibid., 1809–22, p. 78.
26 Below, poor relief to 1837 (Local Act and par. cttee).
27 Vestry mins, 1822–33, p. 325; 1833–9, pp. 33–4.
28 Vestry orders, 1745–71, esp. pp. 103, 148; 1771–90; 1790–1809, esp. pp. 346–7; 1809–22; Vestry mins, 1822–33, esp. p. 321; 1833–9.
29 Faulkner, *Chelsea*, I. 191, II. 119; PRO, E 315/498, f. 2; Guildhall MSS 9537/1, f. 72v.; ibid. /2, f. 102; /3, f. 31v.; /4, ff. [1v.], 68v.; /6, f. 3; /15, f. 49v.; /17, f. 48v.; /20, ff. 30v., 96; 9583/2, pt. 6, f. 44; 9583/3, pt. 3l f. 37; CL, deed 18629; BL, Add. MS 11056, f. 284; Vestry orders, 1662–1718, ff. 4, 38v., 47, 50, 55v., 57.
30 *Middx County Rec. Sess. Bks 1689–1709*, 96, 246.
31 Ibid., 123, 136.
32 Vestry orders, 1745–71, p. 11.
33 e.g. ibid., pp. 11, 27, 154.
34 Ibid., 1771–90, *passim*; 1790–1809, *passim*; 1809–22, *passim*; Vestry mins, 1822–33, pp. 11, 86, 129, 147–8.
35 Vestry mins, 1822–33, pp. 165, 224, 246, 249, 271–3, 290, 302; 1833–9, *passim*; 1839–43, pp. 207, 210.
36 Vestry orders, 1662–1718, ff. 18–19.
37 Vestry mins, 1822–33, pp. [1]64, 166, 191–2, 224, 246, 271, 292, 302; 1833–9, pp. 9, 100, 208.

parish officers,[1] there were two jurats in 1574, two jurats or *oeconomi* in 1577, and two *oeconomi* in 1580 and 1586. Since those officials were additional to the wardens,[2] they may have been the predecessors of the overseers of the poor, who were mentioned from 1632.[3] There were 2 or more in 1637,[4] and 2 in 1706,[5] as in 1745.[6] The statutory procedure of Easter Week nomination and submission of names to the justices seems to have been followed. From 1783 those with the most votes were not necessarily appointed. [7] The number was increased to 4 in 1807.[8] An assistant overseer was elected in 1833, when at least 1,651 parishioners, about 21 per cent of adult males, voted.[9]

Surveyors of the highways were chosen in 1691–2,[10] and by 1696, when Quarter Sessions ordered them to be paid by defaulting ratepayers, there were two, as in 1752.[11] From 1774 the vestry submitted names for their appointment by the magistrates; those with most support in the parish were not always appointed.[12] The number was temporarily increased to three from 1787[13] to 1791.[14] A highways board of 6 was appointed in 1834, suppressed in 1836, and revived in 1838.[15]

SALARIED OFFICIALS

The offices of parish clerk and sexton are treated elsewhere.[16]

There was a vestry clerk, separate from the parish clerk, by 1737.[17] By 1755, when a new clerk was appointed, his salary was £25 and he apparently held office indefinitely. That clerk's successor resigned in 1760, and 50 voted in the ensuing disputed election.[18] The new clerk served until his death in 1783, when another election, at which all landholders could vote, attracted 2 candidates and 424 voters. The salary was raised to £60 and customary fees were suppressed. A deputy served in 1789.[19] The salary was again raised, to 80 guineas, in 1798. The duties then defined included, besides keeping rate books and account books, work for the magistrates and the workhouse. In 1802, following a dispute, it was decided that salary increases for the clerk and other officers should have two vestries' notice to enable interested parishioners to attend. The next year the salary rose to £100,[20] and in 1807, reflecting an alleged great increase in the duties, to 150 guineas, raised by a further 50 guineas in 1814.[21] Under the St Luke Chelsea Poor Rates Act, 1821, the vestry clerk was also clerk of the parochial committee.[22] In 1823 the vestry resolved to elect the clerk annually, though the old clerk could be re-elected.[23] The salary was raised to £300 in 1825, when the clerk might employ a deputy to attend the weekly petty sessions.[24] A review of the duties in 1838 revealed that he had to attend all public vestries, draft notices for them, and take minutes; convene committees of the vestry, and attend when required; summon the parochial committeemen; conduct parochial correspondence, and deal with other records; make out rate books for lighting, poor rates, and highway rates; fill up summonses and warrants against an average of 3,000 defaulters yearly; attend the magistrates; make out indentures of apprenticeship; deal with settlement and removal, including observances required by Poor Law Amendment; maintain lists of county voters and juries; organize the annual election of guardians; and deal with contracts or accounts relating to the poor.[25] The duties were accordingly reduced, being managed by other bodies than the vestry, and the salary cut to £80.[26]

By 1685 there was a beadle, provided with clothes and a bell,[27] and by 1712 with a £5 salary.[28] In 1779, when the salary was £12 besides a uniform, ten candidates contested the post on the incumbent's death, and the winner was decided by ballot. He was to attend all church services, vestries, and workhouse committees, and to take instructions daily from the churchwardens and overseers.[29] In 1784 his required attendance on the officers was reduced, but he was to discourage lodgers and beggars, and perquisites were incorporated in a revised salary of £30.[30] Similar instructions were repeated later, as in 1795.[31] By 1795 the beadle elected in

1 PRO, E 315/498, f. 2.

2 Guildhall MSS 9537/3, f. 31v.; 9537/4, ff.[1v.], 68v.; 9537/6, f. 3.

3 Faulkner, *Chelsea*, II. 141; PRO, PROB 11/272, f. 47; CL, deed 18629.

4 PRO, C 8/327/61.

5 Faulkner, *Chelsea*, I. 255.

6 Vestry orders, 1745–71, p. 5.

7 Ibid., pp. 164, 177, 185, 196, 217, 226, 238, 253, 262, 278, 288, 301, 310, 322, 330, 342; 1771–90, ff. 1, 8, 13, 17, 27 and v., 39v., 102, 168; 1790–1809, p. 122.

8 Vestry orders, 1790–1809, pp. 375, 380–1, 383. A vote to increase it to 3 in 1790 had been reversed: ibid., 1771–90, f. 173; 1790–1809, p. 1.

9 Vestry mins, 1833–9, pp. 17–18; cf. ibid., 1822–33, unpaginated section at back of vol.

10 Vestry orders, 1662–1718, f. 57v.

11 *Middx County Rec. Sess. Bks 1689–1709*, 150, 158, 162; Vestry orders, 1745–71, p. 121.

12 Vestry orders, 1771–90, ff. 20v., 29, 163v.

13 Ibid., ff. 157–9.

14 Ibid., f. 172v; 1790–1809, pp. 13, 30.

15 Vestry mins, 1833–9, pp. 62–3, 76, 135, 138, 174–5, 202.

16 Below, Rel. Life, par. ch.

17 CL, deed 18628; Vestry orders, 1745–71, p. 32.

18 Vestry orders, 1745–71, pp. 167, 228.

19 Ibid., 1771–90, ff. 105–8, 169.

20 Ibid., 1790–1809, pp. 173, 253, 278–80.

21 Ibid., pp. 374–5; 1809–22, p. 115.

22 St Luke Chelsea Poor Rates etc. Act, 1821, 1 & 2 Geo. IV, c. 67, s. 12 (Local and Personal). For the cttee, below, poor relief to 1837 (Local Act and par. cttee).

23 Vestry mins, 1822–33, p. 86.

24 Ibid., p. 149.

25 Ibid., 1833–9, pp. 210–11.

26 Ibid., pp. 218–224.

27 Vestry orders, 1662–1718, ff. 37, 39.

28 Ibid., f. 217v.

29 Ibid., 1771–90, f. 43.

30 Ibid., ff. 111v.–112.

31 S. and B. Webb, *Eng. Local Govt* [I]: *The Par. and the County*, 127 n.

1779 was too old to work and it was resolved to elect the beadle annually; from 1796 he was chosen with the other officers.[1] The contested elections of 1779 and 1795 attracted 312 and 419 voters respectively.[2] A second beadle for Hans Town was elected from 1798, and each beadle was given an apparently additional salary of £10.[3] In 1804 each beadle's salary was increased from £40 to £50. In 1806 a retiring beadle was awarded a salary to keep the church galleries and churchyard in order, but the decision was soon reversed and the beneficiary pensioned off.[4] The beadles' salaries were again raised, to £70, in 1812.[5] A proposal for a third beadle, deflected in 1826, was successfully revived in 1829,[6] but from 1838 the salary of that beadle, who served at the parish chapel, was reduced to £40, effectively a pension, as his post was considered redundant.[7]

Under the St Luke Chelsea Rates Act three collectors of rates were appointed from 1821. At the initial election 3,490 votes were cast for four candidates.[8] Twelve inspectors of lighting were appointed from 1833.[9]

HANS TOWN COMMISSIONERS

After Henry Holland's development of Hans Town in the north-east of the parish,[10] an Act was obtained in 1790 which created the district thereafter officially known as Hans Town to cover the 89 a. leased by Holland. The Act set up a body of commissioners to include all landowners resident in the area who had a rental of at least £30 a year, or lessees rated at £30, or occupiers of buildings rated at £30 who also had £2,000 in personal estate. The commissioners had powers to repair, light, and water the streets there, and to appoint watchmen. The costs were to be met by a rate of 2s. 6d. in the pound on houses and gardens, and 1s. in the pound on other land, according to the poor-rate valuation. The commissioners were to pay yearly to the parish surveyors of the highways £4, the approximate value to which the 89 acres of land had been assessed to the poor rate before development. In 1803 the commissioners were also given powers of street cleaning, which seem to have been accidentally omitted from the earlier Act, and of refuse collection.[11] The services which they provided were regarded as far better than those in what came to be called 'the old part' of the parish. Hans Town's streets were better watched in 1829,[12] and in 1854, in proportion to its area and length of road, it had four times as many public pumps and nearly twice as many lamps as the old part.[13] The commissioners were abolished by the Metropolis Local Management Act of 1855.[14]

POOR RELIEF AND RATES TO 1837

Between 1594 and 1613 regular relief was apparently ineffective: several paupers, not all vagrants, were found dead in barns, stables, and yards.[15] Fines collected from drunken revellers in 1612 were consigned to the use of the poor.[16] In the late 17th century Quarter Sessions was making orders about disputed settlements in Chelsea;[17] weekly pensions were paid, and women were paid to feed pauper children. The poor were badged in 1707. The poor rate in 1696 was £58; £52 was spent on pensions.[18] A rate at 4d. in the pound in 1706 raised £85, and another in 1717 raised £68. Not all was spent on the poor but other sums such as church sacrament offerings were given to them, for example in 1696–7.[19] Quarter Sessions intervened six times between 1708 and 1733 to order payment of debts to or from the overseers or inspection of their accounts.[20]

THE WORKHOUSE

The churchwardens were empowered in 1727 to rent a house for the poor, and under a resolution of 1733 a workhouse, capable of accommodating up to 70, was opened in 1735 and completed in 1737 on land given by Sir Hans Sloane north of the King's Road, next to the burial ground. The site was later bounded by Arthur (later Dovehouse) and Britten streets on the west and north respectively.[21] A new building to serve as a workshop was

1 Vestry orders, 1790–1809, pp. 76–80, 97.
2 Ibid., 1771–90, f. 46; 1790–1809, p. 87.
3 Ibid., 1790–1809, pp. 148, 150–63.
4 Ibid., pp. 296–7, 338, 342–3.
5 Ibid., 1809–22, pp. 89–91.
6 Vestry mins, 1822–33, pp. [1]64–5, 172, 247–8, 248.
7 Ibid., 1833–9, pp. 212–14.
8 Vestry orders, 1809–22, pp. 391–3. For the Act, below, poor relief to 1837.
9 Vestry mins, 1833–9, p. 25; cf. below, pub. svces.
10 Above, Settlement, 1680–1865 (Hans Town).
11 Hans Town (Chelsea) Improvement Act, 30 Geo. III, c. 76; Hans Town (Chelsea) Improvement Amendment Act, 43 Geo. III, c. 11 (Local and Personal).
12 Below, pub. svces (pub. order); Faulkner, *Chelsea*, II. 341–2.
13 *Returns of Paving, Cleansing and Lighting Metropolitan Districts* (Parl. Papers, 1854–5 (127), LIII), p. 15.
14 18 & 19 Vic. c. 120, s. 90.
15 Beaver, *Memorials*, 39.
16 Cal. Middx Sess. Rec. 1612, pt 2, 67.
17 *Middx County Rec. Sess. Bks 1689–1709*, 173, 186, 195, 200, 202.
18 Faulkner, *Chelsea*, II. 151–2.
19 Vestry orders, 1662–1718, ff. 66–7, 70, 129v.–135v., 250–9.
20 *Middx County Rec. Sess. Bks 1689–1709*, 333; Cal. Middx Sess. Bk Jan. 1714–15 Dec. 1718, 120; Jan. 1718/19–March 1721/2, 128; April 1722–Feb. 1726/7, 132; Jan. 1729/30–May 1732, 94; July 1732–Dec. 1735, p. 62.
21 Faulkner, *Chelsea*, II. 24–5; Beaver, *Memorials*, 322; *Chelsea Settlement Examinations 1733–66*, p. xvi (giving 1737 as opening date); LMA, P74/LUK/3; Thompson, *Map* (1836). In 1781, however, the vestry recalled building a large par. workho. in 1743 × 1750: Vestry orders, 1771–90, f. 70v.

approved in 1769, though it had not been begun in 1770.[1] It was probably the new building erected before 1778, when another was ordered to remedy overcrowding.[2] In 1783 the main building had a three storeys and a basement, with 13 rooms; buildings in the courtyard had a further 8 rooms, with two 'back of' the house including an infirmary.[3] A west wing was built in 1788, to replace the infirmary, and enlarged in 1807 to extend the infirmary and provide men's dormitories and committee rooms as well. South-west and south-east wings built in 1792 contained sickrooms and dormitories for males and females respectively.[4] Alterations to the male sickrooms were approved in 1797.[5] In 1800 part of the north-west wing was adapted to the work of the Chelsea Soup Society, aiming to provide the poor with nutritious soup instead of bread.[6] Further repairs were made in 1812.[7] By 1822 many of the inmates had to be lodged in 7 houses in Britten Street, contiguous to the workhouse,[8] so a further large wing designed by James Savage was built in 1822 to provide additional accommodation including workshops, laundry, infirmary, and space for women and girls. Rooms for homeless strangers were built over the gatehouse in 1824, and a new infirmary was added in 1827.[9]

In 1735 the vestry set up a committee to manage the workhouse; in its first year those attending the weekly meetings included the rector, one or both churchwardens, at least one overseer, the doctor, the constable, and from 1 to 6 others.[10] At its reappointment in 1746, besides the rector and officers, a further 38 parishioners were added.[11] Meetings were more erratic in the late 1740s, and attendance low,[12] but then and later formal membership was repeatedly increased.[13] By 1769 it had the officers and 57 parishioners, though only 5 were a quorum; they were to report if the workhouse needed an extra workroom.[14] The committee remained an established institution;[15] in 1807 it again met weekly.[16] Ad hoc committees were also set up, in 1753 to study schemes for farming the poor,[17] in 1782 to examine workhouse bills,[18] in connexion with infirmary and other buildings in 1788, 1797, 1807, and 1812,[19] and for appointments of staff in 1800, 1801, and 1809, though a proposal for one in 1805 was defeated.[20]

The workhouse had a resident salaried master from 1735,[21] and a mistress by 1736, who as in the 1750s was probably the master's wife.[22] Two successive masters in the 1750s left under a cloud.[23] The master and mistress elected after a contest in 1780 were to be paid £20 besides board and lodging.[24] In 1783 the master complained that the poor would not obey orders without payment.[25] On his resignation in 1801, he was appointed clerk to the workhouse; his successor's salary was raised to £30. Both officials were to be elected annually.[26] The master's salary was raised to £50 in 1804 and all perquisites abolished.[27] The next year there was a disputed election, 755 voting;[28] in 1809 the post had 15 candidates, reduced before election to four.[29] The master in 1822 received a large grocery allowance.[30] His successor in 1835 was still paid £50.[31]

The vestry decided in 1792 to appoint a matron, unrelated to the master, to manage the female inmates and train the girls.[32] Her salary was £15 by 1800, when it was reduced in the light of the need for an assistant, then appointed.[33] In 1810, however, there was again a sole matron, whose pay then rose from 20 to 30 guineas.[34] The matron was subject to annual re-election from 1816.[35] Besides the formal staff, paupers were paid to undertake specific roles to keep down costs; in 1826 the parochial committee decided that that was illegal, since if the paupers were capable of earning they should be outside the workhouse. Nevertheless it agreed to pay superintendents of the male and female paupers and of wood cutting, a cook and her male assistant, a coal and cellarman, a nightwatchman, and a schoolmaster and schoolmistress.[36] A subcommittee was appointed to draw up rules for the master and mistress in 1735[37] and

1 Vestry orders, 1745–71, pp. 333, 345.
2 Ibid., 1771–90, f. 41.
3 Ibid., f. 100v.
4 Ibid., ff. 161–2; 1790–1809, pp. 366–8, 377–81; Faulkner, *Chelsea*, II. 25–6.
5 Vestry orders, 1790–1809, pp. 126–8.
6 Ibid., pp. 196–7.
7 Ibid., 1809–22, pp. 83–4.
8 Vestry mins 1822–33, p. 15.
9 Ibid., pp. 15–19; LMA, P 74/LUK/26, pp. 150–1, 160; Faulkner, *Chelsea*, II. 25–6.
10 LMA, P74/LUK/3, pp. 1–61.
11 Vestry orders, 1745–71, p. 19.
12 LMA, P74/LUK/3 [not paginated after 1744].
13 Vestry orders, 1745–71, pp. 54, 123–4.
14 Ibid., p. 333.
15 Ibid., 1790–1809, pp. 167, 173–4.
16 Ibid., p. 366.
17 Ibid., 1745–71, p. 139.
18 Ibid., 1771–90, f. 85.
19 Ibid., ff. 161v.–162; 1790–1809, pp. 127–8, 366–7; 1809–22, pp. 83–4.
20 Ibid., 1790–1809, pp. 207–10, 241–3, 313–14; 1809–22, pp. 5–7.
21 LMA, P74/LUK/3, pp. 10, 13, 17, 58.
22 Ibid., p. 42; Vestry orders, 1745–71, p. 176.
23 Vestry orders, 1745–71, pp. 141–2; LMA, P74/LUK/5, 1 March 1756.
24 Vestry orders, 1771–90, ff. 54v.–57.
25 Ibid., f. 99 and v.
26 Ibid., 1790–1809, pp. 240–2.
27 Ibid., pp. 296–8.
28 Ibid., pp. 315–29.
29 Ibid., 1809–22, pp. 7–16.
30 LMA, P74/LUK/26, p. 191.
31 Vestry mins 1833–9, p. 108.
32 Vestry orders, 1790–1809, pp. 26–8.
33 Ibid., pp. 205–12.
34 Ibid., 1809–22, p. 26.
35 Ibid., pp. 191, 273, 295, 340, 363, 384; Vestry mins 1822–33, pp. 11, 85, 129, 147, [1]64, 189, 221, 246, 271, 290, 301; 1833–9, pp. 3, 36, 100, 137, 171.
36 LMA, P74/LUK/27, pp. 281, 461–2. For the cttee, below.
37 LMA, P74/LUK/3, p. 42.

the vestry laid down rules for the master and matron in 1801,[1] and for the matron in 1815.[2]

Annual contracts for provisions for the workhouse were being let, for meat from 1735, for milk from 1736.[3] The vestry rejected in 1753 a proposal to farm the poor.[4] The diet in the mid 18th century was better, and the mortality rate lower, than in many other parishes in the metropolis.[5] In the 1770s and earlier 1780s most categories of provisions, including meat, flour, beans, beer, greens, turnips, and loaves were supplied by different tradesmen, though some continued to supply their respective commodities for several years.[6] In 1782 the vestry ordered the contracts to be made quarterly; the churchwardens and overseers were to examine samples of articles required before and after delivery;[7] a committee found that year that the parish had been seriously overcharged for many commodities.[8] In 1801 the master was required to keep detailed accounts of all provisions, and the officers were to inspect those accounts weekly.[9] In 1809 the vestry forbade parish officers to be involved in selling provisions to the workhouse, but stipulated that all articles were to be supplied by contract with tradesmen of the parish. A committee of 21 non-tradesmen, renewed annually, was to allot six-monthly contracts on the basis of sealed tenders.[10] The scheme split the vestry, however: it was resisted by a minority who attributed its passage to incomers and it was rescinded, after opposition from the officers, on legal advice that it interfered with the officers' duties.[11] The overseers for 1820–1, amid much alleged waste and peculation, apparently ordered for the sick in the workhouse 'finest' delicacies which they themselves consumed.[12] The parochial committee under the St Luke Chelsea Poor Rates Act, 1821, adopted six-monthly tendering, but allowed contractors outside the parish to compete.[13] In 1823 the committee's bylaws required one overseer to be responsible for workhouse provisioning.[14] Wines and spirits for the sick were recommended weekly by the surgeon.[15]

WORKHOUSE INMATES AND OUTRELIEF

It was claimed in 1740 that the opening of the workhouse had substantially reduced demand for the sacrament offertory charity.[16] There were 131 inmates in 1781, 140 in 1801, 199 in 1816, and 262, including those in rented accommodation, in 1822.[17] In 1802–3 there were 1,978 poor relieved occasionally, 257 adults on permanent out-relief, and 130 in the workhouse.[18] The numbers occasionally relieved rose to 5,636 in 1813–14, falling to 4,773 in 1814–15, compared with 802 for all the other parishes in Kensington division. At that time 332 received permanent out-relief and 197 were in the workhouse.[19] It was claimed in 1819 that there had been over 6,000 paupers in the parish in 1817.[20] By 1834 the workhouse accommodated 450 men, women, and children.[21]

In 1735 the workhouse committee agreed to put the workhouse children to work making thread buttons; by 1736 eight girls aged 6–10 were making them.[22] The inmates were also put to spinning yarn from 1736 to the mid 1750s or later, earning only about 5 per cent of their keep; by 1753 they were also making clothes and stockings.[23] In 1751 young inmates were sent to work with Sprimont at the Chelsea Porcelain works, in the hope of apprenticeships.[24] By 1781 'silk work' was carried on at the workhouse,[25] apparently outwork for the Spitalfields industry,[26] and in 1792 girls spent so much time at it that they became useless for domestic employment.[27] By 1804, however, 31 child inmates were employed in an outside factory, reducing the master's income from silk work.[28] In 1822 male inmates were employed on shoemaking, spinning, and weaving, women on needlework; a report recommended that both should knit. Looms had been bought for a new 'manufactory' at the workhouse.[29] Stonebreaking and woodcutting were planned.[30] A superintendent of the inmates' labour was recruited in 1823.[31] Oakum-picking was evidently also required, since in 1825 a committee advised that it cease.[32]

1 Vestry orders, 1790–1809, pp. 242–5.
2 Ibid., 1809–22, p. 183.
3 LMA, P74/LUK/3, pp. 2, 65.
4 S. and B. Webb, *Eng. Local Govt* [VII]: *Eng. Poor Law Hist.* pt. 1: *The Old Poor Law* (1927), p. 294; Vestry orders, 1745–71, pp. 136–9.
5 *Chelsea Settlement Examinations 1733–66*, p. xvii.
6 LMA, P74/LUK/93.
7 Vestry orders, 1771–90, f. 85.
8 Ibid., f. 97v.
9 Ibid., 1790–1809, p. 243.
10 Ibid., pp. 394–5.
11 Ibid., p. 407.
12 Vestry mins 1822–33, p. 31.
13 1 & 2 Geo. IV c. 67 (Local and Personal); LMA, P74/LUK/26, pp. 17, 21–3, 247; P74/LUK/27, pp. 18–21, 104, 182, 263–5, 343–5, 469–71.
14 LMA, P74/LUK/26, p. 315.
15 Ibid., p. 304; LMA, P74/LUK/27, p. 503.
16 BL, Sloane MS 4034, f. 67. For the char., above.
17 Vestry orders, 1771–90, f. 87v.; 1809–22, p. 199; Vestry mins 1822–33, p. 15.
18 *Poor Law Abstract, 1804* (Parl. Papers, 1803–4 (175), XIII), p. 297.
19 *Poor Law Abstract, 1818* (Parl. Papers, 1818 (82), XIX), pp. 264–5.
20 Vestry orders, 1809–22, p. 345.
21 *Rep. Com. Poor Laws* (Parl. Papers, 1834 (44), XXXV), p. 86g.
22 LMA, P74/LUK/3, pp. 19, 21, 26–8.
23 Ibid., p. 53; Vestry orders, 1745–71, pp. 4–10, 13, 146, 157.
24 LMA, P74/LUK/4, 22 Jan., 5 Feb., 22 Feb. 1750/1.
25 Vestry orders, 1771–90, f. 68v.
26 Ibid., f. 99v.
27 Ibid., 1790–1809, p. 26.
28 Ibid., p. 296.
29 LMA, P74/LUK/26, pp. 223–4, 262–3.
30 Ibid., p. 309.
31 LMA, P74/LUK/27, pp. 133, 136–7.
32 Ibid., pp. 302–3.

POOR RATES

Unequal assessment for poor rates was a grievance in 1721,[1] and the liability of the Royal Hospital to poor rates remained contentious. In 1721 Quarter Sessions forbade rating of Chelsea pensioners,[2] but after protracted litigation from 1747 the Hospital agreed in 1750 to pay a modus of £100 for its contribution to the poor rate.[3] By 1781 the vestry was complaining of the great cost of invalid soldiers and their families, attracted to the parish by the Hospital, who became dependent on casual relief; the cost was five times the modus, the workhouse had had to be extended, while houses were being left empty to avoid rates. After negotiating with the Hospital and the Paymaster-General and petitioning the county MPs, the vestry reluctantly accepted a grant of £200 in 1783.[4] In 1819 the vestry was using the argument of the burden of outpensioners' families in a petition against the second Sturges Bourne bill.[5]

Rates set by the vestry required magistrates' approval. Evasion of rate assessment by overseers, clerks, and others involved in parish administration provoked the justices' intervention in 1747.[6] In 1748 an overseer complained that he was £100 out of pocket because the JP refused to confirm the rate set;[7] in the same year Quarter Sessions dismissed as frivolous an appeal of 37 inhabitants against the rate,[8] while in 1767 the vestry refused a rate until it had seen overseers' accounts.[9] In the 1750s rates were normally set and due twice a year,[10] but in 1773–4 three small rates were set, apparently in dispute with the overseers.[11] In 1797–8 three rates were voted,[12] and from 1798 rates were set quarterly.[13] In 1786 the vestry compensated an overseer for costs in a parishioner's vexatious action against a distress for rates,[14] but an attempt similarly to compensate a collector in 1824 was declared illegal.[15]

THE LOCAL ACT AND THE PAROCHIAL COMMITTEE

By 1795 growing inequities in the poor-rate assessment were resented and a committee to equalize them was set up, its report being gratefully accepted,[16] but the next year Quarter Sessions supported a petition by Lady Mary Coke against the new assessment.[17] In 1811 it was resolved to apply for a local Act to enable better assessment and collection of rates, and to sell dust and household waste to reduce the highway composition. A committee of the rector, churchwardens, overseers, surveyors, and up to 21 others was to prepare the petition and Bill. In 1812, however, the committee's draft bill was rejected by the vestry and the proposal abandoned. It was revived in 1820, when a committee of 37 was appointed to draft the Bill,[18] which became law in 1821. It provided for a committee of 40 substantial householders, half from each end of the parish, to assess and set poor rates, appoint collectors, manage the workhouse and poor relief, and make bylaws. Becoming known as the Parochial Committee, and normally meeting weekly, they were statutorily re-elected in the spring. The Act also required the annual election of five auditors.[19]

The Act's operation was at first riven by faction, with the committee, despite an energetic start, denouncing the outgoing overseers, whose incompetence and waste were exposed in detail in 1822 by an ad hoc committee, the parochial committee and auditors denouncing one another, and the second committee, elected in 1822, denouncing its predecessor, while considerable bills and arrears of rates accumulated. The parish JPs at petty sessions were unable to receive attestation of the overseers' accounts for 1821–2, and thus no action could be taken at Quarter Sessions. The auditors' report on those accounts did not appear until 1824.[20] In 1823, however, a new committee proclaimed its intention to avoid party strife, and for some years rate assessment, the workhouse, and outrelief were managed systematically and conscientiously. From 1822 the meetings were often chaired by JPs. The committee spent most of its time discussing rate assessments and appeals, on weekly supervision of casual and pensioned poor, and checking accounts and bills; poor rate defaulters' lists were published in 1824.[21] It set up standing subcommittees for finance and for buildings,[22] the former meeting regularly and the latter later known as the workhouse committee.[23] A separate committee to equalize poor rates was appointed in 1823, and one of 25 besides the

1 Cal. Middx Sess. Bk Jan. 1718/19–March 1721/2, p. 109.
2 Ibid., pp. 110–11.
3 Vestry orders, 1745–71, pp. 20, 23, 30–1, 84–9, 91–2, 113–14.
4 Ibid., 1771–90, ff. 62–96.
5 Ibid., 1809–22, p. 344.
6 Cal. Middx Sess. Bk Jan. 1744/5–Dec. 1747, p. 117.
7 Vestry orders, 1745–71, pp. 48–50.
8 Cal. Middx Sess. Bk Jan. 1747/8–Dec. 1751, p. 10.
9 Vestry orders, 1745–71, p. 317.
10 Ibid., pp. 130, 144, 152, 160, 163, 173, 175, 179, 183, 188, 195.
11 Ibid., 1771–90, ff. 15–16v.
12 Ibid., 1790–1809, pp. 134, 142, 147.
13 Ibid., pp. 168, 178–80; 1809–22, pp. 348, 350, 352, 360, 377–8.
14 Ibid., 1771–90, f. 142.
15 Vestry mins 1822–33, pp. 131, 135–6.
16 Vestry orders, 1790–1809, pp. 74–5, 89–90.
17 Ibid., pp. 99–101.
18 Ibid., 1809–22, pp. 56–8, 71–2, 367–9.
19 St Luke Chelsea Poor Rates etc. Act, 1 & 2 Geo. IV, c. 67 (Local and Personal); Faulkner, *Chelsea*, II. 27–8; Vestry orders 1809–22, pp. 386–7, 405; Vestry mins 1822–33, pp. 1, 126–7, 148, 168, 187, 291; LMA, P74/LUK/26, pp. 44 seqq.; S. and B. Webb, *Eng. Local Govt* [I]: *The Par. and the County*, 77–8.
20 *The Times*, 15 March 1824; LMA, P74/LUK/26, pp. 56–7, 69, 75, 78–9, 198–9, 211, 232–3, 239; P74/LUK/27, pp. 176–7; Vestry mins 1822–33, pp. 22–54, 101.
21 LMA, P74/LUK/26, pp. 334–6, 363–6, 402; P74/LUK/27; S. and B. Webb, *Eng. Local Govt* [I]: *The Par. and the County*, 77–8.
22 LMA, P74/LUK/26, p. 361; P74/LUK/27, pp. 481–2.
23 LMA, P74/LUK/28; P74/LUK/29, 1834–5.

officers to revise the system in 1836; it appointed a subcommittee.[1] From 1823 rates were set thrice yearly instead of quarterly.[2] The arrangements of the 1821 Act continued until its repeal in 1841.[3] In 1825 the vestry voted to increase the collectors' poundage from the rates.[4]

POOR RELIEF: COSTS AND RATES

The average monthly cost of maintaining the poor between June 1745 and March 1746 was £35 gross, £34 net; two rates of 1s. in the £ were raised.[5] The cost of maintaining the poor in 1776 was £1,310,[6] and in the three years to Easter 1785 it averaged £1,936.[7] In 1802–3 more than that was spent on out-relief and a further £2,236 in the workhouse.[8] From a peak of £9,188 in 1813–14 expenditure fell, the full poor rate being £7,397 in 1816. The rate then increased yearly to £11,908 in 1820–1. Perhaps because of the effects of the St Luke Chelsea Poor Rates Act it then fell, to £8,316 in 1824, but from 1825 to 1835 it fluctuated between £10,608 (1826) and £15,625 (1832). Actual expenditure on the poor was sharply reduced from £9,000 in 1835 to £6,507 in 1836.[9]

PETTY SESSIONS BEFORE 1837

Petty sessions were held approximately monthly from the 1730s or earlier to the 1760s or later to deal with settlement and bastardy cases; after the workhouse was built they took place there.[10] JPs resided in the parish in 1788,[11] and special sessions were held in the vestry room in 1792, 1794, and 1795 and in the Cadogan Arms in 1796 and 1797 to nominate the overseers, and in Saltero's coffee house in 1796 to nominate highway surveyors.[12] In 1799 two resident JPs confirmed a vestry order to incorporate footpaths.[13] An order of two JPs in 1800 referred to the parochial magistrates,[14] and there were 3 parish magistrates in 1804.[15] Three JPs subscribed to the report of vestry's workhouse committee in 1807 recommending enlarging the infirmary.[16] By 1822 a court of petty sessions could be held in the boardroom of the workhouse,[17] and in 1823 petty sessions were held in the parish to deal with rate defaulters.[18] In 1824 the parishioners recommended 3 magistrates to the Lord Lieutenant to form a petty sessions for the parish, and the parochial committee fitted up a room at the workhouse for the court, held on Tuesdays,[19] and still held weekly in 1825.[20] Weekly sessions there may have lapsed later, since in 1828 the parish magistrates were thanked for establishing them.[21]

LOCAL GOVERNMENT FROM 1837

In 1837 the vestry resolved to petition the House of Lords against the introduction of the Poor Law Amendment Act in Chelsea,[22] but the parish was nevertheless included in Kensington Union that year. By early 1838 the vestry was lobbying against Kensington board of guardians, stating that the existing parish arrangements under the 1821 Act for poor relief were sufficient and seeking to leave the union.[23] By autumn 1838 the parochial committee was able to report that the burden on the poor rates had risen sharply after the guardians assumed management.[24] The vestry petitioned the Poor Law Commissioners for release from the union, but the commissioners refused and set up an investigation into the parish and union finances. Meanwhile the vestry alleged that proxy votes for election of the board of guardians had been misused. There were also allegations of unchristian dissection of paupers' bodies.[25] The investigator's report showed that expenditure strictly on poor relief had been reduced by joining the union,[26] a result disputed by the vestry, which sent a memorial signed by 1,960 ratepayers to demand release from the union. It then proceeded to challenge the legality of the formation

1 Vestry mins 1822–33, pp. 91–2; 1833–9, pp. 122–3, 127.
2 LMA, P74/LUK/27, p. 49.
3 LMA, P74/LUK/28; P74/LUK/29; Chelsea Poor Law & Highway Act, 1841 (Local and Personal), 4 Vic. c 17, s. 50.
4 Vestry mins 1822–33, p. [150].
5 Vestry orders, 1745–71, pp. 4–10.
6 *Rep. Cttee on Returns by Overseers, 1776*, p. 101.
7 *Abstract of Returns by Overseers, 1787*, HC, 1st ser. IX, p. 143.
8 *Poor Law Abstract, 1804* (Parl. Papers, 1803–4 (175), XIII), p. 296.
9 Above; *Poor Law Abstract, 1818* (Parl. Papers, 1818 (82), XIX), p. 264; *Poor Rate Returns, 1816–21* (Parl. Papers, 1822 (556), V), p. 100, Supp. App.; *1822–4* (Parl. Papers, 1825 (334), IV), p. 133, Supp. App.; *1825–9*, (Parl. Papers, 1830–1 (83), XI), p. 117; *1830–4* (Parl. Papers, 1835 (444), XLVII), p. 114; *Poor Law Com. 2nd Rep.* (Parl. Papers, 1836 (595-II), XXIX), pp. 214–15.
10 *Chelsea Settlement Examinations 1733–66, passim*, esp. pp. vii, xi–xiv.
11 Vestry orders, 1771–90, f. 160v.
12 Ibid., 1790–1809, pp. 25, 53, 67, 102, 108, 122.
13 Ibid., 189.
14 Ibid., p. 218.
15 Ibid., p. 295.
16 Ibid., pp. 366–8.
17 Vestry mins 1822–33, p. 101.
18 LMA, P74/LUK/27, p. 24.
19 Ibid., p. 284.
20 Vestry mins 1822–33, p. 149.
21 Ibid., p. 226.
22 Ibid., 1833–9, p. 169.
23 Ibid., p. 197; for the Act, above (local Act).
24 Vestry mins, 1833–9, p. 233.
25 Ibid., pp. 237–65.
26 Ibid., pp. 271–7.

of the union.[1] In 1839 a dispute between guardians and parochial committee over access to the workhouse boardroom led to an alleged riot.[2] Later that year the vestry unsuccessfully petitioned first the Home Secretary for release from the union,[3] and then the Poor Law Commissioners to constitute the parochial committee a board of guardians.[4] A proposal in 1840 to seek an Act to separate Chelsea from the union was defeated after dissension in the vestry,[5] but the Poor Law Commissioners eventually offered to consent to a separation on condition of changes to the local Act.[6] A new Act of 1841 abolished the parochial committee and established a separate board of guardians for Chelsea, with 20 members elected from four wards established for the purpose. The Act vested the workhouse in the board of guardians, made it the rating authority, and also transferred to the surveyors of the highways powers of the parochial committee relating to sale of dust in the old part of the parish.[7]

BOARD OF GUARDIANS

The board elected under the local Act of 1841[8] was subject to the standardized rules of the Metropolitan Poor Act from 1867.[9] Besides the 20 elected members there were seven ex officio by 1890;[10] from 1894 the wards were rearranged to correspond with the new wards used to elect vestrymen, and there were 24 elected guardians, and, in 1900, two co-opted.[11] The board ceased to be a rating authority in 1901,[12] and its remaining functions passed to the LCC when it was abolished in 1929.[13]

The parish's recovery of control of its paupers failed to restrain expenditure. The amount spent on the poor increased from £10,159 in 1840, equivalent to a 1s. 8¾d. rate, to £19,193 in 1850, equivalent to a 2s. 3½d. rate. It was better controlled in the 1850s, standing at £19,663 (1s. 10¾d.) in 1857.[14] That March there were 1,481 poor in the workhouse and 4,481 relieved outside.[15] In 1874–5 such spending was only £12,415, less than in most Middlesex parishes; £9,807 of that was spent on workhouse inmates and £2,608 on outdoor relief.[16] Expenditure on out-relief had been very sharply reduced since 1867, though it crept up again.[17] In 1890 the corresponding figures were £10,662 and £3,102, with a further £5,930 to maintain lunatics, a total little more than the officers' salaries and largely offset by grants from the Metropolitan Common Poor fund. By far the greater part of the board's expenditure then consisted of precepts or charges by other bodies.[18] The cost of the poor thereafter increased; by 1900–1 the corresponding figures were £19,407, £4,286, and £9,851.[19] In 1904–5 Chelsea had 35.4 paupers per 1,000 of population, a higher proportion than Bethnal Green (28.7); in January 1905 there were 1,719 in the workhouse (probably including the infirmary), and 669 relieved outdoors, beside 12 vagrants and 321 lunatics.[20] By 1914–15 in-maintenance had been reduced to £15,686 and out-relief to £1,515, but the cost of keeping the insane in asylums had risen to £11,673, not counting a £23,240 contribution to the Metropolitan Asylum district. Chelsea paid £2,504 to the Metropolitan Common Poor fund but recovered £17,065 from the LCC.[21]

WORKHOUSES

Though the vestry had claimed in 1838 that the old Chelsea workhouse in Arthur Street was 'replete with every convenience and in every respect suitable for the purposes of such an establishment',[22] it was not fit to house all its paupers in 1841, and the board took over the Victorian Asylum at Chiswick, formerly occupied by the Children's Friendly Society, to accommodate women.[23] In 1843–4 it greatly enlarged the workhouse, to the designs of W.G. Colman. A plan for a new east range was abandoned; instead old buildings in the yard were demolished, and a new central range was built from east to west across it, including a new master's house, vagrant ward, and dead house, and abutting an older west range on Arthur Street, which was retained, widened, and modernized. There seems also to have been a short east cross-wing.[24] A further enlargement, voted in 1849, was designed by William Hudson and built in 1850. The east wing was heightened and

1 Vestry mins, 1833–9, pp. 282–5, 299–309; 1839–43, p. 2.
2 Ibid., 1839–43, pp. 1, 12, 18.
3 Ibid., pp. 39–44.
4 Ibid., pp. 70–5.
5 Ibid., pp. 122–33.
6 Ibid., pp. 165–71.
7 Ibid., pp. 168–90; Chelsea Poor Law & Highway Act, 4 Vic. c. 17 (Local and Personal).
8 Above.
9 J.F.B. Firth, *Municipal London* (1876), 480–1; *London Gaz.* 11 May 1875, p. 2516; 20 Feb. 1877, pp. 840–51.
10 *Vestry Rep. 1889–90*, pp. xxiii–xxiv.
11 *Vestry Rep. 1894–5*, 1–2; *Vestry Rep. 1899–1900*, pp. xviii–xix; G.L. Gomme, *London in the Reign of Victoria (1837–1897)* (1898), 196; below, metropolitan vestry.
12 Below, metropolitan borough.
13 *Ann. Rep. of Council of MB of Chelsea 1929–30*, pp. xiv–xv.
14 *Poor Rates etc. (Metropolitan Districts)* (Parl. Papers, 1857–8 (208), XLIX(1)), pp. 4–5.
15 *Return relating to Medical Poor Relief in Eng. and Wales* (Parl. Papers, 1857–8 (230), XLIX(1)), pp. 2–3.
16 *Poor Law Expenditure 1874 and 1875* (Parl. Papers, 1876 (277), LXIII), p. 5.
17 LMA, CHBG 212/001.
18 *Vestry Rep. 1889–90*, 218–19.
19 *1st Rep. of Council of MB of Chelsea 1900–1*, 176.
20 LCC, *London Statistics*, XVI (1905–6), pp. 70, 74.
21 *15th Rep. of Council of MB of Chelsea 1914–15*, 146.
22 Vestry mins, 1833–9, p. 243.
23 *The Times*, 4 Aug. 1841.
24 J. Wright, *London and its Environs* (1848); LMA, CHBG 001, p. 38; CHBG 002, pp. 274, 303, 312, 349–50, 357, 417–8, 481, 604, 613, 632, 635; CHBG 003, pp. 3, 7, 21, 25–6, 36, 42–3, 47, 55, 62–3, 74, 80, 82, 86–9, 100, 117, 124, 173, 175, 185–6, 194, 205, 252, 257, 261, 263, 269, 284, 312, 340–1, 344–5, 349, 351, 369, 382, 400; NMR, file 101061, extracts from the *Builder* index, 24 Aug. 1844.

lengthened to make a new men's dormitory; a young men's dayroom was added; the women's (probably the west) wing was extended south to the burial ground. The additions allowed the guardians to introduce the statutory classification and segregation of paupers by sex, age, and sanity.[1] From 1860 to 1865, prompted by complaints of inadequate accommodation for imbeciles, the guardians extensively reconstructed the workhouse to the designs of G.C. Handford. In 1860–1 the north-west wing along Arthur Street was completely rebuilt and extended north to Britten Street. The south-west wing had to be propped up because of dry rot, and in 1864–5 it was rebuilt. The guardians also decided on a southward extension to the east wing, completed in 1865. Extensions to the north-east wing were also planned.[2] The resulting workhouse had an **H**-plan with two long wings extending north-south the whole length of the site.[3] An infirmary, later St Luke's Hospital, was built on a site north of Britten Street in 1872 and repeatedly extended; it was joined to the workhouse by a subway under the road.[4] In 1881 the Local Government Board authorized the purchase of adjoining land to the east to enlarge the workhouse. The new buildings in Britten Street, designed by A. & C. Harston and built 1881–3, included a block for able-bodied men and workshops, and a stoneyard.[5] It was decided to build south to King's Road, where the guardians rented no. 250 for demolition.[6] Two blocks also designed by Harstons were built east of the burial ground in 1882–3 to accommodate old men, a boardroom, and offices.[7] The southern block, still standing in 2001, of yellow stock brick with emphatic grey-brick bands, comprised basement and four main storeys, of double depth, with a short wing at the west end and three main bays. Following further acquisitions of adjoining houses in Robert (later Sydney) Street,[8] a grandiose plan of 1895 by M.J. Lansdell & E.J. Harrison to rebuild almost the entire workhouse on a different alignment[9] was abandoned, but part of it, involving eastward extensions of the 1883 blocks as far as Sydney Street to house aged women and infirm women, was carried out from 1903 to 1905 at a cost of over £41,000.[10] The southern extension, still standing in 2001, of basement and four main storeys, was mainly of plain stock brick but had what the Local Government Board described as an elaborate elevation to Sydney Street, designed to obtain architectural effect and involving unnecessary outlay which was not justified by the result.[11] The elevation, Baroque in style, was in red brick with stone dressings, having flanking twin towers. Other alterations included work on a block in Arthur Street, apparently split from the old master's house.[12] The workhouse passed in 1929 to the LCC, became known as the Chelsea Institution, and was apparently administered as part of St Luke's hospital. It was demolished in the 1970s[13] except for the south-eastern block on Sydney Street, which survived in 2001.

The board itself met at the workhouse.[14] New offices in King's Road, south of the workhouse, were built as part of the 1883 extensions. Of red brick with Portland stone dressings, they had two storeys over a basement and three bays with a central shaped dormer gable, and a front door at the west end.[15] They were extended eastwards to Sydney Street in 1903–5, to designs by Lansdell and Harrison, and included a boardroom. The extension was also of three bays in red brick with stone dressings, and had a central entrance surmounted by the borough arms, and at the east end of the south front a large bay window, surmounted by a brick pedimented gable topped by an aedicule with an inscription. A new boardroom had been planned in 1895 for the façade wing of the adjoining ward block but it seems not to have been so used.[16] In 1929 the offices passed with the workhouse to the LCC, which had by 1960 leased part to the Polytechnic School of Chiropody. The LCC's proposal to demolish the structure failed.[17] After an

1 LMA, CHBG 007, pp. 575, 588, 605, 617, 623–4, 631, 670; CHBG 008, pp. 10, 18, 53, 64, 89, 98–9, 150, 178, 186, 196–7, 201, 214, 225–6, 243–4, 259, 289–90, 302, 444, 591, 598, 644, 670, 711–12; NMR, file 101061, extracts from the *Builder* index, 24 Nov. 1849.

2 LMA, CHBG 015, pp. 139, 177–8, 199–200, 291–2, 318–19, 352, 367–8, 406–7, 417, 425, 468, 476, 489, 539, 559, 579, 597, 601, 613, 620, 673, 693–4; CHBG 016 [part paginated, part foliated], pp. 58, 86, 124, 129, 133, 148, 167, 223, 300–1; ff. 383, 384, 395, 400–1, 406, 409; pp. 447, 456, 467–8, 483, 553–4; CHBG 017, p. 711; CHBG 018, pp. 55, 136, 181, 207, 208, 237, 270, 281–4, 192, 311, 313, 334, 403, 411, 424–5, 452–3, 478, 502–3, 511, 518, 522, 561, 572; CHBG 019, pp. 19, 25–6, 27, 37, 47, 59, 85–6, 104, 110–11, 138, 150, 178, 182, 224, 226, 235, 271, 290, 299, 325, 346, 368–9, 531, 578, 619–20; NMR, file 101061, extracts from the *Builder* index, 31 March 1860, 23 Jan. 1864, 16 Sep. 1865.

3 OS Map 1/2,500, London sheet LIII (1865).

4 LMA, CHBG 026, p. 437; below, pub. svces (medical).

5 LMA, CHBG 030, pp. 286, 585; CHBG 031, p. 438; CHBG 162, plan; PRO, MH 14/7, Chelsea 47028/81.

6 LMA, CHBG 030, p. 745; CHBG 031, pp. 75–6.

7 LMA, CHBG 162, plan; CHBG 030, pp. 622, 726; CHBG 031, pp. 25–6, 518; PRO, MH 14/7, Chelsea 47028/81.

8 LMA, CHBG 031, pp. 75–6; CHBG 040, p. 367.

9 LMA, CHBG 040, pp. 118, 367; PRO, MH 14/47, Lansdell & Harrison drawings.

10 LMA, CHBG 047, pp. 269, 279, 294, 323, 338, 343–4, 410–11, 427–8, 437, 439; CHBG 048, pp. 43, 60, 92, 139, 310, 313, 336, 423, 436; CHBG 049, pp. 76, 98, 277, 314, 318, 349, 376, 408; *Builder*, 29 Nov. 1902, 509; 18 April 1903, 418.

11 LMA, CHBG 046, pp. 443.

12 *Builder*, 18 April 1903, 418; LMA, CHBG 048, pp. 355, 401.

13 *Chelsea Soc. Rep.* (1960), 20; below, pub. svces (medical).

14 LMA, CHBG 001, p. 1. *The Times*, 4 Aug. 1841, states apparently wrongly that it first met at the old vestry room.

15 Beaver, *Memorials*, 321; foundation stone on pilaster; PRO, MH 14/7, Chelsea 47028/81; LMA, CHBG 162, plan; CHBG 031, pp. 66, 78, 91–2, 105, 163, 170, 198, 449, 523; see Fig. 67.

16 *Builder*, 18 April 1903, 418; foundation stone on bldg; LMA, CHBG 048, pp. 338, 355; CHBG 162; PRO, MH 14/47, Lansdell & Harrison drawings.

17 *Chelsea Soc. Rep.* (1960), 20.

67. *Board of Guardians' offices, no. 250 King's Road: western section built 1883, extended to Sydney Street 1903–5*

award-winning conversion in 1998,[1] the building and the surviving ward block behind it were in use as private offices and galleries in 2001, and various small shops and a noodle bar occupied the garden area and basement in between.

Proposed casual wards in Milman's Street, considered in 1888,[2] were still being opposed by the public and the elected guardians in 1893,[3] but seem to have been built by 1895.[4] At some time after 1879 the guardians bought Fairfield House, Lower Tooting (Surrey), as a branch workhouse, and extended it in, and probably before, 1894.[5] They sold it in 1906.[6]

IMPROVEMENT COMMISSIONERS

In 1844 the vestry decided to frame a Bill to obtain extra powers of paving, repairing, and lighting the old part of the parish:[7] the Improvement Act, passed in 1845, excluded the district of Hans Town. For the rest it replaced the existing boards of highway surveyors and lighting inspectors with a board of improvement commissioners, of whom 45 were to be elected by rate-payers by thirds, and 5 appointed by the lord of the manor and owners of four large freeholds. They had powers to levy rates, to make, pave, clean, water, and drain streets, collect waste, and deal with nuisances, and to appoint staff including a treasurer and a clerk.[8] The commissioners, first elected in August 1845, began work energetically that autumn, meeting, at first in St Luke's vestry room, later in the boardroom at the workhouse, far more often than the monthly minimum.[9] Later they occupied a building in King's Road known as the Manor House.[10] Despite their early energy, by the time they were abolished under the Metropolis Management Act, 1855, they had still not brought the standard of services in most of the parish up to those in Hans Town.[11]

THE VESTRY TO 1855

Chelsea vestry remained open after the changes of 1837–1845 had reduced its powers. It seems to have met at first in the old vestry room, perhaps the vestry room mentioned until 1846, but thereafter in the vestry room at the east end of St Luke's.[12] In the late 1830s, besides regular elections of officers its business consisted mainly of its feud with the Kensington Union board of guardians, sorting out the damage caused by a venal vestry clerk, and highway matters.[13] In the early 1840s it gave considerable attention to monitoring the work of its highways and lighting boards, and to a dispute with the Metropolitan Turnpike Trust over King's Road and the removal of turnpike gates.[14] Especially after 1845, it spent time on partisan lobbying over national legislation, usually acting from a radical or Whig viewpoint.[15] It attacked the corn laws, though the most trenchant motions on the subject were rejected.[16] Motions, and elections of officers, still sometimes spawned polls attracting numerous voters: for example nearly 900 votes were cast in electing the highway board in 1845,[17] and 600 on a motion to make a road in 1847.[18] The election for churchwardens was disputed in 1841, when 592 voted; for the next ten years they were elected

1 Plaque on E. wall of bldg.
2 PRO, MH 14/7, Chelsea 88931/88.
3 *The Times*, 4 Jan. 1893.
4 LMA, CHBG 040, pp. 118, 162; PRO, MH 14/72.
5 *PO Dir. London* (1879), not mentioning it; PRO, MH 14/7, Chelsea 22107/94; *Kelly's Dir. London* (1902), 3073.
6 PRO, MH 14/47, L.G.B.O. 49,308, 20 Feb. 1906.
7 Vestry mins, 1843–56, p. 28.
8 8 & 9 Vic. c. 143 (Local and Personal).
9 Improvement com. mins, 1845–6, 1846–8.
10 *Vestry Rep.* 1856–7, 4. Not the original man. ho. (above, Landownership, Chelsea man.) nor that in Smith Street used as consumption hosp. (below, pub. svces (medical)), but perhaps near the Manor House Bath Gardens (below, pub. svces (baths)).
11 Above, Hans Town commissioners; below, pub. svces.
12 Vestry mins, 1843–56, pp. 38–68; cf. ibid., 1839–43, pp. 94, 111.
13 Above; Vestry mins, 1833–9, pp. 140 sqq.; 1839–43, pp. 1–90, 127, 129.
14 Vestry mins, 1839–43, pp. 145–289; 1843–56, pp. 1–29.
15 Ibid., 1839–43, pp. 41–7, 257–60; 1843–56, pp. 104–8, 206–7.
16 Ibid., 1839–43. pp. 215–16.
17 Ibid., 1843–56, pp. 41–3.
18 Ibid., pp. 80–2.

undisputed, but as many as 1,454 voted in an election in 1851.[1]

There were still 3 beadles in 1843, reduced to 2 by 1845; from 1840 or earlier to 1878 they were sworn as constables.[2] In 1879 the number of beadles was reduced to one, sworn as constable until 1891. From 1892 the beadle was merely 'beadle of the Old Church' and from 1895 ceased to be considered a parish official.[3]

METROPOLITAN VESTRY

On 1 January 1856 the functions of the improvement commissioners and Hans Town commissioners, and the next year those of the open vestry, passed to a metropolitan vestry elected under the Metropolis Local Management Act, with powers for paving, lighting, watering, cleansing, building and maintaining sewers and drains, and nuisance removal and public health. The parish was divided into four wards, electing altogether 60 vestrymen: Stanley in the south-west (9 vestrymen), Church in the centre (18), Royal Hospital in the south-east (12), and Hans Town, covering the north-east of the main part of the parish and Kensal Town and electing 21 vestrymen. The ward boundaries seem to have been different from those used for electing guardians under the 1841 Act. The rector and churchwardens were ex officio members of the vestry. Each ward had an auditor. The vestry elected the parish's representative on the Metropolitan Board of Works.[4] In 1894 the wards were increased to five and the number of vestrymen reduced to fifty. Stanley ward had 12, Church and Cheyne (formerly Church) ward 15, Royal Hospital Ward 9, and Hans Town ward 12, the same as Kensal Town ward, newly separated from it.[5]

The vestry in 1855 immediately resolved to appoint six officers (clerk, treasurer, surveyor, inspector of nuisances, foreman of the roads, and messenger) and by 1856 had a medical officer of health.[6] By 1864 there were also a food analyst, a hallkeeper, and two assistant clerks.[7] In 1878 the staff had shrunk by one, but after the retirement of the first vestry clerk in 1879 extra assistants were appointed[8] and by 1889 the staff had more than doubled.[9] By 1856–7 four main committees (works, bylaws, finance, and improvements) had been set up; they and the vestry met 130 times that year.[10] By 1888 there were 13 committees, reduced in 1889–90 to ten.[11] In its last year, 1899–1900, the vestry met 26 times and its ten committees and 3 subcommittees 106 times.[12]

The vestry was not a rating authority and obtained its revenue mainly by precept on the board of guardians.[13] Its total expenditure more than doubled from £15,905 in 1857–8 to £31,744 in 1865–6 and £37,196 in 1872–3. At first the main objects were those inherited from the improvement commissioners – paving, lighting, cleansing, watering, and local sewers – but by 1865–6 the MBW took nearly a third of the total.[14] An informed observer criticized the vestry in the mid 1870s for failing to appoint more inspectors of nuisances even though a third of the houses visited by the inspector required notice.[15]

In 1866 an active ratepayers' association met weekly and was said to monitor the vestry's activities closely. Although there was 'rivalry' in every ward, none had been contested at the last election. The vestrymen were mainly shopkeepers and tradesmen, who were anxious to serve.[16] In the early 1880s the vestry's decisions were almost always unanimous; divisions do not seem to have been consistently on party lines.[17]

METROPOLITAN BOROUGH

A draft report of the LCC's subcommittee for the completion of schemes of local government, leaked in 1890, proposed the merger of Chelsea with Kensington. Although only a draft, the suggestion aroused strong local protests. The vestry opposed it unanimously, and in June organized a public meeting at Queen's Park hall under Sir Charles Dilke's chairmanship, which passed a resolution against it. The strength of the opposition was probably what preserved Chelsea's independence under the 1899 London Government Act.[18] The vestry resolved in 1895 to seek incorporation should any other London parish achieve that.[19]

In 1900 the parish became a metropolitan borough, though Kensal Town (ironically including the site of the 1890 meeting) was excluded and there were minor adjustments to the boundaries of the main part of the parish.[20] Besides taking over the metropolitan vestry's functions and officers, the borough council replaced the board of guardians as the rating authority from 1901.

1 Vestry mins, 1839–43, pp. 207, 210, 246, 275; 1843–56, pp. 11, 38–9, 70, 85–7, 99–100, 118–19, 137–8, 168–9, 171.
2 Chelsea Misc. 849–851; *Vestry Rep. 1878–9*, 65.
3 *Vestry Rep. 1879–80*, 76; *1891–2*, p. xxvii; *1892–3*, p. xxvii; *1895–6*, pp. xxi sqq.
4 *London Gaz.* 20 Oct. 1855, 3888–90; *Vestry Rep. 1856–7*, 3–5, 9–12; *1857–8*, 4, 5, 18–19; Vestry mins, 1839–43, pp. 188–90; 1843–56, pp. 225–36; Firth, *Municipal London*, 300–1; above.
5 *Vestry Rep. 1894–5*, 1–2.
6 Vestry mins, 1843–56, pp. 238–43; *Vestry Rep. 1856–7*, 12.
7 *Ret. of property and no. of officers in each Par.* (Parl. Papers, 1864 (379), L), p. 30.
8 *Vestry Rep. 1879–80*, 14, 44.
9 *Vestry Rep. 1889–90*, pp. xviii–xix.
10 *Vestry Rep. 1856–7*, 5, 13.
11 *Vestry Rep. 1889–90*, 9 and App. 1.
12 *Vestry Rep. 1899–1900*, App. 1.
13 Ibid., 24.
14 *2nd Rep. Sel. Cttee on Metropolitan Local Govt* (Parl. Papers, 1866 (452), XIII), p. 276; Firth, *Municipal London*, 318–19.
15 Firth, *Municipal London*, 312–13.
16 *2nd Rep. Sel. Cttee Metropolitan Local Govt* (Parl. Papers, 1866 (452), XII), pp. 43–4, 148.
17 e.g. *Vestry Mins, 1881–2*, esp. pp. 24, 39.
18 J. Davis, *Reforming London: the London Government Problem, 1855–1900* (Oxford, 1988), 129–31; *Vestry Rep. 1889–90*, 2–3; *The Times*, 9, 18 June, 1 Oct. 1890.
19 Davis, *Reforming London*, 205.
20 *Vestry Rep. 1899–1900*, 125 sqq. , reproducing Boro. of Chelsea Order, 1900; above, Intro.

68. ARMS OF THE METROPOLITAN BOROUGH OF CHELSEA
Gules within a cross voided or a crozier in pale or in the first quarter a winged bull statant in the second a lion rampant regardant both argent in the third a sword point downwards proper pommel and hilt or between two boars' heads couped at the neck argent and in the fourth a stag's head caboched or [Granted 1903]

There were to be 36 councillors for five wards: Stanley and Hans Town wards had 9 each, and Church, Cheyne, and Royal Hospital wards 6 each. There were 6 aldermen. The internal boundaries between wards were substantially those of 1894.[1] Stanley ward was divided into North and South Stanley wards in 1949, and each of the six wards thereafter had six councillors.[2]

The first council elections returned 23 Moderates (conservatives) to 12 Progressives and one Independent.[3] The 5th Earl Cadogan was elected the first mayor. After a slight swing to the Progressives in 1903, the conservative grip steadily strengthened, the Municipal Reformers gaining control of all seats in 1912, with no contests in two wards.[4] A few Liberals were elected after the First World War, and a few Labour councillors in 1945. Nevertheless Municipal Reformers before 1939, and Conservatives after 1945, continued to control the council, and in 1963 the 7th Earl Cadogan was elected its last mayor.[5]

Arms and Insignia. The borough council noted in 1901 that it had no civic regalia and accepted the offer of a mace and mayor's chain from Earl Cadogan.[6] A coat of arms, designed in 1902, was granted in 1903.[7]

TOWN HALLS

Vestry Hall

The first four meetings of the metropolitan vestry were held at St Luke's vestry room, but conflict with church uses brought a move to the improvement commissioners' Manor House, King's Road.[8] The vestry decided in 1856 to build a vestry hall for a total cost of £3,500, and in 1857 to acquire a leasehold of part of Manor Terrace on the south side of King's Road, opposite Robert Street, where Lord Cadogan was willing to give the freehold.[9] The premises were to contain the hallkeeper's

69. *The new Vestry Hall in 1859. The doorway* (left rear) *may be incorporated within later buildings on site*

1 CL, Vestry file, notice of Nov. 1900; *1st Rep. Council MB of Chelsea 1900–1*, pp. ix–x, 176; *2nd Rep. 1901–2*, 35; *Vestry Rep. 1899–1900*, 127 sqq., reproducing Borough of Chelsea (Councillors and Wards) Order, 1900; above, metropolitan vestry.

2 *Census*, 1961; LCC, *London Statistics*, NS, I (1945–54), 20, table 9 note (e).

3 S. Knott, *The Electoral Crucible: the Politics of London 1900–1914* [1977], 68.

4 Knott, *Electoral Crucible*, 82, 94, 110, 122; *The Times*, 2 Nov. 1912; Pearman, *Cadogan Est.* 110.

5 CL, Card cat. 'Elections: Borough: Balance of Parties'; Gerald Rhodes, *The Govt of London: The Struggle for Reform* (1970), 236; *The Times*, 21 Nov. 1963; Pearman, *Cadogan Est.* 110.

6 *The Times*, 25 July 1901.

7 Ibid., 11 Oct. 1902; C.W. Scott-Giles, *Civic Heraldry* (1953 edn), 248–9; *Civic Heraldry of England and Wales-London, county of (Obsolete)*, via web site (www.civicheraldry.co.uk), consulted 5 Feb. 2002; see Fig. 68.

8 *Vestry Rep. 1856–7*, 4; above, improvement commrs.

9 *Vestry Rep. 1857–8*, 64–5.

apartment, cellarage, and a fire-proof store room; offices for the clerk, the surveyor, and the medical officer; committee rooms, and at the rear a hall about 24 feet square. There was a much-criticized and finally abortive competition for the design in 1858.[1] The executed building, with a five-bayed façade on King's Road, was begun in 1859 and completed in 1860. Designed by William Willmer Pocock and built by Piper & Sons, it was of brick, in a neo-Jonesian Italianate style. It had rusticated stone dressings, and a porch with rusticated columns; the first-floor windows had eared surrounds and were surmounted by alternate triangular and segmental pediments. The whole was topped by a balustrade with urns. There appears to have been a plain brick rear wing. The total cost was £12,000.[2] From the first, the hall was used for commercial lettings.[3]

Allegedly because of frost damage following the builder's bankruptcy, the hall walls went askew and by 1885 the building had been pronounced unsafe. The vestry decided to build a new hall and offices behind the old, completed in 1886 to the designs of J.M. Brydon and built by Charles Wall. The extension, much bigger than the original building, faced south to Manor Gardens (later Chelsea Manor Gardens), although it had entrances from King's Road. It included a hall 81 ft by 45 ft, a secondary hall west of it, and committee rooms to the east. Built of brick with stone dressings in a superficially Palladian layout but with Queen Anne detailing, the south façade placed the pedimented hall between two lower ranges.[4] The interior of the hall was decorated with murals showing Chelsea's contribution to history and culture; one panel included a portrait of Oscar Wilde, removed in 1914 after political pressure.[5]

Old Town Hall

In 1903 the borough council appointed a town hall extension committee,[6] which met jointly with a committee to reconstruct the adjoining public baths.[7] In 1904 it recommended an extension on the east side of the vestry hall and apparently the removal of the public baths, which adjoined on the east, to the west side of the site,[8] but appears to have abandoned that scheme soon after. Leonard Stokes was appointed architect for the town hall, and Wills & Anderson were appointed for the baths.[9] A.N. Coles of Plymouth's tender of £21,091 for the building was accepted in 1906.[10] Stokes's surreptitious attempt to include a dome was sternly suppressed.[11] The extension, which replaced the original vestry hall of 1860 but retained the 1886 building to its south, provided extra offices and was completed in 1908. Of brick with stone dressings, it faces north to King's Road and has concave corners with boldly rusticated quoins, three-bay pedimented ends with tetrastyle columns, and 9 bays in between, all in an allegedly 'Renaissance' style. A clock projecting into King's Road was and remained in 2001 a prominent feature. The granite plinth had an inscription, in 1908 as in 2001 barely legible, which cost nine times the estimate.[12] The

70. *Chelsea Town Hall, King's Road*

1 *The Builder*, XVI (1858), 706, 781, 804, 838, 849–51.

2 *Vestry Rep. 1858–9*, 59–64; *1859–60*, 103–7; *1860–1*, 66, 73; *The Times*, 13 Dec. 1859, 1 Dec. 1860; CL, Vestry Hall folder, photograph file print no. L/6770; see Fig. 69.

3 *Vestry Rep. 1860–1*, 66–7.

4 *Vestry Rep. 1885–6*, 11–13, 248, 252–4, and app. 39; *Encyclopaedia Britannica* (11th edn), II. 435 (showing inscription not as built); inscription on frieze.

5 *The Times*, 14 May 1914; *Chelsea Soc. Rep.* (1966), 31–2.

6 *Chelsea BC Mins 1903–4*, 351.

7 Ibid., 594–5.

8 Ibid., 638–9; below, pub. svces (baths).

9 *Chelsea BC Mins 1904–5*, 48, 228, 230.

10 *Chelsea BC Mins 1905–6*, 554; *The Times*, 6 Nov. 1908.

11 *Chelsea BC Mins 1906–7*, 389; see Fig. 70.

12 Inscribed stone on plinth; *Chelsea BC Mins 1907–8*, 217, 471; *1908–9*, 186, 284, 434, 441–2; *The Times*, 6 Nov. 1908.

Old Town Hall became the main Chelsea branch library in 1978,[1] and was still standing in 2003.

LONDON BOROUGH OF KENSINGTON AND CHELSEA

The scheme for uniting Kensington and Chelsea was briefly revived in 1945 and as soon scotched.[2] In 1958 the borough council argued strongly to the Herbert commission for the retention of its boundaries and increase of its powers,[3] and a scheme to merge Chelsea with south Kensington and south Fulham was floated.[4] Nevertheless the commission proposed that it merge with Kensington, and in 1963 the London Government Act confirmed that.[5] Resistance in Chelsea concentrated on retaining its name as part of that of the merged borough, against the wishes of the government, with shoppers queuing up in the King's Road to sign petitions. The demand met with success and the new authority was from 1965 the Royal Borough of Kensington and Chelsea.[6] Chelsea had 14 councillors and retained its six wards within its old boundaries, although there were plans in 1999 to alter them; the number of councillors for those wards had apparently been reduced to 13 by 2002. The new borough continued to be Conservative-controlled.[7] With the immediate building of a new town hall in Kensington, its administrative centre moved outside Chelsea.[8] A coat of arms was granted in 1965.[9]

71. ARMS OF THE ROYAL BOROUGH OF KENSINGTON AND CHELSEA
Gules a mitre or, on a chief ermine, three crowns also or [Granted 1965]

PUBLIC SERVICES

PUBLIC ORDER

In 1658 an assessment for erecting a cage was confirmed.[10] The cage, stocks, and ducking stool once stood in Lordship Yard (off Lawrence Street), part of the old manor house; by 1682 they had been moved to the riverside near the church, but constituted a public nuisance and were to be moved back. In 1705 Lord Cheyne was amerced for not maintaining them.[11] A suspected burglar, lodged at the headborough's house rather than in the cage near by, murdered a servant and escaped in 1754.[12] The cage, on the riverside opposite the old church,[13] still stood in 1816.[14]

A constable and a headborough were mentioned in the late 1740s; in 1762 theirs were certainly separate offices. From 1769 two headboroughs are sometimes recorded.[15] There were several constables by 1800, when their duties included preventing squibs and crackers being thrown on 5 November.[16] In 1802 several constables dispersed a mob assembled to watch two pitched battles on Chelsea common one Sunday.[17] From 1798 the duties of the two beadles, the second being for Hans Town, included preserving order and apprehending offenders.[18]

In 1728 the inhabitants offered a reward for information on robberies,[19] and in the 1750s raised subscriptions for the apprehension of highwaymen, footpads,

1 Below, pub. svces (pub. libs).
2 *The Times*, 4 July 1945; *Chelsea Soc. Rep.* (1945), 17.
3 *Royal Com. on Loc. Govt in Greater London: Mins of Evidence* (HMSO 1959), II. 65–89; *Royal Com. on Local Govt in Greater London: Written Evidence from Local Authorities, Misc. Bodies and Priv. Individuals*, I (HMSO 1962), 156–172.
4 *Chelsea Soc. Rep.* (1960), 17; Rhodes, *Govt of London*, 149–50.
5 Rhodes, *Govt of London*, 93, 256.
6 *The Times*, 7 Oct. 1963, et seqq.; Rhodes, *Govt of London*, 201.
7 *The Times*, 9 May 1964, 4 May 1974, 6 May 1978; *Chelsea Soc. Rep.* (1999), 10; CL, card cat., Elections, 'Elections, Council, May 1974'; C.T. Husbands, 'The London Council Elections of 6 May 1982', *London Jnl*, VIII(2) (1982), 177–90; *Mun. Year Bk.* (2002), I. 542–3.
8 *The Times*, 23 Nov. 1964, 4 Feb. 1966.
9 *Civic Heraldry of England and Wales: Greater London*, via website (www.civicheraldry.co.uk), consulted 5 Feb. 2002; *Boutell's Heraldry*, ed. J.P. Brooke-Little (1983 edn), 288; see Fig. 71.
10 LMA, Brentford Petty Sess. Cal. 1651–1714, p. 23.
11 Beaver, *Memorials*, 86.
12 Chelsea Misc. 1091.
13 Chelsea Misc. 1682.
14 Vestry orders, 1809–22, p. 201.
15 Ibid., 1745–71, pp. 5, 48, 259, 330.
16 Ibid., 1790–1809, p. 218.
17 *The Times*, 8 April 1802.
18 Vestry orders, 1790–1809, pp. 148–67.
19 Chelsea Misc. 1091.

burglars, and robbers.[1] In 1771 such a reward was offered after a notorious robbery at Elizabeth Hutchins's farmhouse in King's Road.[2] Rewards in 1793 aimed to prevent, as well as punish, offences. They were to be paid out of the church rate,[3] but in 1800, as a vestry considered them illegal, they were to be discontinued. However, in 1802 the churchwardens were again to reward the apprehension of offenders.[4] In 1833 the parochial committee offered a reward following a murder.[5]

In 1668 the inhabitants of Chelsea and St Martin-in-the-Fields were ordered jointly, as before, to keep constant watch at the Stone bridge for thieves.[6] In 1692 Chelsea was to set sufficient watches for the safety of inhabitants and travellers.[7] Two watchmen at Chelsea were almost killed in a housebreaking in 1706.[8] In 1712 inhabitants apparently obtained a watch at Little Chelsea, which was remote from those provided by Kensington and Chelsea.[9] At the Royal Hospital pensioners manned the guardhouses, preserved order, and closed the gates at night. They were assisted in 1810 by Bow Street officers. In 1715, at the request of Chelsea inhabitants, the Hospital was ordered to form a patrol of pensioners, who manned sentry boxes on the road to St James's. In 1783, to prevent robberies which were occurring at an alarming rate, their number was increased. The patrol ceased to function in the early 19th century. In 1781 the Hospital agreed to contribute towards watchmen for the road round Burton's Court.[10] Armed patrols on the roads from Ranelagh were advertised in 1769; these, and a guard at the back of the Royal Hospital, were paid for by the proprietors of the pleasure grounds, and comprised Hospital pensioners.[11] Although the inhabitants were in 1771 reportedly determined to procure an Act to settle a watch,[12] none was passed and ad hoc arrangements continued. In 1794 the vestry would only countenance an increase in tolls on the Hyde Park and Kensington turnpikes if the trustees would undertake to light and watch the parish's streets, but in the event proceeded no further, fearing additional expense. In 1798 the watchman of Lindsey Row (later part of Cheyne Walk), although armed with a sword, was assaulted by drunks, whom the vestry required to acknowledge their offence by a newspaper advertisement.[13] Private nightwatchmen on King's Road supplemented the day-time activities of the constables.[14] In 1809 inhabitants were not to illuminate their houses for George III's jubilee year, to avoid 'riot and disturbance'. The vestry resolved in 1811 to raise a subscription and form an association to prevent the many crimes against property and the person,[15] and in 1812 a committee duly proposed night patrols to supplement the regular watchmen.[16] The vestry opposed the inclusion of the parish in a Bill for regulating the nightly watch out of concern for the rates, and in 1816 considered it an inauspicious time for expensive innovation in parish government, including watching, resisting a proposal for further legislation. In 1817, in response to the disturbed state of the metropolis, the vestry solicited inhabitants' enrolment as special constables.[17]

In 1811 rooms for a watchman were to be built adjoining the chapel in the new burial ground, which had its own watchman; payments were made in 1819 for his pistols and his dog. A watchbox was made when the chapel was demolished in 1825. By 1828 there were two watchmen.[18] Watchboxes there remained in the 1830s.[19] In 1822 the appointment of a parish watchhouse keeper was allegedly unnecessary, as the beadles and constables had 'little or nothing to do'; apparently none was appointed.[20] In 1824 soldiers drinking in Hans Town caused an affray which 15 watchmen and two constables could not contain; help was summoned from Knightsbridge barracks.[21] At that period Kensington turnpike trust had arranged patrols on the Fulham Road for several years.[22] An Act of 1826[23] empowered trustees to watch the newly-built districts of eastern Chelsea. In 1828 15 constables and 4 headboroughs were employed by day in Chelsea, with a serjeant of the watch and his assistant in charge of 30 watchmen by night; there were also 27 private patrolmen at night. One watchhouse accommodated the night watch.[24] Hans Town's Local Act empowered commissioners to appoint watchmen,[25] and in 1829 its streets were better watched than the old part of the parish where some inhabitants paid private watchmen.[26] In 1811 there was a watchhouse in Symons Street, still standing in 1852.[27]

1 Beaver, *Memorials*, 52; Chelsea Scraps, 15.
2 Vestry orders, 1771–90, f. 5; Faulkner, *Chelsea*, II. 18–23.
3 Vestry orders, 1790–1809, p. 44, also pp. 62–3, 117, 176–7.
4 Ibid., pp. 221, 272–3.
5 Vestry mins, 1833–9, p. 19.
6 Cal. Middx Sess. Bks, V. 59; E. of Royal Hosp.: above, Intro., comms.
7 *Middx County Rec. Sess. Bks 1689–1709*, 87.
8 HMC 6, *7th Rep., Verney*, p. 506.
9 *Survey of London*, XLI. 162.
10 Dean, *Royal Hosp.* 73, 111, 140–1, 196–8, 231.
11 Faulkner, *Chelsea*, II. 314, 354.
12 Chelsea cuttings: street lighting (TS note from *General Evening Post*, 22/25 June 1771).
13 Vestry orders, 1790–1809, pp. 48, 59, 169–72.
14 Bryan, *Chelsea*, 169.
15 Vestry orders, 1809–22, pp. 18–19, 67–9.
16 Beaver, *Memorials*, 315.
17 Vestry orders, 1809–22, pp. 77–8, 86–8, 208–10, 225–6.
18 LMA, P74/LUK/274, pp. 44, 133, 154, 191, 200, and insert pp. 211–12.
19 Chelsea Misc. 837.
20 Chelsea Scraps, 316; Vestry mins, 1822–33, p. 55.
21 *The Times*, 16 Oct. 1824.
22 *Rep. of Sel. Cttee on Metropolis Turnpike Trusts* (Parl. Papers, 1825 (355), V), p. 56; E. Ffooks, 'Kens. Turnpike Trust', 47 (TS in KL).
23 7 Geo. IV, c. 58 (Local and Personal).
24 *Rep. of Sel. Cttee on Police of Metropolis* (Parl. Papers, 1828 (533), VI), pp. 350, 380.
25 Above, Loc. Govt.
26 Faulkner, *Chelsea*, II. 341–2.
27 Vestry orders, 1809–22, p. 54; Chelsea Misc. 851.

Chelsea was part of the metropolitan police district under the Act of 1829[1] but had no station, and one householder argued that the area (especially outside Hans Town), being close to London, would be vulnerable to criminals, since the only watchmen were private ones, of 'no use'.[2] In 1830 the vestry resolved to petition for a police establishment but wished it to be under parochial control.[3] From 1830 V Division served part of Chelsea, with a station in Milman's Street,[4] on the east side towards the river.[5] In 1852 new premises were built west of the junction with King's Road.[6] The station was rebuilt eastward from that structure[7] and opened in 1897. A new one, opened in Lucan Place in 1939, still in use in 2002. The King's Road premises were used as a community centre[8] but *c.*1985 replaced by offices and shops.[9] Wray House (G. Mackenzie Trench, 1934–7) on Elystan Street contained 114 flats for policemen. Sold by the Metropolitan Police *c.*1986, it was converted in 1989 to a residential development (Crown Lodge).[10] There was a police station in Walton Street by 1851.[11] The station was rebuilt *c.*1895 by R. Norman Shaw, its yellow brick façade in a simple English Baroque style with a curved look-out on one angle. Although old-fashioned for its date, the brickwork shows the façade must be Shaw's.[12] It was closed as a station in the late 1950s,[13] but the building was still used by the police in 2002.

WATER SUPPLY

The Tudor manor house, Chelsea Place,[14] was supplied by a conduit installed by Henry VIII from springs on Kensington moor. Pipes to Gorges House were mentioned in 1624, and in 1652 Buckingham (later Beaufort) House was also served by the conduit. In 1685 the water was allegedly being diverted in Kensington before reaching Chelsea, reducing the supply, and between 1702 and 1721 the supply was subject to a dispute between the owner of the manor house, Lord Cheyne, and the Beaufort family.[15] A copy of a plan of the water system drawn up about that time shows the conduit crossing King's Road to a conduit house just inside the glebe's conduit close and then running south to the manor house and its stables and to the fountain in the great garden, whose water display was noted by John Evelyn in 1696. A branch ran west to outbuildings of Winchester House. The branch to Beaufort House ran from the conduit house to the stable yard and office, supplying Dovehouse Close and the gardens and ended at a tank beside Gorges House; it also supplied a pond at the corner of King's Road and Church Lane.[16] A pump by the King's Road burial ground was associated with the conduit,[17] and subterranean passages found near Cheyne Walk in 1939 were apparently also connected with this Tudor supply.[18] Beaufort House also had a high water tower on its wharf by the Thames in 1620 and a watercourse running from it, presumably to take river water.[19] The Royal Hospital had its own supply from the Thames,[20] and in Blacklands a pump was in use in 1653.[21]

An Act of 1722 allowed water to be taken from the Thames between the Royal Hospital and the Neat Houses (in Westminster) to supply Westminster and adjoining areas, and the Chelsea Waterworks Company, incorporated in 1723, was subsequently empowered to make reservoirs in St James's Park and Hyde Park; by 1726 St James's and Whitehall palaces were among the recipients. Despite its name, the company's works were actually just inside the boundary of St George Hanover Square,[22] and the company was not founded specifically to serve Chelsea, although the parish was among the areas supplied. The volume of water raised daily almost doubled between 1767 and 1809.[23] In 1829 a proposal to form a company to supply the parish with better terms than the Chelsea Waterworks came to nothing.[24] The company supplied 13,000 houses in 1835,[25] although at that period the company's service did not cover all of Chelsea itself.[26] In 1849 Chelsea vestry considered an association with other parishes to obtain a cheaper and purer supply, but nothing was done, perhaps because of the expense.[27] During the cholera crisis of the early 1850s the Chelsea company's supply was apparently among the

1 10 Geo. IV, c. 44.
2 *The Times*, 6 Oct. 1829.
3 Vestry mins, 1822–33, pp. 279–80[A].
4 Chelsea cuttings: police (*The Job*, 2 Sept. 1988, p. 4, with letter).
5 Thompson, *Map* (1836).
6 PRO, HO 45/4262; Old OS Map, London 87 (1865 edn).
7 *Chelsea, Pimlico and Belgravia Dir.* (1896), 121; ibid. (1898), 122; Chelsea cuttings: 395 King's Road (photo) (in fact new sta. was no. 385).
8 Chelsea cuttings: police sta. (printed notice, n.d.).
9 Chelsea cuttings: 385–9 King's Road (sale partics. *c.*1981; details of new development 1985).
10 *Flats: Municipal and Private Enterprise* (1938), 120–5 (copy at CL); Pevsner, *London NW.* 588; Chelsea cuttings: Wray Ho. (*Daily Mail*, 8 Aug. 1935; sale partics. *c.*1986; *Chartered Surveyors Weekly*, 18 Dec. 1987); above, Settlement, twentieth cent.
11 PRO, HO 107/1474/2/3/4, p. 24.
12 A. Saint, *Richard Norman Shaw* (1976), 340, 434; Pevsner, *London NW.* 566; OS Map 25", London LXXIV (1897 edn, with revisions of 1893–4); ibid. London IV.16 (1916 edn).
13 *PO Dir. London* (1955, 1959, 1964).
14 Above, Landownership, Chelsea man.
15 Faulkner, *Chelsea*, II. 13–17; Hunting, *Man. Ho. to Mus.* 15–18, 26; *Images of Chelsea*, 19; PRO, C 5/79/12, 55–6; C 54/3676, no. 12; C 78/1438, no. 9; CP 43/520, m. 5.
16 Plan in CL, reproduced in Hunting, *Man. Ho. to Mus.* 16–17.
17 Holme, *Chelsea*, 228; Beaver, *Memorials*, 322.
18 Chelsea cuttings: conduits (various cuttings 1939 and n.d.).
19 PRO, C 54/2440, no. 38
20 Dean, *Royal Hosp.* 49.
21 PRO, C 10/25/55.
22 H.W. Dickinson, *Water Supply of Gtr London* (1954), 55–7, 68, 70–1, 77, 118; recs listed at LMA, Acc. 2558/CH.
23 R. Sisley, *London Water Supply* (1899), 64.
24 Chelsea Scraps, 357.
25 Dickinson, *Water Supply*, 58, 120–1.
26 PRO, MPF 1/165.
27 Vestry mins, 1843–56, p. 129.

safest.[1] By 1854 there were 8 public pumps in Hans Town and 15 in the rest of Chelsea.[2] By 1868 the company's district covered 6½ square miles, supplying nearly 27,000 houses in Chelsea, Knightsbridge, Belgravia, Pimlico, and other parts of Westminster, the smallest of the eight London companies.[3] In 1874 the company gave a constant supply to less than half a per cent of its houses, and in 1883 it remained the only metropolitan company not considering substituting constant for intermittent supply under an Act of 1871. In 1888 it had still not complied with the Act; consequently only 19 per cent of houses in its district were under constant service, presumably newly-built streets, the lowest proportion of any company.[4] Matters improved in the 1890s, however: 73 per cent under constant supply in 1895 had become 100 per cent by 1899.[5] The company was taken over by the Metropolitan Water Board in 1904, which continued to supply Chelsea from the Thames.[6] The Metropolitan Water Board was replaced by the metropolitan division of the Thames Water Authority in 1974,[7] and the industry was privatized under the Water Act, 1989.[8]

SEWERAGE

The two watercourses that formed Chelsea's eastern and western boundaries, the Westbourne, also known as the Ranelagh sewer at its southern end, and Counter's Creek,[9] were used as common sewers, the former mentioned in 1610[10] and apparently 1651,[11] the latter *c.*1635.[12] In 1770, in addition to Ranelagh and Counter's Creek, another open sewer ran eastward towards Ranelagh from Blacklands.[13] Before *c.*1815 common sewers were supposed to convey surface water only, while cesspools were supposed to receive sewage.[14] The common sewers fell within the jurisdiction of the Westminster Commission of Sewers (WCS) from the early 17th century, although its activities were mainly confined to the city and its immediate environs. Its powers, despite consolidation by an Act of 1807, were limited.[15] The Ranelagh sewer was enlarged in 1817,[16] by which time this open sewer had become effectively a vast cesspit,[17] ten years later polluting the water supply taken by the Grand Junction Water Company from near its mouth in the Thames. The use of such open streams was a problem which constantly worsened with new building, including that north of Hyde Park. The Westbourne still essentially a followed its natural route, but as new housing on the Grosvenor and Lowndes estates on Chelsea's eastern border demanded effective sewerage, the builder Thomas Cubitt in the late 1820s altered the course of the Ranelagh sewer and covered its northern section. In 1846 inhabitants complained about the lower uncovered stretch, running east of Sloane Terrace and towards the Thames.[18]

Apart from Ranelagh and Counter's Creek, sewerage in Chelsea under the WCS was only partial. Most sewers, discharging into the Thames, ran north–south.[19] Manorial courts had some jurisdiction, with presentments for failure to clear ditches in 1543[20] and in the late 17th and early 18th centuries.[21] Although the vestry sometimes concerned itself with sewerage many sewers were provided privately and piecemeal. In 1778 the building of Hans Town necessitated arrangements for drainage, achieved by intersection of a new sewer with the Ranelagh sewer;[22] in 1807 a common sewer ran along Sloane Street.[23] In 1782 standing water around the workhouse made it unpleasant in warm weather. In 1785 the ditch which received its foul water was to be replaced by a cesspool.[24] Drains and cesspools were constructed by inhabitants or proprietors at Turk's Row in 1794, Queen's Elm in 1799, and Riley Street in 1800.[25] The vestry was often reluctant to meet the expense, as in 1819 when the construction of a sewer draining the workhouse was deferred. Before 1822 the trustees of the burial ground and of the new church built sewers to the Thames, which also served the workhouse.[26] In 1824, however, the vestry resolved to drain roads on Chelsea common, and the following year proprietors could pay for their houses to be drained into the new sewer. Its construction necessitated 2,000 feet of new road at parish expense and 2,500 feet at the expense of the commissioners: it was presumably that sewer which benefited many inhabitants in

1 H. Hobhouse, *Thos Cubitt: Master Builder* (1995 edn), 170, 513.
2 *Returns of Paving, Cleansing and Lighting Metropolitan Dists.* (Parl. Papers, 1854–5 (127), LIII), p. 15.
3 *Rep. of Com. on Water Supply* (Parl. Papers, 1868–9 [4169], XXXIII), pp. xlvii, xlix.
4 *Living and Dying in London*, ed. W. F. Bynum and R. Porter (1991), 87–8; *Ann. Rep. of MBW* (Parl. Papers, 1884 (186), LXVIII), p. 41; ibid. (Parl. Papers, 1889 (326), LXVI), pp. 63, 67.
5 Sisley, *London Water Supply*, 70.
6 Chelsea MB, *Official Guide* [1937], 107.
7 R. Trench and E. Hillman, *London under London* (1984), 91.
8 *Whitaker's Almanack* (1999).
9 Above, Intro.
10 BL, Add. Ch. 18205.
11 PRO, C 7/396/9.
12 PRO, E 192/15/3 (presentment, n.d.), E 192/15/8 (jury's verdict, n.d.). This applied even after canalization: 5 Geo. IV, c. 65 (Local and Personal); LMA, WCS PR/84; above, Intro., comms.
13 LMA, WCS P/1/4–5.
14 LCC, *Main Drainage of London* (1909), 1.
15 *Jnl Soc. Archivists*, II(5), 198; Hobhouse, *Thos Cubitt*, 111–12.
16 *Rep. on Public Bridges in Middx* (1826), 175.
17 Trench and Hillman, *London under London*, 44.
18 Chelsea Misc. 305; Hobhouse, *Thos Cubitt*, 119–23; LMA, WCS 756, no. 89.
19 LMA, WCS PR/16, 84.
20 PRO, SC 2/188/42–3.
21 Faulkner, *Chelsea*, II. 156, 160–1.
22 Chelsea Scraps, 1154.
23 KL, deed 26415.
24 Vestry orders, 1771–90, ff. 99v., 116v.
25 Ibid., 1790–1809, pp. 61–3, 186, 198–9, 201–2.
26 Ibid., 1809–22, pp. 353, 403; Vestry mins, 1822–33, pp. 69–70, 72; LMA, P74/LUK/274, pp. 30–1, 33–4, 171–2.

1826.[1] In 1840 the vestry considered helping landlords in the Keppel Street (now Sloane Avenue) neighbourhood to improve its poor drainage, although a minority opposed application of public funds to the improvement of private property. Provision of sewerage had to attempt to keep up with building. In 1841 the WCS ordered that no new streets be taken under parochial management unless proper sewerage was made, preferably when the roads were built, seeking to minimize public expense by placing responsibility upon builders.[2] Under Chelsea's Improvement Act (1845) its commissioners could construct sewers, while not interfering with the WCS's activities,[3] and addressed complaints about drainage.[4]

A single Metropolitan Commission of Sewers (MCS) succeeded the existing sewers commissions including Westminster in 1847. It lacked the power to re-plan London's main drainage,[5] but built some sewers in Chelsea between 1852 and 1855.[6] The inhabitants' wish in 1854 that the MCS cover the open portion of Ranelagh south of Sloane Square, given the cholera and fever in the poor neighbourhoods adjacent,[7] was fulfilled;[8] a new covered Counter's Creek sewer was also formed.[9] In 1855 the MBW succeeded the MCS, and it transformed metropolitan sewerage by building intercepting sewers to divert sewage away from the Thames to outfalls outside London. Its northern low–level sewer, the last section to be built, was housed in Chelsea Embankment (constructed 1871–4). Before its completion west London's sewage was discharged into the Thames via Counter's Creek, but the temporary pumping station near Cremorne in Chelsea, built *c.*1864, was superseded by Grosvenor Road pumping station (St George Hanover Sq.) of 1875;[10] in 1877 the MBW conveyed the Cremorne site to Chelsea vestry as a wharf.[11] The MBW's failure to provide storm outlets was criticized,[12] and a storm relief sewer, for the existing Ranelagh main sewer, was added in 1883–5 and crossed the District underground railway at Sloane Square,[13] where the aqueduct above the platforms[14] survived in 2001. In 1896–7 inhabitants blamed effluvia in Cheyne Walk on the low–level sewer, described in 1891 as taxed beyond capacity by west London's increasing population.[15] The LCC, which succeeded the MBW, made alterations to London's main drainage, including building Lots Road pumping station in 1904 to prevent flooding when the Counter's Creek and low–level sewers could not discharge storm water into the Thames at high tide. The one-storey engine house, of red brick with terracotta dressings, has a symmetrical nine-bay façade with arched windows;[16] Station House adjacent, with similar features, is presumably contemporary. The pumping station passed from the LCC to the GLC.[17] It was used by Thames Water Utilities in 2000.

Under the Metropolis Local Management Act, 1855,[18] which transferred the main sewers to the MBW, responsibility for other sewers reverted to the vestry. In 1857 Chelsea had over 25 miles of covered sewer and 883 yards uncovered. Over a mile of streets were unsewered. Its drainage was said to be generally effective, many new sewers having been built in recent years.[19] Between 1856 and 1872 the vestry financed construction of over 2½ miles of sewers, in addition to almost 3½ miles made by other authorities. 'Very imperfect' cesspool drainage prevailing in 1856 was rare by 1872.[20]

MEDICAL SERVICES

Parish-based Provision to 1870

Payments were made by the parish for the pest house in 1666–7, and to Mr Edwin, surgeon, in 1669–70.[21] An apothecary and a physician for the workhouse were appointed in 1735.[22] Poor in the workhouse were attended in 1743–4 by half a dozen medical men, including Alexander Reid, whose medical practice included *c.*1764 two houses in Danvers Street for inoculating against smallpox;[23] his son Thomas Ranby Reid was appointed surgeon in his place at his death in 1789.[24] In 1766 the apothecaries resident in the parish were to work by rotation and receive six guineas quarterly.[25] In 1796 the apothecary, to be appointed for no more than two quarters, was to receive ten guineas quarterly for attendance at the workhouse at least three times weekly

1 Vestry mins, 1822–33, pp. 140, [1]53–4, [1]61, 183.
2 Ibid., 1839–43, pp. 158–9, 234.
3 8 & 9 Vic. c. 143 (Local and Personal).
4 Improvement com. mins, 1845–6, 1846–8, *passim.*
5 *Jnl Soc. Archivists*, II(5), 198.
6 LMA, MCS 206/7, no. 69, MCS 210/11, no. 99, MCS 211/12, no. 100, MCS 221/22, no. 154, MCS 222/23, nos. 155–6, MCS 223/24, nos. 163–5.
7 *The Times*, 1 Sep. 1854.
8 Beaver, *Memorials*, 10; LMA, MCS 219/20, no. 138.
9 MBW, *Rep. by Bazalgette on Sewage and Main Drainage* (1856), 18; LMA, MCS P23. The Kens. canal remained: above, Intro., comms.
10 *Ann. Rep. of MBW* (Parl. Papers, 1865 (33), XLVII), p. 6; ibid. (Parl. Papers, 1866 (18), LIX), pp. 5, 56; ibid. (Parl. Papers, 1867–8 (45), LVIII), p. 5; ibid. (Parl. Papers, 1872 (294), XLIX), pp. 16, 49; ibid. (Parl. Papers, 1875 (246), LXIV), pp. 16, 70–1; ibid. (Parl. Papers, 1876 (290), LXIII), p. 13.
11 KL, deed 34968.
12 Trench and Hillman, *London under London*, 73.
13 *Ann. Rep. of MBW* (Parl. Papers, 1884–5 (186), LXVII), p. 89; ibid. (Parl. Papers, 1886 (170), LVII), pp. 5–6.
14 LCC, *Opening of Chelsea Bridge 1937*, 5.
15 Chelsea Misc. 37, 41–3.
16 Chelsea Scraps, 649 and v.
17 *Bartholomew's Gtr London Reference Atlas* (1963, 1968 edns).
18 18 & 19 Vic. c. 120.
19 *Metropolitan Drainage* (Parl. Papers, 1857 Sess. 2, (223), XXXVI), pp. 213, 229.
20 *Returns from Vestries on Improvements since 1855* (Parl. Papers, 1872 (298), XLIX), p. 23.
21 Vestry orders, 1662–1718, ff. 6, 8v., 11v.
22 LMA, P74/LUK/3, pp. 1, 4.
23 S.L. Sheffield, 'From Hospice to Hosp.: St Luke's Workho. 1727–1875', 5–8, 20–1 (TS at NMR, file 101061); Faulkner, *Chelsea*, I. 280.
24 Vestry orders, 1771–90, ff. 166–v.
25 Ibid., 1745–71, pp. 298–9.

and on the sick poor. By 1806 two apothecaries, one for the old part of the town, the other for Hans Town, were each to receive 30 guineas annually and attend the workhouse in alternate months. Appointments were to be by six-month rotation. The surgeon's salary was increased from £20 to 30 guineas to reflect his increased duties.[1] For the same reason, in 1810 the apothecaries' and surgeon's salaries were again increased, in 1817 rising to 150 and 80 guineas respectively. Regulations were adopted concerning treatment of the sick poor. In 1819, after the death of T.R. Reid, the apothecaries' and surgeon's duties were united: two medical men were to be appointed half-yearly respectively from the west and east of the parish, with a reduced salary of 200 guineas. A procedure for complaints against them was instituted.[2] Before 1822 many parochial paupers were sent to the Chelsea dispensary.[3] At that date an attendant was appointed exclusively for the sick poor, but some householders criticized the appointment by the parochial committee without vestry approval and questioned the financial necessity and efficacy of the change. The vestry increased his salary to £200 in 1823, his labours having been underestimated, and to £210 in 1824, when he was named as Mr Gaskell. By 1828 it had increased by stages to £300.[4] By 1829 over 2,800 patients a year were attended. There were also nurses for sick paupers; payments were made to midwives.[5] In 1832 some inhabitants censured the committee's failure to prevent Gaskell engaging in private practice, said to have seriously affected the sick poor, and alleged that medical aid was restricted, even during the cholera outbreak; their opponents contrasted his satisfactory attendance with the previous system. The 270 paupers on the medical attendant's list in 1822 had almost doubled by 1832.[6] In 1833 four surgeons were proposed, each with a salary of £40, to attend the poorhouse daily by quarterly rotation; a dispenser, prohibited from private practice, was to have £40 and accommodation in the poorhouse. The midwives would attend as usual. Two medical and surgical attendants for the eastern division of the parish and two for the western were accordingly appointed. In 1834 the dispensary was abolished and the surgeons were to supply medicines and received an increased annual allowance of £280. Two men were appointed for the eastern districts (their salaries £50 annually), two for the western districts, and one for the workhouse (their salaries £60). An honorary physician was appointed for consultation in difficult cases. In 1835, when five medical attendants were again appointed, their duties were efficiently attended to. Their appointment in vestry was not recorded after 1837,[7] when Chelsea was included in Kensington poor law union,[8] but from 1840 three medical officers are documented.[9] In 1844 the sole medical practitioner at the workhouse complained of overwork.[10] Under the Metropolis Management Act, 1855, the vestry appointed a medical officer from 1856.[11]

Because of overcrowding at the workhouse, the vestry, fearing epidemics, resolved on a new building in 1778. Two women acted as nurses in its infirmary and another to the lying-in room in 1783. There was an insane ward. In 1788 the bad state of the infirmary necessitated new accommodation for the infirm poor, which was erected on garden ground near by.[12] An addition to the workhouse of 1792 included two rooms for insane men, and that of 1797 had accommodation for infirm women.[13] In 1807 the infirmary of 1788 was extended at either end, and a storey added.[14] In 1822 a committee warned of the danger of having no separate accommodation. Plans to enlarge the workhouse included a detached infirmary.[15] The 1822 extension included five rooms for insane women, and the new building of 1827 housed male and female sick and infirm, with a dispensary, to which application was by ticket.[16] In 1832 the workhouse housed *c.*150 sick and infirm paupers.[17]

In 1816 expenditure was recorded on lunatics,[18] evidently sent away, but by 1822 six people held at parish expense in a private asylum at Bethnal Green had been moved to the workhouse to reduce expense, although some parishioners still believed specialist care to be more effective. There were still lunatics at the workhouse in 1829.[19] In 1832 a parochial board of health sought to acquire or erect a cholera hospital or house of observation, but the vestry suggested using part of the workhouse recently vacated by lunatic paupers.[20] Expenditure of the parochial committee in the 1830s included the support of lunatics, payment to the asylum at Hanwell being mentioned,[21] and continued in 1838–9. Controversy over inclusion in Kensington union involved in 1839 the poor law commission's claim that Chelsea workhouse did not permit classification of paupers, including the sick and especially the infectious. The vestry counter-claimed that before the union there were separate wards for the aged, the sick, and imbeciles, of each sex.[22] In 1866 there was no detached infirmary and

1 Vestry orders, 1790–1809, pp. 109–10, 344–5, 349–50.
2 Ibid., 1809–22, pp. 32–3, 279, 281–2, 354–5.
3 Chelsea Misc. 821; below, this section.
4 Vestry mins, 1822–33, pp. 56, 93–4, 129–30, [149], 166, 192, [226]; Chelsea Misc. 821–2.
5 Faulkner, *Chelsea*, II. 29, 31, 33.
6 Vestry mins, 1822–33, pp. 308–9; Chelsea Misc. 366–72, 768.
7 Vestry mins, 1833–9, pp. 3, 10–12, 22–3, 36, 39–40, 101, 130, 138–9, 174.
8 Above, Local Govt.
9 Chelsea Misc. 849–50v.
10 Sheffield, 'Hospice to Hosp.', 26–7.
11 Vestry mins, 1843–56, p. 242; *Vestry rep. 1856–7*, 12.
12 Vestry orders, 1771–90, ff. 41, 100–v., 161v.
13 Faulkner, *Chelsea*, II. 25.
14 Vestry orders, 1790–1809, pp. 366–9, 378–82.
15 Vestry mins, 1822–33, pp. 17–18.
16 Faulkner, *Chelsea*, II. 26.
17 Chelsea Misc. 768.
18 Vestry orders, 1809–22, p. 199.
19 Chelsea Misc. 821–2; Faulkner, *Chelsea*, II. 25.
20 Vestry mins, 1822–33, p. 296.
21 Ibid., 1833–9, pp. 258, 273, 281; cf. *VCH Middx*, IV. 42, for Hanwell asylum (Norwood).
22 Vestry mins, 1839–43, pp. 86–7, 95, 108.

the sick, but not the aged and infirm, were mostly in dedicated wards. Fever, smallpox, and venereal cases were generally excluded; there were a few imbeciles distributed through the workhouse. About 140 inmates were on the books of the medical officer, some purely for dietary reasons. There were two paid nurses, besides pauper nurses.[1]

Chelsea Infirmary

A separate-site infirmary known as Chelsea infirmary or, increasingly, St Luke's was built north of Britten Street opposite the workhouse. The first block, by John Giles & Gough, was begun in 1872; to the south was an out-patients' department and dispensary. Another ward block was added in 1885 on Cale Street, by A. & C. Harston, and staff accommodation at the corner of Cale and Sydney streets by Lansdell & Harrison, in 1896. Extensions eastward from the original block towards Sydney Street, apparently of 1921, housed a reception block and additional accommodation. There was also accommodation for sick and infirm inmates in the workhouse. Both were taken over by the LCC in 1930.[2] In 1938 St Luke's hospital had 308 general medical and surgical beds and 82 special beds, including 60 for pulmonary tuberculosis; by 1945 only 230 beds were in use owing to bomb damage.[3] It became part of the NHS in 1948,[4] and 264 beds catered for the chronic sick in 1959. In 1971 it had 202 geriatric beds.[5] The hospital closed in the 1970s and was largely demolished,[6] although the dispensary of 1873[7] on Britten Street survived in 2000. The site was taken over by the Royal Brompton.[8]

St Stephen's Hospital

The workhouse of St George's Union in Fulham Road, which included a large brick infirmary of 1876–8 and later additions, served only the poor of St George's union, and from 1913 of the City of Westminster union, until 1930; it was known as St Stephen's from 1924. It passed to the LCC in 1930 as a municipal hospital with 788 beds in 1931, and to the NHS in 1948.[9] In 1952 operating theatres replaced one of two Victorian ward blocks damaged by bombing. Workhouse buildings made way in 1965 for a three-storeyed out-patient department designed by Richard Mellor, and a new ward block was completed in 1971.[10] St Stephen's closed in 1989 and was demolished: four other hospitals – Westminster; Westminster Children's; West London, Hammersmith; and St Mary Abbot's, Kensington – were

72. *St Stephen's hospital, no. 369 Fulham Road*

united on its site as the Chelsea and Westminster hospital, opened in 1993. Designed by Sheppard Robson the hospital was arranged around a large atrium the height of the building; the 580-bed district general and teaching hospital primarily served the City of Westminster, southern parts of RBKC, Hammersmith, Fulham, and northern Wandsworth. Until 1994 the hospital was run with Charing Cross, but the two were separated and Chelsea and Westminster Healthcare NHS Trust was formed.[11] The adjoining Kobler Centre, opened in 1988 for the treatment of AIDS and later named St Stephen's Centre, was the only part of St Stephen's buildings to survive.[12]

Other Local Medical Services

Medical services aside from hospitals included the Chelsea, Brompton, and Belgrave dispensary established on the south side of Sloane Square in 1812 to give medical and surgical aid to the poor, and assistance at lying-in; doctors served gratuitously. Supported by subscriptions and donations, the dispensary operated on

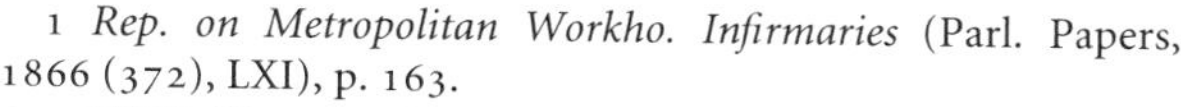

1 *Rep. on Metropolitan Workho. Infirmaries* (Parl. Papers, 1866 (372), LXI), p. 163.
2 NMR, files 101061, 101130.
3 Min. of Health, *Hosp. Survey* (1945), 63, 102.
4 NMR, file 101130.
5 *Hosps Year Bks* (1959), 169; (1971), 184.
6 NMR, file 101130.
7 Foundation stone.
8 Below, this section.

9 C.M. Howgrave-Graham and L.J. Martin, *Hosp. in Lt. Chelsea* (1978), 8–9, 17, 48; *Hosps Year Bk* (1931); see Fig. 72.
10 Howgrave-Graham and Martin, *Hosp. in Lt. Chelsea*, 38–9, 42; Chelsea cuttings: St Stephen's (*Architect and Bldg News*, 20 April 1966, pp. 701–6).
11 *Profile of Chelsea & Westm. Healthcare* (n.d.), 1–4, 9 (copy at CL).
12 Chelsea cuttings: Kobler Centre (*City Limits*, 22–9 Sep. 1988).

a ticket system, although in 1832 cholera suspects were attended without a ticket. In 1848 visiting limits were extended beyond Church (later Old Church) Street, to include the whole parish. The earliest annual average of patients, fewer than 1,200, increased to over 6,000 by 1860,[1] and attendances exceeded 17,000 by 1892.[2] The Sloane Square premises, demolished in 1902, were replaced in 1903 by new premises at no. 1 Manor (later Chelsea Manor) Street.[3] Still voluntarily supported, the dispensary treated its members, not all from Chelsea, and those too poor to subscribe.[4] However, after standing empty for a time,[5] the premises were transferred in 1913 to the Tuberculosis (or Tuberculin) Dispensary League, for use primarily by Chelsea inhabitants. The dispensary, for early diagnosis and tuberculin treatment, reopened in 1914 and was still there in 1920,[6] but had closed by 1927.[7]

St George's Home, Milman's Street, formerly a receiving home for children,[8] was used from 1914 by the Metropolitan Asylums Board as a tuberculosis sanatorium for women.[9] It was transferred to the LCC in 1930 with 50 beds,[10] and became part of the NHS in 1948.[11] The LCC bought it back in 1956 for use as a hostel. It was demolished in the 1980s and replaced by housing by 1989.[12]

Chelsea Health Society was founded in 1911 to promote maternity and infant welfare and was supported by Chelsea MB from 1916. It was housed at no. 1a Manor (later Chelsea Manor) Street from 1922. New premises were opened in 1931 on a site given by Lord Melchett, the chairwoman's husband: the Violet Melchett Infant Welfare Centre housed the Society's clinics and offices, a Mothercraft Training Home, and Chelsea Day Nursery, established in 1915. The Centre, of brick with stone dressings by Buckland & Haywood, stretched between Flood and Chelsea Manor streets. From 1948 the Violet Melchett Centre was aided by the LCC, but was transferred from voluntary control to the RBKC in 1967. The clinic passed to the NHS in 1974,[13] and remained in use in 2000.

From 1927 the Chelsea Babies' Club at no. 35 Danvers Street offered, by subscription, to 'professional' parents the information provided by welfare centres to the working class.[14] It still operated in 1964 but had closed by 1970.[15]

Private and Specialist Medical Provision

Private medical provision existed by the mid 18th century, principally through the work of apothecaries and lunatic asylums. Around 1764 Alexander Reid and his partner Mr Peake, surgeons, administered smallpox inoculations at premises in Danvers Street.[16] No. 6 Cheyne Walk was occupied from 1765 by the notorious physician Dr Bartholomew Dominiceti, whose extensions to the rear housed medicinal baths for ladies and gentlemen. He became bankrupt in 1782 and left the parish.[17]

Michael Duffield maintained two private lunatic asylums at Little Chelsea, one of which in Chelsea parish occupied the mansion built by William Mart in Fulham Road; it was later demolished and replaced by Odell's Place.[18] One treated the critic Montague Bacon before his death in 1749. Alexander Cruden, author of a biblical concordance, complained of barbarous treatment by Duffield's nephew Peter Inskip in 1753.[19] An investigation of 1763 into detainments in madhouses examined a case at Turlington's house in Chelsea.[20] Benjamin Faulkner had a madhouse at Little Chelsea in 1789, uniquely run as a free house where the proprietor provided board, lodging, and attendants but patients saw their own physicians. The commentator on insanity G.M. Burrows kept a small madhouse in Chelsea between 1816 and 1823.[21] In 1830–1 the asylums in Chelsea were the Retreat in King's Road, licensed for 24 females; Blacklands House, for 30 males; and Hollywood House,[22] for 20 inmates; none housed paupers.[23] The Retreat, or Manor Cottage, was between Bramerton Street and Church Street.[24] Elm House asylum at Queen's Elm catered for ladies suffering milder forms of mental disease.[25] Chelsea's two private lunatic asylums in 1841 were presumably Elm House and Blacklands House, north of King's Road, named in 1861. Blacklands had 15 male inmates in 1871 and another asylum, presumably Elm House, housed 7

1 Faulkner, *Chelsea*, II. 351–2; *Rep. of Jubilee Festival* (1862), 15–17 (CL, SR 254/8).

2 *Kelly's London Medical Dir.* (1892), 301.

3 Chelsea Misc. 1746, 2233.

4 Chelsea Scraps, 582, pp. 3–4.

5 CL, SR 250, p. 88.

6 Chelsea Misc. 921v., 1013v.–1014v., 1256v., 1745–6.

7 *PO Dir. London* (1927).

8 Above, Local Govt.

9 K. Morrison, *The Workho.* (1999), 216, 219.

10 G.M. Ayers, *Eng.'s First State Hosps* (1971), 274–5.

11 Howgrave-Graham and Martin, *Hosp. in Lt. Chelsea*, 39.

12 Chelsea cuttings: Milman's Street, St Geo.'s Home (reply to enquiry 1970; *Chelsea News*, 23 April 1983; brochures 1989–90).

13 Chelsea cuttings: Violet Melchett (TS 27 Jan. 1965; *Chelsea News*, 10 Nov. 1967; *Earl's Court Post*, 11 Sep. 1981); Chelsea Misc. 2155.

14 *Chelsea Babies' Club Recipes* (1938), 80, 82 (copy at CL).

15 CL, card index: Babies' Club (*The Times*, 8 Dec. 1964, and MS note).

16 Faulkner, *Chelsea*, II. 280.

17 Faulkner, *Chelsea*, I. 392–5; *Survey of London*, II. 45–9; Chelsea Scraps, 1151.

18 Faulkner, *Chelsea*, I. 142; above, Landownership, later ests (Blake).

19 Beaver, *Memorials*, 334; *DNB*, s.vv. Bacon and Cruden; *Survey of London*, XLI. 181.

20 W. Ll. Parry-Jones, *Trade in Lunacy* (1972), 224–5; Chelsea Misc. 1095.

21 Parry-Jones, *Trade in Lunacy*, 92, 102.

22 Cf. above, Free Cancer hosp., for Hollywood Ho. on Fulham Road (Kens.), but several hos. bore the name, including no. 383 Fulham Road (Chelsea): *Survey of London*, XLI. 184.

23 PRO, HO 44/51.

24 *Images of Chelsea*, 234; Beaver, *Memorials*, 323.

25 Chelsea Misc. 469.

females. Only Blacklands was listed in 1881;[1] it was demolished in 1890, the asylum having removed to Tooting (Surrey).[2]

Several specialist hospitals in Chelsea served a wider population.

Royal Brompton. The Hospital for Consumption and Diseases of the Chest (the Brompton hospital) was started by Philip Rose, a Chelsea solicitor, in 1841 for tubercular patients usually excluded from general hospitals as incurable. In 1842 an out-patients' department opened in Westminster and an in-patients' at Manor House in Smith Street, Chelsea.[3] Admittance was by governor's or subscriber's recommendation, and patients came from London and beyond. A scheme to enlarge Manor House was superseded by the construction 1844–54 of a hospital north of Fulham Road (Kens.). From 1868 the hospital acquired houses, some of which were used for in-patients, south of Fulham Road in Chelsea, connected to the main building by a subway of 1872. These were replaced 1879–82 by the South Block, for out-patients and male in-patients, designed by T.H. Wyatt and completed by his son Matthew. The block, in Queen Anne style with a red-brick and terracotta façade, fronted Fulham Road with its wings extending behind, and added 137 beds to give the hospital over 300. A detached nurses' home of 1898–9 by E.T. Hall in South Parade had a long Free Renaissance front of red brick and stone. Saxon Snell & Phillips extended the South Block westward in matching style and added a floor in the roof of the nurses' home in 1935. In 1948 under the NHS the Brompton was united with the London Chest hospital (Bethnal Green) under one board of governors as a teaching hospital. Further alterations to the South Block by Saxon Snell & Phillips and finished by Adams, Holden, & Pearson, were completed in 1967.[4]

A plan of 1961 for several specialist hospitals on the site of St Luke's and Chelsea Women's hospital proved abortive[5] and after years of debate[6] the Brompton took over the site of St Luke's. St Wilfrid's convent in Cale Street was converted into a research centre in 1985, and a building by Watkins Gray International on the St Luke's site for the Brompton hospital and the National Heart hospital (Marylebone) opened in 1991, for treatment of and research into heart and lung disease.[7] The hospital became the Royal Brompton in 1991;[8] the Royal Brompton NHS Trust was formed in 1994, with 290 beds, and in 1998 merged with Harefield hospital (Uxbridge) to create the Royal Brompton and Harefield NHS Trust.[9] By 1999 the block north of Fulham Road had been converted to residential use, but the hospital retained the South Block, and had taken over the adjacent former fire station on South Parade by 2000.[10] After the construction of the Fulham Road hospital the Brompton's Manor House premises accommodated patients awaiting admission or convalescing;[11] in use in 1881 but not in 1891,[12] the site was built over before 1894.[13]

Free Cancer Hospital. The Free Cancer hospital, founded in 1851 by Dr William Marsden to treat poor sufferers with no admission ticket requirement and to encourage research, opened as a dispensary in Westminster and from 1852 accommodated in-patients at Hollywood House (or Lodge) north of Fulham Road (Kens.). Plans to extend that building were abandoned and a new hospital was built in Chelsea south of Fulham Road 1859–60, designed by David Mocatta of John Young & Sons. It opened in 1862, with wings apparently added 1881–3. It formed the nucleus of the enlarged hospital, by Alexander Graham in 1885, the new façade of red brick with stone mixing Jacobethan and Baroque elements. Further additions included the chapel (1889),[14] nurses' home (1904, demolished after 1951), southwards extension of the east wing (1911), radio-therapeutic department to the south-west (1912, enlarged 1914 and again subsequently), and pay wing on the west side (Granard House, 1932). A full third storey was added and the service towers modified by T.A. Pole *c.*1930; the neo-Georgian wing to the south dated from a similar period. The Cancer Research Institute, founded in 1909, and its original premises opened in 1911, transferred in 1939 as the Chester Beatty Institute (later the Institute of Cancer Research) to the former women's hospital, later Freemasons' hospital,[15] on the south side of Fulham Road, which had been remodelled in 1938–9 by Henry Tanner in red brick and stone, retaining the six storeys but leaving little trace of the Renaissance-style façades. A further building to the east for the Institute replaced older buildings (some belonging to the Brompton Hospital) and was completed in 1999. Often known as the Cancer Hospital (Free), the hospital became the Royal Cancer hospital in 1936 and the Royal

1 *Census*, 1841, 1861, 1871, 1881.
2 Beaver, *Memorials*, 343; Denny, *Chelsea Past*, 119.
3 Not the man. ho. of Chelsea manor, but built in 1780 (NMR, Kens. and Chelsea Red Box: Chelsea Man. Ho.).
4 NMR, file 101058; P.J. Bishop, B.D.B. Lucas, and B.G.B. Lucas, *Seven Ages of the Brompton* (1991), 1–2, 6–10, 14–17, 21–2, 60, 66, 137, 155–6, 179; M. Davidson and F.G. Rouvray, *Brompton Hosp.* (1954), 9–10, 66, 71, 122; *VCH Middx*, XI. 207.
5 G. Rivett, *Development of London Hosp. System 1823–1982* (1986), 296–8.
6 e.g. *Chelsea Soc. Rep.* (1979), 54.
7 Chelsea cuttings: Royal Brompton (*Observer*, 27 Jan. 1985; *The Times*, 7 Feb. 1991).
8 Bishop, Lucas, and Lucas, *Seven Ages*, p. xiii.
9 *Health Svces Year Bk* (1995), p. 13/264; ibid. (1998), 748.
10 Below, fire engines.
11 Bryan, *Chelsea*, 222.
12 *Census*, 1881, 1891.
13 Old OS Map London 87 (1894 edn).
14 Although plaque inside (1995) gives date as 1893.
15 Cf. below, Chelsea Hosp. for Women.

Marsden in 1954.[1] There were 100 beds in 1892[2] and 156 (including 29 private) in 1938, when patients came from London and beyond.[3] The neighbouring Oratory school was adapted for non-patient purposes in the 1970s;[4] the Wallace wing on the west side of the site was perhaps a little earlier. A new hospital block to the rear was added by the George Trew Dunn Partnership 1990–2.[5] With its Sutton (Surrey) branch, the Royal Marsden was a teaching hospital under the NHS.[6] The Royal Marsden NHS Trust succeeded its Special Health Authority in 1994.[7]

Victoria Hospital. The Victoria Hospital for Sick Children was opened in Gough House at the junction of Tite Street and Royal Hospital Road in 1866, initially for out-patients but six in-patient beds opened in 1867, increased to 32 in 1868. Patients came mostly from Chelsea, but also from London and beyond; admission, for a wide range of complaints, was by letter. The hospital also had convalescent homes in Kent: at Margate from 1876 and at Broadstairs from 1891. Gough House, a seven-bay house of *c.*1707 in grounds overlooking the Thames,[8] was considerably altered 1875–6 by extensions and internal re-arrangement, and a single-storeyed isolation block was probably built then, certainly before 1879. A further block to the south by H. Saxon Snell & Sons, 1885–6, included an out-patients' department and accommodation for nurses, who previously had lived in nearby houses; a covered way connected the two buildings by 1893. The hospital absorbed St Gabriel's Hospital for Infants, Westminster (founded 1885), in 1890. An in-patients' block north of Gough House was opened in 1904, and alterations to Gough House itself, with another storey added and an entrance made in Tite Street, were complete by 1905, by which time there were over 100 beds. No. 29 Tite Street was converted for hospital use in 1922, increasing the number of beds to 138 and including a physiotherapy department.[9] Under the NHS Act the hospital became part of St George's Hospital Group.[10] The difficulty of modernizing Tite Street led to the transfer of its activities to St George's Tooting (Surrey) site,[11] and the hospital closed in 1964.[12] It was demolished in 1966 and the site sold to St Wilfrid's convent, so that the latter's Cale Street premises could be used for hospital development.[13]

Chelsea Hospital for Women. The Chelsea Hospital for Women, established by doctors Thomas Chambers and James Aveling in 1871, initially had eight beds in a house at no. 178 King's Road, and catered for gentlewomen in reduced circumstances, respectable poor women, and others. Patients paid a weekly fee, except the poorest supported by a subscriber's letter. In 1875 the hospital had 70 inpatients during the year and 3,235 outpatients, and the need to extend was hindered by lack of room in the neighbourhood.[14] Applications for admission exceeded capacity fivefold and a small hospital was built 1880–3 on a plot on the south side of Fulham Road beside the Jewish cemetery. Designed by J.T. Smith, it was faced in red brick with stone dressings and exuberant decorative elements, and provided 63 beds. It was the first hospital in London built especially for diseases specific to women, and it had a free ward and a samaritan fund.[15] A convalescent home at St Leonards (Sussex) was completed in 1891. An appeal began in 1891 to build a larger hospital, led by Earl Cadogan: the hospital was at that time relieving 500 inpatients and 12,000 outpatients annually.[16] Improvements were made to the existing hospital including an enlarged operating theatre in 1899.[17] In 1911 Earl Cadogan offered a 1¼-acre site in Arthur (later Dovehouse) Street for a larger hospital, which was opened in 1916.[18] After the women's hospital left, the Fulham Road premises were used for the Freemasons' war hospital and masonic nursing home,[19] which continued after the war with 48 private beds in 1931, but was taken over in 1938 by the Chester Beatty Cancer Research Institute.[20]

The new women's hospital, at the south-eastern corner of Dovehouse and Cale streets, was designed by Keith D. Young, 1914–16, with a long front of red brick with stone dressings in a plain neo-Wren style. Unusually for its date, sanitary facilities were incorporated in the main building, not in annexes. The hospital provided 95 beds, of which 18 in 1925 were private. A small pathological block to the rear was later demolished. A nurses' home to the south, by Greenaway & Newberry after a competition, was completed in 1924, and in 1924–5 the

1 NMR, file 101097; *Survey of London*, XLI. 180; Chelsea MB, *Official Guide* [1937], 92–4; *Royal Cancer Hosp. 1851–1951* [1951], 5, 7, 17, 20; Chelsea Misc. 2199; Chelsea Scraps, 780–782; OS Map 25", London LIII (1874 edn); ibid. London LXXXVII (1894 edn); ibid. London VIII.4 (1916 edn; LCC edn [1940]).

2 *Kelly's London Medical Dir.* (1892), 301.

3 Min. of Health, *Hosp. Survey* (1945), 96–7.

4 *Chelsea Soc. Rep.* (1979), 54; below, Soc. Hist., educ.

5 Chelsea cuttings: Royal Marsden (*Evening Standard*, 6 June 1990; *Bldg*, 22 May 1992).

6 *Hosps Year Bk 1960* (1959), 324.

7 *Health Svces Year Bk* (1995), p. 13/269.

8 Above, Landownership, later ests (Gough).

9 G. Edwards, *Victoria Hosp. for Children* (1964), 5–6, 9–10; NMR, file 101094; *Survey of London*, II. 8–9 and plates 7–9; *Kelly's London Medical Dir.* (1892), 318, 323; Chelsea MB, *Official Guide* [1937], 95.

10 Chelsea MB, *Official Guide* [1952], 103.

11 Edwards, *Victoria Hosp.* 3, 14.

12 J. Foster and J. Sheppard, *Brit. Archives* (1995), 373.

13 Chelsea cuttings: Victoria Hosp. (*Chelsea News*, 29 July 1966); also above, Royal Brompton.

14 *The Times*, 8 July 1875.

15 Ibid., 17 May, 17 July 1880.

16 Ibid., 15 Dec. 1891.

17 Ibid., 4 Oct., 23 Nov. 1899.

18 Ibid., 27 March 1912.

19 Ibid., 29 June 1916.

20 Above, Free Cancer hosp.

hospital treated 823 inpatients and 2,199 outpatients. The wards were extended in 1933, and further extensions made in 1938–9 to the hospital, increasing the accommodation to 126, and nurses' home.[1] By 1945 more than half the patients were from outside London.[2] Under the NHS Act the Chelsea Hospital for Women shared a board of governors with Queen Charlotte's maternity hospital (Hammersmith) as a teaching hospital.[3] After the Second World War the hospital had a fertility clinic, treating women from all over London and elsewhere.[4] Two new wings, for research, opened in 1953.[5] The hospital had 84 beds in 1976.[6] In 1988 all the hospital's functions were transferred to the Queen Charlotte's site,[7] and in 1991 the Dovehouse Street building had been taken over by the Royal Brompton,[8] which in 2000 also occupied the nurses' home.

Cheyne Hospital. The Cheyne Hospital for Sick and Incurable Children (known from *c.*1922 as the Cheyne Hospital for Children)[9] was founded in 1875 by Mr and Mrs Wickham Flower at no. 46 Cheyne Walk, expanding into no. 47, also owned by the Flowers, in 1876. Its patients, excluded from general hospitals, suffered chronic or incurable disease such as spinal and hip disorders, but sufferers from cancer, epilepsy, or mental derangement were not admitted; preference was given to subscribers' nominees. Parents were supposed to make a weekly contribution but from 1878 some endowed cots were free. There were 33 beds, but increasing demand led to the acquisition of nos 59–61 Cheyne Walk, part of a late 17th-century row of 5 houses called Prospect Place, which were demolished to make way for a six-bay hospital with 50 beds, of red and yellow brick in Queen Anne style by Beazley & Burrows, 1888–9. The remaining two houses of Prospect Place, nos 62–3 Cheyne Walk, were also acquired by the hospital in 1898 and 1900 and no. 62 served as a nurses' home. A convalescent home at St Nicholas at Wade (Kent) opened in 1910. The Cheyne hospital's pitched roof and part of the gable over the three centre bays were removed *c.*1925 to provide a roof terrace for the treatment of rickets. The hospital, which treated inpatients only, had 67 beds in 1931. A three-storeyed nurses' home to the rear opened in 1939. The hospital was evacuated during the Second World War, and a day nursery was opened in the premises in 1944, impeding the return of the children's hospital, which found alternative accommodation at the

73. *Cheyne Hospital for Children, Cheyne Walk*

Children's Hospital for the Treatment of Hip Diseases at Sevenoaks (Kent) in 1947, becoming part of the NHS in 1948. The day nursery continued in part of the Chelsea premises, but in 1955 the Cheyne Centre for Spastic Children was also opened in the building. A charitable creation, this was administered by the No. 4 (Chelsea) Group Hospital Management Committee although patients came from all over the south of England: its clinic and day nursery offered specialist treatment and research into cerebral palsy.[10] The Centre operated at Cheyne Walk until 1993,[11] but subsequently, as the Cheyne Child Development Service, it was housed by the Chelsea and Westminster hospital.[12] The Cheyne Walk building was sold in 1996 and altered into residential accommodation,[13] the façade surviving relatively unchanged.

1 NMR, files 101059–60; recs. listed at LMA, H27/CW; Chelsea Scraps, 1223; *The Times*, 12 July 1916, 23 Feb. 1923, 23 Feb., 10 Aug., 4 Sep. 1925; *Hosps Year Bk* (1931); Chelsea cuttings: Beatty, Sir A.C. (*The Times*, 27 Jan. 1968); local inf.

2 Min. of Health, *Hosp. Survey* (1945), 92–3.

3 Chelsea MB, *Official Guide* [1952], 103.

4 Chelsea cuttings: Chelsea Hosp. for Women (*Chelsea Post*, 11 Oct. 1968).

5 *The Times*, 17 March 1953.

6 *Hosps Year Bk* (1978), 308.

7 Recs listed at LMA, H27/CW.

8 NMR, file 101059.

9 R. Blunt, *The Watchman's Children* [1922], 8 (CL, SR 106f); see Fig. 73.

10 NMR file 101095; *Survey of London*, II. 84–6 and plates 91–4; *Chelsea Soc. Rep.* (1957), 28–35; LMA, AC.79.55 (deed of settlement, 20 May 1880); *Hosps Year Bk* (1931); J. Saunders and M. Napier, *Spastics in Cheyne Walk* (1957), pp. xiii, 7, 12, 15, 19, 34, 129.

11 *Hosps Year Bk* (1993), p. 2.78; cf. *Health Svces Year Bk* (1994).

12 Above, this section.

13 Chelsea cuttings: 60–2 Cheyne Walk (*Homes and Property*, 30 Sep. 1998).

Ormond Maternity Home. St John's House, a religious community (but not one whose members took vows) which trained nurses, opened a maternity home at Cheyne Walk in 1877, listed at nearby Ashburnham Road in 1878. In 1880–1 St John's House purchased nos 38 and 40 Cheyne Walk. Its home had 11 patients in 1881. Dissension led to the formation of a new community in 1883, when the old community left Cheyne Walk for Battersea. The new Nursing Sisters of St John the Divine held nos 42, 44, and 46 Gunter Grove from 1883. This lying-in house had 12 beds in 1892; admission was free. The sisters left before 1901.[1] In 1937 the Ormond Maternity Home in Blantyre Street trained midwives and served in- and out-patients.[2]

BURIAL GROUNDS

Because of the small size of the churchyard, the vestry considered acquiring a new burial ground from at least 1726. In 1733 Sir Hans Sloane gave a site on the north side of King's Road adjoining the workhouse, consecrated in 1736.[3] In 1782 the vestry imposed fees to prevent so many strangers being buried in the parish. To prevent robberies in the 'exposed' ground, iron rails were to replace some of the wall in 1785, to give workhouse inmates a full view. With the increasing population, part of the workhouse garden adjoining the burial ground to the east was acquired from the owners of the manor and in use from 1790.[4] Although the vestry considered the burial ground sufficiently securely fenced not to lend its support in 1794 to a proposed Act for punishing grave robbers,[5] in 1799 bodies had 'frequently been stolen' and alterations to the walls were again ordered.[6] In 1797 the workhouse committee room was considered sufficient accommodation for the clergyman at the burial ground,[7] presumably for reading the funeral service. In 1807 the vestry considered adding more of the workhouse garden to the burial ground, but decided against it partly because of its limited size; the matter was then shelved because the erection of a new church with a burial ground was under consideration, and meanwhile the sexton was ordered to dig the graves as deep as possible.[8]

By 1810 both the churchyard and the burial ground were 'so full as to render decent interment no longer practicable' because of the growth in population, and an Act of 1810 appointed trustees to acquire and enclose an additional ground.[9] Four acres, rather than the three originally proposed, were acquired to meet the population growth, the rate of building being such that no central site would otherwise be available. The land, mostly acquired from the manorial estate, lay east of Robert (later Sydney) Street, then being laid out for building across former garden ground. It was enclosed and a small chapel for funeral services, designed by the trustees' surveyor Joseph Salway, was erected on the north side; it had Gothic doors, leaded windows, and a turret. The ground was consecrated in 1812, and burials began in 1813. Under an Act of 1819 a central plot, reserved when the burial ground was laid out, formed the site for St Luke's church, built 1820–4, dividing the burial ground into north and south sections; one huge grave in the north-eastern portion housed those buried at parish expense.[10] The funeral chapel was taken down in 1825. There were some problems and irregularities, and in 1832 Sunday afternoon funerals were discontinued to prevent disorderly persons making the grounds a place of resort.[11] The number of burials to *c.*1832, over 600 annually, reflected the rapidly increasing population, although many belonged to adjoining parishes. The only people interred in the King's Road ground after 1812 already had relatives buried there.[12] In 1834 it was reported that the sexton's duties had for years been disgracefully executed, with mourners and clergymen sometimes detained until a grave could be dug. Frauds were perpetrated in charging for depths not dug, and ground was wasted by digging new graves instead of filling old ones; some treatment of the dead was 'too revolting' to be described. In 1835 most of the sexton's fees were transferred to the churchwardens, towards liquidating the debt on the burial ground. In 1838 an allegation that paupers' bodies from Kensington union dissected in anatomical schools did not receive Christian burial was denied.[13] Interments in the burial ground rose from 694 in 1846 to 1,156 in 1849, with 847 in 1852. Following legislation of 1852, burials were to cease in 1854 in the church vaults and, reserving existing rights, in the old and new churchyards and at King's Road. The vestry unsuccessfully countered that the burial ground, which had cost some £6,800 to purchase and lay out, had a further capacity of 30 years or more and posed no danger to public health, even during the cholera outbreak of 1849. In 1854 the vestry considered providing a new ground, but no scheme was endorsed.[14] In 1857 burials were wholly prohibited in

1 LMA, H1/ST/SJ/A44/3–4; other recs listed at ibid. H1/ST/SJ; *Chelsea Dir.* (1878), 30; *Census*, 1881, 1901; PRO, C 54/19193, m. 38; *Kelly's London Medical Dir.* (1892), 311.

2 Chelsea MB, *Official Guide* [1937], 99, 101.

3 Guildhall MS 9184/1/ii; Bryan, *Chelsea*, 150–1; Faulkner, *Chelsea*, II. 37, 43–4 (Faulkner also gives consecration as 1735, but most sources say 1736).

4 Vestry orders, 1771–90, ff. 82–v., 118–v., 167v., 169v.; LMA, P74/LUK/275: unpaginated section at front of vol., and reg. entries following (from 1790).

5 Vestry orders, 1790–1809, pp. 61, 63.

6 Ibid., pp. 194–5 and unpaginated index at front of vol.

7 Ibid., p. 136.

8 Ibid., p. 359.

9 Ibid., 1809–22, pp. 22–3; 50 Geo. III, c. 43 (Local and Personal); subsequent appointments of trustees in e.g. Vestry orders, 1809–22, pp. 103–4 (1813); Vestry mins, 1843–56, p. 245 (1856).

10 Bryan, *Chelsea*, 125–6, 134, 141; CL, SR 94, pp. 9–10, 14, 17; LMA, P74/LUK/274, pp. 28–31, 33–8, 40–55, 58–9, 75–6, 79, 81; P74/LUK/276.

11 LMA, P74/LUK/274, pp. 184, 187–94, 197, 232–7, 247–52, 254–5.

12 Bryan, *Chelsea*, 152.

13 Vestry mins, 1833–9, pp. 77–82, 86–8, 261–5.

14 Ibid., 1843–56, pp. 198–204, 214–16.

the old churchyard and King's Road burial ground, and (excepting vaults and graves existing before 1852) in St Luke's churchyard.[1] Brompton cemetery (Kens.) was later used by the guardians for the parish poor,[2] and inhabitants of Chelsea were buried in Hanwell and Gunnersbury (Ealing) cemeteries.[3]

Chelsea also contained burial grounds reserved for particular groups. The Royal Hospital's burial ground, just north-east of the Hospital buildings, was first used in 1692; it closed in 1855 under the 1852 Act, and the Hospital used a plot in Brompton cemetery until 1893, when it began using Brookwood cemetery (Woking, Surrey).[4] A burial ground for the Moravian church was opened on the stableyard of the demolished Beaufort House near the junction of Milman's Street with King's Road in 1751.[5] A cemetery in Cadogan Street belonging to the Roman Catholic chapel of 1812 was replaced by a mortuary chapel of 1845 which was incorporated in the church of 1877–8.[6] Known as All Souls' cemetery, burials were restricted from 1853 and were completely discontinued in 1858.[7] The Jews' burial ground near Queen's Elm in Fulham Road, purchased for the Westminster Synagogue in 1815,[8] was opened for subscribers in 1816. A small building at the entrance received corpses and housed the keeper,[9] but was demolished in the late 19th century.[10] The ground was closed in 1884,[11] and shops were built on the western side by 1895.[12] The ground was improved by the Metropolitan Public Gardens Association in 1898.[13]

STREET LIGHTING, GAS, AND ELECTRICITY

The Royal Hospital had its own lamplighter from 1691, and wrought-iron lamp standards of that period survive in the East and West Courts. By the early 19th century it had nearly 200 external oil lamps. Gas was laid on in 1823.[14] In the early 18th century patrols from the Royal Hospital on the dangerous roads from Chelsea carried lanterns on long poles.[15]

In 1752 three lamps by the churchyard were to be lit from Michaelmas to Lady Day to prevent accidents on the road and footway.[16] In 1771 the inhabitants reportedly hoped for an Act to have their streets lit,[17] but none was passed.[18] A committee was to negotiate with the commissioners of the turnpike roads about extra lighting and watching in 1790; the parishioners resolved to make no extra payment for lighting in 1794.[19] Ad hoc provision was made for different parts of the parish. In 1799 four lamp irons were to be erected at the King's Road burial ground,[20] but in the early 19th century King's Road itself was poorly lit by a few oil lamps.[21] Lamps were fixed along one side of Battersea Bridge in 1799.[22] From 1806 the Kensington turnpike trust lit Fulham Road as far west as Little Chelsea; in 1815 lamps were added westwards to the parish boundary.[23] The vestry did not wish to be incorporated in a Bill concerning watching and lighting in 1812, and similarly opposed a proposed Local Act in 1816.[24] Though a committee in 1822 recommended discontinuing the surveyors' expenditure on lamps in various parts, made for some years, considering it a 'very partial measure', the vestry resolved to continue.[25] The new burial ground had its own lighting,[26] and in 1822 the churchwardens were to light its lamps for half the year.

From 1824 the trustees substituted eight lamps lit by the Imperial Gas Light Company for the 'common lamps' despite the greater cost; two more were added to improve security in 1825.[27] Gas from Chelsea replaced oil in the Battersea Bridge lamps in 1824.[28] Apparently supplied by the Imperial,[29] other parts of the parish had gas street lights in 1825. Provision followed demand: the surveyors erected one in King's Road after complaints of drunks near the Royal Hospital. Innovations were reported in 1827: 30 gas lamps and 23 oil lamps, where gas could not be used, had been erected, over half the expense defrayed by voluntary contributions. However, the surveyors wanted the commissioners of woods, responsible for King's Road,[30] to light that road. In 1829 the surveyors welcomed the 'systematic plan' of lights being gradually introduced; each year was producing fresh subscribers from streets so far without lamps.[31] Kensington turnpike trust lit Cheyne Walk as well as Fulham Road. By 1829 the Imperial Gas Company had

1 *London Gaz.* 28 Aug. 1857, pp. 2912–13.
2 *Return of Pop. and Burial Places* (Parl. Papers, 1877 (257), LXVI), pp. 194–5.
3 RBKC, *Official Guide* [1967], 63.
4 H. Meller, *London Cemeteries* (1985), 78, 250; Dean, *Royal Hosp.* 88; *London Gaz.* 9 June 1854, p. 1777.
5 Below, Rel. Hist., foreign chs (Moravians).
6 Pevsner, *London NW.* 561; below, Rel. Hist., rom. cathm.
7 *London Gaz.* 29 Nov. 1853, p. 3470; ibid. 17 Nov. 1857, pp. 3852–3.
8 LMA, BRA 641/1/17; PRO, C 54/9678, no. 13.
9 Faulkner, *Chelsea*, II. 2; *Builder*, 2 Nov. 1901, p. 385.
10 Bryan, *Chelsea*, 74; Blunt, *Chelsea*, 154.
11 Meller, *London Cemeteries*, 168.
12 LCC, *Burial Grounds* (1895), 4.
13 *Builder*, 2 Nov. 1901, p. 385.
14 Dean, *Royal Hosp.* 126, 266; Pevsner, *London NW.* 565.
15 Beaver, *Memorials*, 52.
16 Vestry orders, 1745–71, pp. 116, 129.
17 Chelsea cuttings: street lighting (TS note from *General Evening Post*, 22/25 June 1771).
18 Faulkner, *Chelsea*, II. 342n.
19 Vestry orders, 1790–1809, pp. 1, 48, 59.
20 Ibid., p. 194.
21 Bryan, *Chelsea*, 169.
22 Beaver, *Memorials*, 225.
23 Ffooks, 'Kens. Turnpike Trust', 47–8; cf. BL, Add. MS 31326.
24 Vestry orders, 1809–22, pp. 87–8, 208–10.
25 Vestry mins, 1822–33, pp. 63, 67.
26 CL, SR 94, p. 14.
27 LMA, P74/LUK/274, pp. 170, 182, 191, 197.
28 Beaver, *Memorials*, 225.
29 S. Everard, *Hist. Gas Light and Coke Co.* (1949), 160.
30 Above, Intro., comms.
31 Vestry mins, 1822–33, pp. [1]59–60, 206–7, [210], [213]–[14], [218]–19, 254.

apparently extended its supply through Chelsea.[1] However, in 1833 a vestry committee bemoaned the lack of competition: it was forced to accept the company's terms, which included laying down mains where necessary.[2]

Hans Town, lit not by the vestry but by commissioners under its Act,[3] fared better than the old part of the parish. Lit with gas for some years before 1829, it presented in the evenings a 'most brilliant appearance'.[4] In 1834 the London Gas Light Company contracted with the commissioners to lay down mains and supply the streets.[5]

A committee regretted an increase of six gas lamps in the old part of the parish in 1832, as lighting consumed much of the highway rates, recommending that surveyors fund gas and oil lamps only where needed for public safety.[6] It was said that such use of the rate was illegal and that lighting the parish outside Hans Town, while undoubtedly necessary, must be by voluntary subscription pending an Act for lighting,[7] as it was unclear whether existing legislation could be adopted. The vestry wished to ascertain the cost of properly lighting the parish with gas, continuing the present lights meanwhile.[8] In 1833 it approved a proposal that 150 gas lamps light the old part of the parish, including the streets then unlit, by adding 84 lamps. Some of the parish was still lit by oil. The vestry voted funds to 12 inspectors to execute the provisions of new legislation;[9] by 1834 they had paid for 114 lamps, and for lighting 188, aiming to light for the whole year and erect additional lamps. Their priority was to light the thoroughfares, especially King's Road, and then the more frequented areas as funds might allow, attributing a decrease in empty houses to the better lighting. Additional lamps supplemented those of the metropolitan roads[10] at parish expense. A year later more than double the intended number of lamps had been put up, after numerous applications. In 1836 the inspectors had 208 lamps,[11] a number increased by continuing building. In 1841 the metropolitan roads commissioners,[12] because of their declining tolls, refused to light the parish's turnpikes, whereupon the Chelsea inspectors took over their 40 lamps.[13] In 1844, of 291 lamps, 15 were in Hans Town, funded by the inspectors despite being outside their district. The Imperial supplied lamps in the old part of the parish, but Hans Town was lit by a different company, presumably still the London, whose pipes in Chelsea were mentioned in 1845.[14]

A clause in the Chelsea Improvement Bill permitting commissioners to establish a municipal gas supply was successfully opposed by the Imperial:[15] the rights of the London and Imperial companies were reserved by the Act of 1845 which, as the powers of the existing inspectors seemed insufficient, empowered the improvement commissioners to light the streets, again excepting Hans Town.[16] The commissioners continued to add lamps, also lighting Kensal Green for which, as part of Chelsea parish, they were responsible. They regretfully accepted the Imperial's tender, claiming no alternative; its supply was subject to complaints.[17] The commissioners in 1846 allowed for lighting 342 lamps and for an annual increase in their number.[18] That year the board agreed to take on the ten lamps on the Lowndes estate in the north-eastern corner of Chelsea previously lit by trustees under an Act of 1826,[19] and supplied by the London Gas Company, which had 25 lamps in that area in 1847 and also had pipes in western Chelsea in 1846 and 1847. In 1847 the Chelsea commissioners vainly sought tenders from companies other than the Imperial,[20] and in 1850 the vestry sought a reduction in the high price of gas. No better terms were offered by the Imperial or the London, but the Western Company, which lit the adjoining St George Hanover Square at a lower rate, would supply a company formed by the parishioners. A committee was to consult with the improvement commissioners about erecting a gasworks, but the vestry voted down acquisition of the Lots for this purpose.[21] By 1854 the improvement commissioners had 474 public lamps for over nineteen miles of roads; the Hans Town commissioners, with four miles, had 174 lamps.[22]

The Metropolis Management Act, 1855,[23] restored responsibility for lighting to the vestry. Competition between companies, including that between the London and the Imperial in Chelsea, ended in the 1850s and under a territorial arrangement of 1860 Chelsea was served by the London Company.[24] The vestry, dissatisfied with the company's service, believed that lack of competition allowed no control over its supplier,

1 Faulkner, *Chelsea*, I. 31, 52, 138.
2 Vestry mins, 1822–33, p. 324; 1833–9, pp. 12–13, 59.
3 Above, Loc. Govt.
4 Faulkner, *Chelsea*, I. 53; II. 341–2.
5 LMA, B/NTG/1484.
6 Vestry mins, 1822–33, pp. 312–13.
7 Chelsea Scraps, 377.
8 Vestry mins, 1822–33, pp. 316–21, 323–4.
9 3 & 4 Wm. IV, c. 90.
10 Above, Intro., comms.
11 Vestry mins, 1833–9, pp. 12–15, 25–6, 29–30, 58–61, 75, 110–14, 154.
12 Above, Intro., comms.
13 Vestry mins, 1839–43, pp. 161–2, 218–31, 236–44, 251, 285–6, and accounts of Inspectors (1843) at beginning of vol.; M. Searle, *Turnpikes and Toll-Bars* [1930], I. 224–6.
14 Vestry mins, 1843–56, pp. 22–3, 50.
15 Everard, *Gas Light and Coke Co.* 172.
16 8 & 9 Vic. c. 148 (Local and Personal).
17 Improvement com. mins, 1845–6, pp. 23, 28, 31, 37, 50, 53, 63, 79.
18 Ibid., 1846–8, p. [57].
19 7 Geo. IV, c. 58 (Local and Personal).
20 Improvement com. mins, 1845–6, pp. 251, 369; ibid. 1846–8, pp. 208, 254, 294.
21 Vestry mins, 1843–56, pp. 133–4, 143–5, 150–1.
22 *Returns of Paving, Cleansing, and Lighting Metropolitan Districts* (Parl. Papers, 1854–5 (127), LIII), p. 15.
23 18 & 19 Vic. c. 120.
24 *London Jnl*, XI (1985), 42, 47–8; Everard, *Gas Light and Coke Co.* 170, and maps following pp. 176, 192.

but its desire to take over the supply went unfulfilled.[1] Between 1856 and 1872, 165 street lamps were erected.[2] In 1875 responsibility for Chelsea Embankment devolved on the vestry, but under an Act of 1876 the MBW undertook to light the river wall, with 65 lamps, and adjoining footway, on which ornamental lamps had also been erected.[3] The testing places of the Gas Light & Coke Company in 1878 included no. 1 Carlyle Square, still there in 1888.[4] In 1879 Chelsea's 967 lamps were supplied by the London Gas Company; the Gas Light & Coke Company lit 102 lamps at Kensal New Town.[5] The London Company was amalgamated in the Gas Light & Coke Company in 1883,[6] which subsequently supplied the borough.[7] In 1888 Oscar Wilde complained of imperfect lighting in Tite Street; the vestry thought it as well lit as other parts, which was 'not saying much' according to a local newspaper.[8]

In 1911 the borough's decision to award the street-lighting contract to a gas company was controversial in not allowing an equal tender by an electricity company.[9] In the mid 1930s the design of newly erected standards on Chelsea Embankment was criticized. However, the lamp posts of 1874 on the river wall, and elaborate commemorative standards cast at Coalbrookdale, survived. New lamps were also erected by the MB on other main streets.[10] In 1937 more than 1,560 gas lamps lit its 33 miles of roads.[11] Battersea Bridge was lit by electricity from 1951.[12] In the late 1950s the intention to replace standards of Victorian design with lamps lit more cheaply by electricity generated concern for the character of Chelsea's residential streets rather than for where traffic demanded improved lighting, but replacement was in progress in 1960.[13] By 1986, however, some reproduction lampposts (albeit not identical with those removed) had been erected, partly at the expense of residents.[14] In 1993 the RBKC was installing the 'Victorian' design in a rolling programme.[15]

In 1878 a representative sent to Paris to investigate electric lighting advised the vestry to await technical improvements. The distance between gas lamps then varied from 28 yards on the Embankment to 70 yards on King's Road.[16] In 1882 the experiments of a firm of engineers outside their King's Road premises provided the first display of electric lighting in the parish.[17] Various companies were subsequently empowered to supply electricity there. The Metropolitan (Brush) Electric Light and Power Company received authorization in 1883,[18] but nothing more was heard of it. The Chelsea Electricity Supply Company, with premises in Draycott Place, empowered to supply electricity in 1886,[19] commenced supply in 1889, in competition with the London Electric Supply Corporation,[20] authorized to supply Chelsea from 1889.[21] The Cadogan Electric Lighting Company started supplying Chelsea in 1888 but was taken over in 1890 by the New Cadogan and Belgrave Electric Supply Company (with premises at no. 91 Manor Street, later Chelsea Manor Street), permitted to supply electricity from 1891. In 1892 the name was changed to the St Luke Chelsea Electric Lighting Company but in 1893 the company was taken over by the more successful Chelsea Electricity Supply Company,[22] including the Manor Street site. Premises at no. 19 Cadogan Gardens were added *c.*1896 and Draycott Place went out of use soon after; the stations were subsequently at Manor Street and Cadogan Gardens, with offices at the latter. In 1896 the company outlined plans for extending supply, including the erection of substations, to meet the demand arising from the affluence of some districts and from rebuilding. A new generating station, designed by Alfred Roberts, was built 1896–1901 in Flood Street, a two-storeyed structure of brick with arched windows, with larger buildings behind. After 1928 electricity generated there was replaced by supply from the power stations of the London Power Company under an Act of 1925, and a 175-ft chimney shaft of 1905 was demolished; the station thereafter only handled current.[23] The Chelsea company also built a red-brick substation between Carlyle Square and Chelsea Square in 1897, by 1905 occupied by electrical carriage manufacturers and subsequently by motor car works. The building, derelict in

1 PRO, HO 45/6985.

2 *Returns from Vestries on Improvements since 1855* (Parl. Papers, 1872 (298), XLIX), pp. 23–4.

3 *Ann. Rep. of MBW* (Parl. Papers, 1873 (146), LVI), p. 19; ibid. (Parl. Papers, 1875 (246), LXIV), p. 69; ibid. (Parl. Papers, 1876 (290), LXIII), p. 20; ibid. (Parl. Papers, 1877 (225), LXXI), pp. 13, 71.

4 *Ann. Rep. of MBW* (Parl. Papers, 1878–9 (230), LXI), p. 41; ibid. (Parl. Papers, 1889 (326), LXVI), p. 58.

5 *Vestry rep. 1878–9*, 76.

6 Everard, *Gas Light and Coke Co.* 258–62.

7 LCC, *London Statistics*, XVI. 375; Chelsea MB, *Official Guide* [1937], 107, 109.

8 *W. London Press*, 22 Dec. 1888.

9 *The Times*, 1, 15 March 1911.

10 *Chelsea Soc. Rep.* (1934–5), 19; ibid. (1956), 42–[4], 48. Cf. CL, Roll 5(3): designs for original Embankment lamps.

11 Chelsea MB, *Official Guide* [1937], 107, 109.

12 Chelsea cuttings: Battersea bridge (*The Times*, 13 Jan. 1951).

13 *Chelsea Soc. Rep.* (1956), 41–7l; ibid. (1957), 13–14; *The Times*, 30 July 1957; *Archit. Rev.* (Feb. 1960), 81; ibid. (June 1960), 411–16.

14 *Chelsea Soc. Rep.* (1986), 23.

15 Chelsea cuttings: street lighting (*Kens. News*, 13 May 1993).

16 B. Bowers, *Hist. Electric Light and Power* (1982), 105–8.

17 Chelsea Scraps, 196.

18 46 & 47 Vic. c. 213 (Local and Personal).

19 50 Vic. c. 18 (Local and Personal).

20 LCC, *London Statistics*, XVI. 381–2.

21 52 & 53 Vic. c. 178 (Local and Personal).

22 Bowers, *Hist. Electric Light*, 143; PRO, BT 31/4807/31851; Chelsea cuttings: electricity supply companies (reply to enquiry); 54 & 55 Vic. c. 212 (Local and Personal).

23 Chelsea cuttings: electricity supply companies (reply to enquiry); KL, deed 32103; 61 & 62 Vic. c. 233 (Local and Personal); G.B. Harte and G. Stamp, *Temples of Power* (1979), s.v. Flood Street; Chelsea Misc. 241, 2296, 2298; LCC, *London Statistics*, XXXIV. 317.

1992,[1] was demolished before 2000. The Cadogan Gardens building survived in 2001.

The Chelsea Electricity Supply Company served the whole MB, although the London Electricity Supply Corporation was authorized to supply there too. In 1937 the Chelsea company, with several others, was acquired by the Charing Cross Company, subsequently known as Central London Electricity.[2] At nationalization in 1948 the London Electricity Board (LEB) took over all undertakings in London[3] and later supplied the borough.[4] The Flood Street site was still in service in 1979, but only as a substation.[5] The Victorian buildings were demolished before 1992[6] and were replaced by housing by 2000, but later structures on Alpha Place and Chelsea Manor Street, presumably erected by the LEB, survived. London Electricity plc replaced the LEB under the Electricity Act, 1989.[7]

Under the Gas Act, 1948, the assets of existing gas companies were vested in two boards, with Chelsea supplied by the North Thames Gas Board of the Gas Council, replaced in 1972 by the British Gas Corporation, itself privatized in 1986 as British Gas plc. Competition in gas supply was introduced nationally between 1996 and 1998.[8]

FIRE ENGINES

From its foundation into the 19th century the Royal Hospital had its own engines,[9] although in 1834 the parochial engine attended a fire there.[10] In 1748 the parish engine was out of repair, and was to be tested regularly, with 18 leather buckets to replace the old ones.[11] Sir Hans Sloane (d. 1753), the lord of the manor, donated a fire engine to the parish, and in 1750 or 1751 Andrew Millar gave a smaller engine and leather pipes. In 1755 a new engine house immediately east of the cage was to replace the existing one, which stood on the riverside opposite the old church.[12] The decayed parish engine was to be replaced in 1764.[13] In 1811 an engine was to be kept at the watchhouse in Symons Street, in Hans Town off Sloane Square, in addition to existing ones: a committee of the Hans Town commissioners chose an engine, larger than the one then kept in Hans Town, from Messrs Phillips and Hopwood. It was to be worked by 24 men, and with leather pipes and a crane-necked carriage it was estimated to cost about 100 guineas, to be defrayed from the church rate. The same year the workhouse on King's Road was chosen to house the small parochial engine, being near Queen's Elm, Little Chelsea, and the Common – parts of the parish then undergoing development.[14] In 1828 ladders were kept at the old church, Symons Street watch-house, and the workhouse.[15] Petyt School in Church Lane was later used as an engine house until it became too dilapidated.[16] From 1834 three engine keepers are recorded, and three engines explicitly mentioned in 1843.[17] In the late 1830s parish expenditure included repairs to engines, rewards to firemen, and salaries of engine keepers.[18] In 1864 the parish still had three engines and three attendants.[19]

Under the Fire Brigade Act, 1865, the MBW inherited stock and personnel from parishes in 1866 including, in Chelsea, premises in Sloane Square, which presumably became its temporary fire station in 1867 in Draycott Place, off Sloane Square. It subsequently opened permanent stations in Chelsea at South Parade (1868), Pavilion Road (1881), Basil Street (1907), and King's Road (1964).[20]

By 1868 a newly-built station at no. 18 South Parade was operational, and Draycott Place ceased to be used soon afterwards. In 1885 the MBW acquired the freehold of no. 18 South Parade and no. 19 adjoining, and were considering new buildings to accommodate the men, engines, and horses in one place.[21] The cramped station of 1867 passed to the LCC, which in 1891 also acquired no. 17, and a new station, begun in 1892, opened there in 1893; the decorated, gabled façade was of brick with stone and terracotta.[22] By 1938 it was considered out of date,[23] but its replacement, in King's Road, did not open until 1964, whereupon Brompton station, as the South Parade building was known, closed.[24] Representations of fire-fighting equipment on the façade survived in 2001,[25] when the building was used by the Royal Brompton hospital.

In 1879 the MBW proposed to build a station in

1 NMR, file 96614; *Chelsea Dir.* (1905), 75; ibid. (1910), 76.

2 LCC, *London Statistics*, XXXI. 319; ibid. XLI. 375, 396; Chelsea MB, *Official Guide* [1937], 109.

3 LCC, *London Statistics*, NS, I. 189.

4 Chelsea MB, *Official Guide* [1952], 95.

5 Harte and Stamp, *Temples of Power*, s.v. Flood Street.

6 NMR, file 96614.

7 *VCH Middx*, XI. 211. For Lots Rd. power sta., see Intro., comms (rlys).

8 LCC, *London Statistics*, NS, I. 194; *Whitaker's Almanack* (1999).

9 Above, Intro.

10 Dean, *Royal Hosp.* 49, 82, 119, 144, 236, 263–4.

11 Vestry orders, 1745–71, p. 57.

12 Faulkner, *Chelsea*, I. 170; Chelsea Misc. 1681–2 (this map is perhaps *c.*1811, cf. surveyor's other work: BL, Add. MSS 31325–7; LMA, P74/LUK/274, p. 38).

13 *Chelsea Soc. Rep.* (1978), 47; Vestry orders, 1745–71, pp. 94, 169–70, 283.

14 Vestry orders, 1809–22, pp. 48, 54–5, 65.

15 Chelsea Misc. 847.

16 Vestry mins, 1822–33, p. 227; Denny, *Chelsea Past*, 65, 86; cf. Faulkner, *Chelsea*, I. 170.

17 Chelsea Misc. 848v.–851.

18 Vestry mins, 1833–9, pp. 259, 294; 1839–43, pp. 108, 114.

19 *Returns of Fire Engines etc. (Metropolis)*, (Parl. Papers, 1864, (322), L), p. 11.

20 Below.

21 *Ann. Rep. of MBW* (Parl. Papers, 1867 (34), LVIII), pp. 40–1; ibid. (Parl. Papers, 1867–8 (45), LVIII), pp. 33–4; ibid. (Parl. Papers, 1868–9 (23), LI), pp. 35–6; ibid. (Parl. Papers, 1882 (188), LIX), pp. 41–2; ibid. (Parl. Papers, 1886 (170), LVII), p. 33.

22 LMA, LCC/CL/FB/1/60; foundation stone and date on bldg (1892).

23 LMA, LCC/CL/FB/1/60.

24 Below.

25 Figg, *Hidden Chelsea*, 52.

Pavilion Road to serve the Sloane Street neighbourhood, and leased a site from Earl Cadogan in 1880 for a building with accommodation for two engines, seven firemen, and a coachman, which was in use in 1881.[1] It had closed by 1917,[2] probably as a result of the erection of Knightsbridge (below), though the building still survived in 2001.[3] Knightsbridge fire station was built in 1907 in Basil Street,[4] to replace a station in Relton Mews (Kens.), and was designed by the LCC architect W.E. Riley, in red brick with stone dressings in classical style.

A site for a replacement for the South Parade station was acquired in 1939 in King's Road, by the junction with Arthur (later Dovehouse) Street.[5] After the Second World War a Regency terrace there, King's Parade, was demolished by the LCC,[6] which in 1961 approved plans for the station.[7] It opened in 1964, and the Brompton station (South Parade) closed.[8] Basil Street and King's Road remained in use in 2000.

PUBLIC LIBRARIES

In 1887 the parish adopted the Public Libraries Acts, whereupon the town hall housed a temporary reading room. Earl Cadogan gave a site in Manresa Road where J.M. Brydon designed a symmetrical brick and stone structure of five bays with semi-circular Ionic porch, arched windows, and one-bay wings. It was opened in 1891. One reading room converted by Brydon to a gallery commemorating Queen Victoria's jubilee (1897), opened in 1899. An innovation from 1905 was a children's library, converted from the existing boys' reading room. The King's Road front of the old town hall was converted to house the library in 1978, and the Manresa Road building became part of Chelsea College. Chelsea vestry opened temporary library premises in Kensal Town in 1888 and built a library in Harrow Road designed by Karslake & Mortimer, 1890, which passed controversially to Paddington at boundary adjustments in 1900. A scheme of 1901 provided for its maintenance by that borough, which had not adopted the Public Libraries Acts.[9]

BATHS

In 1840 there were public and private hot and cold baths at the Manor House Bath Gardens in King's Road.[10] The Chelsea Swimming Bath Company constructed men's first- and second-class swimming baths and a ladies' swimming bath at no. 171 King's Road in 1877; the company was wound up in 1886.[11]

In 1890 Chelsea vestry sanctioned the purchase by the newly appointed commissioners for baths and wash-houses of the site between King's Road and Manor (later Chelsea Manor) Street, partly occupied by those private baths, from the Cadogan estate.[12] In 1893 private baths for men and women were opened in King's Road, presumably by the commissioners. The baths closed in 1905 for rebuilding.[13] The scheme, drawn up in 1901, was for 100 private baths and 3 swimming baths; they also considered building public washhouses but that was dropped as additional land would be required. As built, however, the new baths, by Wills & Anderson with the engineer Alexander Macdonald, were smaller than planned, and facing only Manor Street so that the King's Road frontage could be used for extensions to the town hall. There were two swimming baths, for men and women, and male and female first- and second-class slipper baths, opened in 1907. The symmetrical 'Renaissance' front of red brick with stone decorations blended well with the town hall. Conversion to provide a sports centre in 1977 or 1978 left only one pool.[14]

The Chelsea commissioners identified a site for baths and washhouses for Kensal Town between Kensal Road and Wedlake Street in 1890.[15] The foundation stone was laid in 1896 and two swimming baths besides private baths for both sexes opened in 1898.[16]

COUNCIL AND PARLIAMENTARY REPRESENTATION

LCC and GLC

Chelsea at first had two members on the London County Council, elected triennially from 1889; from 1949 there were three, also representing Kensington's Brompton ward. Progressives held the seats from 1889 to 1907, except at the 1895 election when they fell to Moderates, including the 5th Earl Cadogan. The 1898 election was marked by allegations of corruption on the part of the Progressives. From 1907 the Municipal Reformers held

1 *Ann. Rep. of MBW* (Parl. Papers, 1880 Sess. 2 (212), LXII), p. 43; ibid. (Parl. Papers, 1881 (240), LXXIX), p. 38; ibid. (Parl. Papers, 1882 (188), LIX), pp. 41–2; ibid. (Parl. Papers, 1886 (170), LVII), p. 33; LMA, LCC/MISC.P/56/1–3.

2 LMA, LCC/CL/FB/1/79; *Chelsea Dir.* (1917), 159, cf. ibid. (1907), 163.

3 Plaque on S identifies bldg, near S end of road.

4 Within ancient par. of Chelsea, but outside MB boundary.

5 LMA, LCC/CL/FB/1/60.

6 *Chelsea Soc. Rep.* (1957), 9, 12–13.

7 *The Times*, 12 May 1961.

8 B. Denny and C. Starren, *Kens. and Chelsea in Old Photographs* (1995), 152.

9 Chelsea Misc. 269, 325–32; Pevsner, *London NW.* 566, 568; B. Curle, *Libs for All* (1987), 8, 12, 29, and inner front cover; memorial plaques in Chelsea Old Town Hall in 2000; *Chelsea Soc. Rep.* (1954), 30–1.

10 *Hand Bk to Chelsea* (1840), 34 (CL, SR 254/1).

11 Chelsea cuttings: public baths (*Bldg News*, 29 Jun. 1877); PRO, BT 31/2215/10439.

12 *Vestry mins, 1890–1*, 520–1, 531.

13 LCC, *London Statistics*, XVI. 138–9.

14 *Archit. Rev.* XX (1907), 30–6; Pevsner, *London NW.* 566; *Chelsea Soc. Rep.* (1977), 16; *The Times*, 16 April 1901; 5 April 1907.

15 *Vestry mins, 1890–1*, 520.

16 Chelsea Misc. 349–50.

both seats. Basil Marsden-Smedley, elected as a Municipal Reformer in 1933, served to 1946, being joined from 1934 by an official Conservative. Conservatives held all three seats from 1949 to the abolition of the LCC in 1965. Thereafter Kensington and Chelsea had joint representation, dominated by Conservatives, on the Greater London Council.[1]

Parliament

Chelsea formed part of the Middlesex county constituency, but from the 1830s agitation for separate representation drew strong local support. A meeting of the inhabitants in 1831 pressed for amendment to the Reform Bill to provide representation for a district including Chelsea, Kensington, Hammersmith, Fulham, and Brompton; Chelsea alone was more populous than 26 districts for which the Bill proposed representation.[2] A motion in the Commons in 1850 to incorporate Chelsea, Kensington, Hammersmith, and Fulham into a two-member parliamentary borough was withdrawn.[3] A public meeting in 1859 attacked the government's reform bill as inadequately representative,[4] and another in 1861 unanimously supported a proposed two-member borough of Kensington and Chelsea.[5] Finally under the Second Reform Act a two-member constituency of Chelsea, including also Kensington, Hammersmith, Fulham, and part of Chiswick, became effective in 1868. In 1885 the constituency was divided and Chelsea became a single-member borough, coinciding with the parish and later, after Kensal Town was excluded in 1918, with the metropolitan borough. It was extended in 1948 by the addition of Kensington's Brompton ward. In 1974 it became the southern division of Kensington and Chelsea, gaining Earl's Court from the former south division of Kensington.[6]

At the 1868 election Chelsea returned two Liberals, Charles Dilke (later Bt) and Sir Henry Hoare, Bt. Dilke remained the leading member while the two-member constituency continued, but in 1874 the second seat fell to William Gordon, a Conservative, the Liberal J.F.B. Firth regaining it in 1880.[7] Dilke was the first member for the single seat in 1885, but following allegations of his adultery he lost it to Charles Algernon Whitmore, a Conservative, in 1886.[8] At the 1906 election Whitmore was ousted by the Liberal Emslie Horniman,[9] but in January 1910 Samuel Hoare (Bt from 1915) won the seat for the Unionists, and Unionists or Conservatives have held it ever since.[10] Hoare, who held in successive Conservative or National governments the posts of air minister, Secretary for India, Foreign Secretary, First Lord of the Admiralty, Home Secretary, and finally air minister again, remained MP for Chelsea until promoted to the peerage as Viscount Templewood in 1944. His picturesque or prominent opponents at general elections included a relative, Hugh Hoare, standing for the Liberals in December 1910;[11] Miss E. Phipps, a feminist independent and ex-president of the National Union of Women Teachers, in 1918;[12] Bertrand Russell for Labour in 1922 and 1923;[13] and Mrs Bertrand Russell in 1924.[14] Though the British Union of Fascists, with a base at Whitelands at the junction of King's Road and Walpole Street,[15] nominated Sir Lionel Berkeley Holt Haworth as their parliamentary candidate in Chelsea in 1936,[16] he apparently did not contest an election.

Sir Samuel Hoare's successor William Sidney, son of a former mayor, returned unopposed in 1944,[17] became Lord de l'Isle and Dudley in 1945[18] and was succeeded by Allan Noble, a junior minister under Churchill and Eden. Capt. John Litchfield was member 1959–66 and Marcus (from 1973 Sir Marcus) Worsley 1966–74. Nicholas (later Sir Nicholas) Scott, MP from 1974 and later a junior minister, narrowly deflected an attempted coup against him in 1977 by his constituency party, which deselected him in 1996 for alleged alcoholic horizontality, probably caused by illness; in 1997 it

1 W.E. Jackson, *Achievement: a Short History of the LCC* (1965), 252–83; *Vestry Rep. 1889–90*, p. xxi; Pearman, *Cadogan Est.* 97; *The Times*, 26 March, 20, 26 April 1898, 23 June 1948; Knott, *Electoral Crucible*, 141; *Royal Com. on Local Govt in Greater London: Written Evidence from Local Authorities, Misc. Bodies and Priv. Individuals*, I (1962), 156; Husbands, 'London Council Elections of 6 May 1982', 186; *Who's Who* (1985), s.vv. Crofton, Sir Malby, and Rugg. *Chelsea Soc. Rep.* (1964), pp. 16–19, states that Marsden-Smedley was elected in 1932.

2 *The Times*, 15 July 1831.

3 *CJ*, CV. 38.

4 *The Times*, 19 March 1859.

5 Ibid., 23 Jan. 1861.

6 P. Arnold, *A Hist. of Britain's Parl. Constituencies: The Constituencies of the Royal Borough of Kensington and Chelsea* (priv. print. 1994; copy in CL), sect. 3 p. 1; LCC, *London Statistics*, XXVI (1915–20), 14; LCC, *Stat. Abstract for London*, XXXI (1939–48), 31, notes (c) (but reading 'latter' for 'later') and (e); *Boundaries of Parl. Constituencies 1885–1972*, comp. and ed. F.W.S. Craig (Chichester, 1972), pp. 3, 49, 127.

7 Roy Jenkins, *Dilke: A Victorian tragedy* (1965, paperback edn 1996), 46, 52, 86, 123; *McCalmont's Parl. Poll Bk of All Elections 1832–1918*, ed. J. Vincent and M. Stenton (1971), part I, p. 54.

8 Jenkins, *Dilke*, 227 seqq.; *McCalmont's Parl. Poll Bk 1832–1918*, part II, p. 39; Arnold, *Hist. Constituencies, Kensington and Chelsea*, sect. 3 p. 1, wrongly giving Witmore; cf. *Vestry Rep. 1899–1900*, p. xxi; G. Noel, 'The scandalous member for Chelsea', *Chelsea Soc. Rep.* (1993), 26–3.

9 *The Times*, 17 Jan. 1906.

10 Rest of this and next para. based unless otherwise stated on Arnold, *Hist. Constituencies, Kensington and Chelsea*, sect. 3, pp. 1–2; *McCalmont's Parl. Poll Bk 1832–1918*, part II, p. 39; part III, pp. 15, 42. For Sam. Hoare, e.g. *Who's Who of Brit. MPs*, ed. M. Stenton and S. Lees, III. 166.

11 *The Times*, 16, 24 Nov., 7 Dec. 1910.

12 Ibid., 26, 27 Nov., 5, 30 Dec. 1918.

13 Ibid., 4, 16 Nov. 1922; 16, 19, 21 Nov., 7 Dec. 1923; B. Barker, 'Two Chelsea Philosophers', *Chelsea Soc. Rep.* (1997), 32.

14 *The Times*, 13, 31 Oct. 1924.

15 L. Lewis, 'Whitelands: From Merry Maidens to Blackshirts', *Chelsea Soc. Rep.* (1994), 50–1.

16 *The Times*, 19 Nov. 1936.

17 Ibid., 3, 18 July, 18, 19 Aug., 12 Oct. 1944.

18 Ibid., 5 May, 19 June 1945.

chose Alan Clark, also a former minister. Clark held the seat that year despite allegations of his adultery, and died in 1999. The ensuing byelection was won by Michael Portillo, former Secretary of State for Defence, who held the seat in the 2001 general election.[1]

Perhaps because of the rebuilding of Chelsea and the lack of a Labour Party in the constituency,[2] turnout at general elections was low by national standards, and generally well below its peaks of 71.1 per cent in October 1924 and 70.6 per cent in February 1950.[3] The Conservative share of the vote, 60.5 per cent in 1910, reached 85 per cent in 1935. After the Second World War, and in the later 20th century, it normally varied between 60 and 67 per cent, rising to 73.4 per cent in 1955 and falling below 60 per cent only in the general elections of 1966 and 1997.[4]

1 *The Times*, 21, 23, 28 Sep. 1977; David Butler and Dennis Kavanagh, *The British General Election of 1997* (1997), 197; Kensington & Chelsea election results, via web site (www.psr.keele.ac.uk/area/uk/constit/020.htm) consulted 5 June 2003; *Evening Standard*, 6 Feb. 2002.

2 Above, Soc. Hist., political clubs.

3 LCC, *Statistical Abstract for London*, XXI (1917–26), p. 37; XXVIII (1926–36), pp. 18 seqq.; LCC, *London Statistics*, NS, III (1947–56), p. 12.

4 Arnold, *Hist. Constituencies, Kensington and Chelsea*, sect. 3, pp. 2–4; Pelling, *Social Geog. of British Elections*, 30–1; *House of Commons Factsheet M15: General Election Results 1 May 1997*, table 11 (web site, consulted 2 Dec. 2001).

RELIGIOUS HISTORY

THE earliest indication of Chelsea as a parish or the existence of a church is in 1157, when as the church of 'Chelcheia' it was among those confirmed to the abbey by Pope Adrian IV.[1] All indications suggest that the medieval parish with its small population was rather poor, and even in the mid 16th century had no lavish plate or rich furnishings.[2] There is little evidence of religious controversies in the 16th or 17th centuries, and the advent of other religious groups, such as the Huguenots in the late 17th century or Roman Catholics in the late 18th, seems to have caused little difficulty.

In 1838 Chelsea was reckoned to have 14 places of worship, 7 of them Anglican and one Roman Catholic; the protestant nonconformists' 6 chapels provided 3,160 places, compared with the Roman Catholics' 600 and the Church of England's 7,350.[3] In 1851 there were estimated to be 28 places of worship in the parish, of which 12 were Anglican, one was Roman Catholic, and the remainder protestant nonconformist.[4] In 1998 in addition to 6 Anglican churches Chelsea had 14 non-Anglican certified places of worship, of which three were Roman Catholic, one was Muslim, and one Jewish. The Church of Scotland and the Moravians still worshipped in the parish together with 6 protestant nonconformist sects.[5]

RELIGIOUS BUILDINGS

This account of the buildings is based on material from the sections of Settlement and Building above, and on accounts of individual churches and chapels and other sources as indicated.

Building to 1820

Chelsea's parish church was an unexceptional late medieval rubble and flint building of a type familiar in many Middlesex villages. In the 16th and early 17th centuries, as medieval houses in the riverside settlement were enlarged or improved, leading parishioners installed substantial funerary monuments in both progressive and conservative taste. In the More chapel, created in 1528, the conventional late medieval tomb of Sir Thomas More contrasts with court-influenced Renaissance ornament.[6] Work done in the late 17th century, including the replacement of the nave with a hipped-roofed brick box designed to be seen from the river, the building of a new west tower, and the erection of a Baroque monument to Viscount Newhaven, belongs to the rapid development of Chelsea between the old village and the new Royal Hospital. Church, Hospital, and the closely-built rows of good quality houses shared the same reticent brick classicism, varied more in the quality of craftsmanship and subtleties of design than in degrees of display.

In the eighteenth-century Chelsea gained only two religious buildings, the chapel of the Moravian colony, established in 1750 in the grounds of Beaufort House where it incorporated 16th-century fabric of the mansion's outbuildings,[7] and a simple brick Anglican proprietary chapel built close to Little Chelsea, perhaps to help stimulate development. Park Chapel was rebuilt in 1810 with aisles, galleries and a two-storeyed Italianate façade, after new houses had begun to appear in Chelsea Park.[8] Several new chapels were built during the first two decades of the 19th century, all in the prevailing Greek Revival style. They included the large galleried nonconformist chapels provided in the fast-developing south-east of the parish – the Congregationalists' Ranelagh chapel of 1818 by W.F. Pocock,[9] and the Methodist church designed in 1812 by the famous minister-architect Revd Jenkins[10] – and the Roman Catholics' chapel, built closer to the better-class part of Hans Town by G.J. Wigley, with funds from leading Catholics families and with an ungalleried interior of some sophistication.[11] The institutional chapel of the period was also Greek, the style of the Royal Military Asylum to which it belonged.[12]

1820–1865

Four out of Chelsea's ten Anglican churches were established in the next three decades of the 19th century, as part of the national church extension scheme to cater for the parish's rapidly expanding population.[13] They were all designed in the Gothic style, favoured by High Church commentators as distinctively Anglican and by the Church Building Commissioners as particularly suitable for additional churches in rural parishes.[14] The

1 BL, Cott. Faust. A. iii, f. 165.

2 Rest of para. based on sections of Rel. Hist. below.

3 *London City Mission Mag.* III. 125.

4 *Religious Census*, 1851.

5 List supplied by ONS (Birkdale). Nos are for Chelsea part of RBKC.

6 Below, par. ch (All Saints or Chelsea Old Ch.).

7 Below, foreign chs (Moravians).

8 Below, Park chapel.

9 Below, prot. nonconf. (Congs.); Colvin, *Brit. Architects*, 649; *Images of Chelsea*, gallery 481–5.

10 Colvin, *Brit. Architects*, 458; below, prot. nonconf. (Methodists).

11 *Images of Chelsea*, gallery 486; below, rom. cathm (St Mary's).

12 Below, institutional chapels.

13 Above, Intro. (pop.).

14 Bradley, 'Gothic Revival', 20, 81.

wealth enjoyed by leading local landowners and residents in the years after 1815 is displayed by the lavish new parish church of St Luke, sited near the centre of the parish and built on parochial initiative and mostly at parish expense. Because of the large budget the requirements of the Commissioners, who contributed one third of the cost, were stretched to include a burial vault, Bath-stone facing, stone ornament throughout, and even a stone vault constructed on authentic Gothic principles. The church designed by the same architect, James Savage, to be a chapel of ease at the east end of the parish, south of Hans Town, was entirely funded by the Commissioners and so followed their strictures regarding economical design and construction.[1] Three large brick district chapels, Christ Church, St Saviour, and St Jude, followed in the late 1830s and early 1840s to serve respectively the south, far north-east, and south-east of the parish, where despite population growth, particularly of lower middle- and working-class parishioners, space was still available for further development.[2] The aisled and galleried plans of all three followed the Commissioners' preferences, though Blore's Christ Church, which served a working-class congregation,[3] was unusual in combining an innovative and influential asymmetrical exterior with a centralized interior dominated by the large pulpit.[4] By the time St Jude's was built in the 1840s, asymmetrical plans were commonplace, and shortage of public funds meant that new solutions, eschewing stone ornament, were tried. At St Jude, Basevi imitated, almost entirely in brick, an English country parish church of the 14th century with a battlemented south-western tower.[5] When first built all three churches had open settings. The south-west front of the same architect's St Saviour's originally faced nurseries, which was still open as the Prince's cricket ground in 1862,[6] but its north-east end had become the termination of the view down Walton Place, also laid out by Basevi, and its west side part of Walton Street. Christ Church, built on garden ground behind houses, had been engulfed by 1865.[7]

In the 30 years after 1845, only one Anglican church was added to the existing stock. St Simon Zelotes was built in 1858–9 to serve a lower middle-class neighbourhood in east Chelsea[8] and asserted a bold presence in streets of modest houses by means of its roguish Gothic style. Its facing of Kentish Rag and the polychrome brick of its interior, roofed elaborately in timber, were a decade out of date and its plan, with broad galleried transepts, low-church.[9] Though most of the non-Anglican congregations established before 1865 adapted existing buildings, the nonconformists and Roman Catholics continued to make noticeable architectural and social contributions to the parish. The Congregationalists, who amongst nonconformists most closely followed Anglican architectural fashions, were responsible for an over-ambitious Gothic church with schoolrooms in Markham Square to succeed their Ranelagh chapel. They built more modestly in Gothic style in West Brompton in 1865–6.[10] The Roman Catholics' efforts, though piecemeal, were architecturally more significant. They commissioned A.W.N. Pugin, who then lived in Cheyne Walk,[11] to build a Gothic cemetery chapel, and his son, E.W. Pugin, to add a Blessed Sacrament chapel to their existing building, as part of a larger complex including school, convent and almshouses.[12]

1865–1914

Red brick, in decorative combination with dressed stone at the Anglican French Gothic St John, Tadema Road,[13] was the material preferred by all denominations from the mid 1870s until well into the next century. The exterior of A. Blomfield's St Andrew's, which replaced Park Chapel in 1912–13, followed much the same formula, as did St Columba's Church of Scotland, designed by J. Macvicar Anderson and opened in 1883–4.[14] J.F. Bentley's St Mary's, with which the Roman Catholics replaced their chapel in 1875–6, differed chiefly in the colour of the brick and the refined design of its interior.[15]

Only two Anglican churches were built between 1875 and 1914. Instead the chief investment was made in enlarging, altering or rebuilding the earlier Gothic boxes, and in modernizing their interiors. The development of the open ground near the church and other improvements on the Cadogan estate were accompanied by the enlargement of St Saviour's in 1878, which was followed in 1890 by a remodelling for Anglo-Catholic usage. High churchmanship also influenced the rebuilding of Holy Trinity in 1888–9[16] to a design by J.D. Sedding that recalled in an enriched late Gothic form its predecessor's twin-turreted façade and incorporated Arts-and-Crafts furnishings of exceptional opulence. Elsewhere churches were extended and remodelled to fill already cramped sites and make them more prominent in the streetscape. Certain alterations, such as the addition in 1888 of a south-western tower and spire at St John's and of a decorative west front at Christ Church in

1 M.H. Port, *Six Hundred New Chs* (1961), 85; *Images of Chelsea*, gallery 474–480.
2 Thompson, *Map* (1836); CL, Tithe Map and Award.
3 Below, dau. chs (Christ Ch.).
4 Bradley, 'Gothic Revival', 406–7.
5 Ibid., 297.
6 Old OS Map, London 74 (1871 edn).
7 Old OS Map, London 87 (1865 edn).
8 Below, dau. chs (St Simon).
9 *The Builder*, XVI (1858), 424; *Images of Chelsea*, gallery 471–3.
10 Below, prot. nonconf. (Congs).
11 A. Wedgwood, *A.W.N. Pugin and the Pugin Family* (1985), 85.
12 Below, rom. cathm (St Mary's); *Images of Chelsea*, gallery 489.
13 Photograph, NMR AA76/909B. See fig. XX.
14 Below, foreign chs (Ch. of Scotland).
15 Below, rom. cathm (St Mary's).
16 Below, dau. chs (Holy Trinity).

1900,[1] also belonged to the amelioration of conditions in those areas. Improvements to the streets north of Cheyne Walk included the building of Goldie's classical Holy Redeemer church for the Roman Catholics in 1894, though street-widening caused changes of plan even before it was complete.[2]

Twentieth-Century Chelsea

After 1900 Anglicans built nothing completely new except St Andrew's, Park Walk, which replaced Park Chapel soon after the area to the east of Park Walk was built up.[3] St Luke's church and churchyard alone remained in almost pristine state, preserved by a huge seating capacity and lack of redevelopment in the immediate area. The most important early 20th-century church building was the Christian Scientists' first branch church in England which, in accordance with the religion's grand vision of its place in the city, was located in a fashionable residential district where it could attract a wealthy congregation and was made conspicuous by means of siting, design, and gleaming white stone.[4]

No Anglican churches were built in the interwar years and St Jude's was demolished for luxury flats. World War II caused more losses – at St John, Tadema Road, which after 20 years of dereliction had to be demolished,[5] at Holy Trinity, Sloane Street, where the roof was replaced,[6] and at St Luke where the original glass was blown-out.[7] Most tragic was the loss of the Old Church, flattened except for the More chapel. It was rebuilt immediately after the war, incorporating salvaged monuments. In all these cases reconstruction was not completed until the late 1950s, together with the rebuilding of the RC convent chapel of the Sisters of Adoration Réparatrice[8] and the Congregationalists' mid 19th-century Edith Grove chapel. The demolition in 1952 of the latter denomination's Markham Square church was unrelated to the war and was a result of a reduction in the local congregation.[9] Only the Church of Scotland rebuilt on a significant scale, to the designs of a conservative English architect, Sir Edward Maufe, who replaced the 19th-century St Columba, bombed in 1941, with a replacement for what was the chief representative of the national church outside Scotland.[10]

Significant change resumed in the last decade of the 20th century. An informal building for less formal worship was adopted at St John's, relocated in the World's End estate.[11] Financial pressures and falling congregations affected churches as diverse as St Saviour, where the building was partly converted to housing,[12] and at the Christian Science church which became offices.[13] Housing was also included in the reconstruction of the Wesleyan Methodists' King's Road church which, remarkably, had exploited its site by incorporating shops along the frontage as early as 1903.[14]

THE PARISH CHURCH

The parish church of Chelsea was known originally as All Saints,[15] but from the late 17th century more commonly as St Luke's,[16] though not, apparently, because of a formal rededication despite the Evangelist's name being inscribed on a bell of 1673.[17] Although also served by institutional or proprietary chapels, the parish remained undivided when the rectory was transferred under an Act of 1819 to a more central church,[18] dedicated to St Luke and opened in 1824. The older building was then left as the 'Parish Chapel', for which the name All Saints was later revived but which has more generally been known as Chelsea Old Church. It was not until 1831 that a division of the ancient parish took place, when the perpetual curacy of a third church, Holy Trinity, was designated a rectory. No district was allotted to the Old Church in 1819, although in 1855 its new incumbent, officially designated the assistant minister of the Parish Chapel, voluntarily took care of certain streets.[49] The Old Church remained a chapel of ease until it was finally assigned a parish called All Saints (Chelsea Old Church) out of St Luke's in 1951.[20] The account below treats church life before 1824 for the parish as a whole, and after 1824 for St Luke's and for the Old Church; it concludes with architectural accounts of both buildings.

PATRONAGE, INCOME AND PROPERTY

Presentations to the rectory were made by the abbot of Westminster,[21] or by the Crown *sede vacante*,[22] until the

1 Below, dau. chs (St John, Tadema Rd).
2 Below, rom. cathm (Our Most Holy Redeemer).
3 Below, dau. chs (St And.).
4 P.E. Ivey, *Prayers in Stone. Christian Science Architecture in the US 1894–1930* (1999). 5, 22–8, 35, 49–50; below, prot. nonconf. (Christ. Sc.).
5 Below, dau. chs (St John).
6 Ibid. (Holy Trinity).
7 Below, par. ch (All Saints).
8 Below, rom. cathm (Sisters of Adoration); below, prot. nonconf. (Congs).
9 Below, prot. nonconf. (Congs).
10 Below, foreign chs (Ch. of Scotland).
11 Below, dau. chs (St John's Community Ch.).
12 Ibid. (St Saviour).
13 Below, prot. nonconf. (Christ. Sc.).
14 Ibid. (Methodists).
15 e.g. *L&P Hen. VIII*, V, p. 207. In 1290 a relaxation was granted to penitents visiting 'Thelchurche' on All Saints' Day: *Cal. Papal Reg.* I. 520.
16 Still All Saints' *c.*1748: Guildhall MS 9556, f. 28.
17 Davies, *Chelsea Old Ch.* 2. Lysons speculated that there might have been a double dedication, to St Luke and All Saints: *Environs*, II. 92 n.
18 Guildhall MS 19224/367(2), copy of 59 Geo. III, c. 35 (Local and Personal).
19 E. Davies, *In Remembrance. A Sketch of the Late Revd R.H. Davies* [*c.*1908], 61.
20 Guildhall MS 19224/33 (inc. map).
21 Hennessy, *Novum Rep.* 119.
22 e.g. *Cal. Pat.* 1313–17, 452, 573.

exchange of the manor together with the advowson in 1536.[1] Thereafter presentations were made by the Crown and then by successive lay lords of the manor or those to whom they had temporarily granted it,[2] Earl Cadogan being patron in 1999.[3] Under the Act of 1819 the rector of the new St Luke's became patron of the Old Church.[4] Under an agreement of 1950 the rector and the patron of St Luke's were to be joint patrons of All Saints (Chelsea Old Church).[5]

The value of the rectory was a modest £8 13s. 4d. (13 marks) in 1291 and 1319[6] and the same in 1535.[7] In 1340 the rector's tithes of corn, wool, and lambs produced within the parish was valued at £6 13s. 4d.: 40s. had been deducted because 30 a. arable and 2 a. meadow belonged to the rectory.[8] The incumbent Robert Richardson, incorrectly recorded as vicar, received £13 6s. 8d. a year in 1548, when Chelsea had 75 communicants, Kensington had 100, and Fulham 444.[9] The living was valued at £120 a year in 1650, of which £60 represented the tithes.[10] The rector took tithes, chiefly on garden ground, in kind, as did his successor Adam Littleton before compounding with his tenants for 3 years at 6s. an acre. In 1694 the new incumbent John King found that Littleton had recently received £182 12s., made up of £7 for seats in the chancel, £15 4s. for house tithes, £51 19s. for glebe tithes, and £103 9s. for fields (garden) tithes.[11] King improved the finances: in 1703, 'tired with the backwardness of the gardeners', he farmed most of the fields tithes. An Exchequer suit against the widowed duchess of Beaufort ensured that tithes, withheld by the duke, would be paid for Beaufort House, and it was agreed with the vestry that the rector should receive at Easter 4d. for every person aged 16 or more, his predecessors having simply appropriated the Communion money. Above all, the value of the glebe was increased by building leases.[12] In 1717 tithes yielded £115 4s. 6d. and glebe rents £157 7s. 6d. out of a total income of over £380.[13]

The living was valued at £390 in the mid 18th century[14] and again slightly later.[15] After his transfer to the new St Luke's the average net income of Chelsea's rector 1828–31 was £1,003, a little less than that of the vicar of Fulham or St Mary Abbots, Kensington.[16] Compositions for tithes in the 1830s were found not to represent their full value. Almost half of the parish, *c.*377 a., was covered by building, roads or waste and so not subject to tithes in 1845, when they were owed on 382 a. and also on *c.*12 a. of glebe not built on. Commutation, after an adjustment in 1846 awarding £3 13s. to the incumbent of Holy Trinity, gave the rector of Chelsea £210 7s. for lands other than the glebe, for which he received a further £7 8s.[17] St Luke's was still Chelsea's richest living in 1866, as it was with £1,400 in 1881;[18] a gross rental of £1,600 was produced by 22 acres of glebe in 1887[19] when the rector still received £217 15s. for commuted tithes.[20] The net income of £1,600 (£2,100 gross) in 1907 was equalled by that of Holy Trinity.[21] About 1¼ acres of glebe on the west side of the Royal Military Asylum was sold to the Crown in 1814 to enlarge the Asylum's grounds,[22] and land at Merton (Surrey) bought for the rectory with the proceeds;[23] the land was sold in the 1860s and the proceeds then used for the expenses of the Chelsea Rectory Act, 1870.[24] That Act and its predecessor of 1825[25] were obtained to facilitate building on the glebe.

The Old Church, left with no entitlement to the glebe, was supported by pew rents and a share in the church rates. Its minister's stipend was to be decided by the trustees of the new St Luke's but was to be not less than £250.[26] Its net income 1828–31 was £300,[27] a figure still given in 1842; for most of the 19th century it was only £250, the gross amount in 1907.[28]

The parsonage house and part of the glebe of Chelsea apparently lay between the later King's Road and the Thames, bounded on the east by land later belonging to Beaufort House and on the west by Hob Lane. The house's location is unknown but probably fronted the road by the Thames near the later Milman's Street.[29] The house, 2 closes adjoining containing 14 a. 22 p., half a rood of meadow, and 3 a. of arable in Eastfield,[30] were conveyed by the rector in 1566 to William Paulet, marquess of Winchester.[31] Paulet in turn conveyed a

1 *L&P Hen. VIII*, XI, p. 84.
2 Hennessy, *Novum Rep.* 120; Chelsea Misc. 1367–8 (abstract of title to advowson).
3 C. Johnston, *Guide to St Luke's Ch.* (1999), 25.
4 59 Geo. III, c. 35 (Local and Personal). Lords of the manor were sometimes listed with the rector as patrons of the Old Ch., e.g. *Mackeson's Guide.*
5 Guildhall MS 19224/33.
6 *Tax. Eccl.* (Rec. Com.), 17a; *Cal. Papal Reg.* II. 184.
7 *Valor Eccl.* (Rec. Com.), I. 433.
8 *Inq. Non.* (Rec. Com.), 197.
9 *Chantry Cert.*, pp. 69, 72–3.
10 Lysons, *Environs*, II. 114, quoting Lambeth Pal. Lib., Parl. Com. Surveys XII a/12, f. 229.
11 Dr King's MS, pp. 157–8.
12 Ibid., pp. 164–5, 167.
13 Ibid., p. 221.
14 Guildhall MS 9556, f. 28v.
15 Guildhall MS 9557A.
16 *Rep. Com. Eccl. Revenues*, 641.
17 CL, map case '1847', drawer 4, nos 34–6.
18 *Clergy List* (1866, 1881).
19 *Return of Glebe Lands* (Parl. Papers, 1887 (307), LXIV), p. 84.
20 *Return of Tithes Commuted* (Parl. Papers, 1887 (214), LXIV), p. 122.
21 *Crockford* (1907).
22 55 Geo. III, c. 66 (Private).
23 Faulkner, *Chelsea*, II. 336.
24 22 & 34 Vic. c. 1 (Private).
25 Chelsea Rectory Act, 1825, 6 Geo. IV, c. 18 (Private).
26 Davies, *Chelsea Old Ch.* 197; 59 Geo. III, c. 35 (Local and Personal).
27 *Rep. Com. Eccl. Revenues*, 641.
28 *Clergy List* (1842, 1859); *Crockford* (1896, 1907).
29 Above, Settlement, to 1680.
30 Newcourt, *Rep.* I. 584. Further specified in Guildhall MS 9531/13, f. 40.
31 *Cal. Pat.* 1563–6, 423.

74. *West front of Chelsea rectory, Old Church Street*

newly-built house, presumably on the site of the 18th-century Rectory in Church Street, with 18 a. adjoining.[1] There was also another 9 acres in Eastfield. House and glebe were thought to be worth £60 a year, half of the total value of the living, in 1650.[2] John King, who claimed to have started his improvements in 1704, has been credited with first augmenting the living by granting building leases.[3] The 18 acres of 1566 had been divided, subleased, and partly built upon by 1724, when the rector had compounded for his tithes at 6s. an acre with tenants who had turned farmland into commercial gardens.[4] Fines for houses on the glebe accounted for £50 of the mid 18th-century income of £390.[5]

The Rectory house, which was owned by the Church until 1980, was a much altered replacement of the parsonage acquired in 1566, which in 1913 was represented, if at all, only by some outhouses and garden walling with possibly 17th-century brickwork.[6] Its dilapidation induced John King to live elsewhere in Church Street in 1694; he took up residence in 1703 but his successor Sloane Elsmere did not immediately do so in 1732 because of the disrepair.[7] In 1724 the parsonage house, new fronted, was two-storeyed and of brick, with 8 rooms to a floor.[8] Perhaps Elsmere's absence was due to work connected with the Rectory's rebuilding, normally attributed to the slightly earlier date of 1727.[9] The wealthy Dr Reginald Heber was said to have carried out partial rebuilding in the 1760s.[10] Later additions, most notably the two early 20th-century Georgian style western wings, obscured the original plan.[11] In 1913 the rectory house included the main part of a substantial early Georgian building, and two large rooms with a passage room between them on the ground floor retained their doors and to certain extent their chimney-pieces, dated to *c.*1725. Two large semi-circular bay windows in brick work were added on the eastern side later in the 18th century, and considerable additions made since 1860 harmonised with the late 18th-century character which house had acquired. In 1913 the house still stood in more than 2 acres of gardens surrounded by a high wall.[12] The two-acre gardens were planted with mature trees and claimed in 1965 as London's largest private garden after that of Buckingham Palace.[13] the Rectory's sale was foreseen in 1979 but proposals to convert the house into offices and build on a portion of the garden proved controversial, in part because they involved the closure of a playground for handicapped children. The property was sold as a residence in 1982 to a Kuwaiti, Sabah Al-Rayes, whose ambitious plans provoked further opposition. After repossession by 1989 by the Banque Arabe et International d'Investissement, it was bought in 1990 by the Japanese Toyoko Metropolitan Company, whose additions included sporting facilities and two wings each larger than the original house. In 1995 it was sold for *c.* £25 million to Gianna Angelopoulos, the owner in 1999. No. 29 Burnsall Street was bought as a smaller Rectory in 1980,[14] and replaced by no. 64A Flood Street *c.*1990.[15]

No residence was reserved in 1819 for the first minister of the Old Church, John Rush 1824–55, who held other livings but by 1847 was at no. 6 South Parade.[16] R.H. Davies, his successor, lived for *c.*50 years

1 Newcourt, *Rep.* I. 584; *Cal. Pat.* 1563–6, 393.
2 Lysons, *Environs*, II. 114, quoting Lambeth Pal. Lib., Parl. Com. Surveys, XII a/12, f. 229.
3 Dr King's MS, p. 164; Faulkner, *Chelsea*, I. 182.
4 Guildhall MS 9628/5/3 (terrier). Plans of different parts of the glebe are in Dr King's MS, pp. 172–88.
5 Guildhall MS 9556, f. 28v.
6 *Survey of London*, IV. 56.
7 Ibid. 57; Guildhall MS 9550.
8 Guildhall MS 9628/5/3.
9 Johnston, *St Luke's*, 33.
10 Faulkner, *Chelsea*, I. 185.
11 *Survey of London*, IV. 56. Mortgage for alterations 1902: Guildhall MS 19224/367(1); plans 1902: ibid. 19224/367(2).
12 *Survey of London*, IV. 56; see Fig. 74.
13 Para. based on Chelsea cuttings: Rectory Gardens; Johnston, *St Luke's*, 33.
14 Guildhall MS 19224/367(1).
15 Inf. from sen. chwdn.
16 *Clerical Guide* (1829); *PO Dir. London* (1847, 1855).

at no. 86 (renumbered 78, then 106) Oakley Street.[1] The incumbent in 1926 lived in Beaufort Mansions, Beaufort Street; in 1935 and 1940 at no. 4 Glebe Place; and in 1947 and 1955–6 at no. 18 Margaretta Terrace.[2] In 1960 a mortgage raised money for supplying the vicar of the newly created parish with a parsonage.[3] Presumably it was no. 4 Old Church Street, the parsonage in 1970 and 1995.[4] In 2001 no. 21 Oakley Gardens served as a temporary Vicarage, while a new house and hall were being built immediately north of the church to replace Petyt House, whose name was to be preserved.[5]

CLERGY AND PARISH OFFICERS

A rector was in dispute with the abbey in 1230.[6] Pre-Reformation rectors, from 1290 until the resignation of the last one in 1530, often held the living only briefly.[7] Three of 41 named are thought to have died at Chelsea: possibly in 1433 and in 1451 and 1470.[8] Reginald of St Albans, rector 1290–9, held a prebend of St Paul's with other preferments and later became archdeacon of London.[9] Richard Martin, 1319–39, held Chelsea as a pluralist without papal dispensation before it was given at Cardinal Gaucelin's request to Nicholas Hosebound, a minor canon of St Paul's.[10] Alexander Brown, 1435–42, was permitted to hold Chelsea with any other living worth not more than 26 marks.[11] William Walesby, who resigned in 1450, was a prebendary of Sarum and former archdeacon of Chichester; a royal chaplain, he went on to further preferments, including the deanery of St Stephen's, Westminster.[12]

In 1530 Sir Thomas More, then Lord Chancellor, nominated his protégé John Larke as rector. Larke, a pluralist, was accused of neglect by the churchwardens in 1540 and plotting against the royal supremacy with the bishop of Winchester's nephew Germain Gardiner and others in 1544.[13] More's son John was pardoned for treasonable words with them after their execution.[14] Robert Richardson, Larke's successor and a royal chaplain, was deprived in 1554 reputedly as a married priest but restored in 1566.[15]

Scholarship, or at least a concern for education, characterized many later rectors. Thomas Browne, 1574–85, who also held an Essex living, had been headmaster of Westminster school and wrote occasional poems.[16] Richard Ward, 1585–1615, was founder of the parochial charity school.[17] George Hampden, 1615–32, was probably the Oxonian of that name who celebrated James I's visit to the university in 1605 with Latin verses.[18] Samuel Wilkinson, 1632–69, declared by parliamentary commissioners to be 'of scandalous report' in 1650, but not apparently deprived, became a canon of Chichester and of St Paul's in the 1660s.[19] The lexicographer Adam Littleton, 1670–94, had been expelled by Parliament from Oxford and had opened a school in Chelsea; he was also a royal chaplain and canon of Westminster.[20] The miscellaneous writer John King, 1694–1732, left a much quoted manuscript account of Chelsea;[21] from 1697 to 1710 he also held the living of Harrold (Beds.) and from 1710 he was a canon of York.[22] Sloane Elsmere, 1732–66, was a benefactor of the girls' charity school.[23]

Later rectors were often well connected. Reginald Heber, 1766–70, who inherited a Shropshire estate,[24] was father and namesake of the bishop of Calcutta (d. 1826).[25] Thomas Drake, 1770–5, held Chelsea together with his family's living of Amersham (Bucks.).[26] The Hon. William Bromley Cadogan, 1775–97, likewise held the vicarage of St Giles in Reading, where he normally lived: the second son of Charles Sloane, created Earl Cadogan (d. 1807), he received both benefices at the age of 24.[27] Charles Sturgess, 1797–1805, who had promoted education when vicar of Ealing, was a canon of St Paul's and chaplain to Earl Cadogan.[28] Gerald Valerian Wellesley, 1805–32, a prime mover in the building of the new St Luke's and fourth son of the earl of Mornington (d. 1781), was younger brother of the first duke of Wellington and married to a daughter of

1 Davies, *In Remembrance*, 62.
2 *PO Dir. London* (1858 and later edns); *Crockford* (1926 and later edns).
3 Guildhall MS 19224/33.
4 *London Diocese Bk* (1970, 1995).
5 Inf. from vicar; above, Soc. Hist., educ. (pub. schs: Petyt's).
6 W.H. Stewart, *Chelsea Old Ch.* (1932), 17; *Hist. of Westm. Abbey by John Flete*, ed. J. Armitage Robinson (1909), 66.
7 Listed in Hennessy, *Nov. Rep.* 119–20. The list is wrongly headed and misplaces some 19th-cent. incumbents of the Old Ch., St Luke's (new) ch., and Holy Trinity, Sloane St.
8 Davies, *Chelsea Old Ch.* 186.
9 Le Neve, *Fasti, 1300–1541, St Paul's, London*, 7, 20, 59, 66; *Cal. Papal Reg.* I. 585.
10 *Cal. Papal Reg.* II. 184; Hennessy, *Nov. Rep.* 60.
11 *Cal. Papal Reg.* IX. 61.
12 Hennessy, *Nov. Rep.* p. lxxii; Le Neve, *Fasti, 1300–1541, Chichester*, 12. A ref. to Cuthbert Tunstal in Guildhall MS 9531/8 is accepted to mean Rob. Tunstal, vicar 1502–3, rather than Cuthbert, bp of Durham: C. Sturge, *Cuthbert Tunstal* (1938), 16n.
13 S. Brigden, *London and the Reformation* (1989), 354.
14 *L&P Hen. VIII*, XIX(1), pp. 277, 285.
15 Ibid., p. 175; Hennessy, *Nov. Rep.* 120; Lysons, *Environs*, II. 114.
16 *DNB.*
17 Above, Soc. Hist., educ. (pub. schs).
18 *Alum. Westmonasterienses*, ed. J. Welch (1852), 67.
19 Lambeth Pal. Lib., Parl. Com. Surveys, XII a/12, ff. 229–30; *Alum. Oxon. 1500–1714*, 1634.
20 Hennessy, *Nov. Rep.*, p. lxxviii; *DNB.*
21 Davies, *Chelsea Old Ch.* p. viii; *DNB.* His MS is in CL.
22 *DNB.* He did not simultaneously hold the rectory of Pertenhall (Beds.), as in *Alum Oxon. 1500–1714*, 853, having surrendered it on acquiring Chelsea.
23 Above, Soc. Hist., educ. (pub. schs).
24 Faulkner, *Chelsea*, I. 185–6.
25 With whom he has been confused: Hennessy, *Nov. Rep.* p. lxxiii; *DNB.*
26 *Alum. Westm.* 325.
27 Guildhall MS 9557, p. 20; *Alum. Oxon. 1715–1886*, 208; Burke, *Peerage & Baronetage* (1904), 256.
28 *VCH Middx*, VII. 150, 165; Le Neve, *Fasti, 1541–1857, St Paul's, London*, 65; Faulkner, *Chelsea*, I. 189.

Earl Cadogan (d. 1807); he was a canon of St Paul's, and later of Durham, and a royal chaplain.[1] Charles Kingsley, 1836–60, domestic chaplain to Earl Cadogan and a canon of Windsor, was father of the authors Charles, George, and Henry,[2] the last of whom described the Old Church in a novel of 1865.[3] Among his successors H.E.J. Bevan, 1902–30, W.G. Arrowsmith, 1930–52, and E.H. Loasby, 1961–82, were all canons of St Paul's; the second was also a royal chaplain. R.S. Hook, 1952–61, became bishop suffragan of Grantham,[4] and Derek Watson, 1982–96, dean of Salisbury.[5]

At the Parish Chapel or Old Church John Rush, 1824–55, was also rector of Hartwell with Little Hampden (Bucks.).[6] W.H. Stewart, 1916–26, was later archdeacon of Jerusalem,[7] and Leighton Thomson, 1950–92, from 1986 was a canon of St Paul's.[8]

An assistant curate was mentioned in 1554,[9] possibly in 1561,[10] and in 1574, 1628, *c.*1630, 1637, and 1664.[11] William King, son of the rector, was curate in 1724[12] and a defeated candidate for the lectureship in 1735.[13] William Gardener, curate in 1758, was controversially appointed by the rector as the first parish clerk in holy orders; he retained the clerkship, with a deputy, but apparently ceased to be curate on securing the disputed lectureship in 1759.[14] Later curates often attended parish meetings in the rector's place, as in 1765, 1769,[15] 1780, 1782,[16] and the 1790s.[17] The author Erasmus Middleton (d. 1805),[18] licensed as a curate at £50 a year in 1786, was unsuccessfully proposed by the rector for the lectureship.[19] John Rush, curate in 1803 and 1806 with a stipend of £70,[20] probably later became the first incumbent of the demoted Old Church.[21] Henry Blunt, licensed as curate in 1825 at £200 a year, to reside in the parish but not at the Rectory,[22] became the first rector of Holy Trinity.[23] The new St Luke's normally had at least two curates until the late 20th century, with 3 in 1859, 7 in 1915, and 4 in 1940; from the 1960s there was usually one curate.[24]

The Old Church normally had no curate, although one was recorded in 1892, presumably after Earl Cadogan, the rector of St Luke's, and a collection from the congregation had each contributed £50 to pay for an assistant to the elderly incumbent.[25] A curate was also recorded in 1961 and 1980.[26]

A lecturer, the Revd Mr Standish, was recorded in 1700.[27] Presumably he was the first to fill an office that in 1786 was claimed to be in the gift of the vestry, having for long been supported by voluntary contributions and filled by ballot.[28] Standish's successor Hugh Shorthouse was chosen in 1708 by 89 votes to 46. Larger votes in 1735 favoured William Rothery, who kept a local school, over William King and in 1759 William Gardener over Dr Martyn, the nominee of Rothery's pupil Thomas Martyn.[29] The 352 voters in 1759, unusually, included several women,[30] as in 1775 when the choice lay between 5 candidates.[31] The winner William Williams in 1786 ascribed his non-attendance to ill health, declaring that the rector W.B. Cadogan had agreed to provide for the afternoon lectureship and collection, whereupon the vestry claimed the exclusive right to make such arrangements. After protests to the absentee rector, in Reading, and lecturer, in Wales, and to the archdeacon, the vestry secured Williams's resignation.[32] A successor John Hutchins was chosen by 319 votes to 217 but was refused a licence by Cadogan, who put forward the curate as his own nominee, and by the bishop, until a compromise led to recognition both of the rector's right to approve and of the successful candidate to preach.[33] Hutchins continued until 1823, when his son and namesake succeeded him.[34]

The clerkship was another, though less important, cause of friction. A parish clerk existed by 1375 and was mentioned in wills in the late 14th century.[35] The rector Richard Ward (d. 1615) built a clerk's house with funds given by Bishop Richard Fletcher (d. 1596), and it was repaired by the parish in 1671. Wages were paid in 1665

1 Le Neve, *Fasti, 1541–1857, St Paul's, London*, 46; *Fasti*, ed. T.D. Hardy, III (1854), 313, 368; Burke, *Peerage & Baronetage* (1904), 1605. Called 'Gerard' in Hennessy, *Nov. Rep.* 121.
2 Hennessy, *Nov. Rep.* p. lxxiii; *DNB*.
3 H. Kingsley, *The Hillyers and the Burtons* (1865), 63–4.
4 *Crockford* (1935 and later edn).
5 *Who's Who, 2000*, 2144.
6 *Alum. Oxon. 1715–1886*, 1235; *Clerical Guide* (1829).
7 Stewart, *Chelsea Old Ch.*, intro.
8 C.E. Leighton Thomson, *Rebuilding of Chelsea Old Ch.* (1992).
9 Guildhall MS 9537/1, f. 72v.
10 Guildhall MS 9537/2, f. 102.
11 Guildhall MSS 9537/3, f. 31v.; 9537/13, f. 54v.; 9537/15, f. 49v.; 9537/16, f. 44v.; BL, Add. MS 11056, f. 285.
12 Guildhall MS 9550.
13 Faulkner, *Chelsea*, II. 89; below.
14 Vestry orders, 1833–9, p. 77; below.
15 Vestry orders, 1745–71, pp. 288, 330.
16 Ibid., 1771–90, ff. 51, 72v., 168.
17 Ibid., 1790–1809, pp. 38, 66, 203, 255.
18 *DNB*; *Gent. Mag.* LXXV. 490.
19 Guildhall MS 9557, p. 20; Vestry orders, 1771–90, ff. 143–4.
20 Vestry orders, 1790–1809, pp. 276, 341; Guildhall MS 9557, p. 20.
21 Below.
22 Vestry orders, 1822–33, p. 152.
23 Below, dau. chs.
24 *Clergy List* (1859 and later edns); *Crockford* (1896 and later edns).
25 Davies, *In Remembrance*, 115.
26 *Crockford* (1961, 1980).
27 Faulkner, *Chelsea*, II. 88.
28 Vestry orders, 1771–90, f. 123. Lecturers were sometimes listed with curates, e.g. Guildhall MS 9557A.
29 Guildhall MS 9537/30, f. 160; ibid. MS 9556, alphabetical list; Faulkner, *Chelsea*, II. 88–90; above, Soc. Hist., educ. (private schs).
30 Vestry orders, 1745–71, pp. 204, 212, 214.
31 Ibid., 1771–90, ff. 22v.–25.
32 Ibid., ff. 120–7.
33 Ibid., ff. 128–45.
34 Ibid., 1822–33, p. 88.
35 Guildhall MS 9171/1, ff. 18v., 95v., 281, 429.

to the clerk; from 1674 to 1681 he was paid for 'wages and washing and mending linen', and in 1681 also for burials.[1] A table of all fees, including the clerk's, was to be displayed in 1699.[2] Fees were payable in 1738 to one individual as clerk and sexton,[3] but in 1758 the offices were separated by the vestry. The clerk was elected unanimously and the sexton by 95 votes to 25 but the rector claimed the right to make both appointments until he conceded over the sexton and it was agreed that the churchwardens rather than the vestry should appoint the clerk. In 1758 the rector appointed his curate as clerk in orders, presumably with few duties since the sexton became deputy parish clerk. The rector's son-in-law Moses Dodd[4] was appointed clerk in orders in 1802 and remained so in 1834; the young Charles Kingsley later filled the office under his father until he resigned it, as a sinecure, in 1849.[5] The office of deputy clerk and sexton was divided in 1828. It was the clerk in orders who appointed the deputy clerk in 1832, whereas the vestry elected the sexton in 1835. Under the Act of 1819 a separate clerk was to be appointed for the Old Church, while the sexton was to be responsible for both churches.[6]

CHURCH LIFE

Chapels flanking the chancel of the Old Church, later known as the Lawrence and More chapels, seem from some stonework to date from the 14th century.[7] John Shoreditch, lord of the manor by 1383, by will proved 1407 was to be buried in 'my chapel' annexed to the north side of the chancel where his wife Helen was buried, leaving money for its fabric and for obits.[8] Gifts in money or kind were made to the priest or church of Chelsea in 1375, 1382, and later,[9] and to the lights of the Holy Cross in 1393, 1394, 1412, and 1441, and of St Katharine in 1394.[10] Margery Lynde in 1484 left money to the high altar, besides two torches, a light before Our Lady, and obits to be sung for 20 years by three priests.[11] A 'batchelors' light' was mentioned in 1518.[12] The church had no chantry lands in 1548.[13] Plate, vestments, and furnishings of the church listed in 1549 suggest a rather poor church. They included two silver chalices and patens, a third having been destroyed by fire, a cross of copper and gilt, two basins and 14 bowl candlesticks of pewter, five candlesticks, a censor, and three lamps all of latten, as well as altar cloths, vestments and cushions, and the altar cloth from 'Lady More's chapel'. Many vestments, the copper-gilt cross, and the latten and pewter were sold, mainly to parishioners, by 1552.[14]

Preaching but not catechizing took place in 1664.[15] Reforms ordered in 1685 included the purchase of a secure chest, a register of strangers who had preached, a table of degrees of marriage, and books of homilies and canons.[16] In the late 18th century services were held twice on Sunday and the sacrament was administered twice monthly and on great festivals to *c.*200 communicants; children were catechized in Lent.[17] There were two Sunday sermons in 1778.[18] Erasmus Middleton, the curate to whom W.B. Cadogan increasingly left the conduct of the parish, was presumably Evangelical, having in his youth been one of six expelled from Oxford for attending or forming conventicles.[19] He may have represented an established tradition: when the next presentation to the new St Luke's was to be put up for sale in 1851, the vestry wished to raise money for trustees to appoint to the next vacancy, 'it being highly important to secure an evangelical ministry'.[20] Candles and fully choral services were nonetheless introduced under G.F. Blunt, rector 1860–1902.[21] By 1881 St Luke's had a paid and surpliced choir; services were thrice on Sunday and once on Wednesday, Friday, and saints' days, with Holy Communion thrice a month.[22] In 1903 worshippers were mainly middle-class, although *c.*200 lower middle-class men attended a so-called Bible class 'stamped with a much wider interest'. In 1999 the church claimed that its services were 'broadly traditional' or 'liberal catholic'.[23]

At the Old Church marriages were forbidden by the Act of 1819 and christenings allowed only by special leave of the rector, for whom the burial fees were also reserved. Other services were those normally provided: on Sunday morning and evening and on great festivals, all with sermons, and Holy Communion at least once a month and on three festivals. By 1881 services were partly choral and held twice on Sunday, with Holy Communion twice a month.[24] In 1903 it was seen as a backwater, of little interest to newcomers.[25]

The strong musical tradition of St Luke's is associated with the new church, perhaps because the fabric of the old building, and its bells and clock, had taken up so much of the vestry's time.[26] In 1745 subscriptions

1 Vestry orders, 1662–1718, ff. 5, 16v., 22v., 26, 27, 28.
2 BL, Add. MS 15609, f. 4.
3 Rest of para. based on Vestry orders, 1745–71, pp. 189–95; 1833–9, pp. 77–91.
4 Probably rector of Fordham (Essex): *Alum. Oxon. 1715–1886*, 375.
5 Johnston, *St Luke's*, 29; *DNB*.
6 59 Geo. III, c. 35 (Local and Personal).
7 Davies, *Chelsea Old Ch.* 3–4; below.
8 Guildhall MS 9171/2, f. 109v.
9 Guildhall MS 9171/1, ff. 18v., 95v., 222, 429.
10 Ibid., ff. 222, 281, 326v.; 9171/2, ff. 227v.; 9171/4, f. 50.
11 Davies, *Chelsea Old Ch.* 13.
12 Guildhall MS 9171/9, f. 101.
13 *Chantry Cert.*, p. 73.
14 PRO, E 315/498, ff 2–4v.
15 Guildhall MS 9583/2, pt. 6, f. 44.
16 Guildhall MS 9537/20, f. 30v.
17 Guildhall MS 9557, p. 20.
18 Guildhall MS 9558.
19 *DNB*.
20 Vestry mins. 1843–56, p. 175.
21 Johnston, *St Luke's*, 9, 15.
22 *Mackeson's Guide* (1881).
23 Lambeth Pal. Lib., Fulham Papers, Creighton 2/1; Booth, *Life and Labour*, III(3), 117; Johnston, *St Luke's*, 36.
24 59 Geo. III, c. 35 (Local and Personal).
25 Booth, *Life and Labour*, III(3), 117.
26 Johnston, *St Luke's*, 15; Vestry orders, *passim*.

enabled an organ to be placed in the west gallery, only to be taken down as unauthorized in 1746. Subscribers sought a faculty in 1752 and obtained it in 1754, after a suit in the Court of Arches, despite opponents claiming lack of space and perpetual expense,[1] but nothing more seems to have been done until 1818. An organ committee was then formed, with Luke Flood as treasurer, and money was raised for an 8-year-old organ.[2] A larger instrument was played by Thomas Attwood (d. 1838) in 1824 at the consecration of the new church, where the composer John (later Sir John) Goss (d. 1880) was elected organist in 1825.[3] A distinguished successor was the composer John Ireland (d. 1962), previously at Holy Trinity, who was organist and choirmaster 1908–30.[4] Maintaining its musical tradition, the church in 1986 offered choral bursaries and in the 1990s was used for recitals and broadcasts.[5]

Charitable bequests from the 17th century onward sometimes benefited the church in addition to the poor. Eventually the six Ecclesiastical charities of Chelsea were established by a Scheme of 1936,[6] with the rector and 4 other trustees appointed by the parochial church council of St Luke's. Richard Gilford's charity, under his will proved 1680, consisted of £58 stock set aside to provide 1s. 6d. to the minister for a sermon on 5 December, 5s. to the ringers, and 2s. 6d. to the parish clerk. Elizabeth Smith by will proved 1828, in addition to bequests to the charity schools and the poor, left 2 guineas to the preacher of an anniversary sermon on 8 August, with one guinea to the officiating clerk. Those sums were payable as part of her Ecclesiastical and Eleemosynary charity under an Order of 1906, which established her Educational foundation. In 1936 her charity (item 14) was divided, £126 stock becoming part of the Ecclesiastical charities to pay for the annual sermon. An endowment of 1856 for Thomas Flood's charity (item 19) was also divided, £8 6s. 8d. being set aside to maintain his memorial tablet in the church. The same Scheme confirmed a fund of £300 established by a deed of 1926 as the Dacre Tomb Maintenance fund. All four charities shared a founder with a Non-Ecclesiastical charity.[7]

In addition Thomas Stewart by will proved 1722 gave £100 for an altarpiece and the interest on £50 for an annual sermon on 15 January on the text of the 50th Psalm, verses 14 and 15; if no sermon was preached, the income was to benefit the boys' charity school. The gift of £50 was said not to have been laid out until Thomas Martin, on whom responsibility for executing the will had devolved, in 1810 reported the purchase of £100 stock.[8] In 1936 the gift (item 5) was still represented by £100 stock to pay for a sermon. Emily Ann Mills by will proved 1911 left stock worth £80 8s. 4d. annually for distribution by the rector and churchwardens every January equally between 10 men and 10 women aged over 60, to be communicants or other members of the Church of England. In 1936 the gift (item 29) was represented by £2,297 16s. 7d. Chelsea's share of Sarah Campbell's gift, excluded from the Scheme of 1936 at the instance of the Church Commissioners, came to be treated as an ecclesiastical charity, spent on such items as payments to the choir.[9]

Chelsea Old Church trust was registered in 1987 for a new fund to maintain buildings or otherwise advance Christian educational or charitable work in the diocese. Its assets in 1995 exceeded £27,000, of which £10,000 was on loan to the Old Church.[10]

ALL SAINTS OR CHELSEA OLD CHURCH

The church of All Saints or Chelsea Old Church, at the south-eastern end of Old Church Street, has been a riverside landmark at least since its partial rebuilding in the 17th century.[11] The three restored medieval parts, the chancel flanked north and south by the so-called Lawrence and More chapels respectively, were for long in different ownership. The Lawrence chapel apparently was built for occupants of the nearby medieval manor house, acquired *c.*1590 by the Lawrence family. Sir John Lawrence, resenting intrusion by Sir Edward Cecil, in 1621 claimed exclusive rights for those 'out of my house' to repair or be buried in the chapel: 'the parson hath nothing to do there'.[12] Also called the lord's chapel,[13] its freehold passed from Lawrence's 18th-century heirs through a succession of owners until sold by the representatives of Henry Lewer to R.H. Davies, incumbent of the Old Church, in 1894. More's chapel went to the Crown, then to the marquess of Winchester and through successive holders to Sir Arthur Gorges, who sold his main house but retained the chapel with a smaller house, both of which passed to the heirs of Sir William Milman. From the Milmans the freehold was acquired by builders, the Flight family and in 1827 Richard Mann, whose son sold it in 1855 to Thomas Francis Crew, from whose mortgagee it was bought by the incumbent in 1874.[14]

A relaxation of penance in 1290 for pilgrims to Chelsea church ('Thelchuche') may have been granted

1 Davies, *Chelsea Old Ch.* 84; Vestry orders, 1745–71, pp. 61, 129; Chelsea Misc. 16(3).

2 Davies, *Chelsea Old Ch.* 34–5; Vestry orders, 1809–22, pp. 288–9.

3 *DNB*; Johnston, *St Luke's*, 14–15; Vestry mins, 1822–33, pp. 134, 141.

4 *DNB*; Johnston, *St Luke's*, 15.

5 Johnston, *St Luke's*, 14; Chelsea cuttings: St Luke's ch. (*Choral Bursaries* leaflet).

6 Para. based on Char. Com. Scheme of 1936.

7 Above, Soc. Hist., chars.

8 *Endowed Chars London* (1901), 220; Faulkner, *Chelsea*, II. 112.

9 Above, Soc. Hist., chars; Char. Com. files.

10 Char. Com. file 297739.

11 e.g. *Images of Chelsea*, nos. 149–56, 159–70; see Fig. 75.

12 Davies, *Chelsea Old Ch.* 4–5, 24–8; *N&Q*, 2nd ser., XI. 13–15.

13 LMA, AC.79.55

14 Davies, *Chelsea Old Ch.* 5–6; *Survey of London*, VII. 2.

75. *South-east view of Chelsea Old Church, with* (left) *Arch House spanning Lombard Street*

to raise funds for a rebuilding.[1] In 1705 remains indicated that the medieval church had been of flint and rough stone, 'confusedly heaped together'.[2] Its appearance can be guessed only from the chancel and the Lawrence chapel, both rebuilt after war damage, and the More chapel. The medieval nave would have been shorter than its 17th-century successor if the east wall of the later tower incorporated part of the west wall of an older tower.[3] Bequests had been made to a bell tower (*campanilis*) in 1389, 1390, and 1393.[4] Encased in brick when the nave was replaced, the chancel in the 1920s was ascribed to the 13th century and the chapels to the 14th, More's perhaps being the earlier. Stonework suggested that the chancel had been lit by 3 lancets, replaced by a larger window itself removed in 1816, and that the chancel roof had been lowered to accord with that of the new brick nave. A surviving arch on the south side of the chancel opening into the More chapel, with its capitals carved with Renaissance motifs and More's arms, is 14th-century and attests that Sir Thomas remodelled rather than built the chapel named after him.[5]

Extensive repairs and alterations were contemplated in 1631, when contributions were to be sought, but apparently to no effect.[6] Subscriptions in 1669–70, presumably including £100 given by George Morley, bishop of Winchester (d. 1684), permitted rebuilding of the nave and the provision of a west tower. Work may not have started until after the funeral in 1669 of Lady Jane Cheyne, who paid the whole cost of a new roof, but it had been finished by early 1672 except on the tower, which had been built by 1674 and, though medieval in silhouette was Gothic only in the details of its openings. It may have received its cupola for a bell given in 1679 and was adorned with a sundial in 1692; a weather vane was added in 1704, removed in 1815.[7] The new classical nave was almost square, as wide as the previous nave and aisles and had a shallow hipped roof on a deep coved cornice. It had north and south doorways, though the south front was more elaborate in acknowledgment of its position on the street. Although chiefly of red brick, the building had 'no exterior appearance of uniformity'.[8]

No major rebuilding took place after the 1670s. An unsightly gallery built by Mr Woodcock for his pupils across the chancel *c.*1703 survived until 1832.[9] Presumably it was the same as, or an enlargement of, a gallery approved in 1698, where pews were allocated in 1702 and whose darkening of the interior had led to the insertion of dormer windows in both the north and south

1 Stewart, *Chelsea Old Ch.* 17.
2 Bowack, *Antiquities*, 1.
3 Stewart, *Chelsea Old Ch.* 18. Building hist. summarized in ibid. 18–21.
4 Guildhall MS 9171/1, ff. 187v., 222, 281.
5 Davies, *Chelsea Old Ch.* 3–4, 7–8; *Survey of London*, VII. 1–2.
6 BL, Add. MS 11056, ff. 292–3.
7 Davies, *Chelsea Old Ch.* 9–11; *Survey of London*, VII. 3–4; BL, Stowe MS 541, f. 136v. Payments and disbursements for rebuilding 1672–3 are in Vestry orders, 1662–1718, ff. 279–80.
8 *Images of Chelsea*, no. 149; *Gent. Mag.* LXXX. 416; L. Matthews, *Chelsea Old Ch. Bombing and Rebuilding* (1993), illus. I.
9 Davies, *Chelsea Old Ch.* 12, 14, 29, 31.

76. *Interior of Chelsea Old Church before destruction by bombing in the Second World War*

roofs of the chancel.[1] A recently erected west gallery for the charity school boys was approved in 1747, when another was to be built for the girls.[2] Already Chelsea had petitioned parliament for one of the promised 50 new churches in 1718, without success.[3] Cracks in the steeple were reported in 1748, when the cupola was strengthened, and a high estimate for repairs in 1751 led to suggestions for complete rebuilding, which were shelved.[4] A new clock was installed in 1761,[5] the walls were whitewashed in 1777, general repairs ordered in 1784, and the pews rearranged in 1784,[6] when the arch between the Lawrence chapel and the chancel was rebuilt. The bells (below) caused increasing anxiety, both for their own condition and, as in 1761 and 1787, for their effect on the cupola and the tower.[7]

Disrepair forced the closure of the church for a month in 1789.[8] Surveyors proposed partial rebuilding, on grounds of safety, in 1802, when peals of bells were banned and the alternative of building a more central church was discussed.[9] A committee's recommendation for an entirely new church was rejected in 1806 and the question was put off in 1807 'until the time of peace'.[10] By 1815 the tower was 'cracked in every direction' and a surveyor warned that drastic but essential repairs might prove to be a waste of money.[11] Minimal repairs were nonetheless ordered, including the removal of the cupola,[12] and it was not until 1818 that a memorial was drawn up to the Church Building Commissioners,[13] preparing the way for the construction of St Luke's.

The Old Church, although cherished for its monuments (below), owed its preservation to the fact that its site did not make rebuilding worthwhile.[14] Workmanship of the 1670s was condemned in 1815 as having been carried out with poor quality bricks laid indiscriminately among rough stone; the walls were too weak for the lead-covered oak roof, and the tower for its cupola.[15] The repairs of 1815 were followed by internal reconstruction in 1832 and conservative restoration by H.H. Burnell, who added a small north-east clergy vestry, in 1857–8.[16] Apart from the rebuilding of the clergy vestry and the provision of a choir vestry in 1908–10, when the floor was relaid and the chancel's timber roof was exposed, the church was unaltered until an air raid in 1941 left only the More chapel standing.[17]

Services were held for *c.*9 years at the Cheyne hospital, although later in 1941 the More chapel was given a temporary roof.[18] The chapel's escape and the salvaging of many memorials proved powerful arguments for the complete rebuilding, despite diocesan misgivings; a new church was approved in principle in 1946 and a temporary extension to the chancel was authorized in 1947.[19] The renovated More chapel was opened in 1950, the

1 Vestry orders, 1662–1718, ff. 77–v., 86v.
2 Ibid., 1745–71, pp. 29, 33.
3 Clarke, *London Chs.* 50.
4 Vestry orders, 1745–71, pp. 58–64, 100–12, 125, 127.
5 Ibid., pp. 231–2.
6 Ibid., 1771–90, ff. 36v., 82, 111v.; Stewart, *Chelsea Old Ch.* 20.
7 Vestry orders, 1745–71, p. 248; 1771–90, ff. 155–6.
8 Ibid., 1771–90, f. 169.
9 Ibid., 1790–1809, pp. 257–8, 265, 336.
10 Ibid., pp. 346, 351–3, 364.
11 Ibid., 1809–22, pp. 137–40.
12 Ibid., pp. 168–9.
13 Ibid., pp. 295, 323–7.
14 Davies, *Chelsea Old Ch.* p. xi.
15 Vestry orders, 1809–22, pp. 138–9.
16 *The Builder*, XVI (1858), 759–60.
17 Clarke, *London Chs.* 50; T.F. Bumpus, *Ancient London Chs.* [1923], 205; *Images of Chelsea*, no. 171; Davies, *Chelsea Old Ch.* 14; Stewart, *Chelsea Old Ch.* 20–1, plate 2; *Survey of London*, VII. 8; Hist. Mon. Com. *W. London*, 7; Thomson, *Rebuilding of Chelsea Old Ch.* illus. p. 19.
18 Thomson, *Rebuilding of Chelsea Old Ch.* 15, illus. p. 23; Matthews, *Chelsea Old Ch.* 22, illus. iv.
19 Matthews, *Chelsea Old Ch.* 21–35.

rebuilt chancel and Lawrence chapel were rededicated in 1954, and the whole church was reconsecrated in the presence of the Queen Mother in 1958,[1] concluding a painstaking and much praised reconstruction by W.H. Godfrey.[2] In 1999 it preserved 'the atmosphere of the pre-Victorian village church crammed full of worthwhile monuments – the most evocative of such interiors in inner London'.[3]

Monuments

The monuments impressed Henry Kingsley as creating a timeless and funereal air.[4] Often they have been seen as more remarkable than the church itself,[5] with the result that the prominent intruders whose numbers made it so inadequate helped to ensure its survival. John Weever in 1631 was the first antiquary to comment on tombs, those of More and the Brays (below),[6] but was soon followed by John Stow, who noted six more,[7] and in 1705 more comprehensively by John Bowack,[8] who considered them, for 'number, structure, and dignity, scarce to be parallelled by any church of its bigness in England'. Fuller lists, also covering the churchyard, included those of Lysons in 1795,[9] of Faulkner in 1810 and 1829,[10] and those in more recent surveys.[11] In 1945 the Diocesan Reorganisation Committee proposed the restoration of only the More chapel, which worshippers feared would be left as a mere museum of ancient monuments. The need to accommodate properly those 'of outstanding merit' was decisive in ensuring a more ambitious rebuilding.[12]

Some rearrangement was made necessary by 17th-century rebuilding: in 1672–3 a churchwarden paid for 'taking down and setting up the Lord Dacre's tomb in part'.[13] Monuments normally were described according to their location in the church until the removal of all that could be salvaged in 1941 for storage in the crypt of St Luke's. The locations given below are those resulting from a further rearrangement on their reinstalment by W.H. Godfrey. Of the ten estimated major monuments, seven are 16th-century.[14]

Among the monuments may be considered the carved hexagonal responds on the two capitals of the chancel arch leading to the chapel which Sir Thomas More remodelled in 1528.[15] Often called the Holbein capitals,[16] since Holbein visited the Mores at Chelsea *c.*1527,[17] they are amongst England's 'earliest and best examples of the new Italian style', although probably the work of masons from France rather than Italy.[18] Against the south wall of the chancel is the oldest tomb, which More prepared for himself, beneath a long Latin epitaph and verses composed by him and inscribed in 1532 as an autobiography and vindication.[19] The unique link with More in itself makes the chapel a national monument.[20]

The chancel contains against the north wall the second oldest monument,[21] the tomb chest of Edmund, Lord Bray (d. 1539),[22] where his son John, Lord Bray, was laid after a lavish funeral in 1557.[23] Also on the north wall is the tablet to Thomas Hungerford (d. 1581). On the south side of the More chapel is the tomb of Jane Guilford, duchess of Northumberland (d. 1555), its figures badly damaged. In the Lawrence chapel are the arched tomb of Richard Jervoise (d. 1563), tablets to Sir Thomas Lawrence (d. 1593) and to Sarah Colvile (d. 1631), 'perhaps the most interesting' where her effigy rises in a shroud,[24] the tomb of Sir Robert Stanley (d. 1632), his bust probably by Edward Marshall, and, over the door to the vestry, a tablet to Sir John Lawrence (d. 1638). In the nave memorials include the ambitious marble wall monuments of Gregory Fiennes, Lord Dacre of the South (d. 1594) and his wife Anne Sackville (d. 1595), ascribed to Nicholas Johnson, which the parish was bound to maintain in order to share in Lady Dacre's charity.[25] It is balanced on the opposite, north, wall by that of the building's benefactress Lady Jane Cheyne (d. 1669) and her husband Charles Cheyne, Viscount Newhaven (d. 1698), said to have been designed by Gian Lorenzo Bernini[26] but later attributed to his son or his nephew, Paolo or Pietro;[27] the figure is by Antonio Raggi. A brass panel from the tomb of Sir Arthur Gorges (d. 1625) shows him in armour, with his children. Among later memorials is the wall tablet in the chancel to the sisters Lucy Smith and Anne Wilton (d. 1781,

1 Thomson, *Rebuilding of Chelsea Old Ch.* 30, 36, 55, 87.
2 Clarke, *London Chs.* 49; Pevsner, *London NW.* 556.
3 Pevsner, *London NW.* 557.
4 Kingsley, *Hillyers and Burtons*, 63–4.
5 e.g. Bumpus, *Ancient London Chs.* 205; Davies, *Chelsea Old Ch.* p. xii.
6 J. Weever, *Ancient Funeral Monuments* (1767), 293–4.
7 J. Stow, *Survey of London* (1633), 786–7.
8 Bowack, *Antiquities*, 1–12.
9 Lysons, *Environs*, II. 93–113.
10 Faulkner, *Chelsea* (1810), 60–105; Faulkner, *Chelsea*, I. 203–53.
11 e.g. Davies, *Chelsea Old Ch.* 219–70; *Survey of London*, VII. 14–83, noting 117 monuments in the ch. and 65 in the churchyard; Hist. Mon. Com. *W. London*, 9–11.
12 Matthews, *Chelsea Old Ch.* 26–7.
13 Vestry orders, 1662–1718, f. 280.
14 Matthews, *Chelsea Old Ch.* 22; M. Blatch, *Guide to London's Chs.* (1978), 346–7.
15 Hist. Mon. Com. *W. London*, pl. 15.
16 e.g. Matthews, *Chelsea Old Ch.* 21, 26–7.
17 R.W. Chambers, *Thos More* (1945), 219.
18 Pevsner, *London NW.* 557; Clarke, *London Chs.* 49–50.
19 Chambers, *Thos More*, 286–7. Inscription in Lysons, *Environs*, II. 83–5; Faulkner, *Chelsea*, I. 207–8, Eng. translation 208–10.
20 Matthews, *Chelsea Old Ch.* 25.
21 Following 3 paras. based on *Survey of London*, VII. 14–82; Clarke, *London Chs.* 50; Blatch, *Guide to London's Chs.* 346–7; Pevsner, *London NW.* 557–8.
22 Edmund requested burial near his uncle Sir Reginald Bray, to whom the tomb has sometimes been ascribed: Faulkner, *Chelsea*, I. 204; Pevsner, *London*, II. 86.
23 Faulkner, *Chelsea*, I. 204–6; *Complete Peerage*, II. 287.
24 Pevsner, *London NW.* 558.
52 Vestry orders, 1745–71, p. 1; above, Soc. Hist., chars.
26 Lysons, *Environs*, II. 106–7.
27 Paolo in Davies, *Chelsea Old Ch.* 64; Hist. Mon. Com. *W. London*, pl. 20.

1787), by Joseph Wilton. Wall plaques commemorate, among others, Henry James (d. 1916) and William de Morgan (d. 1917).

In the churchyard many monuments were recorded in 1795, by which date it had been largely superseded by the King's Road cemetery given by Sir Hans Sloane in 1733.[1] Memorials against the walls of the church itself include those to the Chamberlaine family, Dr Edward Chamberlaine having been allowed to make a vault in consideration of his apprenticing charity.[2] Close to the east wall of the church are an obelisk to Philip Miller (d. 1771) and a stone to William Anderson (d. 1846), both of them curators of the Physic Garden.[3] In the south-east corner of the ground is Joseph Wilton's canopied urn commemorating Sir Hans Sloane (d. 1753); conspicuous from its white Portland stone, its construction was approved in 1764.[4] A controversial seated figure of Sir Thomas More by L. Cubitt Bevis, unveiled in 1969, is outside the railings but so sited for its proximity to the More chapel.[5]

Fittings

Fittings[6] include the baluster font of 1673, with a new cover, late 17th-century communion rails, and 17th-century Flemish glass in the north aisle and chapel. An oak bookcase of 1832 in the south aisle contains London's only surviving chained books, given by Sir Hans Sloane.[7] In the porch has been hung the Ashburnham bell, given in 1679 to celebrate William Ashburnham's escape from drowning; formerly in the cupola, it was rung on winter evenings until *c.*1825, when no more funds could be found.[8]

Three great bells and a little service bell, listed in 1549,[9] may have survived at the church's rebuilding.[10] A fourth great bell was then given in 1673. The physician Baldwin Hamey the younger (d. 1676)[11] gave a bell inscribed to St Luke in 1673 and his nephew Ralph Palmer paid for another bell in 1674. Six bells were recorded in 1705.[12] Recasting of the six old bells into a peal of eight was suggested in 1756 and carried out in 1762 by Thomas Janaway, who was charged with neglecting their wheels and rollers.[13] The bells were to be sold in 1824 towards a peal for the new church but the 4th was retained in order to summon worshippers to the Parish Chapel.[14] The survivor was recast in 1957 and served as the 3rd bell in a peal of eight in 1977, when seven new bells were installed.[15]

The 17th-century plate was transferred to the new church, together with the registers. An electro-plated early 19th-century set of 2 flagons, cups, patens, and almsdishes was in use in 1895.[16] Communion vessels used in 1932 had been given by the father of S.P.T. Prideaux, incumbent 1908–12.[17] All were destroyed in 1941.[18]

CHURCH OF ST LUKE

In 1818 the vestry at last decided to raise money for a large and more central church,[19] to which the rectory was to be transferred under the Act of 1819. It was to be built in the middle of 4 acres east of Robert (later Sydney) Street which had been acquired as an additional burial ground in 1810.[20] Commissioners under the first Church Building Act, 1818, agreed to pay up to one third of the cost; the vestry reduced its total estimate from £30,000 to £20,000 but the architect's estimate of £25,000, in addition to a parliamentary grant of £8,333, was so far exceeded that the final figure came to *c.* £40,000,[21] a tribute to the wealth of local subscribers. The foundation stone was laid in 1820 and the new parish church, dedicated to St Luke, was consecrated in 1824.[22] 'The first stone vaulted church of the Gothic Revival',[23] St Luke's impresses by its height, which is enhanced by spacious surroundings.[24] Its nave, rising to 60 ft, is taller than that of any church in London except St Paul's and Westminster abbey. Designed in patriotic English Perpendicular style by James Savage to seat *c.*2,000,[25] the building of Bath stone was planned as a long rectangle comprising a shallow straight ended chancel, a nave with galleried aisles and triforium and clerestory, and a 142-ft tower springing from the central bay of a porch which spans the west front. Burial vaults strengthened the foundations and a vestry projected beneath the east end. The tower, for which a spire was intended, was crowned by battlements and by pinnacles on its octagonal corner buttresses, echoed by octagonal turrets at the east end. Alterations have been slight: the chancel was decorated by George Goldie and Child in 1874,[26] and its floor raised and extended westward in

1 Lysons, *Environs*, II. 111–12; above, Loc. Govt, pub. svces.
2 Lysons, *Environs*, II. 108–10; Vestry orders, 1662–1718, f. 5v.; above, Soc. Hist., educ. (intro.).
3 *Survey of London*, VII, pl. 87.
4 Vestry orders, 1745–71, p. 273.
5 Chelsea cuttings; More, St Thos.
6 Those in 1921 listed in *Survey of London*, VII. 5–13.
7 Beaver, *Memorials*, 68–9; Denny, *Chelsea Past*, 25.
8 Beaver, *Memorials*, 65, 69, 382.
9 Besides 2 hand bells and a sacring bell.
10 Para. based on Davies, *Chelsea Old Ch.* 19–20.
11 *DNB.*
12 Bowack, *Antiquities*, 1.
13 Vestry orders, 1745–71, pp. 180, 251, 255–6.
14 Vestry mins, 1822–33, pp. 124, 127.
15 Thomson, *Rebuilding of Old Ch.* 111, 123–4.
16 Freshfield, *Communion Plate*, 35; *Survey of London*, VII. 5.
17 Stewart, *Chelsea Old Ch.* 56.
18 Inf. from vicar.
19 Vestry orders, 1809–22, pp. 309, 326–8.
20 59 Geo. III, c. 35 (Local and Personal); above, Loc. Govt, pub. svces (burial).
21 Vestry orders, 1809–22, p. 328; M.H. Port, *Six Hundred New Chs.* (1961), 134–5.
22 *Gent. Mag.* XC(2), 293; ibid. XCIV(2), 291.
23 Clarke, *London Chs.* illus. 33; see Plate 5.
24 Rest of para. based on Clarke, *London Chs.* 51–2; Pevsner, *London NW.* 560; Johnston, *St Luke's, passim.* See Plate 3.
25 *Rep. Com. Eccl. Revenues*, 641; 1,500 and 500 free: *Mackeson's Guide* (1881).
26 C. L. Eastlake, *Hist. of the Gothic Revival*, ed. J.M. Crook (1970), App. 63.

77. *St Luke's Chelsea, from the south-west*

1893; a memorial chapel for the Punjab Frontier Force ('the Piffers') in the south aisle was dedicated in 1951. During repairs to the stonework between 1983 and 1991 the vestry was refurbished and converted into parish offices,[1] the expenditure having been made possible by the sale of the Rectory.[2]

Such an ambitious church has always provoked debate. Savage's plans were criticized by the Crown Architects and realized only because the parish bore so much of the cost.[3] The result was welcomed as a departure from the Grecian style and an example of grandeur, tastefulness, and a correctness of elaborate detail that 'would do honour to a cathedral'.[4] By 1872, however, C.L. Eastlake, while acknowledging the architect's earnestness, found it 'uninteresting in its general effect', with lanky proportions, mechanical decoration, and an overstrained balance in its plan.[5] He was outdone in 1966 when the building, 'one of the most loveless in London', was said to have long got away with fraud on the grounds that it had once been a novelty and cost a fortune.[6] St Luke's has perhaps attracted harsh scrutiny precisely because exact medieval precedents had been followed,[7] and more recently it has received kinder treatment. In 1995 it was recognized as Savage's most important Gothic church, and in 1997 was poetically described as a Gothic Revival ship, sailing parallel to King's Road.[8] Its open site, rare for a London church, gives its soaring height full effect.

Monuments and Fittings

Monuments in the church include one by Chantrey to Lt-Col. Henry Cadogan (d. 1813), formerly in the Old Church, and one considered the best work of W. Pepper the younger, to Luke Thomas Flood (d. 1857).[9] The fittings in Gothic style were designed by Savage, except for the pulpit, replaced in 1893, and the lectern, 1889.[10] His reredos incorporates a painting of the Descent from the Cross by James Northcote (d. 1831), Steven Cox's stone figures of Adam and Eve, installed 1997 in niches on either side. The organ case at the west end echoes the design of the church tower; pipes were added to Nichol's original organ and a new organ by John Compton was installed in 1932. Northcote also designed the glass in the east window, made by T. Willement, for which a subscription was launched in 1823;[11] it was destroyed in the Second World War, and more than 500 square feet of glass, designed by Hugh Easton, replaced it in 1959. A peal of ten bells was cast by Thomas Mears at Whitechapel in 1823[12] and rehung in 1893 and again in 1936.

The plate from the Old Church at St Luke's in 1895 included a paten datemarked 1624, a paten of 1676, and a spoon of 1698, all silver-gilt, two silver flagons of 1680 and two silver cups of 1778, and 18th-century pewter dishes, besides later pieces.[13] In 2003 only the spoon, a funnel wine strainer of 1837, and two churchwarden's staves of 1797 and 1829 were still in the parish's possession.[14] The registers were likewise transferred: those of baptisms and marriages date from 1559 and are irregular for 1644–52; those of burials date from 1559 but are missing for 1564–91.[15] Burials by 1795 had for long exceeded baptisms, owing to the number of nursed children and strangers. Separate registers were kept by the Royal Hospital.[16]

Churchyard

The churchyard since 1887 has served as a public garden, with some gravestones realigned.[17] Burials included that of James Savage (d. 1851),[18] though his

1 Chelsea cuttings: St Luke's ch. (*Restoration Appeal*, 1987).
2 Above.
3 Port, *Six Hundred Chs.* 81; *Chelsea Soc. Rep.* (1988), 46.
4 *Gent Mag.* XCVI(1), 201.
5 Pevsner, *London NW.* 560; Eastlake, *Hist. of Gothic Revival*, 141–4.
6 I. Nairn, *Nairn's London* (1966), 137.
7 Clarke, *London Chs.* 51.
8 Colvin, *Brit. Architects*, 851; Johnston, *St Luke's*, 1.
9 Faulkner, *Chelsea*, I. 228–9; Gunnis, *Sculptors*, 95, 299.
10 Rest of para. based on Johnston, *St Luke's*, *passim.*
11 Vestry mins, 1822–33, pp. 89–90.
12 Weights in Faulkner, *Chelsea*, II. 80.
13 Freshfield, *Communion Plate*, 34.
14 Inf. from sen. chwdn.
15 LMA, P74/LUK/161 et seq.
16 Lysons, *Environs*, II. 117.
17 Above, Soc. Hist., social (other pks); Loc. Govt, pub. svces (burial).
18 *DNB.*

tomb is no longer visible. Among those married in the church were the authors Charles Dickins in 1836 and Jerome K. Jerome in 1888.[1] A church at Chelsea, Massachusetts (USA), founded in 1906, was presented with a block of stone from the Old Church and dedicated to St Luke.[2]

CHURCH EXTENSION

Shortage of space in Chelsea's parish church (later the Old Church) was implied by a carefully recorded exchange of pews in 1626 between the countess of Nottingham and Sir John Danvers.[3] In 1631 enlargement was needed because of recent building and 'the resort and residence of divers great personages', which had deprived many ancient inhabitants of their seats.[4] Similar words were used in 1698, when the church could not hold half of the parishioners after most of it had been rebuilt.[5]

Accommodation eventually was supplemented by the proprietary Park chapel, a little to the north-west, possibly from 1718: the chapel's construction was ascribed to the cessation of services which had been held at Beaufort House.[6] Anglicans in the early 19th century were slower than Roman Catholics or protestant nonconformists to respond to the growth of Hans Town.[7] In 1815 the antiquary Richard Yates, chaplain to the Royal Hospital, was worried particularly by the lack of free places in undivided parishes around London; Chelsea, on the general county average, was populous enough to need 28 churches.[8]

Further provision was made by the more central St Luke's, whose incumbent superseded that of the Old Church as rector of Chelsea in 1824, and by Holy Trinity chapel to the north-east from 1830. St Luke's and Holy Trinity were a response to the Church Building Commissioners' findings in 1821 that Chelsea had places of worship for only 3,200 out of its population of over 26,000.[9]

Both the Old Church and Holy Trinity were intended as chapels of ease to the new parish church, but while the first continued as a perpetual curacy the second in 1831 was given its own parish, sometimes called Upper Chelsea. The rector's conveyance of a site for Trinity chapel and the building commissioners' leasing of pew rents were resented by many vestrymen.[10] Forced to admit the legality of the chapel's construction, in 1834 they appointed a committee to prosecute their grievances over the division of the parish and vainly sought to reverse that 'arbitrary' act.[11]

An additional but modest increase in accommodation was provided by institutional chapels which outsiders could attend: at the Royal Hospital and at the Royal Military Asylum. The sentence of consecration for the first in 1691 confirmed all the rights of Chelsea rectory and that the chapel would remain subject, like the parish as a whole, to the jurisdictions of the bishop of London and the archdeacon of Middlesex.[123]

Mid 19th-century church building was mainly in eastern Chelsea. It started with that of Christ Church, a chapel of ease to St Luke's from 1839 and a separate parish from 1860. The church was the first in Chelsea to benefit from Catherine Elizabeth Hyndman's Bounty to the Church of England, established by her brother in 1836 and largely derived from sugar plantations.[13] In 1838 there were estimated to be 7,350 seats for Anglicans and 3,760 for all other worshippers in the old parish, a total of 11,110 for a population of 46,495. Christ Church was included among the 7 Anglican places of worship, as were the chapels of the Royal Hospital and the Military Asylum which seated 500 and 600 respectively.[14]

There followed the opening of the parish churches of St Saviour, Walton Street, in 1840, St Jude, Turk's Row, in 1844, and St Simon Zelotes, Milner Street, another beneficiary of the Hyndman trust, in 1859.[15] Holy Trinity, claiming to share with St Luke's in the distribution of parochial charities for the poor, was at length allotted a third of the income in 1866, when a further twentieth went to Christ Church.[16] Harriett Burrard by will proved 1867, in addition to a bequest to St Luke's parochial school, left £1,000 stock to be divided between the incumbents of Christ Church and St Jude's, which stock was transferred to the commissioners for Queen Anne's Bounty.[17] In contrast, the less developed western end of Chelsea saw only the opening of the chapel of St Mark's training college in 1843 until the nearby St

1 P. Ackroyd, *Dickens* (1909), 181; J. Connolly, *Jerome K. Jerome* (1982), 49.
2 Stewart, *Chelsea Old Ch.* 22.
3 Except where otherwise stated, section based on inf. in dau. chs below.
4 BL, Add. MS 11056, ff. 290, 294.
5 Davies, *Chelsea Old Ch.* 9; Vestry orders, 1662–1718, ff. 77v.
6 CL, photos. of watercolours 1230–2. The bp of Winchester fitted up a private chapel at Winchester Ho. in the 1660s; it had recently been dismantled in 1822: *Gent. Mag.* XCII. 508; *Survey of London*, XI. 65.
7 *Places of Worship*, 27.
8 R. Yates, *The Ch. in Danger* (1815), 29–30, 63.
9 *London Gaz.* 2 Dec. 1831, p. 2512.
10 Vestry mins, 1822–3, pp. 280A–1, 283–4, 286–8.
11 Ibid., 1833–9, pp. 33, 46–7, 63–4, 86, 97–8.
12 Newcourt, *Rep.* I. 588.
13 H. Reid, *One Hundred Years in a Chelsea Par.* [*c.*1939], 25–6.
14 *London City Mission Mag.* III. 125.
15 Reid, *One Hundred Years*, 27.
16 Above, Soc. Hist., chars.
17 *Vestry rep. 1867–8*, 310; *Endowed Chars London* (1901), 242.

78. *Park Chapel, Park Walk, 1797*

John's, Tadema Road, serving the new but modest streets of World's End, was opened in 1876.[1] Provision may have been found to be over-generous in Eastern or Upper Chelsea, where St Matthew's briefly existed as a temporary church *c.*1878 and where St Jude's was made a chapel of ease to Holy Trinity in 1892.

Chelsea and St Marylebone were distinguished among London's richer parishes for their comparatively modest fall in church attendance, of 9.3 and 9.7 per cent, between 1886 and 1903. Probably a declining population, especially working-class emigration, allowed Chelsea to contrast with Kensington, where the fall was 41.6 per cent.[2] Good relations with protestant nonconformists were claimed in 1900 for St Luke's, St John's, and, with Roman Catholics also, Holy Trinity.[3] At St Simon's, however, there were felt to be too many Roman Catholics, while the vicar of St Saviour's resented the charitable work of the Church of Scotland, which left him ignorant as to who deserved relief. All churches supported social and benevolent societies, St John's in particular sponsoring a wide range of activities which was making the Church popular.[4] Morality was generally seen as good, the worst complaints being of apathy or drunkenness among the poor. Some prosperous eastern districts had their own problems: at Christ Church the wealthy residents lacked interest and at Holy Trinity, where 'educated' parishioners found fault with the preaching, difficulties arose from weekend absences during the Season.

In 1903 Chelsea had 12 Anglican churches or chapels, including those of the Royal Hospital, the Duke of York's schools (formerly the Asylum), and St Mark's college.[5] They were attended on census Sunday by 8,414 worshippers, to whom could be added 1,309 at six Anglican missions to give a total of 9,723, outnumbering that of all other denominations.[6] As only 21.6 per cent of its adult population attended any kind of church, Chelsea ranked 31st on a list of 51 London districts headed by Ealing with an attendance of 47.4 per cent. On a similar list of people attending Anglican services, Chelsea ranked 21st.[7]

Six Chelsea churches had at least one assistant curate in 1896 and 1907, when in both years there were 14 curates in addition to the incumbents. The richest livings in 1896 were those of St Luke's and Holy Trinity, with £1,547 and £1,500 respectively, whereas St John's and St Simon's were each worth only £200.[8] In 1903 the average income of an incumbent in Chelsea was high: £693, compared with £577 in Kensington and £300 or less in most East End parishes.[9]

The rebuilt Park chapel was opened as St Andrew's in 1913. The first closure was that of St Jude's in 1934. After war damage it was proposed in 1947 that the shell of the Old Church be preserved, pending proper restoration, and that a mission hall should serve St John's. Six church buildings were to be retained: those of St Luke, Christ Church, St Andrew, Holy Trinity, St Saviour, and St Simon Zelotes. Together with the Old Church and St John's, they made up Chelsea's 8 parish churches, until in 1973 St John's parish was united with St Andrew's, as had been suggested in 1947, later served by St John's community church at World's End. The 7 parishes were further reduced to 6 when Christ Church was united with St Luke's in 1986.

Expansion at World's End, where St John's clergy worked closely with the Salvation Army and other bodies, was counterbalanced by dwindling congregations farther east. Both of the threatened churches of Holy Trinity and St Saviour served areas whose wealth did not make up for the fact that many residents were transitory, foreign, or part-time; a defender of St Saviour's in 1986, elaborating the complaints of the incumbents in 1900, went so far as to claim that 'most of the residents have country houses to which they repair at weekends'.[10] St Luke's in 1999 drew an 'eclectic congregation' from a 'highly mobile community'.[11] An additional threat to the buildings' survival lay in the value of their sites for redevelopment.

The 6 parishes, with a further 5 in South Kensington, in 1995 formed the deanery of Chelsea. There were also

1 Late 19th-cent. lists, e.g. *Clergy List* and *Crockford*, inc. parishes in Chelsea detached, treated under Paddington in *VCH Middx*, IX, or reserved for treatment under Kensington.

2 H. McLeod, *Class and Religion in the Late Victorian City* (1974), 237–8, 314.

3 Rest of para. based on Lambeth Pal. Lib., Fulham Papers, Creighton 2/1, 3–11.

4 Booth, *Life and Labour*, III(3), 114–15.

5 The Cancer Hosp., Whitelands coll. chapel, and the workho., all listed in the bp's visitation in 1900 (Lambeth Pal. Lib., Fulham Papers, Creighton 2/2, 11,13) were not used for public worship.

6 Mudie-Smith, *Rel. Life*, 113. Similar nos, slightly higher and more approximate, had been reported in 1900: Lambeth Pal. Lib., Fulham Papers, Creighton 2/1, 3–11.

7 McLeod, *Class and Rel.* 299–301.

8 *Crockford* (1896, 1907).

9 McLeod, *Class and Rel.* 122.

10 CCC file, St Saviour, Chelsea.

11 Johnston, *St Luke's*, 36.

79. *West front of Christ Church, Christchurch Street*

4 hospital chaplaincies: that of the Royal Hospital,[1] and those of interdenominational chapels for staff and patients at the Brompton, Royal Marsden, and Chelsea and Westminster hospitals.[2] In 2000 an assistant curate was attached only to St Luke's, with responsibility for Christ Church, while St Saviour's was temporarily served from St Simon's. A total of 6 stipendiary clergy, apart from the hospital chaplains, was left to minister to the entire ancient parish.[3]

DAUGHTER CHURCHES AND PROPRIETARY CHAPEL

Below are brief details, in alphabetical order, about all the Anglican places of worship in Chelsea apart from the parish churches (above). Following the district churches is a section for institutional chapels which allowed the public to attend services.

Inf. about 19th- and 20th-century patrons and clergy is from *Clergy List*, *Crockford*, and *London Diocesan Year Bk* (various edns). Svces, seating, and attendance figs. 1867, 1871, 1881, 1884 are from Mudie-Smith, *Rel. Life*, 113. Liturgical directions are used in all architectural descriptions. The following additional abbreviations are used: a.a., average attendance; aft., afternoon; asst, assistant; consecr., consecrated; Dec., Decorated; dedic., dedicated, dedication; demol., demolished; EE, Early English; Eccl. Com., Ecclesiastical Commission; evg, evening; H.C., Holy Communion; mem., memorial; min., minister; mtg, meeting; R, rector; regs, registers; svce, service; temp., temporarily; V, vicar. Most regs are at LMA.

Christ Church, Paradise (from 1879 Christchurch) Street.[4] Hyndman's trustees decided to build chapel of ease for St Luke's 1837.[5] Listed among chs with seating overestimated at 1,200 in 1838[6] but not consecr. until 1839. Separate par. 1860 with boundaries extended 1861. Patron Hyndman's trustees. Serving poor area and with small endowment and few pew rents, V sought help from Eccl. Com. 1841.[7] Par. more populous and more prosperous from redevelopment by 1890s. Anti-Ritualist under 2nd V 1845–65. Svces twice Sun., with unsurpliced choir, 1867; also Wed. evg, and H.C. 2 or 3 times a month, 1881. Attendance 1903: 257 a.m., 293 evg. Normally one asst curate from 1870s to 1940; 1 in 1961–2. Retained parochial status but shared clergy after formation of combined par. called Chelsea, St Luke and Christ Ch., 1986.

Bldg of yellow stock brick with stone dressings by Edw. Blore 1838–9, seating 800 inc. 250 free in 1881, in EE Gothic style and with an innovative asymmetrical composition with SW. stair tower with bell turret.[8] Shallow chancel, aisled nave with iron pillars and galleries on 3 sides. Built to hold maximum no. of mainly working-class parishioners at minimal cost, ch. was dominated by pulpit and resembled nonconf. chapel in lack of adornment. Extended E. and W. by J. Art. Reeve 1989, when nave roof rebuilt, pillars encased in

1 *London Dioc. Bk* (2001); below.

2 *Places of Worship*, 13, 18, 51.

3 *Crockford* (2000–2001); *London Dioc. Bk* (2001).

4 Based on Reid, *One Hundred Years*, *passim*; Clarke, *London Chs.* 52; Chelsea cuttings: Christ Ch. (inc. *Christ Ch., Chelsea. A Brief Hist.* [pamphlet]).

5 Guildhall MS 19224/56.

6 *London City Mission Mag.* III. 125.

7 *Jnl of Eccl. Hist.* IV. 209.

8 Bradley, 'Gothic Revival', 406–7; V & A Drawings Colln, 8725.10. Architect not known to Reid: *One Hundred Years*, 27; see Fig. 79.

plaster, and 2 SE. vestries replaced smaller vestry; chancel extended and new W. front in Dec. style by W.D. Caröe 1900–1;[1] NW. porch by G. Woodward 1933. 17th-cent. pulpit from St Jas Garlickhithe (London) and organ of 1789 from demol. St Mic. Queenhithe (London) acquired 1876.[2] Vicarage, previously at various hos, built on site at no. 27 Tite St given by Earl Cadogan 1888.[3] Regs from 1839.[4]

Emmanuel. See Park chapel

Holy Trinity, Sloane Street.[5] Inhabitants petitioned for a church in 1819 but disagreed with ch. bldg commrs about cost and plans by Geo. Godwin. Site from E. side of Sloane St to Upper George (later Sedding) St found by par. 1827, and conveyed to commrs by Hen. Blunt, later first incumbent, 1828,[6] where chapel of ease to St Luke's consecr. 1830. Stipend allotted and dist assigned from Chelsea (St Luke's) par. 1831.[7] Blunt formerly asst curate at St Luke's. Bldg financed by large parl. grant (£6,729)[8] but Chelsea vestry's resentment at loss of pew rents[9] and other expenses led to separation as par. with R. to serve Upper Chelsea 1832. Invalidity of division, arising from signature on behalf of Earl Cadogan, a lunatic, led to second order 1832. One twentieth of tithes of St Luke's, besides shares of other fees, assigned to Holy Trinity.[10] Patron Earl Cadogan. Richest ch. in Chelsea after St Luke's, normally with one or two asst curates. Rectory, at hos in Cadogan Pl. 1855, 1863, designed by A.W. Blomfield at no. 141 Sloane St 1874 and there until 1970s.[11]

Svces thrice on Sun., twice on Wed. 1867; fully choral, thrice on Sun. besides H.C., once on Wed., Fri., and saints' days 1881. Attendance 1903: 1,443 a.m., highest at any rel. svce, 808 evg. R. was patron of St Jude's (q.v.) until that par. joined Holy Trinity, its V. moving to Holy Trinity Rectory 1892.[12] Successive rectors Ric. Burgess 1836–70, Rob. Eyton 1884–95, H.E.G. Bevan 1895–1902, H.R. Gamble 1902–16, and Chris. Cheshire 1924–45, were also prebendaries of St Paul's. Bevan became R. of St Luke's and Gamble dean of Exeter. Musical tradition strengthened by appointment of young John Ireland as asst organist and choirmaster 1896–1904.[13] As 'cathedral of the Arts and Crafts movement',[14] ch. survived moves to develop cramped but valuable site.[15] Finances 'desperate' by 1969; R. and many parishioners favoured smaller bldg with rooms for pastoral work 1971; Victorian Soc. alarmed 1972; Sir John Betjeman inspired to address poem to mayor and other worthies as part of campaign to prevent demol. 1974. Living suspended 1997, when electoral roll only 35 and two Sun. svces thinly attended, but bldg given 5 years' reprieve with appointment of Mic. Marshall, who reopened it as base for work as asst bp of Lond. Friends of Holy Trinity formed to seek funds from publicizing relationship between faith and arts 1998. Regs from 1832.[16]

First bldg of brick with stone dressings by Jas Savage 1828–30, seating 1,450 in 1838[17] and 1,600 in 1881, in 'debased' Gothic denounced as 'best example of evils of mixing styles'.[18] Shallow windowless chancel, aisleless nave with square beneath pointed windows and galleries on 3 sides, flat ceiling imitating stone, W. entrance front flanked N. and S. by pinnacled octagonal turrets with spirelets.[19] Closed and demol. as too small 1888. Iron ch. seating 800 erected in Symons St by Lord Cadogan in temp. use 1888–90.

Second church, on same site, built of red brick 1889–90, seating 1,800 in 1907.[20] Fabric cost £20,000 given by Earl Cadogan, while R. sought £7,000 for fittings. Holy Trinity is 'the outstanding London example of the Arts and Crafts movement in ecclesiastical terms'.[21] In plan J.D. Sedding's church is a free rendering of cathedral at Gerona (Spain), but without an apse. It has chancel, NE. chapel with W. baptistery, high wide clerestoreyed nave beneath 5-bay rigged vault, S. aisle narrower than N. but W. entrance front made symmetrical by projection of S. porch; NW. and SW. turrets.[22] Its style is a mixture of English and Continental late Gothic, 'an attempt to take up the threads of the Gothic tradition and weave them into the weft of modern need and thought'.[23] Richness is concentrated on W. front and on eclectic liturgical furnishings by leading designers and craftsmen. Sedding's scheme was

1 J. Freeman, *W.D. Caröe: his architectural achievement* (1990), 246.

2 Photos in NMR organ case dated 1799 in Pevsner, *London NW.* 558.

3 Guildhall MS 19224/56.

4 LMA, P74/CTC/01 et seq.

5 Based on CCC files, inc. M.M. Barber, *Short Hist. of Holy Trinity Ch., Sloane Sq.* [*c.*1951]; F.H. Spicer, *Holy Trinity Ch.* (1956), *passim*.

6 Guildhall MS 19224/126, file 1.

7 LMA, P74/TRI/35; *London Gaz.* 2 Dec. 1831, p. 2512.

8 Port, *Six Hundred New Chs.* 135.

9 Vestry mins, 1822–33, pp. 280–8, 304; 1833–9, pp. 33, 46–7, 86, 97.

10 Guildhall MS 19224/126, file 1. Plan of new par. in LMA, P74/TRI/36.

11 *PO Dir. London* (1855, 1863); Guildhall MS 19224/126, file 2; *Crockford* (1896 and later edns).

12 Guildhall MS 19224/126, file 2.

13 *DNB.*

14 K. Yates, *Holy Trinity, Sloane St, a Brief Guide* [*c.*1993].

15 Details of campaigns to save ch., inc. press articles, pamphlets, letters and adverts., are in CCC file, Holy Trinity, Chelsea, and Chelsea cuttings: Holy Trinity.

16 LMA, P74/TRI/1 seqq.

17 *London City Mission Mag.* III.125.

18 *Gent. Mag.* CI. 299; *Mackeson's Guide* (1881).

19 Port, *Six Hundred New Chs.* 135; NMR (photo.); *Images of Chelsea*, nos. 474–8.

20 *Crockford* (1907).

21 Pevsner, *London NW.* 559; see Plate 5.

22 In addition to CCC files, inf. on bldg and fittings from Clarke, *London Chs*, 54–5; Pevsner, *London NW.* 559; P.F. Anson, *Fashions in Ch. Furnishings 1840–1940* (1960), 249–50; C. Brooks and A. Saint, *The Victorian Ch.* (1988), 207–10.

23 *Archit. Rev.* (1897), reprinted in A. Service, *Edwardian Architecture and its Origins* (1975), 277.

continued after his death in 1891 by his partner, Henry Wilson (d. 1934), though not completed quite as intended,[1] and its Anglo-Catholic programme has been obscured by changes, e.g. to the high altar, and by church's later conventional Anglican life. Original fittings include ironwork designed by Sedding and Wilson; main altar by Harry Bates; chancel stalls and screen by F.W. Pomeroy; partial decoration of nave by Edw. Burne-Jones. E. window by Messrs Powell 1894–5, with 48 figures by Burne-Jones, foliage and surroundings by Wm Morris. Chapel windows by Jas Powell & Sons to design of W.B. Richmond 1904, 1910; S. aisle and other windows by C. Whall from 1900. Main altar reredos by John Tweedsmuir 1912. S. chapel furnished as war memorial by F.C. Eden, glass by Powell, 1921. Lady chapel damaged 1940, but used for svces after nave bombed 1941; blast damage 1944. Temp. roof kept ch. open until repaired with lower roof by V.O. Rees 1950–1,[2] replaced with plaster vault on metal frame by Mic. Farey 1959. Repainting, ascribed to influence of Percy Dearmer (d. 1936), divine, who was hon. curate 1924–9, said in 1960 to have made walls blend too closely with decoration.[3]

Park chapel, Park Walk.[4] Proprietary chapel on E. side of rd originally called Twopenny Walk, at edge of Chelsea Park, built to serve Little Chelsea by accoucheur Sir Ric. Manningham (d. 1759):[5] possibly in 1718,[6] but more likely *c.*1724 when he took lease of pk from Wm Sloane.[7] Lease of chapel made by Manningham to Revd Wm Lacy of Battersea 1730;[8] later held by Sloane Elsmere, R of Chelsea, and by successive, mainly clerical, purchasers for terms of 61 to 81 years, all of them soon assigned.[9] Holders inc. John Owen (d. 1822), R of Paglesham (Essex) and sec. of Brit. and Foreign Bible Soc.,[10] from 1812, whose widow Charlotte was sole proprietor 1829. His son Hen. John Owen was min. at Park chapel 1822–34 before resigning to found Cath. Apostolic ch. in College St.[11] Hen. John and Miss Charlotte Owen conveyed lease 1844–5 to banker John Dean Paul (later Bt).[12] On Paul's bankruptcy 1855 it was bought by cong. and vested in trustees, who remained patrons until demol. of chapel, renamed in 1906 or 1907 *Emmanuel* ch., in 1912.[13]

Noted Evangelical tradition by early 19th cent., with royal attendance at bp's sermon for lying-in hosp. 1810. Large schs for poor built on ground E. of chapel conveyed 1827.[14] John Harding (d. 1874), min. 1834, was later bp of Bombay.[15] Wm Cadman, min. 1846–52, was later a prebendary of St Paul's.[16] Svces thrice on Sun. and Thurs. evg, with H.C. twice monthly, 1867; 'singing entirely congregational'. Under J.G. Gregory, min. 1868–79, ch. had good attendance at 'simplest svce possible in C. of E.'. Gradually came to resemble neighbouring par. chs, surplice being sanctioned *c.*1900. One asst curate 1866, 1881, and, alone with Old Ch., none 1896, 1907; min.'s chief handicap said to be lack of assistance 1900.[17] New mission hall in Ann's Pl. 1899 used for ch. activities and by London City Mission.[18]

First chapel, marked 1745 and mistakenly identified with Huguenots,[19] shown as narrow and tall roofed, with bellcote and small Gothic window over gabled or steeply pedimented W. porch.[20] Previously described as chapel or tabernacle,[21] greatly enlarged or rebuilt by leaseholder Revd John G. Smyth 1810. Plain rectangular bldg lit by 2 rows of round-headed windows, perhaps little altered by early 20th cent. when rendered W. front had central pediment surmounted by bellcote. Bare interior, with deep galleries on 3 sides.[22] Seating for 1,000 in 1838,[23] 1,300 inc. 300 free 1881. Dilapidated by 1897, when freeholder Sloane Stanley conditionally offered site. Smaller ch. on corner of Elm Park Rd planned 1900,[24] but freeholder's offer withdrawn after dispute over patronage. Fund for bldg new ch. spent on necessary repairs and renovations of Park chapel 1906–7, when renamed Emmanuel.[25] Land again offered, if £10,000 could be raised for bldg, securing of which sum led to demol. of chapel and its replacement by St And.'s (q.v.). Regs from 1879.[26]

St Andrew, Park Walk. Freehold of site of Emmanuel ch. (formerly Park chapel) given by R.C.H. Sloane Stanley 1912, 4 neighbouring hos in Park Walk (nos 37–43 odd) given by Miss Birch, and money given by

1 RIBA, Drawings Coll. RAN 71/G/1 (1–6).
2 *Ch. of Holy Trinity, Sloane St, 1939–51* (booklet *c.*1951 in LMA, P74/TRI/176).
3 Anson, *Ch. Furnishings*, 248; *DNB*.
4 Based on LMA, P74/AND/49 (R. Macdonald, MS hist. of chapel, 1977); Chelsea cuttings: Park chapel; Chelsea Misc. 445–9.
5 *DNB*.
6 *Survey of London*, IV. 48 (based on Lysons).
7 Above, Settlement, 1680–1865 (Chelsea Pk); see Fig. 78.
8 Described as 'curate' at Lt. Chelsea *c.*1735: Guildhall MS 9550.
9 Several leaseholders in Faulkner, *Chelsea*, I. 148. Additional names and leases in Guildhall MS 19224/159; LMA, P74/AND/20–1.
10 *DNB*.
11 Below, prot. nonconf. (Cath. Apostolic).
12 Guildhall MS 19224/159; *DNB*.
13 *Financial Statements* 1905–6 for Park chapel, 1906–7 for Emmanuel ch.: LMA, P74/AND/31–2.
14 Above, Soc. Hist., educ. (pub. schs: Park Chapel Nat.).
15 *DNB*.
16 Hennessy, *Nov. Rep.* pp. xxxii, 122.
17 Lambeth Pal. Lib., Fulham Papers, Creighton 2/5.
18 LMA, P74/AND/31–2; below, prot. nonconf. (London City Mission).
19 e.g. *Mackeson's Guide* (1867, 1881).
20 CL, photos of watercolours 1230–2.
21 LMA, P74/AND/20.
22 Faulkner *Chelsea*, I, facing p. 148; NMR photos.
23 *London City Mission Mag.* III.125.
24 LMA, P74/AND/19.
25 LMA, P74/AND/32 (*Financial Statement* 1906–7).
26 Inc. with regs of St And.: LMA, P74/AND/01–28.

80. *St John's, Tadema Road*

Chas Alb. Bannister,[1] for ch. of St And. consecr. 1913. Patron trustees, inc. R of Chelsea, Earl Cadogan, Bannister, Sloane Stanley, and bp.[2] Normally one asst curate between World Wars, but Alf. Abigail, V 1919–44, lived outside par.; his curate S. Newson continued in charge but was not made V until 1962. Plans to absorb part of bombed St John's par. made 1947 but union not effected until 1973, when V of St John's took over combined par. of St John with St And.[3] Patron was Church Pastoral Aid Soc. in 2001, when V assisted by part-time non-stipendiary min. and svces, as stipulated by C.A. Bannister, were evangelical.[4]

Bldg of red brick with stone dressings by Sir A. Blomfield & Son 1912–13 in Dec. style. Chancel, NE. vestry, aisled and clerestoreyed nave, SW. tower with pinnacles and stone spire; plain, spacious interior.[5]

Glebe of both St John's and St And.'s surrendered 1973, when no. 43 Park Walk, given by Miss Birch, became vicarage for combined par.[6] Regs from 1879.[7]

St John, Tadema Rd.[8] Open-air svces held 1873 by John Shaw, later first V, who opened iron ch. 1873 at N. apex of triangular site between Tadema and Ashburnham rds conveyed 1875. Ch. of St John, often described as in Ashburnham Rd and in 1896 as dedic. to St John the Evangelist,[9] consecr. 1876. Dist. chapelry assigned from St Luke's 1877.[10] Patron 5 trustees,[11] appointed with consent of St Luke's and later same as trustees of St And.'s. Min. granted £200 a year from Common Fund 1877.[12] Svces twice on Sun.; also Wed., with H.C. twice a month, 1881. Attendance 1903: 304 a.m., 380 evg. Evangelical in 1883.[13] Normally one or more asst curates, 4 in 1896, necessitated by much missionary and philanthropic work inc. 3 mission halls[14] and 'huge' sun. schs 1902.[15] After bombing amalg. of par. with St And.'s was planned 1947 but mission hall in Blantyre St was fitted up as temp. ch. and used until union was effected 1973.[16]

Bldg of red brick with stone dressings by Newman & Billing 1875–6, seating 777 inc. 400 free 1881, in 'French Gothic' style. Apsidal sanctuary, N. organ transept, aisled and clerestoreyed nave; 140-ft NW. tower with spire by T.R. Pryce dedic. 1888. Interior showed 'mistaken notions of manly vigour' 1883.[17] All save tower bombed 1940. Tower demol. 1949 and site left derelict for 20 yrs. Vicarage ho., 80 on site of iron ch., paid for by grants 1878–80, and in use until *c.*1940.[18] Regs from 1874.[19]

St John's Community church, World's End Pl.[20] Mission of St John, Tadema Rd, at junction of Blantyre St with Dartry Rd built 1880. Sun. evg worship planned *c.*1888 and svces held 1889. Attendance 1903: 183 a.m., 379 evg. Also evg lantern svce. by 1913.[21] Served as temp. par. ch. after bombing of St John's 1940 until union with St And. 1973 and continued in use until 1976. Bldg with steep roof and vaguely Tudor windows, last to be demol. in World's End redevelopment.

Hall replaced by St John's Centre above launderette in

1 Based on LMA, P74/AND/49.
2 Guildhall MS 19224/159.
3 LMA, P74/AND/49; Chelsea cuttings: Diocesan Reorg. Cttee.
4 *Places of Worship*, 39; inf. from V.
5 Pevsner, *London NW.* 560; Clarke, *London Chs*, 55; LMA, P74/AND/48; NMR, photos.
6 LMA, P74/AND/49.
7 LMA, P74/AND/01–8.
8 Based on Chelsea cuttings: St John's ch.; CCC file, St John, Chelsea; Guildhall MS 19224/300.
9 *Crockford* (1896).
10 *London Gaz.* 20 Feb. 1877, p. 817.
11 Named in Guildhall MS 19224/300 (patronage agreement, 1946).
12 *London Gaz.* 15 June 1877, p. 3673.
13 CCC, notes by B.F.L. Clarke.
14 At later St John's Community ch (q.v.), at Gunter Hall, and perhaps at Lacland hall (below, prot. nonconf. (Congs; London City Mission)).
15 Booth, *Life and Labour*, III(3), 115.
16 Chelsea cuttings: Diocesan Reorg.; below, St John's Community ch.
17 CCC, notes by B.F.L. Clarke; see Fig. 80.
18 *London Gaz.* 2 Aug. 1878, p. 4427; 16 May 1879, p. 3387; 23 Jan. 1880, p. 346; *PO Dir. London* (1902 and later edns).
19 LMA, P74/JH/01–19.
20 Based on Chelsea cuttings: St John's ch.
21 *PO Dir. London* (1913); see Fig. 41.

World's End Pl.: St John's Community ch., formerly World's End Community ch. founded by members of Holy Trinity, Brompton (Kens.) and opened in disused studios *c.*1996, had recently moved there in 2000. Brown-brick ch., designed by H.T. Cadbury-Brown & Partners and capable of seating *c.*300, served by clergy of St John with St And. 2000.[1]

St Jude, Turk's Row.[2] Site on N. side of rd bounded N. and E. by grounds of Royal Mil. Asylum, where ch. built with grants from Metropolitan Ch. Fund, bldg commrs, Royal Hosp., and others. Consecr. 1844; dist assigned from Upper Chelsea (Holy Trinity) 1844.30 Patron R of Holy Trinity. Supported 2 city missionaries and 'many other parochial agencies' 1867.[4] Svces twice on Sun. with unsurpliced choir, also Thurs. evg, with H.C. monthly and evg quarterly, 1867; H.C. weekly by 1881. No asst curate 1859, 2 in 1866, one in 1867, 1881. Benefice vacant 1892, when united with Holy Trinity, although svces continued under priest-in-charge until licence withdrawn 1932.[5] Attendance 1903: 216 a.m., 145 evg. John Ireland was official organist while employed at Holy Trinity.

Bldg of stock brick with stone dressings by Geo. Basevi 1843–4, seating 900 free in 1881, in mixed Gothic style. Very shallow chancel continuing aisled and clerestoreyed nave with galleries on 3 sides; 3-stage battlemented SW. tower.[6] Closed 1932 and demol. for York Ho. flats 1934.[7] Proceeds from bldg lease of 1933 given towards construction of St Alban's, N. Harrow.[8] Vicarage hos inc. no. 40 Cadogan Pl.[9] and Stanley Ho., Milner St.[10] Regs from 1844.[11]

St Matthew, Walton Street.[12] Temp. ch. on N. side at corner of Marlborough Rd (later Draycott Ave) opened 1874. Min. attached to London Diocesan Home Mission 1874–81.[13] Served conventional dist within St Saviour's par. 1878, when Metropolitan Dist Rly Co. conveyed nearby freehold plot in Walton St for ch. hall or residence in sole management of clergyman of St Matthew's.[14] Svces twice on Sun., with monthly children's svce, and Wed. evg, with H.C. monthly and at festivals, 1881, when 250 seated free. Despite its own dedic., ch. did not acquire separate par. Serviced by clergy of St Saviour's 1884, 1889, and of St Paul's, Onslow Sq. (Kens.) 1902.[15] 'Very complete premises' but working-class cong. largely outsiders, inc. emigrants to Battersea who wished to maintain Chelsea links.[16] Perhaps identifiable with Church Army Mission, Marlborough Rd, attendance 1903: 42 a.m., 51 evg. Last listed, as St Matthew's mission hall, 1930.[17]

St Saviour, Walton Pl.[18] Part of Quailfield at NE. end of Walton St conveyed by trustees of Hen. Smith's char. to ch. bldg commrs 1838.[19] Commrs made modest grant towards ch. consecr. 1840.[20] Dist chapelry assigned from Upper Chelsea (Holy Trinity) 1842.[21] Patron R of Holy Trinity. Min. assigned £600 a year from pew rents 1843.[22] Svces thrice on Sun. 1867; also twice on Wed., with H.C. monthly and on festivals 1881; paid choir 1884. One or 2 asst curates. Attendance 1903: 429 a.m., 226 evg. St Saviour's had responsibility for mission hall in Marlborough Rd (later Draycott Ave) conveyed by Metropolitan Dist Rly Co. 1878[23] and connected with St Matthew's (q.v.); it may have been the Ch. Army's Marlborough Rd mission, attendance 1903: 42 a.m., 51 evg. Earl Cadogan declined to provide site for vicarage, as ch. was not on his land, but offered £50 a year towards parish work 1881.[24] H.J.R. Osborne, V 1930–52, was prebendary of St Paul's. Redundancy on next vacancy of living proposed 1983 and again, by archdeacon, 1986, when ch. retained svces of 1662.[25] No full-time V by 1992. Ch. temp. closed 1995, when London Diocesan Fund proposed retention of chancel with 2 bays of nave for worship and conversion of rest, inc. ch. hall, for housing. Plan submitted 1996 and work completed by 2003 on ch. to seat *c.*80 designed by Ben Krauze; pars to be served by V of St Simon Zelotes but patronage of united benefices not yet decided in 2001.[26]

Bldg of yellow stock brick with stone dressings by Geo. Basevi 1839–40,[27] seating 1,200 inc. 600 free in 1867, 1881, in EE style. Not oriented. Aisled nave, mostly hidden by external additions, with timbered roof; outer N. aisle and porch by E.P. Loftus Brock 1878; chancel, N. chapel, and S. vestry by Anglo-Cath. Revd Ern. Geldart 1890, presents a main façade of diapered

1 *What in God's Name* [chs millennium pamphlet, 2000]; inf. from V of St John with St And.
2 Based on Spicer, *Holy Trinity*, 133–6; CCC, notes by B.F.L. Clarke; Guildhall MS 19224/355.
3 *London Gaz.* 12 Nov. 1844, p. 3874.
4 *Mackeson's Guide* (1867).
5 LMA, P74/TRI/40–1.
6 Photos in NMR and Chelsea cuttings: St Jude's.
7 *Places of Worship*, 43.
8 *VCH Middx*, IV. 260.
9 *Royal Blue Bk* (1860, 1866).
10 *Royal Blue Bk* (1873); *PO Dir. London* (1879).
11 LMA, P74/JUD/01–09.
12 Based on *Mackeson's Guide* (1881, 1884, 1889).
13 *Clergy List* (1881); *Crockford* (1896), s.v. Sumner, Jos.
14 LMA, P74/SAV/078.
15 *PO Dir. London* (1902).
16 Booth, *Life and Labour*, III(3), 118.
17 *PO Dir. London* (1930).
18 Based on NMR, file no. 93028 (rep. by CCC, 1986).
19 One of several plots given by trustees for pub. purposes: Stroud, *Smith's Char.* 25, 38–9; LMA, P74/SAV/077.
20 Port, *Six Hundred New Chs*, 153; *The Times*, 29 May 1840.
21 *London Gaz.* 12 Aug. 1842, p. 3321.
22 Guildhall MS 19224/633.
23 LMA, P74/SAV/078.
24 Ibid., SAV/076.
25 CCC file, St Saviour, Chelsea; Chelsea cuttings: St Saviour's.
26 CCC file, St Saviour, Chelsea; Chelsea cuttings: St Saviour's; inf. from Mrs Mary McGowan.
27 Summaries of NMR file inf. in Clarke, *London Chs.* 53; Pevsner, *London NW.* 560; see Plate 4.

81. *St Simon Zelotes, Milner Street*

brick with flamboyant tracery to Walton Pl. Fittings inc. altar and probably pulpit by Geldart, glass by Taylor & Clifton in E. window, and by Wm Morris & Co. In the conversion a floor was inserted to accommodate a worship area, meeting room, and flat above a larger foyer and exhibition hall, all part of a Christian Arts Centre. Most furnishings moved to worship area, though NE. chancel chapel retained. Ground abutting liturgical S., conveyed 1888 but never consecr., taken for par. hall 1936[1] and inc. with W. half of ch. in Raven Group's conversion to residential use as St Saviour's Ho.[2] Vicarage ho., for which funds were sought 1843,[3] was at no. 5 Walton Pl. 1847, 1879 and later at various addresses, inc. no. 5 Hans Pl. 1926, 1955.[4] Regs from 1840.[5]

St Simon Zelotes, Milner Street. Site at E. corner of Moore St conveyed to 5 trustees 1858 as means of appropriating legacy of Wm Coles. Ch. of St Simon consecr. 1859,[6] called St Simon Zelotes by 1881.[7] Dist chapelry assigned from Upper Chelsea (Holy Trinity) 1860.[8] Patron trustees, renewed by cooptation.[9] Svces twice on Sun 1867; also twice on Wed., with H.C. twice a month 1881; surpliced choir 1884. Usually one asst curate 1880s–1910s. Attendance 1903: 166 a.m., 94 evg. Among poorest pars in late 19th cent. but benefited later from Hyndman's char.[10] Mic. McGowan (d. 2001), V from 1996 and prebendary of St Paul's was also priest-in-charge of St Saviour's, as was his designated successor.[11]

Bldg of Kentish ragstone with Bath stone dressings designed by Jos. Peacock 1858–9, built by White of Pimlico, in idiosyncratic Dec. style. Shallow sanctuary, aisled and clerestoreyed nave, with higher E. bays of aisles forming transepts galleried until 1896, W. bell turret. Polychrome interior with much naturalistic carving by J.L. Jacquet, and rich E. end with glass by Lavers & Barraud and furnishings by Hailand & Fisher. Organ by Walker.[12] Vicarage ho. built at same time as ch. at no. 5 Milner Terr. (later no. 34 Milner St).[13] Regs from 1860.[14]

Oakley Mission, Manor Street. Earlier, probably undenominational, mission at no. 87,[15] by 1889 was CE and served from St Paul's, Onslow Sq. (Kens.). Svces twice on Sun. with children's svce, also Thurs. evg, with seating for 300 free 1889.[16] Mission room next to St Paul's ch. institute 1902.[17] Attendance 1903: 59 a.m., 125 evg. Listed in 1914, not in 1927.[18]

INSTITUTIONAL CHAPELS

Royal Hospital chapel, Royal Hospital Rd.[19] Begun 1683, 'quite covered' in 1685, fitted out 1687.[20] Consecr. 1691 under royal warrant reserving tithes and all rights of Chelsea par. ch. and providing £100 for chaplain and £80 for curate. No. of chaplains reduced to one in 1833, although an asst still employed until 1892 or later.[21] Patron given as governors of Hosp. 1829, Paymaster-Gen. 1880s, and War Office 1892. Value rarely stated; £300 in 1892.[22] Accn for chaplain in Hosp. Warrant enjoined prayers a.m. and evg, Sun. and feast day sermons, H.C. at least thrice a year; no ref. to baptisms, marriages, or burials, but all performed, weddings only by special licence after 1753. Often inc. in lists of CE chs in 19th cent.[23] Svces partly choral by 1881, twice on Sun., weekday a.m.; H.C. twice a month and on great feasts. Attendance 1903: 225 a.m., 42 evg. Chaplains inc. Chas Ashton (d. 1752), scholar, 1699–1701, Fras Hare (d. 1740), later bp of Chichester, 1703–7, Wm

1 LMA, P74/SAV/077.
2 Advert. board (2000).
3 Guildhall MS 19224/633.
4 *PO Dir. London* (1847 and later edns).
5 LMA, P74/SAV/01–021.
6 Guildhall MS 19224/639; Clarke, *London Chs*, 53.
7 *Mackeson's Guide* (1881).
8 *London Gaz.* 30 Oct. 1860, p. 3941.
9 Inc. R of Upper Chelsea 1858, 1867: Guildhall MS 19224/639; *Mackeson's Guide* (1867).
10 Reid, *One Hundred Yrs*, 27; above, Christ Ch. Patrons sometimes later described as Hyndman's trustees: *Clergy List* (1892, 1915).
11 *Crockford* (2000–2001); inf. from Mrs Mary McGowan.
12 Based on Chelsea cuttings: St Simon; Clarke, *London Chs*, 53; *Builder*, XVI (1858), 424; XVII (1859), 209, 552–3; Pevsner, *London NW.* 561; see Fig. 81.
13 *PO Dir. London* (1863 and later edns).
14 LMA, P74/SIM/1–8.
15 Below, prot. nonconf. (other denoms).
16 *Mackeson's Guide* (1889), addenda, 178.
17 *PO Dir. London* (1902).
18 Harris and Bryant, *Chs and London*, 385; *PO Dir. London* (1927).
19 Based on *Survey of London*, XI, *passim*; Dean, *Royal Hosp.* 53–6, 149–50.
20 *Wren Soc.* XIX (1942), 65, 73.
21 *Mackeson's Guide* (1867); *Clergy List* (1892).
22 *Clerical Guide* (1829); *Mackeson's Guide* (1881); *Clergy List* (1892).
23 Not in *Crockford* (1896 and later edns) but in H.W. Harris and M. Bryant, *Chs and London* [1914], 385.

Barnard (d. 1768), later bp of Derry, 1728, Phil. Francis (d. 1773), miscellaneous writer, 1764–8, and Geo. R. Gleig (d. 1888), later chaplain-gen. of the forces, 1834–46.[1] J.H.S. Moxly in 1900 relied mainly on sermons to combat 'very bad' moral condition arising from drink.[2]

Bldg of brown brick with red-brick and Portland stone dressings, an integral part of Hosp. and with almost the same proportions as hall to W., by Wren. Seating 500 in 1838[3] and *c.*350 in 1880s.[4] Apse with half dome, barrel vaulted plaster ceiling over rectangular chapel lit by 7 tall round-headed windows on N. and S.; oak panelling below windows and at E. end; W. organ gallery and organ case, original organ by Renatus Harris, given by Captain Ingram, first major of Hospital *c.*1692–3. Joinery by Chas Hopson and Ric. Ryley; woodcarving by Wm Emmett and Wm Morgan; plasterwork by Hen. Margetts; fresco of Resurrection in the apse vault by Mario Ricci. Benches rearranged to face E. 1818; rearranged and choir stall added *c.*1920. Pulpit and lectern made from original 3-decker.[5] Plate, silver or silver-gilt hallmarked 1687–8,[6] bought by Hosp. although once believed to have been given by Jas II.[7] Door in apse to pine-panelled vestry, connecting with former chaplain's rooms.[8]

Royal Military Asylum chapel, King's Rd.[9] Svces first held by chaplain in schoolroom at Asylum (from 1892 Duke of York's Royal Mil. Sch.). R of Chelsea conveyed 2 acres of adjacent glebe to governors 1815,[10] where chapel at corner of Cheltenham Terr. was consecr. 1824.[11] Resident chaplain appointed by Sec. of State for War and paid according to rank; duties inc. supervision of educ., first chaplain also being headmaster of sch. All staff required to attend chapel.[12] Svces twice on Sun., with H.C. monthly, unsurpliced choir 1867; H.C. twice monthly 1881. Attendance 1903: 408 a.m., 385 evg. Last svce held 1909, when chapel deconsecr. and fittings moved with sch. to Dover (Kent).

Bldg of yellow brick with stone dressings in plain classical style of Asylum and presumably by its architect John Sanders 1823–4. Rectangular plan, small E. side entrances, Doric W. porch; altar slightly recessed beneath rounded arch, galleries on 3 sides, 2 rows of windows with lower ones in arched recesses.[13] Seating for 600 in 1838;[14] for 500 boys, 60 students and officers, and *c.*150 public in galleries 1867; for 700, inc. 200 in galleries, 1881, 1889. Renovation in progress 2000, when bldg and adjoining Queripel Ho. of 1934 were planned by Cadogan Estates for commercial or gallery use.[15]

St Mark's College chapel, Fulham Rd.[16] Site E. of training college's practising sch.[17] taken for chapel built at same time. Opening accompanied by adoption of St Mark's name for college. Fully choral svces twice on Sun. and feast days, H.C. twice monthly and at greater festivals, choir of students with paid boys and probationers 1867, when all seats free but some appropriated to regular attenders. Surpliced choir and surplice in pulpit 1881. Visitors' attendance 1910: *c.*40 a.m., *c.*80 evg.[18] Total attendance 1903: 180 a.m., 185 evg.

Bldg of stock brick with stone dressings, seating 180 in 1881, in neo-Norman style by Edw. Blore 1841–3.[19] Cruciform plan, E. apse, 2 tiers of windows, bell turrets in angles of shallow transepts; reroofed with round-arched trusses and central lantern after fire 1859.[20] Passed on removal of training college to GLC 1975 and then to Chelsea College and to King's College, London.[21] Bldg, converted into film studio 1990s, externally intact 2001.[22]

1 All in *DNB*.
2 Lambeth Pal. Lib., Fulham Papers, Creighton 2/7.
3 *London City Mission Mag.* III. 125.
4 *Mackeson's Guide* (1881, 1889).
5 *Wren Soc.* XIX (1942), 73–4.
6 *Survey of London*, XI. 30.
7 Hutt, *Royal Hosp.* 99.
8 *Wren Soc.* XIX (1942), 74.
9 Above, Settlement, 1680–1865 (SE Chelsea). Section based on Chelsea cuttings: Duke of York's HQ; L.C. Rudd, *Duke of York's Royal Mil. Sch. 1801–1934* (1935).
10 Guildhall MS 19224/367(1); Act for Sale of Glebe Lands, 55 Geo. II, c. 66 (Private).
11 Faulkner, *Chelsea*, II. 327–8.
12 Chaplain's duties in Faulkner, *Chelsea*, II. 330–1; CL, *Regulations for Establishment of Royal Military Asylum* (1803).
13 RBKC, *Planning Guidelines. Duke of York's HQ* (1999); photos. of interior in Chelsea cuttings: Royal Mil. Asylum. Pevsner implies that chapel was contemporary with asylum of 1801–3: *London NW.* 565.
14 *London City Mission Mag.* III. 125.
15 *Duke of York's News*, July 2000, newsletter in Chelsea cuttings; above, Settlement, twentieth cent.
16 Based on M. Roberts, *Coll. of St Mark and St John, 1840–65* (1946), 27.
17 Above, Soc. Hist., educ. (adult).
18 Lambeth Pal. Lib., Fulham Papers, Creighton, 2/8.
19 Foundation stone 1841: *The Times*, 28 May 1841.
20 Pevsner, *London NW.* 567.
21 Above, Soc. Hist., educ. (adult).
22 *Places of Worship*, 16.

ROMAN CATHOLICISM

George Stanley, his wife, and William Holborne, gentleman, were indicted as recusants in 1583.[1] Holborne was indicted again in 1586, as were Mary, wife of John Lytton, yeoman, in 1610 and Margaret, wife of Francis Kipping, chandler, in 1630 and 1636.[2] It was rumoured in 1627 that Jesuits at court were about to move to the duke of Buckingham's house at Chelsea.[3] Among those presented in 1664 for not attending church, only one, Mr Cooper, was described as papist.[4] There were said to be no papists in 1676.[5] The rector in 1706 listed 22, among them Philip Kemp, a lunatic, with his servant's family, Thomas Humphreys, whose wife kept a small school, and the housekeeper to the dowager duchess of Beaufort; some unknown soldiers at the Royal Hospital were also reputed papists.[6] Seven households and one lodger were listed in 1714[7] and 21 persons, including Thomas Bragg, gentleman, Lady Weston, Kemp, and Humphreys, in 1715.[8] There were said to be 11[9] or 12 papists in 1767, three of them servants and four of them resident for no more than a year.[10] None were known in 1790.[11]

Roman Catholicism owed its later strength in Chelsea to clergy who fled the French Revolution and who presumably found fellow émigrés there. A chapel in Exeter Street was certified in 1798[12] and perhaps short lived, like a house in Wilderness Row which had been 'late a Roman Catholic chapel' in 1802, when it was licensed for protestant dissenters.[13] Local worshippers were served probably by the abbés Tribou, Abraham, and Crespelle from 1798 until 1804 and the abbé Gilles François Thébault from 1804 until 1807. Jean-Nicolas Voyaux de Franous, traditionally seen as the father of Roman Catholicism in Chelsea, had been appointed apostolic missionary there in 1796 but later returned briefly to France and signed acts as missionary only from 1808. Thébault, who also practised medicine, in 1803 lived at no. 12 Lower George Street (later the site of Sloane Gardens). Crespelle lived at Queen's Elm,[14] where by 1799 a house was occupied by Visitandine nuns of the order of St Francis de Sales,[15] to whom Tribou in 1803 acted as chaplain. Services were probably held in Lower George Street.[16]

Funds for a permanent chapel nearby were sought in 1811, after Voyaux de Franous had been leased a site at the east end of Cadogan Street (later Cadogan Gardens) by Lady Charlotte Denys. The abbé himself contributed two-thirds of the cost and was additionally helped by prominent English Catholics and the French nobility. Opened in 1812, St Mary's was seen as a chapel for the French rather than as a mission, although it also served soldiers from the barracks, veterans from the Royal Hospital, and, increasingly, Irish labourers.[17] Chelsea's estimated number of 500 Catholic worshippers in 1814 was double that for any other Middlesex parish outside central London.[18] A charity school was supported from the first, [19] although Voyaux de Franous (d. 1840), who declined a bishopric after the Bourbons' restoration, had no assistant until 1821 and there was no neighbouring religious order to offer help.[20]

Parochial activities increased under Thomas Sisk, Franous's assistant from 1832 and his eventual successor, who doubled the numbers at the school. Benefactions were attracted from, among others, Joseph Knight, a retired nurseryman of King's Road, who bought land for a cemetery and other purposes along the south side of Cadogan Street, which he settled in trust in 1842. St Joseph's convent was opened there in 1845 for Irish Sisters of Mercy from their Bermondsey convent of 1839 and flanked by boys' and girls' schools, the first being staffed by Christian Brothers. Almshouses to the west were built in 1850 and a new church, replacing the chapel of 1812, was opened to the east in 1879.[21] St Mary's, previously still a Mission, was designated a rectory from 1861.[22] The buildings in Cadogan Street, with additions that included St Thomas More's school, thereafter formed a centre of Roman Catholicism in Chelsea.

St Mary's was left to serve a smaller area after the establishment of St Thomas of Canterbury's church at Fulham in 1848 and of the London Oratory at

1 *Middx County Rec.* I. 144.
2 *Middx County Rec.* I. 167; II. 67, 215; III. 32, 139.
3 *Cal. SP Dom.* 1627–8, 230.
4 Guildhall MS 9583/2, pt. 6, f. 44.
5 *Compton Census*, ed. A. Whiteman (Brit. Acad. 1980), 56.
6 Guildhall MS 9800/2, f. 9.
7 LMA, MR/RR/19/24.
8 Ibid., 23/3.
9 *Cath. Ancestor*, VII(2), 59.
10 Lambeth Pal. Lib., Fulham Papers, Terrick 21, f. 92.
11 Guildhall MS 9557, f. 20.
12 LMA, MR/RH/1/27.
13 Guildhall MS 9580/2, p. 102.
14 F.-X. Plasse, *Le Clergé Français Refugié en Angleterre*, II (1886), 154–7, 194, 277–8. For Thébault: D.A. Bellenger, *French Exiled Clergy in the Brit. Isles after 1789* (1986), 249, 279.
15 W.J. Anderson, *Hist. of Cath. Par. of St Mary's, Chelsea* (1938). 16; F.M. Steele (Darley Dale), *Convents of Gt Britain* (1902), p. xix; below.
16 Plasse, *Clergé Français*, 156–7; Anderson, *Hist. St Mary's*, 30.
17 Anderson, *Hist. St Mary's*, 17–20, 22–3, 26, 30, 36. *Laity's Dir.* (1835) attributes foundation to needs of soldiers and veterans.
18 *London Recusant*, III (1), 16.
19 Above, Soc. Hist., educ. (pub. schs: St Mary's).
20 Anderson, *Hist. St Mary's*, 22–3, 33; Bellenger, *French Exiled Clergy*, 53, 70, 256–9, 280, 285.
21 PRO, C 54/12708, m. 22; Anderson, *Hist. St Mary's*, 37 seqq.; above, Soc. Hist., educ. (pub. schs: St Joseph's).
22 Anderson, *Hist. St Mary's*, 63.

Brompton in 1854.[1] The Servites, about to open a temporary chapel and school in Fulham Road, were given part of the Oratorians' parish in Kensington and western Chelsea in 1867;[2] they continued to serve that area after opening the church of Our Lady of Dolours, on the Kensington side of the road, in 1875.[3] The creation of a more central parish for Chelsea itself was foreshadowed by the purchase of a site in Beaufort Street in 1886, eventually taken by Sisters of the Adoration Réparatrice, and effected by the opening of the church later dedicated to Our Most Holy Redeemer and St Thomas More in Cheyne Row in 1895.[4] A total of 1,961 Roman Catholic church attendances on census Sunday 1903 comprised only those at St Mary's, Our Most Holy Redeemer, and the convent chapel in Beaufort Street; it took no account of those who swelled the large congregations at Our Lady of Dolours. St Mary's morning attendance was higher than that of any other place of worship in Chelsea except the Anglicans' Holy Trinity, Sloane Street.[5]

The Sunday behaviour of many 'low' Irish families around Exeter Street attracted censure *c.*1850,[6] when a public meeting denounced the proposed establishment of the see of Westminster.[7] Roman Catholicism perhaps owed its prominence more to individuals and the presence of institutions than to the number of its local adherents.[8] Voyaux de Franous was well connected; he and his successors won widespread support, for much of which Joseph Knight and his wife were commemorated in the names of the convent and its adjoining schools and almshouses. The Sisters of Mercy at St Joseph's, the Sisters at St Wilfrid's (later Servites) by 1861, where they were followed by Daughters of the Cross in 1869, and the Servite Fathers in Fulham Road all came to be responsible for schools, public or private. The Servite Fathers also used social organizations to foster loyalty and even the Sisters of the Adoration, an exclusive order, opened their chapel and offered private retreats. The Sisters' former convent was a seminary in 1999, when St Wilfrid's ran a residential home and when the Church was responsible for St Joseph's Cottages and, through the Servite Housing Association, for flats owned by the Methodists.[9] The Servites were also associated with six other places of worship in western Chelsea, of various denominations.[10]

ROMAN CATHOLIC CHURCHES

The abbreviation reg. denotes registration for worship. Attendance figures 1903 are from Mudie-Smith, *Rel. Life*, 111, 114.

Our Lady of Dolours ch.[11] Originated as first English Mission of Servants of Mary, commonly called Servites, 1864 when Frs Bosio and Morini occupied ho. in Guthrie St (also described as no. 4 Stewart's Grove) adjoining St Wilfrid's convent in Bond (later Cale) St. Served nuns as chaplains and undertook missions, with 2 more Italian priests 1865, until given par. 1867. Moved to no. 78 Park Walk, where 2 rooms were adapted as chapel for 30 reg. 1867[12] and then to Victoria (later Netherton) Grove, Fulham Rd. Temp. ch. of Our Lady of Seven Dolours, for 300, at no. 349A Fulham Rd reg. 1868.[13] Ch., sch., and presbytery called Mount Senario Gdns after order's home near Florence. Site acquired by guardians of St Geo. Hanover Sq. after lawsuit, whereupon Servites moved to Heckfield Lodge, no. 264 on N. side of rd, where new ch. opened 1875, followed by St Mary's convent.[14] Although in Kensington, ch. served much of poorer W. end of Chelsea, supporting many social organizations.[15] Attendance 1903: 1,138 a.m., 345 p.m.

Our Most Holy Redeemer and St Thomas More ch. Originated in purchase of site in Beaufort Street for intended religious community 1886. New parish for central Chelsea formed 1892.[16] Chapel of our Most Holy Redeemer reg. at no. 28 Beaufort Street 1893. Replaced by ch. of same dedication at S. corner of Cheyne Row and Upper Cheyne Row, site of Wm de Morgan's house and pottery, 1895.[17] Marquess of Ripon, statesman (d. 1909), at no. 9 Chelsea Embankment, among benefactors who maintained 2 priests.[18] Bldg of red brick with Bath stone dressings in Renaissance style by Edw. Goldie 1894–5: ornate W. portico with Ionic columns and pilasters and broken pediment flanked by oval windows; Venetian window and triangular pediment above. Aisles and crossing omitted in revised plan because of street widening. No structural division between 2-bay chancel, 4-bay nave, and porch and narthex, bays forming recesses for shrines or altars beneath round-headed windows which break into coved ceiling.[19] Attendance

1 Anderson, *Hist. St Mary's*, 52.
2 G.M. Corr, *Servites in London* (1952), 28–9; below.
3 Booth, *Life and Labour*, III(3), 116; *Survey of London*, XLI. 191.
4 Below; Anderson, *Hist. St Mary's*, 71.
5 Mudie-Smith, *Rel. Life*, 111, 114.
6 *London City Mission Mag.* X. 236; XVII. 219.
7 Vestry mins, 1843–56, pp. 158–60.
8 Para. based on accounts of individual chs and institutions below.
9 Below, prot. nonconf. (Meths).
10 Millennium pamphlet on joint ch. activities (2000).
11 Para. based on Corr, *Servites, passim*; A. Rottmann, *London Cath. Chs* (1926), 43–4; Chelsea cuttings, Servites.
12 ONS Worship Reg. no. 18091.
13 Ibid. no. 18708.
14 *Survey of London*, XLI. 190–1. Reserved for treatment under Kensington.
15 Booth, *Life and Labour*, III(3), 116.
16 Anderson, *Hist. St Mary's*, 71.
17 ONS Worship Reg. nos 34018, 35090; Denny, *Chelsea Past*, 58; see Fig. 82.
18 Chelsea cuttings, Ch. of Holy Redeemer; *PO Dir. London* (1902); DNB.
19 Rottmann, *London Cath. Chs.* 37–8; Chelsea Misc. 106 (cuttings from *Builder*); Chelsea cuttings, Ch. of Holy Redeemer; D. Evinson, *Cath. Chs of London* (1998), 152–3; Loobey, *Chelsea*, 58.

82. *Church of Our Most Holy Redeemer and St Thomas More, Cheyne Row*

1903: 488 a.m., 177 p.m. Dedicated additionally to St Thos More after his canonization in 1935.[1] Parish centre beneath ch. renovated 1972.[2]

St Mary's ch. Originated in appointment of Voyaux de Franous as missionary to local Caths and hosp. veterans 1796. Abbés Abraham, Tribou, and Crespelle served from 1798. Franous, after brief return to France apparently in sole charge from 1808.[3] Chapel in Exeter St reg. 1798.[4] Ho. in Wilderness Row, 'late a Roman Catholic chapel', reg. by prot. dissenters 1802.[5] Svces probably held in Lower George St, between Lt. George St and Chelsea Market, *c.*1803.[6] Funds sought for new chapel 1811 in Cadogan St on part of Pavilion Ho. estate leased for 90 yrs from Lady Charlotte (d. 1835), wife of Peter Denys. Franous paid two-thirds of cost; other subscribers including old Catholic families of Clifford and Jerningham and Franous's former pupil Sir Rob. Peel; foundation stone laid by duchess of Angoulême, dau. of Louis XVI.[7] Chapel opened and reg. as in Pavilion field, Sloane St, 1812.[8] Plain classical bldg with round-headed windows, shallow curved ceiling by G.J. Wigley, side chapel added 1824–5, much later restoration, sanctuary by J.J. Scoles added 1850, chapel of Blessed Sacrament by E.W. Pugin added 1860,[9] new high altar and pulpit by J.F. Bentley, 1864. Closed on opening of new ch. 1879[10] and replaced by flats, no. 105 Cadogan Gdns.[11] Attenders inc. French ambassador 1820s and comte de Chambord, Bourbon claimant, 1840s.[12] Seating said to be for 500 in 1814 and for 600 in 1838 and 1851; attendance 1851: 770 a.m.[13] Franous received £300 a year from French govt until 1830 and was sole missioner until joined 1821–4 by Thos, later Cardinal, Weld (d. 1837).[14]

Former Wellington cricket ground, 2½ a. on S. side of Cadogan St bought by Jos. Knight for Cath. cemetery; part reserved for chapel, convent, and schs, all opened 1845.[15] Chapel seating *c.*100, with altar by A.W.N. Pugin, used for funerals until cemetery superseded by purchase at Kensal Green 1858.[16] Plans for new ch. perhaps delayed by expansion in Fulham and Brompton and by additions to chapel of 1812 (above).[17] Bldg of stock brick with Bath stone dressings in early Eng. style by J.F. Bentley, seating 500, *c.*1877–9. High and finely detailed interior with 2-bay clerestoreyed chancel, 4-bay aisled and clerestoreyed nave, chapel of Blessed Sacrament built out from S. aisle, W. narthex with porch and baptistery, turret intended to have pinnacle beside N.

83. *Interior of St Mary's RC Church, Cadogan Street*

1 Denny, *Chelsea Past*, 58.
2 Chelsea cuttings, Ch. of Holy Redeemer.
3 Plasse, *Clergé Français*, 278.
4 LMA, MR/RH/1/27.
5 Guildhall MS 9580/2, p. 102.
6 Plasse, *Clergé Français*, 157.
7 Anderson, *Hist. St Mary's*, 20, 30; J.H. Harting, *London Cath. Missions to 1850* (1903), 257–8. Lady Charlotte Denys was sis. of earl of Pomfret: *Gent. Mag.* CVI(1), 98.
8 Anderson, *Hist. St Mary's*, 20; LMA, MR/RH/1/49.
9 *Builder*, XVIII (1860), 772.
10 Anderson, *Hist. St Mary's*, 15, 31–2; Evinson, *Cath. Chs.* 149.
11 *Places of Worship*, 9.
12 Ibid., 26; Plasse, *Clergé Français*, 296.
13 *London Recusant*, III(1), 16; *London City Mission Mag.* III. 125; *Religious Census*, 1851.
14 Anderson, *Hist. St Mary's*, 22–3; DNB.
15 Anderson, *Hist. St Mary's*, 47; below, St Joseph's almshos; above, Soc. Hist., educ. (pub. schs: St Joseph's).
16 Anderson, *Hist. St Mary's*, 51.
17 W.J. Anderson, *St Mary's, Cadogan Gdns 1879–1940* (booklet), 5.

door. Much of the internal sculpture was left uncarved. Chapel of St Jos. at E. end of N. aisle with altar from old ch.; A.W.N. Pugin's cemetery chapel incorporated as chapel of St John, later St Thos More, with organ of 1864 and over entrance to vaults, at end of S. aisle; Blessed Sacrament chapel off S. aisle a rebldg of E.W. Pugin's chapel from old ch. and inc. his altar. High altar and pulpit by Bentley. E. window glass by Clayton & Bell.[1] Tablets from former cemetery chapel inc. one to Marie Tussaud (d. 1850), founder of waxwork exhib.[2] Font probably from old chapel.[3] Parish stretched beyond Chelsea to cover dists called Cadogan Sq., Belgravia, Pimlico, and Royal Hosp. 1938. Rectors inc. J.L. Patterson (1881–1902), bp of Emmaus, M.J. Bidwell (1913–30), bp of Miletopolis, and E. Myers, bp auxiliary of Westm. 1932 and coadjutor abp 1951.[4] Attendance 1903: 1,037 a.m., 188 p.m.

Franous in 1838 gave *c.* £6,000 in trust to provide payments of £20 sufficient to raise priests' yearly salaries to £100, besides £12 a year to clothe altar servers, the residue for Rom. Cath. educ. Jean Voyaux de Franous trust, under governing instrument of 1841, was reg. as char. 1966, when gross income was £894 and total expenditure, inc. £38 for clergy and *c.*£22 for servers, was £121. In 1997, after reinvestment, assets totalled £73,332; dividends and interest yielded £2,839, of which only £254 was spent.[5]

RELIGIOUS HOUSES

Sisters of the order of St Francis de Sales. Alternatively described as Visitandines or nuns of the Visitation, in 1799 occupied Salesian Ho., South Row, Queen's Elm. Apparently unconnected with Acton convent opened by 1805, they had probably returned to France by 1808.[6]

Sisters of Mercy. Occupied new St Joseph's convent of Our Lady of Mercy, Cadogan St, opened with adjoining schs 1845 on part of site given by Jos. Knight.[7] First nuns came from Bermondsey (Surrey) convent founded 1839 from Ireland and shared part of bldg with Christian Brothers employed as teachers until 1880. Sisters, who also ran private St Mary's sch., occupied most of original sch. bldgs 1938[8] and presumably left when sch. closed 1954.[9]

St Joseph's almshos. Partly occupied by 1849, stood immediately W. of convent on part of land given by Knight 1842. Bldg funds raised by pub. subscription and by Benevolent Soc. (London's oldest RC char. established 1761). Planned for 24 women but opened for only 18 in 1855; funds for completion still sought 1865. First inmates chosen by subscribers, but management shared by archdiocese and parish 1938.[10] Reg. as char. called St Jos.'s Almshos and Endowment Fund 1965, after Scheme of 1964 vested property in Westm. Rom. Cath. Diocese trustee and management in rector of St Mary's and 2 trustees apptd by abp. Classified as national char., almspeople to be poor Rom. Caths who might be required to contribute up to £1 10s. a week. Trustees to pay at least £20 a year into new Extraordinary Repair fund. Schemes of 1988 assigned at least £1,000 a year to Extraordinary Repair fund and £1,800 a year to new Cyclical Maintenance fund. Char. reg. as housing assoc. 1983, receiving grant and loans from Housing Corp. At end of 1996 char. had current assets in form of investments with market value of £54,549 and fixed assets in form of endowment fund worth £1,268, grant of £269,265, mortgage loan of £26,893, and its own unspecified resources of £13,093. Reserves, inc. repair funds, totalled £62,097.[11]

Architect, who may have built adjacent St Jos.'s sch., probably not A.W.N. Pugin. Courtyard with 4 archways planned, although lack of space and ho. barred egress on 2 sides; only 2 blocks and one archway built. Archway later blocked, reopened 1985–6 when dwellings enlarged but reduced to 10: 2 bed-sitting rooms and 8 one-bedroom flats, all in single occupation in 2000. Two-storeyed range of red brick with stone dressings in Tudor style had frontage of 78 ft to Cadogan St; yellow brick in 3-sided courtyard; plaques commemorated gift of site 1850, reconstruction 1958–65, and renovation 1985–6.[12]

Sisters of the Compassion. Founded in France, built ho. at W. end of Bond (from 1871 Cale) St, on site of no. 4 Stewart's Grove, as convent and orphanage 1857. Bldg work in progress 1859. Our Lady of Dolours was patroness of order and also of Servites, with whom Sisters affiliated in 1864. Remained there, as Servite Sisters, until 1869.[13]

Daughters of the Cross.[14] Founded 1833 in Liège (Belgium), took over Servites' convent and, when growth of fostering reduced demand for orphanages, opened boarding sch. which survived at St Wilfrid's convent until Second World War.[15] Later used as hostel,

1 Anderson, *St Mary's* (booklet), *passim*; Anderson, *Hist. St Mary's*, 79–86; Evinson, *Cath. Chs.* 150–1; Pevsner, *London NW.* 561; Anson, *Ch. Furnishings*, 262; see Fig. 83.

2 Chelsea cuttings, St Mary's Cath. ch.; *DNB*.

3 Evinson, *Cath. Chs*, 152.

4 Anderson, *Hist. St Mary's*, 89, 94, 101, endpaper; *Who Was Who, 1951–60*.

5 Char. Com. Reg., no. 247362.

6 Chelsea cuttings, St Joseph's convent; above, Soc. Hist., educ. (pub. schs: St Joseph's).

7 Plasse, *Clergé Français*, 156; Anderson, *Hist. St Mary's*, 16; *VCH Middx*, VII. 39; *The Times*, 3 April 1845.

8 Anderson, *Hist. St Mary's*, 48, 50.

9 Above, Soc. Hist., educ. (private schs).

10 Anderson, *Hist. St Mary's*, 51, 57, 59; *Cath. Dir.* (1865); inf. from clerk to Trustees.

11 Char. Com. Reg., no. 238993.

12 Ibid. no. 238993; inf. from clerk to trustees; inscriptions on bldg.

13 Corr, *Servites*, 9; Chelsea cuttings, St Wilfrid's; PRO, C 54/15445, m. 10.

14 Para. based on Corr, *Servites*, 9; Chelsea cuttings, St Wilfrid's; PRO, C 54/15445, m. 10.

15 Above, Soc. Hist., educ. (private schs).

having 47 elderly women in 1968 when Min. of Health required Cale St site for post-graduate medical centre.[1] Sisters had been offered former Victoria Hosp. for Sick Children in Tite St,[2] but at first were refused planning permission by LB, which hoped to force govt to clarify proposals. New convent for 15 nuns, with admin. centre for order's 'English' province,[3] training centre, and hostel with 45 bed-sitting rooms, opened on E. side of Tite St 1978: grey-brick bldgs by P.H.F. Stiles of W.J. Gregory and Partners, inc. block of 4 storeys over basement and octagonal chapel with shallow roof and small lantern.

Sisters of the Precious Blood. Came to teach at Servites' first sch.; were at St Joseph's convent, no. 23 Victoria Grove, next to Servites' premises, in 1878–9.[4]

Brotherhood of Expiation. Installed at no. 28 Beaufort St by Fr Kenelm Vaughan, bro. of Cardinal Vaughan, who bought site from Earl Cadogan 1886. Studio was converted into chapel but order proved short lived and was replaced by Sisters of the Adoration (below) 1898.[5]

Sisters of Adoration Réparatrice. Brought from France by Cardinal Vaughan and installed at no. 28 Beaufort St 1898.[6] Convent chapel, of Immaculate Conception, served by priests from ch. of Our Most Holy Redeemer.[7] Attendance 1903: 44 a.m., 27 evg. New chapel of brick with stone dressings in Romanesque style by C.G. Keogh 1912: apse, tall choir enclosed for community, plain nave for public, round-headed windows. Dedicated to Most Holy Sacrament and Blessed Thos More by 1926.[8] Served by Salesians at Battersea (Surrey) 1931, 1969.[9] Bombed 1940. E. end survived while W. end served as garden 1957. Replaced by chapel reg. 1958: tall austere modern bldg, by Corfiato Thompson and Partners, with yellow-brick N. and S. walls, shallow roof, and W. window formed by honeycombed concrete wall facing rd;[10] nave divided, E. part reserved for Sisters, who prayed for conversion of England and numbered 34 in 1926.[11] Order left for London Colney (Herts.) in 1975, when convent and chapel were taken over as Westminster Diocesan Seminary, previously at Old Hall Green (Herts.).[12] Renamed Allen Hall, premises contained 16 candidates for priesthood and inc. study centre for clergy and laity in 1998.[13]

Dawliffe Hall. No. 2 Chelsea Embankment was acquired by Dawliffe Hall Educational Foundation in 1967. Serving as residence for woman university students, under pastoral care of Opus Dei, it was enlarged by acquisition of no. 1 Chelsea Embankment in 1976 and had *c.*34 places in 1999.[14]

Servite Houses. As housing assoc., took 99-year lease from Meth. Ch. of site in Chelsea Manor St. Edith Pope Ho., 21 flats designed in contemporary style by Bernard Lamb, completed 1983. Tenants, aged over 55 and usually with local connections, chosen by assoc.; RBKC entitled to nominate half of new residents in 1999.[15]

OLD ROMAN CATHOLICS

'Old Catholic otherwise Old Roman Catholic Ch.' reg. Sanctuary at no. 23 Basil Street 1927–34,[16] having had several W. London addresses since first reg. at no. 47 Albemarle St (Westm.) in 1917.[17] Ch. of the Good Shepherd was described as Catholic Apostolic when reg. in basement of bombed Chelsea Bapt chapel, Lower Sloane St, 1948,[18] but was recertified as 'Christian Free' ch. 1949 and as 'Ancient Catholic' cathedral ch. 1951–6;[19] later demolished.[20]

PROTESTANT NONCONFORMITY

An assault on the 'minister' of Chelsea during his sermon in 1617 may have indicated some local dissent.[21] So too may a visit to Chelsea by the Puritan William Bradshaw, who died there in 1618.[22] Dr Thomas Harrison (d. 1682), who had lived in Cromwell's family, was described as 'late preacher at Chelsea' in 1663.[23] Two ejected ministers, Gabriel Sangar (d. 1678) and Thomas Pakemen (d. 1691), lived at Brompton, perhaps outside the parish, in the 1660s. The Independent Philip Nye died at Brompton, in Kensington, in 1672.[24] Ten

1 Above, Soc. Hist., educ. (private schs); *The Times*, 9 Aug. 1966; 28 Feb. 1968.
2 Above, Loc. Govt, pub. svces (medical).
3 17 hos in all, inc. 3 in Ireland and 3 in USA.
4 Corr, *Servites*, 36; *Chelsea Dir.* (1878); *PO Dir. London* (1879).
5 Rottmann, *London Cath. Chs*, 39–40.
6 Ibid.
7 *Cath. Dir.* (1900); *PO Dir. London* (1902).
8 *The Times*, 6 Oct. 1910; 13 March 1912; Rottmann, *London Cath. Chs*, 40–1; Loobey, *Chelsea*, 56.
9 *Cath. Dir.* (1931, 1969).
10 ONS Worship Reg. no. 67023; Chelsea cuttings, Convent of Adoration Réparatrice; inf. from rector, Allen Hall.
11 *Places of Worship*, 14; Rottmann, *London Cath. Chs*, 41.
12 *Cath. Dir.* (1976); *VCH Herts.* III. 351; inf. from rector, Allen Hall.
13 *Westm. Year Bk* (1998).
14 Ibid.; inf. from warden.
15 Inf. from regional manager, Servite Hos.
16 ONS Worship Reg. no. 50672.
17 Ibid. nos 47033, 47162, 47774.
18 Ibid. no. 61995; Chelsea cuttings, Bapt chapel.
19 ONS Worship Reg. nos 62366, 63696.
20 *Places of Worship*, 10.
21 *Middx Sess. Rec.* IV. 220.
22 *DNB*.
23 *Cal. SP Dom.* 1663–4, 117.
24 *Calamy Revised*, 370, 379, 427; *DNB*.

nonconformists, and 590 conformists, were reported in 1676.[1] The Congregational writer Samuel Clarke, a great-nephew of the ejected Samuel Clarke (1599–1682), was born at Chelsea in 1684.[2] Zachary Merrill, later a trustee of Dr Daniel Williams's will, was listed as a minister with no fixed congregation, in attendance there on Lady Cheeke as chaplain and tutor in 1690.[3] A house belonging to Sarah Gully was used for meetings by protestant dissenters in 1707.[4]

More prominent in the early years was the role of foreign immigrants. Huguenots met for worship from the 1680s and probably had two chapels in 1718, although neither congregation survived beyond the mid 18th century.[5] Moravians formed a settlement at Lindsey House from 1750 until 1770 and, after its sale, continued to use their chapel until the early 19th century; they retained its burial ground and worshipped in an adjoining hall in 2000.[6]

John Wesley preached at Chelsea in 1741, when he was sharply questioned by a dissenting teacher, and in 1742, when incendiarists failed to smoke him out of the meeting room. He returned in 1748 to commend the Physic Garden as a source for scientific study rather than a mere curiosity.[7] Selina, countess of Huntingdon (d. 1791), in 1748 invited George Whitefield to Chelsea Farm, where within a few months he was preaching 'continuously'. Whitefield, who was thereby able to reach an aristocratic audience including the earl of Chesterfield (d. 1773) and Viscount Bolingbroke (d. 1751), wrote that God's providence had placed the countess at Chelsea. She soon moved away, however, and none of the foundations which came to form her 'Connexion' took place there.[8] Sir Hans Sloane's steward Edmund Howard was a prominent Quaker, but no Friends' meeting house was recorded.[9]

Wesley too had no regular meeting place, although Independents may have had one by 1760, the date of the death of the Revd Benjamin Rogers, 'preacher at the chapel in the Five Fields'.[10] The late rector was said in 1797 to have defended a curate of Methodist sympathies, presumably Erasmus Middleton, expelled from Oxford in 1768.[11] Independents and a dwindling group of Moravians were the only dissenters recorded in 1778; the Independents formed a single meeting[12] and presumably used the surviving former Huguenot chapel which their pastor had taken over in 1773.[13]

In 1790 both Independents and Wesleyans had meeting houses, the latter having been leased a room belonging to Ranelagh House, where John Wesley preached in 1791 shortly before his death.[14] Between 1793 and 1802 seven places of worship were registered: three, in 1793, 1799, and 1801, were for Independents,[15] one in 1798 was for the 'Universal Millennium Church', one in 1802 for Baptists,[16] and two, in 1800 and 1802, were for unspecified dissenters, the first probably being for Methodists.[17] In 1810 Methodists were said to have much increased recently and six meeting houses for them and other dissenters were estimated to hold *c.*2,500, whereas the Church of England's parish church and Park chapel could together accommodate only *c.*1,100.[18]

No new places of worship were registered between 1802 and 1812 but more than 30 were listed between 1812 and 1852. Some were capacious and purpose-built, including the Methodists' Sloane Terrace chapel and the Independents' New Road (Union) and Ranelagh chapels; others were in rooms or converted buildings and often short lived.[19] In 1838 protestant nonconformists had six chapels providing 3,160 places, three Independent (including Ranelagh, described as Countess of Huntingdon's Connexion), 2 Baptist, and one Wesleyan.[20] The undenominational London City Mission was active in much of the parish.[21]

In 1851 15 of the estimated 28 places of worship were nonconformist, of which Wesleyan Methodists had 4, the Wesleyan Association had one, Baptists had 3, Independents (or Congregationalists) 2, Latter-day Saints 2, and Presbyterians, the Catholic Apostolic Church, and an undefined group one each. The most numerous nonconformist worshippers were Wesleyans, with combined attendances of 1,355 in the morning, 300 in the afternoon, and 1,433 in the evening. They were followed by the English Presbyterians, with 550 in the morning and 400 in the evening, and by the Baptists, with combined attendances of 275 in the morning, 85 in the afternoon, and 319 in the evening.[22]

Newcomers in the late 19th century included Welsh Congregationalists from 1860, Brethren from 1869, the Salvation Army from 1881, and the Church of Scotland, against Anglican opposition, from 1884.[23] In 1882 Chelsea, excluding Chelsea detached, was reckoned to have 4 places of worship for Methodists, 6 for

1 *Compton Census*, ed. A. Whiteman (Brit. Acad. 1980), 56.
2 *Calamy Revised*, 119; *DNB*.
3 A. Gordon, *Freedom after Ejection* (1917), 2, 312.
4 *Middx County Rec. Sess. Bks 1689–1709*, 310.
5 Below, foreign chs (Huguenots).
6 Ibid. (Moravians).
7 *John Wesley's Jnl*, ed. N. Curnock (1967), 114, 123, 231.
8 *DNB*; Denny, *Chelsea Past*, 60; *Horace Walpole's Corresp. with Geo. Montagu*, ed. W.S. Lewis and R.S. Brown, I (1941), 73–4; L. Tyerman, *Life of Geo. Whitefield*, II (1877), 193–4.
9 Holme, *Chelsea*, 17.
10 Chelsea Misc. 1094; *Gent. Mag.* XXX. 249.
11 *Gent. Mag.* XXXVIII. 225–6; LXVIII. 288, 461.
12 Guildhall MS 9558, f. 426.
13 Faulkner, *Chelsea*, II. 260; below, foreign chs (Huguenots).
14 Guildhall MS 9558, f. 426; Chelsea Misc. 949 (cutting from *Wes. Meth. Mag.* 3 March 1830).
15 Guildhall MSS 9580/1, p. 88; 9580/2, pp. 21, 75. These and other registrations to 1852 are also in PRO, RG 31/3, passim.
16 Guildhall MSS 9580/1, pp. 171–2; 9580/2, p. 91.
17 Ibid. /2, pp. 51, 102; below, Meths.
18 Guildhall MS 9558, ff. 425v.–6.
19 Guildhall MSS 9580/3–9; below, Meths; Congs.
20 *London City Mission Mag.* III. 125.
21 Ibid., XII, p. xviii.
22 *Religious Census*, 1851.
23 Below; G.C. Cameron, *Scots Kirk in London* (1979), 162; Stroud, *Smith's Char.* 42.

Independents or Congregationalists, one of them the Welsh chapel, and one for Baptists, one for the recently arrived Salvation Army, and 3 for undesignated groups.[1] On census Sunday 1903 nonconformists accounted for almost a third of the worshippers, 5,377 out of a total church attendance of 17,061. No single sect rivalled the Roman Catholics' attendance: Congregationalists totalled 1,366, Baptists 935, Presbyterians 592, and Methodists 491.[2]

Methodism's early strength had brought the formation in 1812 of a Chelsea circuit, from which Westminster separated in 1872. Thereafter the circuit consisted of two chapels in Chelsea, one in Battersea (Surrey), and one in Walham Green (Fulham). Weakened by unspecified social changes, presumably the redevelopment which displaced much of the working class, Methodists by 1902 were said to form a smaller percentage of the population than in any other district in England.[3]

The 20th century saw the arrival of Christian Scientists in 1903, and of Jehovah's Witnesses in 1977. By 1928 Baptists had declined to such an extent that it was asked why Camberwell should be so responsive but Chelsea so hostile.[4] The Second World War led to closures and amalgamations, as elsewhere, and left the Baptists unrepresented in a church of their own.[5] In 1998 Chelsea had 7 certified places of worship for protestant nonconformists: the United Reformed Church, Welsh Congregationalists, Methodists, Christian Scientists, and Jehovah's Witnesses had one each, and the Salvation Army two.[6] Pentecostalists, increasing in many parts of London, had only just opened a centre.[7]

NONCONFORMIST CHAPELS AND CONGREGATIONS

The following abbreviations are used: Bapt, Baptist; cong., congregation; Cong., Congregationalist; Dec., Decorated; dedic., dedicated; demol., demolished; denom., denomination; evg, evening; Ind., Independent; Meth., Methodist; mtg, meeting; min., minister; perm., permanent; prot., protestant; reg., registered, registration; temp., temporarily, temporary; Utd Ref., United Reformed; Wes., Wesleyan. Attendance figs 1851 are from *Religious Census*, 1851; figs 1903 are from Mudie-Smith, *Rel. Life*, 115. Liturgical directions are used in architectural descriptions.

Baptists

School ho., in Little North Street. Belonging to Thos Birks reg. by John Chesney, min., and others 1802.[8] Possibly connected with mtg begun 1800 which acquired Ind. chapel in North (later Basil) St 1812 under min. John Middleton, who was not recorded after 1827. Probably closed *c.*1831.[9]

Lower Sloane Street, Chelsea Baptist Church. Opened 1816[10] on E. side of White Lion (from 1884 southern end of Lower Sloane) St. New plain white-brick bldg by Jas Cubitt[11] reg. as Chelsea chapel 1865 by undesignated worshippers, later styled Bapts.[12] Bldg seated 900 in 1875, when ch. with 389 members and 290 Sun. scholars was in London Assoc. of Bapt Union. Membership fell to 274 in 1893, reached peak of 440 in 1903, and fell to 162 in 1938.[13] Attendance 1903, when sole Bapt chapel: 237 a.m., 698 evg, largest at any prot. nonconf. ch. Damaged in Second World War.[14] Membership, 54, last recorded in 1948, when ch. of Good Shepherd occupied site.[15]

Paradise Walk, Paradise Chapel. Bldg on E. side of rd running SE. from Paradise Row (later Queen's Road W.) reg. for Inds by And. Scott, min., and others 1793.[16] Reported to be Bapt by 1829, when chapel occupied a former schoolroom and managed a Sun. sch. for nearly 100.[17] Seated 500 in 1838.[18] Listed as Bapt until 1863 but apparently closed soon afterwards.[19]

College Street. Rob. Upton from Carmel ch., Westbourne St (Westm.) said to have moved to Chelsea 1824 and with others from Carmel to have founded College St 1830,[20] although no reg. was recorded. Bldg presumably that at SE. end of st 1836.[21] John Nichols, min. from 1838, moved to new Zion chapel, Queen St (q.v.), claiming 1824 as foundation date. Part of cong. presumably left in College St, where Ebenezer Bapt chapel, Oriel Pl., claiming no date, was reg. 1854, existed 1863, and had closed by 1868.[22] Unnamed Bapt chapel on E. side of College St listed as Bapt 1879, 1881, but as Ch. of Christ by 1890.[23]

Eden Place. Chapel in rd E. off Pond Pl. reg. for Bapts by John Shiriston Turner 1838, when it seated 160.[24]

1 *Return of Chs* (Parl. Papers, 1882 (401), L), p. 86.
2 Mudie-Smith, *Rel. Life*, 115.
3 Chelsea Misc. 951–2.
4 W.T. Whitley, *Bapts of London 1612–1928* (1928), 263, 270–1.
5 Below.
6 List supplied by ONS (Birkdale). Nos are for Chelsea part of RBKC.
7 Below, other denoms.
8 Guildhall MS 9580/2, p. 91.
9 Whitley, *Bapts of London*, 141, 271.
10 Whitley, *Bapts of London*, 148. *Bapt Handbk* (1875, 1876) gives 1814; later edns 1817.
11 *Places of Worship*, 10.
12 ONS Worship Reg. no. 16771.
13 *Bapt Handbk* (1871 and later edns).
14 Chelsea cuttings, Bapt chapel.
15 *Bapt Handbk* (1948); above, rom. cathm.
16 Guildhall MS 9580/1, p. 88.
17 Faulkner, *Chelsea*, II. 191.
18 *London City Mission Mag.* III. 125.
19 *PO Dir. London* (1850, 1863).
20 Whitley, *Bapts of London*, 158.
21 Thompson, *Map* (1836).
22 Whitley, *Bapts of London*, 158; ONS Worship Reg. no. 5805; *PO Dir. London* (1863).
23 *PO Dir. London* (1879); *Kelly's Dir. Chelsea* (1881, 1890); below, other denoms.
24 Guildhall MS 9580/8, p. 13; *London City Mission Mag.* III. 125.

Perhaps identifiable with Beulah chapel, said to date from 1836. Probably closed by 1878.[1]

Queen Street, Zion Chapel. Reg. for Bapts by John Nichols as continuation of College St (q.v.) 1842.[2] Nichols recorded as min. to 1851. Wes. Meth. by 1855.[3]

King's Road. Bldg in garden of Mr Brandon's ho. reg. for Bapts by Benj. Barker 1846. Presumably in grounds of china wareho. of Alf. Brandon at no. 4 Beaufort Terr., King's Rd.[4] Perhaps superseded by nearby Grove chapel (q.v.).

Marlborough Road. No. 6 Sydney Terr., SW. side of Marlborough Rd (later Draycott Ave), reg. for Bapts 1852. Bldg occupied by Eden Wilson, carpenter, 1857–8. Reg. cancelled 1866.[5]

Fulham Road, Grove Chapel. Bapt mtg reg. as at Mason's Grove, W. Brompton, 1853; chapel between nos 311 and 313 Fulham Rd.[6] Foundation later dated to 1852, when Alf. Brandon became min. 36 members and 65 Sun. Scholars 1871; seating not recorded.[7] In Fulham Rd 1982 but reg. cancelled 1895.[8] Moved with same name to Drayton Gdns (Kens.), where Brandon was still min. in 1902. Replaced by Grove Ct flats.[9]

King's Road, Cook's Ground. Former Huguenot and then Ind. chapel listed as Bapt 1855. Taken by John Nichols, who moved from Zion chapel (q.v.). Described as both Bapt and Cong. 1863, when ministry vacant. Closed by 1868.[10]

Chelsea Market, Lower Sloane St. 'Subordinate station', est. 1884 and seating 50, presumably in former commercial premises, recorded only in 1886.[11]

Brethren

Victoria hall, Little College St. Reg. by Christian Brethren 1869–76.[12] Former Ind. then Meth. chapel in Radnor St listed as Brethren's Chelsea hall with 2 Sun. and 2 weekday svces 1879 before acquisition by Welsh Congs.[13] Glebe hall, Glebe Pl., King's Rd, reg. by Brethren 1885–90. Gospel hall, no. 108 Church St, reg. 1888–97.[14]

Manresa mission hall. On E. side of Trafalgar Sq., Manresa Rd, leased to Edwin Cook and others for 19¾ years 1889 and reg. by Brethren 1890.[15] Attendance 1903: 73 a.m., 87 evg. Premises included stables, yard, and kiln 1904, when sale was planned to follow expiry of lease. Hall survived 1927 but not as place of worship: nearest Brethren hall was then in Ebury St (Westm.).[16]

Catholic Apostolic Church

Revd Hen. John Owen, recently deprived as min. of CE Park chapel[17] for belief in 'manifestation of tongues', preached probably at Clock Ho. sch. during building of ch. in College St,[18] reg. by him for Prot. dissenters 1833. Owen (d. 1872) reg. bldg while at no. 16 Cheyne Walk,[19] where room perhaps for his use had been reg. 6 weeks earlier by father-in-law John Bayford.[20] Ch. presumably accounted for Cath. Apostolic 200 free sittings 1851, when attendance 150 a.m., 130 p.m., 100 evg.[21] Listed as Cath. Apostolic by 1855.[22] Rebuilding or alterations said in 1870s to have been completed 1861: plain Early Eng. style, no galleries, seating *c.*200 with nearly half the space reserved for ceremonial.[23] Attendance 1903: 188 a.m., 104 evg. One of 7 Cath. Apostolic chs. in London 1913, with 3 Sun. and daily weekday svces.[24] Bldg, on E. side at no. 32 College (later Elystan) St, bombed in Second World War; site sold 1949.[25] Good Shepherd ch. reg. in Lower Sloane St 1949 as Cath. Apostolic but later recorded as Old Cath.[26]

Christian Scientists

Christian Scientists reached London 1891 and reg. branch of First Ch. of Christ, Scientist, Boston (USA), 1899.[27] Former Sloane Terr. chapel reg. as at Wilbraham Pl., Sloane St, 1903–11.[28] Adjoining reading room also opened.[29] Attendance 1903: 342 a.m., 211 evg. Replaced by Christian Scientists' first purpose-built ch. in London,[30] in Sloane Terr., begun 1904; first svce in W. half of bldg 1905, in completed bldg 1907; dedic. 1909[31]

1 Whitley, *Bapts of London*, 162, 271; *Chelsea Dir.* (1878).
2 Guildhall MS 9580/8, p. 151.
3 *PO Dir. London* (1845, 1851, 1855); below, Meths (Queen St).
4 Guildhall MS 9580/8, p. 259; *PO Dir. London* (1845).
5 ONS Worship Reg. no. 545; *PO Dir. London* (1857, 1858).
6 ONS Worship Reg. no. 715; *PO Dir. London* (1863).
7 *Bapt Handbk* (1871 and later edns). Listed under Brompton, like Onslow chapel in S. Kens. Foundation dated 1850 in ibid. (1876).
8 *Bapt Handbk* (1892); ONS Worship Reg. no. 715.
9 *PO Dir. London* (1902, 1942).
10 Whitley, *Bapts of London*, 158; *PO Dir. London* (1863).
11 *Bapt Handbk* (1886).
12 ONS Worship Reg. no. 18857.
13 *PO Dir. London* (1879); below, Congs, Meths.
14 ONS Worship Reg. nos 28585, 31172.
15 Chelsea Misc. 1080; ONS Worship Reg. no. 32123.
16 Chelsea Misc. 1080; *PO Dir. London* (1927).
17 Above, dau. chs (Park chapel).
18 *Alum Cantab. 1752–1900*, IV. 611–12.
19 Ibid., 612.
20 Guildhall MS 9580/7, pp. 119, 126.
21 *Religious Census*, 1851.
22 *PO Dir. London* (1855 and later edns).
23 Chelsea cuttings: Cath. Apostolic Ch.
24 *PO Dir. London* (1913).
25 *The Times*, 18 Oct. 1949.
26 ONS Worship Reg. no. 62366; above, rom. cathm.
27 Char. Com. file 238685.
28 ONS Worship Reg. no. 39628; below, Meths (Sloane Terr.).
29 Char. Com. file 238685.
30 Chelsea MB, *Official Guide* [1937]; see Fig. 84.
31 Char. Com. file 238685; datestone.

84. *First Church of Christ, Scientist, Sloane Terrace*

and reg. 1911.[1] Romanesque elements and tall tower of R. Chisholm's design faintly echo original mother church in Boston.[2] Entrance arcade along Sloane Terr. supports cantilevered gallery of lst-floor auditorium, with raked seats for 1,300, no columns, and shallow barrel vault with roof lights. Spacious offices in semi-basement.[3] Cong. had fallen to *c.*150 by 1990, when it was planned to reduce seating and convert rest of interior for offices or flats. Further fall by 1996, when svces ceased and premises bought by Mohammed Al Fayed, whose Harrods (UK) company sought permission for conversion into single residence 1999 but had sold bldg to Cadogan Estates by 2000.[4] Reading room in Sloane Terr. closed 1966, reopened at no. 109 King's Rd 1967. Move planned 1981 to no. 156 Fulham Rd (Kens.), where it remained in 2000.[5]

Congregationalists (Independents)

Cook's Ground Chapel. Formerly Huguenot,[6] had Ind. min. before 1773, when Revd Mr Traill succeeded by Benj. Fielder.[7] Presumably was mtg ho. of Inds recorded 1778 and 1790.[8] John Bunce min. from 1804, and in 1829.[9] Seated 200 in 1838.[10] Last listed 1853. Replaced by Radnor St (q.v.).[11] Cook's Ground bldg perhaps later reg. as Providence chapel.[12]

Paradise Walk, Paradise Chapel. Reg. for Inds 1793 by And. Scott and others.[13] Bapt by 1829.[14]

Danvers Street. No. 5, ho. of Jas Whitear, reg. for Inds 1799 by Thos Higginbottom, min. at Spa Fields chapel (Clerkenwell), and others. Not recorded later.[15]

Church Lane. Room in ho. occupied by Sarah Dytche reg. for Inds 1801 by group inc. John Bunce, later pastor of Cook's Ground chapel (q.v.).[16]

New Road, Union Chapel. Bldg in New (later Pavilion) Rd, Sloane St, reg. for Prots 1812 by group inc. John Surry, also associated with Meths.[17] Styled Ind. 1829, when bldg 64 ft long and date of erection given as 1813.[18] Seated 500 in 1838.[19] Between nos 29 and 31 New Rd 1857, when svces Sun. a.m. and evg and lectures Wed. evg.[20] Last listed with min. 1872.[21] Taken over by Welsh Congs, who reg. Union chapel 1874 before moving to Cadogan St and then to Radnor St (later Radnor Walk, q.v.).[22]

Lower George Street, Ranelagh Chapel. Built and reg. for Inds 1818 by R.H. Shepherd, who had served cong. from 1813,[23] and to include sch. established 1802.[24] Shepherd, a Calvinist Meth., used CE liturgy in accordance with Ctss of Huntingdon's Connexion a.m. and evg but not afternoons. Commodious, 'best place of worship' in par. 1829.[25] Galleried interior, 6 bays with tall round-headed windows; pedimented street front, 5 bays, projecting Doric porch. Side entrances to B and G schs, lit by windows in basement.[26] Seated 1,000 in 1838.[27] Sold to Eng. Presbs 1845.[28]

1 ONS Worship Reg. no. 44626.
2 P.E. Ivey, *Prayers in Stone: Christian Science Architecture in the US 1894–1930* (1999), 1, 49–50.
3 Pevsner, *London NW.* 561–2; Loobey, Chelsea, 104.
4 Chelsea cuttings, Sloane Terr. (inc. planning appl. 1999); inf. from clerk, First Ch. of Christ, Scientist, London.
5 *PO Dir. London* (1975); Chelsea cuttings, Christian Science Reading Room.
6 Below, foreign chs (Huguenots).
7 Faulkner, *Chelsea*, I. 260.
8 Guildhall MS 9558, f. 426.
9 Faulkner, *Chelsea*, I. 261.
10 *London City Mission Mag.* III. 125.
11 *Cong. Year Bk* (1853).
12 Below, other denoms.
13 Guildhall MS 9580/1, p. 88.
14 Above, Bapts.
15 Guildhall MS 9580/2, p. 21. Spa Fields chapel was the first of the Ctss of Huntingdon's connexion.
16 Guildhall MS 9580/2, p.75; Faulkner, *Chelsea*, I. 261.
17 Guildhall MS 9580/4; below, Meths.
18 Faulkner, *Chelsea*, II. 346. *Cong. Year Bk* (1855) dates bldg from 1800.
19 *London City Mission Mag.* III. 125.
20 *PO Dir. London* (1857); *Cong. Year Bk.* (1857).
21 *Cong. Year Bk.* (1872).
22 ONS Worship Reg. no. 21849.
23 Faulkner, *Chelsea*, II. 316; Guildhall MS 9580/5.
24 Above, Soc. Hist., educ. (pub. schs: Ranelagh Lancasterian).
25 *Chelsea Soc. Rep.* (1956), 11; Faulkner, *Chelsea*, II. 316.
26 Faulkner, *Chelsea*, II, illus. at end. Also Chelsea Misc. 103, 107 (rubbing of foundation plaque), 1961–2; *Images of Chelsea*, nos 481–5.
27 *London City Mission Mag.* III. 125.
28 *Chelsea Soc. Rep.* (1956); below, Eng. Presbs.

Captain Cook's Hall, Chelsea Common. Bldg reg. for Prots 1818 by group inc. Noah Stone of Capt. Cook's Hall and John Sharman.[1] No known connexion with Cook's Ground (q.v.). Presumably Ind., as Sharman later reg. ho. in Turk's Row (q.v.).

Turk's Row. Room in ho. at no. 4 Castle Yard reg. for Inds by John Sharman and others 1831.[2] Not recorded later.

Marlborough Road. 'Lecturing room' at no. 36 Caroline Pl. reg. as preaching ho. for Inds by occupier John Norton 1836.[3] Not recorded later.

White Lion Street. Shop and parlour of John Bosbury at no. 12 to be opened for Inds, cert. by Wm Giles and others 1837.[4] Not recorded later.

Radnor Street, Radnor Congregational Chapel. Mtg served by Fred. Webb, formerly min. at Cook's Ground (q.v.), 1854.[5] Freehold of commercial hall at corner of Radnor St and King's Rd bought by London Cong. Chapel Bldg Soc. 1855,[6] reg. as Radnor Cong. chapel for Inds 1856.[7] J. Clifford Hooper min. 1857, when svces Sun. a.m. and evg and lectures Thurs. evg. Moved to Markham Sq. (q.v.) 1860.[8] Radnor St later served Meths., then Brethren, and finally Welsh Congs.[9]

Gunter Grove, West Brompton Chapel. Reg. for Inds 1859,[10] when mtg formed at Gunter hall, E. side of Gunter Grove. Bldg of white brick with stone dressings, seating 300, by J. Figg of Brentford. Replaced by ch. in Edith Grove (q.v.), although Gunter hall was first mtg place of Uverdale Rd's Ashburnham ch. (q.v.) 1879, remained with Congs as mission rooms 1882, 1887,[11] and was used by St John's CE ch. 1902.[12]

Markham Square, Chelsea Congregational Church. Reg. for Inds 1860[13] in succession to Radnor chapel. Lease for 999 years of site on N. side of sq. bought with help from London Cong. Chapel Bldg Soc. 1858; settled in trust, with 2 hos behind ch. in College Pl., 1859. Third min. was And. Mearns, sec. of London Cong. Union and author of *Guide*. Svces 1882: Sun. a.m. and p.m., Wed. evg.[14] Cited as example of Congs' local rise and decline in late 19th cent., with 890 evg worshippers 1886.[15] Burdened with debt from bldg costs; reports of dissension 1916 and of members joining Wes. 1923. Attendance 1903: 307 a.m., 501 evg, largest at any prot. nonconf. ch. except Chelsea Bapt chapel. 467 ch. members and 333 Sun. scholars 1902; 86 members 180 scholars 1930. Served by father and son J. Lawson Forster from 1882 and W. Lawson Forster from 1918; by G. Doreen Hopewell from 1935; ministry vacant from 1941.[16] Bldg faced in Kentish rag with Bath stone dressings in 'second period of Gothic' by J. Tarring 1858–60, cost £5,006. It had shallow transepts, tower with *c.*130-ft spire on W. side of S. transept; crocketted and pinnacled buttresses; galleried interior with open timber roof seating 1,120; schoolrooms for B and G beneath. Organ and organ front by Bishop & Co.[17] Renovated, with lobby added, by Searle & Hayes *c.*1884.[18] Substitution of smaller ch. debated 1939; open during war but only one Sun. svce, poorly attended, by 1948.[19] Last recorded 1952; demol. for housing, reg. cancelled 1953.[20] Name of Chelsea Cong. ch. adopted by Edith Grove ch. (q.v.) 1960. Additional Sun. evg and Tues., later Wed., svces were held by Markham Sq. ch. at mission hall in College St seating 100 in 1888,[21] at sch. in College St seating 400 in 1891–2, and at Chelsea town hall seating 850 in 1893–4.[22]

New Road, Ebenezer Chapel. Reg. at no. 22½ New Rd (from 1870 Pavilion Rd), Sloane St, 1867 for Inds.[23] Mtg was Welsh Cong., previously at Belgrave hall, Pimlico (Westm.), in New Rd by 1863, later at Union chapel in Pavilion Rd (q.v.), in Cadogan St, and in Radnor St (q.v.).[24]

Edith Grove, West Brompton Church. London Cong. Chapel Bldg Soc. approached about new W. Brompton chapel 1864; opened 1866, reg. as Cong. ch. 1868 for Inds, replacing temp. ch. in Gunter Grove.[25] Burdened with debt from bldg costs, John Morgan, min. from

1 Guildhall MS 9580/5.
2 Ibid. MS 9580/7, p. 20.
3 Signed John Norton, although Wm Norton is wording of cert.: Guildhall MS 9580/7, p. 210.
4 Guildhall MS 9580/7, p. 250.
5 *Cong. Year Bk* (1854, 1855).
6 LMA, N/C/2/2; *PO Dir. London* (1858); A. Mearns, *Guide to Cong. Chs. of London* (1882), 9.
7 ONS Worship Reg. no. 7545.
8 *Cong. Year Bk* (1857); Mearns, *Cong. Chs.* 9.
9 *PO Dir. London* (1863, 1879, 1902); below.
10 ONS Worship Reg. no. 8703.
11 Mearns, *Cong. Chs.* 7, 9, 64; LMA, N/LCU/1/24/43.
12 *PO Dir. London* (1902).
13 ONS Worship Reg. no. 9320.
14 *Cong. Year Bk* (1858); Mearns, *Cong. Chs.* 9; LMA, N/LCU/1/24/44.
15 *Trans. Cong. Hist. Soc.* XX(1), 32.
16 *Cong. Year Bk* (1902 and later edns). LMA, N/LCU/1/24/44.
17 *Builder*, XVIII (1860), 236.
18 Ibid.; *Cong. Year Bk* (1858 and illus. p. 257, 1884); LMA, N/C/2/2; Walford, *Old and New London*, V. 95.
19 LMA, N/LCU/1/24/44.
20 *Cong. Year Bk* (1952); LMA, N/C/2/1; *Chelsea Soc. Rep.* (1953), 25–7; ONS Worship Reg. no. 8703.
21 *Cong. Year Bk* (1880). Called Jubilee mission room, accn 70, in 1889–90 (ibid. 1889, 1890).
22 *Cong. Year Bk* (1891–4).
23 ONS Worship Reg. no. 17805.
24 I.O. Huws, *Hanes Eglwys Radnor Walk* (1959), 10–11; *PO Dir. London* (1863).
25 ONS Worship Reg. no. 18392: LMA, N/LCU/1/24/43; above.

1877, refused resignation requested by London Cong. Union; ch. temp. left Union after controversial appointment of Geo. Sadler 1902. 98 ch. members and 210 Sun. scholars 1902. Attendance 1903: 127 a.m., 248 evg. Bldg in Dec. style, seating 1,100, on E. side of rd 1865–6.[1] Bombed in Second World War and temp. closed 1950, but had 18 members and 80 Sun. scholars 1956, mtg in community centre and being joined by worshippers from London City Mission in Lacland Pl.[2] Replaced by plain brown-brick bldg with tall rectangular windows, datestone 1959, reopened as Chelsea Cong ch. 1960; some funds for furnishing from former Markham Sq. ch. Utd Ref. ch. from 1972 until 1988, when Bapts joined and name changed to Edith Grove Christian Centre.[3] 35 members on roll 1997, when min. was Bapt.[4]

Radnor Walk, Welsh Chapel. Reg. for Inds 1880 by Welsh Congs previously in New Rd,[5] who had moved to Presb. Sun. sch. at no. 1 Halsey Terr. (later a continuation of Cadogan St) by 1879. Freehold of chapel in Radnor St (from 1937 Radnor Walk), reputedly once a music hall, originally Cong. and later Meth., bought by Welsh; cellars leased to adjoining pub. ho. until *c.*1910, thereafter ch. hall and kitchen.[6] Svces 1882: Sun. a.m., p.m., Thurs. evg. Attendance 1903: 59 a.m., 124 evg. 187 ch. members and 101 Sun. scholars 1907.[7] Nos increased by Welsh immigration, to peak of 260 members 1931.[8] Bldg on W. side of rd seating 300 in 1882, 400 in 1894, remodelled 1924 by T.J. Evans, who moved pulpit to opposite end.[9] Styled Eglwys Annibynnol Gymraeg with 60 members and Sun. evg svces in 2000, when stuccoed bldg with shallow cornice and pilasters seated 240 after back part had been made into hall and kitchen, and basement let to clinic.[10]

Uverdale Road, Ashburnham Church. Mtg formed at Gunter hall, Gunter Grove (formerly W. Brompton chapel, q.v.) 1879. Moved 1881 to bldg seating 500 in new Uverdale Rd, W. of Ashburnham Rd. Svces 1882: Sun. a.m. and evg, Wed. evg. Demol. 1885, members moving to Dawes Rd, Fulham, 1887.[11]

Jehovah's Witnesses

Sydney hall, Pond Pl., previously hall of Chelsea Temperance Soc.,[12] used continuously by Jehovah's Witnesses during and after Second World War.[13] Reg. as Kingdom hall 1977.[14] Freehold acquired from UK Temperance Soc. 1999. Main hall seating 150 and rear hall seating 50 used for weekday and 3 Sun. svces rotated between 4 congs named Chelsea, Fulham, Walham Green, and Sign Language in 2000.

Methodists

One of the dancing rooms at Ranelagh converted into chapel 1790, Meths having met previously in upper room of ho. in Royal Hosp. Row. Moved to former levée room 1798.[15]

Lower George Street (later Sloane Gdns), (Ranelagh Chapel). Mtg ho. near market reg. by John Surry and others 1800 as 'new chapel lately built',[16] but may have been converted slaughterho. Gallery added with loan from law bookseller Jos. Butterworth (d. 1826). Superseded chapel at Ranelagh and itself replaced by Sloane Terr. chapel (q.v.).[17]

Sloane Terrace. Reg. for chapel sought by Prots 1811, on leasehold site secured with help from Butterworth. One of Chelsea's 2 Wes. chapels, with Justice Walk (q.v.), by 1858. Plain brick bldg, designed by Revd Wm Jenkins 1812,[18] seating 800 in 1838:[19] 2 storeys over basement, entrance front with 5 bays of round-headed windows, central 3 projecting beneath shallow pediment, and Doric portico; galleries around 3 sides.[20] Served by mins of Wes. Meth. Soc. in rotation 1829.[21] Falling pew rents had impoverished ch. by 1902, when sold and about to be replaced by King's Rd.[22] Site later taken by Christian Scientists.[23]

Mason's Grove, Little Chelsea. Ground floor room in corner bldg occupied by Mary Collins reg. for Meths 1812.[24]

1 LMA, N/LCU/1/24/43; *Cong. Year Bk.* (1902); Mearns, *Cong. Chs.* 7, 59.
2 LMA, N/LCU/1/24/43; Denny, *Chelsea Past,* 59; *Cong. Year Bk* (1950, 1956); below, London City Mission.
3 LMA, N/LCU/1/24/43; Denny, *Chelsea Past,* 59.
4 *Utd Ref. Ch. Year Bk* (1997).
5 ONS Worship Reg. no. 25040; above, Congs., New Rd (Ebenezer chapel; Union chapel).
6 *PO Dir. London* (1879); Huws, *Hanys Eglwys,* 43–4; above, Congs (Radnor St); below, Meths (Radnor St).
7 *Cong. Year Bk* (1882, 1907).
8 Huws, *Hanys Eglwys,* 54.
9 Mearns, *Cong. Chs.* 59; *Cong. Year Bk* (1894); Huws, *Hanys Eglwys,* 54; inf. from ch. sec.
10 Inf. from ch. sec.
11 Mearns, *Cong. Chs.* 9, 59; *Cong. Year Bk* (1886); C.J. Fèret, *Fulham Old and New,* III (1900), 10–11.
12 Datestone.
13 Para. based on inf. from presiding officer, Chelsea Congregation of Jehovah's Witnesses.
14 ONS Worship Reg. no. 74779.
15 Chelsea Misc. 949 (cutting from *Wes. Meth. Mag.* 3 March 1830).
16 Guildhall MS 9580/2, p. 51. No denom. given; Surry was then a Meth., although later associated with Ind. or Cong. chapels.
17 Chelsea Misc. 949; *DNB.*
18 Colvin, *Brit. Architects,* 458.
19 Guildhall MS 9508A; *PO Dir. London* (1858); *London City Mission Mag.* III. 125; Chelsea Misc. 949.
20 Chelsea Misc. 719, 951, 1970.
21 Faulkner, *Chelsea,* II. 348.
22 Chelsea Misc. 951.
23 Below.
24 Guildhall MS 9580A. Two signatories had also reg. Sloane Terr.

Symons Street. Bldg in st W. of Sloane Sq. belonging to John Surry reg. for Meths April 1812.[1] Perhaps temp. mtg place for increased numbers before opening of nearby Union chapel, New Rd, by Surry and others for prots later Inds Dec. 1812.[2]

College Place (later Elystan Rd). Chapel blt. 1838 by John Wm Stacey on ground on S. side of College Pl. belonging to Geo. Downing, a trustee of Ranelagh chapel.[3] Chapel reg. for Wes. by Edw. Ellard 1839.[4] Listed as Dissenting Wes., with King's Rd W. (q.v.) 1858, and as one of 2 Chelsea chapels of Utd Meth. Free Ch. with Marlborough St (q.v.), 1863.[5] Bldg reg. for Utd Meth. Free Ch. 1861 and 1872. Attendance 1903: 16 a.m., 41 p.m. First reg. cancelled 1897 and second, presumably after closure, 1908.[6] Chapel taken by Salvation Army 1909.[7]

Justice Walk. Mission chapel said to have been established *c.*1840. One of 2 Wes. chapels, with Sloane Terr. (q.v.), 1858. Said to have been used as a chapel and Sun. sch. 1843–1903.[8] About to be sold 1902 on amalgamation with King's Rd ch.[9]

Marlborough Street. Chapel on N side, often recorded as in Marlborough Sq., listed as Wes. 1858 and as one of 2 chapels of Utd Meth. Free Ch., with College Pl. (q.v.), 1863.[10] Reg. for Ch. as 'Marlborough chapel' 1872. Attendance 1903: 32 a.m., 54 p.m. Reg. cancelled 1907, when chapel presumably closed. Marlborough hall, nearby in Leader St (later Ixworth Pl.), reg. 1908–13.[11]

Queen (later Flood) Street. Former Bapt chapel[12] at King's Rd end, W. side, listed as Wes. 1855, with Sloane Terr. and Justice Walk 1858, and as Dissenting Wes., with College Pl. and Gunter Grove, 1863. Inc. in Primitive Meths' 9th London circuit 1879, 1881. Probably replaced by undesignated Chelsea mission rooms by 1890.[13]

King's Road West. Chapel or mtg place on S side in Gingell's Terr. listed as Dissenting Wes., with College Pl. (q.v.) 1858.[14] Not listed 1863.

Gunter Grove. Wes. Reform chapel listed, also as Dissenting Wes. with College Pl. and Queen St (qq.v.), 1863.[15] Probably at former Cong. Gunter hall on E. side near N. end, where marked as Cong. chapel 1865 and, after serving as first mtg place of Ashburnham ch., as hall 1894.[16]

Radnor Street. Reg. as 'Radnor chapel' by Meths of New Connexion 1860,[17] presumably former Cong. chapel on W side. Again Cong., as Welsh chapel, from 1880.[18]

King's Road, Chelsea Methodist Church. Ch. on E. corner of Manor (later Chelsea Manor) St reg. by Wes. 1903,[19] after sale of Sloane Terr. Red-brick bldg seating 715, entered from Manor St and inc. 4 shops providing income, at no. 155a King's Rd.[20] Attendance 1903, at 'Chelsea ch., Town Hall', perhaps at new ch.: 131 a.m., 165 evg. Bombed 1940,[21] whereupon svces held in upper room, the adjoining Sun. sch. of 1903, in Chelsea Manor St until reopening 1968.[22] Upper room retained as hall when new ground-floor ch. opened by Cardinal Hume as part of complex inc. shops, pastoral centre for all denoms., and 21 flats for old people 1984. Ch., called sanctuary, by Bernard Lamb in contemporary style, seating *c.*250. Also small chapel originally intended to be open all night but in 1999 reached only through main area. Tenants of flats, managed by Servite Housing Assoc., and shops paid rent to Meth. Ch. 1999.[23]

English Presbyterians (later Presb. Ch. of Eng.)

Ranelagh chapel, Lower George St. Sold by Inds to Presbs 1845.[24] Seated 1,060 in 1851, inc. 60 free; attendance 550 a.m., 400 p.m. One of Eng. Presbs' 8 London chs. 1858. Cong. moved to former Ch. of Scotland ch., Halkin St (Westm.), 1866[25] and, as Belgrave ch., opened Sun. schs at no. 67 Cadogan St, reg. 1883–1934.[26]

Salvation Army

Denyer Street. Reg. as 'Salvation Temple' at corner of Marlborough Rd 1881.[27] Mission hall, attendance 1903: 34 a.m., 56 evg. Replaced by College Pl. (q.v.) 1909.

1 Guildhall MS 9580/4.
2 Ibid.; above, Congs (New Rd).
3 CL, deed 19374.
4 Guildhall MS 9580/8, p. 20.
5 *PO Dir. London* (1858, 1863)
6 ONS Worship Reg. nos 11533, 20622. Baptisms reg. to 1902: LMA, N/C/3/1.
7 Below.
8 *Chelsea Soc. Rep.* (1997), 16.
9 Chelsea Misc. 952.
10 *PO Dir. London* (1858, 1863).
11 ONS Worship Reg. nos 20621, 43375.
12 Above, Bapts (Queen St, Zion).
13 *PO Dir. London* (1858, 1863, 1879); *Kelly's Dir. Chelsea* (1881, 1890).
14 *PO Dir. London* (1858).
15 Ibid. (1863).
16 Above, Congs (Edith Grove; Ashburnham).
17 ONS Worship Reg. no. 9545.
18 Above, Congs. (Markham Sq.; Radnor Walk).
19 ONS Worship Reg. no. 39883.
20 Chelsea Misc. 951; *Places of Worship*, 12; Loobey, *Chelsea*, 43.
21 Chelsea cuttings, Meth. ch. King's Rd.
22 Ibid.; inf. from min.
23 Pevsner, *London NW.* 561; *Places of Worship*, 12; datestones; inf. from min.
24 *Chelsea Soc. Rep.* (1956), 11; above, Congs.
25 *PO Dir. London* (1858); *Chelsea Soc. Rep.* (1956), 12.
26 ONS Worship Reg. no. 27426.
27 Ibid. no. 25801. Not same as Denyer hall: below, other denoms.

Cheyne Row. Salvation Army training depot recorded at no. 15 in 1890. Closed by 1902.[1]

Riley Street. Reg. as barracks 1900. Attendance 1903: 47 a.m., 58 evg. Closed by 1912.[2]

College Place. Hall reg. 1909 as successor to Denyer St in former Utd Meth. Free Ch.; head lease expired 1918 and Wm Bramwell Booth took 5-yr lease from freeholder.[3] Replaced by Flood St (q.v.) 1923.[4]

Flood Street. Hall at rear of no. 23 reg. 1923 as successor to College Pl. Replaced by King's Rd (q.v.) 1931.[5]

King's Road. Hall at no. 461 reg. 1931 as successor to Flood St.[6] Single-storeyed bldg W. of World's End pub. ho.; site later part of open space at World's End Pl.[7]

Blantyre Street. Chelsea Goodwill Centre to serve new World's End estate opened and reg. 1973, renamed Chelsea Corps 1999. Single-storeyed plain brown-brick bldg on E side of rd, with dual-purpose hall seating *c.*75 and used for worship Sun. a.m. and as community centre in 2000. Two-storeyed detached ho., no. 13 Blantyre St, built to N as officer's residence.[8]

United Reformed Church, see Congregationalists, Edith Grove

Other Denominations and Unspecified Missions[9]

'Ho. numbered 4 in Paradise Row' reg. by dissenters called 'Universal Mallienum [*sic*] Ch.' 1798.[10]

Dwellings of Thos Pye, no. 16 Manor Row, Queen St, of Sarah Campleman, no. 1 Cottage Pl., Little Chelsea, of John Abraham, no. 4 Little George St, and of Joshua Rhodes, no. 1 Robinson's Bldgs, Flask Lane, all with premises adjoining, reg. by prots 1816.[11]

Dwellings of John Bowen, no. 9 Seymour Pl., 'Kensington', reg. 1818[12] and of Chas. Eatley, no. 16 New Manor St, reg. 1819. No. 11 Prince's Row, King St, reg. by J. Currie 1820. Dwelling of Wm Pickett, no. 27 Cumberland St, reg. 1824.[13] Sun. sch. room of Wm Edwell of Leader St in Eden Pl., Pond Pl., reg. 1824. Ho. of Rob. Hall, no. 1 Exeter St, reg. 1829.[14] Room in York St, Hans Pl., reg. by Joshua Nettleton of Sloane Sq. 1836.[15] Detached room in York Mews behind York Terr., Queen's Elm Gate, reg. by David Walker of Holles Pl., Brompton, 1844. Room on ground floor of no. 1 Jubilee Ct, Turk's Row, reg. by Ric. Smith, ironmonger, 1848.[16]

'Lloyds', no. 1 Lower George St, reg. by Latter-day Saints 1854–66. Presumably premises of Wm Lloyd, builder, next to Ranelagh chapel.[17]

Oakley Rooms, E. side of Manor St, reg. by 'Ind. Religious Reformers' 1859–66. Oakley mission room at no. 87, perhaps undenom. 1878 but CE for St Paul's, Onslow Sq. (Kens.), by 1889.[18]

Providence chapel, Cook's Ground, reg. by 'Testamentary Cong. Ch. or the Ch. at Chelsea' 1861–95. Listed 1882. Perhaps former Huguenot, then Ind., chapel.[19]

Royal Amphitheatre, Ashburnham Pk, reg. by undesignated worshippers 1869–95. Listed 1882.[20]

College St chapel reg. by undesignated worshippers 1869–1906. Listed 1882.[21]

Denyer hall, Denyer St, reg. by evangelical mission 1880–97. Perhaps Salvation Army temple 1881.[22]

Mission hall, no. 2A Flood St, reg. by Chelsea Gospel Mission 1885–95.[23]

Christian Mission chapel, no. 56 Queen's (later Royal Hospital) Rd, recorded 1878–9.[24]

North (later Basil) St mission hall between nos 60 and 64 in 1878 may have been Sloane chapel recorded 1881.[25]

College St chapel, between nos 50 and 52 (formerly Bapt) listed as Church of Christ 1890–1 and as chapel, with no denom., 1902.[26]

Marlborough Rd mission hall used by Church Army 1902.[27]

The Sanctuary, no. 23 Basil St, presumably a Spiritualist ch., recorded 1934–47.[28]

No. 50 Uverdale Rd, room in basement reg. by undesignated Christians, later altered to 'Slavic Pentecostal Ch.', 1959–70.[29]

Nos 8–10 World's End Pl. served as World's End Community ch. 1998, with Sun. svces and daily activities

1 *Kelly's Dir. Chelsea* (1890, 1891); *PO Dir. London* (1902).
2 ONS Worship Reg. no. 38050.
3 CL, deeds 19374, 19390.
4 ONS Worship Reg. no. 43661.
5 Ibid. no. 48972.
6 Ibid. no. 53356.
7 Inf. from Capt. S. Spry.
8 ONS Worship Reg. no. 73379; inf. from Capt. Spry.
9 Except where otherwise stated, the premises were reg. by undesignated prots. For regs. by Inds, see above, Congs.
10 Guildhall MS 9580/1, pp. 171–2.
11 Guildhall MS 9580/4.
12 Ibid.
13 Guildhall MS 9580/5.
14 Guildhall MS 9580/6, pp. 1–2, 241.
15 Guildhall MS 9580/7, p. 203.
16 Guildhall MS 9580/8, pp. 222, 296.
17 ONS Worship Reg. no. 5861; *PO Dir. London* (1857, 1863).
18 ONS Worship Reg. no. 8665; *Chelsea Dir.* (1878); above, dau. chs (Oakley).
19 ONS Worship Reg. no. 13916; *Return of Chs.* 86; above, Congs (Cook's Ground).
20 ONS Worship Reg. no. 19070; *Return of Chs.* 86.
21 ONS Worship Reg. no. 19279; *Return of Chs.* 86.
22 ONS Worship Reg. no. 25047. Not same as Salvation Army temple, Denyer St: *Return of Chs.* 86.
23 ONS Worship Reg. No. 28610.
24 *Chelsea Dir.* (1878); *PO Dir. London* (1879).
25 *Chelsea Dir.* (1878); *Kelly's Dir. Chelsea* (1881).
26 *Kelly's Dir, Chelsea* (1890–1); *PO Dir. London* (1902); above, Bapts (College St).
27 *PO Dir. London* (1902).
28 Ibid. (1934, 1947).
29 ONS Worship Reg. no. 67574; Chelsea cuttings, Chs.; Kens. and Chelsea.

for neighbouring estate. Listed as one of two Christian centres, together with Edith Grove.[1]

Chelsea Christian Centre,[2] on 1st floor of Kensington and Chelsea coll. in Hortensia Rd, opened as an Elim Pentecostal ch. 1998 by Kensington temple, established since 1930s by Elim Foursquare Gospel Alliance in Kensington Park Rd (Kens.). Sun. a.m. svces and children's programme provided in 2000.[3]

London City Mission

London City Mission, established 1835 and often associated with existing chs,[4] was active by 1847 in W. part of par. and in SE. and NE. corners.[5] District of Kinnerton St (St Geo. Hanover Sq.), stretching into Chelsea and Brompton, described as spiritually destitute in 1844–5: included Exeter Bldgs, with many poor Irish, where missioner helped to establish ragged sch.[6]

Mission at no. 33 Hasker St, off Milner St, 1878–79.[7]

Rooms at no. 19 College St used by London City Mission 1879. Perhaps replaced by Stewart Memorial mission hall at no. 19A, recorded 1902, 1912.[8]

Bedford hall, Upper Manor St, recorded 1878 and used by London City Mission 1902.[9] Attendance 1903: 47 evg.

Ann Pl., off Milman's St, hall reg. as unsectarian 1899–1925 was Park chapel mission hall used by London City Mission 1902.[10] Attendance 1903: 49 evg.

Lacland hall, Lacland Terr. (later Pl.), King's Rd, used by London City Mission, 1902, 1913.[11] Site on west side of Lacland Terrace conveyed to the London City Mission Trust in 1905 by H.J. Veitch.[12] Attendance 1903: 35 a.m., 389 evg. Hall in Lacland Pl. reg. for mission 1930–54.[13] Hall sold to Chelsea MB in 1953;[14] after closure to make way for Cremorne estate, worshippers joined Cong. ch. in Edith Grove.[15]

FOREIGN CHURCHES

CHURCH OF SCOTLAND

Westward movement of many worshippers at the church in Crown Court, Covent Garden (Westm.), led the presbytery of London to seek a site for a new church in 1881,[16] at first without success, perhaps because of opposition from vicar of St Saviour's, Walton Street.[17] An extended site was leased from Henry Smith's charity and Cadogan estates, 1882. Building, at corner of Pont Street and Lennox Gardens, begun as St Andrew's Scottish National church 1883; renamed St Columba's, following objections from St Andrew's, Stepney, soon after opening 1884.[18] Sometimes inaccurately described as in Belgravia. Red-brick building with stone dressings in Early English style,[19] designed by J. Macvicar Anderson who contributed £1,000 to costs: seating 900, it had an aisled and clerestoried nave, tall NW. tower, and hall for 400 beneath. Many social clubs; connexion with London Scottish Rifle Volunteers from 1888. Seen by minister not as dissenters' or mission church but as extension of National Church for exiled Scots, 1902. Attendance 1903: 417 a.m., 175 evg. Bombed 1941, whereupon services moved to Jehangir hall of Imperial Institute, reg. as St Columba's church, no. 7 Lennox Gardens, 1942–50,[20] with some activities at St Saviour's, Walton Street, and then to larger Examination hall seating 800, reg. as St Columba's, no. 57 Cadogan Square, 1950–3.[21]

Foundation stone of new 'cathedral of Presbyterianism in London' laid by queen 1950;[22] adjoining houses in Lennox Gardens acquired 1951,[23] and semi-basement hall seating 800 dedicated 1953. Austere design with Georgian and Romanesque references by Sir Edward Maufe, said to derive 'its significance from its very special Scottish circumstances'.[24] Faced in Portland stone with green tiled roofs; tall entrance to offices and hall. Church above, dedicated 1955 and seating over 1,000,[25] has barrel-vaulted nave, passage aisles, and a shallow sanctuary, with rose window in form of St Andrew's cross, flanked by chapel of London Scottish regiment to N. and by chapel dedicated to servicemen generally to S.; 'Scandinavian modern' tower,[26] on site of former tower, with chapel.

1 Chelsea cuttings, Chs.: Kens. and Chelsea; above, Congs.
2 Additional to two above.
3 ONS, *Official List of Certified Places of Worship* (1998); Millennium pamphlet on joint ch. activities (2000).
4 *VCH Middx*, XI. 238.
5 *London City Mission Mag.* XII, p. xviii.
6 *London City Mission Mag.* X. 235–7; XVII. 219; above, Soc. Hist., educ. (pub. schs: Exeter Bldgs).
7 *Chelsea Dir.* (1878); *PO Dir. London* (1879).
8 *PO Dir. London* (1879, 1902, 1912).
9 *Chelsea Dir.* (1878); *PO Dir. London* (1902).
10 ONS Worship Reg. no. 37203; *PO Dir. London* (1902); above, dau. chs (Park chapel).
11 *PO Dir. London* (1902, 1913).
12 KL, deed 37062.
13 ONS Worship Reg. No. 52383.
14 KL, deed 37062.
15 Denny, *Chelsea Past*, 59; above, Congs (Edith Grove).
16 Para. based on G.C. Cameron, *Scots Kirk in London* (1979), passim.
17 Stroud, *Smith's Char.* 42–3.
18 ONS Worship Reg. no. 27761.
19 Illus. in J.H. McIndoe, *St Columba's: A Brief Guide* (1992).
20 ONS Worship Reg. no. 60256.
21 Ibid. no. 62801.
22 Chelsea cuttings, St Columba's (*Evg Standard*, 18 May 1950).
23 Ibid. (*Star*, 15 Sep. 1951).
24 *Builder* (1956), 293–6; see Fig. 85.
25 Chelsea cuttings, St Columba's (*The Times*, 2 Dec. 1955). Rest of para. based on McIndoe, *St Columba's*, passim.
26 Pevsner, *London NW.* 561; Loobey, *Chelsea*, 100.

85. *St Columba's Church of Scotland, Pont Street*

HUGUENOTS

A chapel may have existed by 1687, French gardeners having settled in Chelsea after Revocation of Edict of Nantes. Sons of minister and schoolmaster John Caizon baptised 1700 and 1702; son of another minister, L'Hirondelle, baptised 1704. Community was recommended by rector Dr King to his successor. Three Frenchmen ministered probably at 2 chapels in 1718, at Cook's Ground and on W. side of Chelsea Park at Little Chelsea.[1] John Narbonne was lessee 1724 of glebe on which Cook's Ground chapel built.[2] Neither congregation later recorded as active. Small Cook's Ground chapel passed to Independents;[3] Little Chelsea building, still marked as chapel 1745, once identified with Huguenots[4] but more probably Park Chapel.[5]

LATVIAN LUTHERAN CHURCH

The hall and first floor of no. 55 Hans Road were registered by the 'Latvian Lutheran Church (Independent)' from 1952 to 1970.[6] The premises, sometimes described as Latvian Church House, were still listed in 1966 but not in 1968.[7]

MORAVIANS

Moravians,[8] originating in Bohemia under John Hus, opened a chapel in Fetter Lane (London) 1742. Count Nikolaus Ludwig von Zinzendorf (d. 1760) bought Lindsey House as residence and international headquarters 1750, intended partly as resting place before colonists and missionaries moved on overseas. Settlement planned on leased land to north formerly attached to Beaufort House, where chapel or hall built on site of Beaufort House stables, with burial ground, also serving Fetter Lane, laid out on stable yard, first used in 1751. Hymn book printed 1752 and English synod held at Chelsea 1754, but settlement not built and numbers declined after founder's departure 1755. Much of the ground sold in building plots after 1770 and Lindsey House sold 1774, but chapel and burial ground were retained.

Moravians, 'greatly diminished' by 1778,[9] held weekday services from 1766, apparently discontinued before 1795[10] but resumed after 1797 until mid 1820s and again in early 20th century. Chapel used by other denominations by 1829, and also served as Clock House school.[11] Moravian attendance 1903: 34 evg. Property leased for 50 years from 1914 to sculptors Ernest and Mary Gillick,[12]

86. *Moravian chapel and burial ground, Milman's Street, 1791*

1 *Proc. of Huguenot Soc. of London*, XXII. 520; Faulkner, *Chelsea*, I. 260; II. 122–3.

2 Guildhall MS 9628/5/3.

3 Above, Congs (Cook's Ground).

4 Rocque, *Map of London* (1741–5), sheet 10; *Proc. of Huguenot Soc. of London*, VIII. 54.

5 Beaver, *Memorials*, 144; above, dau. chs (Park chapel).

6 ONS Worship Reg. no. 63598.

7 Chelsea cuttings, Chs.: Kens. and Chelsea; *PO Dir. London* (1952, 1968).

8 Based on *Survey of London*, IV. 39–40, 46; Faulkner, *Chelsea*, I. 78–84; *Fetter Lane Moravian Cong., London 1742–1992*, ed. C. Podmore (1992); see Fig. 86.

9 Guildhall MS 9558.

10 Lysons, *Environs*, II. 170.

11 Above, Soc. Hist., educ. (pub. schs: Park Chapel Nat.).

12 *Who Was Who, 1951–60*, 422; *1961–70*, 429.

who lived in minister's house, converted chapel into studios, and built additional studio;[1] Moravians worshipped in small burial chapel added in 19th century. Superseded Kingsgate Baptist Chapel, Eagle Street (Holborn) as new home of bombed-out Fetter Lane congregation 1959. City of London's Moravian church, Fetter Lane, registered Chelsea premises 1973.[2] Resident minister 1966–81, part-time thereafter; worshippers largely West Indian and not local.

In 1999 'Moravian Close', behind high brick wall with gateway at no. 381 King's Road, contained former chapel between 'Small Hall' (burial chapel) to E. and early 19th-century minister's house to W., all facing S. across burial ground of nearly one acre. Former chapel a low brick building with 3 tall segmental-headed windows beneath deep roof,[3] by Zinzendorf's architect Sigismund von Gersdorf;[4] divided into 3 studios, of which first had been opened as Moravian Information and Exhibition Centre 1990, other 2 remaining let.[5] Worshippers met in 'Small Hall', seating *c.*50.[6] Tudor brickwork at back of chapel, plastered, and in walls E and S of burial ground.[7] Ground, divided into 4 for married and unmarried of both sexes, exempt from closure under Act of 1855, burials being few and deep. Closed for interments 1888[8] but still used for ashes 1999 and so claimed as sole intra-mural burial ground in London.[9] Graves, marked only by small tablets, include those of divines John Cennick (d. 1755) and James Hutton (d. 1795).[10]

SERBIAN ORTHODOX CHURCH

London's Serbian community[11] worshipped at a Russian Orthodox church in Buckingham Palace Road (Westm.) until Prince Vsevolod, a cousin of King Peter of Yugoslavia, provided a chapel on the first floor of no. 12 Lennox Gardens. A room with a standing capacity for at least 50 was consecrated in 1942 and registered as the Serbian Orthodox church of St Sava from 1943 to 1948.[12] The premises were not retained after the purchase of the larger no. 12 Egerton Gardens (Kens.) by the Yugoslav royal family,[13] where a chapel consecrated in 1947 was used until worshippers moved to Lancaster Road (Kens.), where the church was reregistered in 1982.[14]

NON CHRISTIAN FAITHS

JUDAISM

Although Jew's Row (later Queen's Road West) was built up by the early 19th century,[15] its name was not linked with any Jewish community. The Jews' burial ground at the corner of Fulham Road and Church (later Old Church) Street was not intended for Chelsea residents and served no local place of worship.[16]

Hammersmith and West Kensington synagogue at Brook Green (Hammersmith) was the nearest synagogue after its opening, as a constituent of the United Synagogue, in 1890.[17] Less distant was Fulham town hall, which Ashkenazim attended on high holydays[18] before the opening of Victoria and Chelsea (later Chelsea) synagogue (below). Chelsea's synagogue, which never attained the status of Hammersmith's, thereafter remained the only purpose-built place of worship for Jews in the area.

Chelsea Synagogue, Smith Terrace, Smith St. Worship started in homes of Wolff Adler and Julius Nelken before purchase of 2-storeyed studio with synagogue seating 80 and classrooms,[19] where lst-floor room registered at Red (later Synagogue) Ho. 1916;[20] ground floor used for mtgs.[21] Styled Victoria and Chelsea, admitted as associate of United Synagogue with 52 male seat-holders 1917 and as affiliated synagogue 1949.[22] High holyday worship in larger Welsh ch. in Radnor Walk,[23] and later in Chenil Galleries, no. 183 King's Rd. Rebuilt after purchase of adjoining plot as plain brick bldg, seating 216, in contemporary style by Cyril Adler 1959, when renamed Chelsea synagogue.[24] 75 seat-holders in 1950, 145 in 1960, 125 in 1970, *c.*90 in 2000.[25]

ISLAM

Ahlul Beit Foundation registered ground floor and one room on 1st and 2nd floors of no. 31 Draycott Place, 1978. Still in use 1998,[26] but had closed or moved by 2001, when there were no Islamic places of worship in Chelsea.[27]

1 *Brief Visitors' Guide to Moravian Close* (leaflet *c.*1999).
2 ONS Worship Reg. no. 73526.
3 Chelsea cuttings: Architecture [1947 list]; Chelsea Misc. 1048 postcards.
4 P. Kroyer, *Story of Lindsey Ho.* (1956), 43.
5 *Brief Visitors' Guide.*
6 Inf. from archivist.
7 Hist. Mon. Com. *W. London*, 15; *Brief Visitors' Guide.*
8 18 & 19 Vic. c. 128; B. Holmes, *London Burial Grounds* (1896), 166, 283.
9 *Brief Visitors' Guide.*
10 *DNB.* Other burials recorded in Lysons, *Environs,* II. 170–2, and *Brief Historical Sketch of Lindsey Ho. and Moravian Burial Ground* (booklet revised 1993).
11 Para. based on inf. From Mr N. Petrovic, former chairman of the Church Congregation Council.
12 ONS Worship Reg. no. 60507.
13 Char. Com. file 249616.
14 ONS Worship Reg. no. 76144.
15 *Regency A to Z*, 31.
16 Above, Loc. Govt, pub. svces (burial).
17 A. Newman, *United Synagogue 1870–1970* (1976), 226–7.
18 Inf. from Mr B. Glassner.
19 Ibid.
20 ONS Worship Reg. no. 46804.
21 *Places of Worship*, 11.
22 Newman, *United Syn.* 216, 222–3.
23 Above, prot. nonconf. (Congs).
24 Inf. from Mr B. Glassner.
25 Newman, *United Syn.* 217; inf. from Mr Glassner.
26 ONS Worship Reg. no. 74981; ONS, *Official List of Certified Places of Worship* (1998).
27 *Places of Worship*, 2.

INDEX

NOTE. Page numbers in bold denote the main entry for that item. An italic number denotes a map or illustration. A number preceded by the letters *pl.* refers to one of the colour plates between pages 142 and 143.

Buildings, streets, and localities are in Chelsea except where otherwise stated. Most references to roads, squares, and alleys are to their first occurrence in the text, to subsequent development, or to buildings which do not have individual names. Roads are generally indexed under their modern names, with cross-references. Proper names which occur only incidentally have not been indexed.

CORRIGENDA TO VOLUME XI

Earlier lists of corrigenda will be found in Volumes I and III–XI

page 81*a* Under Roman Catholicism, delete sentence beginning in line 2, 'In 1594 Thomas Leeds', and note 63. (Refers to Wappingthorn House, Steyning, Sussex).

page 126, note 56, add *Bldg. News*, 2 Oct. 1868, 668.
note 58, delete *Bldg. News*, 2 Oct. 1868, 668

page 130*b* line 39, *for* 'Joseph & Smithem' *read* 'F.E. Pilkington'

page 221*a* line 28, *for* 'ST. JOHN' *read* 'ST. JOHN THE EVANGELIST'